CRISIS INTERVENTION BOOK 2

The Practitioner's Sourcebook For Brief Therapy

CRISIS INTERVENTION

BOOK 2

The Practitioner's Sourcebook for Brief Therapy

HOWARD J. PARAD
& LIBBIE G. PARAD
EDITORS

Family Service America
Milwaukee, Wisconsin

The following publishers have given permission to quote from copyrighted works: From the *Encyclopedia of Social Work*, edited by John B. Turner et al.; copyright 1977; reprinted by permission of the National Association of Social Workers, Inc. From *The Experience of Dying*, by E. Mansell Pattison; copyright 1977; reprinted by permission of the publisher, Prentice-Hall, Inc., Englewood Cliffs, New Jersey. From "Help for the Dying," by Carleton Pilsecker, in *Social Work*, 20; copyright 1975; reprinted by permission of the National Association of Social Workers, Inc.

Chapter 3, "The Rape Victim," by Gail Abarbanel and Gloria Richman, is copyrighted by the Rape Treatment Center of Santa Monica Hospital Medical Center, Santa Monica, California.

Library of Congress Cataloging-in-Publication Data

Crisis intervention, book 2 : the practitioner's sourcebook for brief therapy / edited by Howard J. Parad and Libbie G. Parad.

p. cm.

Includes bibliographical references.

ISBN 0-87304-237-9

1. Crisis intervention (Psychiatry) 2. Brief psychotherapy.

I. Parad, Howard J. II. Parad, Libbie G. III. Family Service America

RC480.6.C742 1989

616.89'025—dc20 89-17151

CIP

Printed in the United States

With love and admiration,
to Harry, Jonathan, and Sarah

CONTENTS

PREFACE

This volume, *Crisis Intervention, Book 2: The Practitioner's Sourcebook for Brief Therapy*, responds to many requests from students and practitioners for an updated exposition of brief crisis therapy to serve as a companion volume to our earlier book, *Crisis Intervention: Selected Readings*, originally published in 1965 and reprinted several times to meet the continuing demand for it.

In preparing the present volume, we asked ourselves: How can we provide the reader with state-of-the-art information about the concepts and techniques of brief crisis-oriented therapy? We decided our goal would best be served by compiling a sourcebook with an overview of current crisis intervention theory as well as chapters on the clinical applications of theory to clients receiving time-limited crisis therapy in diverse practice settings. Recognizing the increased utilization of brief crisis treatment by clinical social workers, clinical psychologists, psychiatrists, and other mental health practitioners, we wanted to encompass a multidisciplinary perspective. Finally, we decided a state-of-the-art endeavor should include preventive as well as remedial approaches.

Hence this book is divided into three parts. Part I offers an overview of the evolution of the crisis treatment approach with individuals, families, and groups and an analysis of the multifaceted knowledge base that has contributed to the development of brief crisis services. The major section of the book, Part II, consists of eleven chapters written by experts in various fields of brief crisis intervention who provide in-depth information about commonly encountered situational and developmental crises, including post-traumatic stress disorder, rape, incest and molestation, spousal abuse, life-cycle stresses such as those experienced by college students and adults in transition, catastrophic illness, the plight of the chronically mentally disordered, suicide, and death and dying. No volume on crisis intervention would be complete, however, without attending to the issues surrounding preventive intervention with populations at risk. These issues are considered in Part III, which focuses on crisis consultation, the impact of social support interventions, and the crises of children of divorce and of children with handicapping conditions.

To guide contributors, we asked them to address the following questions in their chapters: What is the magnitude of the specific crisis being considered? What is the relevant literature and research? What guidelines can be offered to frontline practitioners to help them provide their clients with effective services? The contributors have generously illustrated their presentations with practice vignettes that clearly show what the crisis treatment specialist says, does, and thinks.

These case examples illustrate *corrective* crisis intervention (restoring the client to pre-crisis equilibrium, or perhaps to a higher level of psychosocial functioning), *protective* crisis intervention (for example, with victims of rape, abuse, or spousal violence), and *preventive* crisis intervention (aimed at averting crises in vulnerable populations, for example, those affected by disasters, divorce, grief, or handicapping conditions).

No attempt has been made to force an artificial homogeneity on the contributors. Indeed, we are pleased that the contributors, although sharing a common knowledge base and professional value orientation, do not shrink from controversy.

Perhaps more than at any other time in the history of psychotherapy, today's professional climate fosters new theories, new modes of theory development, and new departures from traditional treatment arrangements and techniques in clinical practice. Although this sourcebook is addressed to one specific area of practice innovation, it also reflects many significant contemporary mental health practice trends, including the trend toward eclectic and pluralistic perspectives rather than utilizing a single theory of psychotherapy; the trend toward multidisciplinary collaboration and professional activity; the trend toward interactional therapeutic approaches (couple, family, and group therapy) and away from exclusive reliance on individual treatment; the trend toward mobilizing community support systems rather than institutional care; and the trend toward primary prevention—now more a matter of reality than rhetoric. Most important to the present volume is the trend toward planned brevity in psychotherapy as compared with traditional open-ended, time-unlimited approaches. This trend is influenced not only by economic considerations but also by the realities of trying to provide a meaningful service for clients, most of whom present themselves for brief rather than long-term therapy and who seek services to alleviate a stress with which they cannot cope.

This is a book by practitioners for practitioners, and of this we are proud. Many persons have assisted us in making this volume possible. Our first and greatest debt of gratitude is to the nineteen contributors who have joined us in this enterprise. We also thank the thousands of clients who, over the years, have afforded us the privilege of helping them cope with crises, thereby teaching us constantly to refine and elaborate our treatment approaches to fit their needs, not our ideological or theoretical preferences. And we thank the many students at Harvard University, Smith College, Boston University, University of Southern California, University of Hawaii, and California State University, among other places, who helped us learn by giving us the opportunity to teach.

We also express our appreciation to Ruth Britton, Librarian, University of Southern California, for her assistance; Ralph Burant, Director of Publications of Family Service America, and his editorial staff for keeping us on schedule; and Dr. Alan Levy, Assistant Professor, University of Southern California, for his help in reviewing some of the recent research on crisis intervention. We extend special thanks to Lola Selby, Professor Emerita, University of Southern California, and Jean Allgeyer, of the Benjamin Rush Center in Los Angeles, for their stimulating colleagueship.

H.J.P.
L.G.P.

CONTRIBUTORS

GAIL ABARBANEL, M.S.W.
Founder and Director, Rape Treatment Center
Santa Monica Hospital Medical Center
Santa Monica, California

JOHN BREKKE, PH.D.
Assistant Professor
University of Southern California
School of Social Work, Los Angeles, California

GERALD CAPLAN, M.D., F.R.C. PSYCH.
Scientific Director, Jerusalem Institute for
Study of Psychological Stress and Jerusalem Family
Center, Jerusalem, Israel
Emeritus Professor of Psychiatry
Harvard University, Cambridge, Massachusetts

CHRISTINE A. COURTOIS, PH.D.
Private Practice, Washington, D.C.

MARGARET EPPERSON-SEBOUR, M.S.W.
Director, Psychosocial Services Department
Maryland Institute for Emergency Medical Services Systems
Baltimore, Maryland

NORMAN L. FARBEROW, PH.D.
Co-director, Suicide Prevention Center
A Division of Family Services of Los Angeles
Clinical Professor in Psychiatry (Psychology)
School of Medicine, University of Southern California
Los Angeles, California

JUDITH GREENBAUM, PH.D.
Project Associate
Programs for Educational Opportunity
University of Michigan, Ann Arbor, Michigan

SAMUEL M. HEILIG, M.S.W.
Private Practice, Los Angeles, California

RAY E. LILES, D.S.W.
Private Practice, Blue Jay, California

ALEXANDER C. MCFARLANE, M.D.
Senior Lecturer, Department of Psychiatry, School of Medicine
The Flinders University of South Australia
Bedford Park, South Australia

GERALDINE MARKEL, PH.D.
Senior Research Associate
Reading and Learning Skills Center
University of Michigan, Ann Arbor, Michigan

SHARON MASS, PH.D.
Director of Social Services
Western Medical Center, Santa Ana, California
Lecturer, University of Southern California
School of Social Work, Los Angeles, California

MICHÀL E. MOR-BARAK, D.S.W.
Assistant Professor
University of Southern California
School of Social Work, Los Angeles, California

ANN O'BRIEN, M.S.W.
Coordinator, Riverside Interagency Sexual Abuse
Council, Riverside, California

HOWARD J. PARAD, D.S.W.
Private Practice, West Los Angeles, California
Professor Emeritus, University of Southern California
School of Social Work, Los Angeles, California

LIBBIE G. PARAD, D.S.W.
Private Practice, West Los Angeles, California

HAROLD L. PRUETT, PH.D.
Director, Student Psychological Services
University of California, Los Angeles, California

GLORIA RICHMAN, M.S.W.
Clinical Supervisor, Rape Treatment Center
Santa Monica Hospital Medical Center
Santa Monica, California

NORMAN TABACHNICK, M.D., PH.D.
Clinical Professor of Psychiatry
University of California, Los Angeles
Supervising and Training Analyst
Southern California Psychoanalytical Institute
Los Angeles, California

NANCY BOYD WEBB, D.S.W.
Professor, Graduate School of Social Services
Fordham in Westchester, Tarrytown, New York

RICHARD A. ZUCKERWISE, M.S.W.
Psychiatric Social Worker, Center for Family Living
San Fernando Valley Community Mental Health Center
Van Nuys, California

Part I.

Crisis Intervention: An Introductory Overview

1

Crisis Intervention: An Introductory Overview

HOWARD J. PARAD AND LIBBIE G. PARAD

MENTAL HEALTH professionals and other human services personnel are increasingly attracted to brief crisis intervention as an effective method of delivering readily accessible and rapid services to many people experiencing acute situational and interpersonal stress, life-cycle and other transitional changes, and natural and man-made disasters. These services are offered by various social work agencies, such as family counseling, travelers' aid, neighborhood centers, public social service, and child welfare agencies, as well as in many multidisciplinary settings, such as community mental health centers, emergency walk-in clinics, suicide prevention and hotline services, hospitals, and disaster-aid centers.

In this introductory overview of crisis intervention theory, practice, and research we shall address the following questions:

1. What is a crisis and what is crisis intervention?
2. What are the main elements of the crisis sequence?
3. What roles do timing and time limits play?
4. Why is crisis intervention important in the field of human services?
5. What is the historical background and knowledge base of crisis intervention?
6. What practice implications flow from the crisis approach?
7. What is the connection between crisis intervention and short-term dynamic and other psychotherapies?

What Is a Crisis?

What images does the word *crisis* bring to mind? Urgent? Helpless? Hopeless? Mentally disordered? Dangerous? Upset? Hysterical? Panicky? Off balance? Anxious? Suicidal? Homicidal? (Parad & Resnik, 1975). Or does it perhaps bring to mind a combination of these conditions? And what about the challenges as well as the dangers of the crisis encounter?

We all hear about and cope with crises in our diverse caregiving roles as psychologists, psychiatrists, social workers, teachers, physicians, nurses, physician assistants, emergency medical personnel, police, and firefighters as well as in our everyday roles as mothers, fathers, wives, husbands, lovers, friends, and neighbors. Simply put, a crisis is an upset in a steady state, a turning point leading to better or worse, a disruption or breakdown in a person's or family's normal or usual pattern of functioning. The upset, or disequilibrium, is usually acute in the sense that it is of recent origin. However, when working with a crisis-prone person, a "crisis junkie," acute crises may erupt in a chronic situation (Kagan & Schlosberg, 1989). The pain and discomfort of a crisis may be assessed both subjectively, as perceived by the victim, or "objectively" by an observer. The severity of a crisis may be rated along a continuum from mild to moderate to severe.

How does a crisis differ from a problem or an emergency? Some mental health professionals consider an emergency situation to exist only when a person is thought to be dangerous to self or others or is gravely disabled—a broad term that refers to a person's inability to feed, clothe, or otherwise care for him- or herself. Many professionals, dissatisfied with the imprecision of most formal definitions of crisis, take the practical view that if clients believe they must be seen immediately, they are experiencing an emergency situation; if they can wait twenty-four to seventy-two hours, they are in a crisis; and if they can wait for a longer period, they may merely be experiencing a problem.

Regardless of what definition of crisis is used, professionals generally agree that crisis intervention focuses on a range of phenomena that affect the biopsychosocial functioning of an individual, family, or group, creating a state of disequilibrium. These phenomena include stresses relating to disordered communication patterns, disrupted networks of role relationships, and dissonant values. The causes of these dysfunctional phenomena are as varied as the families and individuals who experience them and as complicated as the neighborhoods and larger social systems in which these individuals, families, and groups live.

In a general sense, crisis intervention is a process for actively influencing psychosocial functioning during a period of disequilibrium in order to alleviate the immediate impact of disruptive stressful events and to help mobilize the manifest and latent psychological capabilities and social resources of persons directly affected by the crisis (and often the key persons in the social environment) for coping adaptively with the effects of stress. More specifically, the crisis clinician's interventive efforts have two principal aims: (1) to cushion the stressful event by immediate or emergency emotional and environmental first aid and (2) to strengthen the person in his or her coping and integrative struggles through immediate therapeutic clarification and guidance during the crisis period.

Concept of Crisis

Crisis is a useful conceptual device for understanding the behavior of individuals and families under stress. However, there has been some confusion regarding terminology. For example, it is difficult to objectively differentiate "stress"—the specific event that may precipitate a crisis—from "strain"—the response to that event. Stress and crisis are often used interchangeably, thus robbing the term "crisis" of precise meaning. Although all people face stress as part of the human condition, not all stressful experiences produce crisis situations.

References to crisis intervention as a theory are another source of confusion. The constructs and techniques of the crisis approach—like virtually all psychotherapeutic modalities—lack the formal attributes of systematically validated scientific theory (Auerbach & Stolberg, 1986). However, a growing body of clinical research concerning stress-response phenomena (Horowitz & Kaltreider, 1980; Horowitz, 1986) provides a promising pathway toward developing a science of crisis intervention. For practice applications of Horowitz's stress-response research, see chapters 2 (post-traumatic stress disorders), 3 (rape), 5 (adult survivors of incest and molestation), and 9 (catastrophic illness) of the present volume.

Another conceptual issue, the difficulty of objectively differentiating a crisis response from ordinary problem-solving behavior, has already been suggested. (This point is elaborated in chapter 8 of the present volume.)

Crisis Sequence

Because the stress–crisis sequence involves a complex set of biopsychosocial forces, crisis, in this volume, is generally viewed as a configuration involving (1) a specific and identifiable *stressful precipitating event*, (2) the *perception* of the event as meaningful and threatening, (3) the disorganization or disequilibrium *response* resulting from the stressful event, and (4) the coping and interventive tasks involved in *resolution*, which may be adaptive or maladaptive. The term "configuration" is used to convey the idea that the phases of the crisis sequence are interlocking. For purposes of analysis, however, it is necessary to separate the components of the configuration. A crisis intervention approach pays attention to the elements of this configuration as well as to the prompt accessibility of treatment, which should be as close as possible to the impact of the stress and crisis response. In essence, then, the crisis state reflects the perception of and response to an internal or external stress that is experienced by the individual or individuals involved as a threat to vital goals such as life, security, and affectional ties.

As noted by Mor-Barak (see chapter 14), other ways of conceptualizing the crisis configuration exist—notably, the formulation of a "hazardous event" disturbing a person's steady state and thus creating a state of "vulnerability." If the ensuing anxiety cannot be "resolved, avoided, or redefined," tension mounts. A "precipitating factor" can then trigger a state of "active crisis," followed by "reintegration" until a new steady state is achieved (Jacobson, 1980; Golan, 1987). We find, however, that the hazardous event is often equated with the "precipitating factor," for example, the sudden loss of a loved one. Frequently, there is a concatenation of predisposing and triggering events, each of which is *perceived* as threatening, thus inducing a cumulative disequilibrium leading to a crisis *response*, followed by adaptive or maladaptive coping aimed at *resolution* of the crisis predicament.

Our definition of the crisis configuration (see Figure 1) is adapted from Hill's (1965) classic formulation of the intervening variables that "transform a stressor event into a crisis" (p. 36). Hill's conceptual framework outlines the following ABCX formula, which is applicable to individuals as well as to families: "A (the stressor event) interacting with B (the family's crisis-meeting resources) → interacting with C (the definition the family makes of the event) → produces X (the crisis)" (p. 36).

FIGURE 1. The crisis intervention "roller coaster."

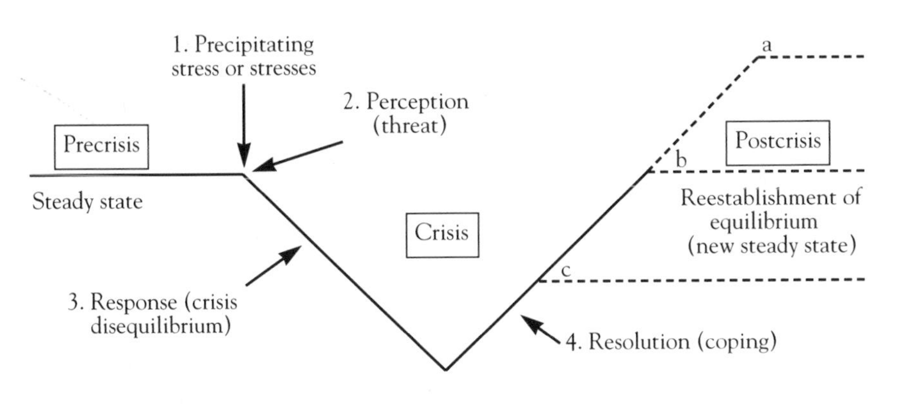

1. Precipitating stress (triggering event or events)
2. Perception (threatening to life goals, affectional ties, security)
3. Response (crisis state, with signs of disequilibrium)
4. Resolution (adaptive or maladaptive coping with crisis tasks)
   a. New postcrisis equilibrium is better than precrisis steady state.
   b. Postcrisis equilibrium is about the same as precrisis state.
   c. New postcrisis equilibrium is less satisfactory than the precrisis state.

Adapted from Hill, R. (1965). Generic features of families under stress. In H. J. Parad (Ed.), *Crisis intervention: Selected readings* (pp. 32–52). New York: Family Service Association of America. Used with permission.

Studying families in crisis, McCubbin and Patterson (1983) and Van Hook (1987) expanded Hill's formula by advancing a "double ABCX model," which focuses over time on the dynamic interactions among participants in the crisis drama and the effects of these interactions on crisis outcome. For example, in her study of distressed farm families, Van Hook points out that during an economic crisis a farmer's wife may seek outside employment. This coping effort leads to an increase in family income, which is adaptive for the family. The wife's employment, however, may create a new stress for the husband if she is less emotionally available to him than she was during the precrisis steady state. The husband may then perceive the wife's new status as threatening to their relationship. Thus a new crisis may be induced as part of the trade-off cost for crisis resolution. Basic to this expanded model of interactional crisis phenomena is the understanding that perceptions of and responses to stress reflect the participants' sense of internal as well as external reality and therefore have reciprocal, reverberating effects within the circularity of the family system (Van Hook, 1987).

Applicable to families as well as to individuals is the useful concept of a "crisis matrix" within which life events requiring coping for extended periods (for example, separation–divorce, immigration to a foreign country) can be viewed in terms of "vulnerable" stages that may or may not reflect a crisis response (Jacobson & Portuges, 1976; Jacobson, 1980). Although the following material focuses on the individual, we shall return to the family in crisis in a later section of this chapter.

The following interconnected assumptions (Parad, 1977), commonly used to explain the phenomena of the crisis sequence, have been discussed in detail by Lindemann (1956) and Caplan (1964)—the two main formulators of the crisis approach.

1. When a stressful event becomes a crisis, there is, by definition, a period of disequilibrium during which the individual or family is both vulnerable to further breakdown and amenable to positive and corrective influence—hence the familiar observation that crisis means both danger and opportunity.

2. The crisis is characterized by a significant turning point (often described as "the point of no return") requiring the use of new coping mechanisms.

3. This turning point, accompanied by mounting anxiety, tension, and struggle, often involves the mobilization of previously hidden resources.

4. The tasks posed by the crisis situation are beyond the normal coping mechanisms of the individual, whose resources (and perhaps those of the primary group network of which he or she is part) are overtaxed.

5. The duration of crisis is more or less limited, depending on the nature and perception of the threatening event, response patterns, and individual and group problem-solving resources. Most crises are self-limiting in that during the crisis-response phase, intense anxiety can be tolerated only temporarily.

6. A new equilibrium arising from a complex of homeostatic mechanisms sets in, often within four to six weeks, leading to a level of mental health and social functioning that theoretically may be the same as, better than, or less satisfactory than the precrisis level (see Figure 1). Hence some families emerge from crises as stronger and more effective units, whereas other families become weaker, and still others become dismembered.

7. The crisis situation imposes various affective, cognitive, and behavioral tasks to be mastered. These tasks vary from stress to stress and have been partially documented through empirical research. For example, mastery of the special tasks involved in coping with the birth of a premature baby is likely to lead to a successful outcome, but unsuccessful coping usually leads to a mentally unhealthy outcome, which may be characterized by maternal overprotectiveness or incomplete bonding. One of these tasks, from the mother's viewpoint, is to face and accept the feeling of failure often associated with premature birth. A related task is to visit and observe the baby in the hospital nursery, thus making the adjustment to the care of the baby at home more manageable. A more common crisis situation is that of bereavement, the successful resolution of which depends on the person's ability to cope with the normal tasks of "grief work." As pointed out by Lindemann (1944), these tasks include (1) disconnecting oneself from psychological bondage to the deceased ("burying the dead") by experiencing the normal misery of mourning (for example, sadness, feelings of somatic distress, weakness, preoccupation with the image of the deceased, temporary feelings of unreality, and guilt), (2) readapting oneself to the environment in which the loved one is missing, and (3) reconnecting oneself to new social relationships. Those who show maladaptive grief reactions, for example, an inability to face the reality of loss or overidentification with the deceased, can often be steered by mental health workers toward adaptive mastery of the grief tasks. The mushrooming literature on death and dying draws heavily on Lindemann's early formulations (1944 & 1956) of the

bereavement crisis (Kübler-Ross, 1969; Parkes, 1972; Davanloo, 1980; Bowlby, 1980; Raphael, 1983).

8. With the overpowering of available coping and adaptive mechanisms, the stressful event typically reactivates old problems from the near or distant past, thereby making it possible to rework previously unresolved problems, which themselves may represent the sequelae of previous crisis situations that were unsuccessfully mastered. Thus the individual has another opportunity—a second chance—to deal with old problems that have erupted under the pressure of the crisis situation.

9. During the crisis period, the individual is in a state of high anxiety. The characteristic signs of crisis response are familiar to anyone who has experienced a life crisis. There are changes and upsets in eating, sleeping, dreaming, lovemaking, feeling, thinking, and doing. The important aspects to note are disruptions in previous behaviors and modes of functioning that signal a person's inability to cope in his or her customary way.

The following nine "senses" have been found useful by crisis workers at the Benjamin Rush Center for Problems of Living.*

1. *Bewilderment*: "I never felt this way before."

2. *Danger*: "I feel so nervous and scared—something terrible is going to happen."

3. *Confusion*: "I can't think clearly. My mind isn't working right."

4. *Impasse*: "I feel stuck. Nothing I do seems to help."

5. *Desperation*: "I've got to do something—don't seem to know what, though."

6. *Apathy*: "I really don't care. I'm in a zero situation."

7. *Helplessness*: "I can't manage this myself. I need help."

8. *Urgency*: "I need help now."

9. *Discomfort*: "I feel miserable, restless, and unsettled."

Thus, the person feels powerless and perhaps hopeless, afraid he or she is headed in the wrong direction. The individual's ego patterns therefore are more likely to be open to influence and corrective intervention. As defenses are lowered during this temporary period of disequilibrium, the individual is usually more accessible to therapeutic influence than he or she was prior to the crisis or will be following the establishment of a new equilibrium, with its accompanying consolidation of defensive patterns. Hence, a minimal preventive or therapeutic force may have a maximal effect during this period.

Typical clinical responses to crises may roughly be classified in terms of dominant affective themes or moods. For example, events that threaten physical well-being lead to anxiety states, loss of object relationships lead to depression, and "growth" or "maturational" crises often evoke a sense of challenge to seize the opportunity for effective mastery of future life situations.

Cumming and Cumming (1962) outlined three broad types of crisis situations that may enhance or endanger personality functioning: (1) those that are "biologically tinged" (such as those that occur during adolescence or menopause) and are therefore inevitable and may be anticipated as part of the

---

*The editors appreciate the contribution of the late Martin Strickler, who formulated this profile material, which has been adopted for use in this chapter.

life cycle; (2) those that are "environmentally tinged" (for example, a change of job or retirement) and are somewhat less inevitable but usually anticipated; and (3) those that are "adventitious" (disasters such as floods and fires, which are attributable to sheer chance and thus cannot be anticipated). Thus the probability of occurrence moves along a biopsychosocial continuum from certainty to random chance.

In this context, some observers refer to the "normal" crisis. For example, Erikson (1959) refers to normal and maturational crises that all human beings experience in the process of growing up. These crises may be prolonged periods of marked physical, psychological, and social change that are characterized by common disturbances in thought and feeling. At puberty, for example, a complex of biopsychosocial stimuli must be successfully mediated if the next maturational stage is to yield its full potential for further growth and development. Erikson's concept of normative or "epigenetic" crisis, referring to years of growth or change in the human life cycle, obviously differs from typical clinical usage, which involves a tighter time frame.

Cumming and Cumming (1962) have defined crisis as "the impact of any event that challenges the assumptive state and forces the individual to change his view of or readapt to the world, himself, or both" (p. 54). The resolution of crisis leads to "new combinations of established (ego) sets" (coping abilities). A problem, in contrast to a crisis, does not necessarily challenge the assumptive state and implies that the available ego sets (and their related adaptation mechanisms and role repertoires) are serviceable. Thus it is generally unnecessary to call into action novel methods of coping. Successful resolution of crises makes it possible to master future vicissitudes with less anxiety and vulnerability. A lifetime of effective mastery of crisis situations ideally contributes to a mature and stable ego state—a concept that seems analogous to Erikson's (1959) life-cycle concept of "generativity," that is, "interest in establishing or guiding the next generation . . . or other forms of altruistic concern or . . . creativity" (p. 97). A few theoreticians have contributed to the development of typologies concerning the severity of the stressor (in terms of aversiveness), probability of occurrence, and strategies for prevention and intervention (Schulberg & Sheldon, 1968; Auerbach & Stolberg, 1986).

Timing and Time Limits

To recapitulate, during the active state of crisis, the person experiences a turning point. Sooner or later, but generally within four to six weeks according to Lindemann and Caplan, things get better or worse because nature abhors a vacuum. Thus a state of crisis is by its very nature time-limited. As stated earlier, a minimum of therapeutic intervention during the brief crisis period can often produce a maximum therapeutic effect through the use of supportive social resources and focused treatment techniques. Hence, crisis intervention services are usually short-term.

Because this chapter presents a time-structured approach to crisis intervention, brief therapy will be considered in general and time limits in particular. Whereas crisis intervention services are usually brief, not all brief therapy is to be equated with crisis intervention. Crisis intervention may involve a specific

TABLE 1. Use of the crisis approach and the time dimension in mental health practice.

PSTT	Non-PSTT
Crisis oriented	
Early accessibility at time of request for help (within twenty-four to seventy-two hours of the "cry for help") Use of PSTT limits (specific number or approximate range of interviews or weeks— determined at intake—to be utilized during crisis response and resolution phases) Use of task-centered techniques Focused attention to crisis configuration (precipitating event, perception of threat, response, and resolution) (+ +)	Early accessibility at time of request for help (within twenty-four to seventy-two hours of the "cry for help") Open-ended orientation toward time dimension; duration of contact may be informally brief (no time contract made during intake phase, that is, first or second interviews; or contact may be "long-term": crisis intervention may be regarded primarily as point of entry into an extended treatment service Some attention to elements of crisis configuration (+ −)
Noncrisis oriented	
May be short or long waiting period Use of PSTT limits: contract for specific predetermined number of interviews, determined at intake Use of task-centered or other goal-oriented techniques No special attention to crisis configuration (− +)	May be short or long waiting period Open-ended orientation toward time dimension; no use of PSTT limits No special attention to crisis configuration May be oriented to specific or diffuse goals (− −)

Adapted from Parad, H. J. (1982). Brief family therapy. In H. Schulberg & M. Killilea (Eds.), *The modern practice of community mental health: A volume in honor of Gerald Caplan* (pp. 419–443). San Francisco: Jossey–Bass. Used with permission.

or approximate number of interviews or weeks of treatment as part of the treatment arrangement. Several rationales have been offered for the desirability of time limits in therapy. One commonly advanced argument is that time limits may increase the client's *and* the worker's motivation.

The seemingly simple question of how brief is brief treatment is actually very complex (Wells, 1982). Some professionals consider brief treatment to consist of a single session; others think it should involve approximately six sessions; still others define brief therapy as extending up to twenty or even forty or more interviews (Budman & Gurman, 1988). A nationwide study of crisis-oriented treatment in family counseling agencies and children's psychiatric services demonstrated that from 80 percent to 90 percent of all planned short-term cases were seen for up to twelve interviews over a period of up to three months (Parad & Parad, 1968). A *planned* short-term treatment (PSTT) approach involves the designation of a predetermined specific number of interviews or weeks of treatment within the first or second session with the client, family, or group.

In reviewing a number of studies of PSTT, Bloom (1980) suggests that the renewal of interest in PSTT has been influenced by at least three developments: issues relating to efficiency, changing concepts of and approaches to psychotherapy, and the conclusion drawn by many researchers that PSTT—in relation to the focal problem—is generally as effective as long-term and open-ended treatment and is often even more effective. A census of family service agencies concluded that formal, planned short-term treatment is generally cost effective, thus suggesting that PSTT not only can reduce the number of dropouts from treatment but can improve treatment outcomes in less time than that involved in traditional open-ended services (Beck & Jones, 1973). In a perceptive article on the historical background and future of brief psychotherapy, Marmor (1979) concludes that "the trend of the future can be expected to be toward short-term therapies" (p. 149). This position is supported by Butcher and Koss (1978) in their conclusion that "comparative studies of brief and unlimited therapies show essentially no difference in results" (p. 758). This finding is reaffirmed in their 1987 review of several approaches to time-limited therapy, including crisis intervention, behavioral, behavioral/cognitive, and psychodynamic orientations (Koss & Butcher, 1987, p. 662).

Thus, time and timing are important in crisis counseling. Practice-derived wisdom suggests that access to help should be available early and that help is best timed at the onset of a crisis experience. However, issues such as how many contacts there should be, how they should be spaced, and for what duration for each individual, family, or other small group are less settled. Mental health practice tends to be flexible and is often based on matters of expediency as well as on the style and temperament of practitioners. There seems to be no magic in the six-week pattern of crisis intervention first suggested by Caplan, although in a nationwide study six was the modal number of interviews used in PSTT crisis-oriented programs (Parad & Parad, 1968). Practice, of course, varies greatly, from marathon groups to once-a-week sessions for six to twelve or more weeks. Empirically derived findings concerning the optimal number, frequency, and spacing of treatment contacts would be useful to those interested in both crisis intervention and brief therapy.

The paradigm presented in Table 1 attempts to clarify the use of the crisis approach and the structured use of time in mental health practice. As indicated in this paradigm, the following are four logical service categories with respect to the dimensions of crisis and time:

1. PSTT crisis-oriented services: a great deal of crisis intervention work falls within this cell.

2. Non-PSTT crisis-oriented services: the crisis may afford entry to open-ended, long-term therapy.

3. PSTT non–crisis-oriented services: many forms of brief therapy are offered in human service programs (see Budman, 1981; Budman & Gurman, 1988).

4. Services that are neither PSTT nor crisis-oriented, that is, most traditional psychodynamic and other open-ended therapies.

This paradigm clarifies a point all too frequently confused by many practitioners—namely, that not all brief-service programs are oriented to a crisis framework and not all crisis-oriented programs are geared exclusively to brief service, let alone to time-structured approaches.

Importance in Human Services

Why is crisis intervention important in the field of human services? This question can be answered by referring to the universality of human experience with life crises causing disruption in people's ability to cope. Crises occur wherever there are people—at home, at school, at work, or at leisure. Informal crisis counseling is usually part of everybody's personal, family, and social functioning in the sense that we help each other by listening, encouraging, and giving information and advice during acutely stressful periods. When offered by trained, sensitive caregivers and professionals, crisis intervention services can be of special importance. People in crisis predicaments are often amenable to preventive, protective, and corrective influences because by definition their defenses are lower during the high-anxiety stages of most crisis experiences than they are before or after a crisis when defenses are in place and they are thus less motivated to change. To cite Bloom (1980), "an hour spent with the client at the time of the crisis has the same potential benefit as perhaps 10 hours spent with that same client after the enhanced state of readiness to change has passed" (p. 114).

Through prompt and effective intervention, practitioners can help prevent the development of more serious psychosocial problems that often occur after the crisis or emergency is over if the crisis is maladaptively rather than adaptively resolved. Hence, the last four chapters of this volume focus on preventive interventions. Most crisis intervention experiences are classified by mental health experts as early secondary prevention. Certain protective interventions, for example, on behalf of children who are potentially at risk but who have shown no obvious signs of difficulty, may be classified as primary prevention. Still other corrective intervention procedures, because they are utilized some time after the onset of the original problem, may be classified as tertiary prevention. Thus crisis intervention services serve both preventive and remedial purposes; they may well strengthen the person's ability to learn from the crisis experience and offer the individual opportunities for growth. Ideally, they prevent or at the very least help reduce human suffering and pain at times of illness, bereavement, divorce, disaster, or other severe stress.

Historical Background

The present section provides a selective overview of the major theoretical, program, legislative, and research developments in the evolution of contemporary crisis intervention. It is not intended as a comprehensive chronicle of the use of the crisis concept or of time-limits in the mental health professions and social and behavioral sciences. Many contributions from psychiatry, psychology, and sociology over the past forty years have been sketched by Golan (1987) in a recent review.

The roots of crisis intervention may be traced to several sources. During World War II and the Korean and the Vietnam wars mental health professionals learned that soldiers suffering from combat fatigue (now called post-traumatic stress disorder) were more likely to be returned to combat duty if they were treated at or near the front lines by immediate brief therapy, thus avoiding regression and secondary gain as well as feelings of failure and guilt about abandoning their buddies (Menninger, 1948; Glass, 1954; Laufer, Frey-Wouters, & Gallops, 1985). The rationale for emergency military psychiatry—similar to today's crisis intervention approach—included the general expectation that the traumatized soldier would soon recompensate and return to active duty if given prompt, supportive therapy with opportunity to ventilate and debrief; reassurance that his symptoms were typical of persons exposed to extreme stress; and proper medication, if needed. It was found that soldiers who were permanently withdrawn from front-line assignments also experienced loss of peer group support, which aggravated their sense of stigma about being a psychiatric casualty.

Lindemann's (1944) classic study of the bereaved disaster victims of a 1942 fire in the Coconut Grove nightclub in Boston was a pioneering contribution to the development of preventive crisis intervention for persons who are unlikely to cope appropriately with the crisis of bereavement. In 1948 Lindemann organized an innovative community mental health program, the Wellesley Human Relations Service, where his colleagues, Gerald Caplan, Donald Klein, and others, stimulated research on primary prevention relating to school entry and other life-cycle transitions (Klein & Ross, 1958).

Although the foundation work was done by Lindemann, Caplan is generally acknowledged as the master architect of preventive crisis intervention. In 1954, under the aegis of the Harvard University School of Public Health, Caplan established the Harvard Family Guidance Center, a multidisciplinary crisis research and consultation project to study the impact of four stressors—premature birth, birth of children with congenital anomalies, birth of twins, and tuberculosis—on ordinary families in a lower- and working-class area of Boston. As the social work member of this mental health–public health team, Howard Parad went beyond the project's research focus to explore and elaborate experimental techniques for preventive and corrective (early secondary) crisis intervention (H. J. Parad, 1961), with consultation from Caplan (Parad & Caplan, 1960).

Caplan's metatheory of preventive psychiatry provided much of the rationale for the community mental health ideology of that era. The Harvard Family Guidance Center and its successor, the Harvard Laboratory of Community Psychiatry, trained leaders in community-oriented psychiatry, psychology, social work, and nursing who, like itinerant preachers, traveled throughout the United States and abroad to spread the gospel of community mental health in general and crisis intervention in particular (Schulberg & Killilea, 1982). A succession of studies concerned with a broad range of health and situational crises and their implications for individual and family functioning as well as for preventive crisis intervention and crisis consultation were initiated. Among the social workers who participated with Caplan in the Harvard studies were Kaplan (Kaplan & Mason, 1960) and Rapoport (1962).

Though sometimes ignored in reviews of crisis intervention, Bellak's contributions to brief emergency psychotherapy (BEP) are important (Bellak & Siegel, 1983). In 1958, Bellak started the first psychiatric emergency twenty-four-hour walk-in clinic in the United States—the Trouble-Shooting Clinic at Elmhurst City Hospital in New York. Based primarily on psychodynamic theory, the BEP approach borrowed selectively from learning and systems theories and was limited to five sessions plus follow-up. While focusing on the patient's crisis predicament, the BEP therapist also attended to the "establishment of causality—of continuity between the present and the past" (Bellak & Siegal, 1983, p. 3).

A few years later, in 1962, Jacobson, influenced by Caplan's theories, launched the Benjamin Rush Center for Problems in Living in Los Angeles. Annually serving approximately 1,750 persons in crisis, the center has been part of the Didi Hirsch Community Mental Health Center since 1975. A walk-in clinic, it offers up to six sessions (the number used by most crisis clinics) to individuals and families coping with life crises. Jacobson and his colleagues have made significant contributions to the literature concerning crisis intervention with individuals, families, groups, and communities (Jacobson, 1980; Strickler & Allgeyer, 1967; Brown, 1976).

The Quick Response Unit of Jewish Family Service of New York City provides a more recent example of an innovative crisis program combining the following components: prompt response to the cry for help, flexible use of time limits (up to six sessions) and spacing of interviews, selective use of home visits, involvement of significant others, and mobilization of social resources (Goldring, 1980).

Brief treatment is not new in psychotherapy or social work, although it has received varying degrees of emphasis reflecting both the evolution of therapeutic techniques and changes in the larger social milieu within which the therapeutic professions function (L. G. Parad, 1971). Bellak and Siegel (1983), in their review of brief and emergency psychotherapy, cite Freud's treatment of conductor Bruno Walter in six sessions for paralysis of his arm and of composer Gustav Mahler for impotence in a marathon four-hour session as support for their allegation that originally Freud often practiced brief therapy. In a review of short-term treatment in psychoanalysis and psychoanalytically oriented psychotherapy, Malan (1963) commented that "the early analysts seem to have possessed the secret of brief psychotherapy, but with increasing experience to have lost it" (p. 9). Although Freud (1933) foresaw the probability that "the application of our therapy to numbers will compel us to alloy the pure gold of analysis plentifully with the copper of direct suggestion" (p. 402), the adaptation of insights from psychoanalysis to brief psychotherapy, which began in the 1920s and took root in the 1930s, came to fruition with the development of ego psychology.

The persistence of long-term intensive treatment as a therapeutic desideratum was challenged in 1938 by the Chicago Institute for Psychoanalysis, under the leadership of Franz Alexander (Alexander & French, 1946). Recognizing there was "no simple correlation between therapeutic results and the length and intensity of treatment" (p. iii), the institute began a collaborative investigation of both the duration and depth of treatment in a search for a shorter and more efficient means of psychotherapy. Planned prior to entry of the United States into World War II, the institute's organization of the Brief Psychotherapy Council, which met in 1942 and 1944, was given additional impetus by the massive need for psychotherapeutic intervention for servicemen and their families (Chicago Institute for Psychoanalysis, 1942). By the third and final meeting in 1946, the name was changed to the Psychotherapy Council, reflecting a temporary decline of interest in brief psychotherapy. Some experimentation with short-term psychoanalytic psychotherapy was also conducted at the Menninger Clinic (Berliner, 1941, 1945). The war brought new awareness of the role of stress in neuroses as well as an opportunity to test the principles of brief psychotherapy (Grinker & Spiegel, 1945; Beck & Robbins, 1946).

The utilization of brief psychotherapy in medical practice, especially in relation to psychosomatic illness, was exemplified by Deutsch's (1949) application of his interviewing technique, the associative anamnesis, to develop what he termed "sector therapy."

During the 1940s most of the articles and books on short-term therapy stressed the following factors: (1) the use of a controlled relationship and modification of the use of transference, with emphasis on positive transference, (2) focus upon a carefully delineated presenting or central problem, (3) focus on the ego and mobilization of its capabilities to deal with stress, (4) the linking of present conflicts with past unresolved conflicts, and (5) the therapeutic goal of restoration to functioning. Emphasis should be on reality factors and on the present rather than on the past. For example, Deutsch (1949) describes the purpose of the associative anamnesis:

> to keep the therapeutic approach within certain strata of the personality. . . . It links up as soon as possible a manifest symptom or a problem of the present with the underlying conflicts and their expression in the past. The free association guides the patient into the past, but the technic confronts him constantly with the reality" (p. 28).

In a review article Charen (1948) sounded a contemporary note—as relevant now as it was revolutionary forty-one years ago—when he linked brief methods of psychotherapy with the need for preventive psychiatry and for therapeutic psychiatry as an integral aspect of public health. Stone (1951) called for empirical research to determine the therapeutic effectiveness, scope of applicability, and techniques that might successfully be used in brief psychotherapy.

From today's perspective, the preoccupation of the clinicians of the late 1950s and 1960s with what were termed the "continuity" studies seems ludicrous. These studies of short-term cases in a variety of clinical settings had diverse emphases, purposes, and methods but a central focus; that is, why were short-term cases not long-term or "continued" cases (Shyne, 1957; Levinger, 1960)? These studies explored motivational, psychological, and sociocultural variables such as appropriateness of referrals, community image of agencies and clinics, discongruity between client and helper, adequacy of communication between client and helper, and the client's attribution of responsibility for the problem to self rather than to others.

Although the continuity studies were chiefly concerned with "unplanned" short-term treatment, the relentless pressure of service demand, combined with the continuing concern over persons who failed to use the therapeutic services offered them, led to experimental efforts to eliminate or reduce the waiting period by offering group application interviews. Primarily intended to screen applicants, the serendipitous effect of these efforts was the discovery that "a large number of cases . . . came to a successful conclusion during the application process because a short-term service was all that was needed" (Dickstein, Young, & Levin, 1961, p. 6).

Throughout the 1950s, much was written about goal-limited treatment based upon concepts from ego psychology. The elements of ego psychology, precipitating stress, crisis, and planned use of time were *combined*, in various configurations, in a series of experimental projects and studies designed to meet increasing service demand and to better utilize scarce therapeutic personnel.

In the United States, national and state legislation further accelerated the need for experimentation to more effectively provide emergency mental health and crisis services, including:

1. The provision in the 1963 Community Mental Health Centers Act (PL-88-174) requiring twenty-four-hour crisis or emergency services as one of the five compulsory program features in community mental health centers financed under this landmark legislation.

2. Policy decisions to depopulate state mental hospitals, thus emphasizing services for the client or patient in his or her own community. The decision to deinstitutionalize challenged the resources of many communities as well as the tolerance threshhold of many families, as the number of patients discharged increased. The discharged patient, who all too often is dismissed from the state hospital without the support of an adequate aftercare plan, therefore often decompensates and requires crisis intervention services (see chapter 10).

3. The Emergency Medical Services System Act of 1973, providing guidelines for medical and psychological emergencies (see chapter 9 for an example of a medical emergency system).

4. The Crisis Counseling Assistance and Training Section of the Federal Disaster Relief Act of 1974 (42 USC-5183), providing funds from the National Institute of Mental Health for brief crisis services to disaster victims as well as short-term training activities—often sponsored by the Red Cross and other rescue organizations—for crisis workers to staff one-stop disaster aid centers.

Research Developments and Knowledge Base

Basic to an historical overview of the crisis approach is an understanding of the many studies that have contributed to the interdisciplinary knowledge base of contemporary crisis intervention. Unfortunately, these studies are mainly exploratory–descriptive rather than experimental in design.

In the early 1960s, a variety of commonly encountered stressful events that may be crisis inducing or potentially hazardous were studied: (1) loss or threatened loss of a significant relationship, (2) addition of one or more new individuals into a social "orbit," and (3) transition in social status and role sets as a consequence of such factors as entry into school or college, marriage, divorce, or horizontal or vertical social mobility (Klein & Lindemann, 1961). All stressful events are obviously patterned by sociocultural arrangements as well as by psychodynamic perceptions.

Later, Holmes and Masuda (1973) developed a promising but yet to be fully validated scale that assigns values to diverse life changes, including events such as retirement (45 points), marital separation (65 points), divorce (73 points), and death of a spouse (100 points). If changes during a year add up to 300 points, a danger point has been reached. In one of Holmes's samples, 80 percent of the subjects who scored more than 300 points experienced severe depressions, heart attacks, or other serious illnesses. As previously mentioned, from a sociological perspective, Hill (1965) developed a highly useful classification scheme for analyzing "stressor events" in terms of their source, their perceptual meaning, and their organizational effects on the family.

Many researchers have grappled with the complex conceptual and methodological problems relating to the measurement of these variables in the crisis configuration. Bloom (1965) studied the rate of agreement of mental health experts in assessing the presence or absence of crisis in terms of a known precipitating event; absence of such an event led to the judgment of "psychiatric disorder" rather than crisis. Partially replicating Bloom's methodology, Neuwelt (1988) recently investigated the responses of 100 practitioners to case analogues. She found that respondents were able to differentiate between crisis and noncrisis situations on the basis of the presence of a specific precipitating stress or stressors as well as the "behavioral indicators of a crisis state" (p. 201). Dyer (1965) used independent judges to arrive at "crisis scores." Freeman, Kalis, and Harris (1965) developed an instrument for studying the precipitating event and the behaviors related to it. And, as peviously indicated, Caplan and his Harvard colleagues found associations between various types of crisis-coping behavior during the disequilibrium "response" phase and the mental health outcome during the "resolution phase" of the crisis sequence (Caplan, Mason, & Kaplan, 1965).

In contrast to most of the above studies, which lack control groups, a few researchers have investigated *experimentally* designed crisis-oriented and time-limited programs in hospitals, psychiatric clinics, family service agencies, police departments, and other settings. From the perspectives of psychiatry and social work, Langsley and Kaplan (1968) combined time-limited approaches, family therapy, and crisis intervention into an experimental action research project that produced an effective community-care alternative to mental hospitalization. Follow-up studies of both experimental and control groups were completed at six- and eighteen-month intervals after discharge from treatment. Follow-up data indicated that family crisis therapy significantly reduced the rate and duration of hospitalization as compared with patients initially receiving traditional hospital care (Langsley, 1980). This investigation of mentally disordered patients (who were randomly assigned to conventional in-patient care or experimental out-patient family-oriented crisis therapy) is notable because it demonstrated both the applicability and cost-effectiveness of crisis intervention.

Similarly, studies by Bill (1969) and by Decker and Stubblebine (1972) indicated the effectiveness of brief crisis intervention techniques in reducing the incidence of hospitalization. Bill compared the rates of psychiatric hospital admissions from four Delaware regions, two of which were served by a new crisis intervention program. The regions thus served showed a significant decrease in the number of state hospital admissions. The research by Decker and Stubblebine not only showed a significant reduction in the hospitalization rate of a sample treated by crisis intervention techniques but also revealed no increase in the patients' disabilities or suicidal potential.

Researchers have also inquired into other topics pertinent to time-limited crisis intervention activities. Driscoll, Meyer, and Schanie (1973) studied the effects of a special training project for police officers in Louisville, Kentucky, dealing with family crisis calls. Patterned after Bard's (1970) New York City police crisis intervention program, the Louisville program confirmed the hypothesis that policemen trained in crisis intervention would perform more effectively than would those who were not trained. Baron and Feeney (1976) and Parsons and Alexander (1973) documented the effectiveness of family crisis therapy programs aimed at reducing recidivism by diverting delinquent and predelinquent adolescents from further involvement with the court and correctional systems.

In their descriptive study of 1,656 cases of planned, short-term, crisis-oriented treatment, Parad and Parad (1968) found that if the clinician's impression was used as a yardstick, two-thirds of the cases showed improvement, at least in relation to the problem for which help was originally sought. According to the client's impression (as reported by clinicians), three-fourths of the cases demonstrated improvement. Parad and Parad concluded that continued experimentation with crisis-oriented, planned, short-term treatment (PSTT) showed promise of serving an increasing number of individuals and families under stress through the redeployment of available professional personnel. In a rigorously controlled study of treatment of distressed marital and parent–child relationships in 120 families at the Community Service Society in New York, Reid and Shyne (1969) found that eight preplanned interviews, conducted according to a "task-centered" approach over a period of three months, produced results that were not only equal but in many instances superior to those achieved in open-ended family counseling. Also impressive was the finding in the 1973 census of family service agencies that PSTT was definitely cost-effective. It reduced the number of dropouts from treatment and improved treatment outcomes in less time than that involved in traditional open-ended treatment services (Beck & Jones, 1973).

Crisis Intervention in Emergency Medical Care

A recent study concerning the role of the social worker in emergency medical service (EMS) in Southern California health care facilities (Parad & Houston, 1984) is relevant to the expanding knowledge base of contemporary crisis intervention. Since World War II, the scope and utilization of general hospital emergency services have increased rapidly. In central city ghetto areas, where emergency medical services provide up to 80 percent of the health care for the surrounding population, a significant proportion of patients exhibit urgent psychosocial needs as well as medical problems. The study indicated that clinical social workers employed in emergency medical departments accorded high priority to crisis intervention activities with patients and their families in relation to such stresses as trauma following accidents, catastrophic illness, impending death of a loved one, loss of a loved one, and other critical incidents. Respondents also indicated that emergency social work personnel needed support to avoid burnout associated with their stressful work. Those who help people in crises are themselves vulnerable to personal and family crises. Thus, those who give support also need support.

Among the program guidelines recommended in the study were around-the clock staff, with bilingual skills where needed; a flexible intake system allowing self-referral by patients or their families and reaching out by the social workers to patients in crisis in addition to the physician referral now mandated in most facilities; orientation to the patient's significant others, thus making conjoint and family-crisis intervention viable as part of an interactional approach; systematic follow-up of patients needing aftercare plans, including the monitoring of referrals; adequate orientation for new EMS social work staff and expanded intra- and extramural educational opportunities to improve skills in developing and implementing specialized crisis intervention protocols, for example, in working with victims of rape, sexual abuse, and family violence; and development of staff debriefing and support systems to reduce staff burnout.

Crisis intervention services are, of course, also relevant for patients who require medical care beyond that which is available in the outpatient emergency room (for examples, see chapter 9). An experimental study of the effectiveness of such services for a large group of patients (N = 280) hospitalized due to illness or accident, contrasted with a similar group who did not receive crisis intervention, indicated that those who received crisis treatment were less anxious and perceived themselves as less helpless and more competent upon discharge than did those who did not receive these services. Following discharge, the significant differences between the experimental and control patients were not only maintained but were widened, as reported by follow-up interviewers (twelve to fifteen months postdischarge) who did not know whether patients were in the experimental or control group (Viney, Clarke, Bunn, & Benjamin, 1985).

In summary, during the past thirty years, the concepts of dynamic ego psychology, crisis-inducing stress, planned use of time limits, task-oriented problem solving, and emergency mental health have been operationalized in both experimental and ongoing crisis intervention programs to rapidly meet the needs of people experiencing interpersonal, maturational, and situational crises and to better utilize mental health personnel in a cost-effective manner.

The proliferation of experimentation with planned, short-term treatment may generally be said to have coincided with the emergence of a rationale—namely, the crisis approach. Because, as earlier stated, most crises are time-limited, crisis intervention provided both a rationale and a method for use in brief treatment. Although during the 1960s crisis intervention helped provide PSTT with a conceptual and program rationale, during the 1970s and 1980s systematic experimental research on the favorable cost effectiveness of PSTT gave crisis intervention increasing credibility. It is also interesting to note that Taft's early formulation of time as a key factor in the therapeutic process, which previously was dismissed due to the professional imbroglio of the Freudians versus the Rankians ("functionalist" social workers influenced by Otto Rank's theories of separation, time, choice, and will), could now be reinvigorated and integrated with the crisis intervention framework that emerged in the 1960s (Taft, 1933; Parad & Parad, 1968).

The following interrelated developments contributed to the widespread acceptance of crisis-oriented, brief-treatment approaches: research on precipitating stress and coping behavior; the imbalance between high demand for therapeutic services and scarce resources; recurrent personnel and financial restraints, including the reluctance of many insurance companies to reimburse therapy vendors for long-term treatment; continued emphasis on accountability and related cost/benefit issues; studies of crisis intervention services to certain ethnic groups; the contributions of the newer cognitive, behavioral, humanistic, and eclectic perspectives regarding problem-solving and action-oriented coping repertoires; and the accelerated interest in family therapy. The burgeoning interest of crisis intervention personnel in nonkinship networks and other social systems, reflected in their thinking about the crisis experience in the context of community social supports, has also been important.

Practice Applications

When does the practitioner use crisis techniques? The pragmatic answer is whenever there is an event that precipitates a significant upset in a steady state. Thus crisis intervention has wide applicability and in many programs is the preferred mode of service delivery, as indicated in subsequent chapters of this volume.

It is useful to differentiate direct from indirect interventions. Both are aimed at crisis resolution and have preventive implications at the primary, secondary, and tertiary levels. Direct intervention, the focus of this chapter, refers to client-centered personal services. Indirect intervention (described in chapter 13) encompasses diverse types of consultation to caretakers (such as clergy, physicians, public health nurses, firefighters, and teachers), who may themselves be in a work-related or personal crisis situation or who may seek help when those with whom they deal in their respective professional roles are in a crisis predicament.

Jacobson, Strickler, & Morley (1968) distinguish between "generic" and "individual" crisis intervention. Generic approaches, broadly applicable as a means of primary prevention by paraprofessionals, are addressed entirely to the acute crisis episode as opposed to its developmental antecedents. They utilize techniques such as direct advice, encouragement of adaptive behavior, anticipatory guidance, and environmental manipulation. In contrast, individual approaches, while using similar sustaining techniques, also deal therapeutically with the dynamic connections between the current crisis experience and previous emotional conflicts. Hence, they require the services of mental health professionals. Mental health professionals can be engaged as consultants to caretakers who are or easily can be trained to use population-oriented generic types of crisis intervention (Caplan, 1989). In this manner, they can obviously influence indirectly a much larger number of people in crisis toward adaptive resolutions than can professionals who are engaged exclusively in individual client-centered clinical activities. Ideally, the professional interested in crisis intervention should assume both roles. (For examples, please see chapters 13–16 on preventive intervention.)

In brief, the crisis-oriented therapist should be attuned to three questions. These questions are, of course, relevant to all intake procedures: What is troubling the client? Why does he or she come for help now? What can I do to help? The first two questions concern the client's presenting problem and his or her perception of the crisis-inducing stress, and the third question concerns the actual methods of clinical intervention. These principles and techniques are substantially the same as those used in long-term therapy, but they require certain modifications in approach and emphasis. Specifically, the therapist changes his or her technique by assuming a more active role in order to foster the client's cognitive awareness of the realistic aspects of the stressful situation as well as to avoid regression in the client and to promote mastery within a brief period. The crisis therapist is more likely than are other therapists to give advice, make disciplined use of confrontation techniques, and to use focused rather than diffuse interviewing techniques.

Crisis therapy also accepts and emphasizes limited but significant clear-cut goals more readily than does traditional, open-ended treatment. Techniques of role rehearsal or anticipatory guidance help clients prepare for stressful situations that they are likely to encounter between interviews or after therapy has ended. Homework assignments (for example, keeping a log of critical incidents, checking a community resource, talking with a significant other), similar to those used in task-centered PSTT, are often given to enhance (1) problem-solving between sessions and (2) the client's sense of mastery and accompanying sense of self-esteem.

During the crisis-resolution period, the client often needs the support of community resources and services to relieve environmental pressures that trigger or aggravate the crisis situation. Thus, it must be emphasized that the full benefits of crisis intervention programs can be realized on a long-range basis only when supplemented by adequate community-support systems (for examples, see chapter 16). Ideally, these include homemaker and legal aid services; employment and job training opportunities; income maintenance provisions; a range of housing resources (including independent living, halfway house, crisis hostel, foster care, and other residential facilities geared to the individual's rehabilitation potential); and involvement of families and significant others in the person's social network (Rueveni, 1975). In addition, mentally disordered persons often need appropriate, medically supervised psychotropic medication, as indicated in chapter 10.

It is also important to utilize adventitious influences that may enhance the therapeutic process, for example, the client's tendency to invest trust and hopeful expectancy in the therapist, often an aspect of positive transference (Frank, 1973). The crisis clinician must be aware of a person's self-help resources and the fact that these natural self-healing efforts are often efficacious.

Theory, practice wisdom, and research point to other familiar principles to guide the crisis counselor in doing planned, brief, goal-oriented therapy (H. J. Parad, 1984).

1. It is important to select a focal problem on which to concentrate. Many authors have stressed that if the worker and client together cannot define a specific workable problem, it is highly unlikely that constructive help can be offered. The worker must differentiate a *general* task (for example, to improve communication between husband and wife) from an *operational* task (for example, an explicit contract between husband and wife specifying that they will talk with each other each evening for at least fifteen minutes in order to maintain an open communicative relationship) (Reid & Epstein, 1972).

2. Planned, brief, goal-oriented crisis intervention assumes that the core conditions originally postulated by Rogers and later investigated by Truax (namely, the worker's positive regard for the client, nonpossessive warmth,

empathic response, and genuine congruence) are necessary but not sufficient conditions for the success of therapy (Truax & Carkhuff, 1967).

3. The worker emphasizes the client's need to experience the successful accomplishment of tasks in order to feel competent, thereby gaining mastery and gradually increasing self-esteem and concurrently the ability to cope with future stress in an adaptive rather than a maladaptive manner.

4. Session by session the worker monitors the outcome of the client's efforts at task fulfillment, reinforcing the client's positive achievements, and exploring obstacles. Although workers must give systematic attention to the agreed-upon tasks in order to stay on course, they must also maintain an open, empathetic, and responsive stance toward the client, lest in their zeal to be goal-focused they are overly rigid. Hence, workers must give balanced attention to both the systematic and responsive elements of the communication process (Reid & Epstein, 1972, 1977).*

Toward an Integrative–Eclectic Orientation

The crisis counselor's basic task is to help clients change those affective (feeling), cognitive (thinking), and behavioral (doing) patterns that hinder effective value clarification and rule making as well as to encourage constructive communication and appropriate role behavior. Thus it is essential to develop a judiciously eclectic approach that attends to these domains of human functioning (feeling, thinking, and doing) in order to help persons in crisis mobilize the resources that will unblock and enhance performance in these vital areas. Eclecticism, which perhaps is regarded pejoratively in some quarters, is a fact of life for most mental health professionals (Jayaratne, 1978; Lazarus, 1976; Fuhriman, Paul, & Burlingame, 1986; L'Abate, 1986).

At the University of Utah Counseling Center, Fuhriman and her colleagues developed a ten-session eclectic, time-limited therapy (ETLT) format based on "principles and themes that were consistently used across a variety of theories and models . . . and were operable in a brief time period" (p. 229). As summarized by Koss and Butcher (1987), these principles include prompt intervention and quick assessment (note the similarity to the early-access requirement of crisis intervention); "quickly established" therapist–client relationship to foster "therapeutic leverage"; structuring the number of sessions; specification of limited goals; active "management of the sessions by the therapist"; development of a guiding focus; adequate opportunity for the client to engage in ventilation and catharsis; and "flexibility in choice of technique" (that is, an eclectic orientation) (p. 662).

Most crisis clinicians would probably subscribe readily to these principles as guidelines for their own practice. Although they may not formally label their theoretical orientations as eclectic or "pluralistic," they pragmatically recognize that (1) no single theory exists to explain all clinical phenomena, nor is such a theory ever likely to exist; (2) different clinical approaches—or different eclectic blends—work well with different clients; and (3) different approaches may be used with the same client at different times. In their book on brief therapy,

*Adapted from H. J. Parad (1984), Time-limited crisis therapy in the workplace: An eclectic perspective. *Social Work Papers, 18*, 20–30. Los Angeles, University of Southern California. Used with permission.

Budman and Gurman (1988) state, "We believe that most brief therapists and even most adherents of psychodynamically-oriented short-term methods are pragmatically eclectic" (p. 10). In our opinion, then, a disciplined eclecticism utilizing *psychodynamic* (Marmor, 1979; Bellak & Siegel, 1983), *existential* (Slaby, 1985), and *cognitive/behavioral* (Alevizos & Liberman, 1976; Kuehnel & Liberman, 1986; Beck, 1976) theories and techniques can facilitate a new synthesis of interlocking modes of clinical intervention. However, unraveling the puzzle of what makes people change and what makes some people responsive to particular approaches is beyond the scope of this chapter.

Because attention is concentrated on the client's current problem in functioning rather than on less immediately relevant childhood antecedents, history taking should be selective in relation to key derivative conflicts. However, a caveat is in order: The crisis clinician should actively explore the connection between the client's current crisis impasse and analogous events, activated by the present crisis, from the recent as well as the remote past. These past events may well represent previous unresolved life crises that the client now has a second chance to resolve adaptively because his or her defenses are more fluid during the "hot" crisis response phase than they will be when the crisis is over. The following case from a crisis clinic dramatically illustrates (1) how the present crisis turmoil may reflect the derepression of unresolved childhood crises and (2) the opportunities for eclectically oriented interventions:

> Mrs. A, a thirty-four-year-old obese woman, visited a walk-in crisis clinic in a panicky state at the urging of her sister. She couldn't stop crying, was "going around in circles," and couldn't get anything done at home. She wanted help because she and her husband were quarreling about unpaid bills. That morning Mr. A left the house and said he would spend the night at a friend's apartment; he had never done this before. Mr. A worked as carpenter for a local contractor. The couple had three children, ages twelve, eleven, and nine. They had been arguing about bills for several weeks. Several days previously, in desperation, Mrs. A pawned Mr. A's shotgun to help pay bills. A few weeks earlier, in the course of one of their fights about money, Mr. A had threatened his wife with the shotgun.
>
> Mrs. A stated that for the past few months she had been unable to take the mail out of the mailbox. When the mail, including bills, was removed by her husband, she was afraid to open and read it, so it was usually left unopened on the dining room table. Hence bills did not get paid. Each person seemed to expect the other to do something about their budget problems.
>
> For the past two months, Mrs. A had had a strange repetitive dream about a casket. She recalled that when she was six, her father, then thirty-five, died suddenly in an accident caused by his drunkenness. (She had been very scared when, at the funeral, her mother had, in reality, told her to kiss her father in the casket.) She had not told her "weird" dream to anyone but the worker because she was scared of her husband's reactions. The casket in the dream reminded her of her mailbox. In three weeks, her husband would be thirty-five. Thinking about his birthday made her anxious. She didn't know why. Crying, she asked for help in getting her husband to return home.

Imagining that we are the intake crisis counselor, let us briefly sketch Mr. and Mrs. A's situation from the perspective of the stress-crisis configuration:

1. *Precipitating stressor(s)*: The immediate triggering event (the "last straw") is Mr. A's threat not to return, preceded by (1) tense quarrels about unpaid bills, (2) Mr. A's disturbing homicidal threat to shoot his wife, and (3) Mrs. A's impulsive pawning of Mr. A's shotgun. Mindful of the difficulty in untangling cause from effect in this not atypical concatenation of domestic disputes, we can at least agree that the above three events represent predisposing stress factors (or "hazardous events").

2. *Perception of stressors*: Panicky, crying, her routines disrupted, Mrs. A clearly feels threatened by the possible loss of her husband's presence in the home, not to mention her surfacing preconscious fear that he may suffer an untimely death, as did her father. Mr. A, we can safely speculate, is furious over the pawning of his shotgun, which he may perceive as a threat to his manliness and status in the family.

3. *Crisis response*: In light of these perceptions, Mrs. A suddenly experiences crisis. Mr. A is probably also experiencing crisis. The typical signs of an active crisis state manifested by Mrs. A are that she can't stop crying and she's immobilized at home—going around in circles. Without seeing Mr. A (he should be involved in treatment, if possible), the counselor may assume that his impulsive departure, which never occurred before, is a sign of crisis and perhaps a cry for help.

4. *Crisis resolution*: Obviously, it is important that the crisis counselor see Mrs. A immediately, consistent with our emphasis on early-access treatment. Of course, intervention choices flow from the counselor's prompt assessment, which is that the couple appears to have a reasonably viable though strained relationship. Using a direct approach, the counselor assures Mrs. A that her dream is very important, while appreciating how frightening it is to her. Although the dream seems "weird," the counselor understands that it relates to her anxiety about her husband's impending birthday.

The counselor might speculate (privately) about oedipal remnants if so inclined (Gardner, 1958). The trauma of her father's death, the counselor later learns, was compounded by Mrs. A's removal to the home of relatives (so she wouldn't be upset!) immediately after the funeral.

This dramatic example of an erupting anniversary syndrome reflects considerable derepression of long-denied bereavement affects, with mounting tension and anxiety about the possible death of her loved/feared/hated husband.

> To foster Mrs. A's coping, the counselor directs Mrs. A to call her husband and tell him about her scary dream. Her sister, who is present for part of the interview, thinks this is a good idea, because Mr. and Mrs. A have a pretty good marriage. The suggestion works: Mr. A listens, not too sympathetically. Thus the couple reestablish contact (which was the worker's goal), and Mr. A returns home.
>
> In the next session, Mrs. A exclaims with tearful agony, "So that's why I don't get the bills from the mailbox—it reminds me of my father's casket in the dream." (The mailbox is of the large "rural delivery" type.) "I'm scared my husband will die when he becomes thirty-five!"

Thus, by affording Mrs. A an opportunity for ventilation and catharsis, and by encouraging her to restore communication with her husband, the counselor helps the couple rapidly achieve equilibrium over a period of four sessions. However, serious unresolved problems obviously remain: the unpaid bills, Mr.

A's threat to use the shotgun, Mrs. A's partially resolved grief regarding her father's traumatic death, Mrs. A's obesity, and Mr. A's tendency to avoid dealing with financial and emotional issues. Thus, this case illustrates both the efficacy and limits of very brief (fewer than six sessions) crisis intervention.

An eclectically skilled therapist would have had the option of treating Mrs. A's phobic reaction to the mailbox through systematic desensitization techniques (guided imagery, muscle relaxation) if the cathartic ventilation used in the crisis counselor's psychodynamic approach had failed to produce quick relief. It is also important to note that according to systematic comparisons of brief behavioral and psychodynamic therapies, symptom substitution, a response often feared by psychodynamic therapists when behavior modification is used, does *not* occur in a statistically significant manner (Sloane, Staples, Cristol, Yorkston, & Whipple, 1975; Wachtel, 1977).

Termination and Follow-up

The planning and implementation of the termination process is another key issue. In crisis-oriented PSTT, the termination is planned at the beginning and anticipated throughout the therapeutic encounter. Structuring the treatment to avoid undue transference dependency, the therapist hopes that the final session—whether it is the sixth, eighth, twelfth, or fourteenth—will be experienced by the client primarily as a summary of what he or she has learned rather than as a serious threat or pervasive loss (Webb, 1985). Ideally, the final session should reinforce the client's accomplishments in dealing with cognitive, affective, and behavioral tasks related to the crisis; afford the client opportunity to express emotions about ending the treatment; consider future tasks, with a sense of challenge and confidence in the client's ability to cope, "knowing that the experience of successful work will continue to guide future behavior despite absence of the ongoing helping relationship" (Webb, 1985, p. 339). We believe that the practice guidelines outlined by Webb facilitate a constructive termination process within a crisis framework (Table 2).

To return to Mr. and Mrs. A: Flushed with enthusiasm about his apparently successful intervention, the relatively inexperienced crisis counselor neglected to plan a follow-up with Mrs. A that, ideally, would involve Mr. A. Such a follow-up would have been more desirable than his simply suggesting that Mrs. A "feel free to call if things don't go well around the time of your husband's birthday." Planned follow-ups—in person, if possible, by telephone, if not—serve three important purposes: (1) They offer a safeguard against undue arbitrariness in structuring time limits—the door should be open for further help or referral if needed, (2) they afford the crisis clinic a chance to get valuable feedback from the client concerning the actual crisis outcome (better than precrisis state? about the same? or worse?), and (3) they offer the crisis clinician an opportunity to bolster and reinforce the client's confidence and future coping ability. Thus, planned follow-ups, anticipated with the client well before the case is closed, should be a vital component of all crisis programs. Although Mann (1973) sternly warns that follow-up sessions should not be mentioned to the client until just before they are conducted, other clinicians who have done preplanned follow-ups have not experienced the disastrous consequences predicted by Mann.

TABLE 2. Termination process.

Crisis principle	Application to termination
Appreciate the crisis time-frame (say 6-8 weeks)	Allow adequate time to work through the crisis of termination
Analyze the underlying meaning of the crisis for the individuals involved	Identify elements of *loss*, *threat*, and *challenge* that the termination precipitates for both client and worker
Deal with the *loss*; promote and facilitate the grief process	Discuss feelings associated with the loss of the therapeutic relationship (anger, deprivation)
Deal with the *threat*; recognize and interpret anxiety, which underlies symptom formation	Review original reason for seeking help; identify progress; confront impulse to regress
Deal with the *challenge*; convey belief that a crisis is an opportunity to learn new coping	Analyze anxiety *vis-à-vis* separation/individuation issues (feelings about independence and autonomy)
Encourage cognitive awareness of significance of feelings	Verbalize ambivalent, fluctuating feelings
Focus on the present	Work on the termination of the helping relationship
Offer anticipatory guidance	Help client rehearse future actions
Communicate therapeutic optimism	Let the client leave with belief in future independent survival

It helps both worker and client say good-bye if each can honestly admit to having had an impact on the other. The work accomplished merits acknowledgment and mutual pride. It is also helpful to anticipate the client's *ongoing* internalization and application of treatment gains after the regular meetings between client and worker cease.

Adapted from Webb, N. (1985). A crisis intervention perspective on the termination process. *Clinical Social Work Journal, 13*, pp. 338–339. Used with permission.

Finally, the counselor should have considered the possibility of referring Mrs. A to a self-help weight-reduction group and to a family counseling agency for aid in budget management. Linkage with self-help and other community support groups (for example, Alcoholics Anonymous, Adult Children of Alcoholics, Recovery, Inc.) often helps clients maintain, even enhance, postcrisis functioning (Langsley & Kaplan, 1968).

Ripple Effect

Increments in the client's self-esteem during the postcrisis period help explain the familiar observation that brief therapy often stimulates a growth process, the positive effects of which may eddy out long after the last session has been completed. The following case example from an Employee Assistance Program (EAP) illustrates this "ripple effect" in addition to the application of various principles of task-oriented PSTT in a crisis situation (H. J. Parad, 1984).

> Linda, a bright twenty-nine-year-old technician, was referred to the EAP by a fellow employee who was concerned about her increasing lack of concentration on the job. Linda emphasized that her job was not in jeopardy, but

she was worried that it might be if she continued to be as preoccupied as she had been the last week or so, ever since she and her fiance, Dan, had started to quarrel. In fact, she sobbed, their relationship was a "mess," and she and Dan might not go through with their plans to get married in five months.

A search for the precipitating event revealed that about ten days earlier Linda had had a "crazy fling" with another man while attending a weekend conference with fellow technicians from the plant. Her friend, Marian, who had also attended the conference, told Linda she was acting crazy. That's why Linda requested counseling. Further exploration indicated that a few weeks ago Linda had loaned almost $1,000 to Dan, ostensibly to help him buy a new car on the installment plan. Just before leaving for the conference, Linda learned that Dan had gone to Las Vegas, gambled, and lost her money as well as some of his own. Linda was furious. Dan, as usual, asked for another chance, stating that he had gambled because the money Linda loaned him was not enough for a down payment on the car he wanted.

With support and focused questions from the counselor, Linda tearfully said that her problem with Dan was similar to problems she had experienced with other men because of her tendency to rescue and mother them. She had to make a decision. Should she break off her engagement with Dan? She knew she could no longer avoid her problem with him. She hesitantly said that she was going to be thirty years old in seven months; she feared she might be too old for marriage if she didn't get married soon—hence her sense of urgency.

Linda agreed to contract for eight sessions of therapy with the counselor; sessions focused on helping Linda to come to a decision about Dan as well as to explore why she had such a low opinion of herself even though her friends, as well as her supervisor and fellow workers, considered her personable, bright, and attractive.

Linda was responsive in her sessions. In her own insightful words, she was having a "crisis of self-esteem." Instead of "hiding" her problems with Dan (denial had been her customary coping device), she had several long talks ("homework" tasks assigned by the worker) with Dan about reasons for her dissatisfaction with their relationship. However, Dan continued "to tell stories and play games." After her fourth session, Linda returned her engagement ring and "surprised" herself by feeling more relieved than sad. Dan did not want to undertake counseling for himself.

With her counselor's active encouragement, Linda began to explore some of the reasons for her unrealistically low sense of self-worth. When the counselor pointed out her tendency to identify with her mother's depressive tendencies, Linda was stunned. After absorbing the worker's comment, she laughingly stated she was having an "Aha!" response—the counselor was on target.

In the follow-up session, scheduled one month after the eighth session, Linda reported that she was "through with Dan," "still relieved," and occasionally dating other men. She had followed the worker's suggestion that she talk more openly with her mother about the possibility of her mother getting therapy for her depression rather than bringing her depression to her daughter. Two months later, Linda called the counselor to share the news that she had just been promoted to the position of assistant supervisor in her department.

Noteworthy in this case is the way the EAP counselor and Linda shared in task definition and monitoring; the counselor's flexible, multimodal approach, blending behavioral and psychodynamic perspectives; the structured use of time limits; the clarity of the treatment focus on Linda's immediate crisis (whether to break her engagement to Dan) as well as on her underlying self-esteem issue; the planned follow-up; and Linda's continued progress (reflected in her job promotion), illustrating the post-treatment ripple effect previously mentioned. A highly intelligent young woman, Linda entered counseling motivated to explore her self-defeating pattern. The positive treatment outcome was due in no small part to her strong motivation and self-observing abilities.

At this point, it is useful to discuss three additional issues relating to our crisis intervention approach: (1) motivation and its operational definition, (2) the perennial riddle of whether a change in outward behavior reflects a change in underlying personality patterns, and (3) the place of crisis intervention in a spectrum of brief therapy services.

The Problem of Motivation

Too often professional counselors bypass certain cases in their daily practice, stereotyping these cases as having "too many reality problems" or being "too crisis-ridden" or "too messy" or "unmotivated." Such labels often serve as a kind of professional rationalization for failure to act in critical situations (H. J. Parad, 1963). Although the difference between needing and wanting help is admittedly crucial in short-term therapy, wherein issues must be faced squarely and time responsibly used, the problem of helping people who need help to want help is equally crucial and hence worthy of the practitioner's best clinical efforts.

Grinker (1960) points out "the need for increasing the number and strength of boosters toward treatment by external social forces and the responsibility of the clinic for increasing the motivational strength by satisfying more of the client's needs" (Lichtenberg, Kohrman, & Macgregor, 1960, p. xii). In this view of motivation, active effort on the part of the therapist is clearly implied. Motivation cannot be assessed in a mechanistic, unilateral sense. It frequently develops even when resistance initially appears very high, if the client's needs are satisfied in a reasonable way and his or her emotional crisis is properly understood and not placed in a social vacuum. The worker's therapeutic zeal and the intensity of his or her positive (but disciplined) investment are of greater than usual importance in this kind of outreach activity. The assessment of motivation and treatability is a transactional interplay—not only of what clients want and how much they want it, but also of what mental health workers want and how much they want it. Thus, a worker's commitment to an early and tangible result is frequently communicated to the client. As latent strengths are identified and fostered, the drive toward help is intensified. In a sense, then, motivation results from the *push* of the client's discomfort and the *pull* of hope instilled by the therapeutic endeavor (Perlman, 1957).

The Problem of Assessing Change

A controversial question inevitably arises: Through crisis intervention are practitioners relieving symptoms and not treating underlying causes? Of necessity, many problems are untreated because efforts are focused on selected, immediately relevant issues. Although the PSTT approach focuses on conscious and preconscious derivatives of specific problems rather than on the core pathology of an individual, is this altogether different from long-term intensive treatment in which some issues are worked on and others ignored (H. J. Parad, 1963)? Even psychoanalysis does not pretend to deal with all issues. It has often been said that the main purpose of analysis is to enable people to face the vicissitudes of life in a mature way, not to provide a talisman for all of life's problems—or to paraphrase Freud, to replace neurotic suffering with ordinary human misery. In the kind of activity described here, it is perhaps artificial to differentiate between outward changes in functioning based on environmental manipulation and changes in ego adaptation and coping patterns based on internal shifts in the defenses, as the two go hand in hand. Typically, alterations in social functioning reflect improvement in such basic ego functions as perception, judgment, control, and mastery.

Although it is possible that certain life crises may pass with improvement in functioning but no change in adaptive patterns, in ordinary human experience people become stronger through successful mastery of crisis situations. Moreover, supportive therapy (Hollis & Woods, 1981) *can* change the quality of the ego's adaptive patterns. Whether previous adaptive patterns are restored through reestablishment of a former equilibrium, whether the client's life situation remains the same (which in a pure scientific sense is impossible, although clinically it may *seem* to be the same), or whether the client's functioning improves, the focused use of both emotional and environmental support is indicated in virtually all crisis situations calling for outside intervention. For purposes of comparison, cases may be arranged along a continuum, extending from those in which techniques of clarification predominate (leading to the client's increased awareness of hidden motivation in his or her behavior) to those in which environmental support is the main dynamic of change. However, this spread in techniques and emphasis is fundamentally no different from ordinary mental health practice, regardless of the setting.

Time Limits

Related to the issue of the nature and depth of therapeutic change is a third question—perhaps deserving a separate chapter in itself—concerning the connection between crisis phenomena and time limits. As discussed earlier, because most crises are self-liquidating—for better or worse—over a relatively short period, the appropriate crisis intervention is also likely to be attuned to the client's struggles during the response and resolution phases and therefore will also be time-limited. Regarding the continuum of time-limited therapies, Bloom (1981) reports the value of single-session therapy; Jacobson (1980) and Caplan (1964)—and most crisis practitioners—apparently favor using up to six sessions; Reid (1978) usually uses eight sessions in PSTT; Mann (1973) uses twelve sessions in dynamic psychotherapy, typically focused on separation–individuation issues; Sifneos (1972) uses approximately fifteen sessions in therapy (targeted to Oedipal issues) for highly selected patients in emotional crisis; Strupp uses twenty-five sessions (considered by most professionals to be the upper limit of brief therapy) in interpersonal dynamic therapy that is not crisis-oriented (Strupp & Binder, 1984). Davanloo (1980), whose controversial role as the self-styled "relentless healer" has attracted wide attention, uses a variable number of sessions from a few to twenty or more. (For example, using Lindemann's formulation of the bereavement crisis, he has detailed a poignant account of brief crisis intervention with a mother whose son strangled in a crib.)

In a recent review of these varied modes of time structuring and their diverse rationales (both crisis and noncrisis related) Budman and Gurman (1988) arrived at the familiar conclusions that (1) brief treatment should be by design, not by default (as in unplanned brief treatment wherein the client aborts therapy) and (2) the terms "time-sensitive" or "time-effective" treatment would perhaps convey the attitudinal intent of the brief therapist better than would the term "time-limited."

Crisis Intervention and Brief Psychotherapy

Many authors have wrestled with the elusive problem of differentiating "crisis intervention" from "short-term dynamic psychotherapy." Marmor (1979), who considers brief therapy as the wave of the future, suggests that the goal of crisis intervention is to reduce stress and *sustain* the client's coping, thus helping the client recuperate enough to return to a precrisis state of functioning. In contrast, short-term dynamic therapy more ambitiously *modifies* the patient's ability to cope and focuses on "only secondarily relieving stress" (p. 154). Mindful that "there are no sharp lines of demarcation" and that "each can merge into the other," Marmor pursues his inquiry:

> Emergency treatment may proceed from the provision of immediate relief to an effort to reduce the precipitating stress situation, and in crisis intervention it is often necessary to help the patient develop more effective coping mechanisms to deal with the presenting stress situation as well as future ones. To the extent that crisis intervention emphasizes the modification of coping mechanisms it moves closer to short-term dynamic psychotherapy.
>
> The differences are primarily in terms of emphasis. Crisis intervention is usually of shorter duration and limited to five or six sessions and dynamic psychotherapy is usually of longer duration. The primary goal of crisis intervention is the restoration of homeostasis. A secondary goal is to improve the patient's adaptive capacity when necessary. The basic goal of short-term dynamic psychotherapy is to improve the patient's coping abilities. The termination point of crisis intervention is when the crisis is resolved. The termination point of short-term dynamic therapy is not dictated by the resolution of the crisis. Crisis intervention involves a more supportive approach than does short-term dynamic psychotherapy. It can also be more directive. In short-term dynamic therapy, the approach is active but nondirective. Crisis intervention deals only with the here and now; short-term dynamic psychotherapy includes the exploration of the past to illuminate the present. Finally, crisis intervention may involve a variety of other techniques (e.g., family therapy, group therapy, and dealing with the social network), but short-term dynamic psychotherapy is essentially a one-to-one approach. However, it may well be that the lessons learned from

> short-term dynamic psychotherapy will find increasing application in conjoint marital, family, and group therapies as time goes on (p. 154).

Marmor is quoted in detail because his inquiry suggests a *continuum* or *blending* of methods of therapy (from support and relief of stressful symptoms to in-depth attempts to alter basic coping mechanisms, including "exploration of the past to illuminate the present") rather than a *dichotomy* of crisis intervention versus brief dynamic therapy. To the extent, then, that crisis therapists try to help clients in the crucible of crisis to alter basic personality patterns and coping styles, their "technique clearly merges into short-term dynamic psychotherapy and differs from it primarily in being of shorter duration and crisis oriented" (Marmor, 1979, p. 154, footnote).

Thus, according to this definition, our brief crisis intervention approach, structured within a flexible time frame of, say, from six to twenty interviews (including one or two preplanned follow-ups), is equivalent in scope to "short-term psychotherapy." The practitioner's orientation may, as indicated earlier, be primarily psychodynamic, behavioral, cognitive, existential, or a prudent integrative blend of two or more of these approaches. By "prudent" we mean that the therapist's approach is based on the client's needs rather than on the therapist's ideological predilections.

Use of Dreams in Brief Therapy

The present section on the use of dreams illustrates how a crisis approach may be incorporated into short-term dynamic psychotherapy.* As indicated in the case of Mr. and Mrs. A, dreams are a valuable tool in time-effective treatment, especially in crisis-oriented psychodynamic therapy with clients demonstrating self-observing abilities and a wish to explore the learning opportunities inherent in the volatile crisis situation. The following guidelines are suggested:

The therapist introduces the idea of brief crisis therapy in the first session, telling the client he or she believes it will help to work intensively for a short period; the therapist asks the client if he or she is willing to do so as well. If the client is reluctant, the therapist may enhance the client's motivation to accept this approach by pointing out obvious advantages, such as saving time and money and the opportunity to accelerate the client's coping ability. The therapist recommends a specific number of sessions, such as twelve, sixteen, or twenty, or may informally propose that the process last a few months. The therapist invites the client's reaction to this recommendation in the hope that a "time-sensitive" agreement may be reached.

The therapist's next step is to suggest that dreams may become an important part of the therapy. In the first session, the therapist asks the client about his or her dreams. The client is told that dreams can be a powerful aid and a rich, creative source of information, that answers to current problems can often be found in dreams, and that progress in therapy can be facilitated by remembering them. For those clients who "erase" their dreams or believe they do not dream, additional help can be offered: they can be reassured that they do dream

*This section is adapted from Wallace & Parad, 1980; the dream material was prepared by H. J. Parad. Used with permission.

every night and can learn to recall them. A suggestion to keep a pad and pencil—or a voice-activated tape recorder, if feasible—next to their bed to remember whatever they can about their dreams is helpful.

Being expectant and hopeful that the client can and will remember dreams and that they will be a positive part of the therapy is usually sufficient to start the flow of dream material by the second session. When dream material is not forthcoming, a sensitively timed reminder about the value of dreams is advisable. If only minimal dream material is presented, the therapist may strongly reinforce whatever is remembered by a positive verbal reaction or by making special notes about the dream. For example,

> Edith, in her second session, said she did not remember any dreams. The therapist said, "Remembering dreams often helps." She said she did remember one weird thing from a dream, "a worm squiggling." The therapist asked what that brought to mind. She said, "Like a snake in the grass . . . that must be that S.O.B. boyfriend of mine" (who had just left her). The therapist pointed out her anger, which she had denied up to this point. She responded by reporting some of the history of her relationship with her boyfriend. As she spoke, she became visibly angry. She talked about what a "snake in the grass" he had been and how she felt as insignificant as a worm after losing him. Excited at first, then appropriately upset by her own revelations, Edith was able to make use of her dream material and was later able to learn more about her true feelings through her dreams.

Targeting dreams serves various therapeutic purposes. The dream material gives the therapist immediate access to information that might take a long time to obtain in other ways, such as by reports of other behaviors or by waiting for key issues to be reflected in transference phenomena. The genetic or developmental origins of the client's core issues, current psychodynamic conflicts, and denied affects may easily be perceived and related to the current psychosocial situation. Attending to dreams facilitates the client's interest in his or her own intrapsychic processes, which improves the quality of other reporting as well. Solutions to problems first conceived in dreams can be recognized and supported by the therapist. Even when dream reports reveal serious defects in problem-solving capacities, the awareness of the deficits gives the therapist a better understanding of how to deal with the total situation and a better appreciation of the client's true struggle. Throughout the process of dream interpretation, the therapist *emphasizes the client's positive intent to solve problems through the dream metaphor*; confrontive interpretations likely to induce a regressive transference are scrupulously avoided in this mode of focused therapy.

Jane

First, a quick overview: Jane had been unable to find anyone to listen to her dreams, neither her husband nor her previous therapist. The current therapist cooperated with Jane's desire to find meaning in her dreams. After a period of improvement, Jane produced new dream material (in the sixth of sixteen planned sessions), but this time she became alarmed by her dream disclosures. The therapist then helped her with her fears in a way that enhanced her self-esteem. As indicated below, after the second session with Jane, the therapist invited her husband for a few conjoint sessions so that Jane's interpersonal environment could be more accepting, thus illustrating the use of an interactional approach in brief psychosocial therapy. Two follow-up sessions indicated that Jane not only held her gains but continued to grow.

Jane was an anxious, sad, thirty-one-year-old woman married to Sid, a "rigid, inflexible" engineer, aged forty-one. She had a lively, twenty-three-month-old daughter, Sandra. Jane asked for brief therapy to deal with "my anxiety, my depression, my relationship with my husband, my relationship with my mother-in-law, my mother, and my baby." She cried throughout the intake interview. She had been sad during the past few days and had been crying more than usual; in fact, she couldn't stop crying at times.

The precipitating event triggering her request for therapy was a quarrel with her husband in which he exclaimed she needed to straighten herself out because she was "exceptionally emotional." She would get angry with him when he overconcentrated on what he was doing, whether reading the paper or watching a TV show. She felt cut off. If she told him how she felt, he seemed to get angrier, which made her angrier as well. She complained of "feeling caught in a vicious circle—the trouble is I get hurt, not he." Therefore, she was keeping everything inside. She had considered taking diazepam (Valium) but thought it would be better to talk with a therapist. She had had a brief period of counseling three years earlier, and it seemed to help to have someone to talk to.

Sid, an only child, had a strong attachment to his mother, aged seventy-two. Jane's problem with her mother-in-law was that "we are totally different." The mother-in-law was a religious person, and Jane was not a churchgoer. Jane felt distant from her own mother as well. She had been, however, close to her father, who died three years previously. His death had precipitated her request for the previous period of counseling.

Her parents were divorced when she was ten. Since that time her mother had had a succession of boyfriends and two unsuccessful marriages. Jane also complained of feeling alienated from her brother, who she said had been jealous of her close relationship with her father. She described her mother as cold and indifferent and mentioned how hard it was to talk with her. "I feel all mixed up and afraid to let out my anger. I don't want to lose Sid because he really is good to me and gives me and our daughter a lot of security." She said the only happy time she could remember in her whole life was a brief period during adolescence when she was a class officer in high school, had a boyfriend, and seemed less dependent on her mother, brother, and father for support.

After hearing all of this, I commented that Jane was obviously in a very unpleasant and painful place, and that I wanted to help her. I asked what bothered her the most. She replied that her husband's distance was "like my mother" and wondered whether she had "married her mother." Yet her husband was also supportive, gave her a lot of freedom, and maybe she shouldn't complain so much. I asked what she was experiencing while she was crying, and she said, "a kind of terrible emptiness and a vague dread that some harm" would come to Sandra. She said she was a prolific dreamer, but her previous therapist, although otherwise sensitive, did not pay any attention to her dreams and was interested only in "problem solving." I told her I was interested in her dreams, that they were a rich source of self-awareness and creativity, and that when properly understood, a source of strength in helping people feel better about themselves.

She seemed visibly relieved, dried her tears, and recalled a dream that she had the night before, in which she felt utterly helpless. She was angry in the dream and seemed overwhelmed with the feeling that "nobody takes me seriously." She went on to say, "I was upset that I allowed myself to be so helpless." She reported the following dream sequence.

> A mason was building a fence out of bricks. However, instead of using mortar, he was using diapers, rags, and other items of clothing. I looked closely at these items of clothing and realized that they were Sandra's clothes. I was trying to control my anger. I first began to talk calmly and rationally to the mason, whose identity seemed vague and inscrutable. The mason looked back at me in an equally vague way. I began to raise my voice louder and louder, but no matter how much I shouted, it made no difference. Other people began to watch. No one was upset; no one flinched. It felt the way it usually does—me against the world.

She began sobbing, saying she felt totally miserable, then became quiet. After a few moments, I asked what she was experiencing, and she said, "misery and helplessness, and a kind of vague anger." I asked what the dream meant to her—"let yourself go and see what comes to mind." She said that it was as if she just couldn't get through to other people. I asked who the mason was, and she said she didn't know. She became anxious. I suggested the mason might be her mother, and she immediately responded to my suggestion and said, "Yes! Now I remember what I thought when the dream awakened me; it was my mother and she wasn't listening to me; it was the way she is when she calls and feels cold and distant. No matter what I try, I don't get through, as I keep saying." I asked what the meaning of using her daughter's clothes as a substitute for mortar was, and she said, "Well, I hate to say it, but my mother is not someone I trust alone with my daughter. She smokes and drinks a lot, and I'm always afraid she's going to harm my daughter the way she harmed me. My mother knows my feelings and gets even angrier when she picks my feelings up. I also have the feeling that my mother is jealous of me because she has never had a relationship as good as the one I have with Sid, despite the problems we have. She said I was being patronizing toward her because I had a husband and she didn't, and that I was more happily married than she had ever been, and compared me also with my brother who was recently divorced." I asked her what her feeling was now, and she said she felt a "powerless rage against my mother." She recalled that the dream was probably precipitated by a phone call in which her mother asked for her husband and paid no attention to her. Drying her tears, she decided immediately that the next time this happened, which would be soon, she would confront her mother directly.

The following week she reported that her mother had indeed called, abruptly asking for Sid. But before Jane turned the phone over to her husband, she confronted her mother with her feelings, and her mother became apologetic. Jane said she began to feel some strength within herself. Instead of crying as she usually does, she expressed her feelings toward her mother, who then seemed to be on the defensive. As she reported this, Jane appeared calm and more self-assured. The crisis was subsiding.

She asked if it would be all right to tell me about a repetitive dream she had been having during the several months before she came for help. She said these dreams were disturbing to her, although her husband made light of them, saying, "They're only dreams, so stop fussing; they have nothing to do with reality." This made her feel furious with him and "freaky." The recurrent dreams consisted of variations on a chasing scene.

> Someone is always after me; I am a fugitive; I am running and running. The chaser has a kind of cloudy quality to me. Whenever I seem to be getting away from the chaser, the chaser gets close to me. If I run into a room and close a strong door against the chaser, the chaser in the dream would turn into a liquid and slip under the door and envelop me that way. It was terrible; I would keep waking up. Funny, since coming to see you, my dream has suddenly gone away, but when I think of the brick and the mason dream with the rags, I am reminded again about the chaser.

Jane paused and seemed thoughtful; I inquired what she thought the dream meant. "Well," she said, "for one thing, I'm glad it's over, but knowing me, I'll start a whole new sequence before our work is done." I repeated that dreams were important to the work we were doing and that by understanding them she would be better able to deal with her helplessness, her anger, and, we hope, could improve her communication with her husband, mother, and mother-in-law. I added that she would probably worry less about her daughter, too. She said that one of the dreams that was especially scary involved her husband getting killed in a hospital. It was because her husband was trying to help her get away from the chaser.

I asked what all of this meant to her. She said it was hard to figure out. She had tried to talk with her husband, but again he belittled the dream and said it was just a dumb nightmare, that she was "too emotional."

I wondered whether the chaser was her mother and if the chaser and the mason were one and the same person. The brick wall was made out of rags instead of solid mortar, symbolizing that the wall was not going to be strong enough to keep her mother away from her. The *positive* meaning was her desire for separateness, her wish to lead her own life. She seemed startled and said she just remembered that her mother, in one of their angry encounters, had accused her of putting a wall between them since she married and had a baby. I said that perhaps the mason partly represented herself as well as her mother. Jane said that her mother was jealous of her relationship with Sid and that Jane was fearful that her "mother would take away anyone who was good for me since I never had anything that was good. The things that are good to me are my husband and my daughter. So I guess I put up a wall against her, too."

After a period of anguished crying, she became silent, wiped her tears, then heaved a sigh of relief, saying she felt better. She realized that she had emphasized to her mother how confident she felt in taking care of Sandra, how great she felt as a homemaker and wife. She acknowledged that her mother probably thought she was "rubbing it in." Then she said, "I guess mother got back at me in the dream, chasing me down and telling me that I couldn't do that to her." Her brother and mother had both said to her, "You're so damn perfect, you're disgusting."

After the first two sessions with Jane, I arranged with her to see her husband, who reluctantly participated in three conjoint sessions. Jane was surprised that Sid, with encouragement from me, was able to listen to her. He indicated that perhaps dreams did have meaning, though he wished she would be more rational and realize how harmless they were. He said, "I do not dream, or if I did, I would not bother to remember." He indicated that there was nothing about himself he wanted to change, but he did love his wife. He was sorry she was hurting so much and was willing to come for a few times to help her.

In our second and third conjoint sessions, tension between Jane and Sid was markedly reduced after their intensive discussions about some of the sources of disagreement between Jane and Sid's mother. They worked out a number of practical solutions to their disagreements, which they said, and I believed, brought them closer together.

During the sixth session Jane reported that, as she had feared, a whole new alarming series of dreams have "come upon me." In the new dream sequence, she kept dreaming of high school. She was very tense and tearful as she spoke.

> "I don't know anyone; I'm a misfit. Here I am, thirty-one, and everybody in the dream is sixteen. I have trouble finding my classes; I can't find my locker; I can't find my key; I'm back working as a waitress doing things I did before, but I don't remember anyone. I go up to people and they don't recognize me. I want them to see how much more confident I am than when I was a class officer, and it's as if no one recognizes me.

I suggested that the dream was actually a very positive one; although it seemed to her like a put-down, there was some important, perhaps hidden, meaning in it. She became reflective rather than tearful, and asked what that meaning might be, commenting that I had earlier stated that dreams could be creative. I reminded her that, as she said, she wanted people to see how much more confident she is now than the insecure girl who had been a class officer, even though as a class officer she felt better than she had before she entered high school. Could it be that it was not they (former fellow students) who could not recognize her, but that Jane, as it were, looking in the mirror, was surprised by her own image of increased self-confidence and couldn't recognize her own accomplishments? After all, during the past two weeks she had not been having prolonged crying episodes, had been able to communicate more effectively with Sid without feeling distant from him, was less intimidated by her mother and mother-in-law, and was no longer panicky or having feelings of dread about Sandra's well-being. She nodded vigorously, said she was very relieved, that maybe she could stop having all these dreams now that she understood they were positive. She said, "Thanks to you, I'm not having any more chasing dreams." I replied, "You had the courage to remember and record your dreams; you were able to work hard with me to master feelings of insecurity. You risked asserting your feelings to your husband, mother, and mother-in-law; *you* did it!"

In two follow-up sessions, Jane indicated that she did not have the heavy, anxious, depressed feeling or the emptiness she experienced before, was sleeping better, and was thinking of devoting more time to volunteer and club activities. She reported that she had a babysitter for Sandra so that she would have more time for herself, and was generally less worried. She promised herself she would keep track of her dreams in her diary. "It's a wonderful feeling to be glad about your dreams instead of scared to death by them the way I used to be." She stopped referring to her dreams as "weird."

Impression

In a crisis state, Jane, an intelligent, introspective young woman, found herself reacting to her husband as if he were her mother, thus reexperiencing fears of abandonment and powerless rage. Recalling her strong feelings of attachment to her father, who had died a few years previously, she became aware of the fact that she thought that her mother and brother would be vengeful toward her because she and her father had been close, whereas her mother and brother were close to each other. It was as if there were two coalitions in the family—Jane and Dad versus Mother and Brother.

Deep within herself, Jane struggled not only with fears of anger but with desires for independence from the negatively perceived mother and fears of success, symbolized in the chasing and high school dreams. Jane's active dream life was, of course, her way of expressing her positive growth strivings as well as finding outlets for these tensions; yet when she wished to share her dreams, her husband seemed critical and again reminded her of her mother. Three conjoint husband/wife interviews—in which I reenforced Sid's willingness to listen to Jane, letting her recount her dreams without being judgmental—seemed to produce a marked reduction in tension, along with problem-solving discussions about areas of disagreement. Sid and Jane began talking more directly with each other about their problems with relatives. Jane's drive toward healthy individuation found expression in a markedly improved self-image. Instead of being panicked by her dreams, Jane was helped to use them as part of her coping repertoire for crisis resolution. Thus work with Jane shows how an initial course of brief crisis therapy can merge into short-term dynamic psychotherapy.

The nature of the transference is also worthy of note. The therapist deliberately played an implicitly benevolent parental role, supportive of Jane's impressive growth efforts but confrontive when necessary. For example, when Jane hesitated to ventilate suppressed feelings of anger against her husband and relatives, the therapist was firm in insisting that Jane become aware of how she depressively turned her hostile feelings against herself.

Discussion and Caveats

Although a dream is an individual psychological event, reporting a dream is an interpersonal one. When the report is made to an interpreter of dreams, the way he or she understands dreams will influence the meaning of the dream in the relationship and to the dreamer. For example, a fortuneteller may recognize the dreamer's wish to use aspects of a dream to predict the future, whereas a brief therapist will use it for a different purpose, to understand aspirations and fears, to detect transference phenomena, and, above all, to improve the client's self-esteem and social functioning.

Brief psychodynamic psychotherapy occurs within a special context, and time is the crucial variable. Typical features include focusing on specific problems, greater variability of technique, and more active solicitation of material, including dreams. In dream interpretation, there is a greater tendency to focus on what the dream reveals about the here and now—the specific person–situation configuration being confronted in the treatment—than about early childhood material. However, even early childhood content can become important when it is specifically relevant to the client's focal problem. Within a psychodynamic context, one may observe that the ego "knows" time while the id does not. A variety of ego functions are involved. Examination of the effects of the brief treatment approach in relation to each function is beyond the scope of this chapter. Yet structuring the therapeutic relationship, using time boundaries and other principles of crisis-oriented brief psychotherapy, influences ego functioning in general, with implications for self-esteem, management and control of affects and impulses, superego functioning, and object relatedness.

In order not to be misunderstood as proposing yet another fad in the gimmick-ridden field of therapy, we conclude this section with four caveats: (1) Although the client's dreams have been emphasized, other communications are equally relevant, whether facts, fantasies, or silences. (2) Although dream solicitation and interpretation are the central focus of the approach described in this section, the therapist obviously utilizes other techniques such as exploratory clarifications, interpretation of other material, persuasion, mobilization of outside resources, and environmental manipulation. (3) Although the dream can be a promising tool in brief therapy, solicitation of dreams is neither a necessary nor a sufficient condition for effective brief crisis therapy to occur, because in the final analysis the therapist can only create a therapeutic milieu within which the client may wish to change him- or herself. (4) Obviously, the observations presented here have been at the practice-wisdom and theoretical level; more systematic research (using random assignment of subjects to therapy in which dreams will be solicited versus a control group) would scientifically test the efficacy of the dream as a central focus in brief psychotherapy.

Family Crisis Therapy

From the foregoing, it is clear that we favor an interactional, systems perspective on crisis and crisis intervention. A crisis is an interpersonal or collective as well as an individual phenomenon in that it can be experienced by both family and nonkinship groups. Significant others in an individual's social network affect crisis resolution efforts and are affected by them. In short, the individual is not viewed in isolation but rather within his or her relevant social milieu.

Crisis practitioners are increasingly turning to modes of family therapy. Family crisis intervention is helpful in solving problems of psychosocial functioning during an acutely stressful period experienced by a relatively intact family as well as during the acute eruption of crisis in a chronically disordered family. In the latter case, only one member of the disordered family may be presented as the emotionally disturbed or mentally ill "identified patient."

A variety of family-oriented crisis modalities are used in situations in which the identified patient is either a child or an adolescent. Morrison (1965), for example, described a tightly structured family crisis service offered by a psychiatric emergency program for children that incorporated an explicit time plan for managing immediate problems. He pointed out the need for prompt intervention involving direct advice to family members for getting through a crisis.

Children's self-destructive behavior is interpreted to family members as a sign of "blocked communication" within the family, culminating in a crisis episode. Others have reported similar attempts at short-term family-crisis intervention in programs concerned with a range of problems (Kaffman, 1965; Alevizos & Liberman, 1976).

Regarding criteria for case selection, families with chronic crisis-ridden disturbances as well as those with less serious problems have evidently been helped by crisis-oriented approaches, provided they are seen during an acutely stressful period. The question of criteria may have more to do with therapeutic goals and the mental health worker's stance than with the niceties of clinical diagnostic labels.

The following case examples reflect H. J. Parad's early attempts to combine action-oriented early secondary prevention with the Harvard Family Guidance Center's research concerning the effects of crisis-inducing stress on family functioning (H. J. Parad, 1963). Although multiple interviews were held with the children as well as with the parents in these families, the case presentations, because of space limitations, focus on work with the mother. The case examples and analyses are adapted from H. J. Parad (1963).

Case Examples

In the following case example, a mother experiences a crisis after giving birth to twins.

> Mrs. B, a shocked, reluctant mother of premature twin girls (she was already struggling with rearing three young children), commented in the seventh of twelve interviews that she had reached, in her own words, "the crisis peak." Gripped with panic, she said, "Either the situation will give or we will break!" The younger children were still in pajamas, although it was already after lunch. She had recently had a very upsetting quarrel with her husband, with whom she had been avoiding sexual relations. Her youngest son, who was suffering from extreme jealousy of the twins, had wandered away from the house and had been taken to a police station by a neighbor. The twins' continued colic had deprived Mrs. B of sleep, and her fatigue was understandably uppermost in her mind—"I've never been so weak or tired in all my life. Next week you'll see me at the State Hospital."
>
> During this interview, I gave Mrs. B an opportunity to discuss her many fears, then focused quite actively on her fear that her aggression might lead her to an act of violence, mentioning specifically her anger at the "extra twin" and her husband. She quickly associated the babies' crying with her husband's sexual interest, saying that she could not respond to him sexually since all she could think of was intercourse produces crying babies. However, in discussing this further she realized that her husband had been deprived of sexual gratification and had been looking forward to the resumption of normal sexual relations following the birth of the babies. Because of her denial tendencies, Mrs. B was strongly urged to begin to admit that it was harder to care for two babies than for the one baby she had originally expected.
>
> Her pervasive helplessness reminded her of her mother's death (when she was seven years old) and her father's subsequent remarriage. Her early experiences and the trauma she suffered then flashed before her as if they had happened yesterday. She poured out in an agonized, tearful, confused

way her guilt about not having gone to her father's funeral. My initial concern—fortunately not substantiated—was that she was about to have a psychotic-like episode.

Treatment efforts focused on relieving some of Mrs. B's guilt by pointing out its unrealistic quality. Concrete environmental supports, which she had previously resisted because of her own fears of helplessness, were utilized. She was able, with considerable support, to seek help from relatives in making plans for the babies' christenings. She permitted herself to accept gifts of clothing from her friends. Her husband was helped to secure supplementary financial assistance, because he was temporarily not working due to a strike.

In her previous visits to the well-baby clinic, Mrs. B had presented an impassive facade to the examining physician. I encouraged her to bring her questions to the doctor and accompanied her to the well-baby clinic, where I remained throughout the examination. The physician told her to feed the babies when they were hungry, without worrying about overfeeding, and urged her to strengthen their formula, suggestions that seemed to have a great deal of psychological significance to her. The net effect of this examination, together with our subsequent discussion, was to reassure her that she had not, in fact, harmed the babies. She seemed able to respond with much less hostility to her stepmother's advice that they arrange a rotating system for feeding the babies instead of trying to feed both at once.

Mr. and Mrs. B were soon able to resume satisfactory sexual relations. Mrs. B was helped to acknowledge her youngest son's jealousy, which was discussed in joint interviews with her and Mr. B, whose supportive efforts were appreciated. The meaning of her son's wandering off was discussed as a reaction to the new babies. As the routine in the family began to settle into a normal pattern, she was able to take her son with her to church and on shopping expeditions, and one day even took him on a private outing. The father dramatically satisfied the child's need for security and a sense of inclusion by taking him on his lap along with the twins, saying, "I have a big lap; there is room for you, too." The crisis was now subsiding.

Regular visits and active support from the public health nurse completed the picture, along with the use of an efficient, but not too motherly, homemaker who permitted Mrs. B to get some rest and throw off the fatigue that had contributed to her deranged appearance.

Over a period of twelve interviews, therapy focused on linking the present situational crisis with previous unresolved problems that erupted under the impact of what Mrs. B herself referred to as a "crisis." Through cognitive restructuring, she was helped first to develop an adequate recognition response to the problems involved in having twins and then to confront her own problems in a way that gave her a better perspective on her relationships with her mother and father, which allowed her to cope with previous unresolved problems in an ego-syntonic manner. Anticipatory guidance was used extensively in preparing her for subsequent relationship adjustments among the children and with her husband. The success of these efforts was demonstrated and reinforced in a number of follow-up visits over a period of several months. Emotional first aid and discussion of previous issues stirred up by the crisis were coordinated with specific environmental supports.

To argue that the environmental support was of greater or lesser importance than the psychological aid would ignore the psychosocial nature of this kind of intervention. Treatment procedures for both the inner and the outer stresses proceed simultaneously and are dovetailed for maximum therapeutic benefit. Ventilation, abreaction, and the clarification of the associative links obviously played an important part in the successful result. Encouraging this family to separate themes interwoven from previous life situations—from a guilt-laden past to a confused present—helped its members to gain a more realistic awareness of their situation. Past, present, and future characteristically merged into a single perception, particularly at the crisis peak. The key issue of the mother's guilt over her hostility toward the extra baby was extracted, her current feelings of helplessness were linked with her old feelings concerning the loss of her parents, and the illogical connections were modified through discussion and abreaction of the associated affects. Thus the central, emotionally relevant issues were selected from a welter of other feelings, observations, and experiences. Intervention focused on the current stress configuration, that is, the stressful event and the perceptions and conflicts relating to it. Previous life-history data were elicited spontaneously and used selectively.

With some clients, the therapist must be willing to risk direct confrontation and interpretation of issues if circular negative reactions are to give way to a more benign pattern of interaction. The following case example describes a family who had to cope with a child's congenital anomaly.

> Mrs. C was an intelligent, somewhat excitable thirty-four-year-old woman, who was reacting with unusual tension to the mild, bilateral club-footedness of her three-week-old daughter. Mrs. C seemed to be constantly hovering over the child, despite positive medical reassurance about the child's prognosis. In response to active confrontation, Mrs. C brought out instances of marked friction with her husband and indicated they were on the verge of separation. Except for a heated discussion about a possible divorce, they were engaged in a war of silence. Her husband, who also suffered from a marked orthopedic handicap, was very attached to his parents. He had infuriated his wife by visiting them late in her pregnancy and thereby not being available when the baby was born. Mrs. C's perception of the stress revealed that she somehow felt at fault for having given birth to a less than perfect baby: "I have been punished for wrongdoing." Subsequent discussion of her "wrongdoing" indicated guilt about premarital sexual relations, a nagging guilt that reemerged after the birth of the baby. "God is punishing me for my sins," she said. Because she had been unable to discuss this feeling with her husband, she was actively encouraged to verbalize her feelings in therapy. Mr. C had also fantasized himself responsible for the child's defect and felt that his "sperm was defective."
>
> Because they were paralyzed by guilt and anger toward each other, I suggested that Mrs. C break the silence and reopen communication with her husband. Joint interviews with the couple provided opportunities to air a number of disagreements about the care of the child; Mr. and Mrs. C were encouraged to discuss their fears with each other. The risks involved in giving each other "the silent treatment" were pointed out to them. Mrs. C's guilt was relieved when I observed that, although she might imagine that previous sexual activities had caused the defect in the baby, she was being hard on herself. Techniques of universalization, which emphasize that many mothers who have babies with anomalies feel this way, bolstered her feelings that she was not a bad person. Communication increased between

> Mr. and Mrs. C, and Mr. C was gradually helped to see the importance of paying more attention to his wife. Both Mr. and Mrs. C were able to emancipate themselves somewhat from their dependent relationships with their respective parents. Follow-up reports confirmed that the family and baby were doing well.

Whereas Mrs. B had an "underrecognition" response to the needs of the "extra twin," Mrs. C's response was overexaggerated. Mrs. C's ego ideal was mirrored in her baby: she had fantasized the child as a ballerina. She was encouraged in treatment to express her own childhood frustrations and to begin to think of her daughter as a person in her own right, thus minimizing her need to live vicariously through the baby. The precipitating stress, the child's mild bilateral club-footedness (highly responsive to orthopedic remediation), elicited unconscious mutilation anxiety in both the husband and wife. I pointed out that they were putting their fears onto the child. Intense emotions of anger and guilt were aroused, as each blamed self and the other as the cause of the baby's defect. The guilt associated with previous life experiences was relieved through careful, detailed discussion. The therapeutic goal was threefold: improvement of the husband–wife relationship by encouraging better communication and direct expression of feelings of guilt, anger, and helplessness; fostering continued efforts at emancipation from dominating, possessive parental ties; and stimulation of more accurate perception and satisfaction of the baby's needs and respect for her as a developing personality in her own right, as opposed to an extension of a narcissistic parental self-image.

The family was actually strengthened in the course of its exposure to a stressful situation. The new equilibrium achieved was better than the old. Their marriage became more meaningful, and the couple were able to deal in a more mature way with subsequent vicissitudes without experiencing debilitating failures in communication. This result would not have occurred had the worker not been flexible in making home visits, keeping in touch through telephone calls, and arranging both single and joint interviews in the office and in the home.

Use of the "unlinking technique" (Caplan, 1955, p. 151) prevented the development of a disordered mother–child relationship. The goal of confining the mother's conflict so that it would be segmented off and not be acted out vicariously in the life of the baby was realized over a period of three months. This technique, variously called "child-centered treatment of the mother," "focal therapy," or "segmental therapy," obviously involves carefully limited goals; it has been used in preventive work and in early treatment of mothers who have unsuccessfully attempted abortions (Caplan, 1954).

Chronic Disequilibrium

Obviously, some outcomes were not as positive as the case examples presented. In a number of situations, the underlying pathology was so persistent that brief intervention, while producing some alleviation of symptoms, was insufficient, and clients were referred for long-term treatment. In a few of these experimental cases, widely spaced interviews were used to encourage mobilization of coping efforts in families that hitherto had passively resigned themselves to a fate of long-term dependency and disability. Techniques of accompaniment often helped to stimulate their faltering motivation for help.

> Mrs. D, a welfare recipient who feared authority figures, greeted the efforts of social and health agencies with a smiling mask, which made it impossible to initiate meaningful help. When Mrs. D's premature baby was born, she seemed unable to follow medical and nursing advice. Although she was eligible for an increase in her public assistance allowance, Mrs. D did not qualify because of her inability to produce a birth certificate for the child. The public welfare worker speculated that Mrs. D refused to submit the required birth certificate because the baby was conceived out of wedlock. I felt there was no real evidence of extramarital sexual activity. I told Mrs. D that I felt she was making things unduly troublesome for herself and suggested that there were other factors involved, which we did not understand, in her refusal to get the birth certificate. Without attempting to probe, I offered to accompany her to the registry of births. She responded with alacrity. The explanation was dramatically revealed when we passed, on our way to the office where births are recorded, another office where the death of a previous child was recorded. Mrs. D had suffered enormous guilt over the death of this stillborn baby and had never discussed it before. With intense pain, she talked about some of these feelings. She indicated that she had not been able to bear the thought of going to this building to get a birth certificate until I offered to go with her.

Although we do not pretend that the technique used in this case and the related discussion of one issue—no matter how central or emotionally relevant—would solve the multiple problems of this family, the experience was a corrective, educational one for Mrs. D and helped to improve her relationships with other health and welfare agencies. Techniques of accompaniment, although time consuming and requiring adaptation on the part of the worker, may be used successfully in many situations. Clearly, they are not magical cure-alls, any more than home visits or family interviews have special magic. When this technique is diagnostically indicated and geared to specific goals, the worker must be willing to leave the sanctity of the office and enter actively into the client's life.

Brief Family Crisis Therapy: A Conceptual Framework

From these early case studies of families in the throes of biopsychosocial crises—and the interventive efforts aimed at crisis resolution—a conceptual framework emerged (Parad & Caplan, 1960). This framework has been subsequently updated and elaborated on the basis of our clinical, teaching, and research experiences. We have found this framework valuable in understanding ongoing family functioning, just as McCubbin and Patterson (1983) have found the "double ABCX model" a useful scheme for studying the phenomenology of family crises.

In this conceptual framework (Figure 2), data about family functioning are analyzed under the following basic classifications (H. J. Parad, 1982):*

1. In relation to the structural and functional parts of family life, three interdependent subsystems are significant: *value orientations, communication styles, and role networks*. Thus, believing, communicating, and doing affect

*The ensuing material on brief family crisis therapy is excerpted and adapted with permission from "Brief Family Therapy" (H. J. Parad, 1982).

and are affected by one another. Collectively, these comprise the family's *life-style*. Values, for example, family rules, are usually implicit, not explicit. They refer to shared premises, commonly held beliefs, and attitudes about what is to be cherished, how much and in what order; thus values influence the family's allocation of time, money, status, and affectional rewards. What the family thinks and believes influences and is influenced by the family's mode of communication.

Assessment of family communication style reveals the messages that are considered important enough to be transmitted and received as well as how they are transmitted. The degree of importance attached to each message unit is determined by the family members' value orientations. Some families are relatively comfortable in expressing angry and judgmental feelings but much less comfortable in expressing the positive feelings that these angry feelings often mask. In many families, analysis of recurrent uproars often reveals that overdetermined, hostile expressions mask areas of tenderness and exquisite vulnerability.

The last interrelated subsystem pertains to the role network. Who expects what of whom? Who does what? This subsystem of reciprocal expectations and loyalties mediates the value subsystem—what people feel and believe—along with the communication network subsystem—what messages and signals are considered worth sending and how they are sent. Overtly? Covertly? What combination of words, symbols, and nonverbal gestures are used?

2. *Intermediate problem-solving mechanisms* are coping devices triggered by the actual impact of crisis. They are called intermediate to emphasize the temporary, dynamic nature of processes in flux, compared with the relative stability of family life-style. Intermediate mechanisms are various transactional and interpersonal methods for coping with the cognitive, emotional, and behavioral tasks associated with stress. These mechanisms may be negative (scapegoating, emotional neglect) or positive (use of family and neighborhood social network resources and adequate worry and grief work). Above all, these mechanisms represent a series of attempts at problem solving through trial and error. In dealing with dysfunctional and disordered families, the clinician's role is to point out that faulty mechanisms involving "error" are often repeatedly used, despite the great pain and discomfort they produce in family members and the identified patient.

3. *The need–response pattern* affords a dynamic assessment of the mental health of an individual family member within the context of the family interaction process, thereby furnishing a conceptual linkage between family functioning and the individual's mental health. Several basic human needs are considered relevant to mental health, including nurturance and love, a balance between support and independence with respect to tasks, a balance between freedom and control with respect to instinctual expression, and the availability of suitable role models. In studying the response to these categories of need, one can observe three separate but interlocking phases: (1) the *perception* of the individual's needs by other family members, (2) the *respect* accorded to these needs as being worthy of attention, and (3) the *satisfaction* of such needs to the extent possible in light of the culture of the family and available family resources. Thus the need–response pattern, which may be altered during a period of crisis, becomes an instrument for assessing the

FIGURE 2. **Theoretical framework for viewing families in crisis.**

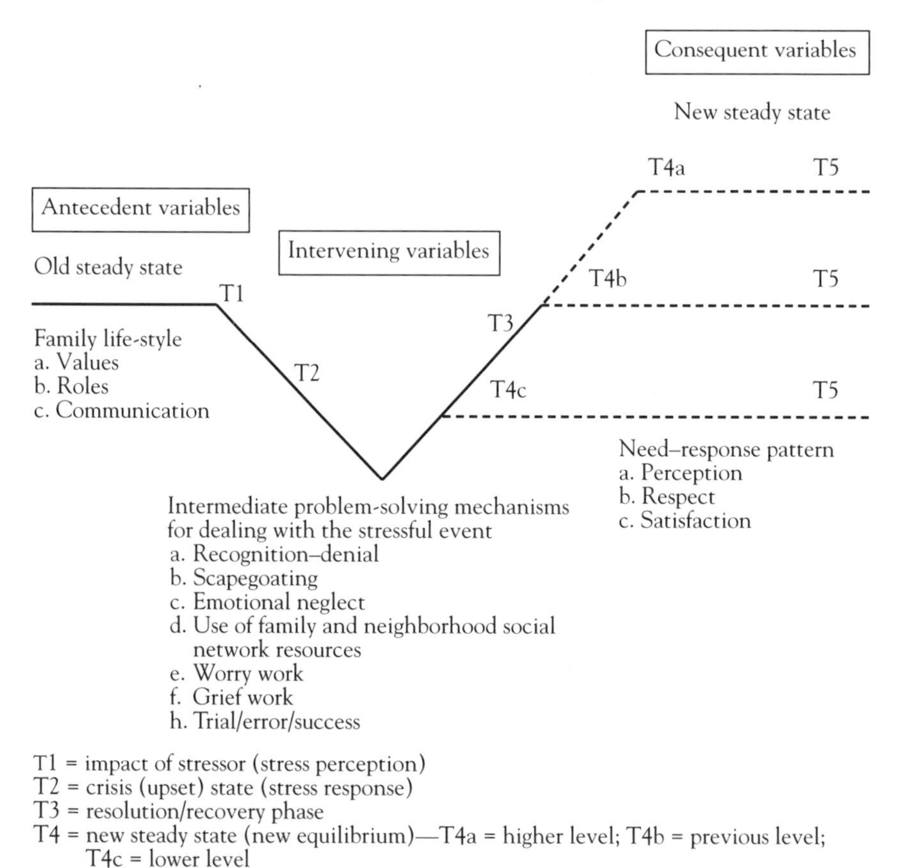

T1 = impact of stressor (stress perception)
T2 = crisis (upset) state (stress response)
T3 = resolution/recovery phase
T4 = new steady state (new equilibrium)—T4a = higher level; T4b = previous level;
T4c = lower level
T5 = follow-up (booster shot)

Adapted from Parad, H. J. (1982). Brief family therapy. In H. Schulberg & M. Killilea (Eds.), *The modern practice of community mental health: A volume in honor of Gerald Caplan* (pp. 419–443). San Francisco: Jossey–Bass. Used with permission.

family's solution of problems posed by the crisis. In research terms, family life-style elements may be considered antecedent variables; intermediate problem-solving mechanisms as intervening variables; and the need–response pattern with its triad of perception, respect, and satisfaction of needs as a consequent or outcome variable. A detailed case illustration of this conceptual framework was presented in an earlier publication (Parad & Caplan, 1960, pp. 61–72.)

Our main thesis is that important changes occur in the family during a crisis period with respect to the future mental and social functioning of individual family members and the family as a group. Thus, as outlined in Table 2, the need-response pattern may be approximately the same (T4b) as that which prevailed prior to the crisis; it may be at a lower level when the crisis adversely affects the family (T4c); or it may reflect a higher level of functioning (T4a) when members respond to crisis in terms of challenge and opportunity rather than in terms of danger only.

Advocating an eclectic approach to family therapy, Steidl and Wexler (1977) underscore the need for different approaches due to the various forms of family structure and pathology, different forms of therapy, and diverse ways in which human change occurs. Concluding that no overarching theory or metatheory of therapy exists, they urge clinicians to "develop a good working knowledge of the variety of models in order to do justice to the variety of families we see" in clinical practice (p. 195). In their overview, they outline the main features of four important models of family therapy: (1) the *communication* approach, emphasizing cognitive and affective themes in the messages sent by family members to one another, as exemplified in the work of Watzlawick and associates at the Mental Research Institute in Palo Alto, California (Watzlawick, Beavin, & Jackson, 1967); (2) the *psychodynamic* approach, also emphasizing cognitive and affective themes, especially those relating to separation-individuation and loss phenomena, as illustrated by the work of Paul (1976) and Framo (1965); (3) the *structural* approach, emphasizing behavioral and affective themes relating to "boundaries" and role enactment, as in Minuchin's (often crisis-inducing) problem-solving mode (Minuchin, 1974; Minuchin & Fishman, 1981); and (4) the *systems* approach, relying heavily on didactic, cognitive, intergenerational, and autonomy themes, exemplified by the work of Bowen (1978).

An Approach to Brief Family Crisis Therapy

Utilizing an integrative-eclectic mix of the elements noted above, this section outlines basic interrelated principles concerning the initiation and implementation of family crisis intervention. Of prime importance is the concept that family crisis treatment must be immediate, easily accessible, and effectively coordinated with early and quick biopsychosocial assessment. In other words, the traditional approach of prolonged history taking and extended diagnostic study is contrary to the crisis approach. In traditional long-term modalities, the clinician may typically elicit information from "healthy" family members about the "ill" patient. With these approaches, an implicit expectation is often aroused in family members that the expert ("doctor–magician") will provide a solution to the family's problem and rid it of either the deviant behavior or the person causing the problems.

By definition, the crisis therapist makes a commitment to treating the family as a group, that is, as a small-scale social system, perhaps in the natural social setting of the home (Langsley & Kaplan, 1968; Whittington, 1985). Except for rare exceptions involving high-risk suicidal or homicidal persons, outpatient family crisis therapy is regarded as a far more desirable treatment alternative than is hospitalization (Langsley & Kaplan, 1968; Pittman, 1987). Ideally, the family, not the identified patient, is the client.

The distressed behavior of the identified patient is conceptualized as a cry for help. It represents blocked communication, absence of warm contact, or lack of subgroup alliances among family members. The patient's presenting problem is regarded as a reflection of treatable problems in family interaction.

The worker confronts the family with the main cognitive, affective, and behavioral tasks that must be addressed and offers advice on how to carry them out. The worker makes liberal use of contracts, encouraging working agreements among family members to deal with problems through a here-and-now interactional approach. The worker uses a variety of techniques, including sculpting, psychodrama, modeling, anticipatory guidance, guided imagery, and videotape playback (Alger, 1976).

Well before the end of the first interview, the worker is likely to plan a second session, which usually will take place in the office or occasionally in the client's home. In order to gain the family's collaboration, the worker seeks sanction from the family power figure, perhaps one of the parents, a grandparent, or an older sibling. The worker reviews goals and specific means for reaching them; encourages feedback concerning what has been accomplished thus far; negotiates family members' expectations; ensures that homework assignments are clear, relevant, and achievable; and, mindful of the power of the self-fulfilling prophecy, arouses hopeful expectancies to help the family improve its functioning.

Intervention Guidelines

When family crisis intervention is implemented, the following specific steps—similar to the generic stages of individual or group crisis counseling—should be taken. Appropriate efforts should be made to involve family members in each phase: (1) search for the precipitating event and its perceptual meaning to the family members; (2) look for the coping means used by the family and appraise the extent to which these have or have not been successful; (3) search for alternative ways of coping and the resources that might improve the situation, while actively soliciting suggestions from family members; (4) review and support the family members' efforts to cope in new ways, with evaluation of results in terms of day-to-day living experiences; (5) assist toward the early termination that was planned in the initial contract with the family; and (6) plan and conduct at least one follow-up or "booster-shot" session. Throughout this process, the worker should actively define the goals of the family crisis session and the means that can be used for goal achievement, while energetically focusing on the relevant issues.

Influenced by the communications and psychodynamic orientations as well as by Bowen's (1978) systemic concepts relating to family fusion and individual autonomy, our approach, based on our assessment of the family, is planfully directive, goal-oriented, and selectively risk-taking, often assuming a problem-solving stance similar to Minuchin's (1974) approach to structural family therapy. To recapitulate, the framework we use involves antecedent (family life-style), intervening (intermediate problem-solving), and consequent (need–response) variables in the observation, study, and treatment of the family in crisis. Follow-up interviews (T5 in the theoretical framework presented in Table 2) can have a reinforcing effect and thus enhance the new postcrisis need–response pattern; provide feedback to increase consumer input into crisis-oriented mental health delivery systems; afford a safeguard if the time limits specified are not adequate for the family's needs; and aid systematic research on cost effectiveness and other issues.

Case Examples

An excerpt from a case history illustrates our theoretical perspectives on family values, roles, and communication as systemic foci in short-term crisis intervention.

> The E family consisted of Sam, who was nineteen, a younger sister, three older brothers, his mother, and his father. Mrs. E earned more money than her husband, which was a source of concern. According to Mrs. E, as adolescents the three older brothers "had serious problems with drugs, wore long hair, and had trouble with the law." The brothers, now married, had moved into homes adjacent to their parents' to settle down with their wives and raise children, forming a family enclave. This enmeshed family illustrated Bowen's (1978) theory of the undifferentiated ego mass, with all four sons working with the mother in a small family business.
>
> Sam was rushed to the local hospital after taking all the pills he could find in his mother's medicine chest. This suicide attempt was Sam's seventh attempt through overdosing. The mother had just given Sam a job in the family business; when Sam did not behave responsibly, his mother angrily threatened that Sam would be fired, which precipitated Sam's suicidal gesture. Immediately after ingesting the pills, Sam called a hotline. Unfortunately, the line was busy. However, he had enough presence of mind to call their minister, a friend of the family, who immediately came to the house and rushed Sam to the hospital where his stomach was pumped. Sam's parents were interviewed by hospital staff only as sources of information for history-taking purposes.
>
> A few days after Sam's brief stay in the hospital, I (H. J. Parad) initiated family crisis therapy with Sam, his parents, and his younger sister. After an initial period of anxious mumbling, Sam began to open up in response to a sculpting exercise in which he was asked to portray his father and mother in relation to himself (Papp, 1976). His first sculpting exercise placed his father in a mildly threatening position, with his father's fist near Sam's head. Impressed by Sam's beginning efforts at communication, the father responded by saying, "I'll show you the way it really is. In your eyes, I think you view me this way," and he proceeded to resculpt the family interaction by making his hands into claws menacing his son's throat. When asked how this felt, Sam was at first quiet. When I insisted, he expressed his anger at his father and his feeling that his mother passed the ammunition to his father, who then "shot" it at him. The father began crying, saying that he and Sam had a long history of fighting and he wanted to end the battle. Sam said, "You always notice what I do that is bad, not when I do something that is good." In an attempt at value clarification, I asked for a discussion of the good/bad issue. The mother said, "My idea of your being good is when you are concerned with us; you're bad when you are concerned with you." I concentrated on this kind of value confrontation for several minutes. It was clear Sam's need for autonomy paralleled the father's emerging need to be free of family enmeshment.
>
> In relation to the *communication subsystem*, I encouraged open expression of feelings, and the father was able gradually to become much less judgmental in his approach toward his son, validating Sam's desire for self-direction. In this interview, the mother was not able to validate her son's feelings beyond a few clichéd responses.
>
> In relation to *role patterning*, it was obvious that expectations were not clear regarding who should do what. Sam's abortive efforts at going to a

> local college were frowned upon because the college he had attended was not his parents' choice. When asked directly what he wanted to do, he told his parents, "to carry out my wishes, not yours!" In subsequent discussions, it became obvious that Sam was, in part, acting out his father's anger at the mother. His suicidal attempt was formulated as a *cry for help*. We discussed how Sam had turned his anger against himself instead of expressing it directly. Did Sam think he was so bad that he had to destroy himself?
>
> Attempts at crisis resolution culminated in a series of problem-solving discussions relating to Sam's proclaimed need to carry out his own wishes to leave home, enroll in an out-of-town college to pursue his studies, and grow up. I supported Sam in his struggle for individuation, and I modeled for the parents how they, too, could encourage Sam in his new efforts at independence.

It is noteworthy that Sam's family was not included in Sam's hospital treatment plan, even though the family would have been responsive to an outreach effort. I attempted to move family functioning away from pseudointegration, which had involved the parents in an unhealthy, wavering alliance against the children, toward a more facilitating and validating type of integration that would lead to greater recognition of Sam's growing autonomy. In a later discussion, while encouraging the parents to deal directly with their own mid-life transitional crises, I emphasized the similarity between the developmental tasks with which the adolescent son and daughter were struggling and those with which the parents were struggling. In this way, treatment assumed an intergenerational problem-solving approach. However, as is typical in brief family crisis intervention (perhaps also in long-term family treatment), I was willing to settle for limited, but positive, goals.

The second case vignette illustrates crisis intervention with a family in which the identified patient, Mrs. K, had been hospitalized with a diagnosis of paranoid schizophrenia.

> The K family consisted of the identified patient, Mrs. K, age thirty-four, who was born in Hungary and raised in a strongly religious family; her son, Tom, age nine, from her previous marriage; and her husband, Mr. K, age thirty-five, also divorced, and self-described as a "backsliding" Irish-Catholic whose parents were both alcoholics.
>
> Videotaped demonstration interviews were held in front of selected staff members at a state hospital (just prior to Mrs. K's anticipated release to home) in order to demonstrate the relevance of a family crisis approach to the staff of the community mental health aftercare program to which Mrs. K was being discharged. Mr. K and Tom had not been previously seen by hospital staff, although they had visited Mrs. K daily during the ten-day period of her hospitalization. Mrs. K had responded well enough to psychotropic medication and the protective milieu of the hospital to be ready for a trial home visit. Mrs. K began the interview by explaining that approximately two weeks ago, she had begun to feel anxious and overwhelmed and was afraid that the "force" (from the movie *Star Wars*) would harm her. She had experienced a psychotic episode approximately two years earlier (at the time of her divorce) and had been on psychotropic medication but stopped taking the pills because she was feeling O.K. To cope with her current fears, she sobbingly revealed, she had called a friend,

who told her not to let her imagination take over. She attempted to cope by drinking coffee and smoking cigarettes to calm her nerves, but to no avail. Despairing, she tore off all her clothes, screamed at Tom, ran out of the house, and with a tube of bright red lipstick scribbled "HELP!" on her car's windshield.

In searching for the stressor that had precipitated Mrs. K's decompensation crisis, I learned that Mrs. K and Mr. K had had terrible fights because Mr. K had been dating another woman since transferring to the night shift at his job. Mrs. K, according to her husband, had been sexually unresponsive and generally distant. He said he really loved her but couldn't communicate with her. Mrs. K said, "You never try!" The following is a brief interview excerpt:

Mr. K (to Mrs. K): I try, but you don't listen.

Mrs. K: I put my faith in the Lord.

Mr. K: [angrily] That's a lot of crap, and you know it!

Therapist: Mr. K, you said when you were a kid your parents would drink and fight?

Mr. K: Yes, you better believe it, and they would throw me and my brother and sister out of the room. Nothing ever got settled.

Therapist: Are you repeating the same patterns?

Mr. K: I don't understand—how do you mean?

Therapist: I mean the pattern of being excluded.

Mrs. K: [touching Tom tenderly] He drinks and smokes pot when he's angry and stays away from me.

Therapist: [observing Mrs. K who is hugging and looking at Tom while talking to Mr. K] Mrs. K, are you aware of what you're doing?

Mrs. K became aware that she was attending to Tom while Mr. K talked to her. And Mr. K immediately noticed that his wife did not make eye contact while talking to him. Mrs. K smiled inappropriately. Mr. K said in a surprised tone, "You don't even look at me!"

Subsequent discussions focused on the couple's *communication* pattern, the *triangulation* that was occurring, and how Mr. K felt shut out. Mr. K related how being shut out made him feel depressed and how he would handle his feelings by drinking, smoking pot, and going out with other women. But, he repeated, I love my wife and son, and don't want to break up the family.

In response to the worker's interpretation of how Mrs. K and Mr. K hurt each other, the two of them engaged in a tender dialogue, embraced, cried, and poignantly discussed plans for the future.

In another discussion, we talked about how Tom, confused by the events that had preceded Mrs. K's hospitalization, had blamed himself for his mother's illness, asking if he had been "bad." Mr. K, talking directly to Tom, explained that Tom had nothing to do with his mother's illness. Tom became visibly relaxed.

The hospital staff agreed to try a biopsychosocial aftercare plan with the K family, including continued medication for Mrs. K, with supervision by the public health nurse; conjoint interviews with Mrs. K and Mr. K by the community care social worker to maintain communication between them;

and family interviews (including Tom) to encourage shared recreational and social activities for the family.*

In the treatment encounter, there should be a balance of support and confrontation to help achieve the goal of action-oriented problem solving at a time of family crisis. The focus is often—but not always—on planned, short-term contracting; on setting specific and achievable goals; on clarifying who will do what; on the use of homework assignments between interviews; and on an exploration of reasons for success and failure in carrying out homework tasks. Flexibly spaced interviews are arranged to support completion of the treatment contracts. Keeping in mind the life cycle through which the family evolves, the therapist focuses on marital, parent–child, and sibling subsystems, in addition to viewing the transactional family system as a whole.

Community Care

In response to the continuing depopulation of state mental hospitals, various innovative attempts have been made to apply a family-oriented crisis approach to the community care of mentally disordered persons (Polak & Jones, 1973). The Southwest Denver Mental Health Services affords a promising example of this trend by using rapid tranquilization; offering nonhospital care through family sponsors (who are on the payroll of the center); making frequent home visits; drawing upon a large cadre of volunteers; arranging special homes for constant observation in the case of acutely psychotic, suicidal, or potentially dangerous clients; and operating within a social system framework rather than following a purely psychodynamic ideology (Polak, 1978). In creatively designing family-oriented care of the mentally disordered, hospitalization gives way to a community system of carefully selected family settings. Mechanic (1980) emphasized the need for comprehensive systems of service to aid the family in meeting crises relating to mental disorder. Other models are needed to incorporate the social system perspectives of Jones and Polak (1968) and to utilize the techniques developed by family crisis workers who are comfortable working with the emotionally disturbed and mentally disordered in their own homes or in substitute community settings.

In recounting his experiences doing family crisis therapy as an alternative to mental hospitalization, Pittman (1987), in a delightfully trenchant theater-of-the-absurd style, comments on his experiences as a collaborator with Langsley, Kaplan, and others at the University of Colorado Department of Psychiatry as well as on his subsequent experience at Grady Hospital in Atlanta:

> What we did in Denver demonstrated that family crisis therapy is far cheaper, quicker, and at least as effective as psychiatric hospitalization for comparable patients, with far fewer long-range disadvantages. The data from the Denver Project was [sic] widely reported . . . and strongly influenced the community mental health movement. Verification that family

*Zuckerwise (see chapter 10) refers to the problems of mentally disordered persons and their family systems, pointing out that their welfare is now a priority issue in mental health legislation and social welfare programs. The National Institute of Mental Health (NIMH) believes that the plight of homeless schizophrenic persons, many of whom have children, requires urgent attention.

> therapy worked was heartening to that movement too, which was gaining momentum at that time but had little data to back it up.
>
> My subsequent experience, applying this approach on an enormous scale as director of Atlanta's public mental health services at Grady Hospital, from 1968 to 1972, demonstrated dramatically that this approach was as practical as it was effective. But, since few professions are seeking a cheaper alternative to themselves, family therapy as an alternative to psychiatric hospitalization has not been widely adopted.
>
> In private practice since 1972, I do what we did in Denver and for Atlanta, but with families that are usually, but not always, less profoundly disorganized and less pressing in their sense of emergency. The differences between families in transition and families in crisis are less than meet the eye. . . .
>
> In Denver, in the process of studying families in crisis, we came up with a framework for understanding the state of crisis in families. That framework has kept me structured through twenty-odd years of dealing with and expanding my understanding of families in transition and crisis. I emerged from Denver with great respect for the ability of family members to drive one another sane if they must, and with the belief that the keys to mental health include responsibility and functioning. A philosophy and technology gradually developed based on family members' taking responsibility for their effects on one another and functioning appropriately (pp. xvi–xvii).

Thus there is great need for further training and administrative changes if the family-oriented community programs suggested here are to achieve fruition. There are formidable obstacles as well. First, senior staff members often resist work with families. Often cast in the role of rebels, new staff members may have to fight to be allowed to do family crisis intervention. Second, involving families at the time they request hospitalization or rehospitalization of the identified patient is particularly difficult in the face of bureaucratic opposition—overt or covert (Framo, 1976). Yet, at times, the initial process of family involvement can be extremely simple.

We recently learned about the typical practices of various staff members in a university-sponsored outpatient emergency walk-in crisis clinic that serves many emotionally disturbed and mentally disordered persons who are variously self-referred, brought in handcuffed by the police, or shepherded into a crowded emergency waiting room by anxious family members. In one situation, for example, a senior staff member would emerge from his office, ask the nurse, "Who is the next patient?" and then interview that person alone in his office, even though the patient had been accompanied to the emergency room by significant others. (Or, as in the case of Sam, the staff may view other family members primarily as sources of background information rather than as collaborative agents of change.) In dramatic contrast, however, a young staff member, trained in the techniques of family crisis intervention, would request that all members of the family who were with the identified patient accompany him or her to the office to discuss and deal with the *family* problem. Thus differences in therapeutic ideology are immediately reflected in therapists' initial approaches to the family.

Ongoing family crisis intervention with emotionally upset and mentally disordered individuals, and particularly with the psychotic-level family, is not easy work (Lieb, Lipsitch, & Slaby, 1973). Constantly expected to give sustenance as they implement the concept of the social support system, family crisis interveners themselves need support. Obviously, there are mental health hazards for practitioners in this work. To cope with these hazards, staff members need opportunities for respite, additional training and supervision, staff development seminars, and a favorable work milieu in which they can share their clinical experiences—both their failures and their successes.

Summary

Drawing on early work in family-oriented crisis intervention with Caplan and other Harvard colleagues, as well as on our experiences as clinicians and as training consultants for the California Department of Mental Health, we have attempted to update the conceptual framework and family crisis intervention principles that characterize our present approach to families in crisis. Our approach relies on the structured use of time limits; understanding family dynamics within a systems perspective; use of the family life-style concept, with attention to its three components (values, roles, and communication); appreciation of the intervening problem-solving mechanisms used by families to cope with crisis events; and the relevance of the need–response pattern as a way of measuring the success of these coping efforts. Finally, we have outlined the integrated use of various action-therapy techniques within an eclectic framework aimed at dealing with the cognitive, affective, and behavioral components comprising the phenomenology of family crisis intervention.

Group Crisis Counseling

The crisis approach is used not only with nuclear and extended families but also with natural friendship or common interest groups, including gangs and clubs that are not kinship-related (H. J. Parad, Selby, & Quinlan, 1976). Crisis intervention is applicable to a broad spectrum of formed groups as well, including groups of children and teachers in school settings, work groups, activity groups, and therapy groups. These groups meet on an intra- or extramural basis—again, the common denominator being the experience with crisis. People who are simultaneously experiencing crisis are usually able to be comfortable with one another in a group setting, despite social factors that would distance them during noncrisis periods. Crisis also serves as a social leveler when communities are struck by natural disasters.

Group crisis intervention is practiced within various institutional settings, including crisis hostels, halfway houses, and detention facilities. In these settings it is often combined with techniques of crisis induction (deliberate confrontation to produce an upset state), which is used as part of delinquency control programs.

New developments include crisis intervention in protective service settings. The precipitating stress is the protective service worker's knock on the door announcing that a complaint requiring investigation has been made. (See chapters 3, 4, 9, 11, 13, and 16 for discussions of varied uses of group process in crisis intervention.)

The group crisis counseling program developed by Strickler and Allgeyer (1967) at the Benjamin Rush Center in Los Angeles, the first of its kind in the country, is particularly interesting. Groups are open to new members who join at a time of crisis, attend up to six sessions, and provide mutual aid to one another. The familiar steps in the ensuing group process, which are similar to those in individual and family crisis therapy, are as follows: (1) search for the precipitating event and its meaning to the member; (2) discuss current means of coping with the crisis; (3) explore alternative, perhaps novel, ways of coping that might better fit the demands of the crisis situation, and review and support, in subsequent group sessions, the member's efforts to cope in new ways; (4) handle feelings about termination and summarize and evaluate efforts at coping with crisis; and (5) consider possible referral to self-help and other resources as well as the need for follow-up to reinforce the member's ability to cope with future stress.

Despite certain methodological problems, an experimental study at the Benjamin Rush Center compared clients receiving group crisis intervention with a control group receiving placebo medication. Results indicated that group crisis counseling clients had less need for additional therapy, showed more awareness of their life situation, demonstrated more effective coping skills, and were judged to be less dependent than were control group clients (Morley, 1974).

More recently, Donovan, Bennett, and McElroy (1981) at the Harvard Community Health Plan have described another apparently effective approach to group crisis intervention; follow-up showed that 91 percent of the participants considered the group "helpful" (p. 290). Fostering a sense of universality about encounters with life crises in order to promote group cohesiveness, the group leader is directive, inquiring, hopeful, friendly, "often confrontive, but supportive" (p. 301).

The following vignette presents a one-year follow-up interview with a group member whose initial precipitating stress was the break-up of a relationship and for whom "the group retained a positive glow, and as predicted further treatment had not been necessary" (Donovan et al., 1981, p. 293). When asked how the group helped him, he replied:

> I had an opportunity to see others in their relationships. This helped me gain a better perspective on my own. I also met some very fine, caring people in the group. It permitted me to relax enough to get back in the swing of my job and personal interests. I had an opportunity to compare and contrast myself to others. It allowed me to reaffirm my self-evaluation and esteem. It helped me realize that I was a good, valuable person even though my relationship was ending (p. 293).

Although candid about the limitations of the crisis group experience (for example, 25 percent of the members dropped out), Donovan's follow-up study of members' perceptions persuaded him that the group format is "usually a superior mode of treatment to individual crisis intervention" (p. 302), because the group can simultaneously enhance independence (individual coping efforts) and interdependence (relatedness to other members). More intensive than the Benjamin Rush groups (whose members met for up to six sessions), the members of the Harvard crisis group met twice a week for four weeks (a total of eight sessions).

A recent study (Joyce, Azim, & Morin, 1988) compared the clinical activities of therapists in brief crisis-oriented group treatment with those in long-term group therapy. As expected, the crisis-oriented therapists were more directive and challenging than were their counterparts in long-term therapy. The crisis group clients, who manifested fewer "resistance behaviors," reported greater improvement than did the long-term group participants. In interpreting these impressive results, one has to note two related methodological problems: (1) it is unclear whether group assignment was random and (2) certain between-group differences were noted, for example, the short-term clients were more likely to be diagnosed as having stress-related adjustment disorders rather than personality disorders. Yet, the power of the crisis-oriented treatment is apparent in the fact that the crisis group clients generally received higher ratings on severity of psychosocial stressors and were more likely to report higher levels of depression than were the long-term clients.

While apparently offering promising results, crisis groups are still a sadly underutilized resource for helping people cope with crisis. True, there are difficult problems to be addressed, as indicated below, but the potential rewards of group support and aid in problem-solving will, we hope, encourage more practitioners to experiment with modes of group crisis counseling. Important questions to be considered when forming groups in crisis intervention programming include:

1. How can a balance of homogeneity and heterogeneity be achieved? Although the crisis experience is a common denominator, problems may occur when members' ages, personality problems, and life-styles are extremely disparate.

2. Is a lengthy pregroup screening interview needed? Donovan et al. (1981) say yes; our experience suggests that a quick rather than a prolonged preliminary interview is often preferable so that the client does not have to retell a detailed story when introducing him- or herself to the group. The Harvard Community Health Plan (Budman & Gurman, 1988) has successfully experimented with a single ninety-minute trial task-oriented workshop to determine a client's suitability for brief group therapy.

3. Should the group membership be open or closed? If open, perhaps one or two new members should be invited to each session, which is optimally attended by six to eight members. If closed, a highly structured format may be used: All members start and end on the same date. However, this format creates a problem when members drop out, possibly threatening the continuation of the group.

4. Is a co-therapist needed? Donovan et al. (1981) say yes; our experience as crisis group leaders suggests that a co-leader is often desirable, but given the drain on staff time, not always cost-effective.

5. Should group members be discouraged from socializing with one another after or between sessions without the therapist's presence? Based on his long-term insight-oriented model, Yalom (1985) would say yes. However, most crisis group practitioners believe that outside social activities facilitate a mutual-aid problems-of-living approach.

Other Interactional Approaches

In addition to forming crisis groups, crisis clinicians who are oriented to the client's "social surround" have unique opportunities to involve significant others during the crisis resolution phase: selected family members (but not necessarily in the context of a plan for ongoing crisis therapy); fellow workers and supervisors in Employee Assistance Programs (EAPs); other caregivers (for example, physicians, nurses, teachers); friends; and, indeed, anyone who is important to the person or persons going through a crisis. The following cases illustrate an interactional approach beyond the typical examples of family and group crisis treatment. In the first case, intergenerational therapy between an adult child and parents was utilized.

> Sue, a very attractive thirty-seven-year-old career business person, came to a brief therapy clinic following a succession of failed relationships with men, the latest of which precipitated a crisis response with accompanying feelings of depression and devastation. I (H. J. Parad) discussed with Sue two interrelated patterns in all of her relationship "breakdowns": (1) Sue picked men who, in her words, were "commitment phobic"—as if she needed to be rejected—and (2) when the relationship failed to prosper, she would overreact to the loss, feeling totally unprepared for what she had already anticipated, namely, the end of an inherently flawed relationship. She was always left with a feeling of exclusion, which counterproductively made her want to refuse dates with other men to protect herself from further rejection.
>
> "Why do I feel this way?" she asked, then began to talk about a "weird" feeling that she had often felt excluded as a child, that her parents were not available to her. Typically, she began to berate herself for such a "distorted" feeling. Approximately two years earlier, she had received individual psychodynamic therapy for about seven months for recurrent anxiety and depression, but found no relief for her problems with men.
>
> Mindful of her tendency to talk about rather than *feel* her feelings, I suggested that we schedule two sessions—one with her mother and one with her father. Our purpose was to try over a period of a few months to experience directly and to address her feelings of exclusion, then work through her maladaptive "push/pull" (approach/avoid) way of currently relating to men. After a lot of reflective indecision (her typical precrisis mode of coping), Sue finally accepted the suggestion to risk asking her parents to attend a session. I reassured her that it was a "no lose" plan: If her parents refused to come, she was no worse off than before; if one or both parents came for a parent–daughter session and little happened, we would still have some grist for our mill; and if we generated excitement, anger, tenderness, or closeness, so much the better. In any event, we would both have a better notion of her "exclusion crisis."
>
> Her father, an obese sixty-seven-year-old retired administrator, came with Sue the following week. After a short warm-up, Sue haltingly and tearfully told him that she often experienced feelings of detachment when he was with her. Defensively, her father replied that nothing could be further from the truth. However, after some discussion and apparently without realizing the importance of his statement, the father said that he and his wife, Terry, sure were glad they had two TVs in the house—one for Mom and Dad and the other for the kids—when Sue and her four sisters were growing up.
>
> Sue began to cry again. I said perhaps Sue felt detached from Dad and Mom because they were detached from Sue. Not knowing what to say or do, Dad's eyes teared up while he unconvincingly commented that he and his wife were in the living room talking and worrying about money and other family problems while "you kids" were watching TV. He began talking about

> his own mother's sudden death when he was only sixteen and how terrible the loss was for him. He began to cry, saying how much he missed his mother—what a lonely empty feeling he often has when he thinks of her.
>
> Later, while Sue's father was reminiscing about his work experiences, I asked what kind of work he did. He became irritable and suddenly excluded me, refusing to talk for a few moments. Apparently, I had inadvertently touched a sensitive spot. Sue later explained that her father was ashamed of not getting promoted at his job—hence his annoyance. He refused to discuss the matter directly with me.
>
> Sue, emboldened by her father's vulnerability and my presence, confronted her father for "purposefully" being late for her birthday party. He accepted her anger and apologized—a rare thing for him. Sue and her father touched hands tenderly; for a while Sue felt close to him, and the session ended on a positive note.
>
> In her next session, two days later, Sue was amazed by what she had learned and felt somewhat elated. Although she did not expect a dramatic transformation in her relationship with her father, at least she was able to understand where some of her exclusion feelings came from and that it wasn't "all me."
>
> The following week Sue brought her sixty-eight-year-old mother, Terry. Sue and her mother talked about the time Terry's mother died. Sue, who was approximately eight years old then, wondered why her mother didn't cry. Weeping openly, Terry described how when her father died when Terry was six years old, family roles were reversed and she became her mother's mother. Sue and her mother talked about Sue's feeling of exclusion. Sue said, "Apparently, it seemed to me as if you weren't there for me when I was growing up!" Terry said, "No 'apparently' about it, *I wasn't* there for you—I was blocked!" Crying, she continued, "Your Dad and I both missed out as kids; we didn't get what we needed and we didn't give you what you needed. I'm sorry."
>
> In the next two sessions, Sue expressed intense feelings regarding her sessions with her parents. She was surprised that so much had happened; she felt hurt and angry but had a better sense of what had caused her exclusion crisis. We talked about her improving sense of self-esteem; I reminded her that she felt excluded because of actual life events, *not* because of some fantasized inner defect on her part.
>
> Now involved in a relationship with a warm, caring man—who "can you believe may actually want to be committed?"—Sue uses a novel way to cope: first, she looks at the people around her to discover who they are and what they do, then she looks inwardly to check her perceptions, without reflexively feeling excluded and judging herself negatively.

This type of short-term interactional dynamic therapy is guided by Bowen's (1978) intergenerational and thinking-versus-feeling formulations as well as by Framo's (1982) emphasis on working through problems by direct, here-and-now experiences with significant others in an effort to understand how these experiences may relate to antecedent events. The therapeutic focus provides a clear and steady strategy for change, using the intensity of the client's exclusion crisis to foster and try out new modes of relating and communicating. Perhaps the therapeutic lesson to be learned is that it is often more effective for adults in crisis to talk directly *with* their parents than *about* them in endless therapy. Of course, intergenerational contacts may apply to long-term therapy as well.

Clearly, it is not always feasible to see significant others in therapy. When (after an appropriate period for developing a therapeutic alliance) the therapist first mentions the prospect of seeing clients' parents, adult clients are often resistive and reluctant initially. The client and clinician must realistically anticipate the likely outcome of such intergenerational encounters. Of course, not all such encounters produce dramatic changes. At the very least, however, they afford the therapist a chance to observe the client's *in vivo* interactions, thereby providing rich data for future sessions focused on change-oriented behaviors.

Pragmatically, it makes sense to try to include persons who are involved with the client in a work-related problem to contribute toward its solution. Such an interactional crisis-oriented approach is illustrated in the case of the F family (H. J. Parad, 1984).

> The F family consisted of Mr. F, a thirty-one-year-old communications installation technician, Mrs. F, a twenty-nine-year-old homemaker, and their two children, Ralph, seven, and Mary, four. An ongoing health problem was dramatically aggravated when Ralph became terminally ill and Mr. F's work attendance became spotty. Indicating that his absenteeism was a serious problem and put his job at risk, Mr. F's supervisor referred him to the Employee Assistance Program (EAP) counselor on an emergency basis.
>
> In the initial interview with Mr. F, it became immediately clear that he was suffering tremendously. His grief and pain overwhelmed his personal, family, and work life. He needed a flexible work schedule to enable him to visit his son and to be with his family. He desperately needed to maintain his job for the money and a sense of belonging. Work was a place where he could escape from the frightening reality of his son's impending death. However, because of heavy work pressures, his supervisor and unit manager were increasingly intolerant of his absences.
>
> Although the counselor felt deep empathy with Mr. F's pain, she also realized that he would have to make tough decisions regarding when to visit his son during the day, when to be with his wife and daughter, and when to go to work. Moreover, he would obviously have to alert his supervisor in advance when he needed to be away instead of just not showing up. As client and counselor talked, Mr. F began to see the company's perspective as well as his own. The counselor obtained a signed release to talk with Mr. F's supervisor and unit manager on his behalf and to invite them to a brief meeting to attempt to resolve the problem. At the meeting (attended by Mr. F, his supervisor, his unit manager, and the counselor) two related goals were achieved: First, the supervisor and manager were sensitized to Mr. F's anguish, isolation, and feelings about his inability to relieve Ralph of his pain and prevent his death. Second, the counselor assured the supervisor and manager that she would be able to assist Mr. F with his work-attendance problems, that Mr. F would communicate with them openly in the future, but that he would, of course, be with his son and family when the end came.
>
> This meeting assisted management to become more sensitive to an employee's crisis while respecting the best interests of the company. The counselor's suggestion that Mr. F be temporarily assigned to another position because climbing for installation work would be hazardous for him in his upset state was rejected by Mr. F, because he wanted to be with his buddies at work, and a job transfer was more than he could bear at this time. As it turned out, Mr. F's climbing partners took the situation in hand; they

climbed while Mr. F did the ground work, a division of labor that seemed to satisfy all concerned. In addition, the counselor had two conjoint interviews with Mr. and Mrs. F, and visited the hospital with Mrs. F to see Ralph. Mr. F's wish to have further interviews on an as-needed basis only was respected. The counselor maintained regular telephone contact with Mrs. F and helped answer her questions about Mrs. F's wish to help her husband and their daughter, Mary, deal with Ralph's illness and subsequent death. Feedback from management and the family indicated that the contacts were helpful in supporting Mr. and Mrs. F during the period following Ralph's death (H. J. Parad, 1984).

Interactional and group crisis counseling have not been sufficiently utilized in the workplace. These methods offer exciting treatment possibilities in that they have been found to be an effective and economical tool for helping people who are experiencing similar life or work crises in a variety of mental health settings. Research increasingly indicates that interactional therapies, including couple, family, and small-group approaches, are generally more effective in dealing with clients' problems in social functioning than are purely individual-centered approaches (Gurman & Kniskern, 1981).

Conclusion

The crisis intervention approach advocated here requires certain administrative procedures to ensure that services are easily and promptly accessible and to provide for clients' needs rather than for the social agency's or clinic's convenience. A number of steps must be taken to meet these goals of proximity, accessibility, and effectiveness: (1) the virtual elimination of waiting lists (in part through the proper utilization of professional and paraprofessional personnel); (2) the avoidance of complex intake screening so that psychosocial treatment will be virtually simultaneous with diagnosis; (3) the development of an open-door policy for persons who may require further services when faced with new unmanageable crises; (4) as previously indicated, the use of a built-in policy of preplanned follow-up interviews (by telephone, if necessary, for reasons of economic expedience) to provide feedback about the effectiveness of service, and to provide ethical safeguards when an arbitrary number of interviews is used in planned, short-term treatment arrangements; and (5) although this position may be controversial, wherever possible, the avoidance of centralized intake, which requires that clients be transferred to another staff member after their initial presentation of their crisis quandaries. Therapists should attempt to imagine how they would feel if they told their intimate story to a strange person, then, having developed some initial trust in a helping relationship, were required to tell their story to a new therapist.

Basic to implementation of these recommendations is an administrative mindset that favors egalitarian rather than purely hierarchical arrangements among interdisciplinary staff members; encourages experimentation with interactional as opposed to purely individual-centered interviews; provides support to counselors in order to avoid staff burnout (especially important in hotline, protective, and other emergency crisis services for high-risk populations); values disciplined, integrative eclecticism; believes in accountability for the effectiveness of services; and above all, respects the special vulnerabilities and strengths of people in crisis.

References

Alexander, F., & French, T. M. (1946). *Psychoanalytic therapy*. New York: Ronald Press.

Alevizos, P., & Liberman, R. P. (1976). Behavioral approaches to family crisis intervention. In H. Parad, H. Resnick, & L. Parad (Eds.), *Emergency and disaster management* (pp. 129–143). Bowie, MD: Charles Press.

Alger, I. E. (1976). Integrating immediate video playback in family therapy. In P. J. Guerin (Ed.), *Family therapy: Theory & Practice* (pp. 530–547). New York: Gardner Press.

Auerbach, S., & Stolberg, A. (Eds.). (1986). *Crisis intervention with children and families*. Washington, DC: Hemisphere Publishing.

Bard, M. (1970). *Training police as specialists in family crisis intervention*. Washington, DC: National Institute of Law Enforcement and Criminal Justice, U.S. Department of Justice.

Baron, R., & Feeney, F. (1976). Crisis intervention and the juvenile court: One project's approach. In H. Parad, H. Resnik, & L. Parad (Eds.), *Emergency and disaster management* (pp. 119–128). Bowie, MD: Charles Press.

Beck, A. T. (1976). *Cognitive therapy and the emotional disorders*. New York: International Universities Press.

Beck, B. M., & Robbins, L. L. (1946). *Short term therapy in an authoritative setting*. New York: Family Service Association of America.

Beck, D. F., & Jones, M. A. (1973). *Progress on family problems*. New York: Family Service Association of America.

Bellak, L., & Siegel, H. (1983). *Handbook of intensive brief and emergency psychotherapy*. Larchmont, NY: C.P.S. Inc.

Berliner, B. (1941). Short psychoanalytic psychotherapy: Its possibilities and its limitations. *Bulletin of the Menninger Clinic*, *5*, 204–213.

Berliner, B. (1945). Short psychoanalytic psychotherapy. *Bulletin of the Menninger Clinic*, 9, 155–161.

Bill, A. (1969). The effectiveness of a psychiatric emergency service, *Delaware Medical Journal*, *41*, p. 241.

Bloom, B. L. (1965). Definitional aspects of the crisis concept. In H. Parad (Ed.), *Crisis Intervention: Selected readings* (pp. 303–311). New York: Family Service Association of America.

Bloom, B. L. (1980). Social and community interventions. *Annual Review of Psychology*, *31*, 111–142.

Bloom, B. L. (1981). Focused single-session therapy: Initial development and evaluation. In S. H. Budman (Ed.), *Forms of brief therapy* (pp. 167–218). New York: Guilford Press.

Bowen, M. (1978). *Family therapy in clinical practice*. New York: Jason Aronson.

Bowlby, J. (1980). *Loss: Sadness and depression* (Vol. 3). New York: Basic Books.

Brown, V. (1976). Community crisis intervention. In H. Parad, H. Resnik, & L. Parad (Eds.), *Emergency and disaster management* (pp. 99–108). Bowie, MD: Charles Press.

Budman, S. D. (Ed.). (1981). *Forms of brief therapy*. New York: Guilford Press.

Budman, S. D., & Gurman, A. (1988). *Theory and practice of brief therapy*. New York: Guilford Press.

Butcher, J. N., & Koss, M. P. (1978). Research on brief and crisis-oriented psychotherapies. In S. L. Garfield & A. E. Bergin (Eds.), *Handbook of psychotherapy and behavior change* (pp. 725–767). New York: John Wiley.

Caplan, G. (1954). The disturbance of the mother–child relationship by unsuccessful attempts at abortion. *Mental Hygiene, 38*(1), 67–80.

Caplan, G. (1955). The role of the social worker in preventive psychiatry. *Medical Social Work, 4*(4), 144–160.

Caplan, G. (1964). *Principles of preventive psychiatry*. New York: Basic Books.

Caplan, G. (1989). *Population-oriented psychiatry*. New York: Human Sciences/Plenum Press.

Caplan, G., Mason, E., & Kaplan, D. (1965). Four studies of crisis in parents of prematures. *Community Mental Health Journal, 2*, 150–159.

Charen, S. (1948). Brief methods of psychotherapy: An overview. *Psychoanalytic Quarterly, 12*, 287–301.

Chicago Institute for Psychoanalysis. (1942, October 25–26). *Psychotherapy for the people*. Proceedings of the Brief Psychotherapy Council, Chicago.

Cumming, J., & Cumming, E. (1962). *Ego and milieu*. New York: Atherton Press.

Davanloo, H. (1980). The technique of crisis evaluation and intervention. In H. Davanloo (Ed.), *Short term dynamic psychotherapy* (pp. 245–281). Northvale, NJ: Jason Aronson.

Decker, J. B., & Stubblebine, J. M. (1972). Crisis intervention and prevention of psychiatric disability: A follow-up study. *American Journal of Psychiatry, 129*, 725–729.

Deutsch, F. (1949). *Applied psychoanalysis*. New York: Grune and Stratton.

Dickstein, G., Young, H., & Levin, H. (1961). Helping applicants become clients. *Child Welfare, 40*, 1–6.

Donovan, J., Bennett, M., & McElroy, C. (1981). The crisis group: Its rationale, format, and outcome. In S. Budman (Ed.), *Forms of brief therapy* (pp. 283–303). New York: Guilford Press.

Driscoll, J. M., Meyer, R. E., & Schanie, C. F. (1973). Training police in family crisis intervention. *Journal of Applied Behavioral Science, 9*, 62–82.

Dyer, E. D. (1965). Parenthood as crisis: A re-study. In H. J. Parad (Ed.), *Crisis intervention: Selected readings* (pp. 312–323). New York: Family Service Association of America .

Erikson, E. (1959). *Identity and the life cycle*. New York: International Universities Press.

Framo, J. (1965). Rationale and techniques of intensive family therapy. In I. Boszormenyi-Nagy (Ed.), *Intensive family therapy* (pp. 143–212). New York: Harper & Row.

Framo, J. (1976). Chronicle of a struggle to establish a family unit within a community mental health center. In P. Guerin (Ed.), *Family therapy* (pp. 23–39). New York: Gardner Press.

Framo, J. (1982). *Explorations in marital and family therapy*. New York: Springer Publishing.

Frank, J. D. (1973). *Persuasion and healing*. Baltimore, MD: Johns Hopkins University Press.

Freeman, E. H., Kalis, B. L., & Harris, M. (1965). Assessing patient characteristics from psychotherapy interviews. In H. J. Parad (Ed.), *Crisis intervention: Selected readings* (pp. 349–365). New York: Family Service Association of America.

Freud, S. (1933). Turnings in the ways of psychoanalysis. *Collected Papers II*. London: Hogarth Press.

Fuhriman, A., Paul, S., & Burlingame, G. (1986). Eclectic time-limited therapy. In J. C. Norcross (Ed.), *Handbook of eclectic psychotherapy* (pp. 226–259). New York: Brunner/Mazel.

Gardner, G. (1958). The balanced expression of oedipal remnants. In H. J. Parad (Ed.), *Ego psychology and dynamic casework* (pp. 159–163). New York: Family Service Association of America.

Glass, A. (1954). Psychotherapy in the combat zone. *American Journal of Psychiatry, 110,* 725–731.

Golan, N. (1987). Crisis intervention. In *Encyclopedia of social work* (18th ed.) (pp. 360–372). Washington, DC: National Association of Social Workers.

Goldring, J. (1980). *Quick response therapy: A time-limited treatment approach.* New York: Human Sciences Press.

Grinker, R. (1960). Preface. In P. Lichtenberg, R. Kohrman, & H. Macgregor (Eds.), *Motivation for child psychiatry treatment.* New York: Russell and Russell.

Grinker, R. R., & Spiegel, J. P. (1945). *Men under stress.* Philadelphia: Blackstone Co.

Gurman, A., & Kniskern, D. (Eds.). (1981). *Handbook of family therapy.* New York: Brunner/Mazel.

Hill, R. (1965). Generic features of families under stress. In H. J. Parad (Ed.), *Crisis intervention: Selected readings* (pp. 32–52). New York: Family Service Association of America.

Hollis, F., & Woods, M. (1981). *Casework: A psychosocial therapy.* New York: Random House.

Holmes, T., & Masuda, M. (1973). Life change and illness susceptibility. In J. P. Scott & E. C. Senay (Eds.), *Separation and depression: Clinical and research aspects* (pp. 161–186). Washington, DC: American Association for the Advancement of Science.

Horowitz, M. J. (1986). *Stress-response syndromes.* New York: Jason Aronson.

Horowitz, M. J., & Kaltreider, N. B. (1980). Brief treatment of post-traumatic stress disorders. In G. Jacobson (Ed.), *Crisis intervention in the 80's* (pp. 67–80). San Francisco: Jossey-Bass.

Jacobson, G. F., Strickler, M., & Morley, W. E. (1968). Generic and individual approaches to crisis intervention. *American Journal of Public Health, 58,* 338–343.

Jacobson, G. (1980). Crisis theory. In G. Jacobson (Ed.), *Crisis intervention in the 80's* (pp. 1–10). San Francisco: Jossey-Bass.

Jacobson, G., & Portuges, S. (1976). Marital separation and divorce. In H. J. Parad, H. Resnik, & L. Parad (Eds.), *Emergency and disaster management* (pp. 433–441). Bowie, MD: Charles Press.

Jayaratne, S. (1978). A study of clinical eclectism. *Social Service Review, 52,* 584–595.

Jones, M., & Polak, P. (1968). Crisis and confrontation. *British Journal of Psychiatry, 129,* 734–736.

Joyce, A. S., Azim, H. F., & Morin, H. (1988). Brief crisis group psychotherapy versus the initial sessions of long term group psychotherapy: An exploratory comparison. *Group, 12,* 3–19.

Kaffman, M. (1965). In H. J. Parad (Ed.), *Crisis intervention: Selected readings* (pp. 202–219). New York: Family Service Association of America.

Kagan, R., & Schlosberg, S. (1989). *Families in perpetual crisis.* New York: W. W. Norton.

Kaplan, D. M., & Mason, E. A. (1960). Maternal reactions to premature birth viewed as an acute emotional disorder. *American Journal of Orthopsychiatry, 30,* 539–552.

Klein, D., & Lindemann, E. (1961). Preventive intervention in individual and family crisis situations. In G. Caplan (Ed.), *Prevention of mental disorders in children* (pp. 283–306). New York: Basic Books.

Klein, D., & Ross, A. (1958). Kindergarten entry: A study of role transition. In M.

Krugman (Ed.), *Orthopsychiatry and the school.* New York: American Orthopsychiatric Association.

Koss, M. P., & Butcher, J. N. (1987). Research on brief psychotherapy. In S. Garfield & A. Bergin (Eds.), *Handbook of psychotherapy and behavior change* (pp. 627–670). New York: John Wiley.

Kübler-Ross, E. (1969). *On death and dying.* New York: Macmillan.

Kuehnel, J. M., & Liberman, R. P. (1986). Behavior modification. In I. L. Kutash & A. Wolf (Eds.). *Psychotherapist's casebook* (pp. 240–262). San Francisco: Jossey-Bass.

L'Abate, L. (1986). *Systematic family therapy.* New York: Brunner/Mazel.

Langsley, D. (1980). Crisis intervention and the avoidance of hospitalization. In G. Jacobson (Ed.), *Crisis intervention in the 80's* (pp. 81–90). San Francisco: Jossey-Bass.

Langsley, D., & Kaplan, D. (1968). *Treatment of families in crisis.* New York: Grune and Stratton.

Laufer, R., Frey-Wouters, E., & Gallops, M. S. (1985). Traumatic stressors in the Vietnam war and post-traumatic stress disorder. In C. Figley (Ed.), *Trauma and its wake* (pp. 73–89). New York: Brunner/Mazel.

Lazarus, A. A. (Ed.). (1976). *Multimodal behavior therapy.* New York: Springer Publishing.

Levinger, G. (1960). Continuance in casework and other helping relationships. *Social Work, 5,* 40–51.

Lichtenberg, P., Kohrman, R., & Macgregor, H. (Eds.). (1960). *Motivation for child psychiatry treatment.* New York: Russell and Russell.

Lieb, J., Lipsitch, I., & Slaby, A. (1973). *The crisis team.* New York: Harper & Row.

Lindemann, E. (1944). Symptomatology and management of acute grief. *American Journal of Psychiatry, 101* (September). Also in H. J. Parad (Ed.). (1965). *Crisis Intervention: Selected Readings* (pp. 7–21). New York: Family Service Association of America.

Lindemann, E. (1956). The meaning of crisis in individual and family living. *Teachers College Record, 57,* 310–315.

Malan, D. H. (1963). *A study of brief psychotherapy.* Springfield, IL: Charles C Thomas.

Mann, J. (1973). *Time-limited psychotherapy.* Cambridge, MA: Harvard University Press.

Marmor, J. (1979). Short-term dynamic psychotherapy. *American Journal of Psychiatry, 136,* 149–155.

McCubbin, H., & Patterson, J. (1983). Family transitions: Adaptations to stress. In H. McCubbin & C. Figley (Eds.), *Stress and the family,* Vol. 1 (pp. 5–25). New York: Brunner/Mazel.

Mechanic, D. (1980). *Mental health and social policy.* Englewood Cliffs, NJ: Prentice-Hall.

Menninger, W. C. (1948). *Psychiatry in a troubled world.* New York: Macmillan.

Minuchin, S. (1974). *Families and family therapy.* Cambridge, MA: Harvard University Press.

Minuchin, S., & Fishman, H. C. (1981). *Family therapy techniques.* Cambridge, MA: Harvard University Press.

Morley, W. E. (1974). *Final report: Outcome of crisis intervention treatment.* National Institute of Mental Health Grant, MH 18846, August 22, 1974.

Morrison, G. C. (October 8, 1965). *Therapeutic intervention in a children's psychiatric emergency service.* Paper presented at the regional meeting of the American Association of Psychiatric Clinics for Children, Cincinnati, Ohio.

Neuwelt, A. (1988). *A study of the measurement of knowledge about crisis intervention among professional social workers*. Unpublished doctoral dissertation, University of Toronto, Toronto.

Papp, P. (1976). Family choreography. In P. Guerin (Ed.), *Family therapy: Theory and practice* (pp. 465–479). New York: Gardner Press.

Parad, H. J. (1961). Preventive casework: Problems and implications. *Social Welfare Forum* (pp. 178–193). New York: Columbia University Press.

Parad, H. J. (1963). Brief ego-oriented casework with families in crisis. In H. Parad & R. Miller (Eds.), *Ego-oriented casework: Problems and perspective* (pp. 145–164). New York: Family Service Association of America.

Parad, H. J. (Ed.) (1965). *Crisis intervention: Selected readings*. New York: Family Service Association of America.

Parad, H. J. (1977). Crisis intervention. In *Encyclopedia of Social Work* (pp. 228–237). Washington, DC: National Association of Social Workers.

Parad, H. J. (1982). Brief family therapy. In H. Schulberg & M. Killilea (Eds.), *The modern practice of community mental health: A volume in honor of Gerald Caplan* (pp. 419–443). San Francisco: Jossey-Bass.

Parad, H. J. (1984). Time-limited crisis therapy in the workplace: An eclectic perspective. *Social Work Papers, 18*, Los Angeles, University of Southern California, 20–30.

Parad, H. J., & Caplan, G. (1960). A framework for studying families in crisis. *Social Work, 5*, 3–15. Also in H. J. Parad (Ed.). (1965). *Crisis intervention: Selected readings*. New York: Family Service Association of America.

Parad, H. J., & Houston, M. K. (1984). *Role of the social worker in emergency medical care: Summary of project findings and recommendations*. Los Angeles, School of Social Work, University of Southern California.

Parad, H. J., & Resnik, H. (1975). A crisis intervention framework. In H. Resnik & H. Ruben (Eds.), *Emergency psychiatric care: The management of mental health crisis* (pp. 3–6). Bowie, MD: Charles Press.

Parad, H. J., Selby, L., & Quinlan, J. (1976). Crisis intervention with families and groups. In R. Roberts & H. Northen (Eds.), *Theories of social work with groups* (pp. 304–330). New York: Columbia University Press.

Parad, L. G. (1971). Short-term treatment: An overview of historical trends, issues, and potentials. *Smith College Studies in Social Work, 41*, 1971, 119–146.

Parad, L. G., & Parad, H. J. (1968). A study of crisis-oriented short-term treatment. *Social Casework, 49*, 418–426.

Parkes, C. (1972). *Bereavement: Studies of grief in adult life*. New York: International Universities Press.

Parsons, B. V., & Alexander, J. F. (1973). Short-term family intervention: A therapy outcome study. *Journal of Consulting and Clinical Psychology, 41*, 195–201.

Paul, N. (1976). Cross-confrontation. In P. Guerin (Ed.), *Family therapy* (pp. 520–529). New York: Gardner Press.

Perlman, H. (1957). *Social casework: A problem-solving process*. Chicago: University of Chicago Press.

Pittman, F. S. (1987). *Turning points: Treating families in transition and crisis*. New York: W. W. Norton.

Polak, P. (1978). A comprehensive system of alternatives to psychiatric hospitalization. In L. Stein & M. A. Test (Eds.), *Alternatives to mental hospital treatment* (pp. 115–138). New York: Plenum Press.

Polak, P., & Jones, M. (1973). The psychiatric non-hospital: A model for change. *Community Mental Health Journal, 9*, 123–132.

Raphael, B. (1983). *Anatomy of bereavement*. New York: Basic Books.

Rapoport, L. (1962). The state of crisis: Some theoretical considerations. *Social Service Review*, *36*, 211–217.

Reid, W. (1978). *The task-centered system*. New York: Columbia University Press.

Reid, W. J., & Epstein, L. (1972). *Task-centered casework*. New York: Columbia University Press.

Reid, W. J., & Epstein, L. (Eds.). (1977). *Task-centered practice*. New York: Columbia University Press.

Reid, W. J., & Shyne, A. (1969). *Brief and extended casework*. New York: Columbia University Press.

Rueveni, V. (1975). Network intervention with a family in crisis. *Family Process*, *14*, 193–204.

Schulberg, H., & Killilea, M. (Eds.). (1982). *The modern practice of community mental health: A volume in honor of Gerald Caplan*. San Francisco, Jossey-Bass.

Schulberg, H., & Sheldon, A. (1968). The probability of crisis and strategies for preventive intervention. *Archives of General Psychiatry*, *18*, 553–558.

Shyne, A. W. (1957). What research tells us about short-term cases in family agencies. *The short-term case in the family agency*. New York: Family Service Association of America.

Sifneos, P. (1972). *Short-term psychotherapy and emotional crisis*. Cambridge, MA: Harvard University Press.

Slaby, A. E. (1985). Crisis-oriented therapy. In F. R. Lipton & S. M. Goldfinger (Eds.), *Emergency psychiatry at the crossroads* (pp. 21–34). San Francisco: Jossey-Bass.

Sloane, R. B., Staples, F. R., Cristol, A. H., Yorkston, N. J., & Whipple, K. (1975). *Psychotherapy versus behavior therapy*. Cambridge, MA: Harvard University Press.

Steidl, J. H., & Wexler, J. P. (1977). What's a clinician to do with so many approaches to family therapy? *The family*, *4*, 190–197.

Stone, L. (1951). Psychoanalysis and brief psychotherapy. *Psychoanalytic Quarterly*, *20*, 215–236.

Strickler, M., & Allgeyer, J. (1967). The crisis group: A new application of crisis theory. *Social Work*, *12*, 28–32.

Strupp, H. H., & Binder, J. L. (1984). *Psychotherapy in a new key: A guide to time-limited dynamic psychotherapy*. New York: Basic Books.

Taft, J. (1933). *The dynamics of therapy in a controlled relationship*. New York: Macmillan.

Truax, C., & Carkhuff, R. (1967). *Toward effective counseling and psychotherapy*. Chicago: Aldine.

Van Hook, M. (1987). Harvest of despair: Using the ABCX model for farm families in crisis. *Social Casework*, *68*, 273–278.

Viney, L. L., Clarke, A. M., Bunn, T. A., & Benjamin, Y. N. (1985). Crisis intervention counseling: An evaluation of long- and short-term effects. *Journal of Counseling Psychology*, *32*, 29–39.

Wachtel, P. (1977). *Psychoanalysis and behavior therapy: Toward an integration*. New York: Basic Books.

Wallace, M. E., & Parad, H. J. (1980). The dream in brief psychotherapy. In J. Natterson (Ed.), *The dream in clinical practice* (pp. 405–426). New York: Jason Aronson.

Watzlawick, P., Beavin, J., & Jackson, D. (1967). *Pragmatics of human communication*. New York: W. W. Norton.

Webb, N. B. (1985). A crisis intervention perspective on the termination process. *Clinical Social Work Journal, 13*, 329–340.

Wells, R. (1982). *Planned short-term treatment*. New York: Free Press.

Whittington, R. (1985). House calls in private practice. *Social Work, 30*, 261–264.

Yalom, I. (1985). *The theory and practice of group psychotherapy*. New York: Basic Books.

Part II.

Clinical Applications

2

Post-Traumatic Stress Syndrome Revisited

ALEXANDER C. MCFARLANE

THE IMPACT OF THE VIETNAM WAR on a generation of veterans has led in the 1980s to greater awareness of the long-term psychological sequelae of traumatic stress. The inclusion of diagnostic criteria for post-traumatic stress disorder (PTSD) in the *Diagnostic and Statistical Manual of Mental Disorders* (DSM-III-R) (American Psychiatric Association, 1987) was the result of better understanding of the effects of extreme stress. However, history documents that this disorder is not unique to the twentieth century. Homer's *Odyssey* records the suffering of Ulysses (Evatt, 1985); Samuel Pepys in his famous diary of the fire that devastated London in 1666 provided a graphic account of his symptoms (Daly, 1983). Although the psychological casualties of two world wars triggered most of the early investigations into the nature and treatment of PTSD, these problems are also common in civilian life (Ettedgui & Bridges, 1985).*

Post-traumatic stress disorder is triggered by psychologically traumatic events outside the usual range of human experience. Such events include a serious threat to a person's life or physical integrity (for example, rape, motor vehicle accident, or violent assault), destruction of a person's home or community (for example, through a natural disaster or fire), or seeing another person who is mutilated, dying, or dead. One need not be too rigid in the definition of a traumatic event because persons' perceptions of the danger or threat posed by an event depend on a range of factors, such as past experience. For example, a Vietnam veteran had coped with serious injury and the death of comrades but developed PTSD when he witnessed the rape of a Vietnamese woman by two soldiers. He had been sodomized by a pedophiliac when he was ten years old, an experience that molded his psychological vulnerability.

The Nature of the Stress Response

Treatment of PTSD requires thorough knowledge of the stress response. The therapist must be attuned to the way the client is haunted and preoccupied by

---

*Examples of PTSD in civilian life are presented in subsequent chapters of this sourcebook, especially those concerning rape, molestation, spousal abuse, catastrophic illness, and disaster.

intrusive memories of the trauma while attempting to avoid these memories and contain the distress they evoke. Horowitz (1976) carefully described the wide range of waking imagery, which varies from dim impressions to vivid, detailed memories that repeatedly enter consciousness and are difficult to dispel, to pseudohallucinations, hallucinations, or hypnogogic phenomena. Earlier descriptions focused largely on nightmares of the trauma (Brett & Ostroff, 1985). In essence, these images occur because the event is new information that the individual must integrate into his or her preexisting view of self, others, and the world. The cognitive and affective reworking of the event fluctuate between intrusion and denial, in an attempt to process the information without the individual becoming overwhelmed by the enormity of the trauma. Horowitz (1976) describes the sequence of this process: outcry, denial, intrusion, working through, and completion.

As the trauma recedes into the past, the intensity and frequency of involuntary recollections decrease until the individual achieves an equilibrium wherein the experience is incorporated into his or her view of the world. These phenomena (involuntary recollections) are a normal adaptive response and indicate that an individual has been traumatized. The process of cognitive and affective mastery of these intrusive memories in PTSD can, like grief (Raphael, 1984), fail to progress to resolution or can be avoided by the individual. The presence of these phenomena is not necessarily a marker of decompensation; this must be judged in relation to the severity of the trauma and the duration of time that has elapsed since the event occurred. In other words, what might be considered an appropriate degree of distress immediately after a traumatic experience might be abnormal at some point in the future (McFarlane, 1985).

Distress versus Disorder

The separation of distress from disorder has important implications for the management of trauma victims because different treatment strategies are required for these two states. The available evidence suggests that the degree of distress caused by an event is the major factor determining the probability of the onset of psychiatric disorder (Tennant & Andrews, 1978; McFarlane, 1988a). Therefore, a crisis intervention approach that aims to lessen the distress of traumatized people and bolster their coping strategies is likely to be useful for the primary prevention of PTSD (Raphael, 1980). There is probably a critical period of several months during which such intervention can be successfully implemented.

The evolution of distress into disorder has been reported in a group of bush fire disaster victims in Australia who requested help from a psychiatric service (McFarlane, 1986a). In the weeks that immediately followed the trauma, these people's distress seemed little different from other victims of the same bush fire. They perceived that their disorder emerged out of their failure to resolve the distress caused by their losses and a sudden awareness of their vulnerability to further trauma. Although acknowledging the extent of their losses, which included the destruction of their home or death of a spouse, these clients recognized that their response differed in degree or duration from the expected distress and grief. Some of these people went to considerable lengths to seek psychiatric treatment, because the welfare and health services they had consulted failed to accept the pathological nature of their symptoms and did not arrange a referral for them (McFarlane, 1984).

Many, if not most, people who undergo trauma experience intrusive recollections and images, which they try to remove from their consciousness. A minority of these people develop full-blown PTSD (McFarlane, 1988a). People with PTSD are differentiated by the presence of two other sets of symptoms: (1) estrangement from others, emotional numbing, or diminished interest in previously pleasurable activities and (2) a disorder of attention and arousal, for example, disturbed concentration and memory (American Psychiatric Association, 1987).

Obviously, the distinctions between persons with the normal stress response and those with PTSD are blurred, particularly soon after the event. Some influential researchers (Quarantelli & Dynes, 1977) have argued that traumatic events such as disasters have little or no long-term effects on the mental health of victims, although such events are an important cause of distress and problems in everyday living. Others (Leopold & Dillon, 1963; Gleser, Green, & Winget, 1981) claim that the levels of disorder are high and long-lasting. This controversy about the prevalence and predictability of PTSD needs to be further examined in that it has major implications for the design of mental health services for traumatized populations.

Prevalence and Etiology

Background Issues

Ongoing debate has questioned whether the trauma or individual vulnerability is the central etiological variable in PTSD. Historically, this issue has been controversial on moral and legal grounds, making it difficult at times to examine the scientific validity of the various claims. Because of the problems that decompensation on the battlefield pose to the military, issues of cowardice and moral inferiority have sometimes become confused with the notion of vulnerability. Furthermore, questions of legal liability often arise in PTSD if negligence or responsibility for the trauma can be proven (Trimble, 1981). The possibility of financial compensation raises suspicions about the genuineness of the sufferer's symptoms. Also, pretrauma vulnerability, if it can be proven to be a major cause of illness, may shift the balance of legal argument against the victims, especially when determining the size of a damages settlement.

The concern in the minds of some mental health workers that investigating the role of individual vulnerability can lead to blaming the victim for his or her suffering should not prevent serious examination of the objective evidence. Although the illness model of mental disorder has received a lot of criticism, a socially sanctioned sick role does relieve sufferers from various responsibilities (Pilowsky, 1969), including the notion that they are to blame for their illness. Furthermore, the biopsychosocial model of illness (Engel, 1980) also promotes a sophisticated perspective of the complex interaction between individual, psychological, and biological characteristics and the social environment in the onset and course of psychiatric disorders, including PTSD.

Finally, the answer to questions regarding the relative importance of the trauma and vulnerability factors affects crisis intervention services that aim to prevent the onset of established PTSD following events such as natural disasters. Does the entire population who were intensely exposed to the trauma require preventive counseling because they are all at equal risk, or is it possible to identify a smaller group of individuals who are especially at risk? Thus the issues of the etiology and the prevalence of PTSD are related: the lower the prevalence of disorder in a traumatized population, the greater the likelihood that vulnerability factors will predict who is at risk. Against this background, it is important to consider carefully the available evidence.

The variable quality of much research that has examined the effects of traumatic events, for example, Green's (1982) study of disasters or Helzer's (1981) study of wars, emphasizes the need to examine evidence from various sources. The body of knowledge documenting the effect of stressful life events that are not extremely adverse is a valuable source of corroborative information and defines a number of important methodological issues (McFarlane, 1985).

Although early studies suggested that life events were a potent cause of mental and physical illness, more systematic and methodologically acceptable research has failed to support the strength of this association (Rabkin & Struening, 1976; Paykel, 1978; Andrews & Tennant, 1978). For example, a number of prospective studies concerning the onset of neurotic disorders such as depression and anxiety failed to demonstrate a central causal link between adversity and neurosis (Tennant, 1983). Therefore, claims about the potency of extreme adversity as a cause of psychological impairment seem at variance with carefully conducted research on life events, which supports the need to consider the view that events such as disasters have no major enduring effect on mental health (Quarantelli, 1985).

Combat. A key issue in interpreting the data from studies examining the impact of combat concerns the appropriateness of the control groups (La Guardia, Smith, Francois, & Backman, 1983). In general, the results from the more rigorous studies suggest that combat alone does not play a large role (Andrews, Christensen, & Hadzi-Pavolovic, 1985). For example, Helzer, Robins, Wish, and Hesselbrock (1979) compared the effects of combat on individuals one and three years after active service. They concluded that the onset of a depressive syndrome was influenced by prior combat experience only to a small degree at the first follow-up (3 percent of the variance) but that these effects were insignificant by the time of the second interview.

A similar follow-up study of Swedish soldiers serving in the United Nations forces in the Congo revealed that the combat veterans did not differ from noncombat veterans in psychiatric morbidity (Kettner, 1972). Also, those soldiers who did succumb to combat exhaustion were defined by several vulnerability factors, such as family psychiatric history. A study of the Yom Kippur War (Levav, Greenfeld, & Baruch, 1979) demonstrated that although the intensity of combat was an important predictor of the number of psychiatric casualties, personality factors influenced who decompensated and the rate of recovery. Van Putten and Yager (1984) have also pointed out that despite the suffering of many veterans of the Vietnam War, many who had similar combat experiences remained well adjusted. However, studies (for example, Foy, Rueger, Sipprelle,

& Carroll, 1984) examining the relations between the symptoms of PTSD and the intensity of combat experience in patient populations found that the trauma was the primary etiological factor. Thus, although decompensation, even in the face of a high combat exposure is not inevitable, we conclude that combat, in conjunction with vulnerability factors, does play an important role in the onset of PTSD.

Disasters. Green (1982) suggested that the methodological problems in disaster research at the time of her review were sufficiently extensive to prevent any accurate generalizations about the psychological consequences of this type of trauma from the existing data. For example, the follow-up study of the Beverly Hills Supper Club fire (Green, Grace, & Gleser, 1985) found that 60 percent of the variance determining vulnerability to PTSD came from the traumatic experience itself, and that only 117 victims of the 2,500 were affected, with no way to determine the representativeness of the sample. A powerful association was found by the same researchers between exposure to the Buffalo Creek flood and psychiatric impairment; 80 percent of the victims were disordered (Gleser et al., 1981). However, the particularly harrowing process of seeking financial compensation for damages in this disaster may have influenced the prevalence of morbidity.

Since Green's 1982 review, three studies have been published that overcame issues of unrepresentative sampling in adult populations. Shore, Tatum, and Vollmer (1986), who investigated the effects of the Mount St. Helen's volcanic eruption, found a correspondence between exposure to the eruption and disorder related to the trauma. Responses included generalized anxiety and depression as well as PTSD. Of those who had the most intense exposure, 40 percent were disordered at some stage (eleven to twelve times the prevalence of disorder in the control group). However, the effects of the trauma largely abated by the third year. Second, Weisaeth's (1984) follow-up of all victims of a Norwegian paint factory fire, which began several days after the fire, also found that the prevalence of acute PTSD was determined by the initial intensity of the exposure. However, the prognosis at four years was influenced more by preaccident psychological functioning than by the intensity of exposure to the explosion. Third, McFarlane's (1986b) investigation of the impact of an Australian bush fire disaster, a longitudinal study of a representative sample of 469 firefighters who had a particularly intense exposure to the fire, found that 14 percent of the firefighters had a pattern of chronic post-traumatic morbidity at twenty-nine months after the disaster. At the most, 10 percent of the variance of disorder in this group could be explained by their exposure to and losses in the fires. As the event receded into the past, the role played by vulnerability factors (such as a family or personal psychiatric history, a tendency not to think through problems, and neuroticism) became more important in the maintenance of this morbidity (McFarlane, 1988b, 1988c). In contrast, a cross-sectional study of all the registered victims of the same disaster, conducted one year after the fire, found that at least 50 percent more of the population had a psychiatric disorder than would have been anticipated by comparison with unaffected groups (Clayer, Brookless-Pratz, & McFarlane, 1985). Finally, a longitudinal study of 808 primary school children (McFarlane, Policansky, & Irwin, 1987) demonstrated that 32 percent of the mothers and 21 percent of the fathers had clinically significant post-traumatic phenomena twenty-six months after the fire (McFarlane, 1987a).

One Perspective on the Issues

Although many important questions remain to be answered, it is possible to reach tentative conclusions with the available evidence. Even after extreme trauma, it seems that only approximately 40 percent of an exposed population develop PTSD (Clayer et al., 1985; Weisaeth, 1985; Shore et al., 1986), although several studies have found higher levels (Gleser et al., 1981). Most studies found that in contrast with distress, PTSD is not universal (Hoiberg & McCaughey, 1984), which consequently emphasizes the importance of the individual's vulnerabilities and strengths in determining the response to extreme adversity. In general, as the event recedes into the past, the role of vulnerability factors in perpetuating PTSD appears to become increasingly important (McFarlane, 1985).

That is not to say that the event does not play a critical role in triggering PTSD. A significant percentage of people who develop a psychiatric disorder after a trauma would not have done so in the absence of the event. Furthermore, a greater percentage of people are distressed and preoccupied by their experience in the weeks immediately following the traumatic event. The experience has a profound impact on their future attitudes and concerns, although a psychiatric disorder is not likely to follow the chronic course (Kolb, 1986) as is typical of PTSD (Archibald, Long, Miller, & Tuddenham, 1963), a differentiation that has implications for treatment.

Thus people's biological predisposition to psychiatric disorder, their coping style, the meaning of the trauma, and their social matrix all influence their responses to trauma. Treatment should in part be based on an assessment of the relative importance of these factors. However, before discussing assessment in detail, it is necessary to examine the treatments that have been recommended for PTSD.

Proposed Treatments

Many approaches have been recommended for the management of PTSD (Kelly, 1985; Figley, 1985; Ettedgui & Bridges, 1985), which poses a major problem for an inexperienced therapist called upon to assist victims of trauma. The problem is compounded because in contrast with most other psychiatric disorders (Quality Assurance Project, 1985), "the available empirical evidence is of such poor quality that it does not allow any conclusive statements to be made about the treatment efficacy" of PTSD (Andrews et al., 1985, p. 1). No study of PTSD meets the criteria for good outcome research (Epstein & Volk, 1981); in particular, no study has randomly assigned subjects to treatment and control groups, a basic requirement of outcome research. Kolb (1986) suggested that the prescription of treatment in this disorder "represents, for the most part, either the ideology or skill of individual therapists" (p. 119).

Individual psychotherapy, guided by various theoretical perspectives, has been the most commonly proposed treatment. For example, Horowitz (1974) emphasized the usefulness of a dynamically oriented approach that assists the person in working through the elements of trauma that cannot be faced and assimilated, thus modifying intrusive recollections and numbing. A second approach, which has been suggested by behavioral therapists, uses implosion and flooding (Keane, Fairbank, Caddell, Zimering, & Bender, 1985) to desensitize the individual to memories of the trauma. Both perspectives emphasize the importance of focusing on people's memories and reexperiencing of the traumatic event.

Hypnosis has long been proposed as a way to confront the memories of the event (Brende, 1985), as have drug-assisted abreactions that encourage catharsis (Perry & Jacobs, 1982). However, some therapists have emphasized the need, particularly among victims of concentration camps, for a more supportive approach that focuses on the immediate issues facing the client within the context of a consistent and warm relationship. They have noted that detailed inquiry into the nature of the traumatic experience often intensifies symptoms without providing any long-term relief (Boehnlein, Kinzie, Ben, & Fleck, 1985).

Group psychotherapy is often proposed as a useful treatment strategy in stress-response syndromes (Walker & Nash, 1981; Brende, 1981). Groups of people who have experienced the same event allow members to share their trauma without taking on a client/patient role, for example "rap groups" initiated by Vietnam veterans (Lifton, 1978). For more severely disabled sufferers, inpatient programs that use various therapeutic approaches as well as group therapy principles have been instituted (Rosenheck, 1984; Berman, Price, & Gusman, 1982).

The impact of PTSD on members of the affected person's family is substantial because of the associated interpersonal estrangement, irritability, and violent behavior; thus family therapy could be potentially beneficial (Marrs, 1985; Stanton & Figley, 1978). Also, if more than one family member has been exposed to the trauma, the effects of the event on all members should be considered, including the possibility that several members have PTSD (McFarlane, 1986a).

A range of pharmacological treatments have been used in PTSD (Van der Kolk, 1983; Walker, 1982). Tricyclic antidepressants (Bleich, Seigel, Garb, & Lerer, 1986) and monoamine oxidase inhibitors (Hogben & Cornfield, 1981) have both been used with some success to decrease intrusive imagery, nightmares, and anxiety symptoms.

Establishing a Therapeutic Alliance

No single treatment approach can be used with every PTSD client. Before specific recommendations are made, it is essential that the client undergo a thorough assessment. Although certain elements of the stress response are predictable, a wide range of reactions and preoccupations can be observed among victims of the same trauma. Therefore, it is useful to emphasize the themes and issues that need to be considered in the treatment process.

Victims of extreme adversity have been notably ambivalent about becoming involved in crisis intervention and treatment programs (Lindy, Grace, & Green,

1981; Haley, 1985). This seems to be particularly the case once the first weeks after the trauma have passed. Weisaeth (1985) has also noted that the most severely affected can be the most reluctant to accept treatment. For example,

> Mr. Grover, a fifty-two-year-old divorced man who owned a small home-building business, developed PTSD following a motor vehicle accident in which he collided with a car that stopped across a freeway lane. He was unable to avoid the accident and remembered the terrified face of the driver in the lights of his car, just before the moment of impact. Fortunately, nobody was seriously injured. Mr. Grover had been convinced just before impact that he was going to kill the woman in the other vehicle, a thought that haunted him after the accident.
>
> His business suffered considerably because he could not concentrate and plan projects with his usual efficiency. The physical symptoms of neck and arm pain made it difficult for him to drive his machinery. He attributed these to a neck injury, despite several orthopedic opinions to the contrary. He had considered remarriage prior to the accident, but this relationship broke up due to his interpersonal withdrawal. Despite the obvious disruption caused by PTSD, he could not accept the idea that he needed treatment.

Mr. Grover's ambivalence about treatment was typical in several ways. First, he took a very judgmental view of his own suffering. He had prided himself on his ability to tolerate pain and suffering in the past. For example, on one occasion he had broken several bones in his foot when he had dropped a pipe, but had only taken one afternoon off from his work, which involved heavy manual labor. He perceived his stress-related symptoms as a sign of weakness and believed that he should be able to control the way he was feeling, despite the fact that his symptoms had changed little in the year following the accident. Such attitudes are common among victims of trauma. (It should be noted that therapists and researchers who emphasize the inevitability and normalcy of PTSD may be attempting to deny that they could take a dismissive attitude toward their own or others' suffering.

Second, Mr. Grover, who felt that his physical symptoms were the major problem, believed that these symptoms were due to injury and hence could not see the relevance of psychological treatment. Physical symptoms are often a prominent feature of PTSD (Weisaeth, 1984; Horowitz, Wilner, Kaltreider, & Alvarez, 1980; Solomon, Milkulincer, & Kotler, 1987) and are often the problem that clients first present for treatment (McFarlane, 1986a). This somatic link can complicate the formation of a therapeutic alliance. Unless these physical complaints are adequately assessed and explained, clients are likely to reject psychological treatment.

Similarly, such clients often have a complex set of attributions and beliefs to explain their distress and physical symptoms. The controversy surrounding whether Agent Orange caused a series of health problems in Vietnam veterans was, in part, based upon veterans' attempts to find an explanation for the many unexplained symptoms caused by PTSD (Hall, 1986).

Until the therapist and the client have negotiated a mutually agreed-upon assessment of the problem, specific treatment cannot begin. Thus assessment, explicit problem formulation, and explanation are central to winning the client's trust and treating PTSD. Their importance is demonstrated by the high rates of noncompliance found in PTSD clients (Burnstein, 1986).

Assessment

Assessment is critical in treatment of PTSD. Often the assessment interview is the first occasion in which a person confides the real nature of his or her trauma. The simple process of unburdening one's distress to another person can play an important role in evoking a sense of hope, in stark contrast with the demoralization and isolation that are part of PTSD.

Treatment is successful only if the individual can be encouraged to challenge the emotional isolation and estrangement typical of PTSD. This process takes time, and the client should be allowed to determine the pace of the work. Excessive enthusiasm on the part of the therapist for clients to disclose the full affective quality of their experience may cause clients to withdraw from treatment. Usually, the successful assessment interview is characterized by brief moments of intense affect, which the client is allowed to modulate. The therapist's awareness and acknowledgment of this process (Strupp, 1972) can be an important vehicle with which to encourage the person to become reinvolved in social and family relationships. Psychotherapy trials have demonstrated how the simple process of assessment can bring about significant beneficial changes, independent of any specific therapeutic intervention (Sloane, Staples, & Cristol, 1975). The importance of the initial interview, therefore, should not be underestimated.

The Assessment Interview

Before discussing the trauma with the client, it is important to establish why the person has chosen to seek professional assistance and ensure that the treatment plan specifically addresses these issues. People seldom seek help simply because the traumatic event happened; rather, they are usually concerned about the way they are feeling and behaving, after having made allowance for what has happened (McFarlane, 1986a). Often clients will describe the nature of the complaint only after questioning. The distress associated with recurring images can prevent the client from reporting or acknowledging the full extent of preoccupation with the trauma. For example,

> Mrs. Stirling, a sixty-year-old housewife, denied having any intrusive thoughts about a recent bush fire disaster that threatened her home, or any fear of the event, although she had many of the associated symptoms of PTSD. However, when she was shown a video report of the disaster, she experienced intense panic and could tolerate it for no longer than one minute. With treatment, she was increasingly able to acknowledge her preoccupation with the disaster.

Associated Psychiatric Disorders

A growing body of evidence suggests that PTSD is associated with another psychiatric disorder in more than 50 percent of clients (Davidson, Swartz, Storck, Krishnan, & Hammett, 1985; Escobar et al., 1983; Sierles, Chen, McFarland, & Taylor, 1983). Often the treatment of PTSD is difficult unless the nature of any coexistant disorder is understood and treated. For example,

> Mr. Mill lost all his stock, fences, sheds, and machinery when his property burned in a bush fire. Although he was initially very distressed by his losses and preoccupied by his confrontation with death, he coped with the immense task of rebuilding his life in the first six months following the disaster. His post-traumatic symptoms became disabling when he developed a major depressive episode. He then struggled for eight months with his nihilism and lack of energy before the problem was diagnosed. Successful treatment of his depression led to a resolution of his post-traumatic symptoms.

Major depressive disorder and panic disorder (American Psychiatric Association, 1987) are the two diagnoses most commonly associated with PTSD. These disorders require specific treatments and often require medication (Quality Assurance Project, 1985).

Account of the Trauma

When the client is describing the event, it is important to explore the person's perceptions and thoughts during and immediately after the trauma, and to discuss the reality of these perceptions in relation to the event. Both the actual events and their meaning need to be explored. Clients may resist this process of exploration because of the intense fear that memories of the trauma can generate in them. However, such discussions can be facilitated by making clients aware of the way in which their traumatic memories arise from the unresolved dilemmas of the event. For example,

> Mr. Keith's farm and home were totally destroyed in a bush fire, and one of his two children was killed trying to rescue a neighbor and his two children. Another daughter had been killed in a motor vehicle accident three years earlier. Six weeks before the disaster, a minor bush fire had occurred in the region; Mr. Keith had tried to take his son, who was later killed, to the site of the fire in order to teach him how bush fires behaved. His son had told Mr. Keith not to be so overconcerned and would not go.
>
> Mr. Keith found his son's body. The tips of his son's shoes and a belt buckle were the only unburnt remains. Mr. Keith identified the body by the belt buckle that lay in the ashes. Nearby, he found the remains of his neighbor and two children sitting upright in the burnt-out shell of their car.
>
> *Mr. Keith*: "The worst thing was the way his body was lying. His arms were held up in the air."
>
> *Psychiatrist*: "Is that what keeps playing on your mind?"
>
> *Mr. Keith*: "Yes . . . (looking away) I keep thinking he died in a state of terror. . . . That is what his posture seemed to show."
>
> *Psychiatrist*: "What do you imagine was going through his mind?"
>
> *Mr. Keith*: "I imagine that he saw something terrible. . . . The noise of the fire was the worst thing. It was like standing behind the engines of a 747 taking off. You could not see anything in the smoke . . . his car got bogged . . . he got out."
>
> *Psychiatrist*: "Do you think he panicked and then may have got bogged?"

> *Mr. Keith*: "I keep wondering if he did . . . his posture . . ."
>
> At this point, Mr. Keith appeared to be struggling with his thoughts and feelings about whether his son had contributed to his own death in some way.
>
> *Psychiatrist*: "You must have wondered whether he might not still be alive if he had taken your advice and thought about survival in a fire."
>
> *Mr. Keith*: "Yes, I always took the threat very seriously. My father used to put the old Chev in the farmyard on hot days, ready to go. He said there was no point in being a hero."
>
> *Psychiatrist*: "Sometimes you must have felt angry with your son about not taking your advice. I guess that you might even blame him for what happened."
>
> *Mr. Keith*: "That . . . the guilt plays on my mind. When my daughter died, the last thing I said to her was 'Drive carefully.' And it was not her fault. It was a bunch of idiots who came around a corner on the wrong side of the road."
>
> *Psychiatrist*: "Have you talked to anybody about your thoughts before?"
>
> *Mr. Keith*: "No. My wife is grief-stricken and she worries about me too much. She keeps talking about all the things they used to do. That does not help."

Mr. Keith's post-traumatic memories were not only tied to his son's death, but also to the way this event had made him experience a sense of impotence with regard to protecting his children, in addition to his anger with his son. The personal context of the tragedy and the meaning of the experience were explored during the recounting of the traumatic experience. Simply going over the event, in the hope of triggering a catharsis, does little more than intensify the client's post-traumatic memories.

Perceived Threat

A person's perception of threat often has little to do with his or her actual experience of a trauma.

> A fifty-four-year-old woman developed chronic PTSD following a bush fire disaster. The fire approached her home, then changed direction because the wind shifted. Her husband was uninjured, although he drove through the fire. The woman had a longstanding fear of some accident befalling her husband and also believed she did not belong in her rented home because it was a temporary accommodation. During treatment she made it clear that the thought of losing her home intensified her feelings of having no roots and was a primary preoccupation during the disaster. She was aware of the irrationality of her subsequent intrusive thoughts about the disaster and her perception of vulnerability.

Many people are unaware of the interaction among their perception of the trauma and their self-image and past experience, particularly people who have been victimized in a relationship at some stage of their lives. Having been a victim in other circumstances may heighten a person's vulnerability to trauma, even if the events have no obvious similarities.

> Mrs. Waters, a fifty-year-old divorcee, had been married to a violent alcoholic man. Feelings of being "attacked" were dramatically rearoused when she was exposed to a devastating fire. Treatment concentrated as much on

her unresolved feelings about her previous marriage as it did on her losses in the fire. She began to understand that if she was going to work through her brush with death in the fire, she must face the terrors she had experienced in her marriage. Initially, she presented to her physician complaining that she had developed asthma. At that point, she denied feeling any sense of trauma in the disaster.

Other Life Events

Intercurrent life events may prolong or intensify the sense of loss or conflict experienced and should always be elicited. Such events can interrupt an adaptive resolution of the trauma and lead to the onset of PTSD. Sometimes even seemingly trivial events can add powerfully to the sense of trauma.

Miss George, a sixteen-year-old girl whose family sustained many losses in a disaster, including their home and pets, was given a dog from the same litter as the pet that had been killed in the disaster. She developed PTSD only when this second dog was run over by a car. This event reevoked all her feelings of loss from the disaster and shattered her confidence that the world was a safe and predictable place where effort and planning were rewarded.

The trauma acts as the trigger of PTSD; the helping professional must help the client place this event within the context of his or her life. It is important to explore the way the person reinterpreted life before and after the event. The trauma may color the individual's past, present, and future by becoming the framework around which perception is organized.

Miss Luke was a twenty-six-year-old woman whose family suffered two major traumas. In the first trauma, their home and farm were destroyed; in the second, the family's third son was killed in an industrial accident. Miss Luke felt that making relationships and trying to better her life through her work were futile efforts. The experiences of her family left her feeling that attachments to people were a liability and that the efforts of a lifetime could be lost in a few brief moments. This sense of impending disaster dominated all her interactions, including her relationship with her therapist. Until she acknowledged and confronted these feelings, it was not possible to explore the trauma or to receive any commitment to treatment.

Generally, trauma has potentially greater impact on the lives of adolescents and young adults who become prematurely aware of the dangers of the world and the transitory nature of human endeavor. They can develop a sense of paralysis at a time when risk-taking is an essential part of their attempts to create an independent and productive life. Furthermore, adolescents do not have a marital relationship or career that they can use to reestablish continuity in their life. In other words, their life cannot be easily balanced against what came before and after the trauma. Therefore, the practitioner should consider the age at which the person experienced the trauma, particularly if a long delay intervened between the event and presentation for assistance.

If the traumatic event resulted from the negligence of a third party, the victim may seek financial compensation. This process can, in itself, become very stressful in that the victim's suffering becomes an issue of public legal debate. The practitioner should discuss the various conflicts that a litigant may face in the judicial process. The client should be aware that a legal case may take years to resolve, thereby keeping the trauma in the forefront of the client's life.

Constricted Affect

Constricted affect is very difficult to assess and manage. A striking characteristic of people with PTSD is the way they recount their experiences without showing emotion. Similarly, they may describe other emotionally important experiences without communicating affective associations.

> Mr. Inns described the experience of being accidentally thrown off a fire truck that was trying to escape to safety down a bush track. The avenue of trees surrounding him exploded into a wall of flames and visibility was reduced to several feet because of the smoke. He managed to escape to safety because he knew the terrain. He slowly made his way back to his farm, only to find its gutted remains. He described this terrifying and tragic sequence very matter of factly, without any mention of his thoughts or fears. His facial expression was passive, and he spoke in a flat, emotionless voice.

Lack of emotional color can easily be misinterpreted to indicate that the person has coped with the event. The individual may be unaware of his or her manner of presentation. The interviewer should make the client aware of this lack of emotional expression with regard to the experience. For example, the practitioner responded to Mr. Inns's description in the following way:

> *Psychiatrist*: I noticed that as you described your experience, you gave very few signs of your feelings about what it must really have been like to come so close to death. Do you notice that you have found it more difficult to show your feelings and reactions since the fire?

This observation is more likely to strike a chord in the client if it is linked to his or her immediate behavior and lack of responsiveness and can be the first step in allowing the client to reveal the true emotional impact of the trauma.

The Importance of the Family

A family's capacity to incorporate and contain the experience of trauma also plays an important role in determining an individual's adjustment. The impact of the event on all family members should be assessed, particularly following events in which more than one family member has been directly exposed to trauma. The intrusive memories of one spouse will often resonate with the pattern of distress in his or her partner, especially if that partner is experiencing PTSD. For example,

> A twenty-five-year-old woman developed acute PTSD following the total destruction of her home and loss of all her possessions by fire. She experienced intense anxiety when returning to the burned ruins of her home. She attempted to put all memories of the fire out of her mind. She avoided working on rebuilding her home, which was a source of conflict with her husband, who was keen to commence reconstruction. She was very distressed when these issues were discussed in an assessment interview. However, she became involved in treatment because her husband sought help

for his intrusive memories of the disaster. Her inability to discuss their losses was an important factor contributing to his preoccupation with the disaster. Paradoxically, she was more disabled than he was.

Thus, in this case, the intrusive thoughts of the husband and the avoidance behavior of his wife played a central role in preventing this couple from mastering their losses. Such patterns are especially important in families with young children, because the children's adjustment to the trauma is determined more by the impact of the trauma on the parents than by their own experiences (Bloch, Silber, & Perry, 1956). Children sense and react to their parents' posttraumatic preoccupations. Moreover, traumatized parents may become anxious, causing the children to become more fearful (McFarlane, 1987b).

The issue of the apportioning of blame should also be considered when working with families. Attribution theory suggests that people make causal attributions that facilitate adaptation by helping them feel as though they are in control of their environment (Wong & Weiner, 1981). Blame is a way of stating that the trauma could have been averted. It is used to protect one's sense of self-control, which is threatened by awareness of vulnerability. In some instances, one family member may be blamed for the others' distress and trauma. It is important that scapegoating be quickly averted, as it can be highly destructive to family relationships. A person who develops PTSD or some other psychiatric illness triggered by the trauma can easily become the family scapegoat because of the distress this disorder may induce in other family members. For example,

Mrs. Summers developed severe PTSD after the family's farm was destroyed by a bush fire. She became irritable and emotionally labile. She had been very angry with her husband after the disaster because he had left the property an hour after the fire front had passed to take his elderly father home. She never discussed her feelings. She coped by burying herself in her career, which made Mr. Summers very angry. He had no knowledge of his wife's suffering.

Mr. Summers developed some features of PTSD. One year after the fire he developed a major depressive illness, at which time he became suicidal. His depression responded quickly to antidepressant medication. He attributed his depression entirely to Mrs. Summers's behavior and denied that the disaster had played any role. His lack of concern about the possibility of another fire occurring was a major source of conflict with his wife, because his lack of precautions aggravated Mrs. Summers's sense of vulnerability. He denied that he would experience any sense of loss if another fire occurred because he had insured the property to cover any damage.

This strategy allowed Mr. Summers to deny that the disaster had had any direct impact on him and that he felt any sense of vulnerability about the future. He saw himself as invulnerable. He was able to project the blame and vulnerability onto his wife, even though his depression had been precipitated by his unresolved and unconscious sense of loss following the disaster. Furthermore, he could not empathize with her because doing so would force him to face the same feelings in himself.

Thus the family is a critical matrix that can mold the trauma response. The roles played by family members should always be considered in treatment.

The Need for a Multidimensional Approach

In PTSD, three sets of problems (intrusive memories, disturbed attention, and estrangment) require attention in treatment. What works for one set of symptoms will not necessarily work for another.

Intrusive Memories versus Denial

A psychotherapeutic approach is crucial to this type of symptom. When the memories of the traumatic event, however intrusive, are split from awareness of the emotional impact of attendant loss, strategies may be designed to attempt to help the client overcome his or her avoidance of pain. Of course, the therapist must sensitively titrate any challenge to the client's defensive avoidance. Thus it is important to differentiate the intrusive and painful traumatic memories from feelings of loss and bereavement. For example,

> Mr. Keith (whose thoughts about the way his son died are described above) clearly separated the horrifying memories about the way his son's body was positioned from his feelings of longing and grief. As he worked to rebuild his farm, he would often recall the activities he shared with his son. Although these thoughts made him sad, Mr. Keith welcomed these recollections, in contrast with the images of his son's death that tormented him.

Thus, the therapist needs to examine both the bereavement process and the victim's sense of traumatization.

Disturbed Attention and Arousal

Control of the client's disturbed attention and arousal is often critical to treatment success. Relief of these symptoms plays an important role in ensuring a client's commitment to the treatment process. After distressing and disabling symptoms are alleviated, clients find it much easier to focus on and think through their traumatic memories outside the treatment setting. Medication, used as a short-term adjunct to psychotherapy, can be particularly useful in this regard.

Tricyclic antidepressants and monoamine oxidase inhibitors are the most effective and commonly used medications (Bleich et al., 1986). Sedatives or tranquilizers are seldom used. The nonmedical practitioner should have a consulting physician discuss the reasons for prescribing these drugs as well as the possible side effects. Medications should be reviewed regularly by the physician.

It has been suggested that the use of medication can interfere with the psychotherapeutic process. However, others believe that the effect of each is enhanced by the other and that these approaches do not necessarily conflict (Conte, Plutchik, Wild, & Karasu, 1986; Weissman, 1979). Similarly, relaxation techniques and hypnotherapy can augment the control of anxiety.

Estrangement and Withdrawal

Estrangement and withdrawal require specific attention in their own right as they do not necessarily respond to the techniques aimed at intrusive memories or anxiety. In an acute disorder, social and interpersonal problems are still evolving and are therefore more amenable to treatment. In long-standing PTSD, however, the underlying disturbance of attention and arousal may be relatively minor problems compared with constricted affect and estrangement. For example,

> Mrs. Hill was a fifty-eight-year-old widow whose husband had died ten years earlier as a result of injuries he received in a mine accident. He had suffered a slow death and had been grossly disfigured, including having both legs amputated. Mrs. Hill's presenting problem was emotional numbing and withdrawal from intimate relationships, despite the fact that she was socially competent and youthful. Treatment focused primarily on the defensive nature of her withdrawal as an attempt to ward off an inner sense of vulnerability to further trauma and loss.

Conceptually, these phenomena are separated because they are likely to have different causes and, as such, to require different treatments (Kolb, 1986). For example, the personality of the individual is likely to play a more important role in explaining interpersonal withdrawal than are disturbed attention and concentration, which are more likely to have a neurophysiological basis. Medications that act on neurophysiological mechanisms are aimed at changing anxiety symptoms. Similarly, family therapy may play an important role in changing relationship conflicts and withdrawal, but may lead to no direct change in the underlying disturbances in attention and arousal. Thus, symptomatic impairments and social handicaps should be assessed separately (World Health Organization, 1980), after which a treatment program aimed at the specific elements of the disorder should be initiated.

Maintaining Client Involvement

Keeping clients involved is a major problem in treating people with PTSD (Lindy, Green, Grace, & Titchner, 1983). This problem has several dimensions.

First, avoidance of situations that lead to an intensification of memories of the trauma is central to the stress response (Horowitz, 1974). Therefore, treatment has the potential of being an anxiety-provoking experience.

Second, trauma victims may be suspicious about the motives of people who want to know about their experience. They may resent what they perceive as a voyeuristic fascination with their plight. Many victims say that it is much easier to share their experience with someone who has been through a similar trauma. Veterans' associations testify to this fact.

Third, some experiences are truly unspeakable. The therapist must guard against the belief that catharsis alone is the central element of treatment (Marmor, 1980). Such a therapeutic technique may add to the client's sense of being a victim. Horowitz (1976) concludes that "for some [victims of catastrophic stress] the damage appears irreversible: the horror was too great and treatment can become only a reliving but not a dispelling of the nightmares" (p. 121). Thus a therapist must be constantly aware of the possibility that treatment may have a negative effect (Hadley & Strupp, 1976). This issue is not easy for practitioners to face and to accept.

Fourth, clients sometimes describe the trauma in a repetitive manner without any change in emphasis. This compulsive going over and over may reflect the client's helplessness during the event or a situation that might have been changed if he or she had behaved differently. The practitioner should avoid going along with the client and not challenging issues of personal responsibility for fear of implying blame and not being empathic.

> Mr. Green was a forty-year-old bank officer whose home had been destroyed in a bush fire. Throughout the day of the disaster, he and his wife denied the risk to their property. Mrs. Green had been agoraphobic for fifteen years and rarely left home without her husband. When the fire front hit, Mr. Green panicked and ran out of the house, calling to his wife to come. She did not follow immediately, and Mr. Green hastily escaped in his car. His wife was burned to death.
>
> In treatment, Mr. Green went over and over the horror of the fire as it hit and his terrifying drive to safety. One could not help empathizing with the terrible predicament that this man faced in thinking about the disaster. At no stage did he make it clear that his wife had agoraphobia or that he had resented the restrictions that this had placed on his life. This information was passed on in confidence by the woman he married five months after the disaster. She urged him (unsuccessfully) to stay in treatment. She also said that he had been married previously, at the age of twenty-one, and had left his first wife without any discussion one week after the wedding.
>
> Mr. Green avoided thinking about his behavior in the fire by emphasizing his helplessness. A clue to this was the repetitive way in which he spoke of his terror. Exploration of his choices during the fire was mistakenly not pursued because the practitioner was afraid of increasing his traumatic imagery and of being perceived as blaming him. Mr. Green projected his guilt onto the therapist and left treatment because he believed it was making him worse. In all probability, the issues were of such enormity that Mr. Green could never have faced his own worst fears about the personal meaning of his behavior.

This example graphically illustrates how past events and relationships can mold the individual's sensitivity to the current trauma.

Issues for the Therapist

Treating victims of trauma is demanding for any therapist and raises personal issues that do not arise in other settings. Lindy et al. (1983) found that therapists who were familiar with the reality of a traumatic event, having accompanied relatives during body identifications after a fire, tended to be more successful at engaging the clients, whereas therapists who had not been through this experience sometimes resisted hearing the details of the disaster.

This finding emphasizes that therapists dealing with trauma victims must face their own personal feelings about the trauma and the way this knowledge might increase their sense of vulnerability. In one sense, therapists can be indirectly affected by the trauma and use the same psychological mechanisms as the victims do to avoid experiencing the horror of the event. For this reason, some form of personal supervision by a colleague who is experienced in PTSD work is helpful. Although discussion of cases can be useful, personal issues may not be as easily acknowledged (see chapter 9 for a discussion of debriefing).

Therapists must also face the painful reality that some of the psychological wounds that they attempt to repair cannot be healed. In such cases, it is important not to prolong treatment because doing so may only increase the client's reliving of the trauma with no benefit. A therapist's overt optimism about the benefits of treatment may indicate that the therapist feels vulnerable to the trauma too. Thus flexibility and sensitivity on the part of the practitioner are important attributes in this work.

Situations may arise in the course of treatment wherein the therapist experiences profound sorrow and distress in response to what a survivor has described. On the one hand, the therapist must not burden the victim with his or her feelings because doing so may make the client feel reluctant to discuss similar events in the future. On the other hand, the therapist's emotional response can be used as a vehicle to challenge the client's constricted affect. For example,

> Mr. Byrd arrived at the top of his driveway to see the roof of his burning home collapse into the walls. His wife and seven-week-old son were in the building and were killed. Mr. Byrd described this event without showing emotion. The therapist responded by saying, "One can only feel deeply upset by hearing about what you have lost and been through, let alone having to cope with it all, in reality."

In this way, the client's felt but unexpressed affect was acknowledged, and the therapist indicated that feelings could be communicated and expressed. At the same time, the statement did not leave the client overburdened with the therapist's feelings.

In contrast to other treatment areas (Strupp & Hadley, 1979), the degree of training and experience of the therapist in the treatment of trauma victims appears to be an important outcome variable (Lindy et al., 1983). This issue needs to be considered when appointing a team to deal with a traumatized population and has implications for the type and frequency of supervision that should be provided.

Finally, on occasion a therapist may feel that words are an inadequate response to what has been described; silence, if appropriately used, may be the only appropriate communication. For example,

> In the days that followed the death of his son and the destruction of his farm, Mr. Keith had to erect temporary fencing to stop his remaining stock from wandering. He felt that his family was cursed and faced the future with a sense of foreboding. As he was fencing in a burnt-out paddock, a huge thunderstorm approached, with lightning frequently striking the ground. Mr. Keith turned to his companion and admitted his fear that he was going to be killed by the lightning, the final chapter in the curse. The other man replied, "God just is not that bad." Having recounted this story, Mr. Keith started crying and admitted that his companion's simple words provided him with a tremendous sense of relief. The therapist and Mr. Keith sat in silence for several minutes.

Conclusion

Many uncertainties surround the etiology and treatment of PTSD. Much of the available evidence is anecdotal and mere opinion. Therefore, future research should pay particular attention to methodological issues. Accurate information is also much needed in the area of treatment methods.

Although patterns of response can be described, it is important not to overgeneralize. People respond to trauma in many ways. Their responses are molded by their individual perception of the event, which, in turn, is influenced by the unique matrix of experiences, personality, and relationships that they bring to the trauma. Although trauma is the focus of the individual's initial reaction, these other characteristics color the long-term adaptation. In fact, the importance of other vulnerability factors has often been underestimated in chronic PTSD (McFarlane, 1989).

Careful assessment of these issues and attention to the individual preoccupations of each client are central to adequate treatment of PTSD. Similarly, treatment programs often use various therapeutic methods concurrently, emphasizing the need for an eclectic, multidimensional approach to this disorder.

Crisis intervention techniques play an important role in guiding recently distressed trauma victims toward a healthy resolution. Hence, crisis intervention principles are essential knowledge for anyone working in this area. However, as indicated in chapter 1 of this book, few experimentally designed studies have examined the effectiveness of crisis intervention. This is not surprising, considering the many practical difficulties faced by people who must work in extremely demanding settings after disasters. Evidence from recent PTSD studies suggests that although crisis intervention has benefits, a significant level of PTSD may remain (Singh & Raphael, 1981; Lindy et al., 1983; Fowlie & Aveline, 1985).

This point is perhaps best demonstrated by Solomon and Benbenishty's (1986) study of the effectiveness of an acute intervention service for treating combat stress reactions in the Israeli armed services. The success of their program enabled soldiers to return to the battlefront. However, approximately 50 percent of the best outcome groups, when followed up one year later, showed persistent, chronic PTSD.

Although many claims have been made about what constitutes the essential ingredients of PTSD treatment, in some treatment situations the nonspecific elements of treatment are more important. Frank (1961) alerted therapists to the value of instilling hope in the distressed and in providing a system for explaining their symptoms. Perhaps the most critical benefit a therapist can offer victims of trauma is a sense of hope to counteract their demoralized and vulnerable state.

References

American Psychiatric Association (1987). *Diagnostic and statistical manual of mental disorders* (3rd ed., rev.). Washington, DC: Author.

Andrews, G., Christensen, H., & Hadzi-Pavolovic, D. (1985). Exhibit 1452, *Royal Commission on the use and effects of chemical agents on Australian personnel in Vietnam.* Canberra, Australia: Australian Government Printing Service.

Andrews, G., & Tennant, C. (1978). Life events and psychiatric illness. *Psychological Medicine, 8*, 545–549.

Archibald, H. D., Long, D. M., Miller, C., & Tuddenham, R. D. (1963). Gross stress reactions in combat—A 15-year follow-up. *American Journal of Psychiatry, 119*, 317–322.

Berman, S., Price, S., & Gusman, F. (1982). An inpatient program for Vietnam combat veterans in a Veterans Administration hospital. *Hospital and Community Psychiatry, 333*, 919–922.

Bleich, A., Seigel, B., Garb, R., & Lerer, B. (1986). Posttraumatic stress disorder following combat exposure: Clinical features and psychopharmacological treatment. *British Journal of Psychiatry, 146*, 493–496.

Bloch, D. A., Silber, E., & Perry, S. E. (1956). Some factors in the emotional reaction of children to disaster. *American Journal of Psychiatry, 138*, 14–19.

Boehnlein, J. K., Kinzie, J. D., Ben, R., & Fleck, J. (1985). One-year follow-up study of posttraumatic stress disorder among survivors of Cambodian concentration camps. *American Journal of Psychiatry, 142*, 956–959.

Brende, J. O. (1981). Combined individual and group therapy for Vietnam veterans. *International Journal of Group Psychotherapy, 31*, 367–378.

Brende, J. O. (1985). The use of hypnosis in post-traumatic conditions. In W. E. Kelly (Ed.), *Post-traumatic stress disorder and the war veteran patient*. New York: Brunner/Mazel.

Brett, E. A., & Ostroff, R. (1985). Imagery and posttraumatic stress disorder: An overview. *American Journal of Psychiatry, 142*, 417–424.

Burnstein, A. (1986). Treatment non-compliance in patients with post-traumatic stress disorder. *Psychosomatics, 27*, 37–40.

Clayer, J. R., Brookless-Pratz, C., & McFarlane, A. C. (1985). *The health and social impact of the Ash Wednesday bushfires: Survey of the 12 months following the bushfires of February 1983*. Adelaide, Australia: Mental Health and Evaluation Centre, South Australian Health Commission.

Conte, H. R., Plutchik, R., Wild, K. V., & Karasu, T. B. (1986). Combined psychotherapy and pharmacotherapy for depression. A systematic analysis of the evidence. *Archives of General Psychiatry, 43*, 471–479.

Daly, R. J. (1983). Samuel Pepys and post-traumautic stress disorder. *British Journal of Psychiatry, 143*, 64–68.

Davidson, J., Swartz, M., Storck, M., Krishnan, R. R., & Hammett, E. (1985). A diagnostic and family study of post-traumatic stress. *American Journal of Psychiatry, 142*, 90–93.

Engel, G. M. (1980). The clinical application of the biopsychosocial model. *American Journal of Psychiatry, 137*, 535–544.

Epstein, N. B., & Volk, V. A. (1981). Research on the results of psychotherapy: A summary of evidence. *American Journal of Psychiatry, 138*, 1027–1035.

Escobar, J. I., Randolph, E. T., Pruente, G., Spiwak, F., Asamen, J. K., Hill, M., & Hough, R. L. (1983). Post-traumatic stress disorder in Hispanic Vietnam veterans. *Journal of Nervous and Mental Disease, 171*, 585–596.

Ettedgui, E., & Bridges, M. (1985). Posttraumatic stress disorder. *Psychiatric Clinics of North America, 8*, 89–103.

Evatt, P. (1985). *Royal Commission on the use and effects of chemical agents on Australian personnel in Vietnam*. Canberra, Australia: Australian Government Printing Service.

Figley, C. R. (1985). *Trauma and its wake: The study and treatment of post-traumatic stress disorder*. New York: Brunner/Mazel.

Fowlie, D. G., & Aveline, M. O. (1985). The emotional consequences of ejection, rescue and rehabilitation in Royal Air Force aircrew. *British Journal of Psychiatry, 146*, 609–613.

Foy, D. W., Rueger, D. B., Sipprelle, R. C., & Carroll, E. M. (1984). Etiology of posttraumatic stress disorder in Vietnam veterans: Analysis of premilitary, military and combat exposure influences. *Journal of Consulting and Clinical Psychology, 52*, 79–87.

Frank, J. (1961). *Persuasion and healing*. Baltimore: Johns Hopkins University Press.

Gleser, G. C., Green, B. L., & Winget, C. (1981). *Prolonged psychosocial effects of a disaster: A study of Buffalo Creek*. New York: Academic Press.

Green, B. L. (1982). Assessing levels of psychological impairment following disaster: Consideration of actual and methodological dimensions. *Journal of Nervous and Mental Disease, 170*, 544–552.

Green, B. L., Grace, M. C., & Gleser, G. C. (1985). Identifying survivors at risk; long-term impairment following the Beverly Hills Supper Club fire. *Journal of Consulting and Clinical Psychology, 53*, 672–678.

Hadley, S. W., & Strupp, H. S. (1976). Contemporary views of negative effects in psychotherapy: An integrated account. *Archives of General Psychiatry, 33*, 1291–1302.

Haley, S. A. (1985). Some of my best friends are dead: Treatment of the PTSD patient and his family. In W. E. Kelly (Ed.), *Post-traumatic stress disorder and the war veteran patient*. New York: Brunner/Mazel.

Hall, W. (1986). The Agent Orange controversy after the Evatt Royal Commission. *Medical Journal of Australia, 145*, 219–225.

Helzer, J. E. (1981). Methodological issues in the interpretations of the consequences of extreme situations. In B. S. Dohrenwend & B. P. Dohrenwend (Eds.), *Stressful life events and their contexts*. New York: Prodist.

Helzer, J. E., Robins, L. E., Wish, E., & Hesselbrock, M. (1979). Depression in Viet Nam veterans and civilian controls. *American Journal of Psychiatry, 136*, 526–529.

Hogben, G. L., & Cornfield, R. B. (1981). Treatment of traumatic neurosis with phenelzine. *Archives of General Psychiatry, 38*, 440–445.

Hoiberg, A., & McCaughey, B. G. (1984). The traumatic aftereffects of collision at sea. *American Journal of Psychiatry, 141*, 70–73.

Horowitz, M. J. (1974). Stress response syndromes: Character style and dynamic psychotherapy. *Archives of General Psychiatry, 31*, 768–781.

Horowitz, M. J. (1976). *Stress response syndromes*. New York: Jason Aronson.

Horowitz, M. J., Wilner, M. E., Kaltreider, N., & Alvarez, W. (1980). Signs and symptoms of post-traumatic stress disorder. *Archives of General Psychiatry, 37*, 85–92.

Keane, T. M., Fairbank, J. A., Caddell, J. M., Zimering, R. T., & Bender, M. E. (1985). A behavioral approach to assessing and treating post-traumatic stress disorders in Vietnam veterans. In C. R. Figley (Ed.), *Trauma and its wake: The study and treatment of post-traumatic stress disorder*. New York: Brunner/Mazel.

Kelly, W. E. (1985). *Post-traumatic stress disorder and the war veteran patient*. New York: Brunner/Mazel.

Kettner, B. (1972). Combat strain and subsequent mental health: A follow-up of Swedish soldiers serving in the United Nations forces 1961–1962. *Acta Psychiatrica Scandinavica Supplementum, 230*.

Kolb, L. C. (1986). Treatment of chronic posttraumatic stress disorder. *Current Psychiatric Therapeutics, 23*, 119–127.

La Guardia, R. L., Smith, G., Francois, R., & Bachman, L. (1983). Incidence of delayed stress disorder among Vietnam era veterans: The effect of priming on response set. *American Journal of Orthopsychiatry, 53*, 18–26.

Leopold, R. L., & Dillon, H. (1963). Psychoanatomy of disaster: A long-term study of posttraumatic neuroses in survivors of a marine explosion. *American Journal of Psychiatry, 119*, 913–921.

Levav, I., Greenfeld, H., & Baruch, E. (1979). Psychiatric combat reactions during the Yom Kippur war. *American Journal of Psychiatry, 136*, 637–641.

Lifton, R. J. (1978). Advocacy and corruption in the healing professions. In C. R. Figley (Ed.), *Stress disorders among Vietnam veterans: Theory, research and treatment*. New York: Brunner/Mazel.

Lindy, J. D., Grace, M. C., & Green, B. L. (1981). Outreach to a reluctant population. *American Journal of Orthopsychiatry, 51*, 468–478.

Lindy, J. D., Green, B. L., Grace, M., & Titchner, J. (1983). Psychotherapy with survivors of the Beverly Hills Supper Club fire. *American Journal of Psychotherapy, 37*, 593–610.

Marmor, J. (1980). Recent trends in psychotherapy. *American Journal of Psychiatry, 137*, 409–416.

Marrs, R. (1985). Why would the pain not stop and what the family can do to help. In W. E. Kelly (Ed.), *Post-traumatic stress disorder and the war veteran patient*. New York: Brunner/Mazel.

McFarlane, A. C. (1984). The Ash Wednesday bushfires in South Australia: Implications for planning future post-disaster services. *Medical Journal of Australia, 141*, 286–291.

McFarlane, A. C. (1985). The effects of stressful life events and disasters; research and theoretical issues. *Australian and New Zealand Journal of Psychiatry, 19*, 409–421.

McFarlane, A. C. (1986a). Posttraumatic morbidity of a disaster: A study of cases presenting for psychiatric treatment. *Journal of Nervous and Mental Disease, 174*, 4–14.

McFarlane, A. C. (1986b). Long-term psychiatric morbidity after a natural disaster: Implications for disaster planners and emergency services. *Medical Journal of Australia, 145*, 561–563.

McFarlane, A. C. (1987a). Family functioning and overprotection following a natural disaster; the longitudinal effects of post-traumatic morbidity. *Australian and New Zealand Journal of Psychiatry, 21*, 210–218.

McFarlane, A. C. (1987b). The relationship between patterns of family interaction and psychiatric disorder in children. *Australian and New Zealand Journal of Psychiatry, 21*, 383–390.

McFarlane, A. C. (1988a). The relationship between psychiatric impairment and a natural disaster; the role of distress. *Psychological Medicine, 18*, 129–139.

McFarlane, A. C. (1988b). The aetiology of posttraumatic stress disorders following a natural disaster. *British Journal of Psychiatry, 152*, 116–121.

McFarlane, A. C. (1988c). The longitudinal course of posttraumatic morbidity: The range of outcomes and their predictors. *Journal of Nervous and Mental Disease, 176*, 30–39.

McFarlane, A. C. (1989). The aetiology of post-traumatic morbidity: Predisposing, precipitating and perpetuating factors. *British Journal of Psychiatry, 154*, 221–228.

McFarlane, A. C., Policansky, S. K., & Irwin, C. (1987). A longitudinal study of the psychological morbidity in children due to a natural disaster. *Psychological Medicine, 5*, 133–141.

Paykel, E. S. (1978). Contribution of life events to the causation of psychiatric illness. *Psychological Medicine, 8*, 245–253.

Pilowsky, I. (1969). Abnormal illness behavior. *British Journal of Medical Psychology, 42*, 347–351.

Perry, J. C., & Jacobs, D. (1982). Overview; clinical applications of the amytal interview in psychiatric emergency settings. *American Journal of Psychiatry, 139*, 552–559.

Quality Assurance Project. (1985). Treatment outlines for the management of anxiety states. *Australian and New Zealand Journal of Psychiatry, 19*, 138–151.

Quarantelli, E. L. (1985). An assessment of conflicting views on mental health: The consequences of traumatic events. In C. R. Figley (Ed.), *Trauma and its wake: The study and treatment of post-traumatic stress disorder*. New York: Brunner/Mazel.

Quarantelli, E. L., & Dynes, R. R. (1977). Response to social crisis and disaster. *Annual Reviews of Sociology, 3*, 23–49.

Rabkin, J. G., & Struening, E. L. (1976). Life events, stress, and illness. *Science, 194*, 1013–1020.

Raphael, B. (1980). Primary prevention; fact or fiction. *Australian and New Zealand Journal of Psychiatry, 14*, 163–174.

Raphael, B. (1984). *The anatomy of bereavement: A handbook for the caring professions.* London: Hutchinson.

Rosenheck, R. (1984). Hospital-based treatment of malignant post Vietnam stress syndrome. *Psychiatric Quarterly, 56*, 259–269.

Shore, J. H., Tatum, E. L., & Vollmer, W. M. (1986). Psychiatric reactions to disaster: The Mount St. Helen's experience. *American Journal of Psychiatry, 143*, 590–595.

Sierles, F. S., Chen, J., McFarland, R. E., & Taylor, M. A. (1983). Post-traumatic stress disorder and concurrent psychiatric illness: Preliminary report. *American Journal of Psychiatry, 140*, 1177–1179.

Singh, B., & Raphael, B. (1981). Postdisaster morbidity of the bereaved: A possible role for preventive psychiatry. *Journal of Nervous and Mental Disease, 169*, 203–212.

Sloane, R. B., Staples, F. R., & Cristol, A. H. (1975). *Psychotherapy versus behavior therapy.* Cambridge, MA: Harvard University Press.

Solomon, Z., & Benbenishty, R. (1986). The role of proximity, immediacy and expectancy in frontline treatment of combat stress reaction among Israelis in the Lebanon war. *American Journal of Psychiatry, 143*, 613–617.

Solomon, Z., Milkulincer, M., & Kotler, M. (1987). A two-year follow-up of somatic complaints among Israeli combat stress reaction casualties. *Journal of Psychosomatic Research, 31*, 463–469.

Stanton, M. D., & Figley, C. R. (1978). Treating the Vietnam veteran within the family system. In C. R. Figley (Ed.), *Stress disorders among Vietnam veterans: Theory, research and treatment.* New York: Brunner/Mazel.

Strupp, H. (1972). On the technology of psychotherapy. *Archives of General Psychiatry, 26*, 270–278.

Strupp, H. S., & Hadley, S. W. (1979). Specific versus non-specific factors in psychotherapy: A controlled study of outcome. *Archives of General Psychiatry, 36*, 1125–1136.

Tennant, C. (1983). Life events and psychological morbidity: The evidence from prospective studies. *Psychological Medicine, 13*, 483–486.

Tennant, C., & Andrews, G. (1978). The pathogenic quality of life events stress in neurotic impairment. *Archives of General Psychiatry, 35*, 859–863.

Trimble, M. R. (1981). *Post-traumatic neurosis.* Chichester, England: John Wiley.

Van der Kolk, B. A. (1983). Psychopharmacological issues in posttraumatic stress disorder. *Hospital and Community Psychiatry, 34*, 683–691.

Van Putten, T., & Yager, J. (1984). Posttraumatic stress disorder: Emerging from the rhetoric. *Archives of General Psychiatry, 41*, 411–413.

Walker, J. L. (1982). Chemotherapy of traumatic war stress. *Military Medicine, 147*, 1029–1033.

Walker, J. L., & Nash, J. L. (1981). Group therapy in the treatment of Vietnam combat veterans. *International Journal of Group Psychotherapy, 31*, 379–389.

Weisaeth, L. (1984). *Stress reactions to an industrial accident.* Doctor of Medicine Thesis, Oslo University, Oslo, Norway.

Weisaeth, L. (1985). Psychiatric studies in victimology in Norway; main findings and recent developments. *Victimology, 10*, 478–487.

Weissman, M. M. (1979). The psychological treatment of depression: Evidence for the efficacy of psychotherapy alone, in comparison with, and in combination with pharmacotherapy. *Archives of General Psychiatry, 36*, 1261–1269.

Wong, P. T. P., & Weiner, B. (1981). When people ask "why" questions, and the heuristics of attributional search. *Journal of Personality and Social Psychology, 40*, 650–663.

World Health Organization. (1980). *The international classification of impairments, disabilities and handicaps*. Geneva, Switzerland: Author.

3

The Rape Victim

GAIL ABARBANEL AND GLORIA RICHMAN

RAPE IS ONE OF THE CRUELEST forms of criminal violence. It has been called "worse than death" (Rose, 1986). The victim suffers profound injury. She is rendered powerless by physical force, threats, or fear, after which she is forced to submit to sexual acts, including vaginal penetration, oral copulation, sodomy, and penetration of a genital opening with an object. Rape is an intrusion into the most private and intimate parts of a woman's body as well as an assault on the core of her self. The most apt descriptions of the impact of rape come from victims themselves. One woman in her twenties, still shaken by the pervasive effects of a rape inflicted upon her several months earlier, said, "It's not just your body that's raped, it's your whole life."

Regardless of whether the victim suffers physical trauma, the psychological impact of a sexual assault is severe. Moreover, the painful, post-trauma symptoms that result from rape are long-lasting. Even victims who appear to have recovered months or years later often find that an overwhelming sense of powerlessness and vulnerability remains close to the surface and can easily, and unexpectedly, be reexperienced. A critical factor in the long-term impact of rape is that the assault radically changes the victim's view of the world. Her basic beliefs about the environment, other people, and herself are shattered. These are devastating losses. Thus, many survivors report that their lives are irrevocably altered by the rapist. He takes something away that the victim can never wholly regain.

This chapter is about the victim: who she is, what she experiences, and how she can be helped to recover.

We have incorporated two general concepts into the material that follows. First, the term "rape" is defined here as it is in common usage, rather than according to the law. The legal definition of rape in most states is limited to forced vaginal penetration. However, in common usage, rape refers to many different forms of sexual assault, including sodomy, oral copulation, and sexual battery. Generally, the impact upon the victim is the same, regardless of the site of abuse or the degree of penetration. Second, the female gender is used to refer to rape victims because the preponderance of rape victims are women. Although males are also victims of sexual assault and they suffer the same profound trauma as do female victims, this chapter focuses on the adult female victim.

A Crime No One Talked About

For centuries, women have suffered the violence of rape as well as the fear of victimization (Brownmiller, 1975). However, rape was noticeably absent in the psychiatric literature until the 1970s. Although it represented a major physical health, mental health, criminal justice, and public safety problem, rape was virtually ignored in both clinical and academic settings. Advocacy and treatment services for victims were almost nonexistent. Prevention programs had not been established. Very little research was conducted to further understanding of the problem. Misconceptions about rape allowed discriminatory laws and practices to persist, leading to inhumane treatment of victims by law-enforcement agencies and the courts. Because of these conditions, most victims remained silent, never reaching out for the help they so desperately needed. The few victims who did come forward were often revictimized by the systems to which they had turned for aid and understanding. There was a vicious cycle of low reporting, low prosecution rates, and escalating rape victimization.

This silence was broken in the early 1970s (Griffin, 1971; Largen, 1976). Women began to talk with one another about their victimization experiences, and gradually they began to speak out. Women formed grass-roots organizations to assist victims; these groups helped bring many previously hidden aspects of the problem to public attention. Finally, the plight of rape victims gained recognition. As a result, changes began to be made, albeit slowly, in the systems and institutions upon which victims must rely for treatment and legal redress, such as hospitals, police departments, and courts.

During the late 1970s and 1980s, treatment of rape victims began to improve. Rape crisis services became available (Abarbanel, 1976). Rape reform legislation was enacted (Largen, 1988). Medical protocols for victim care were developed (Plant & Wood, 1977). Victims were awarded some rights and protections in the criminal justice process. And clinicians and academicians began to focus their skills on the problem (Sutherland Fox & Scherl, 1972; Burgess & Holmstrom, 1974; Symonds, 1976; Notman & Nadelson, 1976; Kilpatrick, Veronen, & Resick, 1976).

Prevalence and Incidence of Rape

With changes in police agencies and the courts and the development of specialized services, more victims came forward and the number of reported rapes rose dramatically. Between 1970 and 1980, the rate at which rapes were reported to police departments across the country increased by 100 percent (FBI, 1971–1981).

A rape is now reported about once every six minutes in the United States (FBI, 1986). Although the number of reported cases is alarming, it still represents only a small fraction of the rapes actually committed (BJS, 1985). Historically, rape has been described as the most underreported of all violent crimes against persons (FBI, 1982). Victimization studies estimate that there are 3.5 to 10 times as many victims as the number who report (FBI, 1979).

The majority of victims remain silent because of feelings of shame; fear of retaliation by the assailant; concern about how they will be treated by law-enforcement and medical personnel; uncertainty about the reactions of significant others; lack of knowledge about where to turn for help; and, finally, because they believe that nothing will be done if they do seek redress. Another critical determinant of the victim's decision about reporting is whether the assailant is a stranger or an acquaintance. Women who are raped by someone they know are generally much more reluctant to make a police report (Abarbanel & Klein, 1981; BJS, 1985).

Various surveys have attempted to measure the actual prevalence of rape and the number of women who have been victimized. These studies consistently find much higher rates of victimization than are reported to the police. For example, in face-to-face interviews with a randomly selected sample of San Francisco women eighteen years of age and older, 41 percent reported being victims of rape or attempted rape. This rate is 13 times higher than the rate reported to the police for the same city (Russell, 1984).

College students are in the age group with the highest risk for rape. In a national study involving 6,000 students from thirty-two colleges throughout the United States, one of every fifteen male students reported committing or attempting rape during the preceding year. One of every six female students reported being a victim of rape or attempted rape during the same period, and 28 percent reported having been victims of rape or attempted rape since the age of fourteen (Koss, Gidycz, & Wisniewski, 1987).

Both of the victimization surveys described above found that more than 90 percent of the women who had been raped never reported their assaults to authorities. Thus, even though there has been a dramatic increase in reported rapes, the true scope of sexual violence in this country still remains hidden. Rape victims continue to suffer discriminatory treatment in many systems and institutions as well as under the law (Estrich, 1987). The persistence of a "blame the victim" mentality in response to rape also keeps victims silent. The problem of rape in our society will never be solved as long as there are silent victims. The secrecy of rape is, in part, what perpetuates it.

Differences between Stranger and Acquaintance Rape

Some of the issues with which the victim struggles in the aftermath of a sexual assault have to do with whether her assailant was a stranger or an acquaintance. Therefore, it is important for clinicians to understand how stranger rapes differ from acquaintance rapes. The differences fall into three general categories: (1) the circumstances surrounding the assault, (2) the attitudes people have toward the victim, and (3) victim reporting patterns.

Circumstances Surrounding the Assault

In a stranger rape, the victim has no prior relationship with the person who assaults her. The attack happens suddenly. The stranger rapist often uses the element of surprise to catch the victim off guard and gain control of the situation. In addition, he usually initiates contact with the victim by using force or threats. In most cases, the victim senses danger immediately.

> Martha, a sixty-two-year old woman, went to the bank in the early afternoon and parked her car in the adjacent parking lot. When she returned to

> her car, she unlocked the door. Suddenly, she felt a gun in her back. The man standing behind her ordered her to get in. He made her lie face down on the seat, drove her to a nearby alley, and raped her.

> Susan lived in a high-security apartment building. She was asleep in her bedroom when she felt someone touching her. She awoke, opened her eyes, and saw a man standing over her bed. He said, "Shut up or I'll kill you."

The most common image people have of rape is that of a stranger wielding a weapon who confronts a woman in a dark alley in a "bad" part of the city. In reality, this is not the most frequent scenario, even in stranger rapes. Many stranger rapes occur in or near the victim's own home (McDermott, 1979). Often they are associated with residential break-ins in the middle of the night. Stranger rapists also accost their victims outside and in public places, such as on the street or in a parking lot, office building, public restroom, or park. Some stranger rapists kidnap their victims, drive them to a secluded location, and rape them in an automobile. Frequently, the victim is threatened with a lethal weapon, such as a gun or a knife. In almost all stranger rapes, even those in which no weapon is brandished, the victim fears death. The rapist uses menace and intimidation to instill this fear.

Acquaintance rapes usually happen in much different circumstances. The rapist rarely carries a weapon. Brute physical force is the most common method used to control the victim. The most likely location is the victim's or the offender's residence. The victim and the attacker have a prior relationship and some history of interaction. The relationship may be new or casual, or the rapist may be someone whom the victim knows quite well. The vast majority of these assaults are "date rapes," although they also occur in the context of other types of relationships. For example, the offender may be a friend, neighbor, teacher, employer, fellow student at school, work colleague, new or casual acquaintance, or social companion.

A critical characteristic of the victim–offender relationship in an acquaintance rape is that the rapist is someone whom the victim has had no reason to fear prior to the rape. In fact, she usually has reason to trust him. The rape occurs in the context of a relationship that has been initiated in a socially acceptable way. Most of us make certain assumptions about people we know from work, school, our neighborhood, or through mutual friends or family relationships. We assume that these people are "safe." We assume that they will not turn against us, assault us, or inflict acts of criminal violence upon us. We make the same assumptions about people with whom we have built a relationship over time. We assume mutual trust and expect personal boundaries to be respected in the context of these relationships. Thus, acquaintance rapes happen in situations in which the victim is understandably not on guard.

> Teresa, a seventy-five-year-old grandmother, returned home alone after attending a family party. As she got ready for bed, she heard a knock at the door. The visitor was an old family friend who had been at the party earlier in the evening. He seemed distressed and said that he needed to talk with her, so she opened the door. He came in and started making sexual advances. When she resisted, he became angry, pushed her down on the couch, and raped her.

Another characteristic of acquaintance rape that differentiates it from stranger rape is that, in many instances, the situation in which the rape occurs begins as a voluntary, consensual encounter. For example, the victim accepts a date with a man, agrees to go to his house to study, or allows him into her home for nonsexual purposes. Then something goes wrong. The assailant violates the boundaries of the victim's consent. He demands sex and he uses force to obtain it.

> At Christina's high school graduation party, she met a young man who seemed very interested in her. He asked her if she would go out with him after the party. She declined because she felt she did not know him well enough. Over the next few weeks, he called frequently and they had long telephone conversations. Finally, she accepted his invitation to go out for dinner. He came to her home to pick her up, met her parents, and took her to a nice restaurant. After dinner, she thought he was driving her home. Instead, he took a turn in another direction and, speeding, drove to a secluded road where he parked the car so that her door was on the edge of a steep cliff. She asked him to take her home. He told her that if she spoke again he would kill her. Then he opened the glove compartment, put on black leather gloves, held her down, and raped her.

> During her freshman year, Karen attended a party off campus with a group of her friends. Her boyfriend was away visiting his family. One of his teammates, Mike, asked her to go with him to a nearby liquor store to get more beer for the party. The clerk asked them for identification, which neither of them had. Mike said he had some six-packs at his house and suggested they go there to get them. When they arrived at Mike's house, he offered Karen a beer. While they were talking, Mike's roommate appeared unexpectedly. The two men went into another room to talk. Then the roommate reappeared with no clothes on. He pinned Karen down on the couch and raped her while Mike watched and verbally abused her. When he was done, Karen screamed, "How could you do this to me?" He raped her again.

These examples demonstrate the profound betrayal suffered by acquaintance-rape victims. As one survivor said, "If you can't trust someone who is supposed to be your friend, whom can you trust?"

Attitudes toward the Victim

Acquaintance rape is one of the most misunderstood forms of criminal violence. Many people believe that it is not "real rape" (Estrich, 1987). It is mistakenly viewed as less violent, less serious, less criminal, and less traumatic for the victim than is stranger rape. These misconceptions lead to discriminatory treatment of rape victims. Women who are raped by someone whom they know are often victimized twice: once by the rapist and again by the system and significant others.

The second-class status of acquaintance-rape victims has many manifestations. People often view their allegations of rape with suspicion. Victims of acquaintance rape are frequently blamed or disbelieved, whereas victims of stranger rape are likely to receive empathy and support. This differential treatment is also reflected in the way stranger- and acquaintance-rape cases are handled in the criminal-justice system. Acquaintance rapes are much more likely than are stranger rapes to be rejected for prosecution.

The attitudes described above obscure the reality of victims' experiences. Victims of acquaintance rape suffer the same violation as do women who are sexually assaulted by strangers. The common, traumatizing element in every rape is the use of force by the offender and the subjection of the victim to a state of powerlessness.

Although the tendency to "blame the victim" and minimize the trauma associated with a sexual assault is more widespread in cases of acquaintance rape, these attitudes also emerge in response to rapes by strangers.

Victim Reporting Patterns

Acquaintance rapes are far more often underreported than are stranger rapes. In a study of the similarities and differences between stranger and acquaintance rape, researchers at the Rape Treatment Center at Santa Monica Hospital Medical Center in California found that only 58 percent of the acquaintance-rape victims had made police reports, whereas 88 percent of the stranger-rape victims had contacted authorities (Abarbanel & Klein, 1981). The ambivalence of acquaintance-rape victims about reporting the crime was also demonstrated in this study. If they report at all, women raped by someone whom they know are much more likely to make delayed or late reports.

Acquaintance-rape victims are the most silent victims primarily because of the prejudicial treatment they receive. They are also reluctant to report an attack because of their intense feelings of guilt and shame. The experience of being raped by someone whom they initially trusted makes them feel that something is wrong with their own judgment. They blame themselves for failing to foresee the dangerousness and violence of the person who attacked them. They fear they will be similarly judged and blamed by others. For some victims, the inability to report stems from discomfort with causing another person to be publicly tried or punished for a criminal act. Another reason for hesitation is the greater risk of being subjected to public scrutiny. It is very difficult to protect the victim's privacy in an acquaintance-rape situation because she and the offender usually share many friends and acquaintances. Upon disclosure, the victim's behavior and character may become the subject of debate.

> Marissa was a freshman in college, carrying a heavy load of science classes. She needed a tutor in chemistry and was assigned a young man who was also a member of the football team. He asked her out several times, but she turned him down. One evening, she went to his dorm room to get help preparing for an exam. He started to kiss her. She forcefully said "No" and "Stop" several times. But her verbal resistance seemed to make him more aggressive. He pushed her down on the bed, held her down with his hands and body, and raped her. She told her roommate about the rape, and the roommate, in turn, told other students. Marissa became the subject of gossip. She was alienated and criticized by her peers for causing trouble. The offender's teammates harassed her for several months by taunting and ridiculing her. She was accused of fabricating the story.

The Assault Encounter

Despite the differences between stranger rape and acquaintance rape, they share many features in common. These similarities are evident in the dynamics of the interaction between the victim and the assailant. Rapists use terror and intimidation to coerce their victims into involuntary acts. Sometimes they also employ actual physical force. Once rendered powerless, the victim becomes an object for abuse. She is no longer a person. One victim said, "It's like you are reduced to a block of wood."

The rapist may use one or more methods to coerce the victim to comply with his demands. These methods include brandishing or using weapons, applying physical force (hitting, choking, pinning the victim down), using restraints (ties, blindfolds), and/or making verbal threats of harm to the victim or significant others, such as the victim's children. Some sexual assault victims are coerced through other forms of intimidation. For example, in sections of the country where there are undocumented immigrants, women may be threatened by a person posing as an immigration officer who says, "If you don't do what I tell you, I'll have you deported," or "I'll have your children taken away." This is called a "badge of authority" rape.

When faced with the threat of being raped, almost all women attempt to defend themselves. They try to avert the attack or dissuade the assailant. Victims use many different strategies for self-defense. Most victims make an assessment of the situation in which they evaluate their position and available options. This happens in an instant. Then they employ one or more strategies in an effort to prevent the rape. For example, the victim may become verbally assertive, saying firmly, "Get away from me." Or the victim may attempt to talk her way out of the situation by persuading or negotiating with the assailant. This is a common response because reasoning with another person works in most interpersonal conflicts. Another strategy is to bargain with the assailant, for example, "Take my money, just don't hurt me." Sometimes victims scream in the hope that they will scare off the attacker or attract the attention of a potential rescuer. Victims may also try to escape or stall for time. Some victims try to physically resist and fight off the assailant.

In some situations, the victim finds that one or a combination of these strategies is successful in warding off the attacker. Nevertheless, the survivor is still a victim of an attempted rape, which is a serious felony. Victims of attempted rape may suffer the same trauma as victims of completed rapes.

In other assault situations, the victim may find that the same tactics only serve to escalate the violence and/or the threats made against her. Her resistance—talking, screaming, stalling, fighting—is countered by more force and/or increased threats. Thus the danger of the situation mounts. Victims usually report that in these circumstances, they fear they will be killed or seriously injured if they continue to resist. They therefore decide to submit to the rape in order to get out of the situation alive and/or without being mutilated or suffering more serious harm. In effect, the victim chooses nonresistance to protect herself. At this point, the victim's goal changes from preventing rape to ensuring survival. Her behavior also changes dramatically. She complies with the rapist's demands.

Another psychological state that also manifests itself in nonresistance is called "frozen fright." Frozen fright is a state of panic in which the victim is immobilized by fear. This combination of shock and terror may be engendered in victims when they fear annihilation and see no avenue of escape. The victim is psychologically paralyzed, reduced to a state of helplessness or "psychological infantilism" (Symonds, 1976). Moreover, the victim senses that her only hope for survival depends on the whims of the rapist because he has control of the situation. She cooperates with him, because she does not want to do anything that will anger, startle, or provoke him. She tries to stay calm. She becomes passive and obedient. She may even become friendly and solicitous. She has one goal: self-preservation. Because the victim perceives the rapist as being unpredictable and capable of the worst imaginable acts, she tries to ensure that she will stay in his good graces.

Frozen fright, passivity, and ingratiating behavior on the part of the victim may persist far beyond the time the initial threats against her are made. The power of the criminal, in large part, comes from the terror he instills in his victim. The victim never loses her view of him as dangerous. Even if he had no weapon, even if he made no verbal threat of death, even if he was an acquaintance who had never been violent before, the experience of being rendered powerless by him, through whatever means, terrorizes the victim. This terror continues to influence her behavior.

> Barbara was kidnapped at gunpoint by two men. They drove her to a vacant lot, raped her, and forced her to orally copulate them. When they were done, they drove her around the city, and stopped on a busy street. Both men left the car and went into a liquor store to buy beer. Barbara did not try to escape from the car, nor did she ask any passerby for help. She was terrified that if she made a move, they would run out of the store and kill her.

Nonresistance and frozen fright are common responses in both stranger and acquaintance rapes. It is critical for therapists as well as the general public to understand the dynamics of these reactions for two reasons. First, in the aftermath of rape, the victim struggles to resolve her feelings about how she reacted under the stress of the assault. She may need help to understand the psychological rationale for her responses. Second, the public, represented by jurors, often confuses behaviors that accompany frozen fright with consent. This confusion can affect the outcome of criminal prosecutions. It can also lead to the victim being blamed without cause by significant others.

Another area of confusion related to victim resistance concerns the expectation of physical injuries. A prevalent misconception about the crime of rape is the belief that if the assault had really been against the victim's will, she would have fought and therefore would have battle scars to prove it. Although this standard is not applied to victims of any other crime, victim resistance and corroborating injuries were for many years almost always required as proof of rape. However, rape can often be accomplished through intimidation. The violence is threatened but not actually inflicted on the victim. The majority of victims survive rape without serious physical trauma. Many have no visible signs of the terror they endured. Even the victim who is held at gunpoint or knife point, or the victim who is pinned down by the rapist's body weight, may emerge from the attack without a visible mark, not even a bruise or a scratch. Therefore, physical injuries should never be used to determine the veracity of a rape charge, nor should they be used as the sole measure of the victim's trauma.

Types of Rapists

The particular style of attack to which a victim is subjected depends upon the type of rapist committing the crime. Our understanding of offenders and their impact on victims has been greatly enhanced by the research of A. N. Groth, a psychologist who has worked extensively with convicted rapists. He developed a typology that categorizes the *modus operandi* of these offenders into three patterns: anger, power, and sadistic rapes (Groth, 1979). The material in this section is based primarily upon his contributions.

The anger rapist uses physical brutality and excessive force. He wants to hurt and humiliate the victim. He inflicts physical and verbal abuse. He employs far more violence than is necessary to control the victim. For example, he may beat the victim after he ties her up. He degrades her with verbal insults, and/or subjugation to multiple sexual acts. He usually rapes someone after experiencing an event in his personal life in which he feels he suffered an injustice. His rapes are impulsive, not preplanned. In an effort to retaliate, he displaces his anger onto an unknowing victim. She experiences an explosion of rage and aggression. She also sustains visible physical injuries.

The power rapist is very different. This type of offender does not want to hurt the victim. Rather, he seeks a conquest. He wants to have a woman and he wants to control her. He also wants her to like him. He wants to "score." The power rapist is usually willing to use whatever means are necessary to force compliance. Thus he is capable of hurting his victims. He may carry a weapon because it is the easiest way to control someone without physically harming her. Power rapists often have fantasies about taking a woman by force as a way of establishing a continuing relationship. Through the rape, he hopes to fulfill his fantasy. He often keeps the victim with him for hours, making normal social conversation. He may even ask her for a date at some future time. Power rapists are usually men who have been unsuccessful in interpersonal relationships and in their lives in general. They feel incompetent and ineffective. They rape to compensate for these feelings of inadequacy. Their victims often survive with no serious physical injuries.

The third type of offender is the sadistic rapist. He is the most dangerous and, fortunately, the rarest type of sex offender. For him, aggression is eroticized. The sadistic rapist gets pleasure from torturing his victims. He uses extreme forms of degradation and abuse, such as bondage, biting, burning, cutting and shaving, penetration with objects, and stabbing. One sadistic rapist ran the blade of a knife all over the victim's body. Then he put the knife in her vagina and slowly turned it. Sadistic rapists commit the most grotesque crimes and may even murder their victims. Therefore, they often get the most publicity, creating the false impression that sadistic rapes are more prevalent than are the other types. Some victims who survive these assaults initially wish that they had not lived through them. They fear that their nightmare will never be over.

Groth's typology of rapists helps explain some of the differences we see in victims. Some people feel that the power rapist, the most prevalent type, is the least dangerous and is far less frightening to the victim. This is wrong. From the victim's point of view, being held captive by a man who rapes her and tries to make normal social conversation is a harrowing, terrifying experience, even if he does not beat her. Every rape victim fears that, in the end, she will be killed or otherwise harmed, because physical harm is the ultimate, underlying threat in all rapes.

Three elements are present in every rape: power, anger, and sexuality. However, most rapists do not rape out of sexual desire or to achieve sexual satisfaction. Sex is their weapon, their means for expressing aggression or power. Their aim is to satisfy nonsexual needs. One of the most prevalent fallacies surrounding the crime of rape is that it is a sexual act. As long as rape is viewed in this way, the victim will be unfairly blamed because she is cast in the role of sexual provocateur.

The Impact of Rape

The impact of rape can be examined in various ways. One perspective takes into consideration the underlying meaning the assault has for the victim. The grave threats and profound losses the victim suffers change her life dramatically, sometimes forever. Another manifestation of the impact of rape is the anguish of the victim. Her psychological and behavioral symptoms of distress are poignant symbols of the destructiveness of the rapist's acts. Yet another way to understand the impact of rape is to compare it to other forms of trauma. Rape is an extreme form of human cruelty that in some ways resembles other overwhelming traumatic events and in other ways is a unique stressor. The rape victim suffers a violent intrusion into the innermost part of herself. She also faces forms of discrimination that other victims do not experience. From all of these perspectives, it is clear that for the victim rape does not stop when the rapist finishes his crime. As one victim said, "Rape doesn't end with rape, it lives on in the victim's heart."

The Meaning of Rape

The significance of rape in a victim's life is illuminated by the following statement: "My life is divided into two parts: before the rape and after the rape."

Rape dramatically challenges the victim's basic world view. It shatters many of her beliefs and assumptions about her environment, herself, and other people (Abarbanel, 1980; Janoff-Bulman, 1985). One's assumptions about the world operate at both the conscious and unconscious levels. They are beliefs that most of us hold. They include a general feeling of personal invulnerability and self-worth, a sense of predictability and order in the world, and confidence in our ability to take care of ourselves and negotiate relationships with other people. Most of us also have a fundamental belief in a just world (Lerner, 1980). We know that bad things happen, but we tend to believe that they happen to other people or to people who use poor judgment or do bad things. In these ways, we feel in control. This is the basis of our sense of security within our environment, within ourselves, and with other people. This security enables us to function in the world.

Rape violates these assumptions. The victim is thrust into a state of cognitive dissonance. The rape experience tells her that the world is not a safe place, that her environment and other people are not predictable. She suddenly learns that one can be subjected to irrational and violent acts without warning. Bad things do happen to good people. Another person can control and invade one's body against one's will. Furthermore, despite the criminality of sexual assaults, society may not support the victim. Therefore, the victim is left feeling vulnerable.

A particularly important determinant of the meaning of rape is the interpersonal nature of the violence. Such an event is unlike a natural disaster, an accident in which the victim is hurt by chance or through someone else's negligence, or a crime committed to gain money or property, such as a robbery. Rape is a deliberate act, committed by one or more persons against the victim with the intent of harming her. Thus rape, like murder, truly is a crime against the person. This personal aspect of the experience plays an important part in how the victim attributes meaning to the event. The event is personalized and internalized. The rape victim may attribute "badness" to herself because she was singled out to become an object of this degrading abuse. She may also feel tainted. Her self-esteem and self-worth may be diminished. Her confidence in her ability to protect herself is shaken, as is her ability to trust other people. People are now seen as potentially dangerous. This may jeopardize her ability to ask for and accept the support of others during the aftermath of the rape.

Another dimension of the meaning of rape for victims is the victim's feeling that a part of her self has been killed. One victim said, "You think you are going to die. And then it's over, and you are still alive. And you have to go on. But a part of you is dead."

Many rape victims experience an explicit or indirect threat of death during the assault. Afterwards they often say, "I thought he was going to kill me." Every rape victim, however, experiences an annihilation of self because that is the essence and the meaning of the rape experience. The victim is reduced to nothing and rendered helpless. It is as if she, the person, is not there. She has no control or autonomy over her own body. She is powerless as she is violated. One victim said, "He killed a part of my soul." Helplessness is the most feared of all human conditions and one of the most traumatic experiences. It is so abhorrent that during the rape, many victims dissociate. They describe a sense of leaving their bodies or of being outside the room where the attack is taking place, instead of being the person undergoing the rape. One victim explained, "I had to keep a part of myself away from what was happening." Another victim described removing herself and fighting back at the same time. She said, "As he was raping me, I concentrated on gathering information I could use as evidence against him. I memorized every detail of his physical description."

Thus a sexual assault causes staggering losses for the victim. The toll of these losses can be long-lasting. Effective treatment must address the scope and depth of the victim's trauma.

Symptoms of Rape Trauma

The meaning of the rape is reflected in the victim's symptomatology. The impact of the assault is immediate and profound. The first researchers to report on the effects of victimization identified stages of victim reactions (Sutherland Fox & Scherl, 1972; Burgess & Holmstrom, 1974). Although most victims experience these reactions in the sequence described below, individual variations exist in the timing, intensity, and duration of the symptoms.

The initial impact of rape is shock and disbelief. In this first stage, the victim feels numb. She may still be terrorized. She may appear stunned or dazed, outwardly calm, and subdued. The seemingly flat affect that accompanies this shock reaction can be misleading. Because many people measure trauma by visible injuries, they may conclude that the rape victim is "not hurt." However, one of the most striking characteristics of rape trauma, especially in its initial stages, is its invisibility. The seemingly contained demeanor of the victim further masks the serious psychological wound she has sustained. Her inner turmoil is reflected in her immobilization as well as in her expressions of disbelief. Many victims say, "I can't believe this happened to me." They already know that their lives have been irrevocably changed.

The second stage is denial. The victim actively tries to block out the experience and ward off the feelings it produces. The experience is too threatening and overwhelming. She may feel she cannot risk losing control. For some victims, this is an adaptive defense that usually serves to postpone dealing with the assault. Attempts at denial may be direct. The victim may say, "I don't want to talk about it," or "I want to forget that it ever happened." Denial may also be evident in the victim's behavior. She may wash or douche as if to cleanse herself of the rape. She may avoid dealing with the traumatic event by not seeking medical care, not making a police report, and not discussing it with others. Victims may also express denial by carrying on with their usual activities as though nothing out of the ordinary has happened. Engaging in familiar, routine tasks is more than avoidance. It is a way of reaffirming her sense of self and competency.

Eventually, almost all victims move into a stage characterized by acute distress. The feelings evoked by rape are so intense that they break through the victim's attempts to suppress them. In this third stage, the victim's symptoms include disturbing fears about personal safety; anxiety; preoccupation with the event (intrusive thoughts and feelings); sleep disturbances (frightening nightmares, insomnia, middle-of-the night awakening); emotional lability (crying jags, irritability, mood swings); helplessness; depression; lowered self-esteem; diminished self-confidence; feelings of guilt, self-blame, shame, and anger; sexual dysfunction; changes in appetite; and somatic complaints, such as soreness, aches, gastrointestinal stress, and gynecological problems. Fatigue is also common. The victim may be as frightened by the flood of symptoms as she was by the rape, because they cause her to relive the feeling of being out of control. Rape victims often say, "I feel like I'm going crazy." Although these symptoms define the acute stage of rape trauma, they may, in some form, become chronic. Several of these reactions are described in more detail below.

For many victims, fear, the most pervasive feeling during the rape, continues to dominate its aftermath. The victim's fears may be generalized or specific to the circumstances of the assault and characteristics of the offender. Victims commonly fear being alone, being in crowds, and revictimization. Their fears are related to heightened feelings of vulnerability to danger and harm; they live in fear of a recurrence. Their fears are evident in their nightmares, anxiety, withdrawal, and other behavioral and life-style changes. The rape victim may be unable to live or sleep alone. She may be unwilling to go out at night. She may never again sit with her back to a door. She may move to a new residence.

Personal safety becomes an overriding concern. Yet, to the victim, it feels like an unattainable goal.

> Pat was a victim of sexual battery and harassment in her workplace. The male employees frequently made unwanted sexual advances to the female employees. They also constantly made comments about the women's breasts and other parts of their bodies. One day, Pat was attacked by a male employee. He pushed her down in the staff lounge, got on top of her, and started to simulate having intercourse with her. Eventually, she fought him off. Two years later, she could not go anywhere alone, even to the grocery store. She is still plagued by nightmares in which she is at the end of a narrow hall and her attacker is coming toward her with a knife. In this dream, she is helpless and cannot move.

Feelings of guilt and self-blame are prominent symptoms. The victim may have exaggerated feelings of personal responsibility for the rape, regardless of the circumstances. These feelings, in part, reflect the victim's search for a reason to explain the arbitrary, traumatic event. She tries to answer the question "Why me?" This is part of the normal process of working through a traumatic event. She replays and reviews what happened. She struggles with feelings that perhaps she could have or should have avoided, escaped, or successfully resisted the attack. Her self-blame may represent an attempt to undo what happened and regain control. It may serve as a defense against being vulnerable. If the rape happened because of something she did or did not do, she can prevent it from happening again. This type of self-blame may be easier for some victims to tolerate emotionally than the reality that rape is a random event. If rape is random, it could happen again.

However, in some victims, self-blame may have another focus, which may be maladaptive. In making this assessment, it is useful to differentiate two types of self-blame: The most common type, described above, is behavioral—"It happened because I made a mistake or did something wrong." The second type of self-blame is characterological—"It happened because I am a bad person or I am inadequate." In this situation, the victim attributes the cause of the problem to a personal defect, rather than to an action or inaction (Janoff-Bulman, 1985). Regardless of the type of self-blame the victim expresses, it is critical for the therapist to explore fully her attributions and to understand the functions of these responses. Ultimately, it is important to help the victim place responsibility for the rape on the rapist—the person who used force. The victim may still choose to make behavioral changes to increase her personal safety and to prevent a future rape, but she should not have to carry the burden of feeling that her rape was punishment for some wrongdoing on her part. Even in situations in which the victim may have used poor judgment, it is important to distinguish poor judgment from asking to be raped.

Rape victims suffer deep, painful feelings of shame. Their shame is evident in lowered or averted eyes, and, all too often, in their secrecy about the rape. Shame is different from self-blame. Whereas self-blame reflects a feeling of responsibility for acts of commission or omission, shame involves a diminished, devalued self. Because of what happened during the rape, the victim is ashamed of herself. Nathanson (1987) discusses shame as a "family of emotions," including humiliation, degradation, embarrassment, disgrace, dishonor, and mortification. Shame has several origins in the rape victim. In part, it stems from the humiliation and degradation to which the victim is subjected during the assault. It is also related to the ways in which the rapist forces the victim to participate in the crime, if only by enduring it. One victim who was ordered by the rapist to act as if she enjoyed what he was doing said, "I became an unwilling participant." Afterward she was filled with a persistent sense of humiliation and disgust. Betrayal, a central element in rape, also produces shame. Another source is the special meaning our society attaches to rape victimization. Because of the rape, the victim may feel that she is "damaged goods." In some cultures, the stigma associated with rape remains strong, and the rape victim is treated as a ruined woman. She not only suffers dishonor herself, she brings disgrace upon her family.

Rape trauma symptoms such as as guilt, shame, and self-blame are also related to other unique burdens placed upon sexual assault victims. Our culture is permeated by misconceptions about rape, such as "Rape happens only to women who ask for it or to women who let it happen," "Rape happens only to certain kinds of (bad) women," or "Honorable women would fight to the death rather than risk dishonor." Women who consciously or unconsciously believe these misconceptions impose these judgments on themselves when they are raped. In addition, the victim's own reactions may be compounded when these attitudes are expressed by significant others or people with whom the victim interacts in law-enforcement agencies and the courts. For these reasons, education is an important component of rape treatment.

Many victims experience sexual dysfunction following rape (Burgess & Holmstrom, 1979b; Gilbert & Cunningham, 1986). Their symptoms include both changes in sexual behavior and diminished sexual satisfaction. Common problems are fear and avoidance of sex, arousal and desire dysfunctions, and the triggering of flashbacks to the assault during sex.

Because of their range and intensity, rape trauma symptoms cause tremendous disruption in the victim's life. Everything is affected, including daily activities of living (eating, sleeping, work, school), relationships with friends and family, and emotional adjustment (feelings, life satisfaction) as well as attitudes, beliefs, and values.

Some symptoms of rape trauma may be long-lasting. Several longitudinal studies have identified chronic symptoms in victims as long as six years after the assault (Burgess & Holmstrom, 1979a; Kilpatrick, 1985). The most common long-term problems are fears about personal safety, anxiety, and related constrictions in the victim's life-style. Many victims continue to have intrusive recollections of the experience, although the images and feelings occur less often than they do during the acute stage of distress. Victims often become more cautious and less spontaneous. Frequently they construct a restrictive lifestyle that enables them to manage their anxiety but fails to eradicate completely the disturbing affects associated with the trauma. One victim who feels she is recovered said, "The world I am in now is a lot more uncomfortable than the world I was in before the rape." Two key factors in victim recovery are the availability of social supports following the rape and effective treatment.

The final stage of rape trauma is the victim's resolution of the event. She responds to the meanings and the impact of the trauma in ways that may be functional or dysfunctional. She may incorporate and integrate the experience and find a new way of being in the world. Or she may remain fixated on the trauma, compartmentalize it, or repress it. No victim will ever be as she was before the rape, although victims do not have to be less than they were before. Some victims emerge from rape treatment with newfound strengths and insights. They feel they have faced one of life's worst possible challenges and met it.

Rape and Other Trauma Victims

It is evident from the symptoms described above that many rape victims, like other victims of extremely terrorizing and traumatic events, are left with post-traumatic stress disorders (American Psychiatric Association, 1987). Post-traumatic stress disorders (PTSD) are caused by traumatic events that are "outside the range of usual human experience," including fires, floods, airplane crashes, and military combat. The stressor usually is an event that subjects the victim to extreme threats, fear, terror, and helplessness. The cluster of symptoms that characterizes PTSD impairs the victim's functioning. The rape victim continually reexperiences the traumatic event in intrusive, recurrent images, flashbacks, and dreams. At the same time, she tries to avoid any stimuli that might remind her of what happened. The victim may significantly constrict her life-style and withdraw from activities that she previously enjoyed. Many victims experience psychic numbing. They become "sealed off." Thus they are less responsive to the external environment. They feel detached. Another PTSD symptom is hyperalertness. The victim stays on guard. Sleep disturbances are common. Victims become hypersensitive to sounds and noises in the environment, to which they respond with alarm. Many of these symptoms intensify with exposure to stimuli that are similar to or symbolic of the traumatic event. These symptoms also cause great disruption in the victim's life, impairing her concentration and disrupting many of her activities and relationships. This syndrome characterizes the symptomatology presented by a large majority of rape victims.

Treatment Models

The Rape Treatment Center (RTC) at Santa Monica Hospital Medical Center was established in 1974 to provide specialized treatment for sexual assault victims. More than 10,000 victims have received twenty-four-hour emergency medical care, evidence collection, crisis intervention, advocacy, court accompaniment, legal assistance, and psychotherapy services from the RTC. Individual treatment (the focus of this chapter), family treatment, and group treatment modalities are utilized. The RTC's model for victim care is used in hospitals and other agencies throughout the United States. Other RTC services include school-based prevention programs that reach 20,000 adolescents each year; public education and victim-assistance programs for businesses and community organizations; training for police, prosecutors, medical, and mental health personnel; and consultation with the media and governmental agencies. The RTC also produces educational films and written materials that are distributed nationwide.

The RTC has developed two models for rape treatment in response to victim needs and the variations in treatment settings in which victims seek services. The first approach is a crisis intervention model that is effective in settings where the helping professional has only one to six contacts with the victim, such as hospital emergency departments, victim/witness programs, rape crisis centers, or community mental health agencies with crisis services. Many rape victims are initially seen in these settings.

The second approach is a short-term psychotherapy model. A more extended and comprehensive treatment model than the crisis intervention approach, it integrates crisis intervention theory and techniques with brief-treatment concepts.

Crisis Intervention Model

Rape victims who report their assaults are brought immediately to hospital emergency departments by law-enforcement personnel for medical care and evidence-collection services. Regardless of whether the victim has sustained any physical injuries, rape trauma represents a psychiatric emergency warranting immediate intervention. Crisis intervention should be an integral part of the victim's care. The protocol described in this section is a common application of the crisis intervention model for rape treatment; it was developed to guide the initial counseling interview in the emergency medical setting. The same protocol is applicable in a rape crisis center or victim/witness program for the initial interview with the victim. It is flexible and may be adapted to meet the particular needs of victims in various situations. For example, every step listed does not have to be implemented, nor is it necessary to follow the steps in the order listed, because the natural flow of an interview may develop in a different sequence.

The primary goal of crisis intervention is to help the victim cope effectively with the rape. Crisis theory delineates three tasks the victim must accomplish: (1) correct cognitive perception of the event, (2) management of her feelings and reactions, and (3) the development of new behavioral patterns of coping.

The counselor's interventions facilitate the accomplishment of these tasks. For example, the counselor assists the victim's cognitive understanding by helping her clarify relevant circumstances and maintain the problem at a conscious level so that it can be worked through. Management of affect is enhanced by supporting and validating the victim's expression of feelings. The development of adequate coping is advanced by providing the victim with relevant information and supportive resources and relationships. The tasks necessary to crisis resolution can only be initiated during the first interview. Most victims will resolve the crisis gradually over time. The effectiveness of the initial crisis intervention interview can be measured by certain observable outcomes:

- The victim begins to express feelings, reactions, and concerns related to the assault.
- The victim begins to conceptualize the loss experience and thereby regains some feelings of control.
- The victim experiences some reduction in anxiety.
- The victim begins to use her own coping skills and problem-solving strategies to resolve problems and concerns related to the assault.

• The victim develops a short-term plan for handling immediate situational needs.

• The victim is aware of the common symptoms that characterize the aftermath of a rape.

• The victim has information regarding alternative ways to handle various aspects of the aftermath.

The specific protocol developed by the RTC (Abarbanel, 1979) for use in hospital emergency departments is described below:

1. *Introduce yourself to the victim.* Explain how you are associated with the treatment setting and the victim's care. For example, explain that you are a counselor and that you work in the hospital's special program for sexual assault victims.

2. *Explain your role and purpose.* Describe how you can assist the victim. This explanation helps clarify the purpose of the crisis intervention counseling interview. You might explain that your role is to help the victim deal with her feelings and reactions and with any concerns or problems she may have because of the assault.

3. *Acknowledge the rape.* Communicate your knowledge and understanding of the violent, traumatic nature of rape and your recognition of its effects. For example, you might say, "I know you have been through a very difficult experience and you are probably having a lot of reactions to what happened."

4. *Encourage the victim to talk with you about the assault.* Explain how and why it will be helpful to talk about the rape, for example, it helps relieve some of the control the event has over the victim. Other ways of encouraging the victim include asking questions or making statements that invite her to tell you what happened. For instance, you might say, "I'd like you to tell me about what happened; it will help me to understand." If the victim does not respond to these approaches, you might ask questions such as "What is bothering you the most?" Encouragement is also given through nonverbal behavior. Be patient and give the victim time to respond to your questions. Listen attentively and maintain eye contact.

5. *Encourage the expression of feelings related to the assault.* As the victim talks about the assault, help her express the associated feelings. You might ask questions such as "How did you feel when that happened?" or "What did it feel like to be so overpowered?" As the victim talks, note which issues seem to evoke the most affect and, if appropriate, ask for more detail about them. For example, you might ask "What are you feeling as you tell me about that?" or respond with "That seems to have been especially difficult for you." For some victims, interpretive statements are necessary or useful. For instance, to encourage the sharing of feelings, you might say "It appears that you are especially worried about your daughter's reaction."

6. *Validate the feelings expressed.* Most victims are relieved to know that the feelings they are experiencing are normal, common reactions to rape. Validation of the victim's feelings also helps her to conceptualize the meaning of the experience. Cognitive understanding reduces anxiety and confusion. The usual affective reactions to rape (shame, fear, guilt, and anxiety) are very distressing to the victim; the victim can better manage these reactions if she knows that the counselor recognizes and understands them. You might say "It's very fright-

ening to lose control" or "I can see why you feel frightened." Clarify that most victims of sexual assault have these feelings and reactions to some degree by saying, "It is usual for victims to feel afraid for a while." You can also validate feelings by nonverbal reactions, such as touching or nodding. If the victim is not expressing feelings that are usual responses to rape, the counselor should prepare her for the possibility of having other feelings later. Helping her to anticipate provides her with a sense of control. Some victims are unable or unwilling to articulate their emotional reactions. The counselor can help them by suggesting that they may have these feelings and acknowledging how difficult it is to talk about them.

7. *Elicit the victim's concerns about the impact of the rape.* Ask the victim what she feels was or will be the most difficult aspect of the experience or whether she is worried about any special problem. As each concern is identified, elicit details and encourage the expression of feelings. For example, many victims express feelings of self-blame with statements such as "Maybe I should have fought harder." You might respond initially with a question or statement that asks for more information and encourages the expression of feelings, such as "It seems that you are feeling responsible for what happened." It is very important to find out what the victim's thoughts are about what she might have done and why she acted as she did, so that you fully understand the nature and source of the self-blame. You might ask "What is it that you think you could have done?" Then, if it is indicated, clarify any distortions that are causing misplaced attributions of blame. Explain that it is common for rape victims to have exaggerated feelings of personal responsibility. Clarify that the victim was not at fault—that she was, in fact, a victim. As the victim begins to express concerns, it is important that you not give false, unrealistic, or facile reassurances. Although you may want to relieve the victim's stress and make her feel better, false reassurances cut off the expression of feelings, contribute to a sense of distrust, and interfere with problem solving. For example, if the victim says she is afraid and anxious about her personal safety, telling her that she will feel more relaxed as time passes is a false reassurance. Assist her instead by helping her to talk about her fears and plan steps she can take to feel safer.

8. *Summarize the concerns the victim has expressed.* Briefly review the issues and concerns the victim has identified as most significant. This step marks a transition in the interview to the problem-solving phase. For example, you might say "You have talked about several of your concerns, including feeling extremely fearful and anxious, having flashbacks, and how you can handle your work commitments this week." You may also begin to conceptualize the issues underlying the concerns the victim has expressed: safety, control, and trust. Doing so helps the victim gain some cognitive understanding of the assault experience.

9. *Help the victim partialize and prioritize her concerns.* You might say "Let's sort out your concerns and choose the ones that are most pressing, the ones that need to be dealt with before you leave here" or "Let's talk about these things one at a time. What is the most important to you now?" It is the counselor's role to direct and focus the interview, which includes helping the victim determine what is manageable and feasible for immediate problem-solving efforts.

10. *Help the victim problem-solve.* Help the victim begin to develop a plan of action for priority needs and problems related to the assault. Use the information you have gathered throughout the interview, including your assessment of the victim's coping style and skills. For each concern or problem you work on, help the victim identify alternative solutions. For example, asking "What would help you feel safer?" will enable her to identify solutions, perhaps having a friend stay with her for a while or getting a new lock for her door. Provide her with information and access to the resources that will help her deal with her identified concerns. Help her regain her sense of control and autonomy by encouraging and allowing her to make her own decisions and take action on her own behalf. Point out assets, personal strengths, coping strategies, and support systems available to her. Help her plan how to use these supports to her advantage.

11. *Assess the victim's ability to cope with the impact of the assault.* The counselor must make a clinical assessment of how the victim will cope with the impact of the rape. This assessment is necessary for planning for the victim's care subsequent to discharge from the hospital. Because support from other people is so crucial to the victim's recovery, this part of the assessment is particularly important. You might ask questions such as "Whom do you feel you can talk with about the assault?" and "How do you think they will respond?" and "Do you need help telling them?" Victims are more likely to seek support from persons close to them if they have had help thinking through how they will ask for that support.

12. *Prepare the victim for future reactions.* The closing steps of the initial interview are directed toward preparing the victim for the period following hospital care. Thus discharge planning includes anticipatory guidance. You may repeat or summarize previous steps and information. For example, it is important to acknowledge again the traumatic nature of rape. It is also important to prepare the victim for the common reactions and feelings most victims experience. Explain that these reactions are normal and that most victims experience them to some degree. Acknowledge that it probably will take a while for the victim to feel like herself again. It is reassuring to the victim to know what to expect. It gives her some control over the situation and provides her with a framework for understanding the experience.

13. *Identify ways for the victim to deal with her feelings, concerns, and future reactions.* Acknowledge and reinforce the victim's strengths, personal resources, coping strategies, and available social supports that have been identified during the interview process. Reaffirm the importance and value of talking about the experience and the feelings related to it with supportive family members and friends. Help the victim think through and plan whom she can and will talk with about the assault, whom she can turn to for support. Ongoing professional counseling resources should be offered routinely as a preventive mental health measure. Additional resources should be provided to meet the victim's other identified needs.

14. *Involve the victim's family or significant others.* It is essential to have the victim's consent for these contacts. Family members and others close to the victim have their own feelings about the assault. These feelings often include anger and guilt. Family and close friends may also have questions and concerns

about the impact of the assault on the victim, which they should be allowed to express privately, away from the victim. They may benefit from the same interventions outlined above. Identify any additional support, counseling, and/or informational needs they have and provide significant others with access to needed resources. Educate them regarding the nature and trauma of sexual assault and the possible delayed reactions the victim may experience. Help them understand their role in helping the victim.

15. *Prepare the victim to leave the hospital.* Before the victim leaves the hospital emergency department, make sure that she has a safe destination, companionship, transportation, and a plan for follow-up assessment and treatment.

The crisis intervention interview described above is a beginning intervention. During this interview, it is important for the counselor to encourage the victim to utilize additional treatment.

Crisis intervention is also effective as a treatment modality for rape victims in a six-session framework. The goal of crisis intervention in this extended context is to help the victim complete the three tasks outlined above, so that she can resolve her crisis and return to her pre-rape level of functioning. The basic principles and techniques used when the victim is in the hospital emergency department also are utilized in short-term psychotherapy.

Short-Term Psychotherapy

For many years, the RTC worked with a crisis intervention model that offered six to eight treatment sessions. Although a great many RTC clients were helped with this model, we found that many victims wanted and needed more treatment to deal effectively with their rape. For these victims, the tight structure of crisis intervention did not allow sufficient flexibility for thorough exploration and resolution of the cognitive, emotional, and behavioral effects of the assault. Therefore, this approach was refined and a second treatment model was developed. The RTC's subsequent experience with thousands of sexual assault victims clearly demonstrates that the present model, which is of longer duration and greater depth, facilitates a greater degree of integration and recovery.

Many compelling arguments support the use of an extended treatment model for rape victims. The deep, profound, and extremely traumatic effects of rape, discussed earlier, cause severe psychological injury. The victim experiences grave threats to her well-being. Her previous view of the world, other people, and herself is dramatically challenged. Her losses are enormous. Her sense of safety and control has been shattered, her ability to trust other people compromised, and her self-confidence and self-esteem diminished. The victim needs adequate time to grieve, work through these losses, and develop adaptive coping responses. In addition, changes in personality and behavior may occur because of the symptoms, conflicts, and defenses produced by the rape, particularly in victims who remain silent and delay seeking help (Rose, 1986). Rape trauma may be further compounded by other factors, such as the lack of support for rape victims within our culture, revictimization by systems that should provide avenues of redress, and victim silence and secrecy. The interaction of these elements accounts for the well-documented psychological morbidity of rape trauma. The rape experience may also activate earlier losses and prior victimization experiences or may exacerbate unresolved, core conflicts that affect the victim's ability to manage the trauma.

The RTC's short-term psychotherapy model addresses the severity and complexity of rape trauma. The goal of this treatment model is to enable the victim to work through the meanings of the traumatic event. The model incorporates crisis intervention theory as well as psychodynamic concepts and tenets of brief treatment. Brief-treatment theorists focus on one central or core problem for intervention (Bauer & Kobos, 1987; Davanloo, 1980; Wells, 1982). Their approach represents a departure from the more global goals undertaken by traditional psychoanalytic therapists and the more limited goals of crisis intervention. Nevertheless, their models are congruent with and inclusive of crisis intervention theory. They use a time-limited structure, specific goals, education, information, and suggestion. They also employ psychoanalytic concepts, such as insight, transference, countertransference, clarification, and interpretation.

The RTC's short-term psychotherapy model is practiced in a setting devoted exclusively to treating victims of sexual assault. Therefore the focus of therapy is defined by the agency's mission as well as by the structure that the therapist provides during the treatment. The RTC's psychotherapy model is time-limited. Victims receive up to sixteen weeks of planned treatment. The model emphasizes a high level of therapist activity. Generally, the treatment falls into three phases: initial phase, middle phase, and termination phase. These phases are not always discrete. Activities and issues that are typically associated with one phase of treatment may continue or reappear in other stages. Some of the important features of this treatment model are discussed below.

1. *The beginning phase of treatment encompasses approximately two sessions during which the therapist quickly engages the client, actively helps her begin to understand and deal with the rape, negotiates the contract for therapy, evaluates her for depression and suicidality, and arrives at a diagnostic formulation to structure ongoing treatment.* The therapist must be particularly sensitive to the ways in which the rape victim's needs for safety, trust, and control are expressed. These needs influence the client's concerns about seemingly unimportant details, such as the time of day for appointments, and the urgency the client attaches to solving concrete problems, such as finding a place to live and being tested for pregnancy and sexually transmitted diseases.

2. *Victims often present for treatment in a crisis state.* Therefore, the therapist employs crisis intervention theory and utilizes techniques described earlier, including clarification of the client's situation, making connections between the client's distress and the traumatic event, education, validation, suggesting available options, and helping the client initiate action plans to deal with identified concerns. The therapist is active, direct, and supportive, quickly demonstrating to the client expertise in rape treatment and understanding of rape trauma. This instills confidence in the client, who often begins therapy with some ambivalence and anxiety about dealing with the rape even though it brought her to treatment. It also helps the client to gain cognitive understanding of the rape and the feelings she is having, thereby providing some immediate relief.

3. *Time is a critical element in planned, short-term psychotherapy.* The specific goals, focus, structure, and time-limited nature of the treatment are discussed

with the client as the contract for therapy is negotiated. Defining the time-limited structure provides hope and helps to defuse transference, reduce dependency on the therapist, and mobilize the client to work on important issues in a timely way. It is also the beginning step in planned termination.

4. *During the initial phase of treatment, the therapist makes a differential diagnosis.* Most rape victims present with symptoms of post-traumatic stress disorder. However, clients with underlying, profound characterological disturbances, such as borderline personalities, do better within the more contained structure of the six-week crisis intervention model. The therapist also utilizes the first few sessions to construct a diagnostic formulation to organize ongoing treatment. The therapist makes an assessment of post-trauma symptoms and reactions, the degree of symptom intrusion versus denial, the client's defenses, coping style and skills, developmental issues, relevant cultural influences, social supports, earlier experiences with loss and trauma, and core unresolved conflicts. These issues affect how the rape is experienced by the victim. They also are indicators of internal and external resources available to support effective coping. The therapist conceptualizes the symbolic meanings of the rape for the client.

5. *The middle phase of treatment focuses on enabling the client to talk about, understand, and work through all aspects of the rape.* The way the client responds to the rape reflects her characteristic defensive style and modes of coping. Some issues and themes surface quickly, others are more threatening. Many of the issues and symptoms dealt with in this phase were identified in the earlier discussion on the impact of rape. The goals include integration of the rape with the totality of the victim's life experience and the development of adaptive strategies for coping with its effects. The therapist must recognize the interrelationships among the cognitive, affective, and behavioral aspects of rape trauma and rape treatment.

6. *A crucial activity in therapy for the therapist and the client is the sharing of every aspect and detail of the rape as well as all the thoughts, feelings, and behaviors it has evoked.* The therapist may find it difficult to listen to this material because it is painful and threatening. It triggers feelings of outrage and vulnerability, sometimes disbelief. Nevertheless, these disclosures are critical to successful rape treatment. Therefore, the therapist cannot avoid or discourage them in any way. Many of the complaints rape victims make about failed therapy have a common theme: "I never talked about my rape."

7. *Although the therapist must encourage the client to talk about the traumatic event, the client can only "remember" and deal with the trauma in tolerable or "manageable" doses* (Horowitz, 1976). Denial or warding off of these painful recollections and their implications serves initially as an adaptive defense. This defense is gradually relinquished throughout treatment. The therapist must allow the client to determine the pace of this process, albeit in the context of a therapeutic relationship that supports the telling of the trauma.

8. *As the client is able to describe the traumatic events associated with horror, shame, powerlessness, terror, and betrayal, these events gradually lose their control over her.* Sharing the experience with another person also lessens the victim's feeling of isolation and begins to diminish her feelings of shame. As long as the victim is silent, the victimization experience remains alive and powerful. This does not mean that the therapist should coerce the client into telling about it.

Rather, if the client remains unable to talk about the experience, the therapist should explore the reasons for her reluctance to talk.

9. *As the client talks about the rape, the therapist helps her access and work through associations to feelings, thoughts, beliefs, behaviors, relationships, life-style issues, self-concept, and prior experiences.* The victim may also relate the rape to thoughts and feelings about the future. The therapist should be active in encouraging, clarifying, validating, supporting, and providing information. As the client begins to gain some understanding of the reasons for her reactions, some of her distressing symptoms (for example, nightmares, unbidden thoughts and feelings) may abate.

10. *The therapist may elicit analogous events.* For example, when the client talks about how demeaned she feels, the therapist may ask, "Have you ever felt this way before?" Or the client may spontaneously share earlier experiences. One client recalled a painful childhood experience: "My father used to always humiliate me by making me stand with my face to the wall and my back to the rest of the family while they ate dinner. This was my punishment for not getting acceptable grades. I was always a bad student." The therapist should help the client connect the feelings from the earlier experience to the rape, which should remain the focus of treatment. The therapist should not interpret unconscious material. Interpretation is used to deal with conscious material related to the memories and meanings of the traumatic event.

11. *Rape trauma activates unresolved, core conflicts and characterological problems that, in turn, affect the client's coping style and ability to manage the rape experience.* Typically, as the acute symptoms subside, the client begins to focus more on core issues that are themes in her life. The therapist may deal with these issues while maintaining a primary focus on the meanings of the rape. Commonly encountered areas of unresolved conflict include dependency, abandonment, and family relationship issues.

> Deborah, a special eucation teacher, was married and the mother of a nine-year-old son. She was away from her family, attending an out-of-state conference on a college campus. As she walked down a corridor, a man approached and said his daughter had gone into the women's restroom and had not come out. He asked Deborah if she would go in and look for her. She agreed to assist him. He then followed her, pulled a knife, and raped and sodomized her inside the restroom. Deborah told no one at the conference. She returned home and remained silent. When she came for treatment, she was adamant that she could not tell anyone. When the therapist asked her why she felt this way, she explained that no one would believe her or give her support. Her behavior at home with her family had changed dramatically since the rape. Her husband was angry and her son seemed frightened. Yet, she maintained her secret. She explained that she grew up in a home where her mother had a succession of husbands and lovers. One of these men raped Deborah when she was twelve. As a child, she never told about her rape because she was afraid her mother would abandon her in the same way as her mother left all of the men in her life. Deborah's silence about her recent rape was related to fears of abandonment.

The therapist should help the client understand the aspects of the rape that evoke feelings similar to those experienced in other contexts. The client is helped to focus on working through the rape-related issues. In the case example described above, Deborah was able to tell her husband, who supported her in making a late police report and pursuing a criminal prosecution.

12. *One task in therapy is the management of rape-trauma symptoms.* The therapist should help the client relate the symptoms to various aspects of the trauma. This facilitates cognitive understanding of the meaning of the event. In addition, the therapist should encourage the client to develop new, adaptive coping (including cognitive and behavioral) strategies. Symptom management is also aided by various techniques, such as relaxation and stress reduction, participation in physical exercise, systematic desensitization, and cognitive restructuring. It is important to recognize the strong cognitive component in rape-trauma symptoms and victim recovery. As the patient understands and resolves the experience on a cognitive level, she is able to regain control. Using symptom-management techniques, the therapist should support the client's reentry into daily routines, thereby helping her behaviorally to regain feelings of mastery and control. This enhances self-confidence and self-esteem.

13. *Education and advocacy are important aspects of rape treatment.* The therapist must be well informed about rape victimization to be effective in helping the client identify and understand misconceptions and attitudes in herself and others that result in victim-blaming responses. Rape victims are often revictimized by casual remarks and actions that imply victim responsibility or by minimization or misunderstanding of the severity of rape trauma. Another role of the therapist in rape treatment is advocacy. In some situations, the therapist should intervene directly to assist the client with concrete problems stemming from the victimization. For example, if the client finds that her employer is uninformed about the nature of rape trauma and therefore refuses to allow for the ways in which the client's symptoms are temporarily interfering with her work, she may ask the therapist to assist with educating the employer. Many victims still experience insensitive and discriminatory treatment when they pursue legal redress. The RTC therapists frequently accompany their clients to court to provide support.

14. *The client is helped to incorporate the rape experience on cognitive, emotional, and behavioral levels.* This involves change and growth. For example, a rape victim must deal with the fact that bad things can happen to good people, which in turn will result in cognitive and behavioral changes. There are many different forms of resolution. She may find a way to explain, minimize, or redefine the event. One client came to view the rape as a traumatic event she managed well: "It could have been worse; I could have been killed." She compares herself with other victims who have been murdered and feels "lucky." On a behavioral level, the victim decreased her feelings of vulnerability and increased her sense of safety by moving to a second-floor apartment and investing in dead-bolt locks. On an emotional level, the victim's damaged self-esteem and ability to trust were repaired when she received strong support and genuine affection from the significant others to whom she turned for help. Her view of other people remains changed by the rape. She says, "I used to think everyone was good. I was a very trusting person. I don't think that anymore." But her feelings of distrust have not become global and generalized to all people and all situations. The therapist guides and supports the client in finding functional resolutions to the trauma.

15. *Planning for termination begins with the initial contract for treatment*. This helps prevent regression and revictimization. The time-limited structure is reiterated throughout the course of treatment. In the eleventh session, the therapist reminds the client that there are five sessions remaining so that issues that have not yet been dealt with can surface and the client can prepare for the loss of therapy and the therapist. The client should experience these losses as planned events and not as arbitrary abandonments. Planned short-term treatment gives the client the opportunity to work through these losses within the therapeutic relationship. During the termination phase, it is important to review what has been learned and accomplished and to provide anticipatory guidance.

Conclusion

The therapist who treats rape victims must bring more to the therapeutic relationship than clinical expertise. The foundation required for this work includes knowledge about the issues that influence victim reporting; similarities and differences between stranger rape and acquaintance rape; circumstances in which sexual assaults typically occur; behavioral patterns of offenders; usual victim responses during and following a sexual assault; symptoms, meanings, and manifestations of rape trauma; prevalent attitudes and misconceptions about the crime of rape; and the history of rape-victim treatment by social institutions, such as hospitals, police departments, and the courts. All of these factors affect the client who asks the therapist for help to deal with the aftermath of a rape. The therapist must also have the capacity to understand the rape experience and empathize with the client. Thus, in addition to acquiring a specialized knowledge base, the therapist must deal with the realization that "this could happen to me or to someone I love."

References

Abarbanel, G. (1976). Helping victims of rape. *Social Work, 21*, 478–482.

Abarbanel, G. (1979). *Protocol: A crisis intervention counseling approach with victims of rape*. Santa Monica, CA: Rape Treatment Center, Santa Monica Hospital Medical Center.

Abarbanel, G. (1980). The role of the clinical social worker in rape treatment. In C. G. Warner (Ed.), *Rape and sexual assault*. Germantown, MD: Aspen Systems.

Abarbanel, G., & Klein, S. (1981 November). *Similarities and differences between stranger and acquaintance rape*. Paper presented at the annual meeting of the American Public Health Association, Los Angeles, CA.

American Psychiatric Association (1987). *Diagnostic and statistical manual of mental disorders* (3rd ed., rev.). Washington, DC: Author.

Bauer, G. P., & Kobos, J. C. (1987). *Brief therapy*. Northvale, NJ: Jason Aronson.

Brownmiller, S. (1975). *Against our will*. New York: Simon and Schuster.

Bureau of Justice Statistics (1985). *The crime of rape*. Washington, DC: Author.

Burgess, A. W., & Holmstrom, L. L. (1974). Rape trauma syndrome. *American Journal of Psychiatry, 131*, 981–986.

Burgess, A. W., & Holmstrom, L. L. (1979a). *Rape: Crisis and recovery*. Bowie, MD: Robert J. Brady.

Burgess, A. W., & Holmstrom, L. L. (1979b). Rape: Sexual disruption and recovery. *American Journal of Orthopsychiatry*, *49*, 648–657.

Davanloo, H. (1980). *Basic principles and techniques in short-term dynamic psychotherapy*. New York: Spectrum.

Estrich, S. (1987). *Real rape*. Cambridge, MA: Harvard University Press.

Federal Bureau of Investigation (1971–1982; 1986). *Crime in the United States*, Washington, DC: Author.

Gilbert, B., & Cunningham, J. (1986). Women's post-rape sexual functioning: Review and implications for counseling. *Journal of Counseling and Development*, *65*, 71–73.

Griffin, S. (1971, September). Rape: The all-American crime. *Ramparts*, *10*, 27–35.

Groth, A. N. (1979). *Men who rape*. New York: Plenum.

Horowitz, M. J. (1976). *Stress response syndromes*. Northvale, NJ: Jason Aronson.

Janoff-Bulman, R. (1985). The aftermath of victimization: Rebuilding shattered assumptions. In C. R. Figley (Ed.), *Trauma and its wake: The study and treatment of post-traumatic stress disorder*. New York: Brunner/Mazel.

Kilpatrick, D. G., Veronen, L. J., & Resick, P. A. (1979). The aftermath of rape: Recent empirical findings. *American Journal of Orthopsychiatry*, *49*, 658–669.

Kilpatrick, D. G. (1985, February 28–March 3). *Research on long-term effects of criminal victimization: Scientific, service delivery, and public policy perspectives*. Paper presented at colloquium titled "The Aftermath of Crime: A Mental Health Crisis," Washington, DC.

Koss, M. P., Gidycz, C. A., Wisniewski, N. (1987). The scope of rape: Incidence and prevalence of sexual aggression and victimization in a national sample of higher education students. *Journal of Consulting and Clinical Psychology*, *55*, 162–170.

Largen, M. A. (1976). History of women's movement in changing attitudes, laws, and treatment towards rape victims. In M. J. Walker & S. L. Brodsky (Eds.) *Sexual assault: The victim and the rapist*. Lexington, MA: Lexington Books.

Largen, M. A. (1988). Rape-reform law: An analysis. In A. W. Burgess (Ed.), *Rape and sexual assault II*. New York: Garland.

Lerner, M. J. (1980). *The belief in a just world*. New York: Plenum.

McDermott, M. J. (1979). *Rape victimization in 26 American cities*. Washington, DC: U.S. Department of Justice.

Nathanson, D. L. (1987). *The many faces of shame*. New York: Guilford Press.

Notman, M. T., & Nadelson, C. C. (1976). The rape victim: Psychodynamic considerations. *American Journal of Psychiatry*, *133*, 408–412.

Plant, J., & Wood, E. (1977). "E.D." involvement grows in audit activities, rape treatment. *Hospitals*, *51*, 107–112.

Rose, D. S. (1986). "Worse than death": Psychodynamics of rape victims and the need for psychotherapy. *American Journal of Psychiatry*, *143*, 817–824.

Russell, D. E. H. (1984). *Sexual exploitation*. Beverly Hills, CA: Sage.

Sutherland Fox, S., & Scherl, D. J. (1972). Crisis intervention with victims of rape. *Social Work*, *17*, 37–42.

Symonds, M. (1976). The rape victim: Psychological patterns of response. *American Journal of Psychoanalysis*, *36*, 27–34.

Wells, R. A. (1982). *Planned short-term treatment*. New York: Free Press.

4

Crisis Intervention in Intrafamilial Child Sexual Abuse

RAY E. LILES AND ANN O'BRIEN

IN RECENT YEARS, child sexual abuse has increasingly become a matter of national concern. A study of college women determined that as many as one in five women and one in eleven men had been sexually molested as children (Finkelhor, 1979). The National Center on Child Abuse and Neglect (NCCAN) estimated that 12 percent of more than one million cases of reported child abuse involved sexual molestation (Mrazek & Kempe, 1981). A recent television movie, "Something about Amelia," stimulated a flood of calls to child abuse hotlines around the country. However, despite efforts to study the incidence and severity of child abuse, such as that of NCCAN (1981), the extent of the problem remains unclear.

Estimates of intrafamilial child sexual abuse vary widely. For example, Russell (1984) found that 16 percent of a random sample of 930 women reported at least one incestuous abuse experience before the age of eighteen years. Other studies suggest that up to 50 percent of all reported cases of child sexual abuse involve sexual activities between family members (DeFrancis, 1969; Sgroi, 1975). Swift (1986) reports that of 816 protective service child sexual abuse cases in fifteen Kansas and Missouri counties, 73 percent involved incest. The preponderance of incest cases was between daughters and fathers or father surrogates.

Nuclear family incest involving a parent and child is one of the most virulent forms of child sexual abuse. Consequently, many specialized intrafamilial child sexual abuse treament programs have been developed in the United States. The Riverside Interagency Sexual Abuse Council (RISAC), one of the first such programs (Liles & Wahlquist, 1981), provides the context for the present chapter. The Council is a joint effort of the Riverside County (California) departments of Public Social Services, Mental Health, and Probation, as well as several private, nonprofit human service agencies, to provide a coordinated interagency approach to treatment.

Crisis intervention is a vitally needed service in helping families deal with the chaos that occurs when incest is disclosed. Because crisis intervention generally occurs shortly after the disclosure of incest, it serves as the first step in what will most probably be long-term treatment. Crisis intervention skills and techniques are also needed at various points during long-term treatment of incestuous families because families generally experience stresses triggered by the complex interactions between the emotional turmoil of family members and the demands of the child protection, juvenile, and criminal court systems.

Because the authors believe incest treatment is most effective in guided "self-help" group settings, a central principle of RISAC is involvement of parents in Parents United and children in Daughters and Sons United (Giaretto, 1982). A parent referred to RISAC is screened by an intake social worker. If the worker feels that the parent is not an appropriate candidate for Parents United, the parent is referred to another treatment resource.

Most Parents United programs offer clients a succession of treatment groups with distinct goals. Clients move from group to group as their treatment progresses. They are exposed to a multimodal treatment approach involving individual, couple or other dyad, and family therapy at various points during the lengthy treatment process. In RISAC, clients first attend an orientation group for three or four months. In this group, they receive support from persons with similar problems while learning about the complex legal and social service systems in which they are now entangled. After the orientation group, clients attend the offenders group or the nonoffending-spouses group, where they may remain for a year while they deal with both the causes and results of the incest. The last group in the program, which participants attend for up to one year, consists of either single males and females or couples. The mixed groups focus on marital relationships, sexual issues, parenting concerns, and other problems of living. Although Parents United programs vary, most are similar to the groups described above. Many programs also have special groups to deal with topics such as sexuality or reunification of the family. For a more complete discussion of the Parents United model, see Giaretto (1982).

Parents United Sponsors

In many Parents United programs, parent sponsors become a valuable adjunct to professional services by providing crisis intervention services to new and ongoing members. Sponsors are living proof to new clients that they are not alone. Because the use of clients as lay helpers raises ethical and quality-control issues, professionally supervised sponsorship is essential.

In RISAC, sponsors are parents who have either completed the treatment program or are far enough along in their own treatment to be able and willing to offer emotional support to parents who are just beginning. Sponsors undergo a formal approval process: they must attend at least four of the monthly sponsors' group meetings; observe two and facilitate two "preorientation" sessions for parents who are attending Parents United for the first time; participate in several role plays of telephone outreach situations that are critiqued by professionals; and obtain the approval of the other sponsors, current group leader, and RISAC coordinator. Sponsors must demonstrate an awareness of the limitations of their outreach activity. Also they must agree to solicit case consultation from one another, the intake social worker, the RISAC coordinator, or another staff member. Male sponsors (who are offenders) agree not to engage in any sponsoring activities with a female Parents United member.

When a parent first calls the Parents United intake social worker after incest has been disclosed, the parent is asked whether he or she would like to be contacted by or would be willing to contact a sponsor. Sponsors who call new clients are given instructions on what to say:

> *Sponsor*: "Hi, my name is Hank. Is this Mr. Smith?"
>
> *Mr. Smith*: "Yes."
>
> *Sponsor*: "Well Mr. Smith, I got your name from Mary Jones. I'm a father and two years ago I molested my daughter. She told the school, police, and everybody about it."
>
> *Mr. Smith*: "You molested your daughter?"
>
> *Sponsor*: "Yes, and after the police took her and my wife threw me out, I had no one to talk to. I was alone and scared and wondering what was going to happen to me. You can't just tell your friends about this. I'm calling you so you won't be as alone as I was. Can you tell me what happened in your family?"
>
> *Mr. Smith*: "Did you go to jail? Did your wife leave you?"
>
> The sponsor then tries to answer Mr. Smith's questions, tells him about Parents United, and encourages him to attend the next meeting. . . .
>
> *Sponsor*: "Well, Mr. Smith, I'm sorry this happened in your family. But you can get through this. Parents United really helps. I'll be there Tuesday night. When you get there, just ask for Hank. I'll show you around. If you want to talk between now and Tuesday my number is. . ."

Mothers who are sponsors in the Parents United program similarly seek to help mothers in families in which incest has recently been disclosed. Parents who are in an extreme state of crisis are informed that they are not alone and that the trauma of incest can be survived. Sponsors offer support, role modeling, and hope. It is one thing for a well-meaning social worker to say "you can get through this," and quite another for a parent to say "my husband molested my daughter; it was tough, but we got through it and we're better now."

Parents attending their first session are greeted either by the sponsor who talked to them on the phone or by another sponsor. They are ushered into a small conference room with other new members (if there are any) for a "preorientation" session conducted by the sponsors. This session includes a short parent-to-parent talk on what Parents United does. The new parents are given a telephone list and are urged to call and talk to other Parents United members during the week. The new parents are then introduced by the sponsors to the professional therapists who facilitate their respective groups.

Screening for Parents Groups

Screening parents of a victim of intrafamilial child sexual abuse for participation in group therapy requires more than merely gathering facts and developing a preliminary assessment. The screening process itself is an essential component of the crisis intervention stage of treatment. It provides an opportunity to learn about a new client; it may also provide the first therapeutic intervention a parent receives after the disclosure of the incest.

Referral to RISAC for group treatment within twenty-four to forty-eight hours of disclosure is optimal. However, this rarely occurs. Referrals are frequently received within one to three weeks of disclosure, at a time when parents are still in a state of extreme crisis and feel as though a new crisis is activated every time they hear about another court date or another interview with a law-enforcement official. Parents interviewed at this time are very confused. They are aware of a multitude of problems, while feeling helpless and unable to think of realistic and constructive ways to approach these problems, let alone solve them. Parents feel alone, ashamed, and cut off from their normal sources of support. They believe no one else has gone through what they are experiencing and that their situation will never be satisfactorily resolved. Even persons who employ defenses such as total denial or gross minimization have many of these feelings.

For some individuals, knowledge that an organization exists to deal with incestuous families provides some comfort or hope. Parents learn of the availability of treatment from various sources, such as an emergency response protective services worker, a juvenile court investigator, a law-enforcement official, other parents, hotlines, therapists, or other professionals from mental health agencies. Some parents find the telephone number through public service advertisements or the telephone book. However parents learn about the groups, few know anything about them. Most call asking about "the parenting class"; none is aware of how many people are coming to weekly treatment groups for families who have experienced incest.

During the gathering of information, other processes occur as well. The screening interviews can be seen as a transition between disclosure and traditional longer-term treatment. During this crisis stage of intervention, parents must face the reality of incest having occurred in their family. They must begin to adjust to new facts about family members, the family composition, and about themselves and their situation. The screening interview provides an opportunity for a professional clinician to help the parent focus on these new facts and their meaning for the parent and other family members and to guide the parent in making some sense out of the diverse reactions of various family members. Throughout the screening process, the therapist informs the client of the significance of the various reactions of child protective services and the juvenile court and helps the client anticipate the requirements of the court and social services in the near future. Perhaps the most valuable byproduct of the screening interview is the opportunity to let parents know that an established way exists to address the problems they are facing. For parents who admit that their child was sexually abused by a parent or parental figure, this information can provide hope for the future. For parents who deny, minimize, or project blame, the screening interviews serve notice that the problem will not be swept under the carpet and that professionals will not accept the statement "It's over now and it will never happen again."

The information gathered during the screening process includes the address where each family member is now living, home and work telephone numbers, brief employment history, and the names and ages of the victims and any other children in the family. The parent is asked to describe exactly how the child was sexually abused; the reaction and attitude of each parent toward the disclosure and allegations are also explored. Information is requested on any juvenile court, criminal court, or social service intervention. Parents are asked for a history of past sexual offenses and violence inside or outside of the home; if they, their spouse, or partner were ever a victim of childhood sexual abuse; and if they have a history of drug or alcohol abuse. Questions concerning when the disclosure of the sexual abuse occurred and who told whom—ultimately leading to the abuse being reported to the authorities—are of particular interest. Whether the victim was able to tell her or his mother of the abuse and whether the mother was effective in immediately protecting the victim from further abuse are important for treatment prognosis (Faller, 1988; Orten & Rich, 1988). Usually, information provided by a parent is corroborated by checking with other professionals and expanded upon by a social worker.

The screening of new clients for the treatment program is not completed in one or two interviews prior to parents' attending their first group meeting. Screening continues for the first few weeks of group attendance. In the case of parents who attend the group therapy program because of court mandate but who do not acknowledge that they or their spouse or partner sexually abused their child, the screening may continue for one month. Parents who do not identify themselves as child abusers or molesters or do not acknowledge that their spouse or partner is a child abuser or molester are not permitted to continue treatment beyond four sessions.

When a parent is not permitted to attend the group therapy program for any reason, an attempt is made to link that parent either with another program more appropriate to his or her needs or with an experienced individual therapist in the community. Other parents, who are appropriate candidates for group treatment, may be reluctant to come to a group or may have been instructed by their attorney not to discuss the allegations. In such situations, a sponsor can provide the most nonthreatening intervention. The work of sponsors may be the deciding factor in whether parents are able to acknowledge the sexual abuse of their child and to attend the group therapy sessions.

Incest Victims in Crisis

Child victims of incest who are at the point of disclosure are in a state of crisis; moreover, the actual disclosure precipitates additional crises for themselves and their family. Victims of incest can be of either sex and the molestations can occur at any age. In father-figure–daughter incest, the mean age at which molestation begins is nine years, with the abuse lasting an average of three years (Liles, 1984). Although each case has its own complexities, the following vignette presents a typical case of incest and the circumstances surrounding disclosure:

> Tina, age thirteen, told her mother that her stepfather had been molesting her for the past four or five years. The disclosure was precipitated by her stepfather's not letting Tina stay overnight at a friend's house. She became very angry with him and screamed, "You're not my father. You have no right to boss me around. I'm going to tell Mom what you've been doing to me." Tina's mother overheard this exchange, which confirmed her suspicions. She later took Tina aside and was able to get her to tell what her stepfather had done. Tina's mother called the police; the police called the emergency response unit of the Department of Public Social Services. A police officer and an emergency response worker interviewed Tina at

home. Tina appeared to be quite affected by her mother's emotional reaction to the disclosure; by the time the interview took place several hours later, Tina was already reluctant to talk about it.

Tina: "Do I have to talk about this? I don't want to talk about it."

Emergency response worker: "I don't blame you. I never met anybody who found it easy to talk about the first time. But it is necessary for you to tell us what happened so we can help you and your family. We want to make sure this doesn't happen to you again."

Tina: "Will I have to go to juvenile hall? I had a friend at school that this happened to and they took her away. I haven't seen her since."

Emergency response worker: "I want you to know that what happened was not your fault. You won't go to juvenile hall because you haven't done anything wrong."

After the interviewers addressed some of Tina's fears and apprehensions, she was able to make a statement about what her stepfather had done to her over the past four years. Tina's mother was also interviewed; the emergency response worker felt that she was able to protect her daughter from the stepfather. The worker noted that Tina's mother believed her daughter's statements and readily agreed to have her husband move out of the family home.

In the early stages of treatment for incest, it is sometimes unclear whether the victim is traumatized more by the incest than by the intervention of the social service and legal systems. For example, in some cases children are made to feel that the incest was their fault. The question "why didn't you tell someone sooner?" often is interpreted by children as implying that they could have stopped the incest somehow and that they must have been willing participants. In other instances a child may be unnecessarily removed from the family home before an assessment is made and it is determined whether the father will leave the home and if the mother can protect the child. Children who are removed and whose fathers remain in the home often feel that they are the guilty ones. For some children, separation from a parent, even during the course of the investigation, can be an extremely painful experience that rivals the pain of the molestation. Thus professionals must respond with sensitivity to the victim in order to facilitate the resolution of the crisis and to prevent the child from being further damaged by the system designed to protect him or her. Appropriate intervention at this early stage should be viewed as the first stage of treatment rather than as merely the "investigation" stage.

Talking to the Victim in Crisis

The first person to talk to the child victim and all other involved persons need to tell the child that she or he is not to blame for the molestation or for what happens to the family as the result of the disclosure. Children need to hear repeatedly: "This was not your fault." Children need to know they are not alone in the experience of having been molested by a family member. The worker might say, "I have talked to many boys and girls your age who have been molested by their fathers and who have told me they feel the same way you do." Or "We have a group of girls [boys] your age who get together after school one day a week and have a chance to talk about what happened and how things are going for them."

If it is possible, the child should be subjected to a minimal number of investigatory interviews. Joint interviews with law-enforcement personnel and district attorneys should be conducted if feasible. Video- and/or audio-recording equipment can be used to record initial interviews that can be reviewed later by district attorneys and treatment staff. The use of recorded interviews with child sexual abuse victims is a relatively new and somewhat problematic development. For instance, defense attorneys sometimes request copies of videotaped interviews to review before the trial. This request often raises anxiety in parents, treatment staff, and prosecuting attorneys over the use and possible misuse of these tapes.

Children who come into contact with the child protection system often experience a great deal of anxiety about what may happen to them and their families. One way to lessen this anxiety is to help children anticipate what may happen to them. For example, the worker might say, "You are going to stay in this shelter home at least until your next court hearing three days from now." When helping children anticipate what is going to happen, it is important not to make promises that one cannot keep. For example, children sometimes want to be reassured that their fathers will not go to jail. However, workers cannot make such a promise. Furthermore, children may ask questions for which workers do not have answers. Workers should say that they do not know rather than give false reassurances. Sexually abused children have been severely betrayed by an important adult; inaccurate information may be interpreted as another betrayal.

When interviewing an incest victim, it is important to be aware of the child's ambivalent feelings about the offender. One should avoid judgmental remarks about the offender. Although children know they did not like being sexually abused, they may still have a strong emotional attachment to the offender, who may have met many of their needs for affection and attention.

In the early stages, interviewers must work to establish a common vocabulary with children. With younger children, this common vocabulary can be constructed by using anatomically correct dolls or drawings. The worker must determine whether the child is more comfortable using his or her own terms or the adult's terms. Even older children, who are assumed to know the conventional terms for parts of the body and sexual acts, frequently have an idiosyncratic vocabulary for sex-related topics. So,workers must be sure that older children understand the meaning of the words.

The experiences these children relate often elicit powerful feelings of outrage, disgust, anger, and sorrow in the listeners. However, conveying these feelings to the children can be countertherapeutic. Workers who convey shock to a child who discloses the details of a molestation may mislead the child into believing that he or she is the only one who has had this kind of experience. Workers who convey extreme disgust may mislead a child into believing that he or she disgusts the worker. It is important for workers to recognize their own reactions, vent their feelings to co-workers and supervisors, and be available to colleagues when their support is needed.

Children who have been molested need an empathic response from the worker. Communicating empathy involves listening attentively for feelings the child is currently experiencing and acknowledging those feelings in a warm and caring manner. An empathic response should facilitate the child's expression of feelings. Obviously, not all children experience trauma in the same way, and not all children progress at the same pace.

Sometimes children first disclose their abuse to a school authority or other person outside the family (Swift, 1986). In such cases, the nonoffending parent (usually the mother) may be called at home or at work by a principal and asked to come to the school for an urgent conference. When this occurs, the child needs to know that his or her mother will be informed. Moreover, the mother should be told about the incest privately to afford her the opportunity to react to the disclosure away from the child. The mother needs to pull herself together before she begins to talk to the child about what happened. Mothers who do not vent their initial reactions of disgust, disbelief, and anger with an appropriate adult risk traumatizing the child if they vent those feelings on the child.

Shame

Shame is one of the first emotions victims feel. They begin to imagine how othe people will feel about them if the incest becomes known. Children who are molested at an early age (preschool through second grade) may become aware that other children do not engage in sexual contact with a parent or parental figure. Many children feel "transparent," as though everyone can see, just by looking at them, that they were molested. They feel that their experiences have made them different from their peers and invest much energy in keeping the secrets of their family. Children who have had premature sexual experiences are often seen as "damaged goods" (Sgroi, 1983). Older children frequently feel ashamed for having lost their virginity. Children who express such concerns should be told, "No one can take your virginity, you can only give it." Putting victims of child sexual abuse into a therapy group with other victims is an important method for addressing and ameliorating the victim's sense of being different.

Some children who have experienced physical pain during the molestation fear that they have suffered permanent physical damage. These children may benefit from a thorough physical examination by a physician who will take the time to discuss any findings and address the child's fears. This type of physical examination should not to be confused with the "suspected child abuse and neglect" examination that is conducted shortly after disclosure and that is often viewed negatively by the child.

Guilt

Incest victims feel guilty for several reasons. A primary cause of guilt is their realization that they have participated in sexual behavior considered to be so wrong that it cannot even be talked about. They may feel guilty for having kept "the secret," even though the offender may have pressured them to do so and they felt that they would not be believed anyway. Sometimes children imagine that they have a personal quality that caused the molestation. Older victims often feel they have been provocative or seductive or may agree with such accusations by the parent (Meiselman, 1978).

Children may also feel guilty about the consequences of the disclosure. If the father is removed or arrested, the victim may feel that it is his or her fault that the father is suffering. Similarly, mothers who show extreme despair over the future of their family or who share their profound personal pain elicit guilt from the victim, who may feel that he or she has destroyed the family. Unfortunately, many incest victims come to believe, and are sometimes told, that they have betrayed their families by failing to prevent the incest and by disclosing the molestation to the authorities.

Again, children need to be told that the incest was not their fault and that what is happening to their fathers and their families is not their responsibility. When a child expresses guilt about what is happening to his or her father, the child should be told, "Your father made some choices when he decided to do what he did. He knew he could get into serious trouble when he decided to molest you." In addition to receiving reassurance in individual therapy, it is helpful for children to hear that they were not responsible for the incest from their peers in a group setting.

Fear and Confusion

The crisis of disclosure and the child's concern about immediate consequences produces a lot of fear and confusion in the child. Children are afraid of the unknown. They are afraid that they will be blamed, that their mother will not love them anymore, that they will have to leave home (or go back home), and that everyone will know what happened to them. In cases in which children are believed and supported by mothers, fear and confusion are sometimes tempered by relief that the secret has at last been exposed. These feelings are best dealt with by anticipating for the child the likely sequence of events and answering questions as honestly as possible.

Betrayal and Anger

Much of the children's anger is caused by their feeling that they have been betrayed; these feelings of betrayal are acted out as anger. Consequently, these emotions are inextricably intertwined. The molester betrayed them by misusing a parental relationship to exploit them sexually. Children who are molested through a process of slow seduction preceded by an initial period of appropriate physical affection begin to question whether any parental affection and caring is genuine. The child wonders whether he or she was really loved or merely used. The intensity of these feelings of betrayal is not necessarily proportionate to the sexual acts that occurred. Children who are "only" fondled still have to deal with the fact that their parent is using them sexually. They have been betrayed. Some of these children are aware of the anger aroused by their betrayal and express it readily and appropriately toward the offender; others cannot. The nonoffending parent betrayed them by failing to protect them or, after disclosure, failing to believe them. From the child's perspective, it may be irrelevant whether the nonoffending parent actually knew about about the molestations as they were occuring; the child still feels betrayed. These children believe that the nonoffending parent should have known. They may believe that they left clues or hinted about what was happening. For example, a child who never seems to want to be left alone with her father is communicating a clue. This child may assume that her behavior will be interpreted by her mother as a statement that incest is occurring.

These feelings of betrayal are acted out by children as anger. Within the family, this anger can appear to be defiance, lack of respect, moodiness, and general lack of cooperation. In an ideal situation, the worker approaches the parents, helping them to understand the nature of and the legitimacy of the child's anger. The worker may say to a parent, "Your child is angry and has a right to be angry about what happened. Your child needs to tell you how mad she is at you. And you need to listen and not attempt to defend or explain your behavior."

The anger is often projected onto social workers and others who become involved in the case. Younger children need the opportunity to express anger indirectly through the use of puppets, dolls, clay, or other playroom equipment. As they symbolically express anger in play, the worker can interpret the child's behavior to him or her. For instance, the worker might say, "The little girl puppet seems really mad at the daddy puppet. Is that how you feel toward your dad right now?" Older children can usually express anger verbally. They need to be reminded that the feelings they are having are normal and to be expected.

In some cases, the parents are either not available or are simply unable or unwilling to tolerate the child's feelings when the child needs to express anger. In such situations, the worker must provide an opportunity for the child to express anger in the playroom, in a group, or directly to the worker. One useful technique is to draw, or have the child draw, a life-size picture of the perpetrator and then allow the child to act out what he or she would like to do to that person. The worker can expect anything from polite defacing of the picture to total mutilation or eradication.

Helplessness

During the molestation, most children initially feel helpless and respond passively (Liles, 1984). Perpetrators often report that the child seemed to be asleep during the molestations; children report that they frequently attempted to feign sleep. However, even children who are passive during the molestation give the perpetrator subtle clues that the molestation makes them feel uncomfortable. These clues include lack of eye contact, depressed affect, avoidance, slight drawing away when touched, and a variety of tense facial expressions. The sense of helplessness incest victims feel stems, in part, from the fact that it is their parent (usually the father or father figure) who is molesting them. One of the two most powerful people in their lives, a person who is supposed to protect them in a threatening situation, is, in fact, the aggressor.

After disclosure, the child's sense of helplessness is exacerbated by the intervention of the juvenile-court and criminal-justice systems. Children often feel responsible for disrupting family life as well as powerless to do anything about it. They may feel that the only option is to recant their allegations.

Several techniques are useful in reducing children's sense of helplessness: (1) give permission to say no to adults who ask them to do something that makes them feel uncomfortable, (2) anticipate for them what is likely to happen in various areas of their life, and (3) guide them through a meeting with their parents in which the child can discuss issues that he or she has been previously unable to discuss. Another useful technique for giving the child a measure of control over his or her life is to allow the child to make choices in as many areas as possible, for example, the selection of meeting time.

Lonely, Sad, and Depressed

For some children, depression is indicated by their sadness; other children, however, reveal their depression by acting out and in other indirect ways. Feeling betrayed, angry, afraid, and helpless, the child is likely to become sad and depressed. Separation from friends and family is another source of pain. Unfortunately, after the secret is revealed many children are removed, for their own protection, from their families, social support network, and familiar surroundings, which increases their sense of being alone. Profound depression may be experienced by children from dysfunctional families in which, in addition to being abused, their most basic emotional needs were not met. These children have little to go back to even if the incest issues can be resolved.

Treatment of the Victim

Therapy with sexually abused children ideally begins with the first contact between a helping professional and the child. Crisis intervention immediately after disclosure can help determine the course of the child's recovery from the trauma. However, most children will need ongoing group and/or individual therapy extending well beyond the scope of crisis intervention.

The child is likely to experience a series of minicrises during subsequent months and years as major decisions are made about the criminal process, juvenile court intervention, and family reunification. In addition, sexually abused children often experience developmental crises during their teenage years and in adulthood due to unresolved issues related to their history of abuse (see chapter 5). Thus victims may require brief, professional intervention at several points in their lives.

Victim Crisis Group

Traditional group treatment for female victims of incest generally extends for months, sometimes years. Issues that are covered in depth include the sexual abuse itself, family relationships, other interpersonal relationships, and issues of self-esteem. Social skills are developed and practiced at events such as pizza parties and birthday celebrations. For many victims, this type of treatment may be the only treatment they receive or contemplate receiving. In recent years, the demand for group therapy in the authors' area for victims of intrafamilial child sexual abuse, especially girls, has exceeded available resources. Victims have waited months for any type of professional therapeutic treatment. Recent changes in juvenile court legislation have exacerbated the need for timely provision of services. In response to this need, crisis groups for female victims of incest were begun.

Crisis groups differ from traditional open-ended or long-term groups in several ways. First, they are limited to six weeks (in our program). Not intended to supplant the longer Daughters United group treatment, crisis group therapy addresses some of the needs of group members in the period immediately following disclosure. A second major difference is the elimination of face-to-face screening. Acceptance is based on information provided by the protective services worker, a referring parent, school outreach worker, or therapist. Few girls are refused participation, although at the end of this group, it may be recommended that they not continue long-term group therapy because they do not benefit from the group process. In dealing with the logistics of starting a new group approximately every two months, the leaders must be flexible in accepting last-minute referrals if the target population is to be properly served. Provision of transportation facilitates attendance, especially for involuntary clients.

The groups are composed of four to eight girls, clustered by age. Age of the participants ranges from eight to seventeen years; girls younger and older are served by other programs in the community with which services are coordinated.

The members of the crisis group live in various settings, which increases the disruption in their lives. Some are still in shelter care; others live in foster care, having already completed the original juvenile court investigation. Some girls may progress from a shelter home to foster care, to the home of a relative, or back to their family home during the course of group treatment. For some, the shelter home stay is very brief, three or four days immediately following disclosure, after which they are returned home. Other victims are never removed from their homes; instead the offending father or stepfather may have left.

In some cases, all or some of the children (usually the girls) are removed from the home. Other victims may be the only one of a sibling group to leave the family home or to remain out of the home after the others have returned. These circumstances make support to children who do not know where they will be living critically important to the treatment process.

Group members also face diverse reactions from their parents following disclosure. The mothers of girls who remain in the home generally believe that their daughters were sexually abused by the father figure in the home and take actions to protect their daughter from further harm, whereas mothers of girls who are removed from the home are more likely not to believe that their daughter was sexually abused. They tend to be unwilling or unable to protect their daughter from further contact with the offender. Some girls must cope with the trauma of sexual abuse and with their subsequent rejection and abandonment by the offender, their mother, siblings, and extended family. The crisis group helps participants deal with the confusion and uncertainty created by the reaction of their parent or parents. In addition, some girls need to prepare for the difficult task of testifying at a criminal hearing, although few criminal cases proceed rapidly enough to cause hearings to be concurrent with the crisis group.

The group has two basic goals: (1) to let the victims hear from the leaders and group members that the incest and what has happened to their families since disclosure are not their fault and (2) to learn through contact and conversation with other victims that other girls have experienced abuse and have reacted in similar ways.

At the first session, the co-leaders introduce themselves and the group members to one another. The leaders make a brief statement about what they do outside the crisis group, as they may also co-lead a group in which the childrens' parents participate. Children need to be given this information up front and not overhear it in a conversation at home or with their social worker. Next, the co-leader discusses confidentiality; it is made clear that what their parents say will not be repeated to them and what they say will not be repeated to their parents. Members are told how long the meetings will be and the number of weeks they will meet. Girls are usually given the co-leaders' telephone numbers and asked to call if they cannot attend one of the weekly sessions.

Early in the first meeting, the co-leaders explain why the girls are attending the group in a statement such as "We're all getting together in this group for the next six weeks because each of you was sexually molested by your dad or stepdad or your mom's boyfriend. We're going to talk about what happened and how it makes you feel." Following this statement, the older girls generally show little reaction other than a few sideways glances. Generally, the older girls understand what the group is about and are aware that other girls in the room are also victims of sexual abuse. For the younger girls (approximately eight to ten years of age), however, this statement often serves as a springboard for productive conversation for the remainder of the session. At this point two co-leaders are essential: one to listen to a girl tell her story or spill out feelings and the other to keep some order in the group after such emotions are elicited. For a group composed only of young girls, a third adult, such as an intern, is helpful.

Occasionally, group activities, such as drawings of themselves, their family, or their offenders, are planned. However, planned activities rarely take place because the girls are usually so anxious to discuss their own issues. Still, there are exceptions, as illustrated by the following example.

> A group of thirteen- and fourteen-year-old girls was dominated verbally by girls who, following disclosure, had recanted because their families would disgrace and abandon them if they maintained their allegations. No direct attempt was made to get these girls to admit that they had been sexually molested, although the group leaders were clear in their statements that they believed the girls had been molested. The group was moved to a playroom, normally used with younger children for individual therapy, where members were free to choose any activity. Their choice to make glitter and glue pictures and plaques prompted much regressive play, including tossing the glitter in the air. Interestingly, they also chose a game with structured role playing, which enabled the group as a whole to face a range of issues. In one vignette, a child wanted her father to go to the authorities to report his involvement in a hit-and-run accident. The analogy was not lost on any of the members; from body language it was clear that even those who had recanted were identifying with the girl who was being strongly pressured by her father not to report him to the authorities.

When it is possible, the meetings are scheduled to allow extra time for a co-leader to meet jointly with a child and parent if a child wishes to discuss a particular issue or to ask a difficult question. These parent–child sessions expedite progress considerably. The timing of the crisis group meetings immediately after disclosure is especially beneficial because the child experiences maximum stress at that time and thus is most open to receiving help. Also, some victims run away before they can begin traditional long-term treatment. Others become resistant after time has elapsed; treatment while they are still in shelter care may be the only help they ever receive. Most of the girls seem to like the crisis group experience; many ask if they can go into a long-term group with other members.

The time-limited groups provide a serendipitous benefit. Because they require only a six-week commitment, talented professionals are willing to volunteer as co-leaders in order to gain treatment experience.

Mothers' Crisis Groups

Mary was the thirty-four-year-old mother of four children, who ranged in ages from five to eleven. The following transcription of a telephone conversation between Mary and Ann, an intake worker who does initial assessment on new incest cases, demonstrates the pain and uncertainty experienced by mothers whose daughters are molested.

> *Mary*: "My social worker said to call you." (Mary speaks very softly and sounds uncertain.) "I think I am supposed to go to parenting class."
>
> *Ann*: "Do you mean Parents United?"
>
> *Mary*: "Yes."
>
> *Ann*: "Do you know what Parents United is for?"
>
> *Mary*: "No."
>
> *Ann*: "It's group therapy for parents of children who have been sexually molested by someone in the home. Does this fit what has happened in your family?"
>
> *Mary*: "Yes." (Mary then talks spontaneously, revealing much of the information necessary for the worker to make a judgment concerning the appropriateness of the couple for group therapy. However, she does not reveal the nature and extent of the sexual acts involved in the molestation.)
>
> *Ann*: "Mary, what did your husband do to your daughter?"
>
> Mary responds that five days ago her daughter, Jennifer, reported to the school outreach counselor, who had just completed a child-abuse prevention presentation in her fifth-grade class, that her father had been fondling her since she was in third grade. Jennifer said that during the past few months "Daddy has been kissing me in my private parts" and that her father told her, "This is our little secret; don't tell anybody."
>
> *Ann*: "Is your husband admitting that he molested your daughter?"
>
> *Mary*: "He won't talk about it."
>
> *Ann*: "Do you believe your daughter?"
>
> *Mary*: "I don't know. We've had so much trouble with Jennifer the past few months I don't know what to believe anymore."
>
> *Ann*: "Why would Jennifer lie about this?"
>
> *Mary*: "I don't know."

It is difficult to imagine a greater crisis than that precipitated by learning that one's spouse has been molesting one's child. Mothers react to the disclosure with great emotional distress and with intense concern over their ability to function independently of their husbands. Not only do they feel betrayed emotionally and sexually, but they are often extremely anxious about possible loss of financial support and economic stability. Mothers sometimes vacillate between feelings of extreme anger at their husbands and excessive dependence.

They worry about how they will be able to pay lawyers' fees or afford counseling for themselves and their children. Many feel caught between wanting to work full time in order to meet the family's basic expenses and wanting to stay home to protect and make restitution to the children.

Mothers are often so shocked by the revelation of the molestation that in their attempts to deal with their own feelings and to ensure the survival of the family, they have few emotional resources remaining to focus on the feelings and experiences of the victims. Some mothers are so overcome with fear and insecurity at the disclosure of the incest that they feel their very survival is threatened; they often deal with this threat by denying the truth of the allegations. Other mothers find themselves in the dilemma of trying to save the family by being advocates for their children while, at the same time, attempting to be supportive of their husbands.

In cases in which children are removed from the home, even temporarily during the investigative stage, mothers may despair at having lost their child. They may fear they will never get the child back and that if they do, the child may be removed in the future. Mothers may feel that they are being judged by the community as being an unfit parent—a feeling that is often reinforced by the wording of juvenile court documents. Some women, who have viewed themselves as good parents, suffer from this stigma for many years.

Being labeled unfit often intensifies the guilt that many of these mothers feel and at times try to deny. They may feel guilty when they remember clues, in hindsight, that something was wrong: "Now it all fits together. Now I know why she never seemed to want to be alone with him." They blame themselves for not having acted on the clues to prevent or stop the incest. The woman may believe she had a role in the marital or family dysfunction that contributed to the likelihood of incest. They ask themselves, "Why didn't my child tell me?" and question the quality of their relationships with their daughters, sons, and husbands.

During the course of the intake interview or the early stages of treatment, women often reveal that they too were victims of child sexual abuse at the hands of their father, stepfather, close friend, or relative. These women rarely told their mothers of their abuse during their childhood; if they did disclose the abuse, they were seldom believed or protected from further abuse. Many of these adult victims choose not to disclose their abuse to their mother even years later.

Adult women who were abused as children tend to react to disclosure of their own child's molestation in one of several ways. Some expect their child to handle abuse the same way they did: They are expected to forget about it, to forgive the offender, or to be unilaterally angry with the offender. Some even doubt the veracity of the child's allegations if the child does not react in the same way they did (see chapter 5 concerning adult survivors of molestation).

Other mothers who were abused as children may have promised themselves that they would never let the same thing happen to their children. When their child's abuse is revealed, they feel doubly guilty because they, more than anyone, should have seen the signs. Some women who were abused as children minimize the effect of the abuse on their lives. They may initially admit that the abuse was unpleasant at the time but deny that it made much difference in their lives. This defense, which they use to protect themselves from their repressed pain and anger, makes it especially difficult for them to be empathetic with the victim. A clue to a mother's own history of molestation is when she blames the victim for seducing the offender or for not preventing the molestation. Mothers who blame themselves for their own molestations frequently project this blame onto their daughters. Fortunately, some women who were themselves molested as children respond empathetically to the victim after disclosure and are motivated to work on issues relating to their own molestation, thus providing good role modeling for their daughters.

Interventions

During the crisis stage, mothers respond well to several interventions.

1. Let the mother know she is not alone by offering her the opportunity to talk with another mother from an incestuous family—a sponsor—prior to attending the first Parents United meeting. The worker might also say, "When you arrive at Parents United the first night, don't be surprised at the number of people in the room. We often have up to a hundred parents at the weekly meeting."

2. Use graphic words and phrases. If mental health professionals are shy about using words such as incest, molest, fondling, sexual intercourse, oral copulation, sodomy, or penis, distraught mothers cannot be expected to communicate clearly what happened to their children. Workers need to let mothers know that what happened to the child can be talked about.

3. Attempt to derail initial denial by requesting specifics about the allegations against the husband or partner. One way to do this is to ask the mother: "What does your daughter say your husband did?" Confront her belief that her daughter is lying by asking why the child would lie. The worker should communicate that he or she believes children who say they have been sexually molested and that the worker's first priority is to see that these children are protected. Let her know at this time that the expected role of a mother is also to believe and protect her daughter.

4. During the initial crisis after disclosure, mothers often reveal that they too were victims of childhood sexual molestation. If they do not spontaneously disclose, then the worker should ask. Understanding what the mother's own molestation meant to her and how it was or was not responded to by her parents is a significant piece of information in understanding the mother's reaction to her daughter's disclosure.

5. Let the mother know that she is experiencing a crisis but will survive. The mother may say, "I don't know what to do. I feel so confused. I cry all the time." Workers need to define this state of mind as a normal reaction and to assure mothers that they are not going crazy—eventually they will feel better and will be better able to handle their situation.

6. Educate the mother about the legal system, Parents United, and other treatment resources. Mothers need to know the difference between juvenile court and criminal court; they should be encouraged to retain an attorney, know the name of their social worker, and ask questions of the various professionals with whom they will be dealing. Such an approach helps the mother to reestablish her problem-solving skills. The information that is provided during initial phone calls should be kept to a minimum because the mother is generally experiencing extreme anxiety, which inhibits learning. Thus much of the material subsequently will need to be repeated and explained.

Offender Crises

Offenders vary in the way they initially present to mental health professionals and sponsors. Some men adamantly deny the molestation; others admit the molestation, assume responsibility, and are remorseful. The offender's response is an important prognostic sign (Faller, 1988; Orten & Rich, 1988). For some offenders, the orientation group at Parents United is their first contact with a professional counselor. Because early intervention by a sponsor may be a key factor in the successful completion of treatment, the offender should be contacted as soon after disclosure as possible. The following vignette illustrates how treatment is initiated:

> Gary, age thirty-nine, arrived at his first Parents United meeting fifteen minutes early. He and his wife joined several other new members for a forty-five-minute sponsors' "preorientation" session. Phone numbers of the sponsors and new members were exchanged. Because Gary had previously refused to be contacted by a sponsor, one was assigned at this time. If he had questions or needed to talk to someone during the week, he could call his sponsor at any time. The sponsor then introduced him to his orientation group leaders.
>
> The meeting started with members being asked to identify themselves (first name only) and to tell the group what had happened in their family that brought them to Parents United. Gary listened to the other men admit to molesting their daughters and express their desire to get their family back together. When it was Gary's turn to speak, he said, "My name is Gary and I molested my son." He did not make eye contact with anyone in the group and said little else in the first session.
>
> The following week, in the second group session, Gary told his story: "My son told his soccer coach, who told the police. They came and talked to my son at school and didn't even tell my wife and me until dinnertime that they were taking him to a shelter home. We didn't get to talk to him until court. Detective Kramer from the Police Department called and told me to come down to the station. We talked for about two hours and I told him everything. I had to spend four hours in jail before my wife bailed me out. I know what I did was wrong, but my son was not really hurt. He never told me to stop and he didn't act like he was afraid of me."

Offenders' Fears

Although the father's initial reaction may be relief that the secret is finally out, his relief is soon dissipated by his realization of the possible consequences of the abuse. He faces the possible loss of his wife, children, job, extended family members, and freedom, not to mention the profound loss of self-respect when he realizes that he has been labeled a child molester.

Offenders must face a succession of professionals who know or suspect what the offender did and who intrude in his life in various ways. Offenders must respond to the demands of the juvenile court, social workers, police, the district attorney's office, defense attorneys, the criminal court, and mental health professionals (Orten & Rich, 1988). As they attempt to meet the sometimes conflicting demands of these professionals and agencies, they must decide whom to trust, where to live, how much to tell their wives and others, and whether to lie or tell the truth about the molestations.

Interventions with the Offender during the Initial Crisis Period

Offenders who call or come in for a screening interview shortly after disclosure present in a state of crisis. Workers must be prepared to deal with offenders who acknowledge their offense, those who deny their offense, and those who remain silent on the advice of their attorneys. Workers need to be both supportive and confrontive of the father while encouraging behavior and attitudes that minimize stress on the victim and family. If the first contact is by telephone, the worker should ascertain where the father is calling from and if he is able to talk freely. Frequently, fathers who leave the home are living with relatives or friends, and it is difficult to have a private conversation. When making their first phone call, offenders are often less than clear about why they are calling, sometimes because people are listening and sometimes because they are unwilling or unable to state their offense. Therefore, it is important to be direct with the father from the very beginning. For example, the worker might ask, "Did you molest your child or have you been accused of molesting your child?" The majority of callers will answer, "Yes," a smaller number will equivocate, and some will say, "No."

Most offenders exhibit massive defenses when forced to face the reality of what they did, its effect on the victim and family, and the motivation behind the offense. At the time of disclosure, some fathers are so remorseful and guilt ridden that they may be suicidal. Offenders may manifest one or more of the following defenses:

- *Lying*: Fathers who molested their child yet accuse the child of lying.
- *Denial*: Fathers who admit they had sexual contact with their child, but claim (and seem to believe) that the child was not hurt. "Yeah, I did it, and maybe I shouldn't have. She's just fine. What's upsetting her is having to go to counseling. Those counselors are trying to get her to hate me."
- *Rationalization*: For example, "I just wanted her first experience with sex to be good." "My wife didn't give me what I needed." "I was drunk."
- *Minimization*: "It only happened once and we didn't go all the way." "Yes, I did it. But the Lord has forgiven me and so has my daughter. I don't need to be here. It will never happen again because I am going to church now."
- *Projection*: "She came to me. She wanted me to. She enjoyed it and didn't want me to stop."
- *Redefining the victim*: "She's a lyin' tramp. She's been a liar since she was six years old. She's just trying to get back at me for grounding her."

During the initial phase of treatment, the worker should combat these defenses, communicating to the offender that he or she believes the child has been molested and that the adult, not the child, is always responsible for any molestation. The denying father must be moved toward admitting what he did and accepting responsibility for it. Simultaneously, the worker must let the molester know that he is not alone. Workers should tell perpetrators that they have worked with other men with this problem and that there is a treatment group for men who have molested their children. If it seems appropriate, the father should be informed about Parents United sponsors who are available to speak with new members. The worker should help the molester define "incest" and child sexual molestation, as these terms are used by child protective services, the juvenile courts, and treatment providers. The perpetrator should understand, for treatment purposes, that incest includes voyeurism, exhibitionism, fondling, and other behaviors not listed in lexicographical or legal code definition. Graphic words and phrases—incest, molest, fondling, sexual intercourse, oral copulation, sodomy, and penis—should be used so that fathers understand that what they did to the child can be talked about.

The worker should be prepared to do a great deal of listening. The offender usually has a tremendous amount to unburden. He frequently needs help in focusing his thoughts and encouragement in identifying and expressing his feelings. For instance, the worker should let him know it is normal to feel as if he is going crazy. If he perceives that his feelings are recognized and understood, the offender is more likely to be motivated to enter treatment.

As workers encourage offenders to express their feelings, they should be especially careful not to reinforce denial or minimization of the offense or aid offenders in their efforts to redefine themselves as the victim.

The offender should be asked whether he has committed or been accused of committing previous sexual offenses. Many incest treatment programs find that treatment is more effective with offenders who have not molested a child outside the family or committed rape. The worker must determine whether the offender has a history of substance abuse because fathers who are recent or current substance abusers need to be referred to specialized drug or alcohol counseling prior to or concurrent with incest treatment (Liles & Childs, 1986). In order to understand the father's situation, the worker needs to know where the children are living, whether the offender has been arrested, if he has legal representation, where he is living, his wife's reaction to the child's disclosure, and whether the offender hopes to reconcile with his family in the future.

The social service and judicial systems in which fathers find themselves are very complex and confusing. Consequently, during the initial interventions with fathers, workers need to begin educating them about these systems. One of the first things an offender needs to understand is the difference between the juvenile and criminal courts. Frequently, offenders falsely believe that they will have to be found guilty by a criminal court before the juvenile court can find their child in need of protection from them.

Workers must address the father's immediate concerns but must also be aware that treatment for incest is a long-term commitment. In the RISAC–Parents United treatment program, the immediate goal of initial contact with offenders is to facilitate linkage with sponsors and involve offenders in treatment groups of Parents United.

Conclusion

The disclosure of parent–child incest has a devastating effect on the family. Not only is the continued existence of the family as a unit threatened, but individual members often wonder if they will survive the crises precipitated by incest disclosure. Moreover, equilibrium that is gained after disclosure is usually disrupted by the subsequent interventions of various professionals who intrude on the family in an attempt to protect the child and offer treatment and support to the family. All members of a family in which incest has been disclosed need sensitive, timely, and informed intervention. Intervention must occur within the context of a coordinated child sexual abuse treatment program; it is most effective when paraprofessional helpers are used to augment professional efforts. Crisis intervention in incest cases should be viewed as a necessary and immediate service that lays the foundation for long-term treatment. Effective crisis intervention offered at the earliest possible time may be the most important variable in determining the outcome of individual, group, and family treatment.

References

DeFrancis, V. (1969). *Protecting the child victim of sex crimes: Final report*. Denver: American Humane Association.

Faller, K. C. (1988). Decision making in cases of intrafamilial child sexual abuse study. *American Journal of Orthopsychiatry*, 58, 121–128.

Finklehor, D. (1979). *Sexually victimized children*. New York: Free Press.

Giaretto, H. (1982). *Integrated treatment of child sexual abuse*. Palo Alto, CA: Science and Behavior Books.

Liles, R. (1984). *Therapist ascription to theoretical statements taken from the literature on father–daughter incest*. Ann Arbor, MI: University Microfilms International.

Liles, R., & Childs, D. (1986). Similarities in family dynamics of incest and alcohol abuse. *Alcohol Health and Research World, 2*, 66–69.

Liles, R., & Wahlquist, D. (1981). Interagency cooperation in the treatment of intrafamilial child sexual abuse. *Social Work Papers, 16*, 24–32.

Meiselman, K. C. (1978). *Incest*. San Francisco: Jossey-Bass.

Mrazek, P., & Kempe, H. (Eds.). (1981). *Sexually abused children and their families*. New York: Pergamon Press.

National Center on Child Abuse and Neglect. (1981). *National study of the incidence and severity of child abuse and neglect*. Washington, DC: U.S. Government Printing Office.

Orten, J. D., & Rich, L. L. (1988). A model for assessment of incestuous families. *Social Casework*, 69, 611–619.

Russell, D. (1984). *Sexual exploitation: Rape, child sexual abuse, and workplace harassment*. Beverly Hills, CA: Sage Publications.

Sgroi, S. M. (1975). Sexual molestation of children. *Children Today*, 4 (3), 18–21.

Sgroi, S. M. (Ed.). (1983). *Handbook of clinical intervention in child sexual abuse*. New York: Lexington Books.

Swift, C. F. (1986). Community intervention in child sexual abuse. In S. M. Auerbach & A. L. Stolberg (Eds.), *Crisis intervention with children and families* (pp. 149–171). Washington, DC: Hemisphere Publishing.

5

Adult Survivors of Incest And Molestation

CHRISTINE A. COURTOIS

ADULT SURVIVORS OF INCEST AND MOLESTATION are well known to mental health practitioners for their broad range of symptoms and the variety and complexities of crises with which they present. Adult survivors seek crisis intervention both from within the mental health system, as therapy clients, and from without, as members of the general populace in need of urgent clinical assistance. In the past, adult survivors were likely to seek therapy or crisis intervention without making an overt disclosure of their abuse history. Currently, it is more common for adult survivors to make an open disclosure of their past (when they have knowledge of its occurrence) or for the clinician to be aware of obvious clues to a history of abuse.

This chapter provides information about the crisis presentations of adult survivors of incest and other forms of child sexual abuse. The first section describes adult survivors as a special population with special needs that must be acknowledged in treatment. The mental health practitioner working with the adult survivor must understand abuse issues and dynamics in order to adequately respond to her needs. (The female gender is used to refer to survivors in this chapter because research indicates that females are victimized more often than are males. This emphasis is not meant to minimize the sexual victimization of males. The issues and counseling approaches discussed in this chapter are applicable to male survivors as well.) This introduction is followed by a description of the most common aftereffects experienced by the child at the time of the abuse and later in adulthood. Because the abuse experienced by adult survivors occurred at a time when child sexual abuse was largely unrecognized, most victims received little or no assistance. Thus, the aftereffects were untreated, a circumstance that often led to the development of other problems commonly referred to as the "secondary elaborations of the original untreated effects" (Gelinas, 1983). These initial and long-term aftereffects and their secondary problems most often meet the criteria for post-traumatic stress disorder (PTSD), acute and/or chronic and delayed, and also for dissociative disorders (American Psychiatric Association, 1987).

Post-traumatic stress reactions account for the vast majority of crisis presentations made by adult survivors of incest; therefore, it is imperative for the clinician to be able to conceptualize the distress within a PTSD framework. The bulk of this chapter outlines and explains the most common crises experienced by this population from such a perspective (see chapter 2). Case examples are used to illustrate the various crises. The final section of the chapter offers suggestions for therapeutic response derived from the principles of crisis intervention theory, victimization/traumatic stress theory, and incest/sexual abuse treatment.

Adult Survivors of Incest and Molestation

Adults who were sexually abused as children have special needs due to the past and present societal attitudes surrounding incest and other forms of molestation, the nature of the victimization they experienced, and their attempts to cope at the time of the abuse and later.

The prevalence and seriousness of child sexual abuse have been acknowledged in the United States only over the past ten years. The taboo on sexual interactions between related individuals (and to a lesser degree between adult and child) has previously been so strong as to inhibit discussion of the problem. This inhibition, along with seriously flawed research investigations, has in turn led to a substantial underestimation of the prevalence of incest and other forms of child sexual abuse.

For many years, incest was believed to be extremely rare and a gross aberration. As recently as 1955, one researcher calculated its prevalence rate at one or two cases per million of population per year (Weinberg, 1955). In contrast, contemporary researchers report that 16 percent of all girls experience at least one incestuous experience before the age of eighteen years (Russell, 1986). Boys are also victimized; research indicates that the rate of abuse of boys within the family is much lower than that of girls but that boys are more likely to be sexually abused outside of the home (Finkelhor, 1984). Available data document that the majority of victims are female, and the majority of perpetrators male (Russell, 1986). Nevertheless, just as some males are victims, some females are perpetrators, possibly with greater frequency than is now documented. The less "typical" forms of abuse are only now coming to light. Male victims and victims abused by females are often reluctant to disclose because of additional feelings of shame.

Individuals who were abused during the period that Summit (1982) has labeled the "age of denial" had less recourse to assistance and intervention because at the time of the abuse there was little acknowledgment of the reality of incest and molestation. Incest is strictly forbidden in most cultures, and its occurrence generally elicits shock, horror, and punishment. Despite such strong prohibitions, researchers have uncovered evidence of incest and other forms of child sexual abuse going back to Biblical times (Rush, 1980).

Incest involves sexual interactions between individuals who are blood relatives or who are related by contract (for example, stepparents, in-laws) or by the role they hold in the family (for example, live-in lover or father's best friend). Incest is abusive and a form of child sexual abuse when it is cross-generational, that is, when an adult is involved with a minor (usually defined as being younger than eighteen years of age). Incest between peers of approximately the same age (for example, siblings or cousins) is considered abusive when it is coercive and nonconsensual.

Like other forms of sexual abuse, incest is human-induced, premeditated (it may have begun accidentally or due to rather unique situational factors, but its continuance is planned), and repeated. Its distinguishing characteristic is that it is perpetrated by a family member or an associate of the family rather than by a stranger, often under the guise of love and affection, or within the context of an otherwise loving relationship. These relationship factors, when combined with the other common characteristics and dynamics of incest, heighten rather than lessen the traumatic potential of the behavior.

Incest is a complex sexual behavior with many permutations. It may range from a single occurrence involving gentle sexual contact to behavior that is addictive and compulsive (occurring as frequently as several times a day for many years) and involving severe sexual violation and extreme violence. The sexual contact usually begins at a prepubertal age and lasts for an average of four years. The average age of onset is eight years, although researchers now speculate that incest frequently occurs at a much younger age. Typically, the victim represses knowledge of onset in early childhood, and its occurrence is therefore not reported to investigators. Although physical violence is not the norm, some form of coercion or misrepresentation is always present. Children may be threatened into compliance and silence through implied violence or with threats of blame, rejection, and abandonment ("Mom will be very upset with you if she finds out," "Daddy will go to jail if you tell," "Nobody will believe you anyway," "If you tell, I'll hurt you, your pet, or Mom," are typical threats used by the perpetrator). The child is often treated as special or given special favors as the price of sexualization. She may be threatened with the loss of this special status if she discloses the abuse. This threat is especially potent when used with an emotionally needy and vulnerable child.

At the onset of the abuse, the sexual behavior is usually mild and often involves flattery, voyeurism, sexual gestures and innuendo, kissing, and fondling. With no deterrent, it typically progresses to mutual disrobing, increasingly intimate fondling, mutual masturbation, oral sex, and vaginal and anal intercourse or penetration with objects. Intercourse usually is introduced with a postpubertal child; however, intercourse is attempted or completed on younger children as well.

Incest involving members of the nuclear family has the greatest potential for harm. Parent–child incest, which in most cases means father– or stepfather–daughter incest, is consistently reported as being the most damaging type, followed by sibling incest perpetrated by brothers. Many aspects of the nuclear family contribute to the traumatic potential: family ties and loyalty; a closer relationship and a greater age difference between victim and perpetrator; and the child's immaturity, dependence, and accessibility. This dependence and accessibility also create the opportunity for incest to last longer and occur more frequently and with greater severity. Incestuous families have norms, defenses, and dynamics that unconsciously support the occurrence of the abuse. Multiple incest among family members both across and within generations and the repeated abuse of one family member by several others (for example, the girl who has been abused by her father and grandfather or her father and brother) occurs fairly frequently in incest cases.

When a child discloses incest to someone within the family, she is often not believed and not assisted because of divided loyalty. It is much easier for a family to blame the child for creating problems or for shaming the family than it is to allow intervention from outsiders. This situation is especially unfortunate and damaging for the child because incestuous abuse usually involves more chronic and serious levels of sexual violation (Russell, 1986; see also chapter 4). Conversely, a child abused by someone outside of the nuclear family is more likely to receive appropriate assistance and intervention from her family because family disruption, shame, and divided loyalty are less likely.

These aspects of abuse within the family, coupled with the child's immaturity and dependence on her parents, entrap her and make her virtually powerless to stop the incest. Although she may have initially liked the activity and any special attention she received, the pressure to maintain secrecy communicates to her that the activity is wrong and activates feelings of guilt and shame. Furthermore, she may increasingly dislike the activity as it escalates and becomes more intrusive and compulsive. In order to cope with both the ongoing abuse and her feelings, the child develops strong defenses and accommodation mechanisms. She often resorts to denial and dissociation, mechanisms also used by family members to defend against the reality of the abuse. With these defenses, the child pretends that the abuse is not happening to her or psychologically removes herself so she doesn't feel it or incorporate it into her reality.

The child must also deal with feelings of self-blame for somehow having "deserved" the abuse and for being so "unlovable" that she does not deserve assistance. The victim may protect her image of having good parents and a good family by telling herself that the incest is the result of her own "badness," which she tries to mitigate by being "good."

Because incest often occurs over the span of a victim's childhood, it influences her maturation and development. For many victim/survivors, the incest, along with its aftereffects and the mechanisms used to cope with its occurrence, influences and becomes incorporated into the personality. Some victims experience developmental deficits as their psychological energy is used for survival rather than for maturation. Other victims become pseudomature and hyperdeveloped, compensating for the abuse and other family problems by becoming little adults and little caretakers in their families. Similar patterns are evident in other types of dysfunctional families, for example, the alcoholic family.

From this abbreviated review of incest and some of its defining characteristics and dynamics, it is clear that incest creates emotional risk for the child victim. Sexual molestation by a stranger may involve many of the same sexual behaviors; however, it does not have the same kinship ties and relational entanglements as incest. Also, the child is not generally as dependent or entrapped, and the abuse is not as constant, serious, or chronic. Nevertheless, because abuse by strangers involves sexual violation, it also holds the potential for emotional damage.

Finkelhor and Browne (1985) completed a comprehensive review of the literature on child sexual abuse and incest to determine those aspects of sexual abuse most related to its traumatic impact. They postulated four "traumagenic dynamics": *traumatic sexualization*—the "process in which a child's sexuality . . . is shaped in a developmentally inappropriate and interpersonally dysfunctional fashion as a result of the sexual abuse" (p. 531); *betrayal*—"the dynamic by which children discover that someone on whom they were vitally dependent has caused them harm" (p. 531); *powerlessness*—"the dynamic of rendering the victim powerless . . . the process in which the child's will, desires, and sense of efficacy are continually contravened" (p. 532); and *stigmatization*—"the negative connotations—e.g., badness, shame, and guilt—that are communicated to the child around the experience and that then become incorporated into the child's self-image" (p. 532).

In earlier periods, adult survivors of incest and molestation were subjected to sexual abuse at a time when the abuse was not acknowledged or discussed and when Freud's theory of the Oedipus complex prevailed. If a victim dared disclose the abuse within the family or to a mental health professional, she was frequently blamed for the situation, told she was imagining the situation, or told to forget it and get on with her life. In such an atmosphere of disbelief, victim/survivors were forced to do just that—forget the situation and get on with their life.

Sexual Abuse Aftereffects as Post-Traumatic Stress Reactions

Sexual abuse frequently engenders the development of various difficulties at the time of its occurrence and later (Browne & Finkelhor, 1986; Courtois, 1988; Russell, 1986). However, not all victims suffer serious consequences either immediately or in the aftermath of the abuse and not all have the same reactions. Just as the experience of incest or sexual molestation varies quite dramatically, so too do its aftereffects. The individual experience and reactions of each victim/survivor must be understood.

Nonetheless, several common negative aftereffects of sexual abuse may be found in women who use or seek mental health services. According to the available research on the sequelae of sexual abuse, 20 to 40 percent of all child victims suffer pathological disturbance at the time of the abuse or shortly afterward (Browne & Finkelhor, 1986; Tufts, 1984). The effects may be transient and remit over time either spontaneously or with assistance. Alternatively, effects may persist over the course of the child's development or have a delayed onset in adolescence or adulthood. Because treatment was generally unavailable when today's adult survivors were abused as children, the initial effects usually were untreated. The effects that persisted and did not remit, either spontaneously or otherwise, caused other problems (known as secondary elaborations) or they remained dormant until triggered by some later life event.

Studies of adult survivors substantiate this pattern. In Russell's (1986) study of incest survivors, the most methodologically sound research of its kind to date, the occurrence of aftereffects was as follows: Approximately 50 percent of the sample reported "little or no lasting effects" and no need for mental health services, 25 percent reported moderate effects that later caused them to seek mental health services either on a regular basis or during periods of stress or crisis, and 25 percent reported serious consequences that caused severe disruptions in personality development and in their ability to function in the world. Russell (1986) and Courtois (1988) strongly suggest that these figures probably underestimate the true damage of incest because survivors often continue to use familiar coping mechanisms and defenses—denial, minimization, rationalization, and dissociation—to soften the effects of the abuse. Moreover, because some effects remain dormant for years, they obviously cannot be reported until they emerge; even then, they are not likely to be associated with prior sexual abuse. The aftereffects can be grouped in the following six categories (Courtois, 1988):

1. *Emotional reactions:* typically includes feelings of anxiety, fear, confusion, guilt, despair, hopelessness, anger, and depression along with loss and grief. Emotional anesthesia is also quite common.

2. *Self-perceptions:* includes feelings of shame, stigma, low self-esteem, malignant power, contamination, and a sense of being different from others.

3. *Physical/somatic effects:* includes gastrointestinal and genitourinary difficulties, neurological abnormalities, psychosomatic symptoms, migraine headaches, depersonalization, derealization and numbness, and conversion reactions as well as flashbacks and other reexperiencing phenomena.

4. *Sexual effects:* includes compulsive sexual behavior or sexual avoidance, both indicative of anxiety concerning sexual functioning. Maltz and Holman (1987) have listed sexual problems under the categories of sexual emergence, sexual identity, and sexual dysfunctions.

5. *Interpersonal relating:* includes impairment in the ability to relate to, be intimate with, and trust others. These effects may manifest differently in interactions with men and women; in intimate and/or committed relationships; in interactions with parents, other family members, and other authority figures; and in relation to children.

6. *Social functioning:* ranges from an impaired ability to function socially or occupationally to antisocial behavior or compulsive overfunctioning. Learning disabilities and behavioral difficulties can result from sexual abuse.

Both the initial and long-term aftereffects have been found to resemble the classic descriptions of traumatic response as first described by Kardiner (1941); yet there are symptoms particular to sexual abuse. The symptom picture, with its psychological and physiological components, variable onset, and associated features of depression, anxiety, impulsive and unpredictable behaviors, and survivor guilt, meets the criteria for the diagnosis of PTSD (American Psychiatric Association, 1987; see also chapter 2). The duration of symptoms must be at least one month. Delayed onset is specified if onset of the symptoms is at least six months after the trauma. Reasons for delay in symptom onset are unknown in all types of trauma response, not only those associated with child sexual abuse.

Post-traumatic symptoms cluster into two main categories or phases, between which victims frequently alternate: (1) *the denial/numbing phase* in which repression, denial, avoidance, withdrawal, and emotional constriction predominate and (2) *the intrusive/repetitive phase* during which aspects of the trauma are psychologically and physiologically remembered and reexperienced during both waking hours and sleep (Horowitz, 1986). The symptoms associated with each phase may themselves lead to secondary elaborations. For example, phobic avoidance of individuals, behaviors, and activities that resemble or symbolize the original trauma may cause serious life-style restriction. "Avoiding emotional involvement further diminishes the significance of life after the trauma, and thus perpetuates the central role of the trauma" (van der Kolk, 1986, p. 3). States of hyperarousal, including flashbacks, nightmares, startle responses, and reenactments of situations resembling the trauma, may cause significant life disturbances as well. Many survivors fear they are going crazy when strong reexperience emerges, especially when the symptoms occur suddenly with no conscious association with the sexual abuse. These symptoms can interfere with the survivor's ability to function interpersonally or occupationally.

Many post-traumatic symptoms are dissociative in nature (Spiegel, 1988). Some of the initial and long-term aftereffects of child sexual abuse also meet the criteria for the diagnosis of dissociative disorder in the *Diagnostic and Statistical Manual of Mental Disorders* (DSM-III-R) (American Psychiatric Association, 1987). The DSM-III-R lists the essential feature of dissociative disorders as a disturbance or alteration in the normally integrative functions of identity, memory, or consciousness (p. 269).

Four forms of dissociative disorder are included: (1) *psychogenic amnesia*, a sudden inability to recall important personal behavior or events that is too extensive to be explained by ordinary forgetfulness; (2) *psychogenic fugue*, sudden unexpected travel away from home or customary place of work, with inability to recall one's previous identity and the assumption of either a partially or completely new identity; (3) *depersonalization disorder*, one or more episodes of depersonalization sufficiently severe to cause marked distress; and (4) *multiple personality disorder*, the existence of two or more distinct personalities or personality states, which recurrently take full control of the person's behavior. *Dissociative disorder, not otherwise specified* is diagnosed in situations in which a dissociative symptom is present, but the total symptom picture does not meet the criteria set forth for the four forms listed above. These symptoms include trance states, derealization unaccompanied by depersonalization, and more prolonged dissociated states that occur in persons subjected to conditions of captivity and other prolonged coercion.

Although dissociative reactions occur with many different traumatic life events, sexual abuse in childhood makes such reactions particularly likely to develop. Dissociation serves many purposes. It acts as a defense against the traumatic experience itself, because it provides the child with a way out of an intolerable physical and psychological situation (many survivors describe floating above their bodies while being abused and being a spectator of the abuse rather than directly experiencing it). Dissociation allows the victim to erect memory barriers (amnesia) to keep painful events and memories out of awareness (survivors may be able to talk about an abusive event without clearly remembering it happening to them). Furthermore, it may function as an analgesic to prevent feelings of pain. Dissociation may be a spontaneous reaction when it first occurs; however, with repeated episodes of abuse, it may become rather automatic.

Dissociation is a survival mechanism that allows the child to cope with a physically and psychologically intolerable situation. Over time, it commonly changes from being functional and adaptive (a survivor skill) to being dysfunctional and disruptive in the individual's life (a symptom). Similarly, Spiegel (1988) noted that "the self which experienced the trauma is detached from the everyday self but continues to exert a demoralizing influence upon it. Thus, dissociation can be understood as a fundamental mechanism through which individuals experience and suffer from trauma" (p. 22).

Dissociative and other post-traumatic symptoms are frequently involved in the development of crises in the lives of adult survivors. Many crises develop as the result of delayed aftereffects of the original trauma, the reexperiencing of the trauma, or exposure to events that symbolize the trauma and trigger symptoms, which can include a variety of common life events and developmental tasks. The reemergence of past trauma and distressing symptomatology is upsetting in any event; it is particularly so for the survivor who has no conscious memory of having been abused. Reemergence and reexperiencing counters the denial and disconnection so characteristic of the dynamics and aftereffects of sexual abuse. These, in turn, can precipitate additional symptoms of anxiety or depression, including decompensation and psychosis and explosive, impulsive, or vegetative behavior.

Common Crisis Presentations of Adult Survivors

Common events that precipitate the crisis presentations of adult survivors are discussed within the following four categories, which are not necessarily mutually exclusive: (1) normative developmental events; (2) exposure to events that symbolize or resemble the original trauma; (3) recollection, disclosure, confrontation, reporting, and criminal-justice crises; and (4) issues within therapy that precipitate crises. Individuals experiencing crises and presenting for help may, at the time, be active therapy clients or may have no current involvement in mental health services. However, given the multitude of serious problems that can result from sexual abuse and the fact that survivors have a high representation in clinical populations (Briere, 1984), very likely a great percentage of survivors have had previous experience as therapy clients and/or as sporadic users of emergency crisis intervention services.

When a crisis occurs with a survivor who is in therapy, management is at least partly assisted by the therapist's knowledge of the client, her dynamics, her history, and the current events in her life. This knowledge may include information about past incest or molestation. Although it is becoming common for survivors who seek treatment to openly discuss their abuse history, the disguised or undisclosed presentation continues to be the norm. The survivor who is not in therapy when seeking crisis or emergency services may likewise not reveal or remember past abuse. A crisis may provide information suggestive of an abuse history or may provide substantiation in the event that abuse has been suspected by the therapist but not remembered by the client.

Normative Developmental Events

Many normative life events and transitions, whether happy and incremental or sad and decremental, have been associated with the onset of symptoms and/or the precipitation of crises for some survivors. Each of these types of events will be explained below and illustrated by case examples.

Incremental events. Incremental life events are generally life-enhancing and give pleasure and happiness. Common examples include the development of a close friendship or an intimate relationship, a marriage or partnership, a pregnancy and the birth of a child, the growth and development of a child, a significant achievement or award, a job promotion, and a stroke of good luck. Incremental events can trigger symptoms in several ways. The first is a paradoxical reaction: The survivor may seek and enjoy the happy events in her life, yet, paradoxically, be extremely discomforted by them. For example, good fortune or good relationships may contradict feelings of being unlovable or undeserving. Success may stimulate fear and anxiety rather than provide satisfaction. Incremental events may further precipitate reactions that lead to a crisis. For example,

> Lois met and fell in love with Doug. After they made plans to marry, she began to feel anxious due to her sense of being worthless and unlovable. She found herself criticizing him and doing other things to distance him. She provoked him to such a degree that within a matter of months he broke their engagement. Lois sought counseling after the break-up for her extreme distress and sense of hopelessness.

> Suzanne was given an achievement award by her professional association upon completion of a research study that made a substantial contribution to her field. Rather than being able to enjoy the regard and appreciation of her peers, she began to experience panic attacks. She would ruminate about mistakes she might have made in her research and the possibility that she would be identified as a fraud. Fearing that this would cause her to lose her job and threaten her independence and safety, she presented in an emergency state at a local clinic for her panic attacks.

Sometimes an incremental event may cause distress by, paradoxically, creating safety and stability so that defenses are lessened.

> Julie and Marge met in college and developed a strong friendship. With Marge, Julie found an accepting and caring relationship that she had never experienced before. While comforting and reassuring, the relationship caused her to begin to admit how emotionally neglected she had been in her family and how abusive members of her family were to one another. She became seriously depressed and suicidal.

Incremental events may stimulate direct recall of abuse experiences or may recreate a circumstance reminiscent of the abuse. For example, an event such as the birth of a child may be joyful, yet stimulate feelings of depression and fear, particularly when the abuser is a family member with access to the child. A marriage or other committed relationship may be experienced as entrapping and obligatory rather than as safe and secure.

> Following the birth of her first child, a daughter, Ellen became inexplicably depressed and terrified, especially when her father visited and held the baby. She began to experience frequent nightmares and flashbacks of a man chasing her and would awaken in a panic. She was terrified that her father would molest her daughter and that she couldn't do anything effective short of killing him to deter him. She was highly agitated when she sought help.

> Anna married the year before she presented in a crisis state. She had dated her husband for years, and they had previously had a satisfying sexual relationship. After they married, however, she began to feel trapped. She came to experience sex as an obligation, with a man who was now a family member. Her husband threatened to divorce her due to their sexual estrangement.

Normal developmental tasks and events might daunt the survivor of incest or molestation because she is developmentally "out of synch" with her peers. Peer-group identification and experimentation with dating, intimacy, and sex can be especially difficult.

> Lorraine's teacher referred her to counseling after noticing that she had gained a significant amount of weight and had become withdrawn, depressed, and unkempt during the course of a semester. She had functioned moderately well until, as she put it, "I hit the college social scene." She had no close girl friends because she didn't trust women and found that "all men were the same and wanted only one thing." She just wanted to be left alone to pursue her studies.

Similarly, the developmental benchmarks of others might provoke crisis reactions.

> Ula had always had a very close relationship with her nephew. She loved caring for him and, over the years, had engaged in many activities with him. Her feelings toward him changed markedly once he reached puberty and his body and voice matured. Whereas once she had experienced her nephew as being innocent, she now experienced him as masculine and threatening. Unconsciously she associated him with her brother, who had molested her when he reached puberty. She sought help in a state of panic and depression.

Decremental events. Decremental events involve loss or diminution and generally cause feelings of hurt, depression, and sorrow. They are usually stressful and often precipitate a state of crisis. Common examples of decremental events include victimizations, accidents, and illness as well as the loss of a relationship through death, separation, or divorce. Decremental events can trigger symptoms in several ways. In some cases, enough distress is created by the loss of a significant person or relationship that dormant affect and memories are dislodged. The current loss may cause the reactivation of old problems from the near or distant past, thus allowing an opportunity to rework an earlier problem. As noted by Parad and Parad in chapter 1, a previously unresolved problem may itself represent the aftermath of an earlier crisis situation that was not mastered. This concept matches the concept of secondary elaboration of the original untreated aftereffect discussed above.

> Liz was involved in a serious car accident that left her physically incapacitated for many months. Being physically out of control caused the reemergence of feelings and memories from childhood—fears of attack, feeling cornered, helpless, and paralyzed.

> Tina had been sexually abused by her grandfather for a number of years. When he died, Tina was overcome with feelings of rage and physical hyperarousal. She felt guilty for being so angry toward a now dead, pathetic old man. Because she had been highly shamed by the abuse, she had never disclosed it to anyone. She was extremely agitated but had no one with whom to talk.

> Mary had been molested by both her father and her older brother. Her mother had been depressed during Mary's childhood, and Mary had carefully kept the abuse a secret in order to protect her mother. Her mother's

death caused the emergence of a major depression with obsessive ruminations about the abuse. She sought help for the depression and the "memories that wouldn't stop."

Following several significant losses and deaths, including a divorce from her husband of fifteen years and the death of a good friend, Pam became reclusive and withdrew from all of her friends. She became obsessed with her abuse history and spent all of her time thinking and writing about it. She drank heavily to cope with the pain and sought help after making a serious suicidal gesture.

In addition to these case examples, two survivor memoirs illustrate how losses can trigger both memories and acute reactions: Fraser's *My Father's House* (1988) and Evert's *When You Are Ready* (1987).

Events That Symbolize or Resemble the Original Trauma

In addition to normative life events, other events may directly symbolize or resemble aspects of the original trauma. The following discussion focuses on events that have a direct resemblance to the abusive event, such as continued victimization by others or abusive behavior toward the self or in interactions with others.

Revictimization. A tragic consequence of incest or molestation is that survivors are more vulnerable to repeat victimizations (Russell, 1986). Several patterns can be observed: survivors who are naive and trusting of others and thus vulnerable when seeking someone to take care of them; those who believe that sex is a trade-off they must make if someone treats them well; those who have little or no knowledge of how to protect themselves and who dissociate when they are approached sexually; and those who provoke others or set up situations in which they are revictimized as a means of self-punishment in order to maintain control or substantiate something they learned in the original victimization (for example, that all men are venal or all women nonprotective).

After being brutally raped by a stranger, Emily developed amnesia. She "came to" months later in a different city using a different name. The rape had resulted in the emergence of a multiple personality disorder. She had a history of brutal physical, psychological, and sexual abuse in childhood, with which she had coped by splitting it off.

From the age of three to eleven years, Lillian had been molested by her brother. During her first gynecological check-up at fourteen years of age, her doctor also molested her. She described feeling numb and in a daze for months afterward and being told by her family that she was "really spacey." She never disclosed these assaults because she was afraid that they were her fault. She felt that the doctor must have found something during the examination that caused him to know that she was already "used and damaged goods" and that it was all right for him to use her too.

Dina sought therapy for a long-standing depression. She came to idealize her male therapist, who was very understanding and caring. She was flattered when he told her that he would teach her how to interact with other men and that he would take good care of her. Sex became a regular part of her therapy sessions. When he attempted to terminate therapy and their sexual contact, she began to mutilate herself, drink exces-

> sively, and have suicidal thoughts. She did not believe that she could live without him.

> Rose was active in her church and became friendly with her minister, who scared her because he was nice to her. She set out to seduce him to prove to herself that he was just like other men and to thank him for having been so nice to her. She succeeded and he subsequently avoided her, causing her to feel depressed and anxious. She felt evil and contaminated, but consoled herself somewhat with her knowledge that he was not as pure as he presented himself to be.

Ongoing abuse within the family of origin. Abuse across and within generations occurs commonly in incestuous families. Sexual contact may continue even into adulthood; the victim may be pressured to continue in return for family support (usually financial or emotional) or in return for the nonabuse of other family members. Counselors in college mental health services may treat victims who live off campus or in a dorm who become "recontaminated" by the family when they return home during school breaks.

> Susan called her college therapist from home during spring break in a decompensated state. She was agitated and having aural and visual hallucinations. Upon returning home, her father had approached her for sex, saying that his continued financing of her education was contingent upon her sexual cooperation.

> Laura's sister sent all members of their immediate family letters documenting her sexual abuse by their stepfather. Although Laura had previously had no recollection of being abused, the letter caused an onslaught of memories and flashbacks. She sought help, saying she was going crazy.

> At a family gathering, Paul was approached by a cousin who asked whether Paul had ever been molested by their grandfather or one of their uncles. All male and female cousins were thus polled. It turned out that eleven cousins had been molested as well as several of their children. The cousins banded together and reported both abusers to the police.

Abuse and/or violence within marriage, partnership, and family of procreation. Survivors are at risk for family violence of all types. They may be battered or sexually abused by spouses or partners, who may also abuse the children. In a minority of cases, the survivor herself becomes an accessory or accomplice to the abuse of her children or abuses them herself. More commonly, however, she is unable to protect them because of her post-traumatic reactions and failure to resolve her own abuse.

> Sarah was chronically beaten and abused by her husband. She sought help at a local shelter when she found her husband in bed with her three-year-old daughter. She later found out that he had molested all four of their other children, including their three sons.

> Ilene's daughter told her teacher that her mother's live-in lover was making her do "funny things." Ilene told the child protection worker, who intervened after the teacher reported the remark, that if her daughter's report were true, it was the daughter's fault for being provocative. She further stated that "it" had happened to her in her childhood, that she had gotten over it, and her daughter would too.

Pat, an attractive seventeen-year-old, sought counseling because "my mother is smothering me." Pat's parents had divorced when she was young, and her mother was excessively dependent on her from then on. She forced Pat to sleep with her because she was afraid. Over the years sexual activity had progressed from holding her to fondling and masturbating her. Pat knew the behavior was inappropriate but didn't talk about it because she was afraid her mother would abandon her.

Self-damaging behavior. According to Courtois (1988), "the goals and motivations of different types of self-damaging behaviors vary markedly and differ by degree of seriousness; however, all involve some measure of self-directed hatred and rage often operating at an unconscious level" (p. 301). Self-damaging behavior is more pronounced in a sexually victimized population (Briere & Runtz, 1986), particularly for female victims, who tend to direct their rage inward, in comparison with males, who tend to direct it outward (Carmen, Rieker, & Mills, 1984). Self-damaging behavior may be either the cause or the consequence of a crisis. For example, a survivor's suicide attempt may cause her to seek help. She may attempt suicide as a consequence of some other crisis or when suffering intensive post-trauma symptomatology. Self-damaging behavior includes self-sabotage, self-defeat, and self-neglect; unnecessary risks and "accidents"; addictive and compulsive behaviors; self-abusive relationships and sexual practices; self-mutilation; suicidality; and death (Courtois, 1988).

Adrienne cut her arms and legs repeatedly with a razor blade because her limbs "had not protected her from being abused." Her father used to pin her down while forcing fellatio and intercourse on her. She made repeated trips to the local emergency room for stitches to repair her cuts. Eventually, she was referred to emergency mental health services for evaluation.

Members of the community mental health emergency response team were shocked and saddened to learn that a sexual abuse survivor who was also a battered woman had been murdered by her husband in front of their children. The team had worked intensively with her for several months as she made numerous unsuccessful attempts to leave him. Tragically, she had always returned because she was "supposed to be with him no matter what."

Pam was addicted to alcohol and drugs. Every year she overdosed during the Christmas holidays and required emergency treatment and detoxification. When this annual holiday pattern was identified and explored, she reported that her mother had died at Christmas when she was seven. Sexual abuse by her father had begun at about that time. Her overdoses were an anniversary reaction to both events. From a very young age, she had used drugs to become numb and to cope.

Other-damaging behavior. Although male survivors are more prone to act out against others than are females (Carmen, Rieker, & Mills, 1984), some female survivors are violent and abusive toward family members and others. Courtois (1988) listed the following behaviors as a continuum of other-damaging acts: inability to sustain an intimate relationship and inadequate parenting; abuse, deprivation, and neglect; physical abuse; sexual abuse; the killing of pets; and homicide. Like self-damaging behavior, other-damaging behavior may be the cause for seeking emergency assistance or may be the consequence of post-traumatic symptoms.

Audrey called her therapist from the local airport to let her know she had booked a flight to her parents' hometown and intended to kill them. She had just learned of her parents' continued physical, sexual, and emotional abuse of other members of the family and felt the only way that she could stop them would be to kill them.

Susan's son and daughter had been reported to child protective services for obvious neglect and apparent physical abuse. They were dirty and unkempt and had bruises on their arms and legs. Susan admitted she was aware of their condition but did not seem overly concerned. She told the investigator that they would have to get by because they were burdens to her and she was doing the best she could do. No one had ever offered her assistance when she had been beaten and sexually violated as a child and she had gotten by. So could they.

Other environmental triggers. Events in the environment can evoke reactions that precipitate crises. For example, the pervasive media attention and coverage of child sexual abuse in recent years has been highly disruptive for some survivors. Although most of them applaud the fact that incest and molestation are finally being discussed, it becomes more difficult for them to repress and dissociate their abuse. Additionally, the particular way a story is reported or the details of a particular case may intensify their reactions.

Other less directly related events can also serve as cues. Anniversary dates, certain geographical locations, activities, gestures, smells, tastes, body styles, body positions (whether sexual or not), and sexual behavior may trigger a strong emotional response. Medical and other physical treatments can also wake kinesthetic memories of abuse, especially when the abuse occurred when the child was at a preverbal level of development. Such treatments include medical examinations (particularly gynecological, rectal, and breast), any type of invasive test or procedure, surgery, hospitalization (psychiatric or medical), drug treatment, acupuncture, massage, psychodrama, and movement therapy.

Elly was molested by her brother and by a male gynecologist. She avoided gynecological check-ups for years because she was afraid of being abused again. At the urging of her therapist, she scheduled an examination. She had flashbacks of both abuse episodes during the exam and for the next several weeks.

JoAnne had a vague recollection that something had happened between her and her uncle when she was a young child. Her uncle is six-feet, two-inches tall and weighs approximately 250 pounds. While riding on the subway one day, a man sat next to her who reminded her of her uncle because he was so large. This event triggered recall of the abuse experience and strong anxiety reactions.

Barbara and her husband waited until marriage to have sex. On the first night of their honeymoon, when they attempted intercourse, Barbara threw her husband off the bed and was paralyzed with fear. She dissociated and it took hours before she returned to normal. This same pattern occurred every time sex was attempted, which caused the couple to seek sex therapy.

Recollection, Disclosure, Confrontation, Reporting and Criminal-Justice Crises

The disclosure of ongoing incest or molestation usually causes a crisis (see chapter 4). Recollection, confrontation, reporting, and involvement in the criminal justice system can also be stressful enough to provoke crisis reactions, because these activities threaten the secrecy and silence of the abuse process.

Recollection. Courtois (1988) states that the recollection or reexperiencing of the abusive event is stressful and anxiety-provoking for many survivors. "For some, it may create a secondary crisis since it symbolizes losing control and losing that which allowed the survivor to function. Loosened control can feel life-threatening and lead to self-destructive or self-mutilative gestures" (p. 140).

> Linda read a newspaper story about a woman in her community who committed suicide after writing about her abuse in her diary. In the diary entry, the woman mentioned lying in bed at night being terrified of the light appearing around her bedroom door as her stepfather entered her room to abuse her. That image—the light around the door—caused Linda's spontaneous recollection of previously repressed aspects of her own abuse at the hands of her brother. She was overwhelmed and felt that she, like the woman in the story, needed to die.

"Remembering may symbolize disloyalty and betrayal of the family, leading to a need for self-punishment. All current relationships, especially those with family members, may be called into question when abuse memories surface" (Courtois, 1988, p. 140). When memories come back, they may be so awful or so distressing to the survivor that she may wish that she had not remembered. It is not uncommon for survivors to "re-forget" some memories after achieving recall.

Disclosure. Issues involving the disclosure of ongoing abuse are discussed in chapter 4. Disclosure of past abuse is discussed here. Although disclosure of incest or molestation is not uncomfortable or stressful for all survivors, it is for most. Because of poor or ineffective responses when the survivors disclosed the abuse in the past, the survivor may experience a crisis state when attempting to disclose. When a child or adolescent discloses and is blamed or receives an ineffective response, she typically recants her story (Summit, 1983), which, in turn, makes later disclosure more difficult. For these reasons, the sexual abuse is often hidden during therapy.

When disclosure occurs or is elicited in therapy, the client may be emotionally overwhelmed and experience a crisis. The therapist should encourage disclosure and react to it in a calm, receptive, nonjudgmental, and empathic way while offering reassurance, validation, and support. The therapist should also forewarn the survivor that disclosures often cause strong emotional reactions and that she is not going crazy if she reacts in this way. The therapist should encourage her to return to therapy to talk about these reactions.

> Joreen disclosed a history of being abused by her brother and uncle to her therapist. She left the session feeling relieved but soon felt afraid that her therapist now thought she was disgusting. She decided never to return to therapy and never to discuss the abuse with anyone again.

Disclosure to family members initiates various reactions. Some disclosure is met with a highly empathic and concerned response and may even result in the disclosure of other abuse in the family. On the other hand, disclosure can also be met with implied or overt hostility on the part of one or more family members and with denial and insinuations that the survivor is crazy to suggest such an awful thing about a member of the family. Ideally, disclosure of past abuse to family members should be carefully prepared and planned. Unfortunately, many disclosures are made impulsively or without regard for the possible consequences. Although a survivor may have changed markedly since the time of the abuse, the family is not likely to have made similar changes unless some type of crisis or intervention has forced them to change.

> After watching a television show on sexual abuse, Charlotte decided to disclose to her mother that her stepfather had abused her throughout childhood. She made this disclosure impulsively without much anticipation of her mother's possible response and without a support system in place. Her mother responded to her disclosure first with shocked silence and then with some support. When her mother confronted the stepfather with the allegation, at first he denied it. Subsequently he made a serious suicide attempt. Charlotte felt an overwhelming sense of guilt for causing such an awful problem in her family.

According to Courtois (1988), *confrontation*

> goes beyond disclosure and builds upon it. While disclosure involves exposing the occurrence of incest, confrontation involves challenging the perpetrator and other family members to face the truth about it. It can involve a diversity of actions: expressing anger, hurt, and other emotions; questioning reasons and motives for the family circumstances, the abuse and any lack of assistance; determining why the survivor was selected for victimization; exposing the toll the incest took on her life; demanding recognition of aftereffects, accountability, apology, and sometimes restitution and family treatment; and preventing further abuse in the family (p. 331).

Because confrontation threatens the *status quo* of the incestuous situation more than disclosure does, it has a greater potential for negative outcome, including violence. Indirect confrontation, whether in group or individual therapy through role play, psychodrama, a letter, or an audio- or videotape, offers a better chance of a positive response than does direct confrontation. In any event, confrontation, like disclosure, should be carefully planned and should include the anticipation of various reactions. As a general rule, confrontation is not recommended when the response is likely to be violent and abusive.

> John returned to his parents' home one night and confronted his drunken father about years of previous sexual and physical abuse of all members of the family. That night his father beat him so viciously that he required medical attention. He also threatened to kill John if he ever said anything like that again.

Reporting of sexual abuse usually leads to the involvement of various social agencies. For adult survivors, reporting most often occurs when another child is currently being abused in the family. The survivor might report the abuse or it might be reported by other family members or by outsiders, for example, the child's teacher. The act of reporting abuse and the ensuing investigation creates a crisis for the family because it stimulates feelings of shame and threatens the denial process. Therapists should inform adult survivors of the possible consequences of reporting, including the fact that it might make the situation worse rather than better. In many communities, child protective services departments are deluged with reports of abuse to the point that staff are not available to investigate allegations adequately. Moreover, most communities have not yet developed comprehensive treatment programs that ensure support and effective treatment to all members of the family.

> Julie's niece, Mary, disclosed to Julie that her father (Julie's brother) had been molesting her. Julie reported the abuse to child protective services. Julie was especially concerned because her brother had abused her when they were adolescents; she was determined that what happened to her should not be allowed to happen to anyone else. The investigation was begun immediately but was not completed for months. Neither Mary nor her father were removed from the home; eventually, Mary said that she had made the whole thing up. She didn't want anyone else asking her questions and she grew quiet and withdrawn. Julie became enraged and depressed about the inadequate response and was frantic for someone to understand her concerns.

Finally, some survivors have filed *lawsuits* against the perpetrator and other nonprotective family members. Despite the fact that these civil actions are currently restricted by the statute of limitations in most states, they have been initiated by increasing numbers of survivors. The survivor who pursues such a course must be fully prepared for possible consequences and for the publicity that might accompany the filing of such a lawsuit. Suing a family member in a public forum is newsworthy in many communities and may lead to intensive media coverage. This attention may cause severe adverse reactions, even in adult survivors who anticipate it.

> Judy sued her stepfather for raping her repeatedly in childhood and sued her mother for negligence and nonprotection. She initially felt good about this action, but when the media in her community began to publicize both the case and the details of her stepfather's abuse, she came under strong family pressure to drop the suit. She was hospitalized because her degree of rage and depression became unmanageable. Finally, she dropped the suit because it was too stressful.

Issues That Arise in Therapy

Issues that arise in therapy, some of which have been discussed, may precipitate a crisis. When symptoms of abuse that are presented in a disguised fashion either at intake or later in treatment cause the therapist to speculate about possible abuse, a crisis may ensue. The survivor may feel threatened by a therapist who is aware of her defenses and who dares to suggest that she speak about the unspeakable.

> Pauline had been in therapy for two years and had never made an overt presentation of her multiple personality disorder (MPD). She presented many dissociative symptoms, causing her therapist to suspect MPD and to attempt to elicit alter personalities. Pauline was relieved that the "secret"

was known but was terrified that her therapist might use this knowledge against her and that she would no longer be able to escape. The diagnosis led to several episodes of self-mutilation.

Sudden recall of repressed memories and reexperiencing phenomena can be traumatic. The knowledge that close relatives and valued individuals perpetrated abuse may cause great distress.

During therapy, Sarah experienced images and body pain indicative of sexual abuse at a very early age. At first, her images were hazy impressions of a woman holding her down. Later, the images and accompanying rectal pain and stomach cramps caused her to recall her mother's excessive use of enemas as a means of punishing her for crying too much. Sarah spent weeks in a shocked state as she struggled to come to terms with these memories. Although her mother had always been cold to her, she recoiled from the thought that she had abused her in this way.

Grief and loss often follow the recollection and acceptance of past abuse and the reattribution of responsibility to the abuser. Adult survivors reexperience pain over the loss of childhood, innocence, trust, and identity ("I'm not the person I might have been"), the loss of potential (interpersonally, sexually, and occupationally), and the loss of family solidarity and responsible parenting. As a survivor resolves past incest issues, she needs to change dysfunctional patterns of relating to others. To do so, she may have to discard relationships that no longer meet her needs. She may need to distance herself from her family of origin, particularly when family members have not changed their old patterns. These losses may in turn stimulate feelings of rejection and abandonment and thus precipitate crisis reactions.

In therapy, Jill went through weeks of crying and grieving for the loss of the "little girl within." Her father had been alcoholic and abusive, and her mother unavailable. As an adult, she had had a series of meaningless, abuse-filled relationships with both men and women. She mourned for the lost potential of her life and for her past inability to find a relationship that was emotionally satisfying.

Finally, the minicrises of the therapy process itself (see chapter 4) and transference reactions to the therapy process and relationship may contribute to the development of larger crises. In fact, some authors (Bass & Davis, 1988; Courtois, 1988) discuss how "symptoms often get worse before they get better" in incest and molestation treatment; such reactions are to be expected as a normal part of the process. Bass and Davis even labeled this part of the process as the "emergency phase" and further noted that as the therapy progresses the emergency phase can be expected to recur. The therapist should prepare clients in advance for this likelihood.

After several months of therapy for past sexual abuse, Angela was obsessed by thoughts, memories, and feelings. She couldn't get the abuse out of her mind. She wrote obsessively but otherwise could not concentrate, eat, or sleep. She was tense and edgy and withdrew from her friends.

Survivors may experience crises related to specific issues in their relationship with the therapist or that they project onto the therapist. For example, if the therapist takes a vacation, the client may experience the therapist's absence as evidence that the therapist does not care about the survivor, or gestures or expressions of the therapist may remind the client of parents or other significant individuals. Survivors may project their own negative self-perception onto the therapist and believe that the therapist rejects, blames, or is disgusted by them for their past abuse experience.

> Carolyn became more and more agitated at the thought of her therapist's upcoming pregnancy leave. She began to believe that her therapist hated her and was trying to get rid of her now that she was going to have a baby. Despite her therapist's reassurances that she was not taking leave because she did not care, Carolyn continued to feel mistrustful and enraged. She began missing her remaining regularly scheduled therapy appointments.

In summary, many events and issues contribute to the crisis reactions and needs of the adult survivor of incest or molestation. It should be noted that many other idiosyncratic reasons may account for crisis reactions.

Guidelines for Crisis Treatment of Adult Survivors

The crisis intervention theory and strategies outlined in other chapters of this volume are certainly applicable to adult survivors of incest or molestation. However, they may require some modification to respond adequately to the post-traumatic component of crisis presentation. The crisis worker optimally receives training in the dynamics of child sexual abuse and its aftereffects and in the psychobiological reactions that make up the traumatic stress response, including the phasic alternation so characteristic of traumatic reactions. The practitioner must assess the survivor's reactions according to the phase—denial–numbing or intrusive–repetitive—in which they fall in order to tailor treatment strategies and respond empathically. The practitioner must also provide information to the survivor in crisis. Many traumatic reactions make the survivor feel as though she is going crazy, or she may have been told repeatedly by the family that "something is wrong with her." Information about sexual abuse and post-traumatic adaptations and responses may significantly assuage a survivor's feelings of anxiety and panic.

As with other crises, the goal of intervention is stabilization. The mental health practitioner attempts to restore the survivor to her precrisis level of functioning as quickly as possible by offering support and the opportunity for ventilation. Strategies are selected according to the severity of the crisis. In an acute crisis, in which suicide, homicide, or battering is possible and the survivor is not capable of acting on her own behalf, psychological first aid with a directive stance on the part of the helper is necessary. Hospitalization or some other protective shelter may be advised. When such risk is low and the survivor appears capable of acting on her own behalf, a more facilitative approach may be used. Slaikeu (1984) has referred to the components of psychological first aid: (1) making psychological contact, (2) exploring the dimensions of the problem, (3) examining possible solutions, (4) assisting in taking concrete action, and (5) follow-up. (These are similar to the guidelines outlined in chapter 1 of this volume.)

Liles and O'Brien (chapter 4) present the types of responses most helpful to the child victim experiencing the crisis of disclosure, reminding practitioners that they are working with persons who are experiencing shame. Consequently, the therapist should approach these clients respectfully and in a noncontrolling manner. Such an approach meets the standards of post-traumatic therapy as articulated by Ochberg (1988) as well as the therapeutic stance of Fossum and Mason (1986) for working with shamed individuals. The helper must be calm, noncondemnatory, accepting, and empathic, even when listening to the horrors of abuse or when responding to a distressing crisis. The specific suggestions made by Liles and O'Brien in chapter 4 for children are applicable for adult survivors as well. Many adult survivors are engulfed in the same feelings they had as children, that is, anxiety, guilt, depression, confusion, and fear.

Crisis therapy or stress response therapy should be used as a follow-up to psychological emergency first aid. These approaches are more extensive in scope and duration and are geared to helping the survivor integrate the crisis and its impact into the various areas of her life—the behavioral, affective, somatic, interpersonal, and cognitive—in a way that increases healthy rather than maladaptive reorganization. Therapy assists the survivor in (1) physically surviving the crisis experience, (2) identifying and expressing feelings that accompany the crisis, (3) gaining cognitive mastery over the crisis, and (4) making behavioral and interpersonal adjustments to the crisis. Crisis therapy is multimodal, utilizing techniques from various therapeutic orientations, and has been found to be most effective when implemented during the period of disorganization caused by the crisis (Slaikeu, 1984, pp. 117–118). Jehu (1988) discusses specific approaches and techniques useful in cognitive restructuring of the belief system of adult survivors and in working with the interpersonal aftereffects of abuse.

Horowitz (1986) emphasizes choosing techniques and ordering treatment priorities according to whether the survivor is in the numbing–denial or intrusive–repetitive phase of the traumatic stress response. In the numbing–denial phase, cathartic–abreactive techniques can be used to help the survivor process the crisis and her reactions to it. Although denial serves as a survival mechanism for the victim, it becomes maladaptive when it impedes processing and resolution of the trauma. To break through the denial–numbing reactions, the practitioner should encourage recollection and description as well as emotional catharsis while informing the survivor of possible emotional repercussions. Educating the survivor about child sexual abuse and post-traumatic stress responses provides her with both information and reassurance.

Survivors in the intrusive–repetitive phase require the practitioner to respond differently because the survivor is being flooded with recall and affect. Rest, containment, and supportive techniques are needed to counter the intensity of flashbacks, sleep disturbances, hyperarousal, and startle responses. Because of the intensity of these symptoms, survivors may be very distraught. These symptoms are especially uncomfortable and frightening when they occur or recur suddenly and appear to be unrelated to an identifiable stimulus. Symptoms are also very upsetting when they interrupt a sustained period of improved mood and functioning. Providing information about the normalcy of alternating symptoms and the likelihood of diminishing intensity over time offers reassurance to the adult survivor. Many stress management techniques can be applied to treat these symptoms: emotional ventilation, external structuring and problem solving, stress inoculation training, social supports, desensitization, and relaxation.

To summarize, the foregoing reviews the most common types of crisis presentation made by adult survivors of incest and molestation. Because of the traumatic nature of child sexual abuse and the lack of effective intervention available to victimized children until recently, most adult survivors suffer both chronic and delayed aftereffects from their abuse. Adult survivors often present in crisis. Practitioners involved in crisis intervention must understand both the dynamics of child sexual abuse and post-traumatic reactions in order to offer appropriate intervention. A calm and accepting response on the part of the practitioner as well as validation and education about incest and molestation offers immediate reassurance to a survivor in crisis. The choice of subsequent intervention strategies depends upon the risk potential of the survivor and the phase of traumatic stress in which the survivor presents. Soothing and containment techniques are appropriate for the intrusive–repetitive phase and expressive and cathartic techniques for the numbing–denial phase.

References

American Psychiatric Association. (1987). *Diagnostic and statistical manual of mental disorders* (3rd ed., rev.). Washington, DC: Author.

Bass, E., & Davis, L. (1988). *The courage to heal: A guide for women survivors of child sexual abuse*. New York: Harper and Row.

Briere, J. (1984, April). *The effects of childhood sexual abuse on later psychological functioning: Defining a postsexual abuse syndrome*. Paper presented at the Third National Conference on the Sexual Victimization of Children, Children's Hospital National Medical Center, Washington, DC.

Briere, J., & Runtz, M. (1986). Suicidal thoughts and behaviors in former sexual abuse victims. *Canadian Journal of Behavioral Science*, *18*, 413–423.

Browne, A., & Finkelhor, D. (1986). Impact of child sexual abuse: A review of the literature. *Psychological Bulletin*, *99*, 66–77.

Carmen, E. H., Rieker, P. R., & Mills, T. (1984). Victims of violence and psychiatric illness. *American Journal of Psychiatry*, *143*, 378–383.

Courtois, C. A. (1988). *Healing the incest wound: Adult survivors in therapy*. New York: W. W. Norton.

Evert, K., & Bijkerk, I. (1987). *When you're ready: A woman's healing from childhood physical and sexual abuse by her mother*. Walnut Creek, CA: Launch Press.

Finkelhor, D. (1984). *Child sexual abuse: New theory and research*. New York: Free Press.

Finkelhor, D., & Browne, A. (1985). The traumatic impact of child sexual abuse: A conceptualization. *American Journal of Orthopsychiatry*, *55*, 530–541.

Fossum, M. A., & Mason, M. J. (1986). *Facing shame*. New York: W. W. Norton.

Fraser, S. (1988). *My father's house: A memoir of incest and healing*. New York: Ticknor and Fields.

Gelinas, D. (1983). The persisting negative effects of incest. *Psychiatry*, *46*, 313–332.

Horowitz, M. J. (1986). *Stress response syndromes*. New York: Jason Aronson.

Jehu, D. (1988). *Beyond sexual abuse: Therapy with women who were childhood victims*. New York: John Wiley.

Kardiner, A. (1941). *The traumatic neuroses of war*. New York: P. Hoeber.

Maltz, W., & Holman, B. (1987). *Incest and sexuality*. Lexington, MA: Lexington Books.

Ochberg, F. M. (Ed.). (1988). *Post–traumatic therapy and victims of violence*. New York: Brunner/Mazel.

Rush, F. (1980). *The best kept secret: Sexual abuse of children*. Englewood Cliffs, NJ: Prentice Hall.

Russell, D. E. (1986). *The secret trauma: Incest in the lives of girls and women*. New York: Basic Books.

Slaikeu, K. A. (1984). *Crisis intervention*. Boston, MA: Allyn and Bacon.

Spiegel, D. (1988). Dissociation and hypnosis in post–traumatic stress disorders. *Journal of Traumatic Stress, 1*, 17–34.

Summit, R. (1982). Beyond belief: The reluctant discovery of incest. In M. Kirkpatrick (Ed.), *Women's sexual experience: Explorations of the dark continent*. New York: Plenum.

Summit, R. (1983). The child sexual abuse accommodation syndrome. *Child Abuse and Neglect, 7*, 177–193.

Tufts New England Medical Center, Division of Child Psychiatry (1984). *Sexually exploited children: Service and research project*. Final report for the Office of Juvenile Justice and Delinquency Prevention. Washington, DC: U.S. Department of Justice.

van der Kolk, B. (1986). *Psychological trauma*. Washington, DC: American Psychiatric Press.

Weinberg, K. (1955). *Incest behavior*. New York: Citadel Press.

6

Crisis Intervention with Victims and Perpetrators of Spouse Abuse

JOHN BREKKE

CRISIS INTERVENTION in the area of spouse abuse presents the clinician with complexities, challenges, and apparent contradictions. It is difficult to understand why a woman whose husband has broken her ribs will not disclose the abuse, leave her husband, or perceive herself to be in crisis. Conversely, it is difficult to comprehend an abuser's insistence that he does not need help after he has recently broken his partner's arm or caused a miscarriage.

Although neither of these scenarios is meant to be prototypical, they do contain elements that are commonly encountered in spouse abuse cases (Coleman, Weinman, & Hsi, 1980; Coleman, 1980; Martin, 1976; Roy, 1982; Walker, 1979, 1984; Gelles & Straus, 1988). They also point to the need to view these situations in context by examining the correlates to spouse abuse and by exploring common and pernicious fallacies about the victims and perpetrators of this crime. Consistent with this orientation, this chapter presents strategies, techniques, and case illustrations of crisis intervention in spouse abuse.

Definitions and Incidence of Spouse Abuse

Spouse abuse is defined as the intentional use of physical force or psychological abuse by one spouse to hurt or attempt to hurt his or her partner. It ranges from threats, slaps, and punches to attacks with a knife or gun. Forms of psychological abuse (for example, screaming, swearing, belittling, and extreme jealousy) are included in this definition because of the debilitating effects of such abuse (Pagelow, 1981, 1984; Walker, 1979) and the tendency for psychological abuse to escalate into physical abuse (Straus, Gelles, & Steinmetz, 1980).

This chapter focuses on wife abuse for the following reasons. First, although some evidence indicates that wives engage in almost as many psychologically and physically aggressive acts as do husbands, husbands use more severe forms of violence more often; wives sustain more physical injuries and require more medical attention as a result of their husband's assaults (Steinmetz, 1977; Straus, 1980). Second, it has been estimated that at least 50 percent to 75 percent of marital violence on the part of women is in self-defense (Straus, 1980; Saunders, 1986). Third, there is evidence to indicate that men underreport their own use of violence to a considerably greater extent than do women (Bulcroft & Straus,

1975). Fourth, women are locked into marriage, both psychologically and materially, to a far greater extent than are men (Straus, 1980; Kalmuss & Straus, 1982). Fifth, evidence indicates that violence against wives is inextricably tied to the oppression of women. Straus (1980) concludes that "women are the predominant victims of marital violence" (p. 681) and Saunders (1986) argues that the term "husband battering" is a misnomer.

How widespread is wife abuse? According to data from a nationally representative sample (Straus et al., 1980), approximately 30 percent of all American marriages experience at least one violent incident; these researchers estimate that 50 percent is a more realistic figure. It is also estimated that 1.8 million wives a year are severely and frequently beaten by their husbands. Thus wife abuse is a widespread problem that cuts across socioeconomic levels. Studies also suggest that similar rates of violence occur in dating relationships (Arias, Samos, & O'Leary, 1987; Carlson, 1987; Cate, Henton, Koval, Christopher, & Lloyd, 1982; Makepeace, 1981). Hence, clinicians are likely to treat many unidentified perpetrators and victims of domestic violence, which has implications for crisis intervention.

Correlates to Wife Abuse

Recent theoretical and empirical reviews of the literature on spouse abuse (Gelles, 1980; Gelles & Straus, 1981, 1988; Saunders & Brekke, 1985) as well as conceptual efforts to organize the correlates to spouse abuse (Carlson 1984) delineate three separate but related levels of influence that account for wife abuse: sociocultural factors, dyadic factors, and individual factors (see also Levine, 1986; Witt, 1987). A brief review of the correlates to wife abuse facilitates discussion of the perplexing situations that workers encounter in this area of practice as well as underscores the importance of crisis intervention strategies that are presented.

At the sociocultural level, cross-cultural studies in the United States indicate that the low status of women and patriarchal norms contribute significantly to the incidence of wife abuse. Interestingly, wife abuse is most prevalent in states where the legal, political, occupational, and educational status of women is high but is also prevalent in states where the patriarchal norms favoring women's subjugation are high (Dobash & Dobash, 1979).

At the dyadic or relationship level, many interesting hypotheses concerning the correlates of wife abuse have been suggested. However, up to now, only two hypotheses have withstood empirical scrutiny: (1) high levels of general marital conflict and nonegalitarian decision-making in marriage contribute to wife abuse and (2) relationships in which the educational and occupational status of the partners is unequal, especially when the woman has greater status than the man or when the male is an underachiever, tend to experience more wife abuse than do relationships in which these conditions do not exist.

Five characteristics seem to typify batterers: (1) aggression in the family of origin in the form of severe physical punishment, child abuse, or witnessing spouse abuse, (2) lack of assertiveness with people in general and with the spouse in particular, which may be manifested as aggression or passivity, (3) rigid stereotypical and patriarchal attitudes toward women, (4) social isolation, and (5) low self-esteem. Clinical observation also suggests that jealousy; dependency on the partner to satisfy emotional needs; and the inability to discriminate among various emotional states, thus causing all emotions to be labeled as anger, are also evident in abusers.

When treating a male batterer, it is important to keep in mind that he is not necessarily a pathological maniac. In fact, the incidence of psychopathology among batterers is no higher than it is in the male population in general (Fagan, Stewart, & Hansen, 1983). He may be a bigoted lawyer or a charming carpenter. Recent evidence, however, suggests that the majority of batterers may have personality disturbances (Hamberger & Hastings, 1986).

Extensive research on battered women has been undertaken. The characteristics of the victim have been examined and compared with nonbattered women in an effort to delineate predisposing factors or to understand the effects of abuse. In both instances the clinician and researcher face the same question: In the absence of accurate historical or longitudinal data, do depression, hostility, passive aggressiveness, or borderline tendencies in the victim represent the causes or effects of abuse? How one interprets such information has a dramatic impact on one's understanding of the problem and on intervention strategies.

Historically, battered women have been blamed for their abuse, as indicated by the empirical and clinical search for factors that predispose these women to victimization. However, no empirical support exists for the "masochism hypothesis" or the notion that battered women enjoy the abuse or seek partners who will abuse them. Furthermore, two studies that examined battered women over time—one based on the retrospective examination of medical records (Stark, Flitcraft, & Frazier, 1981) and the other on personality changes after emancipation from the batterer (Moore, 1982)—found that the mental health problems of the victim began after the onset of the abuse, and that once the woman was removed from the abusive situation, positive personality changes occurred. Evidence also suggests that batterers have a history of violent marriages or relationships more often than do their partners (Walker, 1984).

If workers are not dealing with masochistic women who are predisposed to victimization, then why do victims remain in an abusive relationship? Thanks to the existence of shelters for battered women, many women do leave in an effort to find help and end the abuse (Bowker, 1983; Gondolf, 1988). Unfortunately, shelters can help only a small percentage of women in need at any given time, and many women end up returning to their abusive spouse. Current research indicates that the more severe the abuse and the resulting injuries, the more likely the woman will leave the batterer permanently. On the other hand, the fear of being murdered may keep the woman in the abusive situation.

Other factors that contribute to a woman staying with an abusive partner include psychological and material dependency on the continuation of the marriage, a perceived lack of alternatives, confusion about feminine gender identity, traditional religious beliefs, and lack of employment or employable skills. Another significant factor is the often neglectful, uninformed, and victim-blaming responses of social service, mental health, and legal practitioners and institutions (Bass & Rice, 1979; Davis, 1984).

To summarize, some of the factors that cause wife abuse also contribute to the victim not leaving the abusive male. In order to fully comprehend the demands and strategies of crisis intervention in domestic violence, it is necessary to briefly review the effects of wife abuse on the victim.

Effects of Spouse Abuse on the Woman

Finkelhor (1983) outlined several commonly reported effects of spouse abuse on women. Violence against wives usually occurs in the context of psychological abuse and exploitation—a kind of brainwashing. The perpetrator attempts to gain control of and manipulate the victim's perception of reality. Victims are told that they are incompetent, hysterical, and/or frigid. This distortion of reality and the woman's self-image is one of the most devastating effects of wife abuse. To compound matters, the perpetrator usually threatens the physical well-being of the woman if she reveals the abuse to anyone.

Victims often blame themselves for the abuse, harbor feelings of shame and humiliation, and are unwilling or unable to reveal their victimization to others. After a long period of abuse, a kind of entrapment occurs, in which the victim tends to return to the abuser or even to show an extreme loyalty to him. These effects, however, should be viewed in the context of the pathological responses of institutions to battered women. Battered women are often suspicious and mistrustful of mental health workers or persons in positions of social authority. Victims and perpetrators rarely seek out or encounter mental health professionals soon after the abuse begins. Hence, it is unlikely that victims will be seen who do not show some or all of the long-term effects of abuse. Wife abuse is created and sustained by complex social and individual factors. Services to domestic-violence clients must be viewed in the context of a patriarchal and violent culture that has traditionally turned a blind eye to the problem of wife battering and that has often blamed the victim.

Crisis Intervention with Battered Women

Crisis intervention with battered women occurs in two contexts: (1) when the battering is a part of the presenting problem and (2) when it is not part of the presenting problem but emerges as a result of client disclosure or practitioner detection. In the second instance, the crisis, in a sense, unfolds during treatment. In many instances, the crisis may unfold in the context of problems apparently unrelated to the abuse and, at the beginning of therapy, with no outward signs or symptoms of crisis.

Case Examples

The following case examples illustrate this process of client disclosure and practitioner detection.

> Mary, a thirty-six year-old elementary school teacher, was married and the mother of two children, ages ten and twelve. Mary came to the clinic because of problems with her job and her inability to concentrate. Her principal had suggested that she seek counseling because her performance at school was faltering. She had agitated interactions with parents of stu-

dents. Her job was not in danger, but given her typically good performance, the principal was worried.

During the intake session, Mary concurred with the principal's perception of her work performance and admitted that she, too, was concerned. She said that she was having problems with her oldest child, a son, who was withdrawing at home and acting out at school. He had recently started attending a private school. She thought that his behavior might be merely a phase, but was concerned nonetheless. She also reported a recent loss of sexual interest in her husband.

The second session was spent in assessing the problem and in prioritizing a problem focus. Midway through the third session, when parental interaction with the son was being explored, she began to cry. In response to the counselor's empathy and probing for further problems at home, she revealed that her husband had been abusive to her for the past eight years of their marriage and had recently attacked their son. At this point in the session, she was extremely anxious, unfocused, and angry. Crisis intervention was initiated.

This case example illustrates several points. First, victims of wife abuse learn to cope with violence. Battered wives typically go through a process of "violence norming," wherein they show no overt signs of crisis. However, when the victim feels safe in a therapeutic relationship, she may, as in the case of Mary, experience a state of crisis. Some shelter workers report that after victims resolve the crisis of safety, they may experience a crisis of victimization in which symptoms of their trauma emerge. Second, the abuse is usually a carefully kept secret; victims may go to extreme lengths to deny or conceal it. Although this behavior may appear pathological to the worker, it should be viewed as an effect of abuse. Third, if a crisis emerges in this indirect way, the worker should not attribute the crisis to a problem with his or her professional performance. True, battered women are often subjected to incompetent and insensitive professional responses to their plight. Nevertheless, the fact that the abuse surfaces at all is probably a credit to the worker's sensitivity. Mary later stated that she revealed the abuse because she felt she would not be viewed as pathological. Finally, battered women often show a kind of strength and coping ability that is sometimes inconceivable to mental health professionals. Clearly, the client's coping skill should be used as a crisis intervention tool.

Carol, a twenty-nine-year-old woman who had been married to an accountant for six years, came to the agency complaining that she was not advancing in her secretarial job, about marital conflict over the decision to have children (her husband wanted them, she did not), and long-standing problems with authority figures that she connected to her vocational difficulties. She also stated that her husband did not want her to work full time. After seeing Carol four times, with no clear focus emerging from the sessions, the counselor probed for domestic violence using the procedures outlined by Brekke (1987). Gradually, Carol began to reveal more and more information. The abuse was largely psychological. However, it was severe and had recently escalated, as it had in the past, into pushing and slapping. She began to perceive the connection between the abuse and the problems she initially presented. After the seventh session, a violent incident occurred at home and she called the clinic in crisis.

Battered women sometimes do not label themselves as such and do not perceive the effect that the abuse is having on them. Therefore, the worker must sometimes define or even precipitate a crisis for the victim. Crisis, after all, is the subjective reaction to events in the client's life.

Techniques of Crisis Intervention

The battered woman in crisis is often diagnosed as having a personality or mental disorder. She may appear highly agitated, withdrawn, distracted, depersonalized, or, in extreme cases, exhibit borderline personality symptoms. Whatever her presenting behavioral symptoms, she is likely to be experiencing one or more of the following emotional reactions: helplessness, fear, embarrassment, anger, guilt, and fear of insanity (Resnik, 1976; Ball, 1977). The victim's helplessness may stem from repeated but unsuccessful attempts to change her or her partner's behavior in order to avoid violence. Encounters with insensitive friends, relatives, police, or counselors and living in an environment in which the victim is terrorized also contribute to feelings of helplessness. Fear is a normal reaction to repeated assault. Many battered women are embarrassed by the abuse, are ashamed that they have remained in the abusive situation, and fear life without a man. They are particularly sensitive to the judgments, explicit or tacit, of the worker.

Guilt results from the woman's belief that she has caused or provoked the abuse; she may go to great lengths to perceive her faults. All victims experience anger; some are able to express it and others repress and displace it as depression or somatization. The victim's experience of isolation and helplessness causes her to doubt her sanity; she may ask repeatedly whether the worker thinks she is insane. The woman is likely to be highly ambivalent and tentative in her willingness to self-disclose. It is also difficult for her to accept her partner's responsibility for the abuse, to commit to contracts or plans of action, or to become invested in a counseling relationship.

Sessions

The following sections outline strategies for time-limited crisis intervention with battered women. Session agendas and the corresponding worker tasks and qualities are summarized in tables 1–3.

Session 1. The battered woman typically experiences a range of emotional reactions at the beginning of treatment. She is likely to exhibit doubt concerning her perceptions of reality and the validity of her reactions. Often, she views

TABLE 1. **Session 1.**

Session tasks	*Worker qualities*
Allow client self-disclosure	Validating
Assess safety and danger of suicide	Nonjudgmental, empowering, nonpathologizing
Develop safety plan	Up-to-date with information
Provide information on legal options and social services	Able to balance expressive and instrumental session tasks
Reinforce motivation behind coming for help	

herself as pathological. The first task of the counselor is to allow the woman to disclose her abuse in as much detail as possible and to describe her cognitive and affective reactions to the abuse, including her feelings, thoughts, beliefs, and attributions of blame, no matter how confused, distorted, or irrational they may seem. The goal is to bring into the open that which has festered in isolation and to discover the precipitating event.

The counselor's task is to recognize and be empathic with *all* feelings, including thoughts and feelings that are self-blaming or "pathologizing," such as "I must be crazy" or "there is something terribly wrong with me." All of the victim's perceptions of her problem should be accepted, and *not* challenged until she feels invested in the therapeutic relationship. In addition to validation and reflection, the counselor must try to break through the woman's feelings of isolation by generalizing her plight and relating her reactions to the experiences of other abuse victims and to normal reactions to abuse. Accomplishing these tasks allows the worker to defuse the abuser's most effective weapon, that is, his ability to manipulate the victim's perceptions of reality by playing on her isolation and self-doubt.

An important task at this point is to keep the woman from viewing herself in pathological terms. The counselor should not, for example, ask the victim what she did to deserve the abuse or what she could have done to prevent it. The counselor should be careful to avoid implicitly blaming the victim by questioning the victim too early in the therapeutic relationship about her history of abusive relationships. Such questioning may imply that the victim seeks out abusers. This kind of history, if it exists, can be explored later if it is relevant. Recent research (Walker, 1984) suggests that abusers have a much higher rate of multiple violent relationships than do victims.

The counselor should also avoid pushing the victim into providing information about the abuse. The woman should be allowed to reveal as much as she feels comfortable revealing. Because victims are used to being pushed to their limits by the abuser, the worker must avoid doing the same.

During the first session, the worker should assess with the woman the urgency of her situation, including her present safety and the risk of suicide. The woman may want or need a safe environment. If this is so, she should be referred immediately to a shelter for battered women, or she should stay with a friend or relative. Most shelters will take children, although age or other restrictions may exist. The worker should inform the woman of such restrictions. If the woman decides to stay with a friend or relative, these persons should know about the abuse so that the woman does not feel she must maintain another secret and so that her hosts are better able to accept her condition. The woman should be encouraged to tell her husband that she has left, but should not reveal her location to him.

If the woman does not request or want a safe environment, the worker should develop a safety plan with the woman that allows for quick escape in the event of attack. In devising a safety plan, the victim is helped to protect herself while receiving the message that she does not have to tolerate abuse.

The safety plan consists of four components. The first component—a safe environment—assists the woman in selecting an environment that will be accepting, nonthreatening, and protective. The worker should elicit the details of the environment; that is, which friend or relative she is staying with, where that person lives, and whether she has asked her hosts if it is all right for her to use their home as an emergency shelter.

Second, how does the victim get to the safe environment? The woman should hide a set of car keys somewhere outside the house so that she can drive away even if the abuser takes her keys or purse. If a car is not available, then the bus schedule and correct route should be known. Taxis and friends can also be utilized. Regardless, it is essential that the woman have a strategy.

Third, the woman should have money set aside for an emergency. The money can be hidden outside with the keys. It should be enough to cover bus or taxi fare, and if possible, expenses for several days. If the budget is tight, the woman should attempt to hide a small amount each week.

Fourth, if children are involved, the mother should develop a signal to indicate that the safety plan should be executed, typically, a verbal or hand signal, by which the children are instructed to run to a designated place, for example, a neighbor's house, a schoolyard, or a park, to wait for their mother. Older children should clearly understand their responsibility for very young children.

A stash of clothing kept at the safe environment, and copies of the marriage and birth certificates, in case the woman becomes involved with legal or social service authorities, are also helpful. The abuser should not be told of the safety plan under any circumstances.

The counselor should help the woman organize and implement the safety plan. By helping the woman develop a specific plan, the worker helps engage the woman in actions designed to ensure her own safety and acts as an advocate for her. Although the plan may take time to implement, the first steps should be taken during the initial session.

The victim should also be given information about her legal status and options as well as services available to her. The woman should receive information on spouse-abuse laws, police procedures, and victim options. Many battered women are uninformed or have been misinformed about these issues. Many shelters for battered women have Women's Survival Cards, which consist of a list of relevant and available community resources for the woman in crisis. These cards are usually inexpensive; clinicians can obtain them by contacting a local shelter or feminist organization.

Clearly, the counselor's task is to have current and accurate information regarding formally stated procedures and services and how these services are implemented. For example, some states and counties have explicit spouse-abuse protocols; however, the police often may not implement these protocols and in some cases do not inform the victim of her rights and options. The woman needs to know what will happen so that she can be properly prepared. Again, this information can be obtained from a local shelter or feminist organization. Shelters are generally pleased to share information with sensitive clinicians, although the staff are almost always overworked and underpaid. The worker should provide this information to the woman without pressuring her into taking any particular course of action, although the consequences of each option might be discussed.

Finally, the worker should provide positive reinforcement to the woman for coming in and should restate his or her desire to help the woman develop the best course of action for her and to offer support. The worker should make an appointment with the woman to discuss her plans.

In addition to the tasks already discussed, two other strategies are crucial in work with battered women. First, the worker must be sensitive to maintaining a balance between the expressive and instrumental aspects of the session. In other words, although the woman's need to ventilate must be respected, detailed plans to ensure her safety are vital. The battered woman in crisis also experiences hope when she accomplishes concrete tasks.

Second, the worker should attempt to empower the victim. This term, often used in the feminist literature (Bograd, 1982; Van Den Bergh & Cooper, 1986), implies a style and philosophy of treatment. Empowerment requires counselors to use their implicit and explicit influence in the counseling relationship to nurture, support, and maintain the client's independent decision-making ability. It implies respect for the client's choices, no matter how dysfunctional the clinician may find them. The client should be assisted to make decisions by exploring the consequences of various actions. The counselor should disclose his or her biases, treating them as other options.

Session 2. Various factors work against a woman's leaving an abusive partner: material concerns, self-blame, unsympathetic institutional responses to her plight, and the abuser's loving contrition after a violent episode. Therefore, when beginning the second session with a battered woman, it is important to recognize that her acute reaction to the precipitating event might be over (whether it involved violence or not) and that her ambivalence toward decisive action may emerge. Nevertheless, the worker should reassess her safety and review the safety plan. Asking the victim how safe she feels and what can be done to increase her security is a direct way to begin this process. If the victim has not implemented the safety plan, it should not be assumed that she is sick or resistant. The worker should review the purpose and steps of the plan and discuss any difficulty the woman has had in accomplishing the tasks. Ambivalence and indecisiveness should be treated as effects of the abuse and should be openly discussed as such.

The victim may have numerous questions about the abuser. When these questions arise, it is helpful to remember the following points: (1) The abuser is not a consummate monster and has some endearing qualities (thus the victim is not crazy for caring about him); (2) the batterer is fully responsible for his violence—the victim is not—and nothing outside of self-defense justifies his use of violence; (3) the abuser is not likely to suddenly stop the violence, but will likely get worse unless he gets help; and (4) the most effective remedial action

TABLE 2. Session 2.

Session tasks	*Worker qualities*
Allow ventilation and provide support	Nonjudgmental, empowering, supporting
Reassess safety and adequacy of safety plan	Able to make biases explicit
Provide information and understanding of context and effects of violence	
Assess extent and frequency of violence	
Discuss options and consequences	

a victim can take may be to have her partner arrested or to contact a lawyer for legal assistance (Sherman & Berk, 1984; Bowker, 1983).

In this session, more accurate information about the extent and frequency of the abuse should be gained. Using a modified version of the Conflict Tactics Scale (Straus, 1979; Straus et al., 1980; Brekke, 1987; Saunders, 1982) is helpful. It is also important to obtain information about the victimization of other family members. These efforts may help reduce the victim's denial and reinforce her concerns for her own safety, but might also increase her shame at having remained in an abusive situation. Thus the clinician should convey a nonjudgmental attitude, no matter how severe or pervasive the abuse, while providing positive reinforcement to the victim for seeking help. If it is necessary to report child abuse, the worker must discuss this matter with the woman.

At some point, it is also important to explain the causes and consequences of spouse abuse in an effort to diminish the woman's sense of self-blame, mitigate concerns about her sanity, and to help her see the worker as someone who has more than a superficial understanding of her plight. It is also useful to assess the partner for possible alcoholism. A small percentage of batterers are addicts; such information may dramatically change the woman's strategies.

Finally, it is important to continue to discuss the options that are open to the woman and the consequences of her choices. She may have begun to realize that the worker cannot end the abuse; the ensuing disappointment can be counteracted by focusing on the victim's options, no matter how difficult she may perceive them to be. The worker should attempt to empower the woman throughout these sessions.

Sessions 3–5. During these sessions, the victim makes decisions regarding whether she will leave her partner or, having left, whether she will return. The decision to return to or remain with her partner may be evident when the woman does not return for treatment. If she keeps her appointments and openly discusses her decision to return to or stay with her partner, this decision should be respected and her legal and safety options should be reconsidered. A referral to a battered woman's group for support should be offered as well as continuing support should she wish to see the counselor again. If the victim decides to stay but demands that the batterer receive help, she needs to understand that his motivation will depend on her seriousness and the consequences for him if he fails to comply.

If the woman decides to leave the abuser, the worker should assist her with finding housing, child care, employment, and peer support. Assistance may

TABLE 3. **Sessions 3–5.**

Sessions tasks	*Worker qualities*
Allow emergence of direction with support	Empowering
Facilitate accurate perception of partner's motivation	Able to provide referral information
Make appropriate referrals	
Make client feel welcome to return for treatment	

take the form of referrals or recontracting for more sessions of individual or group work. A group approach is preferable after the crisis phase, but the worker must be sure that the group will meet the specific needs of the client. For example, some groups are designed to help women assert themselves while remaining in the home, whereas other groups are designed to help women consider their options after they have left their partners.

When working with the battered woman in crisis, the following observations and caveats are offered. First, the worker should be ready for surprises, for example, revelations of more serious or pervasive abuse, sudden flights into health, continued sexual contact with the abuser even if they are separated, or abrupt moves toward healthy independence followed by perplexing ambivalence. It is important to remember that the woman has been living in traumatizing circumstances, which may cause her behavior and perceptions to be erratic at times.

Several attitudinal and behavioral pitfalls should be avoided. First, the notion that the victim must leave or that the family must be saved at all costs can be extremely oppressive to the victim. Empowerment based on accurate information and assessment is essential; counselor biases on this issue should be made explicit so that the victim does not have to deal with a manipulative agenda on the part of an authority figure (the counselor).

Second, conjoint family or marital treatment is usually counterproductive to ending the abuse unless the abuse is minor and recent (Saunders, 1984; Bograd, 1982). Finally, if the worker simultaneously recognizes the batterer's violence as well as his qualities, which the woman might cherish, the worker will be able to empathize with the pain that the victim may experience if she decides to leave the batterer.

The clinician must avoid trying to take control of the situation by pushing the victim too hard in any direction. Also, listening to reports and descriptions of violence can sometimes produce extreme anxiety in the worker, regardless of how experienced the worker is. The worker should attempt to use this anxiety to build empathy for the victim, realizing that his or her anxiety is a fraction of the fear and anxiety the woman has experienced. It is appropriate for the worker to inform the client of intense reactions, especially if the worker begins to feel overwhelmed. Finally, it is imperative that the clinician avoid blaming the battered woman, lest the worker become an accomplice to her continuing victimization.

Case Examples

Crisis intervention with the battered woman presents the clinician with a challenging set of demands and opportunities. It must be kept in mind that treatment might not result in the end of the abuse or in treatment for the abuser. However, a nonpathological and empowering counseling experience serves as the initial step in a woman's journey toward recovery, protection, and emancipation.

> Sue, a thirty-seven-year-old mother of two children from a previous marriage, came to the clinic after having asked her husband of six months, Al, to move out of the house. He had abused her once before they were married but promised not to do it again. They had recently moved to a large urban area that presented Al with good job opportunities. He had slapped her and thrown her against a wall before they moved and had broken her nose upon arrival at their new house.

Sue was visibly nervous, perplexed, and feeling guilty during the initial interview. She was preoccupied with thoughts about how stupid she was for marrying Al and moving across the country with him, especially after he had abused her. She felt that asking him to leave the house was a good idea, but was concerned about his welfare and whether she had done all she could before asking him to leave. The precipitating event, in fact, was her ambivalence about whether she should take him back or not.

She was encouraged to focus on her present situation rather than on the wisdom of marrying Al and moving in with him. She said she felt safe in her apartment but that he called her every day to find out what she felt and to try to convince her to take him back. Since moving she had found a good job; the worker praised Sue for her strength and resourcefulness. Sue's options, as she saw them, were to take Al back, to divorce him, or to postpone a decision until he had gone for help. Although she did not have much physical contact with Al, a safety plan was worked out nonetheless. The worker told her of the police and judicial procedures in her area.

An appointment was set for the following week; in the meantime, Sue was asked to consider her options and any problems she had with these options. The worker commented on her strength in asking Al to leave, her ability to continue working through this crisis, and her strong relationship with her children.

Over the next four weeks, Sue vacillated between divorce and taking Al back. They even spent a passionate night together at his apartment. Crisis intervention continued to focus on what Sue wanted to do, the options she had, and the consequences of each course of action. The worker continually told her that the abuse was Al's responsibility. After discussing various facets of Al's abuse and the likelihood that it would recur unless he got help, Sue decided to insist that Al get help before they discussed their future together. She felt defenseless against Al's verbal pressure, so she and the worker role-played conversations. She was able to assert herself, and Al went to a clinic for batterers. Sue was then referred to a group for battered women in transition.

After tiring of Al's insistence that she guarantee that they would live together after he completed treatmen,. Sue went ahead with divorce proceedings. Al dropped out of treatment. Sue remained in the women's group and continued to do well after divorcing A.

Nancy came to the clinic depressed, tearful, and feeling somewhat depersonalized. She had lived with her partner, Jim, for eight years; they had a four-year-old son, Matt. Jim had always been psychologically abusive to Nancy, but had become physically abusive after losing his job two years previously as a result of an industrial accident. Nancy worked as a secretary. She was afraid that Jim might begin hitting Matt, who had recently begun hitting Nancy and acting out at preschool. It was Matt's behavior that precipitated the present crisis; she had been referred to the clinic by another clinician.

Nancy seemed to be in a state of shock, although she denied suicidal thoughts or preoccupation. She cried but did not express anger or fear. Although Jim had been extremely violent with her physically, she said the psychological barrages were the most debilitating. A safety plan was developed, and she was informed of her legal options. She talked haltingly about the abuse, but seemed relieved to be discussing it. A second appointment was set, and she was praised for coming to the clinic.

During the second appointment she was predominantly concerned about her son's love for Jim. She felt guilty that she was unable to stand by Jim when he was down. She was also afraid that she could not support herself if she left Jim. However, she decided that she could not tolerate his abuse and was going to insist that he get help. She felt so guilty about "kicking him when he was down" that the worker thought she might not return for her next appointment. She was told that whatever she decided to do, she was welcome to return and talk it over; another appointment was set.

Nancy canceled the next appointment and did not set another. She was contacted and indicated that she did not want to take any action at this time. She was told that she could return for an appointment at any time, and was also informed about a battered women's group.

Crisis Intervention with Batterers

The man who batters is unlikely to experience a crisis as a result of his violent acts, regardless of their severity. His dilemma after an incident of violence is to convince his partner that he did not mean it, that he is sorry, and that if she behaved properly he wouldn't hit or abuse her. Her reaction to his manipulations may precipitate a crisis for him. If she leaves, threatens to leave, insists that he get help, or has him arrested for wife beating, a crisis may develop and he may seek help.

The batterer's imperviousness to crisis or help-seeking is the result of several factors: (1) the social sanction and neglect of the problem (only a small percentage of states and counties have spouse-abuse laws or mandatory arrest policies for wife-beating); (2) his remarkable denial and minimization of the problem; (3) his belief that the problem is a result of his partner's behavior and the partner's acceptance of this fallacy; (4) his history of being able to get away with violence in the family; and (5) his knowledge, in some instances, that she has few realistic alternatives other than to stay with him.

Crisis intervention with the batterer has three goals: (1) to get him into treatment for his violent behavior, (2) to have him see that the abuse is a function of his behavior and not his partner's, that is, to internalize rather than externalize the motivation, and (3) to teach him two elementary self-control skills—*time-out* and *self-talk*. These skills can be taught quickly and are effective when the batterer feels he is losing control of himself. The fundamental strategies for meeting these goals are support, education, and confrontation—support in terms of recognizing his feelings and perceptions, education regarding the causes and treatment of his problem, and confrontation regarding his denial and refusal to accept responsibility for his behavior.

The batterer usually presents and in fact experiences himself as a victim of a hostile and unsympathetic wife, of unjust law-enforcement procedures, or both. He usually denies and minimizes the seriousness and frequency of the abuse and looks to the worker for sympathy and understanding. Sometimes the batterer may direct hostility toward the worker or he may present as passive or compliant.

The worker must listen to the batterer's story, reflect, empathize, and point out contradictions in a matter-of-fact manner (for example, "You hit your wife, but it was her fault"). Hostility toward the worker should never be tolerated; if requests for respect are ignored, the interview should be terminated (Star, 1983). In addition, verbal hostility toward the victim should be stifled (for example, "Your partner's name is Diane, not 'bitch.' Please use her name"). Maintaining such control during the session prevents hostility from being generalized and directed toward the worker.

The batterer should be assessed for suicidal and homicidal potential and appropriate action taken as needed. Most batterers want the worker to know that they are not wife beaters. The worker should let the batterer know that he or she will not judge the batterer and that the worker's job is to help the batterer control his violence. The overall goal of the first session is to let the batterer know that he can talk without being judged, that the worker understands his perceptions, and that future sessions will focus on his behavior, not his partner's. It is sometimes necessary to let the man know that the worker has no legal authority for getting the man's wife back, and that the worker will not advocate for conjoint counseling until the batterer obtains individual help.

Finally, the batterer should be taught the self-control skills of time-out and self-talk. Time-out is an interactive behavioral skill that consists of four parts: (1) the expression of affective state—"I feel as if I'm going to lose control"; (2) a statement of need for time to cool off—"I need twenty minutes to cool down"; (3) a statement that the batterer will return—"I'll be back in twenty minutes"; and (4) letting his partner know that he is willing to discuss the issue when he (not she) is calmer—"We can talk about this later."

The rationale for self-talk (Novaco, 1983) should be presented to the client, stressing the following points. Thoughts are like talking to oneself, hence the term self-talk. The way we talk to ourselves influences the way we feel and act in all situations. The worker should provide examples that illustrate how self-talk can escalate or deescalate emotional reactions. Asking the client to provide examples from his own experience is also instructive. For both time-out and self-talk, the worker should practice techniques during sessions with the client.

The techniques of time-out and self-talk have two goals: (1) to increase the batterer's self-control and thus protect his partner from harm and (2) to help the client understand that self-control is the key to ending the cycle of violence, which serves to reduce denial and highlights the need for further counseling.

Because batterers usually seek help only under extreme duress, that is, the victim has left, is threatening to leave, or has reported their behavior, one might perceive the batterer as an involuntary client. In some cases, the worker may be asked to document the treatment to legal authorities, or the client may ask the worker to tell the man's wife that he is receiving help. Legal authorities may be advised that the client is being seen and that the outcome of services will depend entirely on his motivation for help. The worker should never make a prognosis unless he or she is an expert in the area of domestic violence. If a prognosis is requested, it should be deferred. The batterer's partner should be advised to seek help. Her judgment of change in her partner, not a professional's opinion, should dictate her decision to stay or leave.

Although the goals for crisis intervention with the batterer are straightforward, achieving the goals can be extremely difficult for the worker. Regardless of what the abuser tells the worker, the worker can assume that the client is denying or minimizing the violence, as is illustrated in the following case examples.

Joe requested help after his wife contacted a shelter and told Joe that he would have to move out if he did not seek counseling. He attended the interview appearing contrite but angry with his wife's demands. He was a successful real estate broker and seemed very engaging. He said he had been "falling apart" recently because of a bad business environment and that the violence was recent and usually associated with drinking. He was very persuasive; it would have been easy for the worker to send him away supporting him in his distortion of the problem. It was later discovered that the client had sporadically, but severely, been violent with his wife throughout their marriage. His constant psychological abuse finally pushed his wife into reporting her problem.

The batterer's crisis can end as quickly as it began, generally when the woman returns, allows him to return, or drops legal charges.

Don visited the clinic in crisis after his wife insisted that he leave their home. Crisis intervention seemed successful with Don; he planned to begin treatment for his violence. He had made good progress and admitted his violence had been a long-standing problem. He said it didn't matter how his relationship turned out, he just wanted help. One week before the treatment group was to begin, he was extremely violent with his wife, who left town permanently. He did not keep his next appointment or attend the group. When contacted, he said that the violence was her problem, not his, and that things would be different with a new woman.

The batterer may present a fascinating prospect for dynamic, insight-oriented therapy. However, the worker should not delve into the batterer's history or dynamic structure unless doing so will enhance the man's confrontation with his violent behavior and his responsibility for changing it. In the case of a man who was abused as a child, it might be necessary for him to express his anger and feelings of violation. However, the primary focus should be on obtaining help for his own violence. Treatment may ultimately have a dual focus: recovery from victimization as well as renouncement of violence. However, allowing a batterer to become too reflective initially may reinforce his tendency to deny his violent behavior, because he is likely to use it to deflect the focus from his present behavior.

Dick entered crisis intervention at the insistence of his girl friend. He had a history of extreme violence with her and had held a loaded gun to her head. He had been severely abused as a child; his father had once hit him with an axe. He was so preoccupied with violence that he had considered becoming a mercenary so that he could capitalize on his special military training. He talked about his own abuse and in counseling realized the connection between his past victimization and present behavior. He expressed great relief and his motivation was enhanced when he realized that ending his own abusive behavior would signify an important phase in his recovery and would relieve him from feeling as though he was just like his father. He eventually entered a batterers' group, remaining highly motivated even though he and his partner separated.

The crisis intervention worker must have a good notion of what treatment for the batterer will be like. It is not enough to refer the batterer to treatment; the worker needs to understand the treatment and the assumptions on which it is based. The most prevalent treatment models are learning-based and do not advocate conjoint treatment until the violence has stopped (Saunders, 1984; Edleson, 1984; Star, 1983; Saunders & Hanusa, 1986; Sonkin, Martin, & Walker, 1985).

Case loads generally contain few batterers in crisis. This state of affairs will continue to exist until judges, prosecutors, and police operate under more effective legal mandates and guidelines and until services to battered women are considered an integral part of community well-being.

Other Treatment Issues

Although some support exists for the use of conjoint treatment of domestic violence cases (Neidig & Friedman, 1984; Margolin, 1979), the present author discourages joint treatment. The worker must remember that it is usually the woman who has made the appointment and that the man is probably there reluctantly. The woman is likely either to be very reticent in order to avoid later retaliation from him or will rage against him, which may lead to further violence after the couple leaves the office. This typical dynamic is very misleading to a counselor who is inexperienced in this area and represents one of many pitfalls in conjoint work (for fuller discussion, see Bograd, 1982). Thus, the preferred mode of intervention is to see the wife and husband separately after the first appointment. If it is possible to do so, the husband or wife should be referred to another staff member or clinician, thus allowing each person to have a safe treatment environment.

Some controversy and disagreement has centered on male counselors working with battered women (Tolman, Mowry, Jones, & Brekke, 1986). The author feels that if agency resources permit, women clients should be seen by women staff members. If it is necessary for men to counsel battered women, it is extremely important for them to examine their own experiences with and biases toward violence against women as well as their own patriarchal attitudes. It may also be useful for men to consult with feminist staff members to detect and correct sexist practices. Both male and female clinicians can be effective crisis counselors for battered women and batterers; however, they must be sensitive to their own experiences and predispositions.

Conclusion

Crisis intervention in the area of spouse abuse is challenging to workers. Unfortunately, work with this population is not always as rewarding as it is demanding. Social and community forces often contribute to the continuing victimization of battered women and the resistance of batterers to help. It can be difficult for the worker not to chastise women for remaining in abusive situations or to despise batterers for their sometimes smug indifference. The suffering in this area is immense and resources are scarce. However, every life that is freed from the mire of spouse abuse is a gift to the generation that follows.

References

Arias, I., Samos, M., & O'Leary, D. (1987). Prevalence and correlates of physical aggression during courtship. *Journal of Interpersonal Violence*, 2, 82–90.

Ball, M. (1977). Issues of violence in family casework. *Social Casework*, 58, 3–12.

Bass, D., & Rice, J. (1979). Agency responses to the abused wife. *Social Casework, 60*, 338–342.

Bograd, M. (1982). Battered women, cultural myths and clinical interventions: A feminist analysis. In New England Association for Women in Psychology (Ed.), *Current feminist issues in psychotherapy*. New York: Haworth Press.

Bowker, L. (1983). *Beating wife-beating*. Lexington, MA: Lexington Press.

Brekke, J. (1987). Detecting wife and child abuse in clinical settings. *Social Casework 68*, 332–338.

Bulcroft, R., & Straus, M. A. (1975). *Validity of husband, wife, and child reports of intrafamily violence and power*. Mimeographed paper, Department of Sociology, University of New Hampshire, Durham, NH.

Carlson, B. (1987). Dating violence: A research review. *Social Casework, 68*, 16–23.

Carlson, B. E. (1984). Causes and maintenance of domestic violence: An ecological analysis. *Social Service Review, 58*, 569–587.

Cate, R. M., Henton, J. M., Koval, J., Christopher, F. S., & Lloyd, S. (1982). Premarital abuse: A social psychological perspective. *Journal of Family Issues, 3*, 79–90.

Coleman, K. H. (1980). Conjugal violence: What 33 men report. *Journal of Marital and Family Therapy, 6*, 207–213.

Coleman, K. H., Weinman, M. L., & Hsi, B. P. (1980). Factors affecting conjugal violence. *Journal of Psychology, 105*, 197–202.

Davis, L. V. (1984). Beliefs of service providers about abused women and abusing men. *Social Work, 46*, 243–250.

Dobash, R. E., & Dobash, R. (1979). *Violence against wives: A case against the patriarchy*. New York: Free Press.

Edleson, J. G. (1984). Working with men who batter. *Social Work, 29*, 237–242.

Fagan, J. A., Stewart, D. K., & Hansen, K. V. (1983). Violent men or violent husbands? Background factors and situational correlates of severity and location of violence. In D. Finkelhor, R. J. Gelles, G. T. Hotaling, & M. A. Straus (Eds.), *The dark side of families*. Beverly Hills, CA: Sage.

Finkelhor, D. (1983). Common features of wife abuse. In D. Finkelhor, R. J. Gelles, G. T. Hotaling, & M. A. Straus, *The dark side of families*. Beverly Hills, CA: Sage.

Gelles, R. J. (1980). Violence in the family: A review of research in the seventies. *Journal of Marriage and the Family, 42*, 873–885.

Gelles, R. J., & Straus, M. A. (1981). Determinants of violence in the family: Toward a theoretical integration. In W. R. Barr, R. Hill, F. I. Nye, & I. L. Reiss (Eds.), *Contemporary theories about the family*. New York: Free Press.

Gelles, R. J., & Straus, M. A. (1988). *Intimate violence*. New York: Simon and Schuster.

Gondolf, E. W. (1988). Battered women as survivors. Lexington, MA: Lexington Books.

Hamberger, H., & Hastings, R. (1986). Personality correlates of men who abuse their partners: A cross-validation study. *Journal of Family Violence, 1*, 323–341.

Kalmuss, D. S., & Straus, M. A. (1982). Wife's marital dependency and wife abuse. *Journal of Marriage and the Family, 44*, 277–287.

Levine, E. (1986). Sociocultural causes of family violence. *Journal of Family Violence, 1*, 3–12.

Makepeace, J. (1981). Courtship violence among college students. *Family Relations, 30*, 97–102.

Margolin, G. (1979). Conjoint marital therapy to enhance anger management and reduce spouse abuse. *American Journal of Family Therapy, 7*(2), 13–24.

Martin, D. (1976). *Battered wives*. New York: Pocket Books.

Moore, J. H. (1982). Sex role stereotyping in battered women: Responses to the Bem Sex-Role Inventory. *Dissertation Abstracts International, 43*, 1663B. (University Microfilms No. DA 82-23, 350).

Neidig, P. H., & Friedman, D. H. (1984). *Spouse abuse: A treatment program for couples.* Champaign, IL: Research Press.

Novaco, R. (1983). Stress inoculation therapy for anger control. In P. A. Keller & L. G. Ritt (Eds.), *Innovations in clinical practice* (Vol. 2).. Sarasota, FL: Professional Resource Exchange.

Pagelow, M. D. (1981). *Women-battering: Victims and their experiences.* Beverly Hills, CA: Sage.

Pagelow, M. D. (1984). *Family violence.* New York: Praeger.

Resnik, M. (1976). *Wife beating: Counselor training manual no. 1.* Ann Arbor, MI: AA NOW/Wife Assault.

Roy, M. (1982). *The abusive partner: An analysis of domestic battering.* New York: Van Nostrand Reinhold.

Saunders, D. G. (1982). Counseling the violent husband, In P. A. Keller & L. G. Ritt (Eds.), *Innovations in clinical practice: A source book* (Vol. 1). Sarasota, FL: Professional Resource Exchange.

Saunders, D. G. (1984). Helping husbands who batter. *Social Casework, 65*, 347–352.

Saunders, D. G. (1986). When battered women use violence: Husband-abuse or self-defense? *Violence and Victims, 1*, 47–60.

Saunders, D. G., & Brekke, J. (1985). *Violence against wives: A review of research findings and needs.* Unpublished manuscript. Family Service, Madison, WI.

Saunders, D. G., & Hanusa, D. (1986). The cognitive-behavioral treatment of men who batter: The short-term effects of group therapy. *Journal of Family Violence, 1*, 357–372.

Sherman, L. W., & Berk, R. A. (1984). The specific deterrent effects of arrest for domestic assault. *American Sociological Review, 49*, 261–272.

Sonkin, D., Martin, D., & Walker, L. (1985). *The male batterer: A treatment approach.* New York: Springer.

Star, B. (1983). *Helping the abuser: Intervening effectively in family violence.* New York: Family Service Association of America.

Stark, E., Flitcraft, A., & Frazier, W. (1981). Medicine and patriarchal violence: The social construction of a "private" event. *International Journal of Health Services, 9*, 461–493.

Steinmetz, S. K. (1977). *The cycle of violence.* New York: Praeger.

Straus, M. A. (1979). Measuring intrafamily conflict and violence: The conflict tactics (CT) scales. *Journal of Marriage and Family, 41*, 75–88.

Straus, M. A. (1980). Victims and aggressors in marital violence. *American Behavioral Scientist, 23*, 681–704.

Straus, M. A., Gelles, R. J., & Steinmetz, S. K. (1980). *Behind closed doors: Violence in the American family.* New York: Doubleday/Anchor.

Tolman, R., Mowry, D., Jones, L., & Brekke, J. (1986). Developing a profeminist commitment among men in social work. In N. Van Den Berg & L. Cooper (Eds.), *Feminist visions for social work practice.* Silver Spring, MD: National Association of Social Workers.

Van Den Bergh, N., & Cooper L. (Eds.). (1986). *Feminist visions for social work practice.* Silver Spring, MD: National Association of Social Workers.

Walker, L. E. (1979). *The battered woman.* New York: Harper and Row.

Walker, L. E. (1984). *The battered woman syndrome.* New York: Springer.

Witt, D. (1987). A conflict theory of family violence. *Journal of Family Violence, 2*, 291–301.

7

Brief Crisis-Oriented Therapy With College Students

HAROLD L. PRUETT

ALTHOUGH LIFE AT A COLLEGE is exciting and challenging for the young adult, it is also fraught with emotional crises that cause many students to seek mental health services. In a recent study, Rimmer, Halikas, and Schucket (1982) indicate that as many as 39 percent of college students will experience psychological impairment at some time during their undergraduate years. The most commonly diagnosed problem will be depression (82–93 percent). Unfortunately, less than one third of the students considered impaired will seek mental health services.

The freshman student enters college with a particular set of coping strategies learned from past experiences of success and failure in tasks and in relationships with peers, parents, and teachers. Some of these strategies are maladaptive (for example, substance misuse, overdependence on parents) and create problems for the new college student who is confronted by new challenges. Even with the best coping mechanisms, the developmental tasks that the student must face in this new and demanding environment may create stresses with which the student cannot adaptively cope.

To help students meet these challenges, a university/college mental health or counseling center needs to develop a model of service delivery that responds to the needs of the college-age adult while taking into account the special characteristics of the college environment and the large demand for services.

Developmental Tasks and the College Environment

The developmental tasks of the late adolescent and young adult years as well as the challenges that face college students have been discussed by several authors (Chickering & Havighurst, 1981; Erikson, 1950; Havighurst, 1972; Levinson, Darrow, Klein, Levinson, & McKee, 1978). Although notable exceptions always exist, the freshman entering the college environment must cope with separation from parents and other family members, high school peers, and "home town" familiarity and must learn to make new friends and acquaintances, live in a new community, and relate to new authorities. Freshman students encounter other students from diverse ethnic, religious, and cultural backgrounds and must reconcile long-cherished and usually unquestioned values and attitudes with the diverse values and attitudes of other students. To a young man or woman without his or her usual supports, this experience can be threatening.

As the new student becomes acquainted with peers and encounters new authority figures, he or she must learn to adjust to other realities, such as competition for grades and classes. The external support structure for the student is limited; no one is around to cajole or support him or her. Moreover, while adjusting to the demands of a new environment, the student must cope with major issues such as: What am I here for? What career will bring me the most enjoyment, money, prestige, security, or challenge? What courses and what major will enable me to accomplish what I want? Who are my friends? Do I choose career, graduate school, marriage?

Grayson (1985) has described the impact of college life on student mental health in some detail. Each year of college requires the student to respond to different tasks. After the first year of transition from the old and familiar to the new and diverse, the sophomore and junior years of college are periods when the student develops a more solid sense of how he or she interacts with others in order to answer questions such as: What are my "true" values? What is the meaning of responsibility and commitment? The student must make important decisions, such as choosing a major and establishing long-range goals. The final year of college finds the student beginning the process of separation all over again. As in the first year, the student must cope with loss and transition in preparation for termination of his or her student status.

In addition to the tasks required of the college student in adapting to the unique environment of the university, various developmental issues emerge. These issues must be confronted and resolved before satisfactory adjustment can occur (Berkovitz, 1983; Erikson, 1950). When a student enters college, he or she is usually an adolescent fresh out of high school and home. The student enters with all the turmoils of adolescence and leaves four years later as a young adult. The studies by Levinson et al. (1978) as well as the report of the Group for the Advancement of Psychiatry (1968) suggest that several tasks must be resolved before this transition can be accomplished: (1) separation from parents and shift from a child–parent to an adult–adult relationship, (2) establishment of a personal sexual identity, (3) commitment to work and choice of a vocation, (4) establishment of a personal value system, and (5) development of the capacity for lasting relationships.

Dependence versus independence is a basic conflict experienced by adolescents when they enter university life. The struggles involved with "letting go" and "holding on," experienced by both the student and the family, are often played out in painful ways. For example, a student may call home less frequently or may no longer come home on the weekends; parents may change the student's room into a sewing room. How the adolescent copes with these changes as well as with other developmental stresses will, in large part, influence his or her growth and development at college and in later years.

In addition to the developmental tasks outlined, the student is often perceived as the "standard bearer" for the family or sometimes for the entire neighborhood or community. This additional burden is often experienced by students from small towns or students who are the first in the family to go to college. Many ethnic minority students also experience this burden.

Harwell (1984), a college administrator, summed up the impact of the college experience on an already vulnerable population:

> with few exceptions, colleges and universities present new, confused students with a cornucopia of available sex (hetero- and homosexual), drugs, and informational feedback that brings into question their previous upbringing and value systems.

In the 1980s, most college students experience enormous pressure, as is evident by the number of suicides that occur in this population. Somehow the student must learn to deal with these challenges. Fortunately, adolescence and young adulthood are periods of rapid change, growth, and physical and psychological resilience. With judicious intervention, profound changes are possible.

The concept of crisis intervention has been very useful in treating college students who face a combination of developmental tasks and situational challenges. Upon entering college, a student is likely to experience crisis as he or she attempts to cope with separation from parents; threats to his or her value system; blows to self-esteem if grades fall below those achieved in high school; threats to independence when interacting with staff, faculty, and peers; and losses in intimate relationships. The student may experience anxiety, depression, or other painful symptoms while struggling with these new challenges. The student may attempt to cope by using previously learned techniques. Some techniques work, some do not. If various attempts at coping fail, the student will experience crisis.

Brief Interventions and the Concept of Crisis

During this period of crisis, it is hoped that the student seeks help from the school's counseling or health center. Brief interventions are most effective during the initial stage of a crisis, because after pathological coping has been established it becomes more difficult, perhaps impossible, for change to occur with brief intervention.

Students often consider brief intervention as the most helpful and least threatening means for dealing with a crisis. Haggerty, Baldwin, and Liptzin (1980) conducted a study of very brief interventions (VBIs) at the University of North Carolina, which replicated a study first performed at Stanford by Dorosin, Gibbs, & Kaplan (1976). Both groups of investigators found that 50 percent of their clients sought treatment for three or fewer visits. Haggerty et al. found that approximately one-half of terminations were made unilaterally by the client. In analyzing the terminations further, they state that "for 'pure' terminations, the decision is twice as likely to be made by the client alone than by the therapist and client together" (p. 328). Furthermore, their follow-up data indicate that only 16 percent of the respondents terminated because they were dissatisfied. The authors conclude that "student mental health clients find the VBI a helpful experience, are likely to finish with a sense of completion, and tend to control the termination themselves" (p. 328). A follow-up study of 140 students who received planned brief therapy (mean = 7.9 sessions) for stress-related problems at the University of Southern California indicated that more than 90 percent of the students believed the treatment was effective, according to ratings by both therapists and clients (Ringstrom, 1981).

At the University of California–Los Angeles, data indicate that consistently from year to year more than 60 percent of clients come for three or fewer visits. Follow-up surveys show an overall satisfaction rate of 80–85 percent with the UCLA Student Psychological Services (SPS). Thus, brief interventions are the rule, not the exception, in most of the studies on client utilization. In many instances, termination is planned by the therapist, but in most it is a unilateral decision made by the client. Upon reviewing several studies on client utilization in various settings, Garfield (1978) reported that the median number of visits was five to six. The Kaiser-Permanente experience (Cummings, 1977) suggests that in a majority of cases, brief intervention strategies are more effective than is long-term psychotherapy. A recent review "found the major positive impact of individual psychotherapy to occur in the first 6–8 sessions" (Budman & Gurman, 1988, p. 9).

The UCLA Student Psychological Services Program (SPS)

As the demand for short-term counseling services has increased and as economic factors demand alternatives to long-term therapy, various brief-therapy models have emerged (Davanloo, 1980; Malan, 1963). In some instances, therapy models have been adapted to the college population specifically (Podolnick, Pass, & Bybee, 1979). The model implemented at UCLA's SPS is based on crisis intervention concepts and is applicable to the majority of clients seen. Most of the requests for help from the approximately 3,000 clients per year are prompted by losses and separations—actual, perceived, or threatened. In addition to providing assistance to students during these situational and developmental crises, the primary objective of SPS is prevention, that is, avoiding maladaptive adjustments and deterioration in response to stresses encountered in a student's daily life. The crisis-oriented format fits well within this prevention framework.

The decision to offer crisis-oriented therapy at SPS evolved out of both administrative and policy concerns. As a service agency of the university, the mission of SPS is to meet the needs of the population of approximately 34,000 full-time students as opposed to simply meeting the needs of students who seek help. Clearly, many high-risk, underserved students did not avail themselves of SPS services, either because they had not heard of the SPS or because they were fearful of losing autonomy or being viewed as "sick."

I was already familiar with the crisis intervention model, having practiced it and supervised counselors using it at the Benjamin Rush Center for Problems of Living in Los Angeles (Jacobson, 1974). The model was an effective, efficient approach to planned short-term therapy; it afforded an appropriate response to many people in distress. However, it was not clear at first whether the crisis-intervention model would be appropriate for students and would fit the SPS mission, although this seemed possible, according to descriptions of its application on a smaller scale (Ichikawa, 1965; Kapp, 1974). Still, crisis-oriented services are often equated with emergency responses and are not viewed as applicable to the broader range of human problems.

In our view, a crisis results from a temporary inability to cope with a problem. The therapist attempts to address the particular crisis or disequilibrium that motivated the student to seek services, to find out why the student's coping repertory broke down or was insufficient, and to help the student modify his or her coping response—that is to *understand* the crisis in a way that allows the student to respond and to behave in a way that potentially is more effective and appropriate. Addressing both the cognitive and affective components of the individual's crisis is crucial. Treatment does not attempt to address long-standing deficits or provide long-term support; rather, services are crisis-specific. If the student is unable to respond to this form of therapy, and learn from it, he or she may be referred to other types of therapy, usually group therapy or intermediate-length individual therapy.

Thus, crisis-oriented therapy, as practiced at UCLA's SPS is a limited but generally appropriate response to students under stress. In keeping with Caplan's (1964) and Lindemann's (1944) basic tenets concerning the self-limiting nature of crisis, we set a time limit for treatment of six sessions. Many mental health professionals tend to offer open-ended rather than time-limited, goal-oriented treatment. However, the time limit set at SPS was not an attempt to truncate traditional, open-ended therapy, but rather to communicate to the students (and staff) the type of brief problem-solving therapy that we wished to offer. Setting time limits also served to maintain focus on the presenting problem and enhance motivation of both student and therapist to achieve goals within the specified time frame, which usually corresponded to an acutely stressful period in the student's life. The six-session limit was not a constraint. As stated above, utilization data over several years indicate that more than 60 percent of our clients consistently come for three or fewer visits; between 85 percent and 90 percent of clients are seen for six or fewer visits. The average number of visits is approximately four. Although some students' ability to cope is severely limited and therefore requires a long-term healing relationship, most clients—if the intervention is timely and well thought out—find brief intervention sufficient and only occasionally return for a "booster" session. Thus the crisis-intervention model addresses the needs of the majority of student clients.

The crisis-intervention approach not only promotes problem-solving skills but also promotes a philosophy of growth and health. Generally, the individual student is the best judge of what is right for him or her and what he or she can do to cope with and resolve a crisis. Helping professionals must be careful not to interfere with the individual's regrouping efforts. It is better for professionals to err on the side of minimizing their contribution as opposed to intervening too much and hindering the individual's progress in solving his or her own problems. The individual in crisis should not be allowed to become dependent on therapists, medication, and hospitals as a means of coping. Crisis intervention facilitates the individual's *progressive* learning and enhances his or her coping repertoire.

From the outset of treatment, staff communicate to the student that therapeutic work should be accomplished within four to six weeks. Students are educated about the stress, stressors, and phenomenon of crisis. Our goal is to help the student realize that the crisis he or she is experiencing is part of the life process. Although efforts are made not to minimize what the student is feeling or experiencing, the student also needs to realize that he or she is not alone, crazy, or sick. Our goal is to get the student to participate in the intervention process and avoid regression. The student should not leave treatment feeling that he or she was a patient who was "treated" by a "doctor" for an "illness." Rather, the student should leave treatment with tools that will help him or her cope with future life stresses.

At UCLA, a walk-in service is offered; most students are accommodated within two or three days of their initial contact. Rapid entry into treatment is essential if the therapist is to take advantage of the client's heightened motivation for assistance. The longer the delay, the more difficult it is to identify what exactly precipitated contact and the emotional hazards experienced by the client. If too much time elapses, the client is likely to become vague as to what prompted him or her to seek assistance. As in most crisis-oriented approaches, intervention focuses on problem-solving methods. After establishing rapport with the client, the therapist helps the student construct a "time line" in an effort to identify the precipitating event(s) that preceded contact with the SPS. Usually the student has just experienced the "final straw" within a day or so of the initial contact. This precipitating event usually can be traced back to some change or life event that occurred within the past one or two weeks, occasionally earlier. This event is termed the "hazardous event." If it appears desirable to do so, the genesis of the "hazardous event" can be traced back further in order to identify underlying conflicts (typically, unfinished issues with parental figures). In keeping with a problem-solving approach, however, staff are ever mindful to focus upon the present situation, the specific problems presented, and the coping strategies necessary to deal with these problems.

Establishing a time line often takes up most of the first session. Finding out how the student usually copes with problems is also important, as is ascertaining why these customary ways of handling things now fail to work. Often students experience a crisis because they have not previously experienced the hazardous event or "final straw" and therefore lack an adequate coping repertoire. Usually, the event involves loss.

Before the end of the first session, the therapist assesses the degree of disequilibrium that the student is experiencing and the possible risks that he or she faces, one of which is suicide (see chapter 11). If such a risk is present, the therapist ensures that a support system is available. The student is asked to do a self-assessment of the degree of risk; a contract is made with the student stating that no intentional (or "accidental") self-destructive behavior will occur prior to the next meeting, according to a procedure outlined by Drye, Goulding, and Goulding (1973).

Adequate supports are important for keeping students at high risk for suicide out of a hospital and for help in resolving crises. Therapists attempt to learn something about the client's support network—where does he or she live? Who are his or her friends? Does the student belong to any organization or club?

In addition to the cognitive work undertaken during the first visit, therapists also focus on the student's emotional state in order to assist the student to become aware of, express, and learn to deal with feelings. Students, like others in crisis, often use vague terms to describe how they feel and why they are upset. Because loss is a major factor in many crises, blocked grief is a common phenomenon. The therapist articulates the student's sadness and anger and in doing so gives permission to express feelings.

At the end of the first session, the therapist hopes not only to understand what brought the student to SPS but to help the student begin to understand why he or she is upset. The therapeutic plan, including the number of remaining sessions, is discussed. The student is told that therapy will focus on helping him or her to understand more fully the nature of the hazardous event; helping him or her explore and develop new coping strategies, if they are needed; and providing support so that the student will be able to manage feelings and thoughts. An appointment is made for a second session, usually within a week. Depending on the therapist's initial assessment of the problem, the second meeting may be scheduled sooner.

When the client returns for subsequent sessions, the therapist, together with the student, assesses the student's functioning and pursues the problem-solving process while enhancing cognitive and affective awareness. The therapist may prescribe homework if it appears that the client would benefit from such activity. Throughout these sessions, the therapist must be mindful of the termination process and be sensitive to both the therapist's and the client's desire to "hang on" after the work is completed.

During the final session, the therapist recounts for the client the events and circumstances that caused the student to seek help, reviews positive gains, and anticipates possible difficulties in the future. The therapist reassures the student that he or she can manage and makes it clear that should a *new* problem emerge, with which the student feels unable to cope, the therapist will be glad to see the student for one or two visits in order to help resolve the problem. Thus, while reinforcing the student's adequacy, the therapist offers support. Generally, students respond positively to this brief crisis-oriented mode of problem-solving.

Case Examples

The following cases were selected to illustrate some of the key aspects of the crisis model. In each instance the therapist's initial "detective work" was critical in identifying the event that precipitated the student's seeking help. Therefore, the first session was critical for progress in subsequent meetings.

Case 1. Jennifer, an eighteen-year-old freshman student in her third quarter at UCLA, walked into SPS and said that she needed to be seen as soon as possible. She appeared calm and collected to the receptionist, although her voice indicated some underlying agitation.

I introduced myself and asked what had brought her to SPS. She replied that she was "very upset" because she had midterms coming up in a couple of weeks and was not able to study. She said that she was not sleeping well and could not seem to relax. I asked her how long she had been experiencing these problems, and she indicated that it seemed like some time. I suggested to her that maybe she was more upset today, because today she had chosen to come to SPS for help.

Becoming tearful, Jennifer responded that she did not have many friends and seemed to be having more difficulties than other students had. She had one good friend, a junior, who she wished were her boyfriend. There had been some problems lately between the two of them; she did not think he was as interested in her as she was in him. I asked her why she thought this was so. She indicated that for the past two months they seemed to be arguing often. She thought he did not pay enough attention to her even though she "hung around him a lot." In the same breath, she also indicated self-disgust, saying she was not a strong person and that he probably did not respect her. Furthermore, she had violated her own basic values. I asked how. She said that at the beginning of the school year, on their first date, she kissed him. She made a vow to herself in high school that she would never kiss on the first date and now she had violated her vow. She cried quietly. I acknowledged how confusing it is at times to know what our values are and that sometimes we need to clarify them and rethink them based on our experiences so that we can decide what values are truly our own. I also said that although I could see this situation upset her, I imagine that she had talked about this problem before and that it was perhaps less of a concern for her now since it had occurred several months ago. She acknowledged that she had talked about it with her mother.

I then asked if perhaps something else had happened recently that upset her. Jennifer responded by talking about her boyfriend and how she hadn't studied since she had been hanging around him more. When asked what that meant, she explained that they both worked at the same place but on different shifts; she stayed at work later in order to get a chance to spend a little time with him on his shift.

Again I asked why she happened to come in today, because the problem she was describing was ongoing. While waiting for her response, I observed how uncomfortable and upset she was and speculated about her problem. She seemed to view herself in a negative way and seemed to be somewhat dependent. I assumed that part of her current difficulties might have to do with recent experiences with her parents, because she had mentioned her mother as someone with whom she talked when worried. Further inquiry indicated she had been a good student until recently and that she had felt "reasonably" popular among her peers. Although her functioning as a freshman was not great, it was adequate. Also, since her difficulty in coping with her boyfriend and school, she confided that she had been drinking in order to relax. Although she did not appear to be drinking a lot, it was certainly more than she had previously.

Again, I pushed for more detail about why she was here now. She explained that approximately one week before, her boyfriend told her that she should start seeing other people, which upset her. I asked her to give me another word for "upset," and she finally indicated that she felt "hurt" by what he said. She talked a little with a roommate about the incident and then called her mother. Jennifer always called her mother when she was upset and her mother had always given her good advice or at least reassured her that things would get better. On this occasion her mother said that perhaps it was time to look for another boyfriend. Jennifer hung up the telephone not feeling as relieved as she ordinarily did after talking with mother. As we further explored a time line concerning the onset of Jennifer's crisis, she indicated through tears that she had called her mother last night and her mother had said to her, "I can't always be here for you. You need to find someone else to talk to about your boyfriend. Don't they have counselors you can see?"

Jennifer had always relied on her mother to be around and described herself and her mother as "good pals." Now mother was withdrawing support and that loss was very frightening to Jennifer. She felt as though she were losing both her mother and her best friend. The possible loss of her boyfriend was even more devastating after her conversation with her mother. Jennifer was unprepared for her changing relationship with her mother. The possible loss of her boyfriend, who had in some ways provided her with similar support, compounded her problems. As we explored together the meaning of her mother's statements and her boyfriend's actions, it was clear that she felt unable to get by without their usual support. Her mother had been particularly important in Jennifer's coping strategy at the university. She was saddened and angry at both her mother and her boyfriend; she could not depend on either of them. She had not found other ways to deal with her feelings. Jennifer and I talked about the importance of the telephone call to her mother and the mother's subsequent suggestion that she visit a counselor at the university. Although Jennifer's relationship with her boyfriend was upsetting, she had found adequate, although not optimal, ways to cope with it. The threatened loss of her boyfriend was difficult for her to deal with, but the threatened loss of her mother was devastating.

Jennifer cried for a while, and we talked about feeling sad and angry at people who matter to us. We engaged in role playing, which helped her express her feelings. As our time was about to end, I told Jennifer I wanted to give her a task: I asked her to identify before the next meeting one person among her peers with whom she would feel comfortable spending time.

During our appointment the following week, she told me that she still felt hurt by her mother but that she had managed to identify someone she met in her swimming club with whom she enjoyed talking. They made plans to attend a swimming event together. She had also talked with her mother about feeling hurt. Her mother pointed out that it wasn't that she didn't want to talk with Jennifer, but that she thought Jennifer relied on her too much. Jennifer felt less threatened and admitted that she did rely on her mother too much. However, she still felt angry. Her mother should not have changed the rules so abruptly!

By our third visit, Jennifer was smiling and apparently doing much better. Although her relationship with her boyfriend was not much better, it had improved somewhat since she had been doing things with her new friend. She was also swimming more and consequently was feeling less tense. She stopped drinking. She took her exams and did reasonably well. She did not think she needed to return and I agreed. We said goodbye, agreeing that she could return if she felt the need to talk.

Although one might argue that more therapy was needed before Jennifer could become less dependent on others and increase her feelings of self-worth, both the willingness of the client and cost factors need to be considered. Subsequent group intervention in a university or community setting might be ideal for someone like Jennifer. However, Jennifer expressed no interest in follow-up and appeared to be managing without undue difficulty. Had intervention not been available to her, she might have continued drinking, been unable to study, and even risked suspension from the university. Crisis-oriented therapy proved effective and practical for her.

Case 2. Paula, a nineteen year-old sophomore who was referred by the student health center, entered SPS appearing very agitated. Because there was a sense of urgency about her, she was seen within a matter of minutes.

She entered my office, smiled, then broke into tears. She sobbed for what seemed like a long time. I softly said that she appeared to be very upset. I asked her if she could tell me what was wrong. She acknowledged that she was upset and that she was in some pain from her stomach. I asked her why she happened to come here today, and she replied she had gone to the student health center earlier because she had awakened this morning with severe stomach pains and diarrhea. She said that she hadn't been able to eat much for almost three days. The health center had given her something for her stomach, made a follow-up appointment for her, and told her that she must be under severe stress and should go to SPS.

When I asked how she felt about all this and about being told to come here, she responded that she really needed some help. I suggested to her that we should work back to what might have happened over the weekend to find out why she was so upset that her stomach was bothering her.

She began by telling me that she and her boyfriend of one year were having difficulties. These difficulties centered on his declaring to her the previous Thursday (today was Monday) that he was thinking about pledging a fraternity. She became angry with him, crying and yelling that he had violated her trust because both had earlier agreed that fraternities and sororities were not for them. Now here he was, talking about pledging. For the next three days she brooded about his possible pledging, thinking that his time would be taken up and that the "little sisters" of the fraternity would flock around him. She finally concluded that their relationship was over. That morning, after a fitful night, she awoke with severe cramps and went directly to the health center.

I explored the meaning of his pledging, her previous relationships, and the importance of the current one. Her current boyfriend was her first "real" boyfriend. Because she had established few other friendships, losing this relationship felt very threatening to her. She did not remember ever feeling anything so painful. Then she began to sob as she recounted the loss of her two older brothers when she was sixteen.

We talked about her two brothers and their deaths. She and her family had been on an outing at a river near her home town. Although all the details were not clear to her, one brother had gone for a swim and experienced difficulty. The other brother jumped in to help. Both drowned. She was watching from the shore, stunned and helpless. She had been very close to her brothers. The threatened loss of the boyfriend stimulated feelings of loss similar to those evoked by the death of her brothers. Why had she experienced such a strong reaction, and how had the threat of loss of her boyfriend reminded her of that earlier loss? Her family, on the day following the brothers' funeral, did not permit any discussion of the tragic accident and had forbidden any mention of the brothers' names. The entire family, including the young woman sitting in front of me, had thus avoided dealing with their grief.

The connection between the threatened loss of the boyfriend and the death of the brothers was apparent to her; her expression of grief continued for a while. We both thought through her "excessive" reaction to her boyfriend's joining a fraternity, considering possible outcomes other than loss. I suggested that she talk with her boyfriend and encouraged her to continue to express her grief over her brothers' death. We scheduled a second session for three days later. When she returned, Paula appeared less tense; her posture was less rigid. She said that she continued to cry and was still mourning. She and her boyfriend had been talking. Although he still expressed interest in pledging a fraternity, the idea was less threatening to her. She also began to reevaluate her life-style and her total reliance on her boyfriend for support.

As we talked, it was clear to her that she had other good friends, as well as other interests apart from her boyfriend. She had even made arrangements to meet a friend to see a movie in a few days.

A third appointment was scheduled for the following week. She came in smiling and said she was doing fine. Her stomach had stopped hurting; the health center had determined that she was physically in good health. She said that her boyfriend had decided to pledge the fraternity; she wasn't happy with his decision, but she knew she was handling it all right. She had even talked to her family about her experience, strongly suggesting that the family needed to see someone to help them mourn the loss of the two brothers.

We agreed that no further appointments were necessary and said goodbye. I saw her several months later when she invited me to a noon concert in which she was performing. Afterward, she said she was doing great and thanked me for seeing her. She was still with her boyfriend but was enjoying some new friends.

Although unfinished grief work is not necessarily a problem for a majority of students, it can be a factor in dealing with students who overreact to loss. Sometimes, incomplete grief work is not the result of failing to mourn a death but is due to repressing feelings concerning changing roles in relationships. Using a time line and detective work, crisis-oriented therapy alerts the therapist to possible antecedents to current reactions.

Case 3. John, a twenty-three-year-old male, walked into SPS one afternoon looking "lost," according to the receptionist. He was well dressed and rather young looking. In my office, he said that he had been very tense lately and was experiencing both stomachaches and headaches. He stated that he had never seen a "shrink" before and probably wouldn't be here now, had not the health center referred him. He went to the health center a couple of days previously, because he was unable to take a midterm examination due to severe nausea. After being examined at the student health center, he was given medication to relieve his discomfort and told that his symptoms were stress-related. He was referred to SPS.

When I questioned him about his background, John informed me that he was a senior and would graduate in December. He should have graduated in June, but because of several incompletes in his course work, his graduation had been delayed.

As I explored the nature of his incompletes, he told me that he was unable to finish his course work because he had become very ill with stomach problems. I responded that it seemed that the same thing was happening again, which he acknowledged. When we looked at the connection between exams and his physical difficulties, it was easy for him to see that they were related. We began to explore why. All he said was that a lot was riding on his exams, because he had to achieve a certain grade point in order to graduate.

I suggested to him that perhaps he also had mixed feelings about graduation. He hesitated at first, then said he could hardly wait to leave UCLA. However, he quickly acknowledged that there were some things he would miss when he left.

> I encouraged him to tell me about his experiences at the university. He had made some good friends, had enjoyed varied dating experiences, and had participated in many campus activities. Tears began to well up in his eyes as he talked about what he feared lay ahead. He came from a small town that he despised. His parents, successful business people who owned a small firm, expected him to return home upon graduation and take his place in the business, just as his older brother had.
>
> We talked further about his tense relationship with his father; John had perceived going away to college as an escape. Now, after four and a half years, he was going to get his due. He had built up such a fear of graduating that he was making himself sick. In part, he was avoiding his exams and hoping, at some level, to avoid graduation. At the same time, he had always prided himself on going to college and his ability to graduate. He experienced ambivalent feelings. On the one hand, graduation meant returning home, perhaps to an environment he disliked. On the other hand, it meant successful mastery of a task that had plagued him for a long time.
>
> I suggested to him that perhaps there were better ways of dealing with his dilemma than making himself sick—to which he agreed. We made an appointment for a second session. I asked him to write down his concerns about returning home and going into business with his father, and to write a dialogue between him and his father that expressed these concerns, before our next meeting.
>
> John returned a week later, saying he was feeling much better since our talk. We went over his assigned task, his concerns, and his dialogue. He quickly saw that he had built up some unrealistic concerns, primarily having to do with how he and his father would relate after his graduation. We also examined his fear of losing two good male friends as well as a young woman he was dating. We agreed that perhaps he needed to discuss his concerns with these people and try to make plans for continuing the relationships. In response to my inquiry about his stomach upsets and headaches, he replied that he had experienced less discomfort during the past week. During our final appointment, John reported that he had had several conversations with his friends and felt satisfied that they would find ways of continuing their relationship. He also talked with his father about some of his concerns. It now seemed possible for him to study without undue stress; however, I asked him to call me before the next set of exams.
>
> I did not hear from John until after final exams and graduation. He called to tell me that he had completed his courses and had graduated. Although he was not happy about returning to his home town, he was proud that he made it through UCLA.

John's concerns about graduating and the dilemmas he experienced are not unique. The experience of loss must be anticipated. John had warded off his true feelings about anticipated losses and was experiencing a threat to his sense of mastery. Although little effort was required to help him to focus on and resolve his dilemma, without intervention he might not have completed his university requirements.

The cases described above illustrate important features of a crisis-oriented approach: establishing a time line to ascertain precipitating stress and antecedent hazards; helping the student understand what went wrong; helping the student find ways to express affect; and establishing new or reestablishing old coping behaviors, often by using social networks. Initial detective work frequently pays off.

Loss is usually a central issue, as is apparent in all three cases. Loss may be particularly apparent for the student who has recently left home. Experience with loss may be new. Moreover, the first loss of an intimate friend often triggers unresolved issues in relationships with parents.

Summary

Colleges and universities are complex environments that challenge entering students. Students often enter college as adolescents, poorly equipped to handle life experiences. If the student is to have a meaningful college experience, he or she must master not only educational requirements but also the developmental tasks of growing into adulthood. For many students these challenges are overwhelming and result in crisis. The SPS crisis program, featuring easy access, prompt assessment, and immediate crisis therapy, assists many students to move successfully through their college experience. However, approximately 15 to 20 percent of student clients clearly require more than the crisis-oriented approach. Often, these students have suffered severe early or multiple losses. Although they may benefit from crisis intervention, they require continued support and, frequently, referral to long-term treatment. Nonetheless, crisis intervention is an important component of the school's mental health program.

The author gratefully acknowledges the assistance of Dr. David Palmer, first director of the SPS, in formulating this chapter's discussion of the UCLA Student Psychological Services Program.

References

Berkovitz, I. H. (1983). Emerging from adolescence: I. Theoretical discussion. *Clinical Update in Adolescent Psychiatry, 1* (14), 2–11.

Budman, S., & Gurman, A. (1988). *Theory and practice of brief therapy*. New York: Guilford Press.

Caplan, G. (1964). *Principles of preventive psychiatry*. New York: Basic Books.

Chickering, A. W., & Havighurst, R. J. (1981). The life cycle. In A. W. Chickering et al. (Eds.), *The modern American college*. San Francisco: Jossey-Bass.

Cummings, N. A. (1977). Prolonged (ideal) versus short-term (realistic) psychotherapy. *Professional Psychologist, 8*, 491–501.

Davanloo, H. (Ed.). (1980). *Short-term dynamic psychotherapy*. New York: Jason Aronson.

Dorosin, D., Gibbs, J., & Kaplan, L. (1976). Very brief interventions—a pilot evaluation. *Journal of the American College Health Association, 24*, 191–194.

Drye, R. C., Goulding, R. L., & Goulding, M. E. (1973). No-suicide decisions: Patient monitoring of suicidal risk. *American Journal of Psychiatry, 130*, 171–174.

Erikson, E. H. (1950). *Childhood and society*. New York: Norton.

Garfield, S. L. (1978). Research on client variables in psychotherapy. In S. L. Garfield & A. E. Bergin (Eds.), *Handbook of psychotherapy and behavior change*. New York: John Wiley.

Grayson, P. A. (1985). College time: Implications for student mental health services. *Journal of American College Health Association, 33*, 198–204.

Group for the Advancement of Psychiatry (1968). *Normal adolescence*. New York: author.

Haggerty, Jr., J. J., Baldwin, B. A., & Liptzin, M. B. (1980). Very brief interventions in college mental health. *Journal of American College Health Association, 28*, 326–329.

Harwell, J. S. (1984). Student mental health from a layman's perspective. *Journal of American College Health Association, 33*, 131–133.

Havighurst, R. J. (1972). *Developmental tasks and education* (3d ed.). New York: McKay.

Ichikawa, A. (1965). Observations of college students in acute distress. In H. J. Parad (Ed.), *Crisis intervention: Selected readings*. New York: Family Service Association of America.

Jacobson, G. F. (1974). Programs and techniques of crisis intervention. In S. Arieti (Ed.), *American handbook of psychiatry* (2d ed.). New York: Basic Books.

Kapp, R. A. (1974). An interdisciplinary campus mental health program specializing in crisis-oriented services. *Professional Psychologist, 2*, 25–32.

Levinson, D. J., Darrow, C. D., Klein, E. B., Levinson, M. N., & McKee, B. (1978). *The seasons of a man's life*. New York: Alfred A. Knopf.

Lindemann, E. (1965). Symptomatology and management of acute grief. In H. J. Parad, *Crisis intervention: Selected readings*. New York: Family Service Association of America.

Malan, D. H. (1963). *A study of brief psychotherapy*. London: Tavistock Publications.

Podolnick, E. E., Pass, H. L., & Bybee, D. M. (1979). A psychodynamic approach to brief therapy. *Journal of American College Health Association, 28*, 109–113.

Rimmer, J., Halikas, J. A., & Schucket, M. A. (1982). Prevalence and incidence of psychiatric illness in college students: A four-year prospective study. *Journal of American College Health Association, 30*, 207–211.

Ringstrom, P. A. (1981). Short-term treatment: A study of characteristics and outcome. Unpublished doctoral dissertation, University of Southern California, Los Angeles.

8

Crisis and Adult Development: A Psychoanalyst's Perspective

NORMAN TABACHNICK

CRISES AND CRISIS RESOLUTION play important roles in adult development. However, because psychological development can be described without emphasizing aspects of crisis, what rationale can be used to link the two?

Human life consists of continuous interactions with people and situations. Many of these interactions involve behaviors whose essential characteristics proceed from established psychic structures. However, people sometimes encounter circumstances for which they are poorly or not at all prepared. These situations constitute *crises* and often lead to the formation of new coping mechanisms.

In other words, the crises of adult life affect adult development, and successful resolution of crises creates a sense of competence, integration, and personal value. Success creates new biopsychosocial modes of reacting—the hallmarks of successful adult development.

Theory

As indicated in chapter 1, crisis is defined, at least in part, by its call for rapid response. From the standpoint of dynamic psychology, this urgency can be understood as due to an *absence of functioning character structure*. As human beings develop, they accumulate a repertoire of adaptational mechanisms that help balance their individual needs (for bodily survival, human relationships, and internal balance) with the environment.

Although a new situation may produce a state of uncertainty, individuals usually draw from their repertoire of available adaptive mechanisms to resolve this uncertainty. And although the individual may experience a sense of impatience, the situation is not urgent. In other words, the individual experiences a *problem* for which he or she is confident a solution will be achieved.

Sometimes, however, the individual does not possess a specific adaptational mechanism or group of mechanisms sufficient to the task. When this occurs, the person experiences a sense of intense urgency and *crisis*. Of course, it is easier to make these distinctions abstractly than when one is immersed in the problematical situation.

Although crises are sometimes resolved through outside assistance, the individual often participates in formulating and effecting a resolution of the crisis.

When the individual plays an active role in crisis resolution, a new adaptive mechanism is created and character developed.

Early psychoanalytic theory postulated the occurrence of *regular developmental crises*. For example, according to Freud, the oral, anal, phallic, and genital stages were inevitable passages in every individual's life. Variability in how character developed was dependent upon constitutional and environmental differences. The crux of the theory, however, was that individuals moved through identifiable stages of development and that certain elements of character were present in all individuals. Other psychoanalysts added significant new concepts to this theoretical outline. Erikson (1959), for example, postulated that certain *modes of behaving* were important outcomes of "stages of development."

However, among early developmental theorists, the universality of developmental stages was a given. Theorists believed that resolution of early crises left a permanent stamp upon the individual's personality. In other words, characteristics forged in the heat of crises would be strong, persistent, and resistant to change. Freud believed that psychoanalysis could do little to change character. He thought that at best psychoanalysis could help people understand themselves better, which, in turn, would make life more tolerable.

One problem with early psychoanalytic thinking is that it placed excessive emphasis on the genetic inevitability of early developmental stages. Freud and others believed that universal genetic patterns meant that all individuals would go through roughly similar developmental experiences. However, cultural relativists were quick to point out that development varied widely among cultures. The values and superegos of South Sea Islanders were quite different from those of the Europeans from whom Freud derived his data. Thus it appeared that cultural influences, shaped by local geography, history, philosophy, and so forth, were as important, perhaps more important, than genetic components in shaping character development.

Another problem with early psychoanalytic thought is its postulate that childhood developmental experience has an overwhelming shaping influence. Numerous thinkers, both from within the psychoanalytic school (Erikson, 1950, 1959; Levenson, Darrow, Klein, Levenson, & McKee, 1978) and outside (Kagan, 1984), have shown how post–childhood developmental experience may strongly affect new character development. In addition, most contemporary psychoanalysts do not agree with Freud that therapeutic psychoanalysis seldom changes character. They feel that change is possible and is often realized.

Thus current thought has revised earlier views that postulated the immutable consequences of genetic and early childhood influence. It now appears possible that all stages of the life cycle are susceptible to psychological crises, which, in turn, can lead to developmental change.

If crises are not inevitable, if they are not preordained, how do they arise? To answer this question, it is helpful to understand good parenting skills. Good parents appreciate the need for children to master new developmental tasks. They help the child identify and meet the challenges of these tasks by offering hope, confidence, and support.

The child experiments in his or her efforts to overcome the challenges of these tasks. Ideally, the parents attempt to help the child confront problems while respecting the child's developmental abilities and special characteristics. For example, if a child who is learning to walk has weak musculature, the parent may provide extra physical support. However, if the child is particularly strong, the parent may provide less physical support and encouragement. If these elements are well fitted to one another, the child experiences walking as a challenge, not a crisis. On the other hand, if a parent is insensitive to a child's development and forgets that the child has muscular weakness, the parent's expectations may be inappropriate. The child's capacities become strained, and the child experiences a crisis due to lack of parental support.

At all ages and all developmental stages, certain circumstances may create crisis situations. Others' expectations may exceed an individual's capacity, or an individual may be suddenly placed in a situation in which he or she has no support and no means of coping. In a more abstract context, crisis occurs when the biological, psychological, and social spheres interact in ways such that the individual experiences more uncertainty and anxiety than he or she can master.

Cath (1965) identified pertinent problems of adult development. In the middle years, individuals experience an awareness of limitation and/or decline of their physical and mental abilities, a sense that their life course is set and opportunities for change are few, an awareness that cherished internal and external goals may not be accomplished, and a sense that their life is closer to its end. In addition, individuals increasingly experience loss as family and friends become independent, move away, or die. Utilizing concepts of developmental diagnosis and adult developmental lines, Nemiroff and Colarusso (1985) focused on several critical issues, including changing body image, midlife sexuality, the race against time, relations with grown children and grandchildren, transmitting values and skills, refining work identity, and continuing familiar and building new relationships.

In one's later years, these issues and problems increase in intensity. Difficult questions arise, such as, "What kind of person have I become? How self-sustaining? How much of a burden? How crippled and restricting of others? How healthy or capable? What respect is due me? What has happened to my plans? What next?" (Cath, 1965, p. 185).

However, these problems are not limited to middle and older age but are often present during earlier stages of the life cycle. Conversely, problems that are frequently associated with earlier stages in the life cycle may be present in middle and older age. Most therapists would agree that the occurrence of specific stresses is not irrevocably linked to specific life-cycle stages. Indeed, the combination of several stressors, perhaps originating in different stages of the life cycle, is common.

Finally, one must question to what degree the appearance of particular stressors in middle and older age is caused by sociocultural factors. For example, in societies in which physical death is not equated with the end of "life," concerns about loss, extinction, and "summing up" occur infrequently or not at all. In her literature review concerning transitional life-cycle crises, Golan, borrowing from Neugarten, reminds us that "social clocks . . . are becoming more significant than biological or chronological ones" (Golan, 1986, p. 6).

As a final theoretical guideline, consider the concept of "RIGs," which stands for *representations of interactions that have been generalized* (Stern, 1985). In *The Interpersonal World of the Infant*, Stern presents recent findings and theories on infant development. Interestingly, however, the concepts are relevant to other stages of life, including adult development. The concept of RIGs can be useful in understanding crisis in that it helps explain what occurs when an individual enters a state of crisis as well as the steps that are taken to overcome crisis.

How are RIGs formed? In infants, RIGs encompass both interpersonal interactions and the feelings that accompany interactions. For example, when an infant plays with his or her mother over an extended period, a "feeling" experience develops and actions and feelings are melded together. Stern notes that not all of the experiences that constitute a given RIG are identical; some are more pleasant, some less so. Also, interactions vary. However, all of the actions, interactions, and feelings are generalized and a certain type of experience takes on meaning. Although this concept is not new in dynamic psychology, Stern has provided an explicit formulation and has cited infant research data in support of the concept.

Adults also utilize RIGs. When RIGs with positive, self-sustaining meaning for the individual are operative, the individual experiences a positive sense of self. Conversely, when RIGs are negative, the individual experiences a negative sense of self. For example, in an important, sustaining relationship, RIGs both qualitatively and quantitatively sustain an individual's positive sense of self. However, if the significant other leaves, the sustaining RIGs are no longer available and self-esteem plunges. Such changes precipitate crisis. The concept of RIGs can also be applied to one's relationship with nonhuman entities, for example, crises that are experienced due to an earthquake or loss of fortune.

Crisis Treatment

Crisis treatment should be approached in the following way: (1) deciding whether a crisis exists (diagnosis), (2) deciding whether the therapist should intervene, and (3) determining the appropriate interventions. Ideally, the first two steps—deciding whether a crisis exists and deciding whether to intervene—should occur simultaneously, although it is not always possible for this to happen.

First, the therapist must differentiate between a *crisis* and a *problem*. Feelings of uncertainty, anxiety, and apprehension often accompany problems, thus making it possible to mistake problems for crises. Such misdiagnoses are regrettable in that the client believes that he or she *requires* outside help, when in fact the client may be entirely capable of dealing with the problem alone. Such misdiagnoses are harmful to the client's self-esteem.

Even if crisis is present, the therapist must decide whether it calls for intervention. Outside intervention is not always necessary. For example, a client may already be taking helpful actions leading toward crisis resolution. Overtreating a crisis may be counterproductive; the ability of the individual to resolve his or her own crisis should not be underestimated.

Diagnostic criteria can be divided into three categories: (1) objective signs, (2) subjective symptoms, and (3) information from significant others.

Signs of crisis. As explained in chapter 1, an individual in crisis shows a decreasing ability to cope in daily and interpersonal functioning. The person experiences anxiety and fear; phobias, illusions, or delusions are sometimes present. Victims describe anxieties that under normal circumstances may be suppressed. Judgment is poor. For example, a man who was acutely suicidal agreed after anxious discussion that he should enter a hospital. However, he asked to defer his admission for twenty-hour hours because he needed to pick up his laundry. Memory and general integrative ability deteriorate. The person may become immobilized and unable to make decisions. The victim may feel exhausted because of the strain of choosing among conflicting courses of action.

Subjective symptoms and feelings. The crisis victim may experience intense discomfort and feelings of depression and failure. The client may feel a sense of impending doom, hopelessness, and worthlessness and may long for surcease from pain and wish for death. Such feelings increase dramatically as the crisis continues. Conversely, a decrease in the intensity of such feelings suggests that the course of the crisis is being reversed.

Crisis victims are caught in a vicious cycle. Less able to accomplish important goals, they cannot alleviate the crisis situation, which makes them feel inadequate and desperate. Desperation triggers increased, often frantic, efforts to accomplish something. Due to the chaotic condition of their lives, however, their efforts generally fail, which creates more desperation. Crisis victims often become exhausted and eventually immobilized as repeated failures take their toll.

Significant others. Frequently crisis victims do not want help. At the beginning of the crisis, a sense of shame may accompany feelings of inadequacy. The person's first impulse may be to work harder. A crisis victim may not wish others to see him or her in such an inadequate state and may fear rejection. As the cycle progresses, the crisis victim may become too disorganized to initiate meaningful contact with helpers. Thus concerned relatives, friends, and coworkers may help connect the crisis victim with a therapist.

The therapist should spend time with these significant others. In crisis treatment, the therapist's stance toward significant others is usually different from that of dynamic therapies. In dynamic therapies, the therapist attempts to emphasize that the work is being undertaken at the wish of the client and to support the client's initiative. In crisis treatment, the reverse may be true, and the therapist may have to help the client acknowledge that he or she is too disorganized at present to take responsibility for his or her life. The client's responsibility is to recognize a need for help. The therapist attempts to make the client aware of his or her disorganization and to direct the client to significant others for assistance. Of course, the victim's own resources should also be enlisted to the extent possible. However, in emergency situations the therapist may reach out to mobilize the help of significant others.

Significant others can be helpful in detailing the origin and progression of the crisis, which is particularly important because the client is often unable to provide such information. Moreover, significant others may figure in the origin of the crisis. Because crisis is often the result of ruptures in interpersonal relationships, significant others may also be enlisted in the reestablishment or healing of a ruptured relationship.

Active Psychotherapeutic Intervention

Crisis therapy is guided by four principles:

- Direct help to a disintegrating or disorganized person
- Rebuilding the client's diminished self-esteem
- Reactivation and strengthening of the client's existing coping mechanisms
- Development of new coping mechanisms

However, before discussing each of these in detail, two general observations are in order: First, in crisis treatment timing is critical. Anxiety, disorganization, and despair are hallmarks of crisis, and there is no time for lengthy evaluations. Although one runs the risk of making wrong decisions, one also runs the greater risk of having the client deteriorate further if the evaluation is prolonged.

Second, although crisis therapy often draws on psychodynamic theory, it is *not* an analytic therapy; rather, it is a supportive, directive psychotherapy. The following case example illustrates the inappropriate use of analytic therapy at a time of crisis:

> A man subject to disorganized psychotic states had been coping successfully for a number of years. He lived with his parents and periodically saw a psychiatrist, who prescribed antipsychotic medication. When the parents moved to a distant city, the son initially stayed behind. He felt less secure but was able to maintain control with his doctor's support and the medication. However, he then decided to follow his parents to their new home where he contacted another therapist. The new therapist elected to treat the patient using an uncovering "analytic" psychotherapy. Medication was not prescribed. The patient became anxious and deteriorated into psychosis. The therapist judged that the patient was being resistant and manipulative, and prescribed increased uncovering sessions and no medication. The patient committed suicide.

Direct Help

Direct *personal support* should be immediately established. The therapist must indicate that he or she will be there for the client, that the client is no longer alone but has a firm, decisive ally. In crisis therapy, the therapist may have to press hard to establish a relationship. The therapist should operate with the understanding that the client is unclear, disorganized, and unable to settle on the best course of action and that someone must make decisions for the client. As the client becomes stronger and the crisis diminishes, this assumption will change and the client will begin to assume more responsibility.

Rebuilding Self-Esteem

The therapist should offer encouragement and hope and let the client know that he or she is feeling more despondent and self-critical than is appropriate. The client needs to understand that everyone experiences periods when things do not go well and that it is important to accept disappointments and to deal with them. As previously stated, the client should be encouraged to turn to others for help. The therapist should point out the capabilities that the client has demonstrated in the past as well as current capabilities in an effort to repair self-esteem. Such comments help establish and strengthen an ongoing, caring relationship.

Reactivation and Strengthening of Coping Mechanisms

The therapist should identify the coping mechanisms that the client is currently using and has used before. For example, if a client says that he feels good only at work, the therapist should try to find out what there is about work that produces a good feeling, then encourage the client to increase such activities. The therapist should elicit the help of relatives and friends to create situations that make the client feel good about him- or herself.

Developing New Coping Mechanisms

In a similar way, the therapist looks for and creates new coping possibilities. One suggests them, and sometimes urges them strongly on the client. If they can be utilized, that is progress; if not, they are discarded and one goes on to a new possibility. For example, if the therapist believes that the client feels comfortable at work in the presence of same-gender friends and suggests that the client become closer with these friends, the client may experience a reduction in crisis symptoms. However, if the client complains of increased anxiety with regard to these work associates, the therapist may decide that the value of peer group contacts is more apparent than real.

All four therapeutic principles share a common thread, that is, a stronger individual offering closeness and suggestions to a weaker person. Most people in crisis respond to and are strengthened by such help. Interactions between the therapist and client simultaneously indicate human concern while providing a bridge to a stronger self. The process is similar to that at work in early infant development. If an infant loses its mother and the implications of such loss are not counteracted by society, that infant will sink into an "anaclitic depression" (Spitz, 1945). However, when society responds to the significance of this loss, the infant moves along a healthy developmental path.

Clinical Cases

The crises that are presented here are intended to be representative of common adult predicaments. The disorganization and discomfort an individual experiences during crisis stem from external and internal losses. External losses include stressors such as the loss of a significant relationship, good fortune, food and shelter, and so forth. Internal losses may be conceptualized as loss of confidence in one's self and, consequently, one's ability to cope with the external loss. Internal and external losses are probably present to some degree in all crisis situations.

Crisis victims obviously differ in their receptiveness to outside help. Some victims wish no outside help, believing they can manage by themselves—an accurate assessment in some instances. Other victims seek outside help or will accept it quickly when it is offered.

The personality of the victim obviously plays an important part in the crisis and its subsequent course. Although some individuals' response to crisis treatment is so quick that issues of character need not be considered in depth, with most victims the crisis is dependent upon the victim's general character and coping style, which, in turn, affect the course of treatment.

Case 1: A Resistant Client

A woman called the local suicide prevention center concerning a sixty-three-year-old man, James, with whom she had been romantically involved. She had decided to leave him. James had been depressed and had talked of suicide even before her leaving. She called him once or twice following the separation. She stated that he still had suicidal feelings and that perhaps they were increasing. She said that she did not wish to be further involved but hoped his life could be saved.

A worker at the center called James and arranged a meeting. At the meeting, after hearing that his friend did not want to reestablish their relationship, James refused to come in again. The worker called each week. James continued to live an isolated life, making no attempt to leave his room except for food and cigarettes. His depression did not subside. Approximately six months later, a worker at the center saw a news item about a fire at a boarding house in which someone had died. The victim, James, had been drinking and smoking in bed.

It seems likely that his accident was related to James's depression and state of crisis. The center was unable to establish a close connection. The only thing James wanted was for his friend to return. In this case, the victim was unable to find new coping behaviors.

Although he received slight support from the center, it was not sufficient to change his patterns of behavior.

Case 2: Overcoming Crisis through Inner Strength

Some individuals attempt to overcome crisis by looking within themselves. The biographies of artists and other creative individuals provide numerous examples of persons who deal with crisis in this way.

In his study of the life, career, and psychodynamics of the nineteenth-century author Herman Melville, Murray (1968) concluded that Melville's success as a writer was related to psychological tragedies. During the first two or three years of his writing career, Melville experienced happy and exuberant periods. However, the subsequent forty years of his life were characterized by frequent bouts of depression, despair, and suicidal thinking, as indicated in chronicles of Melville's life, autobiographical material, and his writing itself.

Murray believes that Melville experienced great psychological pain at not receiving love from his mother, who was either indifferent to him or whom he perceived as indifferent to him. Murray hypothesizes that Melville turned to writing partly to build inner strength and to create a vehicle for expressing and dealing with feelings of rejection. Although Melville experienced despair throughout his life, he never succumbed to that despair. His creative life as a writer, although marked by lack of commercial success, sustained him.

Of course, in clinical practice few persons solve their problems by developing their creative writing talents. However, in work with crisis victims, a client may sometimes develop a special skill in the course of treatment, a skill that helps sustain the victim. Thus some people rescue themselves from crisis by developing an inner talent, others depend on external help and support, and still others receive external help while simultaneously developing an inner skill.

Case 3: Loss of a Longtime Companion

A fifty-year-old single woman, Margie, came to the suicide prevention center because of her increasing depression and suicidal thoughts following her mother's death. Margie had lived with her mother. The two of them had served as each other's chief support, and their life together had been satisfactory. Even while Margie's mother suffered her final illness, the two of them had much emotional interaction, which sustained Margie. She valued herself for taking care of her mother.

After Margie's mother died, she reported feeling lost. She stated, "Coming back from the funeral was like closing a chapter in my life. I came back to nothing."

Margie had had some contact with friends and social groups before her mother's death. However, these activities seemed to have lost meaning for her. She was despondent, but wished to live and hoped that the center could help her. As her therapist, I worked with her for eight individual sessions and had five subsequent telephone calls.

Initially, I saw her three days in a row. Because she was depressed, I prescribed antidepressant medication. I reassured and supported her, telling her that depression was common and normal under these circumstances. Her mother had meant a great deal to her, and Margie had centered her life on her mother. Now she felt as though her life no longer had purpose. She needed to understand that mourning is normal, and that although she would always be sad to some degree when she thought of her mother, her grief would eventually become manageable and her life would become more rewarding.

Margie had lived a good life and had accomplished many things. She was still young and vigorous. The key to treatment was getting Margie to become reinvolved in life. To do so, contacts with friends and organizations that had been important had to be reestablished. Margie needed to push herself to be with these people and groups so that when she felt bad, she had a support network to which she could turn.

Margie improved gradually over a period of several months. In addition to encouraging her to become connected with the outside world, I made calls to some of her friends and to community groups, who responded by encouraging her, grieving with her, and caring for her.

Margie was pleased and followed my suggestions. She said it was hard at the beginning but that she knew I was interested in her, which meant a great deal. She said, "When I'm feeling bad, I think of what you would tell me to do, then I do it."

Subsequent phone calls indicated that Margie continued developing a renewed interest in life. She said that she still grieved for her mother and knew that she would never forget her. Then she talked about "Dr. Tabachnick." She would discuss him with me as if he were a third person. It seemed that she was internalizing this "third person" and having him take the place of her mother.

This case illustrates development of self based upon coping with a loss. Although the loss had seemed overwhelming at first, it had not extinguished Margie's desire to live. During treatment, I confronted that desire directly and vigorously, replacing Margie's loss with an optimistic "something." At the same time, Margie learned how to deal with loss. A new RIG model was established, which gave Margie strength and hope. A growth cycle was set in motion.

Case 4: Losing a Father

A forty-year-old professor of history, Jack, was concerned about his persistent "nervousness" and wanted a consultation. Jack arrived at the office in a state of anxiety. His discomfort, which I initially thought was related to loss, was in part embarrassment. He was ashamed of being depressed for so long. His father had died three months previously. After his father's death, he had at first accepted his grief as normal under the circumstances. However, as time went on and his depression persisted, he became increasingly uncomfortable and felt something was wrong with him. He had always handled life in a rational way and felt that he should be able to adjust to this loss in his life.

Jack felt embarrassed at wanting to talk to friends and relatives about his loss. He felt his credit had run out, particularly with friends. Although they had been willing to support him for a while, they expected him to pull himself together. This combination of feeling defective and wanting to get help without feeling guilty brought him to a psychiatrist.

Jack's father, an energetic, competent, organized man, had worked for an international firm. His job was to initiate new branch offices, work with them for the first six months or year, then move on. Jack and his siblings had rarely stayed in one location for longer than two years when they were growing up. Consequently, the family was quite close—"the only game in town."

Jack felt that his mother was a good caretaker, but he did not love her as much as he loved his father. He idealized his father, who had great energy and loved all of his children. In fact, Jack's father loved everybody, which was a problem because Jack felt left out—he simply did not get enough from his father. Even though Jack wanted more from his father, he treasured what he received. He felt that his father had breathed the "essence of life" into him. He had hoped that his father, while growing older, would be more available for him. Jack talked about having children and looked forward to his father's infusing them with life as he had infused Jack with life.

Thus his father's death not only represented a loss of a loved one, it represented the loss of someone who was to be important in the life of Jack's children. At this point, Jack wondered whether he should even have children. Furthermore, he wondered whether it was possible for him to live meaningfully.

Initially I saw Jack two times a week, but that soon increased to three times a week. The crisis therapy lasted for nine weeks. He used medication for anxiety during the early part of treatment. The medication was later reduced.

Jack's anxiety and concern quickly diminished. It was important for him to tell me about his life. Throughout the sessions his idealization of his father remained strong, but he began to question his relationship with his mother.

Although he felt cheated by her, he could not really blame her. As he saw it, she raised a family and took care of the household under difficult circumstances. The family was always moving to new countries and new homes. She had six children to care for. She took care of the essentials and saw to it that everyone was fed, clothed, and had a decent place to live.

However, she was sorely beset by her trials and treated her responsibilities and children as necessary but irksome burdens. When the children complained, she let them know that she was doing as much as she could and that she expected them to be quiet. Jack accepted this situation as a given in his life. Before treatment, he generally did not seem to know that he resented his mother, and whenever he was aware of resentment, he thought that such feelings were inappropriate. His father, on the other hand, was willing to listen. Indeed, he *liked* to listen. However, his father was often absent.

Nevertheless, Jack and his siblings applied themselves to their lives and their careers. They were successful in their careers and were either married or had long-standing relationships that would probably lead to marriage.

I provided Jack with warm and encouraging support as I do for all clients who are victims of crisis. However, I soon realized that the support I was giving Jack encouraged him to perceive me as a father figure. I concluded that a goal of treatment was for Jack to lose an idealized father figure without losing his zest for life. He needed to "de-idealize" his father.

We began working on Jack's recognition and expression of anger toward supportive people in his life. Because Jack had already accepted his feelings of displeasure with his mother and because she was not living with him, I felt it was safe to encourage stronger expression of his feelings toward her. Although Jack made some attempts to excuse her, he began to see how deprived he felt and how angry he was with her.

Next we focused on similar feelings directed toward colleagues at the university. He had developed a relatively independent life and had few close relationships. He indicated that he "didn't mind" the various frustrations he experienced with colleagues because, as he saw it, his colleagues did not mean a great deal to him. As we continued our work, he began to see that he did want to establish closer relationships with his colleagues, despite the fact that he would have to deal with the inevitable irritations that occur among friends.

Finally, we dealt with his irritation with me, which was difficult for Jack. He felt that if he expressed displeasure toward me I would leave, just as his mother had distanced herself when he made demands as a child. Eventually, Jack was able to express his irritation toward me. He appeared anxious when he did so, but because I did not leave him, the anxiety was tolerable.

Throughout this period, Jack gradually resolved his feelings of depression and crisis. He felt more comfortable at work. He began developing closer relationships with his colleagues, which included getting angry at them. Throughout his life he had tended to be a rather Spartan, self-depriving individual; rather suddenly he became interested in stereo equipment, and to everyone's surprise, purchased a good system. One day he told me that he and his wife were planning to have a child. Clearly, his crisis was ending. Jack decided he wanted to continue work on building self-confidence and involvement with others. He wanted to learn how to differ with others while maintaining a relationship with them.

Jack's initial RIG involved suppressing his irritation. If he did this, then his father, although somewhat distant, would one day return and give him the positive infusions that would make life possible. His father's death shattered his dream. He went into crisis because he had nothing to serve as a substitute for that dream. He literally did not know how he could continue functioning. Using this scenario as his initial RIG, he made contact with a new potential father—me.

A new RIG was then developed that allowed Jack to be self-assertive, express his anger, and make demands of other people. Sometimes this new expression of self would succeed, but even if it didn't, Jack would maintain his integrity. As this new RIG was developing, his sense of panic subsided and was replaced by a feeling of optimism.

This case example dramatically illustrates a spectrum of crisis intervention endeavors, beginning with immediate emotional first aid, accompanied by the use of anti-anxiety medication to avoid decompensation in a crisis-ridden client. Therapy then evolved into short-term psychodynamic treatment aimed at solving problems in living related to the crisis. The therapy concluded with an extended period of help aimed at personality restructuring to enhance the client's view of himself as well as his future coping ability. Drawing on Marmor's (1979) contribution, Parad and Parad discuss this continuum concept of crisis intervention in chapter 1.

Case 5: Willingly Accepting a Loss

Most often crisis is caused by loss; replacing what was lost is usually important in reversing the crisis. However, giving up a cherished relationship without replacement sometimes helps to resolve a crisis.

Margaret was a thirty-seven-year-old woman whom I had previously treated. I considered her to be "borderline," that is, a personality that was stable under some conditions but disintegrated quickly under stress.

In my initial (precrisis) therapeutic encounter with Margaret, she was contemplating marriage and was under pressure from her family to cancel her planned wedding. During her previous dating, she had had high and low points, but she had never before come close to marriage. Her parents regarded her as emotionally backward and in need of constant counseling. They steered her toward men of distinction in appearance, social status, and fortune. Although Margaret agreed that such men were desirable, she felt uncomfortable with them.

About one year before she came to treatment, she met a man whose social status was lower than hers. He had emotional difficulties, but most of the time was able to sustain himself. They got along quite well and decided to marry. Margaret's parents attempted to dissuade her; that interpersonal struggle initially brought her to treatment. During this first episode of therapy, I supported Margaret with advice that she had the right to make her own choices based on her own best interests. I interceded with her parents, who finally and reluctantly agreed to the union. The marriage went surprisingly well. The parents withdrew their objections and the family began to draw together. Margaret and I decided our work was done.

Two years later, Margaret reappeared in considerable turmoil. Her crisis centered on the impending birth of a child (in three months). Although her husband had not been as enthusiastic as she about having a child, he had agreed. At first her parents were ambivalent, wondering whether the new stress would prove too much for Margaret. The parents finally supported her having a child.

As the pregnancy progressed, Margaret became increasingly anxious. She tried to reassure herself by telling herself that her anxiety was normal. She wondered if she was too weak emotionally to become a mother. She wanted to have the child and to overcome her anxiety so that she could be a good mother. Her parents were supportive of her and suggested that she enter therapy. They supported her financially so that she could stop work and devote all her energies to the child. Margaret started to decompensate. She entered my office in crisis.

At first I attempted to point out her strengths, for example, projects she had completed, her successes at work and school. If she could do all this, she would be able to raise the child. I believe I had a narcissistic interest in seeing Margaret become a successful mother.

After a short time, it became clear that Margaret was not getting stronger and that my efforts were unsuccessful. She became increasingly anxious and had trouble sleeping. Indeed, I had the disheartening experience of watching my patient crumble before my eyes. I considered taking another direction in therapy. Perhaps Margaret should acknowledge her limitation in raising children and opt for a more meaningful life for herself, her family, and her child by considering adoption. This position was difficult for me. I contacted a consultant, who concurred with my decision.

When I suggested this idea to Margaret, she protested and expressed guilt. At the same time, however, her anxiety noticeably decreased. In addition, I saw a regrouping and strengthening of her usual coping characteristics. Her anxiety decreased; she began expressing her ideas and feelings more confidently and convincingly. Her sleep patterns improved.

Margaret was still reluctant to give up her child, so we struck a deal. We would make initial plans for adoption. If, during the first few weeks of the child's life, it became clear that the situation was not working, we would implement the adoption plan. However, if Margaret was able to deal with motherhood, we would abandon the plan.

The child was born, and Margaret experienced increasing distress, which she was able to acknowledge. The adoption took place. Margaret began to improve and has sustained her improvement.

In this case example, the crisis victim had to accept a loss in order to sustain a meaningful life. The client gained developmentally in that she was forced to acknowledge her limitations. This RIG had been initiated earlier in her life when she struggled with conflict between her parents' wishes for her and her own desires. In crisis therapy, this RIG was further elaborated in that she learned that even an ideal that she had set up for herself might need to be changed. I supported her in her decision, and eventually her parents did as well.

Case 6: Loss of Self-Esteem

Lance, a fifty-four-year-old physician, entered psychoanalysis because of increasing depression, the impending breakup of his marriage, and difficulty at work. He described several previous brief psychotherapies. When things had gone badly, he had sought help. Although he felt somewhat improved by these contacts, he felt that "nothing much had come of them." He thought that psychoanalysis, which he believed was the best therapy, was his last chance to "put it together."

A trial analysis was initiated to identify important issues and to ascertain if analysis would work. His depression lifted rapidly, perhaps because he was seeing me frequently and because my attitude was uncritical and friendly. In addition, his relationship with his wife (from whom he was separated) improved, and they decided to live together again.

Although he felt a little better about work, difficulties continued. As therapy progressed, he developed new ideas about the significance of his job in his troubles. He realized that the judgment of "poor work," which had been delivered by his medical group, was in fact a notification of impending termination. He believed that he had committed so many errors at work that his colleagues' opinions could not be reversed. Then he received a formal pronouncement that he should seek other employment.

Feeling anxious but with uplifted spirits, he began to look for another job. He found one with a new medical group, and he began to feel better. After six months of treatment, he felt no need to continue. Although he understood that analysis took longer and that his personality was not completely changed, he felt that his interests lay in his new position, being with his family, and other enjoyable pursuits.

In retrospect, what appeared to be a request for analysis was actually a plea for help in a developing crisis. His work situation was the central concern. He needed the self-esteem that comes from doing a good job, not analysis.

Although six months of treatment is not typical for most crisis situations, this case is instructive for three reasons. First, it indicates that a crisis may be resolved over an extended period. Second, it illustrates how various areas of life must be integrated to foster self-esteem. Third, it shows how a developmental RIG was either established or reinforced; that is, as simplistic as it may seem, it is never too late to try something new. Even though one may fear failure, taking a chance often empowers the individual and provides opportunities for something new and good.

Case 7: Significance of the Family

Florence, a thirty-eight-year-old woman dying of terminal metastatic cancer, entered treatment because she was despondent and thinking of suicide. She felt anxious, depressed, and hopeless. It would be best, she thought, if she were dead; she wanted to kill herself, but didn't know how. In the last two months, she had become increasingly physically debilitated. Because of her disabilities, her husband felt she needed to be in a convalescent home, which increased Florence's depression. He did not see how he could work and also take care of his wife, who needed constant attention. Florence was also unable to take care of their two children. The entire family was distraught.

I spoke to Florence, her husband, the children, and a relative. The children, and particularly the husband, were depressed and anxious over the ordeal of dealing with Florence's impending death.

I felt that the husband's anxiety might be reversed by frank discussion of his fears and losses. He broke down and expressed grief for himself and his wife at having lost so much. I suggested that it might be better if Florence lived at home, indicating that help could be found to deal with the practical difficulties. On balance, this solution seemed better than to separate the family and reject the wife. Economic difficulties, which were the reason for placing Florence in a home, were overcome with the help of friends and relatives. Florence returned home, and her depression and anxiety receded. The family felt that the last months of her life were worthwhile. When Florence died, the family coped with grief in an adaptive, open manner..

Conclusion

This chapter focused on adult development through mastery of crisis. In a crisis situation, in contrast with a problem that is manageable, the self must deal with the disintegration of its adaptational responses and defenses that sustain identity. The individual is sometimes able to resolve the crisis by utilizing inner strengths—as did Herman Melville—or by drawing upon the support of family and friends. Or the individual or family in crisis may seek or be brought to a therapist for aid in crisis resolution. The crisis intervention mode may be emergency psychological first aid or short-term dynamic therapy. The latter may, in certain cases, lead to long-term therapy.

Especially frustrating to the practitioner are situations similar to that of James, who refused to accept help. For most clients, however, dissolution of defenses opens them to learning new adaptations and new ways of interacting with their environment.

All of the case examples presented here deal with the resolution of loss: loss of a mother to whom the daughter was bonded; loss of father, wife, child; and loss of self-esteem. Margaret, who gave up the baby with whom she could not cope, and Jack, who lost the father he never had, experienced a dual loss of the person and the dream.

In the case of Florence, there was initially a maladaptive response to the crisis. Florence's husband attempted to deal with the impending object loss by removing his wife to a convalescent home to die. In this case example, we see the importance of familial support and anticipatory grief work in discovering meaning in loss.

It is both a cliché and a truism that loss is inevitable for all humans. In the case examples presented here, crises were resolved by the development of a new RIG that enabled the individual(s) to relate to others in different, more positive ways. Moreover, new coping mechanisms, important additions to the psychic structure, were created that would help the individual face future life crises.

References

Cath, S. H. (1965). Some dynamics of the middle and later years. In H. J. Parad (Ed.), *Crisis Intervention, Selected Readings* (pp. 174–190). New York: Family Service Association of America.

Erikson, E. H. (1950). *Childhood and society*. New York: Norton.

Erikson, E. H. (1959). *Identity and the life cycle*. New York: International Universities Press.

Golan, N. (1986). *The perilous bridge: Helping clients through mid-life transitions*. New York: Free Press.

Kagan, J. (1984). *The nature of the child*. New York: Basic Books.

Levenson, D. J., Darrow, C., Klein, E., Levenson, M., & McKee, B. (1978). *The seasons of a man's life*. New York: Ballantine Books.

Marmor, J. (1979). Short-term dynamic psychotherapy. *American Journal of Psychiatry*, *136*, 149–155.

Murray, H. A. (1968). Dead to the world: The passions of Herman Melville. In E. S. Schneidman (Ed.), *Essays in self-destruction*. New York: Science House.

Nemiroff, R. A., & Colarusso, C. A. (1985). *The race against time: Psychotherapy and psychoanalysis in the second half of life*. New York: Plenum Press.

Spitz, R. (1945). Hospitalism. In A. Freud, H. Hartmann, & E. Kris (Eds.), *The psychoanalytic study of the child* (Vol. 1). New York: International Universities Press.

Stern, D. (1985). *The interpersonal world of the infant*. New York: Basic Books.

9

Psychosocial Crisis Services in the Maryland Emergency Medical Services System

MARGARET EPPERSON-SEBOUR

TRAUMA, THE LEADING CAUSE of death and disability for persons between the ages of one and forty-four, is the third leading cause of mortality for persons of all ages. It has been characterized as the neglected disease of modern society (National Academy of Science, 1966). Injuries destroy the health, lives, and livelihoods of millions of people, yet little attention is paid to trauma compared with diseases and other hazards.

More years of work are lost to injury than are lost to heart disease and cancer combined. Each year more than 4 million years of future work are lost due to trauma, compared with 2.1 million to heart disease and 1.7 million to cancer. Disability due to injury has a similar impact on work life (*Injury in America*, 1985).

To combat the impact of trauma in twentieth-century America, trauma-care systems have been developed. The objective of these systems is to get the patient to the right hospital at the right time and to provide a continuum of care that will enable the traumatically injured person to return to a satisfying, productive life-style.

Development of trauma systems began in 1922 with the appointment of a trauma committee by the American College of Surgeons (Hampton, 1972). The National Academy of Science's report on accidental death and disability (1966), the Emergency Medical Services (EMS) Systems Act of 1973, and the Department of Transportation ambulance standards (1974) publications were other initial attempts to mandate systemized care for seriously injured persons in the United States.

Today, trauma-care systems across the country provide a preplanned response for meeting the needs of seriously injured victims with a continuum of care. The three essential elements in these emergency systems are accessible prehospital treatment; regionalized, specialized acute hospital care; and multidisciplinary rehabilitation efforts (Cales & Heilig, 1986).

Within these newly developing systems of care, which treat a predominately young patient population, lie the need and the opportunity for developing a multifaceted program specifically designed for the psychosocial care of trauma victims and their families. The present chapter deals with the short-term crisis intervention services provided by social workers and other mental health professionals within the various programs of the internationally recognized Maryland Emergency Medical Services (EMS) system, with its lead agency, the Maryland Institute for Emergency Medical Services Systems (MIEMSS). One of the medical facilities within MIEMSS is the Level I Shock Trauma Center in Baltimore, which provides the highest level of care for critically ill or injured adults in the state.

History

The first shock trauma unit in the country, established in 1961 and supported by a U.S. Army grant, was a two-bed clinical research unit at the University of Maryland Hospital. In 1963, a National Research Center grant was awarded to build the Center for the Study of Trauma, a five-floor, self-contained facility devoted exclusively to the care of the most critically injured patients in Maryland. The center was completed and officially opened in 1969. This same year, U.S. Department of Transportation funding was obtained for State Police Med-Evac helicopter service. In 1970, the first trauma patient was transported by Med-Evac helicopter to the center.

In 1973, the governor of Maryland issued an executive order mandating the first statewide EMS system in the country. This statewide system has two interrelated branches: (1) the clinical component (medical specialty referral centers and trauma centers) consisting of acute trauma medical care and trauma rehabilitation and (2) the field operations program, consisting of prehospital providers, training and certification, transportation, and communications. To date, the MIEMSS clinical component has eleven areawide trauma centers, twenty medical specialty referral centers, two rehabilitation programs, and six consultation centers. The system includes 450 ambulances, 23 central alarms, and a fleet of 10 Maryland State Police Med-Evac helicopters.

In the late 1970s, MIEMSS began addressing the unmet rehabilitation needs of severely injured persons. The Center for Living (CFL) was established by the MIEMSS Psychosocial Services Division in 1981. Directed by a social worker, the CFL is a posthospital, community-based facility providing psychosocial/cognitive reintegration services and day-treatment programs for trauma recoverees and their families.

A comprehensive trauma rehabilitation program for polyinjured patients was implemented in 1982. Utilizing a fifty-bed unit at the state's Montebello Rehabilitation Center, this program continued the early rehabilitation efforts begun in the acute-care setting at the Shock Trauma Center. A specialized head-injury unit was opened at the Montebello Center in 1983.

The MIEMSS Field Operations Program is responsible for the statewide EMS communications system and for training and certifying prehospital EMS providers: emergency medical technicians, paramedics, and other EMS personnel. These professional and volunteer prehospital providers, all of whom are certified by MIEMSS, spend at least 36.8 hours a year in EMS training for delivery of prehospital emergency medical care. Since 1970, more than 29,000 patients have been treated and stabilized at the accident scene by the prehospital personnel and transported by Med-Evac helicopter or by land ambulance to acute trauma care centers throughout the state.

Maryland has five EMS regions, each with at least one trauma center. Every year the MIEMSS Level I Shock Trauma Center in Baltimore receives about 3,500 of Maryland's most severely injured persons. Most of these patients are young males between the ages of sixteen and thirty-five. Eighty-six percent of these patients were employed or in school at the time of their accidents (MIEMSS, 1985–1986).

Effective EMS systems have dramatically increased the survival rate for seriously injured patients. The resulting high costs of the patients' acute medical care and the physical, psychosocial, and vocational rehabilitation needed to regain a satisfactory life-style have created new challenges for the medical community. Because the average age of trauma patients is in the mid-twenties, with a normal life expectancy in the mid-seventies, means must be found within the system to alleviate the social and financial burdens that can result from disability due to trauma (Epperson-SeBour & Rifkin, 1986). The Psychosocial Services Department program is designed, in part, to meet this challenge.

Psychosocial Services

The Psychosocial Services Department, a component of the MIEMSS Shock Trauma Center in Baltimore, is under the direction of a social worker. The department has three divisions: (1) the Family Services Division in the Shock Trauma Center, (2) the Center for Living, and (3) the Crisis Intervention Programs in the MIEMSS Field Operations branch, consisting of the Maryland State Critical Incident Stress Debriefing Program (CISD) and the Crisis Intervention Preparedness Team (CIP). (Each of these divisions is described in detail in the following sections of this chapter.) Crisis and crisis response form the threads of the fabric of the EMS system; all three divisions of the Psychosocial Services Department utilize crisis intervention either as the primary treatment modality or as part of a broader treatment plan.

The goal of the Psychosocial Services Department is to provide cost-effective services to trauma patients and their families by means of a continuum-of-care model. Prevention of individual or family breakdown that can occur due to the stress of a slow, long-term recovery process (Harris, 1987) is a primary focus of clinical activity. Clinical activity also focuses on the successful recovery of the family system whose members face the sudden and unexpected loss of a loved one and the need to work through the grieving process. Crisis intervention efforts are designed to prevent the disabling effects of sudden severe stress and/or post-traumatic stress disorder (PTSD) (Figley, 1985) in patients, families, and EMS workers (see chapter 2). Through effective early intervention, crisis states can be resolved, coping skills can be reactivated or learned, and persons can be helped to make the adjustments necessary to resume a normal life.

The department is concerned not only with the well-being of patients and families but also with the emotional needs of prehospital care providers, nurses, and physicians, who are confronted daily with human tragedy and suffering (Epperson-SeBour, 1981, 1985). Crisis intervention services for fire/rescue and other EMS workers help ensure high-quality care for emergency patients by attempting to maintain the mental health of personnel who work in a stressful environment.

Family Services Division

Severe stress caused by life-threatening situations precipitates a state of acute crisis in families when a member is critically injured in a catastrophic event such as a road accident, violent criminal assault, industrial mishap, recreational accident, or domestic violence. Families who come to the Shock Trauma Center must deal with the fact that a loved one may die, as is illustrated by the following case example.

> Mr. and Mrs. J, the middle-aged parents of three teenagers (eighteen, sixteen, and thirteen years of age) were unpacking from an early spring weekend trip with their two youngest children when they received a late-night phone call from the Maryland State Police. Mary, their bright and talented eighteen-year-old daughter, had been in a serious car accident and was flown by helicopter to the MIEMSS Shock Trauma Center in Baltimore. In critical condition, Mary had a severe head injury, multiple fractures, and a lacerated spleen. The driver of the car and another passenger were killed.
>
> The Js and their two other children drove from their home in southern Maryland to Baltimore, a ninety-minute trip. They were met in the family waiting area by a family counselor, a social worker specially prepared to work with families in crisis.
>
> The long drive, the fear of losing their oldest child and sister, the unfamiliar city and hospital setting, the death of Mary's friends, their fatigue, and their total unpreparedness for such a catastrophic event were stresses with which the family had to cope. Upon arrival at the center, the family members appeared agitated, anxious, and tearful, behaviors indicating that they were all in crisis.

The experience of the Js is typical of families thrown into a sudden crisis state. They needed external help in coping with their unanticipated situation until they were able to mobilize their own adaptive capacities and inner resources and eventually reestablish their precrisis "steady state." As indicated below and in Table 1, crisis intervention was provided immediately upon their arrival at the Shock Trauma Center.

Over a period of twelve months from 1973 to 1974, 230 families of MIEMSS patients were observed. As the behaviors of these families were charted and their verbal responses noted, certain recurrent behavioral patterns emerged. The investigator was able to identify a process of recovery from the crisis state and to develop crisis-intervention techniques to help families through the various phases. Each family's treatment time averaged two and one-half interviews, or approximately five hours of intervention (Epperson, 1977).

Family members of severely injured persons experience sudden and severe stress. In general, members appear to go through six distinct phases (high anxiety, denial, anger, remorse, grief, and reconciliation) before the family system is able to reorganize, reintegrate, and regain its homeostatic state. Families differ in both the sequence of phases experienced and in the rate whereby family members pass through the various stages. Some families may skip or eliminate a given stage. Furthermore, all family members do not move through the phases at the same time, and each member completes the process in his or her unique way. Family members, like family groups, have individual styles in working through the adaptive process. Despite this diversity, a

TABLE 1. Family interventions and outcomes.

Phase	Intervention	Desired result
High anxiety	Give brief, accurate information about the patient, including general medical condition, location of patient (admitting area, operating room, etc.), time of admission.	Family knows someone is in control.
	Assure family that the medical team will meet with them as soon as possible to discuss fully the medical status and treatment plan.	Family knows active treatment is in process.
	Explain life-saving methods and advanced technology of the institute.	Family knows patient has every advantage modern medicine has to offer.
	Encourage family members to ventilate about the initial impact of this event on them (where they were, what they were doing, what they were told about the accident, what they did).	Family knows they are the focus of care, as is the patient. Family has assessment opportunity.
	Introduce the medical team caring for the patient to present a complete medical report to the family.	Control begins to be reestablished. Knowledge of the patient's status helps the family know what they must begin to do.
Denial	Maintain a balance in the situation by recognizing the family members' need for denial as well as the need to deal with reality.	Family members are helped to understand and accept their struggle with the reality of the situation.
Anger	Encourage ventilation of angry feelings. Help the family focus on the real source of their anger. Validate angry feelings as an appropriate response to the situation.	Family is helped to understand that they are trying to find meaning for the event. (Often there is none and frustration turns to blame.) Family understands it is O.K. to be angry at the patient when anger is focused there.
Remorse	Listen to expressions of remorse ("if only . . .") and inject some reality as to how much responsibility family members can really take for the accident.	Family members are helped to understand they could have done little, if anything, to prevent the accident.
	Reassure the family that they are worthy persons in spite of what has happened.	Family members are freed from unfounded feelings of negligence and helped in maintaining self-esteem.
	Protect family from media and press representatives who can focus on family members' remorseful feelings and publish or provide inaccurate reports.	Avoid public censure.

Table continued on next page

TABLE 1. **Family interventions and outcomes, continued.**

Phase	Intervention	Desired result
Grief	Recognize expressions of sadness and provide a quiet, supportive presence.	Family members recognize the meaning of their loss or threatened loss.
	Be physically close as appropriate.	Conveys empathy and an understanding of what family members are experiencing.
	Allow tears to flow.	Releases deep emotional feelings of loss, either a permanent loss due to death or a temporary one due to long-term hospitalization.
Reconciliation	Help the family think about and begin to develop a feasible plan of action.	Family members take active control and begin problem solving.
	Suggest and/or bring in outside support resources if appropriate (extended family members, friends, clergy, etc.).	Family will identify those persons who could be helpful to them in coping with their current situation.
	Make referrals to appropriate community agencies.	Family members will know that persons in their community can help them.

distinct, identifiable course of recovery to a steady state may be observed (Epperson, 1977).

At MIEMSS the family counselor's task is to help family members regain their precrisis equilibrium. Table 1 briefly outlines interventions and desired outcomes.

Through intensive intervention in the acute crisis stage, family members develop a realistic sense of hope that the family can and will survive, despite the hardship and pain the tragedy may impose upon them.

> The Js indicated that they were adjusting to the reality of Mary's injuries by statements such as "We've been through hard times before and we've made it," "We are good at making the best of a bad situation," and "We are a strong family. We'll pull together and take each day as it comes."
>
> The family counselor acted as family advocate as Mary improved by helping the family deal with the complex medical shock trauma system. The family relied on the counselor to assist in problem solving and to facilitate communication with medical staff. The family counselor planned and facilitated regular family conferences and helped the family prepare for Mary's discharge to a rehabilitation facility.

The Family Services Division at the Shock Trauma Center assists more than 2,500 families a year. The numerous letters, cards, and small gifts received annually are indicative of families' appreciation of the staff members' assistance. However, appreciation is not a true measure of effectiveness. Periodic family evaluation tools are utilized to measure general family satisfaction with the overall performance of the Shock Trauma Center. The results are usually favorable.

To measure the true effectiveness of the Family Service Division's interventions, a formal study is currently being undertaken. One of the goals of the Psychosocial Services Department is to complete outcome studies on all its divisions by 1990. The Center for Living has completed its initial outcome study (Epperson-SeBour & Rifkin, 1985) and the Field Operations Crisis Intervention Program study (concerning the effectiveness of the debriefing process on emergency workers) is in progress.

The Center for Living (CFL)

The Trauma Recovery self-help group (now a network), established by MIEMSS Family Services in 1979, facilitated collaboratively by a social worker and a nurse, served as the precursor of the CFL (Scanlon & Levesque, 1981). The early trauma recoverees, young adults who had been through the shock trauma system, met bimonthly to offer support to one another, to socialize, and to take advantage of educational presentations provided by family services personnel and other MIEMSS staff.

During 1979–1980, the director of the Psychosocial Services Department met on a regular basis with the Trauma Recovery group to determine posthospital needs and to assess available state and community resources for this population. The success of the CFL stems from the direct input from these recoverees and their families. The plan that emerged from their input was to develop a community-based facility with specially designed programs for persons recovering from trauma and to implement these programs incrementally over a five-year period according to priority of needs. Grant monies were obtained from the private sector; an accessible building was found to house the program. Due to client response, the time frame for full program implementation was reduced from five to three years.

By 1984, the CFL had initiated two twelve-week, group day-treatment programs: the psychosocial Life Enhancement and Education (LEEP) Program and the educational Cognitive Relearning (CORE) Program (a specialized academic program for persons recovering from head injuries). The center also offered a drug/alcohol education program as well as full counseling services, including crisis intervention, and a complete battery of diagnostic and rehabilitative services, including job training and placement services (Epperson-SeBour & Rifkin, 1984). The CFL serves 275 recoverees and their families every year. Expansion of this program into the five Maryland EMS regions is in the planning process. The following illustrates how these programs serve trauma victims and their families:

> Twelve weeks after her accident, Mary J was transferred to the MIEMSS rehabilitation program at Montebello Rehabilitation Center in Baltimore. After fifteen weeks of intensive therapy, Mary was ready for discharge from the rehabilitation center. Having known for some time of her need for follow-up outpatient treatment, she and her family arranged for an evaluation visit at the CFL one week after discharge. Because of her head injury, it was recommended that Mary undergo an extensive diagnostic evaluation to more accurately determine areas of cognitive dysfunction as well as the intact functions that could be strengthened by a therapy program.

> Mr. and Mrs. J had been looking forward to Mary's entry into college in the fall. She had received a scholarship to a prestigious university in the Northeast; the family had visited the university and had completed the necessary arrangements for her leaving home. Mary's recovery was slow and difficult; college was not possible now. The Js experienced conflicting emotions revolving around their frustration over Mary's apparent lack of progress and legal problems stemming from the accident. Mr. J experienced periods of depression that interfered with his work. The Js were especially concerned about their thirteen year-old daughter, who was having nightmares and did not want to return to school.

The social worker who performed the family evaluation at the CFL recognized that the Js were experiencing another adjustment crisis. Episodic crisis states are common for families of trauma recoverees. However, the clinical staff has noted that families who have successfully resolved earlier traumatic life/death crises are better able to resolve the long-term adjustment crises. These observations are compatible with crisis theory; that is, persons can be strengthened by successful resolution of crises.

> The worker recommended that the J family participate in immediate short-term family therapy to help resolve their current adjustment problems. Because of Mary's lack of impulse control and inability to concentrate, she was enrolled in an individual behavior-management program as part of her overall treatment plan until she was cognitively able to participate in family sessions.

The CFL continues to follow Mary and her family (as it does all clients) for three years after their active participation in the center's programs. The center is designed to offer lifelong support and to serve as "home port" for many graduates who participate in the center's ongoing social activities and groups. A trauma study undertaken at Johns Hopkins University demonstrates that trauma recoverees with continuous, identifiable social supports have the best outcomes (MacKenzie, 1985).

Prehospital Provider Crisis Intervention Programs

The Prehospital Provider Crisis Intervention Program includes two related services: The Critical Incident Stress Debriefing (CISD) Program, a crisis intervention service for prehospital EMS workers; and the Crisis Intervention Preparedness (CIP) Team, which responds to disasters.

CISD. The following case example (the J family) describes how the CISD provides support to "first response" personnel, that is, those workers, including firemen, police, and paramedics, who respond to emergency situations.

> A young Maryland State Police officer was first to arrive at the scene of the accident. A car with three occupants had been traveling at high speed. It went out of control while the driver was trying to negotiate a turn. The car apparently hit a guard rail, rolled over, and plummeted into a ravine. The officer radioed for medical assistance and fire personnel in order to extricate the victims.
>
> The fire/rescue team arrived within ten minutes. Two occupants were alive; the driver, a male, appeared to be dead. All three were trapped inside the crushed car. One paramedic was able to crawl close enough to one

> occupant, a young woman, to insert intravenous lines. The other paramedic radioed for a Med-Evac helicopter. Meanwhile, the extrication crew worked on cutting away the mangled metal that entrapped the third victim, another young woman. The crew worked for thirty minutes to open space sufficient for the paramedics to gain access to the victims. It was too late; one young woman had died. The other young woman, Mary J, was stabilized and made ready for air transport to the Shock Trauma Center in Baltimore.
>
> The young police officer was responsible for notifying the families. The officer had had to do this once before, but the victim was much older and the accident less severe. Even so, he had experienced difficulty in telling the family of the accident. He had participated in a CISD session and knew he needed support to communicate the bad news to the families this time. He radioed a fellow officer, who willingly went with him to visit the families of the deceased victims.
>
> Back at the fire station, the fire/rescue teams reviewed the incident and informally evaluated what they could have done to save the other young woman. Two young members of the team had never experienced such a horrible accident and expressed frustration over "junk" tools that "wouldn't cut paper, let alone metal." A paramedic remarked about how much the dead woman looked like his sister; at first he had thought she was.
>
> The next day, personnel talked continuously about the incident, sometimes making macabre remarks or jokes. It became obvious to the unit leader that his personnel were having a difficult time dealing with the incident, now almost two days past. The supervisor called the MIEMSS Psychosocial Services Department and requested a CISD session for the personnel who had responded to the accident. The following evening, three regional CISD team members—a leader and a co-leader (both mental health professionals) and a peer support person (a firefighter)—conducted a debriefing for the thirteen fire/rescue personnel and the two state troopers who responded to the accident.

The CISD program is a short-term (one or two sessions), intensive crisis intervention program provided without charge to help "first response" personnel cope with their stressful psychological reactions to the emergency event. Such incidents may involve multiple deaths, the death of a colleague, or injury to or death of children. These voluntary sessions are provided statewide as needed and have a structured format (Table 2) that allows maximum participation and stress reduction for those who attend (Mitchell, 1983). The sessions, optimally held within seventy-two hours of the incident, can last from two to five hours, depending on the size of the group and the severity of the stress response. They take place in an informal setting with a circular seating pattern to facilitate group interaction.

A debriefing provides many advantages for emergency and disaster organizations. By offering specific, focused procedures designed to release intense stress in participants, the debriefing process allows group members to express feelings and provides emotional support to distressed workers (Hartsough, 1985). The format used by CISD helps some response units to open channels of communication; for others it provides a supportive group setting in which members can share personal feelings about traumatic events. The CISD program is always proactive; preservation of mental health is its goal. Participants learn to recog-

TABLE 2. **Critical incident stress debriefing format.**

Session	Action	Desired outcome
Introductory phase	Introduce CISD team members and explain structure of the session.	Establishes rapport and trust.
	Outline confidentiality requirement.	Clarifies group "rules."
	Explain purpose of session.	
Fact phase	Go around the circle and briefly elicit the following from participants: 1. Name 2. Activities performed at the incident 3. What they heard, saw, smelled, etc. 4. Any other observations about the incident	Members actively share in group process.
Feeling phase	The team leader encourages members to share with others feelings they had at the scene and that they are having now about the incident.	Pertinent emotional issues emerge.
Symptom phase	The team leader focuses on and reframes the psychological and physical effects that the participants have described.	Participants recognize the universality of stress reactions.
Teaching phase	The participants are reminded that the symptoms they describe are normal reactions to extraordinary circumstances.	Participants learn what normal stress reactions are.
	The physiology of the stress response may be explained or clarified.	Participants will be better able to monitor their own stress responses.
	Stress management skills are introduced.	
Reentry phase	The team leader summarizes the group's activity and answers questions.	Closure is given to the group process.
	The facilitator assists the group in drawing a plan of action if it wishes.	
	Counseling referral sources are provided.	
	Stress information handouts are provided.	
Follow-up	The team leader makes a follow-up call to unit supervisor within 48 hours.	Ensures that participants' needs are met and that the goals of the session are attained.
	The peer support person makes a drop-in visit within 72 hours.	
	Within 24 hours, the co-leader makes follow-up calls to individuals who asked for counseling referrals.	

TABLE 3. **Critical incident stress debriefing team (3 persons).**

Title	Qualifications	Function
Team leader	Master's degree or Ph.D. in mental health field CISD training Experienced group worker EMS work-related experience Background in stress management	Conducts debriefing Does debriefing follow-up Makes referrals Completes debriefing report Does stress-related education
Co-leader	Master's degree or Ph.D. in mental health field CISD training Experienced group worker	Helps facilitate the debriefing process Does follow-up calls to individuals seeking counseling referrals
Peer support person	Active emergency services worker CISD training Leadership capability Superior interpersonal skills	Notifies CISD team coordinator of need for debriefing Assists with arrangements for the debriefing Participates in the debriefing process

nize and manage their stress symptoms under the guidance of mental health professionals so that a prolonged crisis is avoided or minimized. Finally, CISD presents an opportunity for participants to request assistance if they feel further help is needed. The mental health professionals on the CISD team provide individual crisis counseling when appropriate or direct persons who seek individual help to the team's referral sources.

The Maryland CISD team consists of thirty master's- or doctoral-level mental health professionals, mostly social workers, and fifty-five peer-support persons, who are specially trained first-response personnel selected from the five Maryland EMS regions (Table 3). The team is centralized in Baltimore, but responds to disasters statewide. Both the professional and peer-support team members must meet specific criteria as outlined in the Maryland CISD Team Policies Booklet. They attend a two-day training session and pass the selection board requirements before being accepted as team members. All team members throughout the state meet quarterly for general business and debriefing critiques and receive two in-service education sessions per year. Team members from each region meet locally every other month. The Psychosocial Services Department is completing a certification process for team members. The team responds to approximately seventy-five debriefing requests per year. Following the Baltimore County Amtrak train disaster, the team provided valuable and much-needed services, as described on the following pages.

The Crisis Intervention Preparedness (CIP) Team. The CIP team is an "at-ready" group of four master's-level social workers and two doctoral-level clinical psychologists who are specially trained in crisis intervention and disaster response. Part of the MIEMSS Disaster Emergency Medical Assistance Team, these personnel are called to disasters by the MIEMSS medical command at the disaster site. The team is dispatched from the Shock Trauma Center. The purposes of the team are threefold:

1. To provide psychological support to disaster victims who are physically unharmed and to the "walking wounded"

2. To assist disaster command in monitoring stress reactions in the rescue workers and recommend appropriate rest times for workers

3. To provide psychological "defusings," or brief group crisis intervention sessions, primarily educational, for rescue workers before they are relieved of duty

The CIP team is assisted by members of the CISD team when backup support is needed at the disaster scene. Psychiatric consultation is available through the EMS system's communication network.

Crisis Response to Disaster: A Case Report

Approximately 1:30 P.M. on Sunday, January 4, 1987, the Amtrak Colonial, a twelve-car passenger train heading north from Baltimore at approximately 120 mph, crashed into the back of a three-engine Conrail locomotive that had crossed into its path from another track. The impact destroyed the lead Amtrak engine and caused the first four passenger cars to pile on top of one another, crushing the bottom car (a café car) into a four-foot-high entanglement of metal. The other passenger cars were derailed at various angles to the track.

The first emergency personnel to respond were confronted with a fire involving the Conrail locomotives and several of the front Amtrak cars, hundreds of passengers who had exited the train on both sides of the tracks, and screams for help from victims trapped in the wreckage. During the following thirty hours, hundreds of EMS and fire personnel processed more than 350 victims through a triage area, transporting more than 180 victims to area hospitals. Sixteen people died from injuries sustained in the crash.

The director for the psychosocial services program was called at home at approximately 2:40 P.M. and was informed that a train wreck had occurred, involving perhaps 300 to 500 persons. The MIEMSS disaster plan was put into effect. The department call-down procedure was activated and within forty minutes the director and four members of the CIP team (three family services clinical staff persons and the MIEMSS chaplain) had reported in; within two hours, the remaining two members of the team and the department secretary arrived at the department office.

According to disaster protocol, upon arrival at MIEMSS the director of psychosocial services reported to the administrator. At approximately 3:15 P.M. the director was asked to dispatch the CIP team to the disaster scene. Three CIP team members were sent immediately to the site, to be joined later by a fourth team member. (One of these team members is also a State Police chaplain.) Before being dispatched, one team member was designated team leader. The CIP team leader, according to protocol, reported to the MIEMSS medical command post and to disaster command upon arrival, at approximately 3:45 P.M. The team then began working with both the crash victims and the rescue personnel.

In-Hospital Activity

In-hospital activity escalated. The department director acted as coordinator, working with hospital security, the designated Amtrak official, the University of Maryland Medical System's (UMMS) Department of Social Work, the Department of Psychiatry, and blood donor centers to meet the needs of the victim's relatives and friends, who had either come to the hospital or were telephoning.

Three family services clinicians and the chaplain worked in various settings, doing crisis intervention with families, while the department secretary answered continuous calls from families of victims, persons from the community, outside agencies, and numerous individuals offering to help. Office phone lines were tied up, making it difficult to make outside calls.

To protect families from disaster-related activity and to ensure that the MIEMSS "red line" patient route was clear for incoming disaster patients, family members of non–disaster-related patients were escorted from the small waiting area on the ground floor of MIEMSS to a large, centrally located space on the first floor of University Hospital. This large waiting area, with many amenities and close-at-hand necessities (large windows, comfortable chairs, restrooms, telephones, and a drinking fountain), was also used by families of disaster victims. Families of MIEMSS patients whose condition was stable were encouraged to go home; all patient visiting was suspended during the disaster.

The administrator from the UMMS Psychiatric Institute called at approximately 4:15 P.M. to report that five psychiatrists were in-house to respond to any disaster-related psychiatric emergencies. This protocol for psychiatric coverage was a result of the critique of a disaster exercise held the previous summer, which cited the need for psychiatric backup. The director of the UMMS Department of Social Work also called to report that four social workers were ready to respond in whatever capacity needed. Further, three UMMS hospital chaplains were in-house and available to respond.

Two UMMS social workers were assigned to the family waiting area to free up the MIEMSS workers who were needed elsewhere. These social workers assisted a total of twenty-five patients and their families before being relieved from their duties at midnight. The MIEMSS family services clinicians remained until 1:15 A.M., when it was established that family needs were met, no more patients would arrive, and the disaster response for MIEMSS was concluded.

Off-Site Response

The department director received a call from Amtrak officials at approximately 10:30 P.M., asking for assistance with distressed families of victims at a Baltimore hotel and at the Baltimore train station. Two family service clinicians were dispatched to those locations. At 12:50 A.M., the clinicians called in to report that there was no further need for their services at those sites; they were sent home.

The local chapter of the American Red Cross assisted Amtrak in setting up a bereavement center at a hotel a few miles from the disaster scene. At approximately 11:15 P.M., a Red Cross official called the director, requesting assistance with families at that site. Two family service workers responded; with assistance from the mental health professionals on the CISD teams, a rotation plan for the night and for the following day was set up.

Because of radio communication problems, the director had not been in touch with the CIP team leader at the disaster scene since shortly before 10:00 P.M. At approximately 1:20 A.M. Monday morning, she went to the scene on a return helicopter flight from MIEMSS to assess CIP team functions and needs.

On-Site Activity

At the accident scene, the four CIP team members who had reported in shortly before 4:00 P.M. began work. After an initial assessment of the situation, the team leader dispatched two persons to assist victims who were assembled at the Harewood Park Community Center, two blocks from the scene. The leader and the third team member remained at the crash site to assess the stress response of workers; to assist the commanding officer in monitoring the need for relief forces; and to begin psychological defusing of rescue squads, brief sessions designed to educate rescue personnel about normal stress response to abnormal events, post-traumatic stress symptoms, awareness of one's own stress reaction, and what to do if symptoms arose. Rescue personnel were also advised that opportunities to participate in formal psychological debriefings would be available to them during the weeks following the incident.

At approximately 4:20 P.M., the CIP team leader contacted the department director via radio through the Maryland EMS system communications network and requested help with the psychological "demobilizations" (small groups, focused on stress-management education, preliminary to subsequent extensive psychological debriefing). Three CISD team members were dispatched and reported to the scene at different times between 5:00 P.M. and 6:45 P.M. Two team members were sent to Chase Fire Station 54 to work with victims and fire/rescue personnel. The other team member was dispatched to the Air National Guard Station at Glenn L. Martin Airport, where a demobilization center had been set up. The latter site provided quiet, comfortable accommodations that facilitated the educational stress-management sessions.

Members of the CIP team, the CISD program, and a clinical psychologist from the Baltimore County Fire Department Psychological Services Unit continued their work with rescue personnel at the National Guard site until approximately 1:00 A.M. Monday morning, when it was determined that the center was no longer needed. Work with rescue personnel continued at Station 54 until approximately 9:00 P.M. Monday evening, when the disaster was officially over.

The CIP team members at the disaster scene were relieved by a psychologist from the fire service at approximately 5:30 A.M. Monday morning but returned later that morning and remained at the scene until the disaster was over and all rescue workers had left.

Collaborative Effort

By mid-morning Monday, January 5, many requests had been received from Chase community residents for help in dealing with the emotional impact of the disaster on themselves and their families. The director contacted the Baltimore County Eastern Community Health Center. It was arranged for the National Organization for Victim Assistance (NOVA), which had offered its services to Baltimore County, to work with the Health Center staff to organize and provide services for the three Chase communities of Harewood Park, Twin Rivers, and Oliver Beach.

Meanwhile, the Baltimore County Police Community Oriented Police Enforcement (COPE) Unit began canvassing the three neighborhoods to assess property damage as well as the psychological impact of the incident on residents. Personnel from COPE conducted 1,274 interviews with community families.

On Tuesday morning, January 6, a strategy meeting was held in Baltimore County Fire Department headquarters to develop a plan for community intervention. Personnel from NOVA, mental health staff, and a fire service psychologist attended this meeting. A series of community group sessions were planned as were other services for children and school personnel.

At an interorganizational meeting on Wednesday morning, January 7, it was decided that the MIEMSS CISD program would be responsible for formal psychological debriefings of volunteer fire/rescue units, Red Cross volunteers, the State Police, and personnel from any other agencies that requested debriefings. The career fire/rescue units were debriefed by the Fire Department psychologists. Also, the Fire Department's Psychological Service Unit and the Maryland CISD program communicated with each other regarding requests for debriefings in order to facilitate an organized, systematic response to these requests. Any career firefighter needing individual help was referred to the Psychological Service Unit. Individuals in the volunteer force who requested individual counseling were directed to referral sources, including the Psychological Service Unit. A total of twenty-eight formal debriefings for various disaster response groups were conducted during the three weeks following the event.

Psychological Support Services

Psychological support services were provided to five categories of people: victims and their families (approximately 250); fire/rescue personnel (approximately 710); community residents (42); personnel from other disaster-related agencies; and other individuals affected by the disaster. In all, more than 1,099 persons affected by the disaster were served.

The types of services varied according to the group served. The victims and their families received crisis intervention, including bereavement counseling when required, as well as assistance in locating resources and in problem-solving. Language translators were made available as needed. Community members also received crisis intervention services. Advocacy services included letters and phone calls to employers on behalf of both community members and rescue workers who experienced work-related difficulties due to the disaster. Services to fire/rescue personnel included brief on-site psychological demobilization, formal psychological debriefing, and individual crisis counseling. Information and referral services were available to all groups.

Services extended from immediately after the crash to weeks later. Ongoing individual crisis counseling for some fire/rescue personnel and a few community members continued for several months, as did COPE's work with the Chase community.

Impact of Disaster on Ongoing Services

For eight working days after the disaster, the MIEMSS Family Services staff was stretched to the limit. The director and one clinician spent approximately

90 percent of their time providing direct or indirect disaster-related psychological services and consultations. One other clinician and the office secretary devoted approximately 30 percent of their time to disaster-related activities. In all, MIEMSS psychosocial service personnel—including the director (182 hours), four family counselors (62 hours), four CIP team members (78 hours), eighteen CISD team members (161 hours), and the secretary (18 hours)—spent 501 hours on the Amtrak/Conrail disaster. Although the time devoted to disaster response gradually diminished, disaster-related activities continued for several months.

During the high-impact period, the division's normal activities were carried out by three family services clinicians. These clinicians covered cases for their colleagues who were involved in disaster services. No decline in ordinary division functions was evident. The volume and duration of disaster activity were far beyond the department's expectations and took a toll in terms of staff stress and fatigue.

Conclusion

On January 14, 1987, all Psychosocial Services personnel who were involved at the disaster scene met to debrief themselves and to critique their response efforts. It was agreed that although the team functioned effectively and efficiently, existing policies and procedures needed to be refined or developed for responding to a disaster of such magnitude.

Personnel also agreed that collaboration and cooperation with other agencies, namely Baltimore County Fire Department Psychological Service Unit, NOVA, COPE, and the Baltimore County Eastern Community Health Center, were excellent. Disaster-aid personnel concluded that a well-organized, highly effective response to psychological trauma was available during the disaster and the weeks following it.

The services provided were primarily preventive in design and were delivered with the intent that early intervention and continued support services would decrease the incidence of post-traumatic stress disorder and/or mitigate the general psychological impact that such a catastrophic event can have on victims, rescue workers, and members of the community. This preventive approach is consistent with recommendations for a model disaster aid program emerging from a number of disaster studies (Parad, Resnik, & Parad, 1976).

Summary

Statewide emergency medical services systems are the wave of the future. This chapter focuses on the utilization of the crisis intervention model in both the clinical and field components of the Maryland state EMS system. For the past sixteen years, the model has provided effective services to multiple trauma patients and their families. At the system's community-based Center for Living (CFL), crisis intervention is provided for trauma recoverees and their families who experience the crisis of physical and/or cognitive disability.

In the EMS field-operations component, an adaptation of the crisis model is used by the Crisis Intervention Preparedness (CIP) team in work with victims and rescue workers during a disaster. The Maryland Critical Incident Stress

Debriefing (CISD) team provides short-term, outreach intervention to fire/rescue and other frontline workers who respond to emergency situations and seek help in working through the emotional impact of the event.

In the Maryland system, immediate crisis intervention services consist of proactive measures to ensure good mental health for victims and workers who are confronted with human tragedy. The effectiveness of these services continues to be evaluated.

References

Accident facts (1984). Chicago: National Safety Council.

Cales, R. H., & Heilig, R. W. (Eds.). (1986). *Trauma care systems; a guide to planning, implementation, operation, and evaluation*. Rockville, MD: Aspen.

Emergency Medical Systems Act of 1973. Public Law 93–154. (1973). 93rd U.S. Congress. Title XII, United States Code, Vol. 1, 660–672. St. Paul, MN: West Publishing.

Epperson, M. M. (1977). Families in sudden crisis: Process and intervention in a critical care center. *Social Work in Health Care, 2*, 265–273.

Epperson-SeBour, M. M. (1981). Responding to a home emergency. In J. T. Mitchell & H. L. P. Resnick (Eds.), *Emergency response to crisis*. Laurel, MD: Brady Co.

Epperson-SeBour, M. M. (1985). Prevention of stress; response. In Center for Mental Health Studies of Emergencies, *Role stressors and supports for emergency workers* (pp. 140–145). Washington, DC: U.S. Department of Health and Human Services, National Institute of Mental Health.

Epperson-SeBour, M. M., & Rifkin, E. W. (1984). *Center for Living standards*. Baltimore, MD: Maryland Institute for Emergency Medical Services Systems.

Epperson-SeBour, M. M., & Rifkin, E. W. (1985). Center for living: Trauma aftercare and outcomes. *Maryland Medical Journal, 34* (12), 1187–1192.

Epperson-SeBour, M. M., & Rifkin, E. W. (1986). Psychosocial rehabilitation. In R. H. Cales & R. W. Heilig, Jr. (Eds.), *Trauma care systems*. Rockville, MD: Aspen.

Figley, C. R. (Ed.). (1985). *Trauma and its wake: The study and treatment of post-traumatic stress disorder*. New York: Brunner/Mazel.

Hampton, O. P., Jr. (1972). The Committee on Trauma of the American College of Surgeons, *57* (6), 7–13.

Harris, J. C. (1987). Survivor grief following a drunk driving crash. *Death Studies, 11* (6), 413–435. New York: Hemisphere Publishing.

Hartsough, D. M. (1985). Emergency organization role. In Center for Mental Health Studies of Emergencies, *Role stressors and supports for emergency workers* (pp. 48–58). Washington, DC: U.S. Department of Health and Human Services, National Institute of Mental Health.

Injury in America: A continuing public health problem (1985). Committee on Trauma Research, Commission on Life Sciences, National Research Council and the Institute of Medicine, Washington, DC: National Academy Press.

MacKenzie, E. (1985). *Changes in functional status of trauma patients following hospital discharge*. Baltimore, MD: Health Services Research and Development Center, Johns Hopkins University School of Hygiene and Public Health.

Maryland Institute for Emergency Medical Services Systems (1985–1986). *Annual Report*. Baltimore, MD: Author.

Mitchell, J. T. (1983). When disaster strikes: The critical incident stress debriefing process. *Journal of Emergency Medical Services*, 8, 36–39.

National Academy of Science. (1966). *Accidental death and disability: The neglected disease of modern society*. Washington, DC: Department of Health, Education and Welfare.

Parad, H. J., Resnik, H. L., & Parad, L. G. (Eds.). (1976). *Emergency and disaster management*. Bowie, MD: Charles Press.

Scanlon, A., & Levesque, J. (1981). Helping the patient cope with the sequelae of trauma through the self-help group approach. *Journal of Trauma, 2l*, 135–139.

U.S. Department of Transportation (1974). *Federal specifications, ambulance, emergency medical care service vehicles: KKK-A-1822*. Washington, DC: General Administration Distribution Center.

10

The Chronically Mentally Ill: A Perspective from the Firing Line

RICHARD A. ZUCKERWISE

A SOCIAL WORKER on the emergency psychiatric service of a major urban health center interviewed a thirty-four-year-old white male. The man appeared to be older than his stated age. He was unkempt, disheveled, and had been sleeping in the downtown alleys of skid row since arriving in the city a few weeks previously. Occasionally he would stop at one of the missions for a meal; usually, however, he begged for spare change or foraged in the garbage for food. He refused to seek shelter in the missions because he felt that conditions there were "worse than the gutter." When asked why he failed to apply for public assistance benefits, he replied that he had "gone there but they'd given him the runaround." He was unable to state more specifically what had happened. At one time, he had received Supplemental Security Income (SSI), for which persons determined to be physically or mentally disabled may be eligible, but he had "moved about" and the funding had been terminated. Initiating proceedings to restore benefits was clearly beyond his capacities.

The patient sought to be admitted to the hospital because he was "hungry and tired and the messages [hallucinations] were starting up again." He believed that a computer chip had been planted in his ear and that a secret government agency was transmitting messages to him. He felt persecuted. When the messages increased, he would go to the nearest hospital; he had been admitted to various psychiatric wards, then discharged onto the streets when the acute psychiatric episode ended.

The crisis therapist listened intently to the patient's description of his life situation. Without challenging the patient's delusional system or unduly arousing his paranoia, the worker let the patient know that help was available. In consultation with the staff psychiatrist, antipsychotic medications were administered. The patient was advised that the "messages" would be less troublesome and easier to deal with if he agreed to take his medication.

The therapist learned that the patient had a brother in another city, whom he contacted after obtaining permission. The brother, who had not known how to reach the patient, provided additional information and agreed to see him the following week.

The patient reluctantly agreed to be evaluated for a residential treatment program. He had been in board-and-care homes in the past but had received no therapy or rehabilitation efforts. The treatment program's interviewer determined that the patient was indeed eligible for the program because he had no history of violence or substance abuse. However, an opening would not be available for another two days. The crisis therapist placed calls to the welfare office; a temporary hotel placement was arranged, and a food voucher was issued to the patient.

Transportation was arranged to the temporary placement so that the patient would not become confused and give up. He had been accustomed to simply being hospitalized, so taking a measure of responsibility for his own treatment was a new experience for him. The crisis therapist maintained contact with the patient both during the two-day waiting period and after he entered the residential treatment program. Consequently, the patient became aware that he could turn to the crisis service whenever he needed to and that he had an alternative to the endless cycle of the hospital and the streets.

The preceding case illustrates the enormous problems experienced by the chronically mentally ill as well as the ways in which a crisis intervention approach can resolve some of these problems.

In response to governmental policies to deinstitutionalize the mentally ill, mental health professionals have been called upon to help care for the chronically mentally disordered in the community without having access to adequate social, medical, housing, legal, and job-training resources. In a profile of this group of at-risk clients, Applebaum (1986) states that soon after their last hospitalization, patients stop taking their psychotropic medication; they frequently break or cease outpatient therapy appointments; they gradually or rapidly decompensate into psychotic crises and often need to be assessed for possible rehospitalization—only to repeat the cycle of discharge, decompensation, and possible readmission.

In any urban area today, the chronically mentally ill account for a major portion of the homeless population, sleeping in streets and alleys, frequenting the rescue missions and skid row hotels (Lamb, 1984). Some are more fortunate and live with family members or in alternative treatment settings, but all pose challenges and opportunities for the crisis practitioner.

Historical Background

Traditionally, the chronically mentally ill (CMI) patient was maintained on a more or less permanent basis in state- or county-supported mental hospitals. By 1955, nearly 600,000 patients were in such facilities, and by 1957 the total population in all psychiatric hospitals (including VA and private facilities) was 1,241,000, of which 840,000 patients were in state institutions (Bloom, 1984).

In the 1950s, however, a series of developments set the stage for major changes in psychiatric care. First, as the development of psychotropic drugs made patients' symptoms more manageable, many former inpatients were able to function in the community as outpatients. Second, hospitals began to change as a result of new psychosocial approaches to treatment. The therapeutic community within hospitals adopted an interdisciplinary team approach designed to maximize the patient's potential for rehabilitation, and the back wards where the less hopeful patients previously had languished were virtually eliminated.

Through the past three decades, these developments combined to bring about a dramatic reduction in the number of hospitalized psychiatric patients. In fact, by 1979 the total psychiatric inpatient population had decreased to 230,000 patients, of whom approximately 140,000 were in state or county hospitals (U.S. Bureau of the Census, 1984, p. 112). These figures have fluctuated slightly in recent years, with a low of 214,000 hospitalized patients in 1981 and an increase to slightly more than 221,000 in 1985, half of whom were in state or county facilities (U.S. Bureau of the Census, 1988, p. 104).

In 1963, President Kennedy signed the Community Mental Health Centers Act. A major purpose of this act was to make treatment and supportive services available to the deinstitutionalized CMI patient. However, the expenditures needed to support such social programs never fully materialized. The Vietnam War and defense spending consumed much of the federal budget, and successive administrations deemphasized funding for public mental health. During the Carter administration (1977–80), the Community Mental Health movement managed to hold its own without suffering major funding cutbacks. Through the 1980 Mental Health Systems Act (Jansson, 1984), authorization was given to increase federal spending on mental health services during a five-year period. However, with the advent of the Reagan administration and passage of tax-cutting measures such as Proposition 13 in California and Proposition 2 1/2 in Massachusetts, cutbacks in existing services became the rule. As the "safety net" of social programs weakened, the plight of the chronically mentally ill worsened.

Within the Community Mental Health movement, innovative treatment strategies have been implemented, and there is an increasing social consciousness about mental illness and the civil rights of psychiatric patients. Mental health programs are being established on foundations that are stronger both empirically and cost effectively. Accordingly, it is becoming easier to defend the need for resources to continue clinical treatment and research. Bloom (1984) points out that a side effect of the Reagan administration's block-grant strategy is the increased influence of the state and local community on resource-allocation issues that once belonged to the federal government.

The preceding discussion emphasizes the changing societal context in which the practitioner attempts to meet the needs of the CMI population. In addition to addressing clinical issues and techniques, practitioners should maintain an active involvement in the larger sociopolitical context in an effort to effect change.

Defining the Chronically Mentally Ill

The term "chronically mentally ill" refers to individuals who experience serious impediments in their day-to-day functioning due to a mental disorder (Turner, 1977). Included are patients who have never been institutionalized as well as those who frequently or intermittently receive inpatient treatment at psychiatric facilities. Typically, the CMI patient has a long duration of illness, characterized by periods of relative stability interrupted by acute exacerbations of symptomatology (Goldman, Gattozzi, & Taube, 1981). During such decompensations any or all of the following may be present: disorganized and confused thought processes, hallucinations, grandiose or persecutory delusions, or, as is frequently noted in therapists' records, a "response to internal stimuli."

Schizophrenia, the most significant of the chronic mental disorders, accounts for nearly one-third of all patients admitted to psychiatric hospitals (Smolar, 1984). With an estimated one percent of the population diagnosed as schizophrenic, problems in developing an effective treatment strategy for this group must be continually addressed. In reviewing research on the effectiveness of treatment of schizophrenia, Smolar (1984) concluded that the therapist's capacity to provide empathy and support is more important than the theory or modality of treatment. Schizophrenic patients can be helped to gain self-understanding and acceptance; to recognize their boundaries, experiences, and goals; and to feel that they can turn to people who care and can help. The chronically ill schizophrenic patient often needs crisis intervention services, including hospital emergency rooms, walk-in clinics, and related mental health facilities where counseling, support, referrals, and medication are available.

Experts generally agree that the psychotic disorders (organic brain syndrome, schizophrenia, major affective disorders, and paranoia) predominate among the CMI. However, other disorders may also lead to chronic disability, including some Axis II disorders listed in DSM-III-R (American Psychiatric Association, 1987), especially borderline and antisocial syndromes, and habitual alcohol and/or other substance abuse. Impairment may exist in all aspects of daily life, such as being able to maintain adequate personal hygiene, social relationships, and economic self-sufficiency. The CMI may need assistance in all these areas, particularly in ensuring that they receive governmental supports, such as SSI, to which they are entitled.

The CMI population encompasses a broad spectrum of individuals whose life situations and levels of functioning differ widely. Whereas some clients require frequent or continuous maintenance in facilities such as board-and-care homes, many are able to live in relative independence if sufficient psychosocial supports are extended (Mendel, 1975). Posthospital services, which are crucial to successful community functioning of CMI patients, must provide continuity and be available and accessible. The sooner an aftercare program serves a patient upon discharge, the greater the likelihood of avoiding hospitalization (Wolkon, 1972). Leaving the hospital is a time of crisis when the connection between service provider and patient is vitally important. Services should allow maximum face-to-face contact between provider and patient; a personalized therapeutic relationship strengthens the bond between the discharged patient and the new support system. Hopefully, in future crises, this support system will be viewed as a primary source of help.

Role of Crisis Intervention

Crisis intervention is particularly relevant to the CMI individual who is unable to provide basic self-care without periodic assistance. Frequently, such patients cannot wait for or keep track of the date and time of a regularly scheduled therapeutic appointment.

When a chronic psychiatric patient is in crisis, the availability of therapeutic intervention may be crucial in resolving the crisis and avoiding hospitalization. The crisis worker's first task is to provide immediate treatment, well coordinated with early and quick diagnostic assessment (Parad, 1976). Issues concerning the need for taking appropriate medications are addressed, and when indicated, a psychiatrist is consulted. The therapist may involve significant others—friends or family members who can lend support to the individual (Aguilera, 1983). If the patient resides in a board-and-care or residential facility, the therapist should determine to what extent its staff is prepared to work with the therapist to help the individual through the crisis. If there are no situational supports, the therapist must fill that role until the patient can again assume responsibility for self-management.

Gers (1979) points out that many CMI patients brought to an emergency service have no ongoing relationships with anyone. This may be a function of their illness, in that CMI patients tend to withdraw, lose contact with significant others, and either refuse or lack the skills to establish new relationships. Without a social support system, the hospital's emergency service is one of the few places to which these patients can turn (see chapter 1). A challenge for the crisis practitioner is to make use of whatever support systems may presently exist, to reestablish contact between isolated patients and former support networks, or, if it is necessary, to create new supportive networks that will maximize the patient's level of independent functioning.

Often a patient is brought to a treatment center by family members because pathological behaviors, which may have been under control, are reemerging. The crisis clinician should explore with all family members the precipitating factors that led to the present decompensation. Whenever it is feasible to do so, the worker should attempt to engage the family as part of the treatment plan for the chronic patient; their understanding and support may be critical to the patient's successful readjustment to community living. The worker should meet with the family in as natural a setting as possible. Maladaptive or disordered behaviors of the patient should be viewed as a cry for help. Blocked communications, lack of warm contacts, and intrafamily dynamics are explored in the context of the family interaction. The therapist's understanding of the family system should be used to produce change in the interactional patterns that reinforce the patient's pathology. Family members can learn to relate to one another in ways that promote crisis resolution. By engaging the family in the treatment process, the patient can also learn that he or she is not alone when the symptomatology erupts, that the family is available as a support (Rubenstein, 1972).

Thus the family as well as the identified patient becomes the client. The crisis worker should clarify the main tasks to be addressed and may offer concrete advice and support. With the help of a here-and-now interaction emphasis, pathological behavior patterns are pointed out, and contracts, that is, working agreements between family members, are encouraged. The worker needs to elicit sanction from the family's "power" figure and plan a subsequent session before the first one is completed. Thus crisis intervention with the CMI patient can be viewed as following the basic principles of family crisis intervention (Parad, 1982) (see chapter 1).

In Asia, the family unit is considered very important in the treatment process. Families have the primary responsibility to ensure that the clinician's instructions are implemented. Viewing the mentally ill patient as the family's responsibility obviously affects the need for alternative residential settings.

The effectiveness of family crisis intervention in reducing the need for psychiatric hospitalization has been confirmed in research programs by Langsley, Machotka, and Flomenhaft (1971) and Langsley and Yarvis (1976). They found that patients treated with this approach were significantly less likely to be rehospitalized than were patients in a control group. For patients who received family crisis intervention and were then readmitted to a hospital, the length of hospital stay was significantly shorter.

In an era when the daily cost of hospitalization is prohibitive, the cost benefits of a crisis treatment program are obvious. In addition, the social stigma associated with psychiatric hospitalization as well as the dependency and regression that such a stay engenders can be reduced. The crisis intervention service, with its twenty-four-hour accessibility, linkage with community resources, and interactional, here-and-now orientation, is uniquely qualified to manage and resolve a patient's crisis (Yarvis, 1975). Without such services, there may be no alternative but hospitalization.

Crisis Intervention Principles

In working with the seriously disturbed individual, a series of general principles of crisis intervention emerge. The maintenance of a positive working alliance and empathic interest on the part of the therapist establish a basic transference (Langsley, 1980). Treatment emphasizes the present situation rather than insight into the underlying origins of the conflict; goals include a strategy to deal with the current crisis. To the extent required, the therapist actively provides reassurance, suggestion, advice, and guidance, while enhancing the patient's self-esteem. As successful coping behaviors are reinforced, the patient again assumes a measure of self-control and competence.

Langsley (1980) delineates a series of steps that can be implemented in working with the seriously mentally ill patient:

Immediate aid. By having treatment available at all times, the patient (and family) knows that there is someone to turn to and that the problem is not unsolvable.

Definition of the crisis as a family problem. If it is possible to do so, family members are called in so that the problem can be viewed in the context of the family system. Hospitalization, which locates the problem in the identified patient, is discouraged.

Focus on the present. To understand the current crisis, recent events are examined. Although past histories are not discarded, they are viewed in terms of what is happening with the patient right now. Emphasizing past strengths and successful coping help restore a sense of control and mastery during the present crisis.

Reduction of tension. Because underlying, intrapsychic causes can be ascertained only speculatively in crisis treatment, symptom reduction and relief of stress are primary concerns. By using reassurance and support, pathological regression is blocked, as is the decompensation process.

Active intervention. The crisis therapist intervenes directly with the problem by giving advice and, if it is necessary, assuming a decision-making role. In family situations, the therapist may need to confront family members regarding their responsibilities to compromise or make changes in their behaviors in order to cope with the situation.

Management of future crises. It is made clear that help is available for future problems, and the patient and/or family may return as needed. Referrals can be given for ongoing treatment, but the door is left open for further crisis services.

The Psychotherapeutic Relationship

With the so-called "normal neurotic," that is, the patient who seeks psychotherapy to gain personal insight and fulfillment, crisis intervention can be clearly separated from ongoing treatment. For the CMI patient, however, the tasks involved in daily living can make each change from the routine a crisis in itself. For these patients, it is more appropriate to distinguish between levels of crisis, from the acute episode to what may be referred to as the chronic, ongoing crisis experience.

The patient's need for a sense of mastery, the feeling that he or she can cope with his or her symptomatology and demands of daily life have been described by Fenichel (1946). Lamb (1982) discusses working with the "well" part of the ego, that is, the part that maintains contact with reality and is relatively stable. Insight must be redefined in terms of helping the patient tap ego strengths so that he or she can confront psychotic features without being overwhelmed by them.

The therapist should help the patient to understand symptoms such as hallucinations and delusions as responses to stress, as an indication that medication may need adjustment, and as a cue that it is time to see the therapist. If the patient understands the symptoms, he or she is less likely to experience an overwhelming panic or loss of control, and patient and therapist together can devise an appropriate treatment plan. Insight, then, consists of helping the patient become aware of what is happening and the reasons behind his or her actions. Over time, the patient may come to recognize this process and to cope more successfully with stressful situations, using the therapeutic relationship as an anchor.

For the chronic schizophrenic, traditional therapeutic notions of "expressing one's anger" or being permitted to regress should be considered with caution (Lamb, 1982). It may be preferable to promote a strengthening rather than release of ego controls in a patient who so easily lapses into psychosis. Structure is important in order to create a life situation that is both bearable and manageable. The therapist can support ego controls by setting limits on the patient's behavior, including promptness for appointments and instructions regarding appropriate behavior. Self-destructive behaviors should be pointed out and discouraged.

Bellak and Siegel (1983) outline specific factors in the therapeutic management of acute psychotic states. Because the acutely disturbed CMI patient is often in a decompensated, agitated, or panic state, the therapist must try to comprehend the patient's way of thinking to enable the patient to feel more secure, not alone, and understood. Ascertaining what precipitated the psychotic break may allow the use of limited interpretations, thus reassuring the patient that help is at hand. Schizophrenics are more apt to lack synthetic ego function and hence be disorganized and repressed, whereas manics may exercise denial and avoidance. Bellak and Siegel suggest that the therapist employ "splinting," that is, direct intervention into the patient's environment to lessen or remove the stressful conditions that have overburdened the patient, thus allowing the ego to make use of its capacity for self-healing and reconstitution. Possible neurological or genetic factors in psychopathology should be explored and pharmacology used to facilitate the patient's receptivity to the therapist's interventions. If symptomatology is too severe, brief hospitalization may be necessary.

The therapist serves as a kind of auxiliary ego when the patient is unable to resolve problems for him- or herself. Appropriate case-management services can be provided so that the daily aspects of life are taken care of until the patient is able to do so on his or her own. The therapist must remain available to the CMI patient to the greatest extent possible, even if only by brief telephone contact. This support provides a measure of continuity and reassurance in the patient's life. When the therapist is unavailable, the crisis treatment center may take on this role. Finally, flexibility is perhaps the key factor in working with the chronically mentally ill. Adapting psychodynamic principles to current realities, the therapist may move back and forth from reflective to active involvement. A supportive but not intimidating relationship can be instrumental in achieving remission and avoiding hospitalization (Lamb, 1982).

> Betty, a twenty-seven-year-old woman, was interviewed by the crisis therapist. She had good secretarial skills and had no trouble obtaining a job. In fact, she had held four jobs in the past eight months. Shortly after starting each new position, she would begin seeing Egyptian men following her, in the elevators, across the street, pursuing her. They were agents of the Antichrist who wanted to attack her so she would become one of them. Betty admitted that a part of her believed it was "all in her mind," but she could not shake these overwhelming feelings.
>
> The therapist listened empathically, reflecting Betty's fears and concerns while reassuring her that she would be helped. In consultation with the psychiatrist, a low dosage of haloperidol (an antipsychotic medication) was prescribed. She was reassured that her symptoms were both understandable and manageable, and she did not need to be locked up in the psychiatric hospital.
>
> Over a period of several sessions, her relationship with her ex-husband was explored, and a cautious interpretation was offered relating her delusions to her history of negative involvements with men. She was advised that because her fears seemed greater in crowded downtown office buildings, she might seek employment in a suburban environment.
>
> Betty called the therapist twice from her current place of employment to express her fears of occult forces. She seemed to draw strength from the reassurance and support she received. After six sessions, the delusions had diminished. Although they occasionally recurred, she was able to deal with them on her own. She left treatment with the understanding that she was welcome to return to the crisis clinic whenever she felt the need.

Crisis Intervention Settings

Crisis intervention with the CMI patient may occur in various settings, including the general hospital emergency room, a hospital-based crisis unit (general or psychiatric hospital), the mobile emergency crisis response service of a psychiatric emergency team (PET), residential crisis treatment centers, and community walk-in crisis centers.

The general hospital emergency room may be the first place an individual in crisis turns to. Indeed, many of the patients who seek out emergency rooms are diagnosed as being primarily in need of psychiatric treatment. A patient may have made a suicidal gesture, for example, such as slightly cutting his or her wrists, and may require only brief medical attention. However, the patient clearly needs more than a bandage; thus a crisis therapist is made available. In some hospitals, crisis treatment is available in the medical emergency room itself. However, the vast number of "psychiatric emergencies" (crises) has led many of the larger facilities to provide a specialized crisis evaluation unit in a separate area. For example, crisis treatment is available for Los Angeles County residents on a twenty-four-hour basis at four major centers and at outpatient mental health clinics during regular working hours. However, even this limited response capability has been threatened by recent fiscal cutbacks. Unfortunately, the situation in Los Angeles County may well be indicative of similar situations throughout the United States.

Hospital-Based Crisis Unit

At Los Angeles County–USC Medical Center, the emergency psychiatric service is located on the ground floor of the psychiatric hospital. It is easily reachable from the downtown and inner-city areas where many chronically mentally ill persons are found. An outpatient mental health clinic, where patients can arrange for ongoing treatment, is located in an adjacent building. Across the street is a pharmacy, where patients can have some prescriptions filled at no personal cost.

Patients enter the service in several ways. Those who are brought in involuntarily on police "holds" (in California under Section 5250 of the Lanterman-Petris-Short Act, a patient can be held for up to seventy-two hours) or who are too agitated to wait cooperatively are taken directly to a locked admitting/evaluation area where they can receive immediate medication and attention. If they come in voluntarily or in the company of family or friends, they register and wait to be seen by the crisis therapist—a social worker, psychologist, or psychiatric resident.

In preparing for the interview, the therapist briefly reviews the patient's file, if one exists, containing records from any previous visits. The patient and persons accompanying him or her are greeted and escorted to an interview room. In an empathic yet direct manner, the reasons for seeking treatment are explored. The therapist makes sure that the patient and companions all have an opportunity to present their versions of the crisis; to do this, sometimes each person must be seen separately as well.

The crisis therapist must simultaneously make a diagnostic assessment while providing crisis intervention. The problem is defined, the family (if available) is engaged, and immediate help is given. Help may include reinforcing the patient's coping abilities, helping the patient to organize his or her thoughts, and developing a plan of action. Often, the therapist will consult with a patient's regular therapist, parole officer, board-and-care manager, welfare worker, or concerned family members via telephone in an effort to resolve any communication breakdown or maladaptive interaction. Specific advice may be given both to the patient and to his or her caregiving network.

During the course of this crisis session, the therapist gathers information that forms the basis of a diagnostic assessment. This mental status evaluation is not simply a series of formal questions put to the patient; it should be part of the treatment process itself. By asking relevant questions, the therapist lets the patient know he or she is concerned and interested in the patient's situation. Often, the patient fails to volunteer information that proves crucial to the intervention, for example, recurrent paranoid delusions or a history of cocaine abuse. However, if the therapist asks about such issues, an outpouring of new information may occur.

With the CMI patient, medication issues generally need to be considered. The nonphysician specialist must have a working knowledge of psychopharmacology. The patient's history of taking medications, or failing to do so, must be explored. On the psychiatric emergency service, a psychiatrist is available for consultation when medication or hospitalization are needed.

Perlmutter and Jones (1985) provide a conceptual model of the crisis interview. During the initial assessment phase, the key tasks are engagement of the family, thus allowing members to express their concerns, reducing the overall anxiety level, and identifying what kind of help is being sought. A differential diagnosis is formulated, suicidal or homicidal ideation explored, and a determination made about the patient's ability to care for him- or herself. Problems are viewed not only in terms of individual pathology, but in the context of the surrounding social system.

Following the assessment phase, crisis intervention, consultation, and referral are provided. In families displaying communication deviance (patterns of communication in which the speaker's unfocused style works against the interviewer's goal of obtaining clear, meaningful information), clarification of these patterns may succeed in altering the family's negative interactional style or, at least, in getting the needed information. The crisis therapist reformulates the problem so that it can be constructively addressed and decides whether to hospitalize the patient or provide an alternative arrangement.

The crisis therapist must be flexible in coping with conflicting demands (individual and conjoint meetings, medication considerations, mental status of patient, family and environmental stresses) while remaining empathically involved with the patient and family and formulating the most appropriate treatment plan (Perlmutter & Jones, 1985). Clearly, the emergency family crisis interview offers both rewards and challenges for the practitioner.

In summary, the emergency psychiatric service offers a kind of therapeutic first-aid station where the CMI patient can always receive some help, even if he or she is unable to keep an appointment or know what day it is. The availability of such a service may prevent the patient from decompensating further or lapsing into an acute psychotic state with no recourse but hospitalization.

> Soonja, a thirty-six-year-old Korean woman, came into the crisis service voluntarily, seeking "somebody just to talk to." She had married an American GI stationed in Korea, who brought her to the United States ten years previously. The marriage broke up after her second hospitalization for

"depression"; her husband and children were in a city thousands of miles away. Soonja lived in and around several shopping malls, where kindly security guards were aware of her and occasionally gave her money. However, she never asked for help unless it was offered first. She would enter a restaurant, order food, and eat, then inform the management that she had no money. If the police were called, she made no attempt to flee, but would serve time in jail.

Soonja evoked a measure of sympathy from the crisis therapist, as she did from many people who met her, but she declined all suggestions for placement or medication evaluation. She did not wish to have her husband contacted; she felt her family was "doing better without her," and she had no other relatives in the United States. The therapist suggested that perhaps the Korean community would become involved in her situation, but this offer too was declined.

Ultimately, the therapist was giving Soonja what she asked for—someone to whom she could talk and who would express concern about her situation. The therapist gave Soonja a list of shelters and resources, despite her statement that she would not utilize them. Soonja could not be treated against her will, because despite her bizarre life-style, she was not dangerous to herself or others. The crisis therapist did provide direct human contact with Soonja, engaged her in an exchange of feelings, and let her know that help was available if she should choose to accept it and that the door was open if she should decide to return. The therapist was able to secure a few dollars in emergency funds for Soonja, which she accepted and then went on her way.

Although the ultimate outcome of this case is unknown, Soonja can be viewed from several perspectives. She was a failure in the short-term sense of being "hooked into the system," and no case-management strategies for linkage and ongoing treatment had been implemented. However, her problem of "needing someone to talk to" was resolved, and the way was paved for her to avail herself of crisis intervention services in the future.

Partial Hospitalization

In addition to emergency crisis intervention services, all programs should have an intensive care unit to stabilize persons suffering from acute, severe symptomatology (Test, 1981). This unit may be simply an area set aside where partial hospitalization is available. Such a unit can provide a structured setting where the distressed CMI patient can receive more intensive intervention over a longer period than an outpatient setting allows, but generally not receive overnight hospital care. For approximately 15 percent to 25 percent of the CMI population treated, brief in-hospital admissions appear to be essential. The goal is to avoid lengthy hospitalization and promote a rapid return of the patient to the community (Hanssen & Rosewall, 1976). The crisis situation is dealt with initially, and appropriate treatment resources are provided for aftercare and long-range resolution of the problem. Thus inpatient care is deemphasized as the treatment of choice for acute crisis states; rather, treatment aims at restoring the patient's previous level of functioning and arranging for continuing care services in the community.

Joe, a twenty-one-year-old man, was literally dragged into the triage (screening) area of the crisis evaluation unit by two of his friends. He was moaning, yelling, singing, laughing, and cursing his friends as well as the attending staff. Due to his incoherent presentation and unpredictable, bizarre behavior, he was placed in restraints in the partial hospitalization area. His friends stated that he had smoked some "sherm," the drug phencyclidine (PCP) (Slaby, 1981). The patient had required emergency treatment for PCP intoxication many times before, but he had never been so uncontrollable.

Joe was medicated with haloperidol intramuscularly; within an hour he had stopped thrashing about. Shortly thereafter he was able to respond to questions and felt sufficiently under control to be released from restraints. He had little recollection of what had transpired since he had smoked the PCP. Because symptoms occasionally reappear with PCP, Joe was held overnight for observation. His family was contacted, and both patient and family were given referrals to several drug treatment programs. It is unknown whether Joe followed through; unfortunately, such patients have a fairly high rate of noncompliance and recidivism.

Bill, a thirty-year-old black male, was dressed in a suit and tie. His mother said he had not removed this clothing for the past three days. He was carrying a Bible and seemed quite euphoric, singing praises of the Lord and clearly having a direct, two-way conversation with God, Mary, and Jesus. His mother, a Christian fundamentalist herself, recognized that her son was delusional and sought the crisis unit's help. Bill had previously been diagnosed as bipolar-manic and was supposed to be taking lithium and thiothixene (Navane) for this condition. It was unclear whether a rapid decompensation prevented compliance or whether he had simply stopped his medication. It was clear that he required emergency intervention.

Because Bill was unmanageable at home in his present condition, he was held for one day on the partial hospitalization unit. His religious beliefs were not challenged, but he was given medication and a structured environment where he calmed down enough to go home.

The Mobile Emergency Response Service

When chronically mentally ill persons are in crisis, they may be far from the nearest treatment center; their regular therapist, if there is one, may not be available; and they may be in no condition to seek help on their own. Frequently, these individuals are decompensating or suicidal and present in a bizarre or agitated manner. The Mobile Emergency Response Service, or Psychiatric Emergency Team (PET), responds to these crises.

The PET, which may be part of a mental health center or of a hospital-based crisis evaluation unit (CEU), consists of an interdisciplinary staff of social workers, psychologists, psychiatric technicians, nurses, and other professionals who make telephone assessments of crisis situations and go directly to the scene if necessary. Calls may be initiated by the person in distress or by concerned relatives, neighbors, or other parties. Major precipitating factors for calls include family conflicts, psychotic symptoms, suicidal threats, and episodes related to substance abuse. Team members assess the situation and provide immediate advice or referrals over the telephone. If the patient's crisis is still unmanageable, usually two team members drive to the scene. Police back-up may be required if the patient is agitated or belligerent. Sometimes the presence of two professionals has an immediate therapeutic effect, causing the patient in crisis and other involved parties to become calmer and more receptive to intervention. The problems and concerns of the patient and significant others are explored, and steps are taken toward resolving the immediate crisis. Referrals to the nearest clinic or agency are provided, and follow-up phone calls or visits help to ensure that the patient's ongoing needs are being met.

When the CMI person's problems are too severe to be treated fully at the scene, the PET is authorized to commit the person to a hospital for further evaluation and treatment. This action can be taken either with the patient's cooperation or, if legal criteria are met, on an involuntary basis. California's Lanterman-Petris-Short Act (Segal, Watson, & Nelson, 1985), which has served as a model for other states' mental health legislation, sets the criteria for involuntary commitment. A person can be placed on a seventy-two-hour hold if the authorized clinician or peace officer determines that the person is dangerous to others, to him- or herself, or gravely disabled. Thus the PET's task is to make this determination. Hospitalization may be implemented either by the PET transporting the patient or, if there is any question of violence, by supporting police or ambulance service.

Foxman (1976) noted that despite many clinicians' initial reluctance to participate in the program, one PET became a close-knit and dedicated group, deriving great satisfaction from their work. Most crises could be satisfactorily resolved through direct intervention at the scene of the incident. Often, the team's intervention and referrals provided an alternative to hospitalization. Psychiatric Emergency Team members generally took a more assertive stance toward crisis management, therapy, and consultation than did more traditionally oriented therapists. As crisis response units became established in their communities, they gained increasing acceptance among the populations they served. Police officers, who still are the primary interveners with the chronically mentally ill when no other help is available, have found it advantageous to work closely with PETs. A psychiatric population is more appropriately served by trained professionals in a mental health system than by police offices in a criminal justice system.

> Juan, a forty-five-year-old Hispanic male, lived with his mother, several relatives, and their children. He had been previously hospitalized several times, sometimes for depression and suicidal feelings and other times for grandiose delusions, hallucinations, and agitation. Diagnosed as having a schizoaffective disorder, he had been prescribed lithium, thiothixene, and benztropine (Cogentin) upon his last discharge nearly a year previously. Initially, Juan had gone to an outpatient clinic and had complied with the treatment plan. However, he missed several appointments; no one seemed to notice, so he dropped out of treatment. Over the past month, he became increasingly restless, often wandering the streets for hours, eating poorly, not sleeping, and quarreling with his family.
>
> Juan was agitated and began shouting at his cousin to get out of his mother's home. He kicked over the furniture and paced rapidly through the house, muttering loudly that no one gave him the respect he deserved. Sometimes he appeared to be talking to an imaginary person in the room.
>
> Upon receiving the call from the mother, the PET member gathered as much information as possible over the phone. She briefly consulted with a colleague, and the decision was made that two team members should go

> directly to the scene. Because the patient was not overtly violent, police back-up was not requested, although this remained an option.
>
> At the scene, frightened family members were given assurance that help was available. The presence of the PET team members had a stabilizing effect both on the family and on Juan. Initially, he was somewhat suspicious and hostile, but as the team members empathized with his problems, he began a dialogue with them. He described his frustration over being unemployed, unmarried, and dependent on his mother at age forty-five. Ultimately, he agreed to accept medication at the mental health center and was given a ride there by the PET. Appointments were arranged for him to see a therapist/case manager, who would contact the patient directly to ensure follow-up.

Had Juan not responded to the PET's interventions, hospitalization could have been arranged for the patient. Often, PET staff are unable to resolve the crisis at the scene, but a brief stay at the crisis evaluation unit avoids the need for long-term inpatient treatment. Working with concerned family members and significant others, the PET can intervene not only to resolve the crisis at hand, but to provide new coping strategies to avoid similar crises in the future. Referrals to appropriate community resources can also be provided.

Residential Crisis Treatment Center

A number of programs offer short-term residential treatment to CMI patients. These programs are designed primarily for patients who are not violent or acutely suicidal but who need close attention on a full-time basis in order to prevent further decompensation.

One program, sponsored by the Massachusetts Mental Health Center (MMHC) (Gudeman & Shore, 1984), includes a two-day hospital service, a thirty-day intensive care unit to stabilize acute psychotic episodes, and an "inn" that provides transitional housing. A continuing-care program consists of graduated levels of residences and day-treatment programs, with approximately 500 severely ill patients receiving treatment and care each day in the combined residential and hospital settings. Chronically mentally ill patients can move back and forth between levels of care within this system; some eventually move on to community living, whereas others are more or less permanent residents of the center.

Using the MMHC as a model, Gudeman and Shore propose the development of a new genre of specialized care services. This model recognizes that although the goal is for each patient to become able to make it on his or her own, some patients will always require a degree of institutionalization. Ideally, the patient should be provided with the least amount of structure necessary for functioning. Gudeman and Shore would locate facilities on the grounds of state hospitals or nursing homes, although facilities could also be on separate grounds. Political realities would be attended to in order to win family, community, and governmental support. Benefits of their plan would include consolidation of services under one umbrella, leading to more focused and effective interventions. In addition to the potentially prohibitive funding considerations that plague nearly all proposed solutions, drawbacks are that patients are once again isolated to some extent from the community, albeit in a modified institutional setting.

In Los Angeles County, such programs as the University of Southern California's Alternatives to Hospitalization, Compass House, and Transitional Living Center offer short-term living arrangements in which individual and group treatment, vocational counseling, and medication are provided. The length of stay varies from a few days up to three months, depending on the program and the needs of the patient.

A Los Angeles-based service, the Community Living Program, designed to facilitate the transition between the CMI patient's residence in a board-and-care facility to an independent living situation is described in a videotape titled "Apartment 3" (Parad & Hart, 1984). In a typical board-and-care home, patients are asked to do little to provide for themselves. Meals are served; the principal activities often consist of smoking cigarettes and watching television. In such an unstimulating environment, residents tend to become passive and sedentary; although they are not confined to a back ward of a hospital, they are nonetheless isolated and dependent. It should be pointed out that the level of services at board-and-care facilities varies widely; indeed, some facilities have regular activity programs and ongoing rehabilitation training. However, too many have become warehouses for chronic psychiatric patients.

In the model "Apartment 3," patients who had been languishing at their board-and-care homes are given support and encouragement as they are taught skills such as budgeting, keeping a bank account, and using public transportation. Patients who had never before prepared a meal learn to plan meals, shop, and cook; maintain their own apartments; and make appropriate choices, thus developing confidence in their own abilities. The treatment rationale is to give a resident as much help as needed but not to smother him or her. The goal is to enable the resident to function on his or her own. Of the ninety-eight graduates since 1981, a recent follow-up showed that 76 percent were maintaining a satisfactory adjustment in independent living arrangements (Wallace, 1989).

The Southwest Denver Community Mental Health Center, a community-based crisis intervention program offering an alternative to psychiatric hospitalization provides still another residential model (Kirby, Polak, & Weerts, 1983). A system of private sponsor homes has been implemented, in which CMI patients who require separation from their families can be placed in a "normal" family setting that is closely monitored by a clinical team. In the supportive, personalized environment of the sponsor home, patients form close personal attachments to the sponsor family members, increase their level of performance expectations, and lessen their dependence on institutional settings. As part of this program, staff members emphasize the treatment of the patient's social system and not merely the identified patient. Throughout the treatment process, therapists coordinate all activities for their patients. A longitudinal evaluation of this alternative to a hospitalization program found that the need for inpatient admissions was reduced, patients were more satisfied with their treatment, and patients were more likely to be employed than were patients in a comparable group who had been hospitalized.

Although this program supports the effectiveness of a comprehensive case management and community support system in avoiding hospitalization and providing services to CMI patients, the model assumes that sufficient high-quality sponsor homes can be found and monitored, that patients will be behaviorally manageable and motivated to cooperate with the treatment, and that adequate funding exists to maintain such a program.

Role of Case Management

For a highly functioning individual, dealing with the complexities of public service agencies can be challenging at best. For the CMI patient who tends to respond to stress or frustration with passivity or withdrawal, it may be impossible. Proper case management with this population forms an integral part of the treatment process. Case management serves a coordinating function with therapeutic facets, including identification of clients and their needs, service planning, and linkage to ensure that available resources are appropriately utilized. Monitoring and evaluation of both clients and service delivery are key tasks (Weil & Karls, 1985). The crisis therapist is uniquely suited to take on the role of case manager for CMI patients, guiding them through the bureaucratic mazes so that desperately needed services can be obtained.

Because funding for social and mental health services is scarce, specific goals must be set for each client. Although the goal remains helping patients obtain their highest feasible level of independent functioning (Levine & Fleming, 1984), provisions for accountability ensure that services are provided on a timely and cost-effective basis. By encouraging the patient to share in the case-management process, individual responsibility and efficiency are enhanced.

The crisis intervention specialist who is skilled in case management can initiate steps to reduce the likelihood of future crises. By making direct contact with the disability worker or the vocational rehabilitation program director, red tape can be reduced and the patient is less apt to get lost in the shuffle. Coordination between staff of these agencies and the case manager not only makes the delivery of services more efficient, but gives the patient the sense that something can and will be done, heightens the patient's self-confidence, and lessens the chance of another decompensation.

A distressing phenomenon observed by mental health professionals is the failure of a client to make or keep a referral appointment. The case manager ensures linkage of patient and service (Levine & Fleming, 1984; O'Connor, 1988; Libassi, 1988) by whatever means necessary. This effort may involve telephone follow-ups or even physical transportation of the patient. Although concrete services may be carried out by paraprofessionals or volunteers, the case manager oversees these arrangements.

Various models have been proposed for the provision of case management services, ranging from the generalist, in which the case manager acts as a broker for all services, to the case manager as primary therapist (Weil, 1985). In the latter model, the case-management function is an extension of the therapeutic relationship (Lamb, 1980). Polak, Kirby, and Deitchman (1979) describe an integrated mental health delivery system in which a team of experts provides all the needed services within a specific community. Such a comprehensive approach could eliminate the lack of coordination between diverse, unrelated programs and services.

The advantages of intensive programs stressing the teaching of living skills in a supportive, carefully structured environment are demonstrable. Funding considerations, unfortunately, make the large-scale implementation of such programs problematic. In addition, many CMI patients may lack the motivational capacity to participate in such programs, or their degree of pathology may be too severe. However, residential crisis-treatment centers provide an optimal treatment milieu. Research confirms that community treatment programs that incorporate these kinds of assistance have stimulated higher levels of functioning in patients (Stein & Test, 1980) than have typical hospital or residential facilities.

The State of Oregon has developed a community support program called Living in the Community (LINC) (Cutler, Terwillinger, Faulkner, Field, & Bray, 1984) that demonstrates effective collaboration between a state hospital and community treatment programs for CMI patients. The program's strategy includes identifying and assisting inpatients who potentially can live in the community in a supportive, small-group environment if provided continuity of care and availability of a full range of services, for example, case management, crisis response availability, and daily structure. A comprehensive program of living-skill training activities, vocational rehabilitation, and financial and housing services is provided for each CMI patient. The program is evaluated constantly. Goals are reset daily at team meetings, and data are kept on hospital recidivism, social behaviors, and levels of functioning. Ideological support within the state's political system, strong local and professional leadership, and adequate funding have been crucial to the LINC project's effectiveness. As with the Southwest Denver study, it appears that given sufficient funding and with provisions for evaluation and accountability, comprehensive community support programs can be developed that enable CMI patients to live outside the hospital with a measure of autonomy. Case-management services are a critical aspect in the operation of such programs.

Honnard and Wolkon (1985) address the issues involved in case-management program evaluation. Experts on evaluation research need to be involved throughout an evaluation effort, offering technical consultation and methodology. Structure, process, and linkage evaluations ultimately assess whether the CMI patient is effectively utilizing the services that are available, and if not, what changes are necessary. The use of a computer tracking system is one technological advance that theoretically makes possible up-to-date monitoring and tracking of treatment episodes, which the clinician/case manager utilizes as an integral part of the treatment plan. Unfortunately, such computerized systems are only as efficient and useful as the information with which they are programmed. Information within such systems is frequently incomplete, not current, or not readily available to the crisis therapist.

To develop an effective case-management system, concrete operational definitions must be developed that address structure of organizations and authorities, staffing patterns, accountability, interagency relationships, and criteria for what constitutes success (Honnard, 1985). Effectiveness of different case-management programs and models can be compared, and what approaches best help different types of CMI patients improve or maintain their current levels of functioning can be determined. Although specific programs have been evaluated and found to be effective according to each study's criteria, further evidence that case-management services significantly improve care for CMI patients is needed (Johnson & Rubin, 1983). Otherwise, case management may be viewed as one more layer in the bureaucratic morass.

Another issue in the provision of case-management services is the training and education of case managers. Differing models and approaches call for varying levels of professional training, depending upon the needs of a given situation. Whereas paraprofessionals may carry out many practical interventions, the crisis therapist must possess the skills to diagnose and assess a patient's psychosocial functioning and to ensure that appropriate psychiatric care is provided. Social work, with its traditional person-in-situation orientation, has an underlying practice framework that has been suggested as being most amenable to case-management principles (Johnson & Rubin, 1983). However, despite their philosophical underpinnings, many social workers in direct practice emphasize in-depth psychotherapy at the expense of ecological perspectives (Libassi, 1988). With the prevailing ideology that one's sophistication in clinical skills is the mark of one's professionalism, models that emphasize service brokerage and advocacy are viewed as less prestigious. Honnard (1985) calls for a balance between psychosocial and rehabilitation functions with treatment approaches based on psychiatry. Integration of clinical and managerial skills so that the CMI patient may be effectively helped poses both a challenge and opportunity for the crisis therapist.

Summary and Critique

The deinstitutionalization movement, with its roots in a combination of civil libertarian and fiscally conservative values, is highly complex. In a sense, it has been half successful; that is, it has met its objective of releasing the chronically mentally ill from the hospitals. Unfortunately, the original objective of returning the patient to the community has often meant releasing the patient to the streets (Surber, Dwyer, Ryan, Goldfinger, & Kelly, 1988; First, Roth, & Arewa, 1988) Thus deinstitutionalization is a mix of occasional successes and a succession of horror stories—bag ladies freezing to death by the curbside, transients drifting from one skid row to another. Although much of the research literature addresses specific programs and treatment strategies, it is evident that no panacea to the plight of the chronically mentally ill has been found. Not to be underemphasized, however, is the power of the therapeutic alliance between the CMI client and the rehabilitation therapist (Goering & Stylianos, 1988).

Crisis intervention services should be given top priority in public mental health systems. The availability of crisis evaluation units, including walk-in facilities, partial hospitalization, and PETs, has repeatedly been shown to reduce the need for psychiatric hospitalization (Langsley, 1980). When the CMI person faces an acute problem, he or she must have help available on a twenty-four-hour basis. Crisis services fill that function. As the first point of contact, when assessment, referral, and treatment are offered, crisis services provide effective interventions that set the stage for more permanent resolutions to a presenting problem that represents only the acute exacerbation of a chronic situation.

Short-term or emergency crisis intervention services fulfill a crucial function. However, they are but one facet of the treatment process for the CMI patient. Key needs of chronic patients include direct assistance with daily living skills (for example, how to plan a budget, ride the bus, cook or eat at a restaurant). These needs are often neglected or overlooked (Walsh, 1988) and require ongoing case-management services that address daily problems of living. In a sense, the CMI patient is in permanent crisis, requiring treatment plans that include food and shelter, income maintenance, and follow-up psychiatric treatment, support, and medication.

If we recognize that temporary solutions are inadequate to meet the needs of the long-term mentally ill, a shift toward permanent solutions can be initiated. Greater consideration should be given to nontransitional living arrangements, because the beneficial effects of halfway houses and time-limited programs are often lost when patients move on (Test, 1981). Within all such arrangements, the care provider's expectations must be geared to the resident's capacity for psychosocial adjustment in order to promote opportunities for achieving higher levels of functioning without overwhelming the individual's ability to cope with the stresses of daily living.

Not all CMI patients can achieve the ideal of normalization (Lamb & Peele, 1984). A characteristic of the schizophrenic process may be a life-style that avoids excessive social stimuli and depends on a consistent, structured environment. Thus, for some CMI patients, maintaining a consistent level of functioning should be deemed success. In other words, recognizing and accepting a patient's limitations as well as strengths can serve as both protection and support for the patient. The need for an appropriately supportive and structured living situation, then, becomes a crucial element in providing a treatment plan for the CMI population.

I concur with Jansson's (1984) call for a massive nationally funded program to be established specifically for the needs of the mentally ill. Funds could be channeled through regional authorities to devise and orchestrate a range of services such as those discussed in the present chapter. In a cogent acknowledgment of the need for further funding, Lamb (1984) concludes that a marked increase in services is needed to improve the quality, quantity, and range of suitable services to this population. Many of the homeless CMI patients could be helped to find and remain in stable living situations. With adequate funding, better providers will enter the field, and regulatory agencies can expect more from them. Unfortunately, current political realities militate against putting such ideas into practice. Increasing attention has been given to the private sector's involvement in social services. But without sufficient financial incentives, this sector will never provide the quality of services and professional staff needed. This, in essence, is the Catch-22 of current politics—calling upon private sources to supplement the so-called "safety net" while channeling funds away from the public sector so that there is no safety net.

Problems of high vulnerability to stress, poor interpersonal skills, lack of motivation, passivity, and dependency in CMI patients lead to a failure of available services to reach their target population (Stein & Test, 1980). If services are made "assertively available"—in other words, the therapist or provider seeks out persons who are in need of them—patients can be engaged in treatment who otherwise would be left out. Coordination between financial assistance offices and mental health services would help to ensure that patients do not get lost in the shuffle. Aggressive case management is an important tool in ensuring that patients take advantage of available services. The case manager's functions serve to link the patient and the range of needed services on an ongoing, continuous basis. When continuity of care is maintained, the quality of a CMI patient's life is enhanced. Unfortunately, this principle is more often breached than it is honored.

A phenomenon evident to all who deal with the homeless mentally ill is their tendency to drift from one city to another or from one living situation to another (Lamb, 1984). The CMI typically suffer from an inability to establish bonding (Hansell, 1982), drifting in search of autonomy, denying their dependency, and preferring an isolated life-style. Having no money, minimal social skills, poor hygiene, and psychotic features makes them undesirable to family members or potential supportive networks. They may have had unpleasant experiences with board-and-care homes, shelters, or hospitals, and often do not want any part of the mental health system. Substance abusers and patients with characterological problems may be unmotivated to change such behaviors, despite the efforts of a skilled and sensitive therapist.

I agree with researchers who believe that the question of liberty must be reconsidered in terms of the pathology of the CMI population (Jansson, 1984; Lamb, 1984). A small but significant percentage of severely ill patients are unable to control their own impulses; they may refuse medications, abuse alcohol and drugs, and be subject to belligerent or destructive episodes. Proposals have been made to institute certain involuntary outpatient commitment provisions for such persons (Wilk, 1988). In the crisis-treatment units of Los Angeles County and elsewhere, the same patients are frequently seen again and again, brought in by families, police, or board-and-care operators for antisocial, unmanageable outbursts. With state mental health laws such as California's Lanterman-Petris-Short Act (Segal et al., 1985) severely limiting criteria for involuntary psychiatric commitment, patients may "stabilize" within a three-day period, deny all problems at a brief civil hearing, and be promptly discharged against the staff's recommendations. Thus the cycle soon repeats itself, and the patients are back in the hospital. Staff morale is lowered as a disproportionate amount of time and energy is invested in what is perceived as an ultimately futile endeavor.

Legal mechanisms such as conservatorship, by which the CMI patient with a documented history of unstable behaviors is assigned a qualified public or private guardian (often a family member), exist but are difficult to implement. Legal procedures need to be clarified and red tape reduced. The rights of CMI patients must be carefully spelled out and protected, but not at the expense of impeding necessary treatment. Locked residential treatment facilities, with high staff–patient ratios and a structured therapeutic milieu, can serve to break this negative cycle and ensure that a patient's pathology does not result in treatment being denied. For patients who do not require such facilities, but decline crucial therapeutic interventions, mandatory aftercare could be legislated (Wilk, 1988). Services could be implemented with the assistance of an assigned case manager.

The crisis therapist must come to accept the limitations of the CMI patient as well as the rewards inherent in working with this population. Successes must be measured by standards different from those used in the treatment of so-called "normal neurotics." High staff–patient ratios, support groups for clinicians, and balancing one's case load with patients at different levels of functioning are ways to maintain staff commitment and morale. Flexibility is perhaps the key factor in working therapeutically with these patients.

In conclusion, although a simple solution does not exist, much is known about the ways in which the quality of life for the CMI patient can be improved and sustained. Optimal utilization of present resources can go a long way toward making a difference in the care and treatment of this population. From the level of individual treatment to exerting influence on local, state, and national governments, by involvement on macro as well as micro levels, crisis therapists and their professional colleagues can make a significant impact on resolving the problems of the chronically mentally ill.

References

Aguilera, D. C. (1983). The role of crisis intervention in the management of the chronic psychiatric patient. In I. Barofsky & R. D. Budson (Eds.), *The chronic psychiatric patient in the community* (pp. 181–204). New York: SP Medical and Scientific.

American Psychiatric Association. (1987). Diagnostic criteria from DSM-III-R. Washington, DC: Author.

Applebaum, P. S. (1986). Outpatient commitment: The problems and the promise. *American Journal of Psychiatry, 143*, 1270–1272.

Bellak, L., & Siegel, H. (1983). *Handbook of intensive brief and emergency psychotherapy*. Larchmont, NY: C.P.S.

Bloom, B. (1984). *Community mental health: A general introduction*. Monterey, CA: Brooks/Cole.

Cutler, D. L., Terwillinger, W., Faulkner, F., Field, G., & Bray, D. (1984). Disseminating the principles of a community support program. *Hospital and Community Psychiatry, 35*, 51–55.

Fenichel, A. (1946). *The psychoanalytic theory of neurosis*. London: Routledge and Kegan Paul.

First, R. J., Roth, D., & Arewa, B. D. (1988). Homelessness: Understanding the dimensions of the problems for minorities. *Social Work, 33*, 120–124.

Foxman, J. (1976). The mobile psychiatric emergency team. In H. J. Parad, H. L. P. Resnik, & L. G. Parad (Eds.), *Emergency and disaster management* (pp. 35–44). Bowie, MD: Charles Press.

Gers, S. (1979). Emergency psychiatric care in municipal hospitals. *Psychiatric Annals, 9*, 31–46.

Goering, P. N., & Stylianos, S. K. (1988). Exploring the helping relationship between the schizophrenic client and rehabilitation therapist. *American Journal of Orthopsychiatry, 58*, 271–280.

Goldman, H. H., Gattozzi, A. A., & Taube, C. A. (1981). Defining and counting the chronically mentally ill. *Hospital and Community Psychiatry, 32*, 21–27.

Gudeman, J. E., & Shore, M. F. (1984). Beyond deinstitutionalization. *New England Journal of Medicine, 311*, 832–836.

Hansell, N. (1982). Serving the chronically mentally ill. In H. Schulberg & M. Killilea (Eds.), *The modern practice of community mental health* (pp. 358–371). San Francisco: Jossey-Bass.

Hanssen, C. C., & Rosewall, C. R. (1976). The crisis evaluation unit: A ripple in the pond. In H. J. Parad, H. L. P. Resnik, & L. G. Parad (Eds.), *Emergency and disaster management* (pp. 75–85). Bowie, MD: Charles Press.

Honnard, R. (1985). The chronically mentally ill in the community. In M. Weils & J. Karls (Eds.), *Case management in human services practice* (pp. 204–232). San Francisco: Jossey-Bass.

Honnard, R., & Wolkon, G. (1985). Evaluation for decision making and program accountability. In M. Weils & J. Karls (Eds.), *Case management in human services practice* (pp. 94–118). San Francisco: Jossey-Bass.

Jansson, B. S. (1984). *Theory and practice of social welfare policy*. Belmont, CA: Wadsworth.

Johnson, J., & Rubin, A. (1983). Case management in mental health: A social work domain? *Social Work, 28*, 49–54.

Kirby, M. W., Polak, P. R., & Weerts, T. C. (1983). Family crisis intervention and the prevention of psychiatric hospitalization. In L. Cohen, W. Claiborn, & G. A. Specter (Eds.), *Crisis Intervention* (2nd ed.) (pp. 111–125). New York: Human Sciences Press.

Lamb, H. R. (1980). Therapist–case managers: More than brokers of services. *Hospital and Community Psychiatry, 32*, 393–397.

Lamb, H. R. (1982). *Treating the long-term mentally ill*. San Francisco: Jossey-Bass.

Lamb, H. R. (1984). Deinstitutionalization and the homeless mentally ill. *Hospital and Community Psychiatry, 5*, 899–907.

Lamb, H. R., & Peele, R. (1984). The need for continuing asylum and sanctuary. *Hospital and Community Psychiatry, 35*, 798–801.

Langsley, D. G. (1980). Crisis intervention and the avoidance of hospitalization. In H. R. Lamb (Ed.), *New directions for mental health services: No. 6. Crisis intervention in the 1980s* (pp. 81–97). San Francisco: Jossey-Bass.

Langsley, D. G., Machotka, P., & Flomenhaft, K. (1971). Avoiding mental hospital admission: A follow-up study. *American Journal of Psychiatry, 127*, 1391–1394.

Langsley, D. G., & Yarvis, R. M. (1976). Crisis prevention prevents hospitalization. In H. J. Parad, H. L. P. Resnik, & L. G. Parad (Eds.), *Emergency and disaster management* (pp. 25–34). Bowie, MD: Charles Press.

Levine, I. S., & Fleming, M. (1984). *Human resource development: Issues in case management*. Baltimore: Center of Rehabilitation and Manpower Services, University of Maryland.

Libassi, M. F. (1988). The chronically mentally ill: A practice approach. *Social Casework, 69*, 88–96.

Mendel, W. M. (1975). *Supportive care*. Santa Monica, CA: Mara Books.

O'Connor, G. (1988). Case management: Systems and practice. *Social Casework, 69*, 97–106.

Parad, H. J. (1976). Crisis intervention in mental health emergencies: Theory and technique in work with the emotionally disturbed and mentally disordered. In M. R. Olsen (Ed.), *Differential approaches in social work with the mentally disordered* (pp. 41–50). Birmingham, England: British Association of Social Workers.

Parad, H. J. (1982). Brief family crisis therapy. In H. C. Schulberg & M. Killilea (Eds.), *The modern practice of community mental health* (pp. 419–444). San Francisco: Jossey-Bass.

Parad, H. J. (Producer), & Hart, J. (Director). (1984). *Apartment 3* (Film). School of Social Work, University of Southern California, Los Angeles.

Perlmutter, R. A., & Jones, J. E. (1985). Assessment of families in psychiatric emergencies. *American Journal of Orthopsychiatry, 55*, 130–139.

Polak, P. R., Kirby, M. W., & Deitchman, W. S. (1979). Treating acutely psychotic patients in private homes. In H. R. Lamb (Ed.), *New directions in mental health services; No. 6. Alternatives to acute hospitalization*. San Francisco: Jossey-Bass.

Rubenstein, D. (1972). Rehospitalization versus family crisis intervention. *American Journal of Psychiatry, 129*, 91–96.

Segal, S. P., Watson, M. A., & Nelson, L. S. (1985). Application of involuntary criteria in psychiatric emergency rooms. *Social Work, 30*, 160–165.

Slaby, A. E. (1981). Emergency psychiatry: An update. *Hospital and Community Psychiatry, 32*, 687–698.

Smolar, T. (1984). Schizophrenic disorders. In F. J. Turner (Ed.), *Adult psychopathology* (pp. 119–147). New York: Free Press.

Stein, L. I., & Test, M. A. (1980). Alternatives to mental hospital treatment. *Archives of General Psychiatry, 37*, 392–397.

Surber, R. W., Dwyer, E., Ryan, K. J., Goldfinger, S. M., & Kelly, J. T. (1988). Medical and psychiatric needs of the homeless. *Social Work, 33*, 116–119.

Test, M. A. (1981). Effective community treatment of the chronically mentally ill: What is necessary? *Journal of Social Issues, 37*, 71–86.

Turner, J. C. (1977). Comprehensive community support systems for severely mentally disabled adults. *Psychological Rehabilitation Journal, 1*, 39–47.

U.S. Bureau of the Census. (1984). *Statistical abstract of the U.S.: 1985* (105th ed.). Washington, DC: U.S. Government Printing Office.

U.S. Bureau of the Census. (1988). *Statistical abstract of the U.S.: 1987* (108th ed.). Washington, DC: U.S. Government Printing Office.

Wallace, B. (1989). Personal communication to editors.

Walsh, J. (1988). Social workers as family educators about schizophrenia. *Social Work, 33*, 138–141.

Weil, M. (1985). Key components in providing efficient and effective services. In M. Weil & J. M. Karls (Eds.), *Case management in human services practice* (pp. 29–71). San Francisco: Jossey-Bass.

Weil, M., & Karls, J. M. (1985). *Case management in human service practice*. San Francisco: Jossey-Bass.

Wilk, R. J. (1988). Involuntary outpatient commitment of the mentally ill. *Social Work, 33*, 133–137.

Wolkon, G. H. (1972). Crisis theory, the application for treatment, and dependency. *Comprehensive Psychiatry, 13*, 459–464.

Yarvis, R. (1975). Crisis intervention as a first line of defense. *Psychiatric Annals Reprint*. New York: Insight Communications.

11

The Suicide Prevention Center: Concepts and Clinical Functions

NORMAN L. FARBEROW, SAMUEL M. HEILIG, AND HOWARD J. PARAD

THE MODERN ERA of suicide prevention began in the United States in 1958 with the establishment of the Los Angeles Suicide Prevention Center (LASPC). In the succeeding three decades, the LASPC has changed considerably, although its basic principles remain the same. The first part of this chapter briefly reviews these changes and describes current practices; the second part focuses on the clinical functioning of a suicide prevention center (SPC) telephone crisis service, presenting examples of the people who use its services and the kinds of demands that are made upon the center and staff. The final section illustrates "in-person" crisis therapy with a suicidal client and summarizes guidelines for suicide prevention.

The LASPC was established as a result of comprehensive research on the status of suicide in Los Angeles County from 1954 to 1957 (Farberow & Shneidman, 1961). Information was obtained about suicides, suicide attempts, and other self-destructive behaviors from mental hospitals, psychiatric clinics, emergency rooms, and mental health professionals and general practitioners throughout Los Angeles County. As the data were collected, it became evident that no agency in the county provided immediate response to suicidal crisis.

The First Decade

The first conceptualization of a suicide prevention center (proposed to the National Institute of Mental Health) was an evaluation unit within the Los Angeles County Hospital through which all hospitalized persons who had attempted suicide would be processed before discharge. The principal aim was to evaluate the suicide potential of the individual upon discharge and to provide the person with an appropriate resource in the community from which continuing treatment could be obtained. While functioning in this way during its first five years, the LASPC gathered information and experience about suicidal persons and their treatment.

In an overview of the field of suicide prevention, Farberow (1968) described the changes that occurred in the first decade. The initial concept of evaluation and referral before hospital discharge changed radically as the community became aware of the agency and its services. The first major change was due to burgeoning telephone calls by persons calling for help before attempting suicide. What had been a 9 A.M. to 5 P.M., five-day-a-week operation became a crisis or emergency service that operated twenty-four hours a day, seven days a week, every day of the year. Professional resistance to the use of the telephone in working with highly disturbed persons was overcome by the growing recognition that the telephone provided an early and readily available means of contact for desperate people seeking immediate help. Thus the service was reconceptualized as a crisis-oriented response center, part of a network of helping resources. The focus was on resolution of the emergency followed by help in finding the resources in the community most suitable for the person's specific needs.

A second major change occurred in 1966 with the introduction of nonprofessional volunteers to respond to telephone callers (Heilig, Farberow, Litman, & Shneidman, 1968), the only way the center could function on a full-time twenty-four-hour basis within budget constraints. Although this change was initiated reluctantly, the selection, training, and supervision of volunteers and their performance in providing the services of the LASPC proved to be highly successful. By 1968 a number of SPCs had been established throughout the country, and a range of models with considerable variation in staffing, forms of support, places of operation, and types of service were developed according to the needs of the individual communities.

At that time, the major clinical problems for suicide prevention were identified as the development of effective evaluation criteria, responding to the needs of the chronic borderline suicidal person who required continually available but not constant care, reaching the persons at highest risk (for example, the elderly, white, sick male) who were not making use of the services, and dispelling the taboo against discussion of suicide that prevented people from asking for help as well as their significant others from responding to a cry for help. Ideas for prevention of suicide, such as teaching suicide prevention in schools, were just beginning to appear; possibilities for primary prevention were being explored; and interventive activities prior to a suicidal crisis were being developed.

The Second Decade

The second decade witnessed continued expansion of clinical and research activities as well as a growing sense of professional identity in the field of suicide and suicide prevention. Motto (1979) summarized specific changes that occurred using a survey of seventy suicide prevention and crisis intervention centers—forty-seven in the United States and twenty-three abroad. Questionnaires asked each of the centers to describe services or activities that had been added to or that had modified the traditional model of a twenty-four-hour crisis service offering telephone counseling and referral. Additional services for a variety of crisis situations were reported, including programs for treatment of disturbed adolescents, drug and alcohol abusers, victims of rape (see chapter 3) and crime, sexual abuse (see chapters 4 and 5), and wife battering (see chapter 6). Respondents reported that ancillary programs were developed for parents concerned with child abuse, for single-parent families, and for the special needs of the deaf and mentally retarded. Some centers had formed clubs and social groups for repeat callers and were offering the use of a meeting place within the center.

Many of the agencies had extended their services with family counseling for suicide problems, sex counseling, marital counseling, and face-to-face as well as telephone hotline counseling offered in their own agencies. Group therapy used traditional insight and supportive methods, but also developed nontraditional methods such as open-end, drop-in, socialization, and art therapy groups (Farberow, 1976). An innovative center in Australia reported an arrangement to provide group interaction by telephone.

Some outreach programs included special groups that visited hospitals to provide emotional support for rape victims undergoing the required medical procedures; crisis counseling for inmates on referral from the jail chaplain; and crisis counseling for hospitalized patients who had attempted suicide. In the Orient special efforts were made to meet with at-risk students who failed their studies or encountered difficulty in school and were afraid to tell their parents.

Emphasis on the emergency aspect of suicide prevention was reported in many SPCs. In some places the evaluation and disposition of evening and weekend emergency psychiatric requests to the county emergency medical services were handled by the emergency telephone lines of the local SPC. These centers were empowered to dispatch an ambulance to an emergency anywhere in the county. In one center, crisis intervention staff covered the hospital psychiatric emergency service during nights and weekends. They also made home visits to patients who declined alternative resources. Conspicuously absent were programs for special populations (such as the elderly or survivors of a significant other who committed suicide) and bereavement counseling following deaths due to accidental and natural causes as well as suicidal deaths.

Motto (1979) summarized the trends over the decade by noting that the services of the SPC were now broader in scope, had increased in depth, and were less dependent on referral sources. Services were less passive in that staff took a more active case-finding approach toward suicide prevention; programs had greater visibility and were more available. In addition, centers became a more integral part of the community care system by collaborating closely with key elements of the community's crisis-response network. At the same time they continued to conform to the important original characteristics of the SPC, that is, accessibility, availability, and unquestioning acceptance of the caller's need.

The 1980s

The third decade has seen the emergence of focused concern for specific groups in the field of suicide prevention: youth, AIDS victims, and family survivors.

Youth

The suicide rate among the young in the United States, especially among the fifteen-to-twenty-four-year-old age group, increased from 4.5 per 100,000 in 1950 to a peak of 13.3 per 100,000 in 1977, an increase of 196 percent, nearly triple the 1950 rate (Farberow, Litman, & Nelson, 1987). Although the rate declined slightly to about 12.8 in 1988, it continues to be distressingly high. Suicide is the second-leading cause of death among fifteen- to twenty-four-year-olds (accidents are first). It is the eighth-leading cause of death among persons of all ages in the United States (Lamb, 1988).

To meet the challenge of the precipitous rise in suicide rates among the young, programs have been developed to teach suicide prevention in schools (California State Department of Education, 1987). The most common signs of suicidal feelings are taught along with simple recommendations of what to do, such as listening with understanding, not being judgmental, and encouraging the individual to talk to parents and/or a responsible adult in the school. Information is provided about possible resources in the community. Suicide prevention centers, available for consultation, service, and training, are identified as a primary resource for the schools. In most programs a major aim has been to enlist the aid of students in the identification of at-risk students. A primary source of resistance is the reluctance to reveal the "secret" of a friend, especially if sworn to secrecy. The students soon see, however, that it is better to get help and to keep their friend alive than to keep the secret and lose the friend.

AIDS

Another population increasingly at risk for suicide consists of persons with AIDS and their families (Frierson & Lippman, 1988). Although the extent of the problem of suicide among AIDS patients is unknown, it is anticipated that the rate will be high due to the guilt and shame, the loss of social status and supportive networks, the extensive medical and physical debilitation, and the accompanying financial pressures that stress the patient. Although systematic data are not yet available, the risk of suicide is probably also greater among persons with AIDS-related complex (ARC) and the "waiting well," that is, those individuals in groups at high risk for the disease because of their prior sexual activities, who are apprehensively waiting to see if symptoms will appear. Calls to SPCs from persons affected by AIDS are rising.

Survivors after Suicide

Increasing attention has been focused on survivors—family members who experience a crisis of bereavement after the suicide of a loved one (Dunne, McIntosh, & Dunne-Maxim, 1987). Family members have been found to be more vulnerable to stress reactions, including prolonged unresolved grief and ongoing depressive disorders, and at higher risk for suicide themselves.

Survivor groups, a specialized type of bereavement group, now number approximately eighty across the country. Most groups have been started by survivors who felt a need for help not available through traditional facilities. Groups usually meet monthly for indefinite periods.

At the LASPC, a "Survivors after Suicide" program was developed according to a crisis intervention model. Groups of six to ten members meet for eight weekly sessions to deal with the following problems: reactions to the loss of a loved one, shame due to attitudes about suicide, guilt about not having done something to prevent the suicide, and anger that the deceased chose to die this way. Family and social relationships change because many family members, friends, and colleagues are too embarrassed to talk about a suicide, thus weakening the usual sources of support. A special problem experienced by survivors is that of disbelief or puzzlement: Why did he or she do this?

It is helpful for survivors to meet in a group with others who share the same trauma. Group members always report that they feel less alone, less shame, and more understood after attending. The group is co-led by a professional and a survivor, the latter having gone through the group experience and received training in group process. The survivor–facilitator serves as a positive role model, exemplifying the success of the program and the fact that it is possible to live through and overcome the grief despite the intensity of the current pain.

When the eight-week program is concluded, members are invited to participate in monthly meetings. Some feel they need additional time and help. Grief is often aroused around anniversaries and holidays, or members may simply need the ongoing support offered by the group.

Standard Setting

The American Association of Suicidology (AAS) had assumed as one of its primary responsibilities the development of standards for the certification of its member agencies and individual members (AAS, 1984). The criteria for certification do not attempt to assess outcome of intervention but rather focus on "adequate functioning" of an SPC, defined in terms such as organization, operation, and role in the community. The criteria establish levels of functioning (unacceptable, minimal, and optimal) that may exist in the various operations of the SPC. Two components of the SPC—the general service delivery system and service in life-threatening crisis—are summarized below.

General Service Delivery

The general service delivery category is evaluated in terms of the response the crisis program provides to its clients. It determines the availability of the five components of the service delivery system as well as the levels at which they operate: telephone service, walk-in crisis service, outreach crisis service, the degree to which crisis cases can be followed up, and client record keeping. The last component evaluates the completeness of the record-keeping system, the availability of the records, and the confidentiality with which they are maintained.

Services in a Life-Threatening Crisis

The components that are evaluated in the area of services in a life-threatening crisis include whether an assessment of lethality is routinely made, the capability of rescue, the degree to which follow-up occurs of persons attempting or threatening suicide or violence, provision of services to survivors of suicide, follow-up for victims of violence, and involvement in community education. Rescue capability is not necessarily required of the agency itself but liaison with other community resources such as telephone company tracing services, police and ambulance services, and other types of rescue services should be evident. The follow-up for victims of violence includes victims of assault, such as rape, child abuse, or battering, and the survivors of victims of traumatic death.

Clinical Principles and Procedures

The basic principles and clinical procedures in suicide prevention have broadened as the field has expanded over the past three decades. First developed with the aim of crisis intervention and resolution, the early procedures were emergency-oriented and directed toward resolution of problems. Their objective was to provide immediate relief from tension by evaluating the lethality of the situation through structured interviewing and focused fact gathering, identifying and rallying resources, developing an action plan, and authoritative management. The broadened concept now includes the acceptance of an ongoing relationship (especially with persons who make repeat attempts) and the use of modified long-term techniques to accommodate the large group of borderline, poorly adjusted, relatively fragile, chronically suicide-prone persons who become the responsibility of the SPC after having exhausted virtually all the other treatment resources in the community. Additional treatment procedures, such as controlled and limited use of the telephone for regular contacts, maintenance of the relationship by telephone outreach, and varied forms of brief and long-term group therapy have been developed to address the special needs of this latter group.

Despite the involvement of many other kinds of medical and community helpers, mental health personnel still have the primary responsibility of providing care to suicidal people. The additional helpers, often termed "gatekeepers" because they are among the first to come in contact with persons whose suicidal impulses are surfacing, include probation officers, school counselors, clergy, physicians, and others involved in ongoing care in the human services sector. Psychological autopsy studies have indicated that many persons who committed suicide had received some type of treatment or counseling just before their death. These cases indicate missed opportunities for early recognition and treatment that might have prevented a suicide.

There are three core elements in suicide prevention: (1) recognition, (2) evaluation of risk, and (3) treatment. Suicidal thinking and behavior is so prevalent that it is useful to ask all clients who are interviewed for counseling or therapy whether they have thought about suicide or have ever felt suicidal. The ubiquity of such thoughts was demonstrated in a study in which youngsters were asked whether they had ever made a suicide attempt or thought about suicide (Farberow, Litman, & Nelson, 1987). The results indicated that 3 percent to 5 percent of high school students ages sixteen to nineteen years had made a suicide attempt, whereas approximately 10 percent had thought about it in the previous week. Also striking was the finding that 40 percent to 60 percent were aware of suicidal activity among their peers. These findings are even more disturbing when one realizes that they relate to young people who had not previously been identified as troubled.

Persons with certain kinds of problems are at higher risk for suicide. These problems include one or more of the following: borderline personality disorders, alcohol and drug addiction, chronic life-threatening illness, and severe emotional and mental disturbance. People who are deeply depressed and feeling helpless and/or hopeless; who are psychotic, isolated, withdrawn, and detached; or who are chemically dependent and acutely agitated are at greater risk for succumbing to suicidal impulses than are persons who are more capable of responding to and accepting offers of help.

It is important to listen carefully to what people say when they come for help. Verbal statements range from remarks that can be understood as indirect suicidal comments to overt suicide threats: "I can't stand this pain," "I can't go on like this," "I can't live without her/him," "I'd be better off dead," "I wish I were dead," "I'm going to kill myself." Suicidal comments need to be explored. However, such comments are often resisted by therapists and counselors because they fear taking responsibility for a case in which death is a real possibility. Such cases can provoke a lot of anxiety as well as demand extra time, energy, and work from the therapist.

After a suicidal problem is identified, it is important to talk openly and directly about it. Most people who think or behave in a suicidal fashion are not at immediate high risk; most people who think about suicide will not try to kill themselves. Moreover, most people who make suicide attempts will not die. Suicidal feelings can best be understood as an indication of the depth of a person's feelings about his or her problems. The important question is how to evaluate the more serious risks within a population already identified as suicidal (Farberow, Heilig, & Litman, 1968). Over the past twenty-five years many experts in the field of suicidology have developed various suicide lethality scales that are helpful to clinicians. However, the best use of these scales is in conjunction with clinical judgment. Although various criteria are useful in evaluating the seriousness of risk for suicide, the following three criteria are most important:

1. *Prior suicidal behaviors*. A history of prior suicide attempts greatly heightens a person's risk for suicide. Moreover, if past attempts have been of high lethality as reflected by the method (gunshot or jumping from high places) or circumstances (cases in which the person survived a suicide attempt due to fortunate and unforeseeable circumstances), the risk is even further heightened. In general, people who have continuing, chronic struggles with suicidal impulses make increasingly serious suicide attempts. Frequently, a suicide attempt is used as a means to put the crisis behind the person; that is, it serves as an ordeal or test to determine whether to live or die. When clients have a history of suicidal behavior, it is useful to learn what brought them to the point of overt suicidal behavior. If the aim was to die or to manipulate responsive behavior from significant others, this information will be important in planning current treatment.

2. *Suicide plan*. People who have arranged a plan to kill themselves, for example, by buying pills or a gun and ammunition, selecting a place and time when they will kill themselves, writing farewell notes or preparing a will, and taking care of last-minute affairs, are obviously at higher risk than are those who have no specific plan. When a person reports that he or she has acquired the means to kill him- or herself, such as a loaded gun, it is extremely important to offer to take the gun for safekeeping or to urge that it be given to someone else so that the person can be protected from his or her own lethal impulse. Surprisingly, many suicidal persons respond favorably to such requests. Most suicidal people are ambivalent and would rather find a solution other than suicide. The opportunity to be protected from their own impulses as well as the offer of help in solving problems can be a life-saving combination.

People who exhibit psychotic symptoms and who act impulsively or unpredictably need external controls and should be evaluated for hospitalization or appropriate medication. A significant clue is the client's responsiveness to an offer of help. Being able to accept help is a positive sign that militates against the hopelessness that frequently characterizes the suicidal person. It is also important to observe the progress of the symptoms. If symptoms remain or get worse, one must be concerned about the possible occurrence of a suicide attempt, and the treatment program should be modified or strengthened.

3. *Resources.* The resources of the suicidal person represent the third most significant factor in evaluating lethality. If the person indicates that he or she has money, a therapist, a close and caring family, and good friends, the risk of suicide lessens considerably. When people are isolated and have no helpful network, the risk increases. Available resources should be enlisted as quickly as possible, especially when risk is high. Suicidal people feel lonely, isolated, and rejected. When feasible, the involvement of friends and family is preferred, but even incorporating community and social services helps to break through the client's feelings that he or she is unworthy and no one cares.

The criteria outlined above should be considered interrelated rather than independent factors. In treatment, the practitioner should remember that although the problems are serious, most suicide cases are not life-threatening emergencies. Rather, they often represent an expression of desperation about the person's inability to cope with life events or perceived existential meaninglessness. The person's feelings progress through stages of depression, anxiety, guilt, and anger to the end stages of feeling worthless, helpless, and hopeless. Most cases are identified and in some kind of care long before the final stages are reached. The greatest risk is associated with feelings of helplessness and hopelessness. Regardless of stage or degree of risk, it is important for the therapist to convey a sense of hope to counteract the client's feelings of hopelessness.

The suicidal person must feel that his or her communication about suicide has been heard and that his or her feelings and predicament are understood, recognized, and taken seriously. The problems precipitating the suicidal reaction may then be explored, for example, losses through separation or divorce, the death of a spouse, a life-threatening or painful physical illness, a serious personal humiliation. Such problems occur within the context of the patient's personality and possible psychiatric conditions, such as depression, borderline personality disorder, alcoholism, manic–depressive disorder, and schizophrenia. Often these conditions are preceded by a lack of success in jobs and personal relationships, and a diminished sense of well being. Approximately 75 percent of the people who call an SPC come from diagnostic groups characterized by failures in living and disordered relationships. The remaining 25 percent who call an SPC are reacting to an unusual life crisis, for example, the death of a loved one. In general, persons who have had a successful life course but are reacting to an extreme, sudden life stress with depression and a suicidal response are good candidates for therapy. With some relief from the stress, they can usually return to a well-functioning life-style.

With chronic suicidal persons who have a history of failure in prior treatment, the therapist should take a long-term, maintenance/supportive approach, with minimal expectations for improvement. These clients need ongoing contact with a therapeutic agent rather than actual therapy. Such clients make repeat suicide attempts and call the SPC when they become disturbed and suicidal. Simply knowing that someone is available to talk with them when they become confused, depressed, or are struggling with a problem helps them get through these episodes. These people are often involved with a number of different helping agencies. Knowing this relieves the full burden from the therapist who is treating these difficult clients. Coordination among the various helping agencies, however, is vital.

It is important to remember that the potential for suicide continues to be present even though the context of the call to the SPC may have shifted to other matters. Clients should be asked if they still have suicidal thoughts. When a chronically suicidal person drops out of long-term counseling, the therapist should question whether the patient is depressed or discouraged about the therapy and/or has been feeling hopeless and suicidal. Effort should be made to locate the person, possibly through one of the other agencies with which the person has contact, to make certain that the person at least stays in contact with a helping professional.

Case Examples

The following examples of suicide calls present brief diagnostic information on each caller and the evaluation and treatment plan for various cases. Although each caller is unique, some callers fall into categories that may be readily recognized and that most mental health professionals can identify in terms of diagnosis and difficulty. The first category, chronic repeat callers, presents the most difficulties for telephone counselors.

The Chronic Repeat Caller

Brenda. A repeat caller for a number of years, Brenda lost her supervisory job three years ago when she falsely accused her own supervisor of sexual harassment. On discovery that the charge was false, she was told that she could be reinstated if she made a formal apology to her colleague. She refused and was subsequently discharged. In discussing this incident she vacillated between blaming the other supervisor and blaming herself. Most of the time her calls focused on regrets over her actions, her wish to undo her "mistakes," and her ruined career. Currently, she works in another business setting but shows much anxiety over her performance.

Because Brenda has high expectations of herself as an achiever, any failure is a source of much anxiety. Diagnosed as manic–depressive, she has been hospitalized seven times since the first incident three years ago. She takes lithium regularly, has a therapist, and indicates that she calls many other crisis lines. Her father is deceased, but her mother continues to be supportive. She has a boyfriend who lives nearby, and she frequently spends the night with him.

Brenda was viewed as an obsessive, highly anxious person with an alternative manic–depressive diagnosis. Her suicide risk has continued to be high, especially in light of a recent serious suicide attempt when she took more than fifty sleeping pills. However, Brenda has received adequate support from a long-time therapist and a supportive mother and boyfriend. Her use of the suicide prevention telephone service is attributed to her need to have a service available at any hour of the day or night and her fear that she will be without such support. Counselors were instructed to encourage Brenda to call her therapist when she is in crisis and to persuade her to use her outside resources as well as her own inner capabilities. They were told to gently remind her that the SPC's purpose is not to do ongoing therapy over the telephone but to help people in crisis find and work with their own resources. Her calls were to be limited to no longer than five minutes unless there was a high suicide risk, in which case the therapist was to be informed and rescue procedures were to be initiated.

Marvin. A forty-five-year-old white male who had been a truck driver, Marvin had brain damage and seizures as a result of being mugged eight years before. Following the mugging, his wife divorced him and he lost his home and child. Currently, he lives with his parents and several pets.

For many years Marvin was permitted to call the SPC for support because he was so lonely. However, in recent years he has learned to make other contacts and now has a much wider social network. Classes at a nearby adult school have provided additional social stimulation. He takes care of his own needs, including grocery shopping and family errands. Even though his abilities and resources have expanded, he continues to call the SPC for social contact.

Marvin's calls have generally been social as opposed to crisis oriented. He talks about his activities, his classes, his walking the dog, and his conversations with others. He has never reported being suicidal. Although he often sounded as if he had been drinking, he always denied it and stated that it was caused by his medication. He has been easy to talk to except that he becomes belligerent when drinking.

During a case conference, SPC counselors decided that their objective with Marvin should be changed from providing a social outlet to weaning him gradually from the service, because he was not suicidal. He had widened his social activities, which needed to be reinforced and encouraged. Workers would also provide him with referrals to new resources such as church, adult day-care, and other organizations. It was decided that an important new resource might be Alcoholics Anonymous, where he could meet many new people and learn to control his drinking. He did not have to be alcoholic to attend the meetings. If it was determined that he was drinking when he called, he was to be told that counselors would not talk with him while he was drinking. No calls were to go beyond five minutes; if he called on a busy shift, he was to be told firmly that the lines had to be kept open for crisis calls.

Loss

Among the most common problems presented to a suicide prevention counselor is that of loss of a significant other, most often through separation or divorce, sometimes by death. The following two cases illustrate the loss of a best friend and a lover.

Bill. Bill indicated that he was a suicide survivor; his "best friend," Mary, had killed herself two days prior to his call. Mary's funeral was scheduled for the next day, and he was anxious about the funeral and unsure how he would behave. He did not want to attend the funeral but felt that it was necessary for him to do so. Most of the discussion revolved around Mary's suicide and the pain he felt at her action, along with his feelings of anger, resentment, and love. It was difficult for him to talk about his feelings of resentment, and he needed reassurance that such feelings were not unusual.

Bill had not anticipated that Mary would commit suicide and was angry, particularly that she had succeeded in killing herself, whereas he had failed in his six previous attempts. He reported strong feelings of guilt because when she called him the night before she had killed herself, he told her that he was very busy and cut their conversation short. She had not told him about her suicidal intentions. He felt he could have helped if he had only known, although they had not been as close as they once had been.

Mary was a victim of incest, both by her father and brother. This experience served as a close bond between them because Bill also had been incestuously maltreated by his father when he was young. His anger at Mary centered partly on her inability to deal with the problem, which made him feel that he was unable to overcome his own. He assumed that the incest was the reason for Mary's suicide.

Bill was not currently in therapy or on any medication. He was urged to attend the funeral and told that he would feel worse if he did not attend. He was advised to seek outpatient counseling and was asked to call back after the funeral to tell counselors how things had gone. He called back within five days to report that he continued to feel very suicidal and that the only thing that kept him from killing himself was the possibility of hurting his friends. He revealed for the first time that he was bisexual and that he accepted his orientation. He did have a close friend with whom he was able to talk and other friends who were quite supportive. He continued to feel guilt about not having talked with Mary when she called.

Bill initially failed to follow through on the advice to seek outpatient counseling and was again urged to do so. He was given a specific referral to an agency in his area and invited to apply to the Survivors After Suicide program conducted by the center. Bill applied to the agency for continuing outpatient therapy but did not take advantage of the suicide survivor program. He stated that he would not commit suicide because a friend had threatened to kill himself if Bill committed suicide, and he did not want to feel responsible for another person's death.

Bill was considered a moderate risk for suicide. Although he continued to feel some guilt over Mary's suicide, he had an excellent network of supportive friends. Moreover, he finally entered therapy.

Tom. Tom, who was gay, said that his lover, an AIDS victim, had died two months previously. Tom said that they had had a "good" relationship for over two years. Although Tom expressed thoughts of suicide, he had no plans to kill himself; the first lethality rating was moderate to low. Tom showed no indication of substance abuse and stated that he had good family support, although his family was not close geographically. He talked about the possibility of visiting his lover's sister and family in another city.

On a second call four days later, Tom indicated he still had suicidal thoughts, but careful inquiry indicated that he had not formulated a specific plan. However, his ambivalence about his homosexuality had increased, apparently as a result of contact with his family, who rejected his life-style and told him that it was just as well that his lover had died because it indicated the error of Tom's ways. Tom continued to talk about his plans to visit his lover's family, who accepted his gay life-style.

Two weeks later Tom called to say that he was leaving the city and he wanted to thank the counselors for their help. He did not wish to talk any further and terminated the call quickly. On a second call two days later, Tom's pain from his loss seemed to be deepening. He was now talking about dying and admitted that he possessed an unloaded gun that he kept in the trunk of his car. He was still in contact with his lover's family, who were urging him to visit. Tom's suicidal risk was considered much higher after this call; he was urged to accept a referral to a therapist in Los Angeles or to find one after he had visited his lover's family. Later that day a counselor from another SPC telephone service in the city called and reported that Tom was threatening to kill himself by drowning; the counselor was trying to get him to come to the office for help. He refused. The counselor was told to remind Tom that he had promised his lover, who had died slowly of AIDS, that he would take care of himself. Tom continued to feel extremely depressed and to refuse all offers of help. He had never provided any telephone number or address and thus could not be traced.

Two weeks later Tom's family called to report that Tom had killed himself the night before. The family felt guilty and angry. Tom had called the family from Canada but had hung up on them. He refused to accept their suggestions for seeking help. There was no information on how Tom had killed himself.

The staff discussed at length how this case might have been handled differently or how Tom might have been persuaded to seek help. Because he had never given identifying information that would allow staff to contact him, any outreach or rescue activity was impossible. His deepening depression and increasing determination to kill himself, which became evident over the succession of calls, was especially frustrating to counselors in that he did not allow any intervention. He was only twenty-three; his death was sad and needless—and especially difficult for a suicide prevention staff to bear because a series of contacts had occurred. In the staff meetings that followed, it was emphasized repeatedly that Tom had refused all help and that the center had exhausted every avenue in its efforts to help.

Borderline Personality Disorder

Dan. A forty-three-year-old Vietnam veteran, Dan worked as a salesperson after the war but had deteriorated over the past three or four years. He lost his job and fiancee, and attempts to find work had been disastrous. He lived with a disturbed father and was supported financially by public assistance.

According to the Veteran's Administration (VA), Dan's diagnosis was borderline personality disorder. The VA claimed that his problems started before Vietnam and therefore limited its services to him. Dan felt that he had been treated badly and became very angry when talking about his experience with the VA.

Dan had been prescribed antipsychotic and antidepressant medication but took his pills irregularly. When he was depressed, he preferred to diet and exercise. He often turned to nontraditional treatments such as yoga, dianetics, and fasting.

Dan had attempted suicide several times. Although some of these attempts were relatively serious, he claimed that he had intended to injure rather than to kill himself. He had a history of alcohol use but tended to deny it was a problem. He had been hospitalized several times over the past half-dozen years.

Dan was depressed and exhibited moderate psychomotor retardation. He felt hopeless and lacked energy. He felt that he no longer fit in or belonged to society. He described Vietnam flashbacks and felt guilty because he was the only man in his squad to survive a fire fight. Lacking finances, he could not afford to move out of his father's house. His suicidal status varied from moderate to high. His history of suicide attempts and his rejection of help from resources that were available to him indicated a higher risk for suicide. However, he did not seem to have any suicidal plan worked out, and his suicidal behavior in the past was more or less impulsive.

Dan continued to use the VA, although he resented the VA's efforts to limit its responsibility to help him. He continued to seek help from the SPC as well as other agencies but was not able to feel comfortable with any single source of help. Currently, he continues to rely primarily on his inner resources, a philosophical and somewhat spiritual approach to life; he is involved in reading, meditating, exercising, and yoga.

The SPC counselors were urged to validate Dan for the growth and progress that he had made and to reassure him that he was not a failure. He was encouraged to use the VA as an always available, no-cost resource, especially when he felt depressed and had impulses to injure or kill himself.

The Abusive Violent Caller

Jim. A forty-four-year-old white male, Jim had called the SPC for several years, usually to complain about the women he met in Los Angeles, how terrible Los Angeles was, and how difficult it was to meet nice women. Frequently, his calls would start out controlled; however, as they progressed he would become more abusive and enraged.

Information was difficult to obtain, because Jim was a nonstop talker and did not answer many questions. Both his father and mother were deceased; he had siblings in other cities. Jim seemed to be active in the community and to participate in several community clubs. He stated that he paid for his sex and did not have any steady female companion. He had one male friend with whom he spent time.

Jim, a clerical worker who had been unemployed for the past five to six years, lived on Social Security disability benefits. He had been fired from his last job after an altercation with a female employee who pressed charges against him. He did not go to prison, but he continued to complain bitterly about the woman and to express angry, violent feelings toward her. He stated that he had harassed her on the telephone for a long time after he was discharged.

Jim first called the SPC six years ago, after which there was a four-year gap about which he would provide no information other than to hint that he had been in a mental hospital for a while. He indicated that he has been in counseling for more than fifteen years and was currently attending a group at a local mental health center. Diagnosed as manic–depressive, he was taking both antipsychotic and antidepressant medication.

Jim had a history of several prior suicide attempts but provided no detailed information about them. When he called, he either threatened to kill himself or someone else. His anger toward women was general and nonspecific, and his threats against women were either to kill or rape them because that was what they deserved.

A case conference about Jim clarified the appropriate responses to take with him. Because of his abusiveness, especially toward women counselors, he was to be told that he could call only during certain shifts and that there would be a particular counselor (male) who would be available to talk to him. If he called at any other time, he was to be told that it was impossible to speak with him now but that someone would be willing to talk with him at the specified times. Confrontations were to be avoided, and statements to him were to be impersonalized; that is, the SPC, as opposed to an individual, would make decisions and establish the procedures for him to follow. In addition, he was to be referred back to his therapist with the reminder that the center could not conduct therapy with him and that he should take advantage of his therapeutic relationship to work through his feelings about women. This plan was approved by Jim's therapist, who stated that Jim's continuous venting of his feelings to the SPC had seemed to impede his progress in therapy.

The objective was to wean Jim away from using SPC services because its counselors, rather than helping him, were providing an outlet for him to be hyperabusive.

The Psychotic Caller

Nan. A thirty-year-old black female, Nan had been diagnosed schizophrenic and was taking medication irregularly. Her alcoholic mother had been unable to take care of her, so Nan had been placed in foster care at an early age. She stated that she had been disabled since childhood. Her history of hospitalization was confusing. At one time she stated that she was first hospitalized at age ten; another report said age sixteen.

She lived in board and care homes and on the streets, although recently she had been living with a boyfriend in a halfway house operated by the state. She reported that she would have to leave the halfway house at the end of the week and was not sure where she would live—either on the street or in her boyfriend's car. Nan depended on her boyfriend to provide for her. He paid for her stay in the home and for her medication.

Unable to read or write, she stated that she received no help from community agencies because she could not fill out the necessary forms. She could not get to the agency offices because she would not take the bus and was unable to drive. Nan called the SPC to complain about her boyfriend's abuse of her. He beat her because she could not work and he had to support her.

Nan frustrated the counselor because she rejected offers of help or referrals. She always terminated her calls very abruptly, possibly because someone came into the room and made her hang up. At other times, it seems she just tired of the conversation and chose to hang up on her own.

Nan was viewed as a high-risk caller, based partly on her statement that she had made more than fourteen suicide attempts using methods such as overdoses and cutting her wrists. Her mental illness, lack of support system, chronic suicide history, and generally chaotic life-style made her a high risk for suicide under any kind of stress.

The Elderly Caller

Rose. Rose, a sixty-one-year-old woman living with her husband and stepdaughter, called several times within a period of two weeks. She had been married to her second husband for ten years; he was an alcoholic and was physically and psychologically abusive. Rose's children by her first marriage were grown and lived elsewhere. They offered no support in her present situation; Rose expressed much bitterness about their lack of support.

She said that she had no friends because she and her husband moved so often that it was difficult to form lasting relationships. She was unable to work; they lived primarily on her husband's Social Security and occasional odd jobs. Her husband retained tight control over finances and did not give her any money for the house or to spend on herself. She had a continuing medical problem of herpes.

At first, Rose refused to identify herself when she called. Eventually, she provided her first name and the area in which she lived. Her calls generally focused on her feelings of loneliness and helplessness. Her husband frequently spent his evenings with friends and often did not return home until morning. Often she called while he was out. Although she was willing to talk about various options for helping herself, she usually ended up rejecting them. She left her husband a number of times but always went back to him. She felt incapable of supporting herself and living alone.

Rose never attempted suicide and never described a suicide plan. However, she stated that she thought of suicide often and felt very depressed. She had nowhere to go, no one to help her, and no way to help herself.

Rose was evaluated as having moderate to low suicide potential in light of her lack of prior suicidal behavior and any suicide plan. She had relatively few resources and stayed in the relationship with her abusive husband for support. Although referred to various community resources, such as Al-Anon, Women Helping Women, and a psychiatric clinic in her neighborhood, she did not follow through on any of these recommendations. Even though it was unlikely that she would do so, the counselors were instructed to continue to urge her to take advantage of the community resources in her area and to point out her opportunities for increasing her social supports through them.

Sharon. A seventy-two-year-old white woman, Sharon was semiretired, working part time as a substitute bookkeeper. She is representative of a group of elderly, lonely, angry callers who are not so much suicidal as depressed, unhappy, and feeling rejected.

Although Sharon claimed she was active and in good health, she also stated that she had no friends and could not seem to get help from the numerous physicians whom she consulted. When the therapist to whom she was referred prescribed medications, Sharon stopped seeing him. She also refused medications prescribed by her physician, claiming bitterly that they could only offer pills but not any evidence that they cared.

Sharon reported suicidal thoughts but never any attempts. She stated that she would either use a gun or overdose on drugs; however, she did not own a gun and had refused all prescriptions offered by her physician.

Sharon was angry and hostile; she rebuffed the counselor's efforts to help the first time she called, which was early in the morning. When she called again later in the day, she complained about the counselor she had spoken with earlier, stating that she did not like all the questions. She said that she wanted to let the center know that if she killed herself it would be the center's fault because the counselors did not help her. However, she promised to call back later that day.

Sharon's suicidal risk was rated low because she had no prior suicidal behavior and her suicidal thoughts were vague and unformed. However, her anger, bitterness, and depression put her at some risk. She had no friends and challenged anyone who might care about her. Because she had a therapist, it was recommended that counselors listen to Sharon for a short period, then urge her to continue with her therapist.

Youthful Callers

Cecily. Fifteen-year-old Cecily called twice. Her presenting problems revolved around the recent loss of her boyfriend and some delinquent acting out. She felt that she received little support from her family because her brother, who was in poor health, required constant attention. She had few friends. She attended high school and worked part time as a clerk in a clothing store.

She had been cutting school for the past several months as well as drinking and smoking marijuana. Recently, she had been dating men in their late twenties. Once she had stayed out all night on one of her dates.

Cecily complained of depression and described feeling lonely and being unable to communicate with her parents. She claimed that her mother blamed her for the breakup of her first marriage because her natural father left when her mother became pregnant with Cecily. Information about prior suicidal behavior was conflicting. At one point she stated that she had made no suicide attempts, but on another call she indicated that she had made one attempt. She reported frequent suicidal thoughts and indicated that she would use drugs to kill herself, although she had none on hand. She had had no counseling and rejected all efforts to get her to talk to her school counselor, her teachers, or her physician. She "knew" that her mother would not go with her to counseling.

It was apparent that Cecily was living a confused and disorganized life that could possibly lead to delinquency and suicidal behavior. The staff considered her to be at moderate risk at this time but at high risk for eventual suicide. Her friends seemed to contribute to her self-destructive behavior and she felt alienated from her family. Reconnecting Cecily with her family was the counselors' highest priority, but she would not provide a telephone number or any information that would let the counselors establish contact with her family. She was urged to call Teen Lines, whose teen workers might be able to establish a more direct relationship with her. Meanwhile, she was urged to call the SPC, where someone would always be available to talk to her. Counselors told her that they considered her situation serious and that they would be there to help her.

Stewart. A single, twenty-four-year-old man, Stewart lived with a roommate and was recently unemployed. His parents were separated; his only brother lived in another city. Stewart called the SPC because he felt completely overwhelmed by all the bad things that were happening in his life. His girl friend of six months had just broken up with him because she felt too young to commit herself to a permanent relationship. In addition, Stewart lost his job, and another job that he had anticipated had not come through. He felt that it never would.

During the call, Stewart reported that he had had no prior suicidal behavior but that he now wished that he had a gun. He talked about jumping off an overpass into the freeway traffic below. However, he was hesitant about doing this because he was afraid that he might hurt someone and might cause an accident on the freeway.

Stewart's parents were only recently separated. He was angry at both of them because he felt that they used him to get back at each other. He resented this but was afraid to say anything to his parents for fear he might alienate them. Stewart's mother was alcoholic and could not be counted on for support.

Stewart was rated relatively low in suicide risk because he had no prior suicidal behavior. The counselor felt that his jumping off a bridge was more a fantasy than a possibility. Despite feeling overwhelmed, he had resources; his father was still available to him and his roommate could also be counted on to assist him. Stewart was urged to apply at one of the several psychiatric clinics in the area where he lived and was assured that although he felt very unhappy and depressed at this point, depressions were usually of brief duration and that he could help himself considerably by talking with a therapist.

Barbara. Barbara, a twenty-eight-year-old white woman who lived with her father and her four-year-old son, worked full time as an executive secretary. Her husband had died within the previous month after a serious industrial accident. She was extremely angry and bitter at his physicians because they did not prepare her for his death. She felt alone, empty, and panic stricken by the immensity of her loss.

Barbara called because she had begun to experience frightening suicidal thoughts within the past week. When questioned closely, however, she had no history of suicide attempts, nor did she have a suicide plan. She appeared to need support, which she felt that she could not get from her family at that point.

Barbara was reassured that her thoughts were normal, considering the immensity of her loss and the suddenness with which it had occurred. She was assured that help was available for her grief and that her bereavement could be made more easy to bear with counseling. She was referred to counseling at the psychiatric clinics in her area and to the Widow-to-Widow hotline.

Evaluation and Treatment in a Clinical Setting

Most of the above case examples illustrate problems of assessment and management by a telephone crisis service of suicidal risk in chronically disordered crisis-prone persons. The following case example by H. Parad illustrates the evaluation and treatment of suicidal risk presented by a relatively high-functioning client experiencing an acute crisis state of loss following betrayal by her boyfriend.

Ann. Ann, a divorced thirty-three-year-old fashion designer, had apparently coped well in her everyday work and social life, despite considerable childhood deprivation and trauma at the hands of her abusive alcoholic father. A few days previously she had learned that Jim, her fifty-one-year-old lover, had deceived her by having an affair with another woman. Discovering her lover's duplicity suddenly activated old and painful memories of her former husband's infidelity as well as her father's womanizing (which led to her mother's nervous breakdown). Jim had falsely assured Ann of his intent to marry her and his desire for children, but now her dreams were shattered. She was having trouble sleeping, had little or no appetite, was avoiding her friends, and was barely able to concentrate on her job. Ann described feeling worthless, unlovable, and suicidal. She had a loaded pistol at home and said she had been about to blow her brains out the previous night but had called a friend instead. The friend calmed her and referred her for immediate crisis therapy.

In the first session, Ann refused to (1) bring in the pistol, (2) give the bullets for safekeeping to her girl friend (who had referred her to the crisis clinic), (3) consider hospitalization, (4) permit the therapist to communicate either with her girl friend who lived in the apartment next door or her mother who lived nearby. Mindful of Ann's extremely high risk for suicide, the therapist offered to see her in frequent therapy sessions to help her cope with her despair and agitation. The therapist said decisively, "Ann, you are in a severe and overwhelming crisis. I don't think you really want to die—what you want is to stop hurting inside. I'm here to help you."

Sobbing, Ann gradually responded to the therapist's overtures and reluctantly agreed to call the SPC round-the-clock hotline if she felt like using the pistol. But she would not surrender the pistol until she had time to sort out her thoughts. She felt miserable and unlovable. She was having flashbacks to her adolescence, when her father, after being especially abusive toward her and her mother, suddenly abandoned the family to live with another woman. Ann also flashed back to the nanny who had raised her and who often slapped her face cruelly. "When I was eight, Nanny burned me by putting my hand on an electric stove." Ann then confided she had taken an overdose of pills when she was fifteen after her father had called her a bitch because she had behaved assertively toward him. Medical help had been called and her stomach pumped out, but apparently she had not been hospitalized.

Ann cried as she talked about her father's death last year from cirrhosis of the liver. She said she was through with Jim, all that she had now were her two dogs ("my babies"), a few friends, and a job she could barely perform.

An unusually thoughtful and self-observing client, despite the intensity of her pain, Ann requested that we tape record the sessions so that she could review (between sessions) what she and the therapist had said. The following verbatim vignettes convey the intense interplay between Ann (A) and the therapist (T):

A (crying): I asked Jim outright, "Were you with another woman when you went out of town?" and he finally said, "Yes."

T: Your feelings were badly hurt. Any woman would be hurt by that. You were lied to. You're entitled to feel hurt and angry.

A: And betrayed.

T: How do you make the leap from what happened with Jim to thinking of killing yourself?

A: Oh, it's not just that. That's just one more thing. That would be overreacting if that were the only thing. This is just the stone gathering up the moss.

T: This is the way life is? Every time you meet a man and are disappointed?

A: This is what continues to happen to me. This is the pain. This is just . . . this is the end of another thing that I put my hopes into, to have something nice in my life. This is another painful thing in my life. I just looked around, no more, I cannot do it, I can't do it anymore. . . . I'm not talking about just this one thing. . . . The problem is I have nothing good in my life. . . . There is nothing! All I see is more pain coming down, all failure, more problems. True, there have been some nice things that have happened in my life, but I've always been in pain and, as you've said, there are no buffers between me and the pain. . . . I'm beginning to believe that this is my destiny. . . . I'm beginning to believe the way it was yesterday is not what a human being can do. I can't . . . I can't do it. I can't continue. . . . I need a sign. I need a little something, some hope. I need a little something nice, not a lot, just a little something and I don't think that's greedy (sobbing).

T: Of course not.

A: Yesterday the pain didn't stop. It went on and on. So many hours. I took a tranquilizer but that didn't stop it. It went on all night. There is an enormity to it that frightens me.

T: Enormity?

A: It's unbearable. It doesn't stop. The enormity of the hopelessness.

T: Could it be that the pain you're experiencing is the little girl in you that feels rejected?

A: It's all the pain of everything.

T: You have successes in your life. You've been a really first-class fashion designer.

A: Yes, that's true.

T: You have lots of friends.

A: Yes, that's right too.

T: Right now you don't have a relationship with a man.

A: No. I have men friends but not on a sexual basis.

T: You've done a lot of things in your life, so how come a man is given so much power—in his greed and betrayal—that he has the power of life and death over you?

A (firmly): He doesn't have that power over me. It's just proof positive. It's not these things. It's that there is nothing in my life. . . . But I'm all right today. I'm alive today. I'm coping today. I'm trying to get positive again. What I'm trying to say to you is I'm trying to push myself in that mode. There's a part of me that yearns to be healthy, yearns to be O.K. And I'm here and I'm listening to you.

T: And you called me yesterday twice.

A (proudly): That's right. And better than that, I got through the day without seeing you in the office. I got through it without anyone.

T: So there really is a thrust toward life and healing in you.

A: There is! There is a thrust, every bit as strong as the other thrust [death]. I wouldn't give one more power than the other. They are both very strong in me and very equal and at different times. And one of them is going to win—and one of them is going to win really big—because when I get very healthy, if that's what happens, I won't feel this way anymore. . . . And if I do away with my life I won't have the other [the thrust toward life]. Maybe they are the same thing, that is, different ways of getting healthy.

T: I want to ask you some important questions.

A (interrupts): Yesterday, as the pain increased, I liked it. I knew where I'd be. I was going to take care of my dogs. I was going to give them to two neighbors.

T: You were going to blow your brains out?

A nods.

T: How many bullets do you have?

A (defiantly): Enough.

T: Do you know how to use the pistol?

A: Yes. I took lessons.

T: So you're very much at risk.

A (quietly): But I didn't use it [the pistol].

T: That's right! And I'm glad you didn't! It's not good for you to be alone. It's good for you to be with people.

A: I called some people I thought could help me by giving me some advice. A girl friend wanted to come over. I didn't want to talk with her.

T: Did you tell her you were thinking of killing yourself?

A: No, but I told her today that I was frightened. I insinuated that there was a danger, a dangerous situation.

T: That's right. It is dangerous.

A: I don't want to be this way.

T: You have a dangerous weapon. Can you give it to me? I want you to bring me the pistol today after our session. I don't want you to kill yourself. I can only try to imagine the depth of what you're feeling. No matter how much it hurts, and only you know how painful it really is, I don't want you to kill yourself.

A maintains eye contact.

T: You believe you have a spirit [previously discussed by A] that will live on in your next life and that your next life will be better, which neither of us can prove or disprove. That's why I try to stay with what we know in this life. You have friends and a career. You have very high intelligence. You have many, many talents and, in my opinion, much to live for. [Therapist waits for Ann's comments. She nods and tells therapist to go on.]

T: And the thing that seems to have stirred up your pain is Jim's affair, which reminds you of the little girl in you that felt abandoned, rejected, and unloved years ago. That's what I think your pain is about to a very significant degree.

A: I haven't dissociated all this from my father.

T: Yes, you say your father left your mother for another woman. Did she try to harm herself after that?

A: She had a nervous breakdown, but I don't think she tried to kill herself.

Toward the end of her next session, Ann gave the therapist the pistol and the bullets; the therapist agreed to provide "safekeeping" for the weapon until further notice. Ann carries a card with the SPC hotline number; although she hasn't called the hotline, she is reassured by the knowledge that someone will always be there to listen to her. Although she declined psychiatric evaluation for antidepressant medication, Ann did agree that she would now consider hospitalization if her suicidal thoughts made her feel out of control again. Like the hotline, the availability of the protective milieu of the hospital was a source of comfort to her. She did not use either resource.

Working closely with the therapist, Ann undertook the following actions, which were discussed over the next four sessions: (1) She confronted Jim about his affair, expressed her outrage at him, and angrily terminated the relationship. (2) She phoned and later visited her mother, with whom she shared her recollections of her father's abusive and tyrannical behavior. The mother and daughter cried and hugged each other. Ann's stepfather, Frank, was unusually supportive toward her, which meant a lot to Ann. (3) She resumed her relationship with three of her closest friends, started swimming lessons, and briefly discussed with her supervisor at work the fact that she had been under a lot of stress due to the breakup of her relationship with Jim. (4) Through frequent role plays, she ventilated her rage against Jim and her father.

Ann gradually began to understand that her depression was triggered by (1) feelings of loss and abandonment and (2) turning her rage against herself instead of expressing it in an appropriate way to the targets of her anger. A prolific dreamer, she kept a dream book; in discussing her dreams, she was able to see that her attraction to older men (Jim, among others) was, in her words, "a wish and a longing for a father." Similarly, she thought of the therapist as "a good dad."

In subsequent sessions, Ann shared the following notes, which she wrote after listening to the tape recordings of the sessions under the heading: "Things that helped me in my sessions":

1. Experiencing my natural state as one of vitality and happiness.
2. Unexpressed rage (which is against others), which I turned against myself and would finally destroy me. Target the rage outward.
3. Expressing yourself empowers yourself.
4. Curse from my father: "I don't have a right to be." "As long as you feel you don't have a right to be, you'll hold on to the depression" (said by therapist).
5. Wallowing. Turning away from inside pain to the world outside would help.
6. Reidentifying myself as myself. Not identifying with my father, who killed himself through alcoholism.

These interrelated notes were reviewed in a therapy session. Ann submitted another account of her observations of the therapy sessions two weeks later:

1. Confrontation. Proving to myself that I can confront and *have the power to no longer be a victim!*
2. Your [therapist's] concern for me! (That helps.)
3. When the therapist said, "You don't want to be dead, you just don't want to hurt so much," that helped a lot too. Then I found out there was a way to avoid pain.
4. I felt you [therapist] understand my pain as much as another person could. Your sympathy meant a lot.
5. Understanding that I am not really a victim and that I don't have to spend my life in victimization.

Within three months Ann resumed dating. In her words, the themes in therapy were "mourning, men, and mother." She regained her enthusiasm about work, resumed an active social life, and, at the time of termination, was involved in a positive relationship with a recently divorced man who was interested in having a family with her.

Last Christmas, Ann sent the following note to the therapist:

> May this Christmas and the coming year be joyous and fruitful for you and your family. My boyfriend and his children by his former marriage and I are doing very well. We never get to see enough of each other and I'm occasionally intimidated by his small son but for the most part I'm thrilled with him. His daughter and I have developed a wonderful relationship, and I'm extremely fond of her and I think I've taken an important place in her life too. She, my boyfriend, and I had a family confrontation one day, instigated and led by me, and in my best therapy-like tradition (learned in our sessions), I got all of us to air our feelings; and as a result we are communicating beautifully. Some things happened between my boyfriend and his daughter that I think represent a turning point for them and maybe for me too. She's a changed girl, definitely less moody and much happier. Bravo, your influence stretches even farther than you imagine! Again, I wish you the best and send you all my thanks again for our work together. Its success shows in the loving and communicative relationship I now enjoy with my boyfriend. Best, Ann.

In a recent follow-up interview, Ann indicated that she would probably remarry soon, looked forward to having a family, was doing well in her work, and had not had any preoccupation with suicide for the past two years.

At Ann's request, her pistol and bullets (she had a license to use the pistol for self-defense) were returned. Both therapist and client felt comfortable with this arrangement.

Guidelines: A Summary

The following guidelines are generally helpful to the mental health professional doing crisis intervention work with suicide-prone clients.

1. Directly explore the possibility of suicidal thoughts with all depressed and distressed clients. Do not be afraid to ask the client if he or she has had self-destructive thoughts or has ever tried to harm him- or herself. Consider suicidal thoughts and behavior as a cry for help.

2. If the client has suicidal thoughts or plans, evaluate the degree of suicidal risk by checking the client's health, history of psychiatric disorder, marital and employment status, attachments to significant others, chemical dependency, previous suicidal attempts, suicidal thoughts or suicidal behavior, and, most important, whether the client has a specific suicide plan, the lethal means (pills, weapons, automobile) and the intention to carry out the plan.

3. If the suicidal plan includes potentially lethal medication, knives, or guns, try to persuade the client to surrender them to you or other reliable person(s).

4. If the client is isolated and if hospitalization is not desirable or feasible, actively reach out to his or her significant others; alert them to the danger of the client being alone; encourage the client to communicate his or her suicidal thoughts and plans. Remember, talking about suicide is healthier than doing it!

5. Contract with the client to call you (or a hotline) if he or she feels like carrying out a suicidal intent. Be sure to have back-up help. Do not be overly

heroic. Make sure you give your at-risk client the number of a reliable twenty-four-hour hotline; instruct the client to call the hotline at any time of the night or day if you are not available at a time of need.

6. Seek consultation from colleagues who are knowledgeable about lethality assessment and suicide prevention. Remember, those who give support must also receive support to avoid burnout.

7. When it is possible to do so, refer suicidal clients to self-help support groups (for example, Alcoholics Anonymous) while continuing your therapeutic contact with them. If you are not able to offer the client short-term therapy beyond your initial emergency assessment and intervention, refer the client to an appropriate crisis clinic or other mental health service for short-term or ongoing individual and/or group therapy.

8. Although most suicide-prone persons do not kill themselves, always take suicidal gestures seriously, even if the client seems to act manipulatively.

9. Finally, and perhaps most important, remember that the healing power of the volunteer's and mental health professional's caring, concerned availability, and reaching out is crucial to the suicidal client's struggle for and affirmation of life.

Conclusion

The LASPC program and clinical approach described here are to some degree representative of SPC programs throughout the United States and in other countries. Suicide prevention centers serve all ages, from the adolescent to the elderly. Volunteers who staff the telephone lines experience many frustrations, especially when they deal with young, high-risk callers who will not provide identifying information to enable contact with their family or other possible sources of support. Loss of loved ones, health, jobs, and self-esteem are pervasive themes that run through all of the clinical examples. Despite the fact that many callers refuse help, the knowledge that the center may make the difference between life and death sustains staff and volunteers in their efforts.

References

American Association of Suicidology. (1984). *Certification Standards Manual,* 3rd ed. Denver: Author.

Dunne, E. J., McIntosh, J. L., & Dunne-Maxim, K. (Eds.). (1987). *Suicide and its aftermath: Understanding and counseling the survivors.* New York: W. W. Norton.

Farberow, N. L. (1968). Suicide prevention: A view from the bridge. *Community Mental Health Journal, 4,* 469–474.

Farberow, N. L. (1976). Group psychotherapy for self-destructive persons. In H. J. Parad, H. L. P. Resnik, & L. Parad (Eds.), *Emergency mental health and disaster management: A mental health source book.* Bowie, MD: Charles Press.

Farberow, N. L., Heilig, S. M., & Litman, R. E. (1968). *Techniques in crisis management: A training manual.* Los Angeles: Suicide Prevention Center.

Farberow, N. L., Litman, R. E., & Nelson, F. L. (1987). *Youth suicide in California.* Paper presented at American Association of Suicidology/International Association for Suicide Prevention Meeting, San Francisco.

Farberow, N. L., & Shneidman, E. S. (Eds.). (1961). *The cry for help*. New York: McGraw Hill.

Frierson, R. L., & Lippman, S. B. (1988). Suicide and AIDS. *Psychosomatics, 29*, 226–231.

Heilig, S. M., Farberow, N. L., Litman, R. E., & Shneidman, E. S. (1968). Role of nonprofessionals in the suicide prevention center. *Community Mental Health Journal, 4*, 287–295.

Lamb, D. (1988, December 6). Support groups help: Rugged West—A climate for suicide. *Los Angeles Times*.

Motto, J. A. (1979). New approaches to crisis intervention. *Suicide and Life-Threatening Behavior*, 9, 173–184.

Suicide Prevention Programs for California Public Schools. (1987). California State Department of Education, P.O. Box 271, Sacramento, CA 95802.

12

A Crisis Intervention Model for Dying Patients and Their Families

SHARON MASS

DEATH, WHICH HAS BEEN called the final stage of growth, is a major life event that underscores the finite nature of human existence. Failure to cope appropriately with death and to resolve the subsequent emotions of loss and grief will likely lead to emotional disorder, regardless of the stage of the life cycle in which the event occurs (Bowlby, 1980). The loss of a parent during childhood is a severe stress that may profoundly compromise healthy development (Bowlby, 1960). An adult's experiences of loss of significant others may precipitate depression as well as neurotic and psychotic reactions. (Schoenberg, Carr, Peretz, & Kutscher, 1972). Parkes (1972) suggested that the loss of a spouse in old age is likely to precipitate illness and death in the surviving spouse. In his seminal work on the importance of grief, Lindemann (1944) reported that the failure to mourn appropriately precipitated neurotic reactions. Three decades later, Meyer (1975) summarized evidence indicating that failure to cope with death is the seedbed of neurosis.

In recent years, it has become evident that mental health professionals need to become knowledgeable about the death process, including the psychosocial aspects of dying and accompanying problems of grief work and situational adjustments that confront the dying and their survivors (Raphael, 1983). Because issues of loss and death permeate mental health practice, workers who are unaware of these issues and how they may affect clients may overlook the dynamics that influence their clients' behavior.

As a result of medical advancements and technology, more people are living longer and dying from conditions other than accidents or acute, sudden diseases. This phenomenon has led to the recognition of the need for services, especially social work and other mental health services, for dying patients and their families.

Social workers and other mental health professionals can contribute to the study of thanatology (death phenomena) through their knowledge of personality development and social functioning as well as through practice methods designed to help people who face actual or potentially incapacitating difficulties (Caroff, 1980; Lister & Gochros, 1976; Prichard, 1977; Smith, 1982; Zelinsky & Thorson, 1983). Assessment of intrapsychic, interpersonal, and environmental factors as well as cultural components of personality and functioning provides prognostic indicators in determining the impact of stress and the coping resources of both the patient and family (Germain, 1984). More recently, investigators have developed promising instruments for assessing grief (Faschingbauer, Zisook, & DeVaul, 1987) and for predicting the outcome of bereavement (Shanfield, 1987).

Theoretical Perspective

The crisis approach helps people cope with the emotional and social impact of loss. The most challenging crisis humans face is death and its threat to the family structure and the life roles of individual family members. Following Parad's (1965) crisis framework, Pattison (1977) discusses the knowledge of death as a crisis event:

> 1. This stressful event poses a problem that by definition is unsolvable in the immediate future. In this sense, dying is the most stressful crisis because it is a crisis to which we bow but do not solve.
> 2. The problem taxes one's psychological resources since it is beyond one's traditional problem-solving methods. One is faced with a new experience with no prior experience to fall back on, for although one has lived amidst death, that is far different from one's own death.
> 3. The situation is perceived as a threat or danger to the life goals of the person. Dying interrupts a person in the midst of life, and even in old age it abruptly confronts one with the goals one set in life.
> 4. The crisis period is characterized by a tension that mounts to a peak, then falls. As one faces the crisis of death knowledge, there is mobilization of either integrative or disintegrative mechanisms. The peak of anxiety usually occurs considerably before death.
> 5. The crisis situation awakens unresolved key problems from both the near and distant past. Problems of dependency, passivity, narcissism, identity, and more may be activated during the dying process. Hence, one is faced not only with the immediate dying process but also the unresolved feelings from one's own lifetime and its inevitable conflicts (p. 47).

Thus, during the crisis of death, the dying patient and family's feelings of competence are severely taxed and compromised. Professional counselors must be sensitive to the newly aroused vulnerabilities of the dying patient and his or her family so that interventions can be initiated that will enhance their ability to cope. Briefly, crisis theory presents a treatment rationale for enhancing individual and interpersonal integrity, even when death is a likely outcome (Caroff & Dobrof, 1974).

The Process of Dying

The process of dying, viewed as a psychological event, has been dealt with by many authors. Various stages of adaptation and their inherent coping behaviors and conflicts have been identified. The most widely known and influential studies of the psychological needs of the terminally ill have been discussed by Kübler-Ross (1969), Weisman (1976), and Pattison (1977).

Kübler-Ross describes a sequence of five "stages of dying" through which patients approach their fate. The patient's initial response to awareness of terminal illness is denial. Denial serves as a buffer and safety valve that cushions the impact of a sudden, emotional upheaval and helps patients develop a state of mind that allows them to maintain some degree of normalcy in their lives. The second stage, anger, derives from the helplessness caused by feeling unable to control what is happening. At this stage, patients may enter the subsequent stages of bargaining, depression, and acceptance.

To illustrate these stages, the patient initially responds in a "It can't be" or "This is not really happening to me" manner, followed by hostility, helplessness, and anger as the reality of the situation becomes clear. The bargaining stage follows: "Let's make a deal" or "I don't care what happens to me after May's wedding. I just want to be able to go." Bargaining helps the individual face death by providing the dying individual with a goal and helping him or her to gain control over his or her life again. Bargaining brings peace, purpose, and interest in life. It provides hope and prepares the dying individual for the pervasive sadness and diminished physical and mental processes typical of depression. This preparatory grief work ideally leads to acceptance and allows the individual to say farewell, not only to loved ones but to life.

Analyzing the process of illness, Weisman (1979) identifies four phases: Phase I begins when the person begins to notice some stressful symptoms and lasts until the diagnosis is confirmed, at which time efforts to protect the status quo by denial, rationalization, and seeking reassurance are evident. Phase II encompasses the time between diagnosis and initial treatment. Phase III is characterized by advanced illness with accompanying deterioration and disability. Phase IV marks the point of final decline and terminality. Here Weisman concurs with Glasser and Straus's (1965) succinct statement "certainty must precede preparation" (p. 79). In other words, the reaction to the death and its concomitant losses cannot begin until the death is perceived as inevitable.

In his model of the "dying trajectory," Pattison (1977) outlines three phases: acute crisis, chronic living–dying, and terminal. Each phase presents different needs for the patient and family and calls for a different style of response from the mental health worker. In the acute crisis phase, professionals are confronted with the issue of extreme anxiety. In the chronic living–dying phase, they are faced with helping the patient resolve issues regarding interpersonal relationships and coping with problems of daily living. In the terminal phase, professionals must help patients face their need for support and for achieving separation and withdrawal from significant others. The crisis of knowledge of death (being confronted with a fatal illness) alters the dying person's perception and orientation to the future.

Pattison's work provides a guide to understanding the kinds of behavior likely to appear in a dying patient and his or her family during various phases of a fatal illness. Confrontation with the inevitability of death, be it immediate or indeterminate, causes the patient to experience conflict in four areas: (1) impaired self-esteem, (2) feelings of endangerment (pain), (3) fear of annihilation (cessation of self), and (4) fear of alienation (loss of relationships with others). The dying individual reacts to these four basic fears while experiencing the acute crisis, chronic living–dying, and terminal states. Weisman (1976) believes that threats to self-esteem are important in that a person who feels worthless, as opposed to worthwhile, experiences greater fear of endangerment, annihilation, and alienation.

The most important factor throughout the adaptation process is hope. Hope is not perceived as a static state but as an everchanging, multifaceted component that each person must define for him- or herself (Kübler-Ross, 1969; Pattison, 1977; LeShan, 1971). Maintaining hope within a realistic context requires the patient to hope for something attainable within a brief span of time, as is illustrated by the following case:

> A sixty-six-year-old woman was informed that she had an inoperable uterine tumor that was quite likely to take her life. She was initially depressed, but rallied to focus her hopes on a course of chemotherapy. Although her doctors cautioned her to temper her optimistic expectations, she steadfastly maintained that she would "beat the odds." When her disease continued to advance, her family and physicians feared she would collapse emotionally. Instead, after a depression that was briefer than her initial one, she turned her hopes toward surviving to see the birth of her fifth grandchild. Against medical odds, she lived the intervening five months and died peacefully less than a week after welcoming her granddaughter into the world. In retrospect, all involved realized that this woman knew that she needed to have hope in order to cope (Gonda & Ruark, 1984, p. 90).*

Some terminal patients seem to accept their impending death. For many people, the completion of unfinished business, for example, economic and work-related tasks, exploration of psychological and other issues relating to self-esteem, or coming to terms with interpersonal and religious issues, may enhance their acceptance of death. The ability to derive a sense of purpose and meaning from life and perhaps from death, to have "an appropriate rather than an appropriated death," is viewed by Weisman as integral to any self-accepting experience of terminality. He further proposes that the task of psychosocial clinicians is to help patients "die their own deaths. An appropriate death is one that a person might choose, had he a choice" (Weisman, 1972, pp. 162–172).

According to Pattison (1977), if a patient is able to integrate the following tasks into his or her life, he or she will have come to terms with his or her impending death:

> 1. The person is able to face and resolve the initial crisis of acute anxiety without disintegration.
> 2. The person is able to reconcile the reality of his or her life as it is to his or her ego ideal image of life as he or she wanted it to be.
> 3. The person is able to preserve or restore the continuity of important relationships during the living-dying interval and gradually achieve separation from loved ones as death approaches.
> 4. The person is able to experience reasonably the emergence of basic instincts, wishes, and fantasies that lead without undue conflict to gradual withdrawal and the final acceptance of death (p. 319).

Knowledge of what the terminally ill patient experiences physically and psychologically as well as understanding the gamut of feelings and defenses the patient uses to cope with impending death allows the worker to mitigate the bur-

*Reprinted with permission from Gonda, T., & Ruark, J. (1984). *Dying dignified: The health professional's guide to care*. Menlo Park, CA: Addison Wesley.

den of the crisis and perhaps transform a potentially chaotic situation into a period that Pattison calls "integrated dying." The following case illustrates this point:

> Mrs. Benning had almost a year to make preparations before her death. Although she often denied that she was unwell, she sold her large home and moved into a small apartment. Then she invited all her children, family, and in-laws to visit, asking them which of her possessions they wanted. Her family knew she was getting ready to die, but did not want to face this fact. Although her preparations took place intermittently, Mrs. Benning often expressed to her daughter that she was really looking forward to spending time with her next summer so that they could do all the things she loved to do, such as shop and visit the museum. Although she was gradually giving away her things and thus breaking ties with possessions she loved, Mrs. Benning still clung to the hope that "next summer" she would be strong enough to go shopping.

Issues in Terminal Illness

Clinical practice emphasizes the importance of a patient's individuality, autonomy, and right to be respected as a person. Several authors have suggested that a dying person's behavior reflects or parallels his or her behavior in response to earlier situations of threat, stress, or failure (Shneidman, 1978). The manner in which the individual faced past crises will determine how he or she deals with the crisis of death. The individual who has been a hostile, defensive, angry person all his or her life may feel that his or her fears have been warranted, that no one understands or cares, and that he or she has been abandoned. In other words, people die the way they live. On a more positive note, the strength and courage with which some persons (including children) and their families encounter death leaves behind a reservoir of inspiration.

Jaffe (1980) lists the following issues as being the most critical in terminal illness: the theme of loss; recognition that the family is also the patient; the concept of time as a framework that makes the death and dying crisis more critical than are other life stresses; anticipatory grief with its concomitant stress, anger, and guilt; and the patient's and family's need for support systems (see chapter 14). Identification of these issues helps establish and facilitate open communication.

Pilsecker (1975) conceptualizes work with the terminally ill "in terms of five basic categories: planning for living during the terminal process, exploration of feelings about impending death, living with the prospect of death, planning for death, and planning for the family after death" (p. 190).

Recognizing that a dying person does not have the luxury of time, the worker must set finite intervention goals. Shneidman (1978) delineates aspects of thanatological work, the overarching goal of which is to assist the patient to achieve psychological comfort. Developing insight is not the goal of psychotherapy with the dying. Helping a dying person is a flexible process, characterized by rapport, conversation, listening to reminiscences, and communicative silences. Interventions must always be in the dying patient's best interest. "No one has to die in a state of psychoanalytic grace" (Shneidman, 1978, p. 211). Interventions can take the form of interpretation, suggestions, advice, interaction with other health care professionals, and acting as the patient's ombudsman. The focus is on benign intervention.

The familiar social work dictum "begin where the client is" should be kept in mind when working with dying patients. The terminal patient should set the pace of therapeutic work and should make the decision as to whether the topic of death is even mentioned. Denial is an ever-present factor in the dying process. Shneidman (1978) suggests that when clinicians go along with the patient's transient denial, the dying person will usually abandon denial and return to the reality of the moment. Denial is sometimes suppressed, sometimes on the surface. In the previous case example, Mrs. Benning talked about "next summer" and "shopping," knowing full well that her remaining time could be counted in weeks.

A Way of Thinking about Death

Talking about death and working with the dying is stressful for the clinician because intense personal feelings are aroused. The possibility of extinction, helplessness, abandonment, disfigurement, and loss of self-esteem are difficult issues for everyone (Pattison, 1977; Shneidman, 1978; Weisman, 1974). If the worker can perceive death as the final developmental stage of the life cycle, he or she will find work with the terminally ill more rewarding and meaningful.

Of course, premature death and the need to deal with termination issues at a young age is a tragic experience. Regardless, dying should not be viewed as a pathological problem that requires treatment (Engel, 1961; Pattison, 1977), but should be perceived as part of the normal life cycle (Beaty, 1980).

"Psychosocial helping" describes a response to the terminal client that is corrective, supportive, inquisitive, challenging, and two-directional (Pattison, 1977). Helping is not so much "doing" as "being." When working with clients who are not terminally ill, the worker attempts to help them engage more fully with life; when a clinician works with a dying person, he or she helps the patient to disengage from life.

Clinicians who work with terminally ill persons need to develop their own philosophy of death and dying. It is important that they have to some extent worked out their own anxiety regarding death. If they do not confront these issues, they may feel uncomfortable with the subject of death and fear the dying patient. Because a clinical interview is a reciprocal process, patients can easily perceive a worker's discomfort with their terminal condition. Empathy, warmth, and genuineness must be combined with self-knowledge if the worker is to be an objective, sensitive counselor to the dying patient and his or her family.

Helping the Dying Person

Communicate Effectively

Open and honest communication is a paramount need of the dying patient and the family. Discussions of death arouse strong feelings, and the worker must prepare him- or herself for such communication. Creating a relaxed, unhurried environment is essential before discussing difficult issues. By calmly sitting at the patient's bedside, the worker communicates to the patient that he or she is there to listen, assess, understand, and empathize. The mental health worker is in the unique position of being the only member of the health care team who does not "lay on hands" or prescribe diet, physical care, or treatment. Thus the worker is not perceived as an "invasive" treatment professional. This distinction often allows the patient to express him- or herself without fear of retribution:

> . . . aside from my immediate family and my own personal friends, the social worker was the only human being on the hospital staff with whom I could confide my own fears, convey some of my rage and express my tears. It was pretty important to have somebody who could acknowledge that I may be facing death. I can't underestimate the importance of that fact (Hanlan, 1984, p. 253).

Dying persons need to express and to resolve difficult and painful feelings. The clinician's willingness to listen allows the patient to discuss his or her relevant past, information that provides the clinician with insight regarding previous coping patterns. Although listening offers direct comfort and support, the intensity of feelings evoked by death and dying engender nonverbal communication as well. Eye contact, body position, body movement, simple nods, and appropriate sounds encourage the patient to communicate by reassuring the patient that he or she is important and being listened to. Intense emotional communication in turn facilitates emotional healing in the terminal patient (Gonda & Ruark, 1984). With appropriate emotional support, the patient and family can focus on reality issues in the here and now as well as plan for the future.

Powerful feelings of anger, remorse, fear, and guilt arouse anxiety in the patient and family. If the patient is tension ridden, he or she will not hear or be willing to engage in discussion. Moreover, cultural taboos decry demonstrations of vulnerability in public. Western society admires coolness under pressure. The therapist should consider doing relaxation exercises with the patient in an effort to facilitate communication of strong feelings.

Discussing feelings of dependency and fears of abandonment helps universalize these feelings and makes them more acceptable. The patient and family should be encouraged to express their fear of and anger concerning the burdens confronting them. Longstanding and unresolved family conflicts may tend to surface violently during this time. Emotional fatigue caused by strain makes it difficult for family members to act "reasonably." The clinician may assist family members by directing their anger toward "safer" vehicles of expression. Articulation of feelings frees energies and channels efforts toward improving the quality of the terminal patient's life (Smith, 1981).

The following example illustrates the positive results that can emerge when feelings are expressed:

> A thirty-four year-old woman, Susan, who was recently estranged from her husband, was hospitalized for the terminal phase of a metastatic malignant condition. Her husband was an executive who had physically and emotionally abused her during their eight years of marriage. She had never revealed this to her parents because they were opposed to her marriage to this older man. When her parents came to visit, she would pretend that all was well and never shared her feelings about her circumstances. However, during

individual contacts with the social worker, Susan would express her fear of abandonment and of not having anyone to stay with her when she died. The parents sought out the social worker because they could not understand their daughter's aloof attitude. After several individual contacts with Susan and her parents, a joint meeting was agreed upon by both parties. At this meeting emotions were expressed, tears flowed, the parents expressed their desire to forget the past and be with Susan whenever she so desired. Six months after Susan's death, her parents wrote the social worker to express their appreciation for his encouragement that they take the risk and confront their daughter. They stated that the sadness they felt over the loss of their daughter was easier to live with because they had shared their feelings and heard her express her great relief and appreciation that she would not die alone.

Although the following case did not reflect the desired goal of facilitating communication between the patient and spouse, therapy did renew an intimacy between the father and son. Unexpected reunions are common when communication systems are developed.

Sally and Dave had been married for thirty-six years. Two years earlier, Sally was treated for breast cancer. She and her husband were seen by the social worker during the initial and treatment phases of her illness. They appeared to have a good marital relationship; they showed consideration and support for each other. After discovery of widespread metastasis, Sally was hospitalized for the terminal phase of her illness. She became totally withdrawn and would not speak to anyone other than her doctor. She ignored her husband and the social worker and refused to see visitors. After many days of this silent treatment, Dave told the social worker he would not visit his wife again. He didn't understand her behavior; he felt that he had been a good husband and that they had enjoyed a good life together. The social worker spent much time explaining to him the anger Sally was experiencing. Dave was encouraged to continue his daily visits, to speak to his wife, and to express his feelings. She died in silence. Shortly after her death, the worker received a letter from Dave's son, who lived out of town. The son wrote that he and his father had never been very close. When the son came to visit his mother in the hospital, he overheard his father telling his mother how much he loved her, elaborating on all the reasons that she had made his life so enjoyable and how sad he was feeling that at this final time she was not her usual self.

After the funeral the son returned home with Dave. During a long talk, the son revealed how poignant and touching that moment in the hospital was for him. Dave confessed that he had not ever wanted to visit Sally again but that he had been counseled to go back repeatedly in hopes that he would reach her. The son wrote to thank the social worker for having encouraged Dave to pour out his emotions, a factor that helped renew their own relationship.

Be a Knowledgeable Clinician

In addition to having basic knowledge about human behavior, the clinician must be knowledgeable about the process of dying, defense and coping mechanisms, and the patient's various medical treatments. By educating patients and their families about what they might expect emotionally and by translating medical terminology into lay terms, the worker advocates for patients and helps them sort out what is real from what is unreal. The "unknown," which is usually more frightening to the patient than what he or she knows, may cause the patient to create elaborate and devastating fantasies. Knowledge dissipates harmful fallacies, for example, the untruth that addiction is a serious complication in terminal illness (Klein, 1971). Most patients who develop adequate coping mechanisms are able to comprehend truth more readily than they are to face uncertainty. Whether a dying patient should be told that he or she has a serious and probably fatal illness is a controversial issue. In my opinion—and in the opinion of the overwhelming majority of patients and professionals—a dying patient needs to know that his or her remaining time is brief (Hinton, 1972). Individuals who are not told of their imminent death or made aware of the unpredictability of their future are robbed of their opportunity to prepare for death and make the most of their remaining time.

Family members' involvement in the decision-making process helps them to address issues of helplessness. By imparting relevant information to the dying patient and family, the clinician offers timely support that helps mitigate the pain of crisis. The worker should listen to the patient and family carefully and sensitively. Workers should familiarize themselves with the state's written instructions that allow terminally ill persons to instruct their physicians not to extend the process of dying via artificial means and should make this information available to patients and their families. These "advance directives" differ from state to state and are commonly called the Living Will, Natural Death Act Directive, or a Durable Power of Attorney for Health Decisions. Time taken to discuss medical intervention issues, such as extension of living versus prolongation of dying, helps ensure that the patient's wishes will be carried out. The more the family members are involved in this process, the less likely it is that they will undermine the patient's wishes. Workers need to participate in the ethics committee at their hospital in order to advocate on behalf of patients and their families. The following case example illustrates such a situation.

> Mrs. Edgerton, a sixty-year-old widow with one child, a thirty-five-year-old son, was terminally ill in the hospital. She was a devout member of the Jehovah's Witnesses and followed her church's dictum prohibiting blood transfusion. In a written directive (Durable Power of Attorney for Health Decisions), she authorized her son to make medical decisions on her behalf in the event she was no longer competent. A few days after she lost consciousness, her doctors recommended that she be given a blood transfusion. Her son did not follow his mother's religious belief and gave permission for the transfusion. The nursing staff consulted the social worker to enlist support to prevent the transfusion as they perceived it was a violation of the patient's wishes. After several difficult meetings with the son, whose wish was to keep his mother alive at all costs, the social worker consulted the ethics committee to advocate on behalf of the patient. The social worker involved the son in the committee process in an effort to clarify the conflict between his needs and his mother's wishes. Eventually, he accepted the reality of his mother's impending death and was able to let her go.

In addition to understanding the psychological needs of terminally ill patients and their families, a clinician must be aware of the specialized community facilities that are available to the terminally ill patient and the family. Hospice care for the terminally ill has developed into many different models: the wholly volunteer program; home care programs; freestanding, full-service, autonomous institutions (such as that developed at St. Christopher's Hospice in London and duplicated in many North American cities); hospital-based palliative care units; and continuum-care sub-acute units (Wass, Berardo, & Neimeyer, 1988). Regardless of the model, the hospice concept provides needed services to terminally ill patients.

Empower the Patient

Death forces people to confront their own limitations in life. Terminal illness reminds people of their finite ability to influence what happens to them and their loved ones and evokes a sense of powerlessness and loss of control. Isolation and loneliness often become linked with issues of power and control and serve to amplify feelings of powerlessness. Poor communication can lead to anger, confusion, and fear. Workers need to reinforce a sense of mastery and control in both the patient and the family. Kübler-Ross (1969) tells the story of a rich, important, powerful man whose wife sought out a clinician because her husband was treating her so badly. The clinician visited the man in the hospital:

> I walked in and right away he was saying, "I didn't ask to see you, did I? All that's wrong with me is malnutrition." Now what was the man saying? What does it mean for a wealthy man to say he's got malnutrition? He had leukemia, but malnutrition is something he could control. He couldn't accept being sick because he had to feel that he was in charge of his situation (p. 180).

The clinician devised a treatment plan, which she subsequently shared with all the health care professionals involved in this case. Instead of simply giving the man a back rub at the specific time, the nurse would ask him when it would be most convenient. His wife followed the same pattern by calling to ask when she should visit and whether she should bring the children. This routine gave the patient some control over what was happening to him in the hospital and eventually enabled him to acknowledge his illness and learn to cope with it.

Most people feel that they have value, worth, and meaning in their life. They fortify this perspective by carving out a place in the world; by building a life, a home, and a family, they hope to create something that will extend beyond their death. Part of being human is searching for self-esteem. Every person has a will and a right to find such meaning. By acknowledging the importance of the dying patient's words, the clinician affirms that person's sense of identity and self-esteem. The worker must react in a flexible, responsible manner in order to help the patient to find meaning in the final stage of life. Brief but frequent contacts with the dying patient and family help convey a sense of sharing. The comfort derived from sharing delivers a consistent message to the patient and his or her family: (1) they are cared about, (2) they are not alone, and (3) meaning can be found in the sharing of this difficult situation (Achs, 1976). Sometimes the mere presence of a silent worker, that is, "being," offers more support for patients and their families than does the frenetic activity of "doing." When no more can be done or said, simply holding the patient's hand, shedding tears, will help the patient in finally letting go of life.

> Katy, a sixty-three-year-old married woman, had been hospitalized twelve times in as many months since she was diagnosed with lung cancer. She would come to the hospital with her husband, Paul, and he would attend to her every need. Throughout the course of the year, I met with them many times. Initially, I met with them when she received the diagnosis of lung cancer to facilitate the expression of her fears and concerns, to offer hope and my availability to the two of them. I also met with their two married daughters for the same purpose. In the early stages of her disease, Katy was actively involved in her treatment, complying with her physician's orders and receiving a great deal of support from her family network. As the disease progressed and she became dependent on a portable oxygen system, she became very dependent upon her husband and frightened about being left alone. Paul was a positive, assertive man who was receptive to my suggestion that he play a role in the care of his wife. The three of us would practice relaxation exercises together so that Paul would learn to help Katy relax and breathe in a calm manner. Her fear of choking or suffocating exacerbated her anxiety and made it difficult for her to breathe. Katy was visibly more comfortable after the relaxation sessions. I wanted to involve Paul because shared care responsibilities remove some of the helplessness family members experience during this time. During Katy's final days, I became a visitor, watching my "pupil" go through the relaxation exercises with his wife. Paul was with Katy when she died, gently whispering his learned instructions about breathing and focusing on a pleasant distant place. A month after Katy died, Paul came to see me to express his gratitude for having been taught to do something that made his wife more comfortable. After some discussion, he quietly confided that my silent presence in the room relieved much of his anxiety and that the sharing helped to diminish some of the emotional distress he felt.

It is important, to the extent possible, to encourage the dying patient to retain authority and control over daily tasks and decisions. For as long as possible, the patient should be allowed to retain autonomy, a sense of identity, and self-esteem in the face of his or her dependency needs (Krant, 1974; Pattison, 1977).

> Lionel, a twenty-five-year-old man dying of a rare tumor in the neck (thymoma), was admitted to the hospital. It became apparent that severe conflicts existed between the patient and his parents. The clinician established contact with the patient and learned that the patient felt that his father had always compared him unfavorably with his older brother and had taken an authoritarian attitude toward him, particularly regarding his illness. The parents, in order to gain a sense of control over the impending loss of their son, dictated orders to both the patient and staff. After the worker made several contacts with the patient and separately with his parents, the patient was able to assert himself, express his feelings, and make his own wishes known. The physician responded to him in a way that allowed the patient to be the decision maker, rather than deferring to his parents.

Prepare the Family

Prolonged illness leading to death poses major adjustment problems for both the patient and family members. The family system may be thrown out of its customary equilibrium; tensions are likely to be reflected in breakdown of communication, social isolation of members, redistribution of roles, and personal confusion (Hamovitch, 1964; Kaplan, Smith, Grobstein, & Fischman, 1973; Pattison, 1977; Smith, 1982). Intervention must be designed to assist the family in coping with the dying person's needs during his or her remaining days. Enabling family members to share feelings is an important task during this period. Often the worker must act as interpreter and mediator, clarifying what family members know, why they may be angry or withdrawn, and how they perceive their own situation and the actions of others. The task of the mental health worker is to assist the family in anticipating and preparing for their final separation from their loved one.

Facilitate Grieving

Physicians throughout the ages have suspected that grief is a significant cause of sickness and death. Although this hypothesis has been borne out in studies that indicate exceptionally high rates of morbidity and mortality among certain populations of bereaved adults (Parkes, 1972; Bowlby, 1960), a recent review of the literature indicates that the epidemiological evidence of breavement-related mortality and morbidity is equivocal (Osterweis, Solomon, & Green, 1984).

Almost from the beginning of work with the dying person, the family members must be considered victims and eventually patients as much as the dying person (Shneidman, 1978). The loss of a loved one disrupts family members' expectations about and sense of the meaning of life, and threatens their identity (Smith, 1982). Each family member will be affected differently by a loved one's death, depending upon personality, relationship with the dying person, age, previous experience with death, and cultural and religious traditions. For the family to achieve a new functional equilibrium, members must be encouraged to grieve and mourn, which will allow them to assimilate their loss. The basic task of grief and mourning is to "give up" one's relationship with the dead loved one and to redirect energies toward establishing new ties. The entire family system must work through its grief; it is not enough for individual members to mourn the loss.

Clinicians who counsel family members in mourning need to educate members about the process of grief—specifically, that grief is painful, that it takes time, and that it must be shared (Simos, 1979). Clinicians should encourage the bereaved to express their feelings, which may include yearning, anger, fear, depression, panic, helplessness, hopelessness, or emptiness. Intervention techniques aimed at ventilation, exploration, and clarification of key issues facilitate the grief process. The psychological tasks of the bereaved—talking, crying, and sharing—require the clinician to support the grief process through his or her investment of time, energy, and patience. Referral to mutual support or self-help groups is often advisable. Groups such as the Widow to Widow program or Candlelighters have proven to be effective vehicles for the prevention or alleviation of the detrimental consequences of bereavement (Osterweis et al., 1984). Regardless, it is essential that grieving persons have someone to whom they can turn for support.

The following example highlights counseling work with bereaved persons:

> Margie, who was twenty-five, had been married eight years when her twenty-eight-year-old husband, Mickey, succumbed to a virulent metastatic lung cancer diagnosed two months before he died. Although contact with a social worker was initiated immediately upon diagnosis, Mickey was too ill and weak to be receptive. Thus the contact focused primarily on Margie in an effort to help her cope with the enormity of her situation. During this two-month death vigil, Margie was encouraged to talk about all kinds of details regarding her life with Mickey. She had known him since childhood. They graduated from high school, obtained blue-collar jobs, saved all their earnings, and realized their goal of purchasing a home so that they could begin to consider raising a family. Margie was a sheltered young woman, protected by her parents and then by her husband. Although she enjoyed her role of homemaker, Mickey handled all the financial matters and made all the important decisions.
>
> Following the funeral and the acute mourning period, Margie began weekly contacts with the social worker in an effort to resolve her grief. The early sessions were spent encouraging Margie to express her feelings of anger and guilt, which are universal components of grief. The social worker spent many sessions detailing the various emotional states that Margie would likely experience in an attempt to help her cope with the anger, denial, and sadness she was feeling. Her yearning and desire for her husband caused her to believe she would see him in a store, in church, or walking on the street. When she learned that this reaction was normal, she felt reassured that she was not losing her mind.
>
> The worker assigned specific tasks to Margie in an effort to restore her self-esteem and mastery of her life. She learned to balance the bank statement, to make decisions related to daily life, and to assume responsibility for herself. Eventually Margie was able to accept her loss and to restore her self-esteem.
>
> Margie has written the social worker every year for the past four years. After her father's death two years ago, Margie stated, "You would have been proud of me—the way I could be there for my mother and brother while handling my own grief." In a recent note, she indicated that she was happily married and had a child. Thus, Margie was able to reconnect with others, refocus on the present, and once again look to the future.

The goal of grief work is to help clients release emotions so that they can relinquish their ties to the loved one. A severe loss makes life seem empty. The grieving person's ability to overcome grief depends on availability of support as well as development of his or her renewed self-esteem and sense of meaning. Loss, if mourned successfully, strengthens and enhances the ego, thus serving as an important aspect of development.

Conclusion

Work with a dying patient and family is challenging and difficult. Like dying patients and their families, clinicians need to engage in the tasks of grief and mourning. They must develop their own support systems at work—whether group sessions or individual friendships—where they can share their feelings and shed their tears. To be able to treat this population successfully, clinicians must face their own feelings about death, avoid rejecting the dying person, and avoid the counterphobic mechanism of identification with the dying person. Only when these tasks have been accomplished can clinicians communicate detached compassion. It is important that clinicians identify their own personal limits. When the clinician becomes aware of his or her countertransference behavior, he or she should withdraw in order to regain perspective and to avoid burnout. In order to help patients, clinicians must also help themselves. It is essential that workers take vacations and spend time in joyful and pleasant activities with friends and loved ones.

Mental health professionals have been in the forefront of disciplines that confront and seek to resolve the many difficult problems of human existence. The challenge of psychosocial clinicians is to make dying a dignified final stage of growth.

Although an increasing number of "grief curricula" have been developed for groups of bereaved children and other at-risk clients ("Children Grieving the Death of a Parent: A Discussion Series Curriculum Guide," 1986), the curricula of most educational institutions do not require courses in death education (Corr, 1978). As helping professionals, all mental health workers need knowledge and training on how to work with the dying and their families. We should work toward the goal of mandating such courses in all professional schools.

References

Achs, S. (1976, April). *Cancer surgery as a human experience*. Paper presented at the meeting of the Brooklyn Psychiatric Society, Brooklyn, NY.

Beaty, N. (1980). *The craft of dying: A study in the tradition of the Ars Moriendi in England*. New Haven, CT: Yale University Press.

Bowlby, J. (1980). *Loss, sadness, and depression*. New York, Basic Books.

Bowlby, J. (1960). Separation anxiety: A critical review of the literature. *Journal of Child Psychology and Psychiatry, 1*, 251–275.

Caroff, P. (1980). Education for social work practice with the terminally ill and their families. In B. Orcutt, E. Prichard, J. Collard, E. Cooper, A. Kutscher, & I. Seeland (Eds.), *Social work and thanatology* (pp. 59–67). New York: Arno.

Caroff, P., & Dobrof, R. (1974). Social work: Its institutional role. In B. Schoenberg, A. Carr, A. Kutscher, D. Peretz, & I. Goldberg (Eds.), *Anticipatory grief* (pp. 251–263). New York: Columbia University Press.

Children grieving the death of a parent: A discussion series curriculum guide. (1986). Seattle, WA: Widowed Information and Consultation Services, Family Services of Seattle.

Corr, C. (1978). A model syllabus for death and dying. *Death Education, 1*, 433–457.

Engel, G. (1961). Is grief a disease? *Psychosomatic Medicine, 23*, 19–22.

Faschingbauer, T., Zisook, S., & DeVaul, R. (1987). The Texas revised inventory of grief. In S. Zisook (Ed.), *Biopsychosocial aspects of bereavement* (pp. 109–123). Washington, DC: American Psychiatric Association.

Germain, C. (1984). Social work practice in health care: An ecological perspective. New York: Free Press.

Glasser, B., & Strauss, A. (1965). *Awareness of dying*. New York: Aldine.

Gonda, T., & Ruark, J. (1984). *Dying dignified: The health professional's guide to care*. Menlo Park, CA: Addison-Wesley.

Hamovitch, M. (1964). *The parent and the fatally ill child.* Los Angeles: Delmar.

Hinton, J. (1972). *Dying.* New York: Penguin Books.

Hanlan, A. (1984). Notes of a dying professor. In T. Carlton, *Clinical social work in health settings* (pp. 245–258). New York: Springer.

Jaffe, L. (1980). Critical issues in terminal illness. In B. Orcutt, E. Prichard, J. Collard, E. Cooper, A. Kutscher, & I. Seeland (Eds.), *Social work and thanatology* (pp. 68–73). New York: Arno.

Kaplan, D., Smith, A., Grobstein, R., & Fischman, S. (1973). Family mediation of stress. *Social Work, 18*, 60–69.

Klein, R. (1971). A crisis to grow on. *Cancer, 28*, 1960–1965.

Krant, M. (1974). *Dying and dignity.* Springfield, IL: Charles C Thomas.

Kübler-Ross, E. (1969). *On death and dying.* Englewood Cliffs, NJ: Prentice Hall.

LeShan, L. (1971). *You can fight for your life.* New York: Jove.

Lindemann, E. (1944). Symptomatology and management of acute grief. *American Journal of Psychiatry, 101*, 141–148.

Lister, L., & Gochros, H. (1976). Preparing students for effective social work practice related to death. *Journal of Education for Social Work, 12*, 85–90.

Meyer, J. (1975). *Death and neurosis.* New York: International Universities Press.

Osterweis, M., Solomon, F., & Green, M. (1984). *Bereavement: Reactions, consequences and care.* Washington, DC : National Academy Press.

Parad, H. J. (Ed.) (1965). *Crisis intervention: Selected readings.* New York: Family Service Association of America.

Parkes, C. (1972). *Bereavement: Studies of grief in adult life.* New York: International Universities Press.

Pattison, E. M. (1977). *The experience of dying.* Englewood Cliffs, NJ: Prentice-Hall.

Pilsecker, C. (1975). Help for the dying. *Social Work, 20*, 190–194.

Prichard, E. (1977). Preface. In E. Prichard, J. Collard, B. Orcutt, A. Kutscher, I. Seeland, & N. Lefowitz (Eds.), *Social work with the dying patient and the family* (pp. xi-xiv). New York: Columbia University Press.

Raphael, B. (1983). *Anatomy of bereavement.* New York: Basic Books.

Schoenberg, B., Carr, A., Peretz, D., & Kutscher, A. (Eds.). (1972). *Psychosocial aspects of terminal care.* New York: Columbia University Press.

Shanfield, S. (1987). The prediction of outcome in bereavement. In S. Zisook (Ed.), *Biopsychosocial aspects of bereavement* (pp. 97–108). Washington, DC: American Psychiatric Association.

Shneidman, E. (1978). Some aspects of psychotherapy with dying persons. In C. Cargield (Ed.), *Psychosocial care of the dying patient* (pp. 201–226). New York: McGraw-Hill.

Simos, B. (1979). *A time to grieve.* New York: Family Service Association of America.

Smith, C. (1982). *Social work with the dying and bereaved.* London: Macmillan.

Smith, E. (1981). Dealing with dying patients. *British Medical Journal, 282*, 1778.

Wass, H., Berardo, S., & Neimeyer, R. (Eds.) (1988). *Dying facing the facts.* New York: Hemisphere Publishing.

Weisman, A. (1972). Psychosocial considerations in terminal care. In B. Schoenberg, A. Carr, D. Peretz, & A. Kutscher (Eds.), *Psychosocial aspects of terminal care* (pp. 162–182). New York: Columbia University Press.

Weisman, A. (1974). *The realization of death*. New York: Aronson.

Weisman, A. (1976). Denial and middle knowledge. In E. Shneidman (Ed.), *Death: Current perspectives* (pp. 452–468). Palo Alto, CA: Mayfield.

Weisman, A. (1979). Misgivings and misconceptions in the psychiatric care of terminal patients. In C. Garfield (Ed.). *Psychosocial care of the dying patient* (pp. 185–200). New York: McGraw-Hill.

Zelinsky, L., & Thorson, J. (1983). Educational approaches to preparing social work students for practice related to death and dying. *Death Education*, 6, 313–322.

Part III.

Preventive Interventions

13

Consultation in Crisis Situations: Behind-the-Scenes Help for the Helpers

NANCY BOYD WEBB

THE WORK OF CONSULTANTS in crisis situations deserves to be spotlighted, even though it is usually upstaged by the more active, visible, and dramatic role of direct service practitioners. Like off-stage theatrical directors who inspire actors to deliver dramatic performances, consultants in crisis situations also work behind the scenes, preparing and helping crisis workers to provide essential services to individuals, families, and communities in crisis.

Consultation is considered an *indirect* service because the consultant generally works with the service providers rather than with the recipients. The consultant only occasionally provides direct service to persons in crisis (Kadushin, 1977; Bloom, 1984; Shulman, 1987). The consultant's typical role is that of an experienced and knowledgeable expert who offers guidance, support, and information to consultees who, in turn, provide direct service to clients in need. Briar (1987) points out that the designation of consultation as "indirect practice" is somewhat confusing when conducted by social workers whose primary work is direct practice. Nonetheless, the consultant usually does not have direct contact with the client. Rather, in a "time-limited, purposeful, contractual relationship" (Rapoport, 1977), the consultant assumes the roles of catalyst, facilitator, motivator, and role model (Kadushin, 1977). When a crisis is anticipated, for example, typical repercussions following parental divorce (see chapter 15), the consultant to a school may help teachers and other staff anticipate the range of a child's probable reactions and plan helpful interventions. When a crisis is unanticipated, for example, a rape or mugging, the consultant helps the consultees deal with their own feelings about the crisis event and then focuses on predictable reactions of the victim, the family, and the community.

Consultants may work with consultees before, during, or after a crisis, depending on the consultee's perceived needs and request. Consultation *before* the crisis provides an opportunity to offer anticipatory guidance to help consultees prepare emotionally and concretely for their helping role during the expected crisis. This model is not the most frequently used model of consultation because resources often limit consultation to actual, as opposed to anticipated, need. Working with hospital social service staff members to help them deal with the anticipated deaths of hospitalized AIDS victims is an example of consultation before a crisis.

Requests for consultation as a result of crisis events usually occur shortly after or *during* the crisis. Ideally, consultants who provide crisis consultation are able to respond within twenty-four hours. An example of this type of consultation is the Good Grief Program (Fox, 1985), which offers timely services to schools and community groups following the death of a child's friend. The Good Grief Program is modeled after the Situational Crisis Service of the Center for Preventive Psychiatry, which is discussed more fully in the section on consultation to a child protective service staff.

Consultation *after* a crisis involves the debriefing of professionals who have been involved in a crisis, allowing them to ventilate their feelings about the crisis situation and to analyze retrospectively the effectiveness of their helping efforts (for example, following reported incidents of child abuse involving children enrolled in a day care center). For other examples of debriefing, see chapter 9.

Intervention with individuals, families, or communities in the midst of crisis requires *immediate* action. Providers of such crisis services must be prepared to plunge into situations as diverse as natural disasters (Birnbaum, Coplon, & Scharff, 1973; Blaufarb & Levine, 1972; Seroka, Knapp, Knight, Siemon, & Starbuck, 1986; Siporin, 1987), train crashes (Grossman, 1973), rape (Fox & Scherl, 1972), and divorce (Wiseman, 1975). Obviously, provision of crisis intervention services during crises such as those listed above may occur directly without the benefit of consultation. However, consultation to crisis workers and caregivers before, during, and after crises can make an important contribution to the morale, stamina, and effectiveness of the helpers. Although consultants are generally one step removed from the actual crisis situation, their role must not be overlooked or minimized.

Unfortunately, the literature often disregards the natural partnership between consultants and crisis workers and community caregivers. A noteworthy exception to this is the work of Karp and Karls (1966) in a community mental health program that used "the same staff members to participate in both the mental health consultation and crisis therapy aspects of the program simultaneously" (p. 542). Regrettably, neither the Rapoport (1977) nor the Shulman (1987) articles on consultation in the *Encyclopedia of Social Work* specifically addresses the use of consultation in crisis situations. Moreover, no reference is made to crisis in the indexes of either Caplan's *The Theory and Practice of Mental Health Consultation* (1970) or Kadushin's *Consultation in Social Work* (1977). The article on crisis intervention by Parad in the *Encyclopedia of Social Work* (1977) only briefly mentions consultation to caregivers and Golan's article on crisis intervention in the 1987 edition makes only one reference (Webb, 1981) to community consultation in crisis situations. Golan's *Treatment in Crisis Situations* (1978) discusses the role of the crisis worker as consultant in a scant two paragraphs.

Perhaps the profession's lack of conceptualization of the specific role and function of crisis consultation accounts for its neglect in the literature. Kadushin (1977) points out that although social work consultation has existed as long as has the profession itself, it was not identified and recognized as a specific endeavor until after World War II. Consultation in crisis situations continues to be taken for granted and underreported, clearly taking a back seat to direct services.

The present chapter redresses this oversight by offering examples of consultation services provided by social workers to individuals, agencies or organizations, and communities in crisis situations. The role of social workers as *providers* as opposed to receivers of consultation services has been recently noted (Shulman, 1987). The present chapter focuses on consultation as provided by social workers in a field that has traditionally been, and still remains, strongly interdisciplinary.

Consultation and Crisis

According to Kadushin (1977) social work consultation is

> a problem-solving process in which help, purely advisory in nature, is offered by the social work consultant to a consultee (individual, group, organization, community) faced with a job-related problem. The problem with which the social work consultant is called upon to help has a social work component. The social work consultant brings to the consultation that expertise which derives from specialized social work education and practice (p. 37).

Kadushin distinguishes social work consultation from related processes such as supervision, staff development and in-service training, and collaboration. Key differences derive from the specific focus of consultation on "circumscribed problems which can be dealt with in a limited span of time" (p. 38), the voluntary nature of the consultee–consultant relationship, the consultant's focus on actual job-related problems that have already occurred, and recognition by both consultant and consultee that the ultimate responsibility for case or program outcome rests with the consultee.

Despite these attempts to specify the nature of consultation, however, Kadushin concludes his book by concurring with Erickson (1966) that "there is no generally accepted definition of consultation and no common terminology among its practitioners" (pp. 284–285). The ambiguity in the field doubtless contributes to confusion about the expected roles and functions of consultants. For example, whereas Kadushin indicates that the consultant is generally engaged on a time-limited basis to work on a specific problem, consultation activities based in community mental health centers frequently have sought to establish ongoing, continuous consultation involvements with community agencies (Webb, 1981). Similarly, nursing homes in some states are mandated to employ consultants who meet regularly with their staff (Gutheil, 1984).

Shulman (1987) defines consultation as "an interaction between two or more people in which the consultant's special competence in a particular area is used to help the consultee with a current work problem" (p. 326).

Rapoport (1977) defines consultation as a "a professional method of problem-solving involving a time-limited, purposeful, contractual relationship between a knowledgeable expert, the consultant, and a less knowledgeable professional worker, the consultee" (p. 193). The description of the consultant as an expert with special competence who creates a relationship characterized by purposeful focus on the consultee's work, using problem-solving techniques, is common to all of these definitions.

Consultation, in general, may occur between peers or members of different disciplines; may be ongoing or *ad hoc*; may or may not be crisis-oriented; and may be client-centered (case), program-centered (administrative) (Caplan, 1970), a combination of case- and program-centered (Shulman, 1987), or individual or group/team.

Consultation that occurs between peers or members of different disciplines, may take the form of, for example, a family agency requesting consultation from a social work faculty member who is an expert on gerontology in order to help the agency staff better understand and treat elder abuse cases being referred to them. Between-peers consultation differs from between-professions consultation—for example, in the case of a police department request for guidance in dealing with family violence situations—in that the social work consultant must be able to communicate without relying on professional jargon and a shared set of professional values.

Consultation activities may be ongoing or, more typically, discontinuous and *ad hoc*. Crisis consultation usually occurs extemporaneously in response to an unanticipated crisis situation, such as following an earthquake or the death of a teacher. However, crises may occur within the context of an ongoing consultation relationship. In such instances, which are analogous to the emergence of a crisis in ongoing therapy, the consultant must be prepared to provide crisis consultation.

In a crisis, consultants generally offer indirect help, guidance, support, and information to the crisis workers or caregivers, who in turn deal directly with the clients. Occasionally, however, the crisis consultant moves into a direct-practice role, intervening directly with clients due to the urgency of the situation and the modeling/teaching opportunity that direct involvement allows. Webb (1981) describes the usefulness of such activity on the part of the crisis consultant following a neighborhood fire in which the consultant helped a day-care staff deal with their feelings, then joined the staff in meeting with the children's parents. Follow-up sessions with the consultant allowed the staff to identify and discuss the consultant's approach to the crisis, which had clearly served as a learning experience for the staff.

The most common type of consultation—*client-centered (case) consultation*—deals with problems regarding a particular client or group of clients. For example, a practitioner working with a family in which an adolescent boy has been killed might turn for advice to a professional colleague experienced in grief work. In such a case, the crisis consultant might help the worker understand and work with the grief responses of the family as well as offer the worker the opportunity to discuss his or her feelings regarding the traumatic event.

In *program-centered (administrative) consultation*, the consultant works with the administrator alone or with staff to effect changes in a delivery system or a program. An example of this type of consultation is work with a juvenile fire-prevention program to help staff communicate more effectively with children and family members when a juvenile is implicated in a fire.

Shulman (1987) refers to consultation that combines case and program consultation. It is the author's experience that much consultation combines the two forms, as was the case in the day-care example cited above, in which the consultant met regularly with the director to discuss both programmatic matters and concerns related to the management of individual children.

Although consultation is usually provided by a single consultant, in large-scale crises such as a natural disaster, a team of consultants may work together. The team approach offers mutual support among team members.

The following general principles guide consultation practice (Kadushin, 1977; Caplan, 1970; Webb, 1981):

1. The *primary objective* of consultation is to provide more effective service to agency clients.

2. A *secondary objective* relates to the professional development of the worker. "As a consequence of having learned how to deal with some specific problem with the help of the consultant, the consultee is subsequently better prepared to deal with similar problems" (Kadushin, 1977, p. 26). Thus, consultation serves future as well as present needs.

3. The consultant has no administrative authority over the consultee, who is free to use or reject the consultant's advice (Caplan, 1970, p. 28).

4. The consultant must have specialized expertise in the area under discussion.

5. The effects of consultation extend beyond the immediate nucleus of consultees to include the clients of the consultees and populations in the community who profit tangentially from the consultant's interventions. This phenomenon has been referred to as the "ripple effect" (Webb, 1981; Golan, 1987).

6. Consultation activities serve as opportunities for prevention at the primary, secondary, and tertiary levels. Crisis consultation is particularly effective at the primary and secondary levels due to its being an immediate response to problems.

Crisis Consultation

The following definition identifies and describes the role and function of consultants in crisis situations based upon the author's knowledge of such activities and practice experience in providing crisis consultation:

> Crisis consultation is a focused method of providing job-related help to caregivers in a crisis situation in which an expert consultant who is knowledgeable about crisis intervention responds rapidly to the consultee's request for guidance in the provision of services to individuals, families, agencies, and/or communities in crisis. The role and function of the crisis consultant is similar to that of other consultants, except that a rapid response (usually within twenty-four hours), a specific focus on crisis intervention techniques, and knowledge about behavior of people in crisis are expected.

The following case examples illustrate consultation in its various forms:

Individual Consultation

A recent MSW graduate contacted her former crisis intervention professor, requesting consultation regarding a case involving the death of a sixteen-year-old youth in a car accident. The consultee (worker) had been working with the parents and four siblings in family therapy since the death; after five sessions, she was concerned that the father seemed ready to terminate. The consultee did not have access to consultation through her agency and felt sufficiently concerned about the progress of this case to request private consultation. An appointment was made. The consultant asked the worker to bring a genogram of the family and a psychosocial summary of the case to their meeting. (In retrospect, it would have been more beneficial if the worker had prepared a list of questions about the case to serve as the focus for the consultation.)

Based on the information obtained in the telephone conversation with the worker, the consultant made the following notes:

> ● What is the real reason behind this request for consultation at this time? The consultee has a solid knowledge base concerning the stages of grief and, in fact, had spontaneously mentioned the family's grief work. The consultee did not call after the first or second session, but after the fifth session, so it seems unlikely that anxiety related to the traumatic death is the source of her concern. Perhaps the father's "pulling away" from therapy is threatening.
>
> Note: In crisis intervention, we must understand the meaning of the crisis event to the client. Similarly, in crisis consultation, the consultant must understand the meaning behind the consultee's request for consultation.
>
> ● The number of people (two parents and four siblings, age range eleven to twenty years) involved make this case complex. The consultee expressed some misgivings when asked to prepare the outline, stating, "I don't know how much I can give you." The consultee conveyed a sense of being overwhelmed; she was carrying thirty-five to forty cases, with infrequent supervision.
>
> Note: Does the consultee's discouragement with this case reflect a general discouragement with her job? Is part of her unstated, perhaps unrecognized, agenda a plea for help in managing her work load?

The consultation lasted fifty minutes, focusing primarily on the consultee's management of the case and her fear that if the father "pulled out" she would lose the case. Losing the case represented a personal failure to the worker. "This family needs so much help and I really want to work with them!" An additional concern was that her professional competence was on the line due to the notoriety of the case; the consultee felt that her performance would be criticized by agency staff if the family withdrew. When the consultee provided this information, the consultant understood the reason for her request for private consultation.

The consultant and consultee reviewed the grief work of each family member, which appeared adequate although clearly individualized in nature. The father, a private, self-contained person, was uncomfortable with the more open expressions of grief of his wife and some of his children. Nonetheless, he had written several letters to his dead son that the family read. He seemed to be coping fairly well.

The consultant suggested that perhaps the worker should see subgroups of the family or individuals, instead of always working with the family as a unit. The parents, in particular, might benefit from father's ventilation of anger toward the dead son, which he seemed reluctant to express in front of the other children. Also, a sibling was having problems academically and socially and needed individual attention. The consultee began to reconsider how restructuring contacts with various family members might meet their individual needs.

The consultant and consultee reviewed the gains that had been made in the case so far. As these gains were identified, the consultant noticed visible relief in the consultee. Although the consultee had planned to work with the family as a unit for twelve weeks, the idea of renegotiating with family members around individual needs seemed like a logical and reassuring course of action at the present time.

With respect to the consultee's work load, the consultant suggested the possible need for the consultee to renegotiate her case load with her administrator. The consultant's recognition of the consultee's basic abilities served to support and validate the consultee's work. The consultee left the meeting with an optimistic attitude regarding her work with this family and her other cases.

In this instance, consultation closely paralleled supervision, except that the consultant was further removed from the consultee's work-related concerns than a supervisor would be. Furthermore, the consultee was free to accept or reject the consultant's suggestions. The role of the consultant as an acknowledged "expert" who had previous knowledge of the consultee as an "A" student enhanced the consultant's ability to support and mobilize this consultee.

Group Consultation

The Situational Crisis Intervention Program of the Center for Preventive Psychiatry (CPP) in White Plains, New York, provides both direct and indirect consultation services to individuals, agencies, and schools during crises such as bereavement, suicide, homicide, physical and sexual abuse, separation and divorce, and illness and hospitalization (Kliman, 1978). The center has a national reputation and is highly regarded in Westchester County for its broad array of programs aimed at the early identification and treatment of emotional problems. When allegations of sexual abuse were made against a day-care center in Mount Vernon, New York, the director of the Child Protective Service (CPS), whose staff was investigating the charges, sought consultation from the Situational Crisis Intervention Program of CPP. The following discussion of this crisis consultation is based on interviews with the director of the Situational Crisis Program and the director of CPS.

According to an article in the *New York Times* ("Woman Is Acquitted," 1987), eighteen children in a day-care center in Mount Vernon, New York, testified that in 1986 they had been victims of or witnesses to sexual attacks in the center. They were five to nine years old when the abuse allegedly occurred. Several employees, including the director of the center, were alleged to have been involved in some aspect of the abuse, for which two employees were subsequently convicted and imprisoned.

The reactions of the community to child sexual abuse is typically intense. In the Mount Vernon situation, denial that the abuses occurred was prevalent, due to the reputation of the day-care center director, a mature woman known as a "respected church-goer." Denial, however, is common in most situations of child sexual abuse because the sexual victimization of young children offends and horrifies most people's sensibilities (see chapter 4). Unlike natural disasters, accidents, or terminal illness, crises involving the sexual abuse of children involve a deliberate human act that stimulates profound feelings of outrage.

Such reactions are not only true of the community at large but also for professional workers whose task is to investigate allegations. Moreover, the inevitable legal proceedings subject practitioners' work to the scrutiny of defense lawyers who seek to disprove or discredit their findings. Thus, workers involved in such cases experience internal pressures due to the emotional conflicts stirred up by the case as well as external pressure associated with exposure of their work to the public.

The literature has slowly recognized the impact of stress on rescue workers in disaster situations (Raphael, 1983–84; Mantell & Huntting, 1987). Raphael asks "who helps the helpers?"—and argues for a social policy that mandates debriefing sessions to assist workers in recognizing and assimilating their experiences of danger and stress connected with their work in traumatic situations (see chapter 9). Work with children, families, and day-care staff amid allegations of child sexual abuse certainly causes high stress in the investigators. These workers need a support system that allows them to ventilate their feelings and ask questions about the aftereffects of the experience on the children. This discussion must occur in a safe environment where confidentiality is maintained.

In the Mount Vernon case, the director of CPS realized after one week that her staff was being overwhelmed by their findings, which included rape, sodomy, and other forms of sexual abuse involving numerous children. A crisis consultation was arranged with the director of the Situational Crisis Program of CPP, the thirteen CPS workers who were directly involved with the investigations, their two supervisors, and the director of CPS. The purpose of the consultation was (1) to allow CPS workers the opportunity to ventilate and share their feelings about the child-abuse revelations so that they could proceed more effectively with their work and (2) to formulate and implement a plan for working with the parents of the children, who, early in the investigation, either denied that the abuse had occurred or were consumed with rage and a desire for vengeance. Because the workers were obliged to interview all the children who had been enrolled in the center during the previous three years, they needed the cooperation of the parents.

The crisis intervention consultant understood the importance of helping the parents help their children in this crisis situation. Clearly, consultation had to take a strong preventive stance. The workers needed to deal with their own denial and rage before they could help the parents deal with their reactions. The parents needed to control their rage sufficiently if they were to provide comfort and support to their children throughout the investigation and trial.

The crisis consultant from CPP agreed to lead a parents' meeting during which a plan for ongoing weekly meetings was formulated. These meetings, which continued for a year, provided an arena in which parents could ventilate their feelings and find emotional support. Thus, in this situation, the crisis consultant moved into a direct-practice role in her work with the parents. She later described her role as being very difficult because of the intensity and range of feelings among some parents, whose own personality problems compounded their difficulty in coping with the crisis.

Consultation with the CPS staff continued on a weekly basis for several months. It was especially beneficial during the early phase of the investigation, during which 104 children were interviewed in a four-month period. Evidence of abuse was found in forty-eight children, although only eighteen children testified in court. The workers felt overwhelmed by the scope of the crisis, which included the need to locate suitable treatment resources for the children and the families. The Center for Preventive Psychiatry provided direct crisis services to many of the children and families, as did three other mental health agencies in the county.

Most of the consultation occurred during the initial six-month period of the investigations. The staff's need for ongoing support lessened with time, and they returned to their precrisis level of functioning. The parent groups did not need professional leadership beyond the initial seven-month period. During the trial, which lasted several months, the parents met irregularly and informally. The consultants offered to meet again with the parents at the time of the sentencing, but the parents declined.

When the consultants conducted follow-up sessions with CPS staff (who had been involved with the early stages of the investigation), they learned that some CPS workers believed that the parents were angry with them because they felt the sentences were too lenient. This may have been the reason for the parents' unwillingness to meet with the consultants following the sentencing. It was helpful for CPS workers to share these reactions with the CPP consultants.

The aftereffects of a crisis such as this linger in a community for a long time. In this situation, it was fortunate that the crisis consultation agency was nearby and available for future collaboration on an "as needed" basis. When a crisis team outside the community is used, follow-up might not be as feasible. One disadvantage in using a local crisis consultant team, however, is that the team members may feel the stress of the crisis more personally because they are part of the community. In this instance, a mandated, ongoing, weekly group-support meeting has been an integral part of the crisis program of CPP since its inception in 1965. Thus the helpers who help other helpers are also able to tend to their own needs.

Consultation to Adults in Schools and Community Settings

When faced with the sudden death of a student, colleague, or student's parent, teachers may be uncertain whether they should discuss the death with the children in their classrooms and, if so, how they should approach this task. Teachers are often afraid that such a discussion will upset the children and that they are ill-prepared to deal with the children's inevitable questions. A survey of teachers (Henney & Barnhart, 1980) reported that 92 percent of teachers had not received preparation for helping children deal with death and dying (see chapter 12).

The Good Grief Program, founded in Boston in 1983 by Sandra Fox Sutherland under the auspices of the Judge Baker Guidance Center and the Junior League, helps teachers and other adults help children cope with death. Through a multifaceted program that includes crisis intervention, in-service training, community education, resource materials, and consultation, the program targets the adults whom the bereaved children know and trust. The goal of the program is to improve the ability of the adults to help bereaved children with their questions, concerns, and feelings so that grief work is accomplished and future emotional problems are averted.

The preventive philosophy of the program flows from Fox's (1985) belief that death can cause emotional and behavioral disturbances in survivors both at the time of the death and in the future. Children are especially vulnerable, according to Fox, because few adults are prepared to help children grieve and to deal directly with the subject of death.

The Good Grief Program provides immediate response to schools or community groups who call for assistance. Help often consists of a single consultation meeting with the concerned personnel (consultees) as soon as possible after the death. During this meeting, the crisis consultant, in the role of expert on bereaved children's reactions and behavior, answers questions of consultees and helps them prepare to talk about the death with the children. The crisis consultant provides the consultees with specific guidelines for helping the children and offers to remain in telephone contact with the consultees, depending on their needs and desires. Typically, the consultant will make a follow-up telephone call one month after the consultation. In the Good Grief Program, consultation is carried out so as not to create dependence on the part of the consultees. Its goal is to help the consultee discover and draw upon his or her own strengths. The consultation services of the Good Grief Program have been extended to include camps, scouts, community centers—any program in which a child may encounter an experience with death.

Consultation with a Host Organization

The author was asked to give a one-day training session to a group of twelve fire marshals who were involved in a pilot program to intervene with juvenile fire setters. Their work brought them into contact with families whose child was involved with a fire. The fire marshal's task was to conduct a structured interview with the child and family and to make referrals to mental health agencies if appropriate. The program had been operating for about six months, and the marshals had received extensive training at the beginning of the program on topics such as the dysfunctional family, communication and interviewing skills, and the juvenile justice system. The ultimate objective of the program was to reduce the number of fires set by juveniles through referrals to a network of concerned agencies, coordinated by a cadre of fire marshals and administrative staff. A clinical social worker was also involved with the program, initially to assist the fire marshals in family intervention techniques and later to work on the evaluation report.

At the time of the consultation/training session, the first phase of the program was ending; a request for extension and refunding had been submitted. The fire marshals had investigated a total of seventy-two juvenile firesetting incidents during the previous six months; therefore, they had clear ideas about the areas in which they wanted further training and help. These areas related to (1) the extensive twelve-page family interview evaluation form and data sheet they had been using to collect statistical data and referral information and (2) skill development with regard to interviewing young children. The author's area of expertise was in interviewing young children. Another consultant was hired to focus specifically on the interview questionnaire.

Entering an unfamiliar organizational system and working with a group of professionals whose background and training are drastically different from one's own present special challenges to a consultant. Kadushin's (1977) breakdown of the consultation process into the phases of preparing and beginning, working through, and terminating is useful for analysis of the process of consultation in this situation.

Preparation. The request for consultation was issued three weeks prior to the consultation. Although this lead time does not conform to the usual pattern of immediate response in crisis consultation, circumstances in this instance required sufficient time to schedule meetings with a group of consultees who were not themselves experiencing a crisis. Rather, the consultation was to address ongoing, serial crises, with which the consultees cope routinely in their daily work. Just as a surgeon cannot cringe at the sight of blood, a fire fighter must not panic at the sight of an apartment house in flames. In fact, these consultees tended to minimize the crisis impact of fires on the multiproblem families in their district. The incidence of fires in this community occurred with sufficient frequency that their shock value, in the opinion of the fire marshals, was reduced. Not having the firsthand experience of the consultees, the author nonetheless believed that the considerable losses and disruptions that occur in the aftermath of fires must inevitably upset family and community equilibrium and thus should be considered a crisis. The importance of not minimizing the impact of urban fires on community residents has been pointed out by Krim (1976).

After the initial request, the consultant reflected on the subject area. Although she had considerable expertise in working with children and families, her experience with juvenile firesetting was limited to two cases in which this symptom was combined with other acting-out behaviors. The consultant also considered how she might translate her expertise into terms that would be useful to the fire marshals. She wondered what their feelings toward social workers would be and how the social worker in their program would feel about the presence of an outsider.

To prepare for the consultation, the author reviewed juvenile books on fire at the local library, selecting two books to take to the consultation. She also did a search of the professional literature on juvenile firesetters, selecting the most recent to take to the consultation.

The consultant requested copies of the interview currently being used by the fire marshals, as well as reports and other information about the program. In retrospect, the consultant felt that it would have been useful to obtain the names of the fire marshals and their supervisors in advance as well as an administrative chart showing the placement of this program within the organization. This would have facilitated the engagement process during introductions and helped the consultant understand who held decision-making power. Such knowledge would be useful in making future follow-up contacts. After determining the name of the social worker, the consultant called the worker to solicit her suggestions regarding how the consultant could be helpful to the program. This effort helped establish an alliance with the worker on a peer basis prior to the consultation.

The consultant discussed the upcoming consultation with two colleagues in an effort to clarify her own thoughts and feelings on the subject. The consultant became intrigued with the notion of prevention work with preschool children who have little impulse control, concluding that parents should be the target of intervention when the firesetter was younger than seven years of age. The consultant collected vignettes and other data that supported this view to take to the consultation.

Consultation. The consultant arranged the seats in a circle. After the group assembled, the coordinator introduced herself, describing her experience in working with children in crisis. She acknowledged the fire marshals' expertise with regard to firesetters and indicated that she was eager to hear their descriptions of the program after having read the informational materials. She also asked the fire marshals what they hoped to gain from the day's consultation.

The natural leaders of the group did most of the talking, and the consultant had to solicit responses from the quieter members of the group. In retrospect, the consultant felt it would have been beneficial to have each fire marshal introduce himself and to describe his particular area of interest.

The consultant asked how many fire marshals were fathers (they all raised their hands) and further asked about the nature of their involvement in the program. They indicated that they had been selected for the program from a large pool of applicants. They discussed their concerns about onging support for the program and its continuation. The consultant sensed a strong sense of bonding within the group and affirmed their cohesiveness by saying, "You are really a very select group." This statement helped establish a relationship between the consultant and the fire marshals based on mutual appreciation and respect.

The consultant took notes as various fire marshals identified their main areas of concern in interviewing young children and their families. The consultant did not respond to these concerns as they were mentioned, but indicated that she would try to do so during the course of the day.

Based on preliminary information obtained during the planning telephone contacts (which was confirmed by the consultees in their discussion of concerns), the consultant had prepared to talk with the fire marshals about characteristics of child development and its implications for fire setting. For example, preschoolers may distort causality and thus be unable to connect a lighted match with the conflagration that follows.

The consultant explained the normal developmental characteristics of the early, middle, and late latency-age stages as well as selected techniques for communicating with children of different ages (puppets, art, stories). The consultant engaged the group in puppet role play and storytelling in a manner that could be replicated by the fire marshals in their interviews with children.

The consultant encouraged the fire marshals to interrupt with questions, comments, and their own examples. The fire marshals contributed freely, using their own examples to illustrate the consultant's points.

During the lunch break, the social worker informally told the consultant that the fire marshals were very pleased with the morning session. The consultant was relieved to hear this because she had wondered whether the material she was presenting was relevant to the consultees' experiences. After the lunch break, the consultant made an effort to obtain feedback from the consultees regarding the consultation. This type of "recontracting" is essential at some point during the middle phase of the consultation so that minor or major concerns and less vocal members of the group are not overlooked.

Out of this effort to obtain feedback, some difficult and challenging issues emerged. Discussions focused on the older juvenile who "cons" and manipulates social agencies after referral, and how to handle the possibility of family punishment of the child who confesses fire-setting behavior to the fire marshal.

Toward the end of the consultation, the consultant was asked how she would treat a child and family referred to her. This question pointed at the need of the consultees for follow-up information from referral agencies. Agencies were not providing this information because of their policies concerning client confidentiality. The consultant affirmed the need for improved and ongoing collaboration with the social agency network and encouraged the fire marshals to request more follow-up information.

During the final hour of the day, the consultant summarized their work and identified areas of ongoing concern. She expressed interest in meeting again with the consultees in order to hear about the effectiveness of the play-therapy techniques. She left business cards and suggested that individual consultees contact her if they so desired.

Follow-up. The consultant sent a follow-up letter to the program coordinator reiterating her interest in follow-up consultation and suggesting specific areas in which further work might be helpful. Several days after the consultation, the consultant took notes on the content of this experience and on her assessment of achievements and areas for future work. This review process, which assesses the performances of both the consultant and the consultees, serves as a helpful guide in the event future work with the same consultee system is undertaken.

One-year follow-up. Lack of funding prevented ongoing consultation in the manner suggested by the consultant. However, collaboration occurred in a different manner through the co-authorship of a professional paper and a panel presentation at the annual program meeting of the American Orthopsychiatric Association in 1989 (Webb, Sakheim, Towns-Miranda, & Wagner, in press).

Case and Program Consultation

During a sabbatical in Australia, the author was engaged as a consultant by the social work department of a large general hospital. In the course of two consultation meetings, five cases were presented to the consultant that dealt with issues concerning patients' relatives and patients who were terminally ill or deceased.

Approximately twelve of the sixteen social work professionals on the hospital staff attended the two meetings. Three cases exemplified the need to engage family members and the dying patient in plans for the care of their young children or dependent family members. The consultant's role was to help staff with their clinical skills, especially in the area of bereavement.

In retrospect, the consultant felt the staff members were more skilled in helping patients and families with practical issues than they were in helping them deal with their feelings about the terminal illness. This impression became significant in the fifth case presented for consultation, which involved a conflict regarding the role and function of a social worker on the interdisciplinary hospital team.

The social worker presented a case involving a married couple in their thirties who were separated when the husband was hospitalized with a diagnosis of bowel and liver cancer. The wife conferred with the social worker and decided, after discussing her marital problems, to reunite with her husband and nurse him during the short time he was expected to live. The social worker arranged hospice nursing care to assist the wife, and the patient was discharged.

The medical social worker wanted help in dealing with her dismay and anger at the nursing staff for not notifying her when the patient was readmitted to the hospital several months later. The consultee learned by accident that the patient had been readmitted. When she arrived at the patient's room, the patient's wife and the hospital chaplain (whom the nurses had notified) were sitting at the patient's bedside. The wife spoke quietly to the social worker indicating that her husband was dying and that she would prefer to be left alone with him. The social worker suggested to the chaplain that they leave the couple alone, but he refused, stating that his role was to help the dying and their relatives. The chaplain then tried to engage the wife in planning where she would stay that night, because the hospital was some distance from her home.

The consultant and staff acknowledged the chaplain's apparent insensitivity, and sympathized with the worker about the nurses' disregard of the worker's wish to be notified when the patient was readmitted to the hospital. At this point, the focus of the consultation shifted from the specific case to the issues raised by the case, namely, the role and function of the social work staff in the hospital. The consultant suggested that the staff consider whether the problems illustrated by this case were unique or typical. Several staff members gave examples of similar conflicts with nurses and clergy; the group consensus seemed to be that other professionals neither understood nor appreciated the role of social workers with dying patients and their family (see chapter 12). When the consultant asked the worker how she thought this case should have been handled, the worker stated that because she had a previously established relationship with the wife, she should have been the designated staff person contacted upon readmission. The chaplain had never met the family before.

It soon became apparent that no prescribed procedure existed for staff notification when a patient was dying. Matters were left to the judgment of the nurse in charge. The consultant helped the social work director identify a hospital committee that could address this matter. Clearly, fighting for turf over a death bed was not appropriate. However, the issue of having "too many helpers" merited careful administrative attention.

The consultant encouraged the staff to work together to clarify for themselves what they considered to be the ideal role and function of the social worker in situations involving the terminally ill. She reviewed several of the cases presented, commenting that the expertise of the social workers in helping with referrals and plans for children and other family members had been clearly demonstrated. Less evident were instances wherein workers had helped family members with their anticipatory and actual grief processes. The consultant noted that because they saw this as an appropriate function, the workers must find a way to highlight it through chart notes, treatment summaries, statements about their goals in each case, and case reviews. The consultant indicated that the workers would feel more confident in conveying their role and function to staff of other disciplines after they had achieved consensus among themselves. She also advocated the building of informal relationships with other staff by inviting professionals from other disciplines to lunch with social work staff and to case conferences. The various disciplines were too competitive and needed to understand and appreciate their respective contributions. Finally, the consultant indicated that service to the patient and family should guide decisions regarding role allocations.

In this example, the consultation utilized case consultations to deal with program issues. Shulman (1987) refers to the blending of individual and program issues as an "integrated approach" to consultation. Although the first consultation session had focused on the development of clinical skills in the area of bereavement (in accordance with the initial request of the director), it became evident during the second consultation session that systemic constraints were working against the successful implementation of these skills. Thus, the consultation needed to refocus on the more basic, underlying issues. This example also demonstrates the value of a two-session consultation in order to develop a trusting relationship in which consultees can reveal internal obstacles and conflicts.

Consultation to a Community

A social worker participated in a six-member crisis team that was formed after the mass shooting of post office employees in Edmond, Oklahoma, on August 20, 1986. At the request of the Oklahoma attorney general, the National Organization for Victim Assistance (NOVA) assembled a team led by a psychologist from the San Diego Police Department. The social worker on the team was a consultant for NOVA and had been herself the victim of a shooting five years earlier. The account that follows is based on an article in *NASW News* ("Aftermath of a Massacre," 1986), telephone interviews with the social worker and NOVA staff, and on written reports by NOVA (1987) and the team leader, Michael R. Mantell (Mantell & Huntting, 1987).

In this community tragedy, twenty people were shot, fourteen people died, the perpetrator committed suicide, and fifty other individuals hid, played dead, or fled the scene. According to NOVA's working paper (1987),

> This act of wanton terrorism caused more than medical injuries and death. It also left hundreds of other postal employees and their loved ones in a state of emotional trauma, as were a great many others in that community of 60,000 (p. 1).

The crisis consultation team of experts from outside the community had a clear mission "to work with the leaders and caregivers of Edmond to help them mobilize an effective response to the concentric circles of individuals directly and indirectly victimized by the shootings" (NOVA, 1987, p. 2). The team included two victim advocates (one of whom was the social worker), two NOVA staff members, a minister, and a master's-level crisis counselor. The team members came from different parts of the county and, with the exception of the NOVA staff members, did not know one another.

The primary objective of the team was to offer support, guidance, and direction to the caretakers. Mantell and Huntting (1987) defined the goals of crisis response teams more specifically: "to help victims deal with the symptoms they experience, to minimize the emotional pain they feel, to prevent the 'secondary injury' they may be subject to, and to help restore a sense of power and control" (p. 2).

This episode was the first known instance of an outside crisis consultation team used to help a community cope with a horrifying crime. The team members were in Edmond only two and one-half days; some members of the team left after one day. Their work included initial planning meetings, the actual interventions, and a follow-up by two team members five weeks after the consultation.

The team arrived in Edmond approximately thirty hours after the shootings. Although the community had already mobilized itself and had had previous experience working with disaster situations, the local leaders did not feel confident about the appropriate response to this violent tragedy (Mantell & Hunting, 1987). Quoting NOVA, a national publication for Chamber of Commerce professionals, the *Chamber Executive* ("Problem Solvers," 1987), states that

> even if the affected community already has a skilled team of caregivers in place, experienced "outsiders" can be of enormous support [because] the caregivers themselves are in crisis. . . . Part of [the job of the crisis team] is propping up and reminding the caregivers that they are doing a good job (p. 8).

An important factor in the success of crisis consultation is the leader's ability to coordinate efforts with local leadership and to delegate responsibilities and tasks among his or her own team. This task was accomplished through a planning meeting held with the team and local officials at the airport immediately upon the team's arrival in Edmond. The purpose of this meeting was to confer with the local community leaders, who had already scheduled several meetings with community groups for the consultation team.

Three target groups were identified as needing service (Mantell & Hunting, 1987):

1. The ninety employees who survived the attack, their families, and the families of persons who had been shot
2. The public safety personnel, who responded to the crisis situation (police, emergency medical personnel, hospital staff, coroners, FBI, and the U.S. Postal Service management)
3. The community of Edmond

Individually and in pairs, team members were assigned to work with various target groups, according to the members' qualifications, experience, and areas of expertise. The social worker, for example, attended a ninety-minute debriefing meeting for more than ninety Postal Service personnel and their families. Three members of the local community mental health center were present to assist as needed and to clarify the role of the center. The notion that the mental health center could be used as a resource for persons who were *not* suffering from a mental illness was unfamiliar to this community and had to be emphasized in other meetings with police and government officials.

One of the major responsibilities of the social worker was to meet with the staff of the mental health center to assist them in working with the families of the murdered victims. These meetings were videotaped for staff who could not attend. The worker encouraged the staff to voice their questions and concerns. Many staff members had experience in working with people in grief and in crisis, but had little or no experience in dealing with victims of violent crime. Thus, the consultation meeting, in which the consultees were psychologists, nurses, and social workers, was educational. In fact, the team referred to these meetings as "training sessions" for service-provider groups.

Eckert (1986) summarized the work of the consultation team:

> By late afternoon of the second day following the shootings, in-service training sessions had been conducted for local counselors and mental health professionals, consultation had been provided to the staff of local hospitals tending to the injured; the community mental health center staff had provided crisis care to over a dozen of the families and victims involved in the trauma; and pastoral counseling was available around the clock (p. 5).

In responding to a community crisis such as this, several principles guide the activities of the crisis consultation team.

1. Mental health services should assume a preventive role in helping individuals deal with the high stress associated with a sensational crime. Use of mental health services at the time of crisis situations does not signify the presence of pathology because crisis is defined as "an upset of a steady state" (Rapoport, 1977). Individuals in the throes of crisis may indeed feel "crazy," disoriented, and unable to fully comprehend their experience, but these reactions are considered normal under the circumstances. Typically, individuals revert to their steady state (normalcy) in time. Part of the intervention consists of providing education, support, and reassurance to crisis victims regarding their typical reactions.

2. Because the impact of a sensational crime reverberates throughout the community, the local caregivers probably experience crisis themselves and are therefore less able to perform their usual functions. Thus, an independent team of outside consultants who can guide, support, and validate the local caregivers is helpful.

3. The meaning of a crisis must be understood in specific, individual terms. Sudden, violent death complicates normal grieving and typically leads to a more prolonged recovery process ("Problem Solvers," 1987). The crisis consultation team should educate local caregivers about this complicated grieving process.

4. The crisis consultation team works indirectly to "empower those who will remain as permanent caregivers in the community" (Eckert, 1986, p. 3). The team in Edmond was commended for providing guidance and support in the background while not seeking or taking a central role. The local caregivers must assume responsibility for the ongoing needs of their community; the role of the crisis consultant is to restore the local service providers to their helping roles as quickly as possible.

5. The crisis consultation team must provide service as soon as possible following a crisis. Because the community in crisis is generally open to receiving help, crisis consultants generally work for a short, intensive period, then leave the area. The team remains in telephone contact with local caregivers and ideally returns for a follow-up debriefing several weeks after the crisis.

Evaluation of Consultation

Assessing the effectiveness of mental health consultation is a formidable task because of the "exceedingly complex research problems which make it so difficult to document its validity as a practice method" (Mannino, 1981, pp. 153–154). Bloom (1984) states that given the complexities of the consultation process, it is understandable that only a few well-controlled studies evaluating either consultee or client outcomes have been reported.

How do we judge the success of a consultation? Does it depend on changed behavior on the part of the consultees' clients? Or is it more appropriate to expect changed attitudes on the part of the consultees? Or perhaps the establishment of a new program in response to the consultant's identification of unmet needs demonstrates that the consultation was effective.

Clearly, the purpose and focus of the consultation dictate the target for evaluation. However, the indirect nature of consultation and its vague, but perceivable, "ripple effects" complicate the assessment process. As Bloom (1984) points out, if it is difficult to demonstrate the effectiveness of individual psychotherapy, it is even more difficult to demonstrate the effectiveness of a consultant working with a consultee on behalf of third parties. Indeed, Caplan (1970) expressed considerable reservations about the prospects for future exploratory studies to improve evaluation research methodology because funding practices favor proposals likely to achieve demonstrable results. Specific outcomes cannot yet be predicted for consultation.

In crisis situations, outcomes depend on many variables that are difficult, if not impossible, to identify, measure, and control. Data rarely exist on the precrisis state of consultees or their clients; the need to provide effective and immediate services equitably to clients usually precludes setting up matched control groups for comparison purposes.

In the author's opinion, evaluation of consultation is an appropriate focus for qualitative as opposed to quantitative research. Qualitative research is useful in exploratory studies that seek to derive hypotheses that can later be tested with the help of quantitative techniques. For example, Bloom (1984) recognizes the influence of the personality traits of the consultant on the process and outcome of consultation, although no research has been done on how personality factors interact with professional skill in producing an effective consultation. Qualitative research that provides an in-depth examination of the interacting influence of these sets of factors could generate valuable hypotheses regarding the relevance and the balance of these variables.

Recent evaluation studies report positive perceptions in approximately 60 percent of consultees and 40 percent of clients as a result of mental health consultations (Bloom, 1984). Thus the perceived usefulness of consultation has been substantiated, despite the problems inherent in precisely documenting its positive effects on consultees' clients. Mannino (1981) concludes that mental health consultation

> continues to be one of the most useful approaches to community mental health practice. Its relevance covers each of the levels of public health prevention, i.e., primary, secondary, and tertiary,* and extends even further to the promotion of mentally healthy environments and communities. . . . If we are to advance the field, it is crucial that [research] efforts continue (pp. 153–154).

*Editor's note: Primary prevention seeks to avoid dysfunctional behavior in at-risk populations through consultation and educational guidance aimed at strengthening their understanding and ability to cope with stress. Secondary prevention, illustrated in Part II of this volume, includes "casefinding" and offering prompt treatment during the incipient signs of crisis response. Tertiary prevention aims to limit the spread of disability in already treated clients with severe or chronic problems. In primary prevention, our hope is to reduce the incidence of psychological disorder by reducing the number of new cases in a given population. Obviously, the more we focus our professional energies on primary prevention, the less the need for secondary and costly tertiary endeavors.

Summary

The six practice examples in this chapter, although diverse, do not encompass the broad scope of crisis consultation activities. Wherever individuals, groups, and communities are in crisis, crisis consultation can be used to help the helpers perform their duties more effectively.

The examples in this chapter depict the consultant working behind the scenes, enhancing the abilities of the designated caregivers as opposed to taking over direct-service functions. The guiding philosophy of crisis consultation is to respect the consultees' abilities and talents; crisis consultants work to restore the abilities of consultees to their precrisis level of functioning. The caregivers' inability to perform is often tied to their need to recognize and deal with their own feelings in the face of the crisis event. The crisis consultant, who typically is from outside the system in crisis, provides objectivity, information, and support in an effort to restore local caregivers to their appropriate roles.

Although crisis consultation focuses on the crises of the present moment, the future effectiveness of consultees is also enhanced through consultation. Consultation empowers and strengthens consultees, thus preventing dysfunction in the future. Depending on the situation, the crisis consultant may remain in contact with the consultees to ensure their ongoing progress. When it is possible, the consultant arranges for a follow-up to learn details about the outcome of the crisis.

The consultant's response to a crisis must be immediate. If the response is timely, a crisis situation may be turned into a positive growth experience for the helpers, clients, and community.

References

Aftermath of a massacre. (1986 October). *NASW News*, pp. 1–8.

Birnbaum, F., Coplon, J., & Scharff, I. (1973). Crisis intervention after a natural disaster. *Social Casework, 54*, 545–551.

Blaufarb, H., & Levine, J. (1972). Crisis intervention in an earthquake. *Social Work, 17*, 16–19.

Bloom, B. L. (1984). *Community mental health: A general introduction*, Monterey, CA: Brooks/Cole Publishing.

Briar, S. (1987). Direct practice: Trends and issues. In A. Minahan (Ed.), *Encyclopedia of Social Work* (18th ed., pp. 393–398). Washington, DC: National Association of Social Workers.

Caplan, G. (1970). *The theory and practice of mental health consultation*. New York: Basic Books.

Eckert, d.' A. C. (1986). *Community mental health in Oklahoma responds to August tragedy*. Oklahoma City, OK: Oklahoma Department of Mental Health.

Erickson, M. H. (1966). *Consultation practice in community mental health services*. Unpublished D.S.W. dissertation. Los Angeles, CA: University of Southern California.

Fire Department, City of New York (1987). *Juvenile firesetters intervention program: First annual report*. New York: Bureau of Fire Investigations.

Fox, S. S. (1985). *Good grief: Helping groups of children when a friend dies*. Boston: New England Association for the Education of Young Children.

Fox, S. S., & Scherl, D. J. (1972). Crisis intervention with victims of rape. *Social Work, 17*, 37–42.

Golan, N. (1987). Crisis intervention. In A. Minahan (Ed.), *Encyclopedia of Social Work* (18th ed.) (pp. 360–372). Washington, DC: National Association of Social Workers.

Golan, N. (1978). *Treatment in crisis situations*. New York: Free Press.

Grossman, L. (1973). Train crash: Social work and disaster services. *Social Work, 18*, 38–44.

Gutheil, I. (1984). The problem of resistance in nursing home consultation. *Social Casework, 65*, 40–44.

Henney, M., & Barnhart, R. S. (1980). Death education: Do we need it? *Psychological Reports, 43*, 996–998.

Kadushin, A. (1977). *Consultation in social work*. New York: Columbia University Press.

Karp, N., & Karls, J. (1966). Combining crisis therapy and mental health consultation. *Archives of General Psychiatry, 14*, 536–542.

Kliman, A. S. (1978). *Crisis: Psychological first aid for recovery and growth*. New York: Holt, Rinehart, and Winston.

Krim, A. (1976). Urban disaster: Victims of fire. In H. Parad et al. (Eds.), *Emergency and disaster management* (pp. 337–352). Bowie, MD: Charles Press.

Mannino, F. U. (1981). Empirical perspectives in mental health consultation. *Journal of Prevention, 1*, 147–155.

Mantell, M. R., & Huntting, K. D. (1987). The crisis response team reports on Edmond, Oklahoma, massacre. *NOVA Newsletter, 11* (1), 1–6.

NOVA (1987). *Toward the development of regional "crisis response teams": A working paper of the National Organization for Victim Assistance*. Washington, DC: Author.

Parad, H. J. (1977). Crisis intervention. In J. Turner (Ed.), *Encyclopedia of Social Work* (17th ed.) (pp. 228–237). Washington, DC: National Association of Social Workers.

Problem solvers. (April 1987). A community in crisis: The story of Mt. Pleasant, Iowa. *Chamber Executive: The Authoritative Journal for Chamber of Commerce Professionals*, pp. 6–8.

Raphael, B. (1983–84). Who helps the helpers? The effects of a disaster on the rescue workers. *Omega, 14* (1), 9–20.

Rapoport, L. (1977). Consultation in social work. In J. Turner (Ed.), *Encyclopedia of Social Work* (17th ed.) (pp. 193–197). Washington, DC: National Association of Social Workers.

Seroka, C. M., Knapp, C., Knight, S., Siemon, C. R., & Starbuck, S. (1986). A comprehensive program for postdisaster counseling. *Social Casework, 67*, 37–44.

Shulman, L. (1987). Consultation. In A. Minahan (Ed.), *Encyclopedia of Social Work* (18th ed.) (pp. 326–331). Washington, DC: National Association of Social Workers.

Siporin, M. (1987). Disasters and disaster aid. In A. Minahan (Ed.), *Encyclopedia of Social Work* (18th ed.) (pp. 438–449). Washington, DC: National Association of Social Workers.

Webb, N. B. (1981). Crisis consultation: Preventive implications. *Social Casework, 62*, 465–471.

Webb, N. B., Sakheim, G., Towns-Miranda, L., & Wagner, C. (in press). Collaborative treatment of juvenile firesetters: Assessment and outreach. *American Journal of Orthopsychiatry, 60*.

Wiseman, R. S. (1975). Crisis theory and the process of divorce. *Social Casework, 56*, 205–212.

Woman is acquitted in child-abuse case. (10 February 1987). *New York Times*, p. B-2.

14

Social Support Intervention in Crisis Situations: A Case of Maritime Disaster

Michàl E. Mor-Barak

Much has been written in recent years about how social supports moderate or buffer the impact of psychosocial stress on physical and mental health (Ell, 1984; Auslander & Litwin, 1987). The deleterious effects of psychosocial stress on health may be lessened or even eliminated in the presence of social support. However, the literature dealing with social support systems has not yet fully explored the use of these systems through the various stages of crisis. Conversely, crisis intervention literature has not yet examined thoroughly the functions of the social support systems, despite the fact that the importance of these systems in the intervention process has been acknowledged (Caplan, 1974; Caplan, 1989).

The present chapter explores the connection between crisis stages and the use of support systems.* More specifically, it focuses on the cooperation and combination of formal and informal support systems in the process of moving people from the stage of crisis to the stage of adjustment to a painful life change. The first section examines theory and research concerning the relationship among social support, stress, and health. In the second section, practice applications of social support theory are reviewed. A case of maritime disaster—the sinking of a ship (the *Masada*) and the bereavement process for the seamen's families—is presented and the support intervention analyzed; a detailed description of the crisis stages and the intervention with the bereaved families is provided within the framework of an employee assistance program (EAP). Finally, a general model for the use of formal and informal support systems in crisis intervention is suggested. The case illustrations throughout this chapter are from the author's experience as a consultant to an EAP in a large shipping company.

Social Support, Stress, and Health: Theory and Research

The importance of social support to individuals' health and well-being was brought into sharp focus by four influential papers published in the mid-1970s

*This chapter is adapted from two previously published articles: Mor-Barak, M. E. (1988). Support systems intervention in crisis situations: Theory, strategies, and a case illustration. *International Social Work, 31*, 285–303; Sharlin, S., & Mor-Barak, M. E. (1983). Bereavement and mourning after a shipping disaster: The case for intervention. *Disaster, 7*, 142–147.

(Cassel, 1974, 1976; Cobb, 1976; Kaplan, Cassel, & Gore, 1977). The papers reviewed findings of several studies dealing with social environment and health and laid the foundation for what has come to be known as "social support theory." They all provided evidence supporting the hypothesis that social support can protect one's health in the presence of stressful life events. This proposition, generally referred to as "the buffering hypothesis," suggests that one's social ties to others provide protection from the consequences of exposure to stressful situations (Figure 1).

To varying degrees, the research that followed these early theoretical formulations indicated that the absence of social support is related to increased rates of disease in diverse groups: middle-aged and elderly men (Graham et al., 1978; Medalie, Synder, Groen, Neufeld, Goldbourt, & Riss, 1973), adult community residents (Berkman & Syme, 1979; House, Robbins, & Metzner, 1982), noninstitutionalized elderly (Stephens, Blau, Oser, & Millar, 1978; Blazer, 1982; Mor-Barak, 1986), women at various stages of the life cycle (Barrera, 1981; Turner, 1981; Sosa, Kennell, & Klaus, 1980; Brown, Bhrolchain, & Harris, 1975), parents (Morrow, Hoagland, & Carnrike, 1981), employees (LaRocco, House, & French, 1980), Japanese–Americans (Reed, McGee, Yano, & Feinleib, 1983), and pregnant women (Nuckolls, Cassel, & Kaplan, 1972; Sosa et al., 1980).

Although this accumulating empirical evidence indicates the importance of social support to health, it is problematic because most of the studies are flawed both conceptually and methodologically (Thoits, 1982). Unfortunately, the literature does not provide a consistent and well-conceptualized body of knowledge. In addition, although health is associated with social support, researchers still do not understand *how* social support affects health. Despite these problems, most of the studies conclude that *social support does, in fact, affect health.* Moreover, evidence indicates that the effect is not simply due to risk factors such as smoking or obesity, because the majority of the studies controlled for these factors. These studies show that the effect of social support is not specific to any one disease state or organ system and that it includes both mental and physical illness. (For reviews of theory and empirical evidence, see Broadhead et al., 1983; House, Landis, & Umberson, 1988.)

Building on the accumulating research findings indicated above, and to overcome the confusion concerning the conceptualization and measurement of social support, House and Kahn (1985) offer a more comprehensive model of this relationship. This model includes three concepts under the "domain of social support": social relationships, social support, and social network. The model also indicates a direct effect of the "domain of social support" on stress and on health, whereas in the original "buffering hypothesis" model (see Figure 1) it was hypothesized that social support may buffer individuals against the harmful effects of stress on health, but it does not have any direct effect on either stress or health. The House and Kahn (1985) model suggests that social supports may play a more powerful role in affecting both stress and health than was originally hypothesized, thus highlighting social support as an especially desirable target for intervention.

In summary, despite conceptual and methodological flaws, the social support literature presents accumulating empirical evidence that the association between lack of social support and disease is not spurious and that the presence

FIGURE 1. The buffering hypothesis.

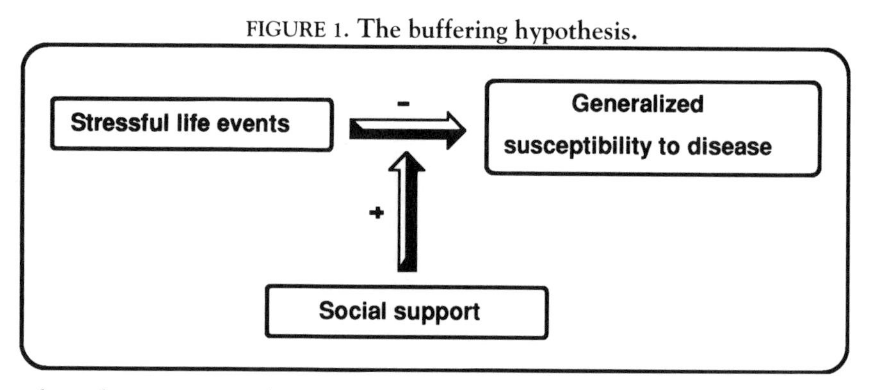

of social support is good for one's health. This empirical evidence has important implications for the interventions described in the following section.

Practice Applications of Social Support Theory

Before describing intervention strategies, a few terms need to be defined. *Social support* is broadly defined as the resources—potentially useful information, services, or material things—routinely provided by others (Cohen & Syme, 1985). *Social network* is defined as a group of people who are important to a person's affective life, such as family members, friends, and co-workers (Gottlieb, 1983). It is important to remember that these people may generate both support and stress at different times and in response to different life demands. A *support system* is defined as all people who routinely provide social support and is a subset of people in the individual's total social network, upon whom he or she relies for socioemotional aid, instrumental aid, or both.

Social support interventions are primarily based on the theoretical and empirical social support literature previously described. Some of these techniques are new, whereas others have been used in the past under different names. The model depicted in Figure 2 expands on Gottlieb's (1983) notion of social network and social support intervention techniques and assigns the various social network intervention strategies to one of the following stages of the helping process:

- *Problem assessment*: assessing the problem and the individual's potential support for coping with it
- *Prevention*: initiating intervention before a stressor has created an actual problem in order to prevent a harmful development
- *Clinical intervention*: when a stressor has already caused a problem, helping individuals cope with the problem by using their social support network
- *Follow-up*: using network members to stabilize the intervention achievement and to detect any regression

Problem Assessment

The social network can influence reaction to a stressful situation in two ways: It can be a source of support or a source of stress, depending on the individual's relationship with different members of the network. A worker who is

FIGURE 2. A general model for
social support and social network assessment and intervention strategies.

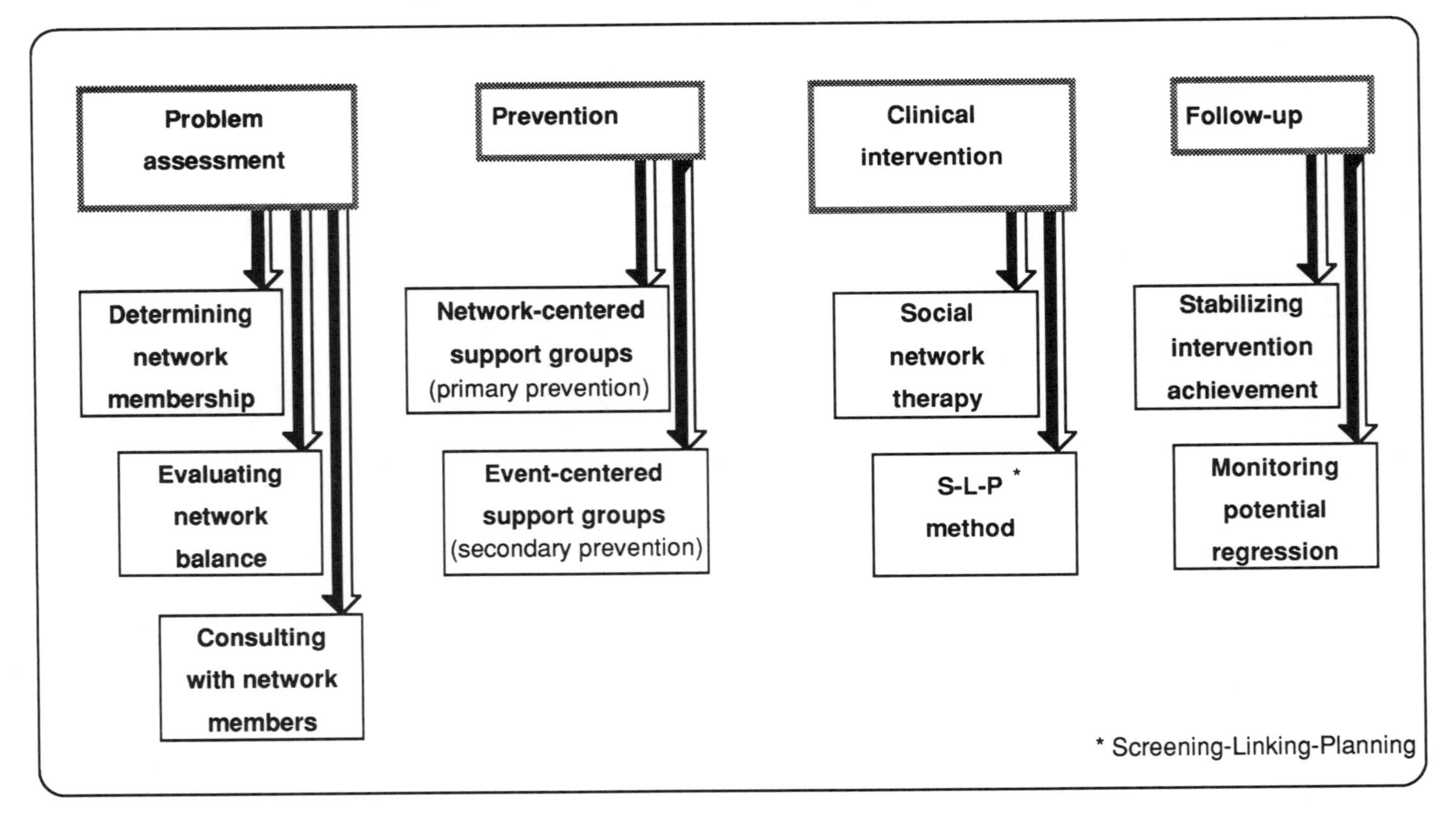

depressed after being passed up for promotion, for example, may receive support from family members ("You'll get it next time, Dear"), or may not, in which case the family members become an additional source of stress ("You didn't work hard enough. It's all your fault"). Thus, it is important to study systematically the social network by the following:

Determining network membership. This information can be obtained by simply asking the employee (or client) who are the most significant people in his or her life with whom he or she has regular, face-to-face contact. A technique for getting at this information is to ask the individual to draw a map of his or her social network and to position network members on the map according to members' emotional closeness. The lines indicate direct relationships among the members of this personal network.

Evaluating network balance. The second task in assessing the social network is to learn about the network's characteristics by studying the balance between support and stress in the network. The network map described above is a particularly good tool for doing this because it identifies the network's members as well as their relationships with one another. For example, an employee who is offered a promotion but must move to another town in which a branch of the company is located may be unable to make such a decision. Drawing a map like the one noted above can help the individual gain some insight into his or her network relationships. The employee may, for example, realize that his or her mother supports the move, whereas the father opposes it. The individual may further realize (perhaps with the help of a counselor) that this conflict has little or nothing to do with the move and promotion but rather indicates that the parents have a poor relationship. Seeing this conflict graphically may help the client decide to have a family conference to confront the issue and discuss the problem with the parents.

Consulting with network members. Sometimes evaluating a problem may require that a counselor or therapist, with the employee's permission, talk to other network members. For example, a female employee may feel that she has to quit a job because her teenage son has problems at school. A conversation with the son may reveal that his problems are the result of an inappropriate choice of school. The son expresses his wish to transfer from his academically oriented school to a vocational one. The solution to the problem does not, in fact, require that the mother quit her employment as she thought, but rather calls for a few meetings involving the mother, the son, and his teachers, and perhaps a transfer of the teenager to a more suitable school.

Prevention

Preventive strategies use the social support system to improve coping and to enhance physical and mental health. In may cases, early intervention can minimize the adverse effects of exposure to life stressors and abrupt transitions. There are two types of preventive strategies: (1) network-centered support groups and (2) event-centered support groups.

Network-centered support groups. The idea of such groups is to reconstruct existing social networks and/or optimize their capabilities so that they reach more people and more adequately fulfill people's need for support. Examples of the groups mobilized are informal community caregivers, such as hairdressers or bartenders, family members and friends, or people who are interested in learning more about their own social support systems and the way they can use them more effectively.

The following example is based on the experience of a shipping company's EAP. It describes an intervention strategy aimed at informal community caregivers, in this case radio officers.

> One of the things the EAP workers realized about seamen's life was that the sailors had no one to turn to, other than their peers, to discuss emotional or family problems. The peer most frequently chosen for informal counseling on the ship was the radio officer. The radio officer, who made the wireless telephone connections between seamen and their families at home, often literally stood by the seamen when they heard either good or bad news from home. He was, therefore, the most natural confidant for sharing emotions afterward. Therefore EAP counselors met with radio officers as a group and talked to them about their role as informal support providers on the ship. The session included expression of their feelings about this role and some basic instruction about how to help the seamen get the assistance they needed by referring them to professional sources for counseling.

Similar interventions can be planned in other work situations to mobilize supportive relationships, to enhance existing ones, and to ensure referral to professional sources when needed. It should be remembered, however, that this type of intervention is focused on teaching peers how to help others. A fine line exists between enhancing supportive relationships and turning the workplace into a pseudotherapeutic environment. The first is a positive goal that can enhance workers' productivity as well as their mental health; the second is an undesired result and potentially destructive to the interests of the employer and the individual employee.

Event-centered support groups. These groups are convened on behalf of specific groups of people who are at risk because certain typically stressful life events have occurred that require social readjustment. Examples of such support groups are those convened to help recently widowed persons, parents of disabled children (see chapter 16), or depressed adolescents. The following illustration is also drawn from the author's experience in the shipping company.

> Several seamen who were married to foreign wives expressed concern about their wives to the EAP counselors. Many of the wives had left their family and friends in their native countries and thus had no support when their husbands were at sea. Consequently, the wives felt lonely and isolated. Some of the husbands were so concerned they considered quitting their jobs and changing their occupation in order to stay with their wives. A support group, led by two experienced counselors, was formed for these women. The women used this forum to discuss their special problems and to provide support to one another. After several meetings of the group, the women began to meet outside the formal meetings to help one another by providing advice, companionship, and performing tasks, such as babysitting or shopping, in times of need. After four months, group members became part of one another's social networks. The women felt that the group's support enabled them to cope with the difficulties of everyday life when their husbands were away from home and, more important, they felt they had somebody to whom they could turn for help when they needed it.

Event-centered support groups can be useful in other work situations as well, for example, support groups for workers who are facing layoffs (in addition to retraining or placement), groups for employed single parents, and groups for workers preparing for retirement.

Clinical Intervention

Clinical intervention includes various forms of social network therapy, an extension of family therapy in which all or key significant others are seen. The techniques may include assembling the whole network for all the treatment sessions or working with subgroups of the network during some sessions of the intervention. This type of intense therapy should not be part of the workplace, but can be performed by professionals to whom employees are referred. A brief description of these therapies follows.

One form of social network therapy is assembling the entire network for a therapy session (Speck & Rueveni, 1969; Speck & Attneave, 1971; Rueveni, 1975). In this type of intervention, everyone who is of significance to the identified client's problem, all members of the kinship system, all friends, and neighbors of the family, are assembled. A typical middle-class urban family potentially can assemble approximately forty persons for such a meeting. However, network therapy is neither widely practiced nor extensively evaluated. It makes heavy demands on the therapist's time and skills and is inappropriate for families who are unwilling to participate because they are afraid that the process will prove embarrassing and place a greater distance between them and their kin.

Other therapeutic interventions use network resources but do not involve the entire network simultaneously in the psychotherapeutic process (Pattison, 1973, 1977). One of these techniques (Garrison, 1974) is the "Screening–Linking–Planning Conference." This technique encourages the social network of the person in crisis to cluster around that person in a supportive way, to express positive expectations, and to provide positive feedback for "identity-repair" purposes. Experience shows that this method is most effective when applied at the height of a crisis, when the individual is in serious trouble, perhaps at risk of psychiatric hospitalization. For example, if an employee's adolescent son is hospitalized after an attempted suicide, gathering parts of the network for a series of therapeutic sessions can provide reassurance to the adolescent that he is loved despite his problems and suicide attempts. It can also help the adolescent and his family establish goals. This technique is not a form of insight-oriented group psychotherapy like the network therapy described above. More directive, it aims to restore the individual's role in the network.

Again, it should be stressed that the above techniques are generally not appropriate for practice in the workplace but may be used by well-trained extramural professionals to whom employees are referred.

Follow-up

Finally, the social network is helpful in the follow-up process. The network should be encouraged to continue providing support when needed and to detect signs of recurrence of the problem. For example,

> Mr. S had a heart attack while on duty on one of the company's ships. This experience was especially frightening because it happened when the ship was at sea and Mr. S had to be flown by helicopter to the nearest hospital, which took more than an hour. Mr. S saw one of the company's social workers for counseling while he was recovering from the heart attack, and after a few months both he and his physicians felt he was fine and ready to go back to work. However, his wife, who participated in some of the therapy sessions, came to the social worker two months later and told her that her husband was having nightmares about having a heart attack on the ship and not getting to the hospital on time. She encouraged her husband to seek counseling again.

Without the support system's intervention in this case, Mr. S might not have come back to therapy, although he obviously needed more help.

Social Support Intervention in a Case of Maritime Disaster

A few years ago, an Israeli bulk carrier, the *Masada*, belonging to a merchant shipping company, was crossing the treacherous waters of the Bermuda Triangle en route to the United States. Thirty-four crew members and one passenger, the radio officer's wife, were on board. Storms caused the ship to sink on a Sunday morning. Twenty-four of the crew were drowned, eleven were saved. This disaster was the worst in the history of Israel's merchant shipping fleet and created a very painful crisis for the families of the crew members who were lost at sea.

Before analyzing the intervention in this crisis, it is useful to describe the framework for analysis of this case. An important aspect of analyzing the process of support systems intervention is to identify the various types of needs and the appropriate help that can meet each need. Barrera and Aimly (1983) offer an empirically derived typology of support functions. In their study they found four important functions of support:

1. Directive guidance: Actions on the part of the helpers to provide support of a practical nature aimed at helping the recipient improve his or her performance through increased understanding and skill (teaching skills, providing feedback, and giving advice)
2. Nondirective support: Expressions of intimacy, unconditional availability, esteem, trust, physical affection, and listening to talk about private feelings
3. Positive social interaction: Joking and kidding, talking about interests, and engaging in diversionary activities
4. Tangible assistance: Physical assistance (sharing tasks), providing shelter, money, and material objects of value

The analysis also follows the five phases of crisis described by Golan (1978): the hazardous event, the vulnerable state, the precipitating factor, the state of active crisis, and reintegration. Integrating the crisis stages defined by Golan, with Barrera and Aimly's (1983) classification of support systems, the following outlines the contribution of both the informal and formal support systems in helping the grieving families of the seamen who were lost at sea.

The Hazardous Event

The first stage of crisis, according to Golan's classification, involves a specific stressor affecting an individual in a relatively stable biopsychological state, which in turn initiates a chain of reverberating actions. Golan further divides these events into anticipated and unanticipated occurrences.

In the *Masada* disaster, the hazardous event was totally unanticipated. The ship was on its way to the United States on a routine voyage, one it had taken many times before. The initial news received at the company's head offices at noon on Sunday was restrained and rather optimistic, as was the message delivered to the families. Family members were told that one of the ship's stores was flooded, that the crew had left the ship in the lifeboats, and that rescue operations were under way. Accordingly, the families' reactions were also restrained. They were worried and asked for further information the moment it was received.

The families' needs at this stage can be described, according to Barrera and Aimly (1983), as a need for directive guidance or, in other words, more information. A team of six EAP department staff was organized to offer the necessary help; all members of the team were experienced social workers. A twenty-four-hour hotline was immediately established to provide information to the families as soon as it arrived at the office. At this early stage, which lasted only a few hours, most of the aid was provided by the formal support system—namely, the company's social workers.

The Vulnerable State

The second stage in a crisis is the vulnerable or upset state, the individual's subjective reaction to the initial blow. Each person responds to the hazardous event in his or her own way, depending on his or her own perception of it.

Throughout Sunday evening and the following days, Israeli television, radio, and newspapers continued to supply news about the *Masada* disaster, which painted an increasingly severe picture of stormy seas and difficulties in the rescue operations. The news reports received by the office were the same: The seamen's situation was becoming more and more desperate. Members of the families came to the office in hope of getting news of survivors as it arrived. Small groups of relatives (parents, wives, brothers, sisters) and friends filled the office; the atmosphere was tense, nervous, and very strained. The extreme tension and uncertainty to which the families were subjected affected each family differently. For example Mrs. H, surrounded by family members trying to calm her, cried incessantly. At intervals she wailed, "So now I am going to be a widow and my children orphans. Who will provide and care for us?" On the other hand, Mrs. T reacted with restraint. She sat quietly in a corner, withdrawn and silent, obviously repelled by the hysterical reactions of other women. At this stage the families needed not only directive guidance, as before, but also nondirective support—such as someone to listen to their worries, calm them, and provide expressions of intimacy and comfort.

The company's social workers tried to provide both kinds of assistance. Family members and relatives tried their best to help the wives and children, but many of them were too shocked and bewildered to help. One of the wives' mothers said, "How can I comfort my daughter when I am sick from worrying about her husband?" The social workers tried to help relatives and friends in supporting the wives and children by expressing sympathy for their feelings and advising them. This stage lasted approximately two days, which seemed endless to both the families and the social workers. The formal system was still the main provider of support; it had begun to help the informal system to provide support. Clearly, however, the informal support system, which included significant others who had intimate relationships with the families, was far more important than was the formal system.

The Precipitating Factor

The precipitating factor or event is the link in the chain of stress-provoking events that converts the vulnerable state into the state of disequilibrium. It is "the straw that breaks the camel's back."

After three days of rescue operations and after the good news that eleven *Masada* seamen were saved had been delivered to their families, a committee of experts was assembled by the company to evaluate the situation and give advice about what actions should be taken next. The committee was composed of shipping experts, the company's physician, rehabilitation experts from the Defense Ministry, a psychologist, and representatives from the Israeli Social Welfare Department's staff. The shipping experts and the physician described the current situation at the disaster site. Their judgment was unequivocal: there was no chance of finding more survivors or bodies of drowned seamen (seven bodies had been found by that time).

The rehabilitation personnel from the Defense Ministry contributed their experience in dealing with the families of soldiers missing in war. They noted that in Judaism a special significance is attributed to the condition of missing persons and specific religious regulations govern their families. For instance, families cannot begin the religious ritual of mourning unless granted permission by the highest religious authority. A missing person is not considered dead for seven years; the widow cannot remarry for that period unless given special permission by rabbinic authorities who require convincing evidence. The rehabilitation consultants believed the present state of uncertainty would be unbearable for the families and might delay the grieving process.

To prevent further fantasies of rescue and survival, it was decided to make announcements of "no hope" to each family by visiting their homes. Special teams were formed to deliver the message. Each team consisted of an experienced ship captain (who volunteered for this duty), a social worker from the family's community, and a high-ranking company official. The teams were thoroughly briefed. Their mission was painful but clear: to clarify beyond doubt the hopelessness of finding the family's loved one alive and to help the family start the bereavement process.

The need to have volunteers and community representatives was clear. Not only were the company's social workers unable to continue shouldering all the burden, but also it was apparent that other team members had a unique contribution. The ship captains could be very persuasive in explaining the sea conditions and the hopeless situation. High-ranking officials in the company could reassure the families of the continuing responsibility of the company to provide for them in the absence of the family breadwinner. Community representatives could help in practical everyday problems such as finding a babysitter or someone to do the shopping.

The precipitating factor is not a stage in the process; it is the trigger that initiates the next phase—the active crisis state. In this disaster situation, it was important to enlarge the existing support system by adding people from the community and volunteers to help the families and the families' own natural networks to cope with the pain of the impending bereavement. However, this disaster was different from most crises in that it did not have a "natural" precipitating factor because of the uncertainty about the fate of most seamen on board. Thus the precipitating event was "planned"—announcements of "no hope" were made.

Active Crisis State

The state of active or acute crisis describes the individual's distressed condition, after his or her homeostatic mechanisms have broken down, tension has peaked, and disequilibrium has begun. In the *Masada* disaster, the most important event in this phase occurred when the Chief Rabbi of Israel gave the families permission to sit *Shiv'aa*, the Jewish religious custom in which close family members mourn the dead for seven days. During this period family members receive condolences, talk about the deceased, repeat certain prayers, and eat special food. One is not allowed to sit *Shiv'aa* when the body of the dead person cannot be found, unless the Chief Rabbi gives his approval. The permission to sit *Shiv'aa* seemed to make families realize that their loved ones were really dead and therefore helped them start the bereavement process.

At this stage the families primarily needed nondirective support from significant others so that family members could talk about their losses, discuss their fears of being widows and orphans, and experience feelings of intimacy and a sense of belonging. Also, the need for tangible assistance became evident: a babysitter for the children when the house was full of visitors offering condolence, help in preparing food for the family and the guests, aid in shopping, and so forth.

During this stage, family and friends (the informal natural support group) provided most of the help. Some families still needed help from volunteers because their families and friends could not provide all the necessary support. Most families still needed to maintain the relationship with company volunteers, who gave them a sense of belonging and reassurance ("we still belong to the company"). The social workers continued to provide nondirective support in helping the families undergo the mourning process. They also provided guidance and help to the informal support system—family, friends, and volunteers. For example, one of the widows cried and shouted in her grief, which alarmed her family. They consulted the social worker, who listened to their fears and reassured them her behavior was normal in mourning and that they should not be frightened by it.

Also, the company provided an extra sum of money for the families' expenses during the *Shiv'aa*, and arrangements were made for the families to receive a monthly salary for the rest of their lives (tangible support). The length of this stage of acute bereavement crisis varied among families, lasting, for most of them, between four to six weeks.

Reintegration

The state of reintegration or restoration of equilibrium is an extension of the state of active crisis. Tension and anxiety gradually subside and some reorganization of the individual's ability to function occurs. Because the stage of imbalance cannot continue for an extended period, some new form of adjustment, either adaptive or maladaptive, begins.

After approximately four to six weeks, most of the families entered the reintegration phase, moving gradually through the substages of this phase: correct cognitive perception, management of affect, and development of new patterns of coping. Their need for tangible support decreased as they gradually resumed their predisaster daily routines; because the husbands had been absent from home for long periods working as seamen, the families were used to functioning independently. The families had less need for both directive and nondirective support. Gradually, an increasing need for positive social interaction emerged: talking about interests other than the relationship with the deceased and engaging in diversionary activities. After approximately six months to a year, some wives began to find new occupations and activities. Although social workers were still in touch with the families, their contact was much less frequent than before. The social workers provided information and help concerning occupational rehabilitation. The main providers of help at this point were family, friends, and other people in the community. The informal support system had begun to take over.

A General Model of Social Support Intervention in Crisis Situations

The intervention process in the *Masada* disaster developed gradually, moving from formal to informal support systems. Each stage merged into the next stage, involving more informal support and less formal support as helpers responded to the changing needs of the families in crisis. At the same time, the size of the network changed in order to adapt to the changing needs of the families. For most of the families, the network expanded and was at its largest at the point of active crisis, when the families' needs were greatest and most diverse. The support network then gradually shrank to its original size (or close to it) as the families experienced the reintegration phase. Based on this process, a general outline for the use of social support systems in crisis intervention can be drawn (see Figure 3).

Clearly, the most important aspect of social support intervention in crisis is the partnership between the formal and the informal support systems. The importance of the informal helpers' role should not be underestimated by professionals when planning their intervention. In crisis situations, the closest support people are often also affected by the crisis. Often, the bereaved families' relatives also need help. Many family members and friends found it impossible to help the widows because they themselves were shocked and bewildered. They felt the need to mourn their own loss and were unable to find strength to help the widows when they needed it the most. Professionals who confront such situations should avoid putting demands on these helpers and should, instead, listen to the helpers' own agony. Such support can strengthen the entire support system and, eventually, the bereaved family. For example, one of the widow's mothers tried but was unable to help her daughter. The social worker talked with the mother who, it was discovered, had been widowed at

FIGURE 3. Crisis stages, families' needs, and support systems intervention.

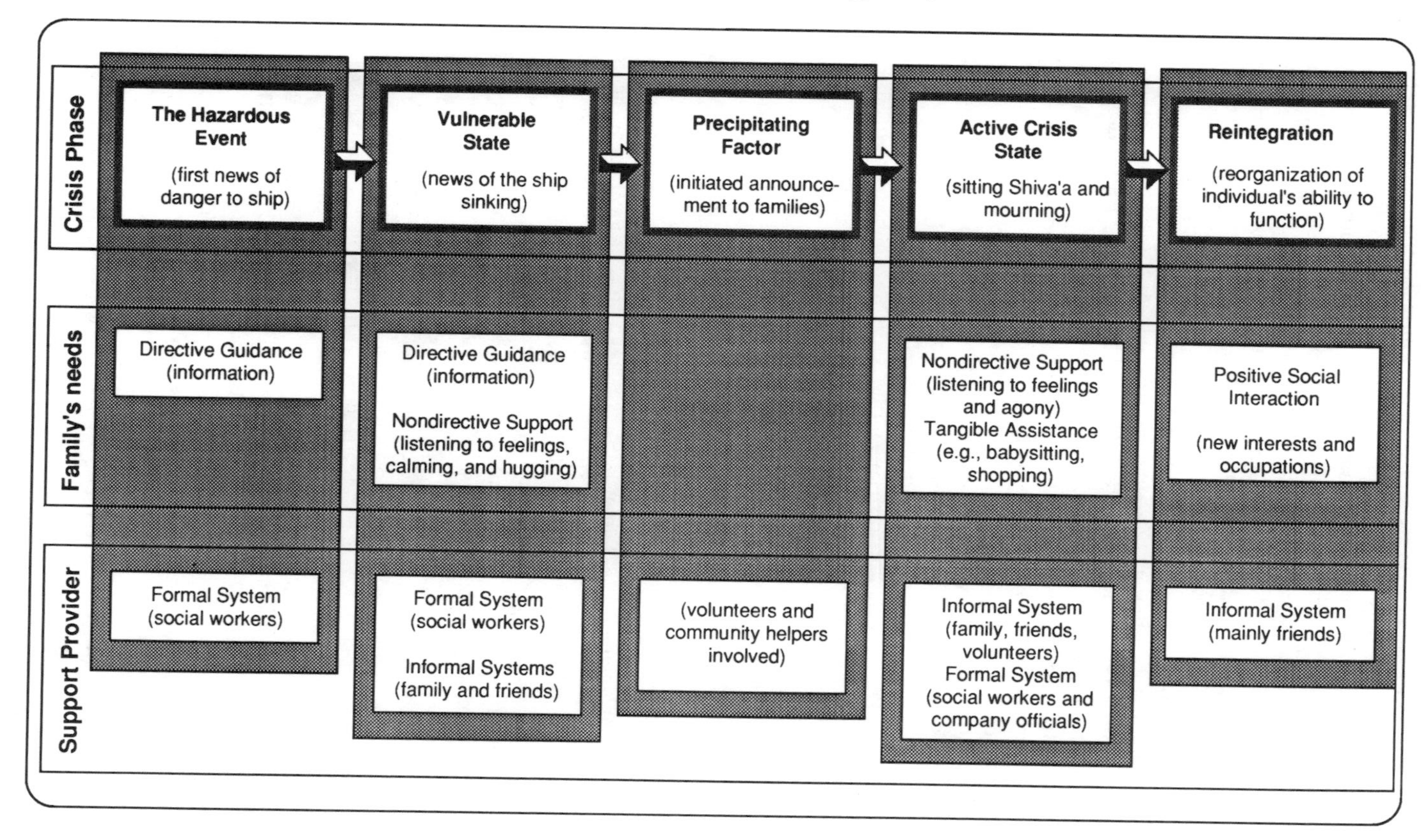

about the same age as her daughter. She identified so closely with her daughter that she was unable to provide help. However, after she realized she was reliving her own crisis, she was able to partially separate the two events and help her daughter more.

The volunteers faced other types of difficulties; like the bereaved families' relatives, they also needed help. Initially, the volunteers found it emotionally draining to face the families' feelings of uncertainty and fear and later their agony and pain. The situation was especially difficult for company officials who were sometimes attacked and blamed by some of the families, who felt that the disaster could have been prevented. One official was severely attacked verbally and almost physically by a family who did not wish to accept his explanations; they accused him of hiding the truth from them.

It was difficult to help these helpers because many of them were not ready to admit the emotional difficulties they were experiencing. As high-ranking officials or ship masters, they felt they should keep a strong facade and not expose their emotions. The company's social workers were creative in overcoming this problem. They asked volunteers to make a report after every visit to the families and bring it back to the employee-assistance department. After they were back in the department, they were gathered in small groups, with a social worker leading the discussion. Each volunteer described his or her experience so that others could learn from it. These discussions provided an excellent opportunity for ventilation without requiring volunteers to admit the need for it.

Summary and Conclusions

The helping process in the *Masada* case can be described as an event-centered type of preventive intervention carried out on behalf of a group of at-risk persons exposed to a commonly encountered stressful event—the loss of a loved one. During the bereavement crisis the families of the seamen were steered toward adaptive grief work and away from maladaptive coping with their tragic losses (Lindemann, 1965).

The literature dealing with this type of disaster aid generally refers to group-oriented intervention (Parad, Resnik, & Parad, 1976). At an early stage of the crisis, this option was considered but was rejected because of the risk of retarding progress rather than encouraging it. On several occasions when the widows and their families met with the other families, we observed that the group encounter was a stressful rather than a helpful experience for most of the families. Therefore, the EAP staff felt that a group intervention could only delay their recovery. The strategies that were actually used resembled in some ways the strategies described under "clinical intervention" techniques, especially the Screening–Linking–Planning model (Figure 3). However, as is the case in many treatment interventions, the creative use of different strategies enabled caregivers to respond flexibly to the client's needs.

How successful was this intervention in terms of preventing mental health problems? Success is difficult to determine because the intervention was not designed as a research project and no systematic instruments were used to evaluate the results. Rather, the intervention developed somewhat spontaneously as the crisis developed. However, all eleven wives who became widows as a result of this disaster and their families have now (five years later) overcome the crisis and have developed new relationships and activities in their lives. Of course, they still suffer the painful agony ensuing from the loss of a loved one, but none of them has developed serious psychological problems.

The model generated from this specific intervention experience can be applied to any crisis situation and is useful in guiding professionals in planning their intervention with support systems. Of course, each crisis needs to be individually examined and evaluated. However, the general intervention strategy can follow the pattern of moving gradually from formal to informal support systems, as described in the present chapter. Professionals should bear in mind that the informal support system is the more important support network, in that informal caregivers were there before the intervention and will continue to be there after the professionals are gone. Professionals need to establish a partnership with the informal support system. They should support informal caregivers, then leave the scene when they are no longer needed.

References

Auslander, G., & Litwin, H. (1987). The parameters of network intervention: A social work application. *Social Service Review, 61*, 305–318.

Barrera, M., Jr. (1981). Social support in the adjustment of pregnant adolescents: Assessment issues. In B. H. Gottlieb (Ed.), *Social networks and social support*. Beverly Hills, CA: Sage Publications, 69–96.

Barrera, M., Jr., & Aimly, S. L. (1983). The structure of social support: A conceptual and empirical analysis. *Journal of Community Psychology, 11*, 133–143.

Berkman, L., & Syme, S. L. (1979). Social networks, host resistance, and mortality: A nine-year follow-up study of Alameda County residents. *American Journal of Epidemiology, 109*, 186–204.

Blazer, D. G. (1982). Social support and mortality in an elderly community population. *American Journal of Epidemiology, 115*, 684–694.

Broadhead, W. E., Kaplan, B. H., James, S. A., Wagner, E. H., Schoenbach, V. J, Grimson, R., Heyden, S., Tibblin, G., & Gehlbach, S. H. (1983). The epidemiologic evidence for a relationship between social support and health. *American Journal of Epidemiology, 117*, 521–537.

Brown, G. W., Bhrolchain, M. N., & Harris, T. (1975). Social class and psychiatric disturbance among women in an urban population. *Sociology*, 9, 225–254.

Caplan, G. (1974). *Support systems and community mental health*. New York: Behavioral Publications.

Caplan, G. (1989). *Population-centered psychiatry*. New York: Human Sciences/Plenum Press.

Cassel, J. (1974). Psychological processes and "stress": Theoretical formulations. *International Journal of Health Services*, 4, 471–482.

Cassel, J. (1976). The contribution of the social environment to host resistance. *American Journal of Epidemiology, 104*, 107–122.

Cobb, S. (1976). Social support as a mediator of life stress. *Psychosomatic Medicine, 38*, 300–313.

Cohen, S., & Syme, L. S. (1985). *Social support and health*. New York: Academic Press.

Ell, K. (1984). Social networks, social support, and health status: A review. *Social Service Review, 58*, 133–149.

Garrison J. (1974). Network techniques: Case studies in the screening–linking–planning conference method. *Family Process, 13*, 337–354.

Golan, N. (1978). *Treatment in crisis situations*. New York: Free Press.

Gottlieb, B. H. (1983). *Social support strategies*, Beverly Hills, CA: Sage Publications.

Graham, T. W., Kaplan B. H., Cornoni-Huntley, J. C., James, S. A., Becker, C., Hames, C. G., & Heyden, S. (1978). Frequency of church attendance and blood pressure elevation. *Journal of Behavioral Medicine, 1*, 37–43.

House, J. S., & Kahn, R. L. (1985). Measures and concepts of social support (pp. 83–108). In S. Cohen & S. L. Syme (Eds.), *Social support and health*. New York: Academic Press.

House, J. S., Landis, K. R., & Umberson, D. (1988). Social relationships and health. *Science, 241*, 540–545.

House, J. S., Robbins, C., & Metzner, H. (1982). The association of social relationships and activities with mortality: Prospective evidence from the Tecumseh Community Health Study. *American Journal of Epidemiology, 116*, 123–140.

Kaplan, B. H., Cassel, J. C., & Gore, S. (1977). Social support and health. *Medical Care, 15*, 47–58.

LaRocco, J. M., House, J. S., & French, J. R. P., Jr. (1980). Social support, occupational stress, and health. *Journal of Health and Social Behavior, 21*, 202–218.

Lindemann, E. (1965). Symptomatology and management of acute grief. In H. J. Parad (Ed.), *Crisis Intervention: Selected Readings*. New York: Family Service Association of America.

Medalie, J. H., Synder, M., Groen, J. J., Neufeld, H. N., Goldbourt, V., & Riss, E. (1973). Angina pectoris among 10,000 men: 5 year incidence and univariate analysis. *American Journal of Medicine, 55*, 583–594.

Mor-Barak, M. (1986). *The dynamics of the joint relationship between social network, life events, and health of the poor frail elderly*. Doctoral dissertation, University of California, Berkeley.

Morrow, G. R., Hoagland, A., & Carnrike, C. L. M., Jr. (1981). Social support and parental adjustment to pediatric cancer. *Journal of Consulting Clinical Psychology, 49*, 763–775.

Nuckolls, K. B., Cassel, J., & Kaplan, B. H. (1972). Psychosocial assets, life crisis, and the prognosis of pregnancy. *American Journal of Epidemiology, 95*, 431–441.

Parad, H., Resnik, H., & Parad, L. (Eds.) (1976). *Emergency and disaster management*. Bowie, MD: Charles Press.

Pattison, E. M. (1973). Social system psychotherapy, *American Journal of Psychotherapy, 18*, 396–409.

Pattison, E. M. (1977). A theoretical–empirical base for social system therapy. In E. F. Foulks, R. M. Witrob, J. Westermeyer, & A. R. Favazzo (Eds.), *Current perspectives in cultural psychiatry*. New York: Spectrum.

Reed, D., McGee, D., Yano, K., & Feinleib, M. (1983). Social networks and coronary heart disease among Japanese men in Hawaii. *American Journal of Epidemiology, 117*, 384–396.

Rueveni, U. (1975). Network intervention with a family in crisis. *Family Process, 14*, 193–203.

Sosa, R., Kennell, J., & Klaus, M. (1980). The effects of a supportive companion on perinatal problems, length of labor and mother–infant interaction. *New England Journal of Medicine, 303*, 597–600.

Speck, R. V., & Attneave, C. L. (1971). Social network intervention, In J. Haley (Ed.), *Changing families: A family reader*. New York: Grune and Stratton.

Speck, R. V., & Rueveni, U. (1969). Network therapy—A developing concept. *Family Process*, *8*, 182–191.

Stephens, R. C., Blau, Z. S., Oser, G. T., & Millar, M. D. (1978). Aging, social support systems, and social policy. *Journal of Gerontological Social Work*, *1*, 33–45.

Thoits, P. A. (1982). Conceptual, methodological, and theoretical problems in studying social support as a buffer against life stress. *Journal of Health and Social Behavior*, *23*, 145–159.

Turner, R. J. (1981). Social support as contingency in psychological well-being. *Journal of Health and Social Behavior*, *22*, 357–367.

15

The Prevention of Psychological Disorder in Children of Divorce

GERALD CAPLAN

MY CLINICAL PRACTICE as a child psychiatrist has convinced me of the increasing significance of parental divorce as a major threat to the mental health of today's children. Therefore, in 1985, I helped establish the Jerusalem Family Center, which seeks to prevent child psychopathology and maladjustment by intervening in families at the time of divorce and afterward. Although the divorce rate is lower in Israel than it is in many Western countries—only one marriage in five ends in divorce compared with, for example, one in three in Britain and one in two in the United States—divorce is still a major problem.

My work at the Family Center has been the most fascinating in my entire career. The intensity of emotional arousal in parents and children during and after the divorce crisis and the victimization of children caught up in the parental battles are capable of provoking profound empathic involvement. It has been particularly exciting to participate in the unfolding of dramatic events of obvious significance for the well-being of the children. In certain cases, I was also able to intervene actively in their family drama to modify the balance of forces and thus fulfill my basic mission of primary prevention.

This work has taught me to study and treat each case according to its own complicated idiosyncratic elements and to beware of premature generalizations that may oversimplify the case. Nonetheless, some common patterns can be seen across a range of cases.

Harmful Sequelae of Parental Divorce

Kalter (1977) reviewed the records of 400 children treated between 1974 and 1975 in the Department of Psychiatry at the University of Michigan. He found that children of divorced parents appeared in the outpatient clinic at double the rate of children in the general population—32.6 percent compared with 16 percent, respectively. He reported that the children of divorce suffered

---

This chapter is based on Caplan, G. (1989). The prevention of psychopathology and maladjustment in the children of divorce. In *Population-oriented psychiatry*. New York: Human Sciences/Plenum Press, 1989. Used with permission.

principally from symptoms associated with poor control over aggression. In the younger children, the hostility was directed inside the home against parents and siblings. In the older children and adolescents, the aggressive behavior took the form of antisocial acts and delinquency, as well as alcoholism, drug addiction, and, in girls, sexual promiscuity. The study was repeated with a new sample of 500 cases seen at the University of Michigan psychiatric outpatient clinic during the period 1976–77, and similar results were obtained (Kalter & Rembar, 1981).

McDermott (1970) emphasized the prevalence of depression in children whose parents were divorced at least two years earlier. He found moderate or severe depression in 34.3 percent of his sample of 116 child psychiatry outpatient clinic cases whose parents had been divorced.

A long-term follow-up study of a national sample of 5,362 children born during one week in Britain in 1946 reported that 36.5 percent of men whose families had been disrupted by parental divorce, separation, or death before they reached five years of age suffered from psychopathology (hospitalization before age twenty-six for affective psychiatric illness or for stomach ulcers or colitis) or social maladjustment (delinquency by age of twenty-one) compared with 17.9 percent of men from intact families. The researchers also found that 23.3 percent of women whose families were disrupted by parental divorce, separation, or death before age five suffered from psychopathology (hospitalized before age twenty-six for affective psychiatric illness or for stomach ulcers or colitis) or social maladjustment (operationally defined as delinquency by age twenty-one or divorce or separation or out-of-wedlock children by age twenty-six) compared with 9.6 percent of women from intact families (Wadsworth, Peckham, & Taylor, 1985).

Wadsworth (1979) tabulated other findings of the 1946 longitudinal cohort study that permit the following recalculation: 29 percent of men whose families were disrupted by parental divorce, separation, or death before they had reached sixteen years of age suffered from psychopathology (hospitalization for affective psychiatric illness) or social maladjustment (defined for purposes of this study as delinquency or divorce or separation by age twenty-six) compared with 18 percent of men from intact families. Twenty-one percent of women whose families were disrupted by parental divorce, separation, or death before the children reached age sixteen suffered from psychopathology or social maladjustment (as previously defined) by age twenty-six compared with 10.1 percent of women from intact families. The British data (29 percent for men and 21 percent for women) can be compared with the findings of Wallerstein and Kelly (1980) in the United States that 35 percent of the sons and daughters of divorced parents they studied suffered from psychopathology or delinquency.

Wadsworth and Maclean (1986) analyzed other data from the 1946 longitudinal cohort study, finding that men from working-class families had significantly lower income at age twenty-six if their parents had divorced or separated before they were sixteen compared with men from intact families. They also found that children of both sexes of divorced or separated parents had significantly lower educational qualifications, such as matriculation or university attendance by the age of twenty-six years, compared with children of intact families. By comparison, parental death had very little impact on a child's later educational achievements and may even have increased the probability of working-class children going to college. These findings indicate that parental divorce or separation has a considerably harmful impact on the lives of children, which is expressed not only in psychopathology or social maladjustment but also in lower educational attainment in both sexes and lower socioeconomic achievement in males.

Psychosocial Hazards

In order to understand why parental divorce is associated with an increased likelihood that the children will develop psychopathology or social maladjustment during childhood or in later adult life, it is necessary to focus on the following factors.

Parental Quarreling

Most divorces are preceded by months or even years of quarreling. These quarrels often go through three phases:

Phase I. This phase is linked with disappointments and frustrations in the expectations of each that motivated the marriage, with incompatibilities of temperament that became salient between spouses, or in a minority of cases with manifestations of psychopathology in one or both spouses. Mutual provocations typically lead to escalation of hostility and to episodes of irrational shouting, screaming, and verbal or physical abuse. The children may be involved as bystanders. The younger children are frightened by these scenes, and whatever their age, the children are burdened and upset by the breakdown of rational control in their parents. Most children, however, do not appear to take sides in these conflicts during this stage.

Phase II. This phase begins when one or both parents decide to start the process of divorce. They begin an adversarial process to wrest from each other an optimal share of their joint property and to safeguard their links with their children. Often, their hostility intensifies, and they inflict mental or physical wounds on each other. Consequently, they may become increasingly bitter and vengeful, especially if this phase lasts for a protracted period. Often, they actively try to recruit their children to side with them by maligning the other parent and by inciting the children against the other parent.

Phase III. This phase begins when the parents separate or divorce. In many cases, the separation of the combatants leads to a period of relative tranquility. Because a contract has been signed or the case has been adjudicated, the immediate conflict of interests has been terminated. Previous animosities become a fading memory of past pains, and the former spouses begin to adjust to the burdens of reestablishing their homes and dealing with the adaptive problems of their children.

Often, however, the hatred and bitterness stimulated by the narcissistic wounds inflicted in the previous phases, or in certain cases by the image of the former spouse having been introjected to play an enduring part in the individual's psychopathological inner world, may lead to long-term vengeful hostility. In these cases the plight of the children may become worse than it was before the divorce. The children are likely to be recruited as protagonists in the fight, particularly as the bone of contention between the parents is often about implementing the terms of the divorce contract in regard to custody and visitation. The other major factor is that the separated parents can no longer vent their hatred through face-to-face contact or even through the medium of a telephone conversation; therefore, they send their hostile message through their children.

Conflict of Interests between Parents and Children

Spouses who continually quarrel with each other may feel that they should cut their losses and end their marriage. Their children, however, will rarely be in favor of divorce. In my experience, although most children of quarreling parents feel burdened by the conflict, very few accept divorce as a solution, because they feel that the splitting of their home and their separation from one of their parents will involve them in worse burdens. Even in cases of physical violence, many children say they prefer their present painful reality to becoming involved in an unknown and frightening future after divorce. For instance, a nine-year-old boy told me, "It is often pretty bad at home, especially when Dad comes home drunk and starts beating us up. But I still love him and I don't want my mother to throw him out of the house for good."

Many children feel that their interests were ignored by their parents and that they were passive victims of adult decisions about adult issues. Shimon, aged fourteen, said, "Our parents have decided to divorce. We feel angry that they didn't pay any attention to what this will mean to us children. They never even talked to us about it till after they had decided." Existentially, the children may be right, which is not to say that if their parents had been fully aware of the needs and views of their children they would have changed their decision to divorce. However, the parents might have found ways to reduce the feelings of passivity and helplessness of the children, which impose a major additional burden on them.

Communication Issues

Children's feelings of passive victimization are often exacerbated by the parents' not preparing them ahead of time and not explaining to them what is happening during and after the divorce, information that at least provides the children with an opportunity to gain cognitive mastery over their predicament. This lack of explanation is particularly problematical with preschoolers and young school-age children. Henry James, in his 1897 novel *What Maisie Knew* illustrates this point most poignantly. For instance, Esther, a five-year old girl, told me, "Three months ago I woke up one morning and found that Daddy had disappeared. Mummy told me he had gone off to do his army reserve duty; but this can't be true because he always comes back from army service at the end of a month. She won't tell me where he has gone!" This lack of authentic communication often leads to the child's developing fearful fantasies that the departing parent no longer loves him or her and has left home because of the child's badness. Esther said, "I think he has left us because I used to make so much noise and he couldn't stand it."

As suggested earlier, another, more serious hazard, particularly for older children, is being used by parents to carry messages. These messages are usually heavily loaded with hatred and disparagement. Even for children who have not been recruited to take sides, conveying such hostile messages is very disturbing. This hazard becomes exaggerated when, as often happens, a child rebels against the feeling of passivity by choosing to play an active role in the parental conflict. The child will then modify the messages he or she carries between the parents—sometimes toning down the hostile elements in order to reduce the animosity between the parents or distorting the messages as well as the stories he or she tells each parent about the other in an effort to stir up further trouble. In either instance, the child's manipulations give him or her the feeling of exercising some active mastery over the situation. Fourteen-year-old Haviv said, "I can't bear to see how much it hurts Mother when I give her Father's messages, so I change them. That makes everyone happier. I wish my parents wouldn't behave so childishly that I have to quiet them down."

Partisanship of Children

A child may begin to hate one of the parents because he or she has been brainwashed and incited to hate by the other parent. The child may also take sides because of his or her interpretation of the relative merits of the adversaries, particularly if one parent was repeatedly violent or was the one the child felt caused the family breakup. For example, an eleven-year-old girl, Talia, said, "Mother suddenly changed. She began to make hysterical scenes and to call the police to stop Father hitting her. But it was she who attacked him, and she also scratched my brother's arm. She shamed us in front of the neighbors. I began to hate her. She was the cause of all the trouble in the home." The child is likely to develop a stereotyped view of one parent as being ideally *all good* and the other parent as being *all bad*. Perceptions and expectations of the "bad" parent usually become colored by fantasy elements that increase the child's rejection and fear. When this occurs, the child typically tries to reduce his or her interactions with the bad parent or may behave provocatively when meetings do occur, which often stimulates hostile reactions in the parent that reinforce the child's prejudices. Talia said, "Mother takes it out on me because she knows I'm on Father's side." Talia's mother said, "She's impossible; she continually attacks me and behaves like a rebellious brat!" Such behavior leads to an escalation of animosity that results in the child, and often the parent, cutting links with the other. In effect, the child divorces that parent or is abandoned by him or her.

Courts have limited power to force a recalcitrant child, even as young as eight or nine years old, to visit a rejected parent. Rifka, aged ten, said, "I absolutely refuse to visit that man. He is no longer my father. Even if you send police to take me by force I won't go; I'll jump off the balcony and kill myself. If you invite me to your office and I know he's coming I will not come to you."

The net result is most unfortunate. Absence of contact allows the child's fantasies about the satanic "evils" of the hated parent to flourish without an opportunity for the child to modify his or her stereotypes by real experience. This promotes the continuation in the child of splitting or ambivalence, wherein the child not only perceives one parent as all good and the other as all bad, but projects this view on all people, the child included. The child may also introject the evil image as a rejected part of his or her own psychic structure, inherited from the bad parent. Rifka, a deeply religious girl, genteel, shy, and fastidious, said, "A couple of years ago, when I used to visit him, he and the whore he lives with used to lie together half naked on the living room couch and behave in a disgusting manner. They also used to have competitions as to who could make the loudest noise by expelling gases." Later, she said, "He is an absolute monster. He once tried to strangle my mother when she was weak after an illness." In fact, her father is an uncouth, insensitive, and brutal man, but he is eager to renew links with his children, although he does not know how to behave with them. Because the internalized bad object is likely to be highly colored by hostile and sexually aggressive elements linked with actual or imaginary aspects of the conflicts between the parents, the situation is conducive to the development of antisocial violence, substance abuse, and sexual promiscuity in adolescence, when the child's psychic equilibrium becomes upset and his or her previously rejected impulses become dominant.

Abandonment

Abandonment may take various forms. In a number of cases a noncustodial parent deserted the children. In one case, a mother, without prior warning, ran off to Australia with her lover, leaving behind three small children with her husband, whom she subsequently divorced. In several cases, a divorced father refused to see his children because they had chosen to live with their mother. In other cases, the father took revenge on his former wife by severing his links with their children on the grounds that she was living in sin with another man. In some cases, the father stopped visiting the children because he claimed the mother had turned them against him and had put obstacles in the way of his visits. Sometimes, the father visited the children irregularly and after long intervals in contravention of the divorce agreement. In all cases the children suffered greatly.

> David, a six-year-old boy, said, "Daddy has gone off and left us. It makes me very, very sad. I can't fall asleep at night and I have bad dreams. In school I think about him the whole time instead of doing my lessons. I long for him and I cry a lot."

> Myriam, a four-year-old girl, said, "Daddy doesn't live with us any more. I don't know what I have done to drive him away. Sometimes he telephones, and I beg him to visit us. He promises to come, but he never keeps his promises."

Many of these deserting parents are psychiatrically disturbed, usually suffering from major personality disorders—paranoid, narcissistic, or borderline. Before they deserted, they behaved cruelly to their children—behavior linked with their lack of capacity to love. Although I believe that ideally children should be given the opportunity to recognize the reality of their parents as human beings, I feel that some children might be worse off if I were to engineer contacts between them and a sick parent. For instance,

> Leah, a fourteen-year-old girl, told me, "I went to see Daddy last week. I had thought that after not seeing me for a year he'd be nicer than in the past. But he spent the whole visit shouting and screaming. He said that he had evidence that Mother was having affairs with several different men and that she has brainwashed me to become his enemy. He demand-

> ed that I leave her at once and come to live with him, because otherwise I will become a whore like her. He says that if I don't come to him, he will no longer accept me as his daughter, and as far as he is concerned I will be dead."

Her father suffers from a borderline personality disorder with paranoid features. In such cases, the therapist should not be doctrinaire about fostering contact between children and a sick parent, but should weigh the evidence very carefully to avoid making a bad situation worse.

Loss of a Parent: The One-Parent Home

Children of divorce usually suffer from a significant reduction in regular contact with one of their parents. Intermittent contact of a few hours a week with a noncustodial parent does not effectively make up for this interruption of parenting. Adequate parenting requires that on a continuing basis the father or mother nurture, control, guide, and support the child by active involvement in the child's daily life. A child needs two parents who play complementary roles in child care and education, who support each other while supporting the child in mastering the expectable stresses of growing up, and who provide the child with two differentiated sexual role models on which to base the identifications that form the core of the child's identity. Weiss (1975), reporting on research at the Harvard Laboratory of Community Psychiatry, documented the burdens of the one-parent home for both the parent and the children. It is important to emphasize that divorce leads not to "one-parent *families*," but to *split two-parent families*, and to *one-parent homes*. If the divorced parents live close to each other, communicate freely, and are able to collaborate well in joint parenting tasks, some of their children's burdens may be reduced by joint-custody arrangements that allow the children to live part of each week or alternate weeks with each parent. When such custody arrangements succeed, this pattern allows the children to relate in more healthy ways to both parents and allows both parents to fulfill their child-rearing roles. However, when animosities and disorders of communication continue between the parents after the divorce, this arrangement can be particularly burdensome to the children.

Divorcing parents often try to solve conflicts over child custody by dividing up their children. Such arrangements do not solve the children's problem of losing daily contact with the nonresidential parent. Furthermore, the children lose the support of a stable sibling group and may be burdened by longings for absent siblings as well as for the absent parent.

After divorce, many children lose their conviction that until they grow up they will be nurtured and protected by their parents. The breakup of their home and the fact that they feel they have lost one parent often arouses the fear that they will lose the other parent. This fear may be exacerbated if the residential parent, usually the mother, is away from the home during the day, comes home tired and irritable after work, and is depressed because of the failure of her marriage and the burdens of running a one-parent home. In such instances, the child may feel that he or she has lost or will lose both parents, which leads to feelings of being alone, of being without support, and of being less able to face and master adverse situations (Rutter, 1985).

Loss of Income

Two homes cost more than one. Almost all families are economically worse off after divorce, despite the efforts of the mother, the parent with whom the children usually live, to increase her earnings and thus make up the deficit and despite governmental family welfare allowances in some Western countries to reduce financial deprivation. Wadsworth and Maclean (1986) confirmed the findings of Fogelman (1983) that family income is almost certain to be reduced after divorce and that this reduction is likely to lead to downward social mobility, a socioeconomically disadvantaged status for children, lower educational achievements, and reduced future earning power in their adult life.

Moving

A child, especially a young child, derives a significant part of his or her feelings of basic security from the stability of a familiar home and neighborhood and from continuing relationships with neighborhood friends and the children and adults he or she meets daily in school. Divorce often leads to the children and the parent with whom they live being forced to move. The mother may have to take the children to live temporarily with relatives. The downwardly mobile family may be forced to move repeatedly so that the mother can find accessible work or a home they can afford. These moves may take place in the middle of the school year, which interrupts schooling and separates the children from their friends. Thus, the children are faced with the burdens of adjustment to new classrooms and new teachers, and with the task of making new friends. These frequent moves further erode the children's sense of security.

Stigma

The increasing incidence of divorce is related to and has resulted in a reduction in the social and religious stigma that used to be associated with it even a generation ago. And yet, apart from places like California, where perhaps two out of three children may become children of divorce, this status is generally not the norm. School-aged children of divorced parents are particularly sensitive to being regarded as different and hence inferior; they are likely to suffer from being stigmatized by their peers.

Sex

Marital conflicts that lead to divorce frequently focus on sexual dissatisfactions. Angry accusations of sexual infidelity or misconduct are recurring features of verbal battles between parents. The children may also often overhear a parent complaining bitterly to a friend about the sexual misconduct of his or her spouse. Small children may not at first understand the meaning of these complaints but will fill out the story from their own fantasies. Their sexual curiosity is likely to be stimulated by these passionate complaints.

After divorce, parents may become sexually overactive to counteract feelings of inferiority about not having succeeded in marriage. Eventually, each parent may begin exploratory dating with a succession of prospective sexual partners with a view to remarriage.

These situations are likely to stimulate precocious development of sexual curiosity in the children and to their taking upon themselves the unnatural role of critic or intervener in the sex life of their parents. Especially during adolescence, when parents normally have a sensitive role to play in helping their child grapple in a socially acceptable way with the complexities of their tumultuous sexual awakening, a child's lack of respect for the sexual maturity of the parents erodes an important source of support and control inside the family.

Adjustment Reactions

In reaction to these psychosocial burdens and to reductions in parental support, children typically show signs of strain that persist for several weeks or months after divorce. These symptoms vary somewhat with age and developmental level. Younger children are confused, frightened, or clinging, and older children tend to be angry, irritable, and restless. They have difficulty concentrating in school because they are worried about parental battles and the breakup of their home. Children of all ages often have difficulty falling asleep, and their sleep is disturbed by frightening dreams. After divorce many children become sad and depressed. Most children are aggressive with their siblings and with peers at school and in the neighborhood. Adolescents have difficulty with impulse control and tend to be more rebellious than the norm.

In my Jerusalem case load, these immediate adjustment reactions have generally cleared up by the end of the first year; but in 15 percent of cases, these reactions have been succeeded by signs of psychopathology described earlier in this chapter. A follow-up study might show that another 15 percent to 20 percent of cases will develop signs of similar psychiatric illness in the future, but on the basis of the clients' present clinical picture and pattern of adjustment, I cannot predict which these will be. Such predictions must await the results of further research. Until such research is undertaken, however, the acute adjustment reactions should be regarded as normal signs of strain and should not be interpreted to be prodromata of eventual psychopathology.

Ethical and Political Aspects of Preventive Intervention

Primary prevention of psychopathology and maladjustment in children of divorced parents requires *proactive* intervention to modify the life conditions of the children, namely, reaching out by caregivers who seek to initiate changes in the family without having received a prior invitation by the parents to intervene. At the Jerusalem Family Center, our goal is to identify harmful factors in the family and to modify them, or to introduce supportive factors. Many parents overlook the risks to their children in their preoccupation with their own conflicts and the complications of the divorce process and are less motivated and able than usual to focus attention on the needs of their children. Intervention in this context raises important ethical and political questions.

In democratic societies, the care and protection of children is largely left in the private domain of parents. Representatives of society are permitted to penetrate the boundaries of this domain only if convincing evidence suggests that a parent is maltreating, battering, neglecting, or depriving a child. This philosophy is justified; the vast majority of parents care adequately for their children on their own or with help that they themselves seek from others. In most societies, the rights of the parents to privacy regarding how they fulfill their responsibilities to their children are protected by law and by public opinion; these rights are defended politically against governmental or professional encroachment by advocates of civil liberty.

These rights are altered, however, when parents voluntarily approach the courts to dissolve their marriage. Parents explicitly open up their private domain to public scrutiny and intervention. Their request for divorce is a formal statement that their marriage has broken down and constitutes an invitation to the representatives of society to assess the consequences for themselves and their children. Most laws governing the procedure of divorce make explicit provisions to protect the interests of the children, who may be endangered by the upheavals of the divorce and its aftermath. I have already cited evidence that the children are in significantly greater danger than are children in intact families. Divorce should be perceived as a marker indicating the need for societal intervention to protect the children. We must avoid being persuaded by the arguments of zealous political advocates of civil liberty to romanticize the competence of all parents, including those who have failed to maintain a stable marriage and have thus placed the mental health of their children at risk.

On the other hand, although adjudication by the courts may be essential in determining the pattern of child care following divorce, the details of how children will be cared for in their family throughout their years of dependency after the divorce cannot be completely determined by court prescriptions. Sooner or later responsibility for the welfare of the children must be returned to the parents. Intervention by agents of society must necessarily be temporary. It should be as short as possible, and the invoking of authoritarian coercion, or its threat, should be minimal, lest it have a counterproductive effect when the care of the children inevitably is returned to the parents.

Although it may sometimes be necessary during divorce proceedings (or subsequent court action to change custody or visitation) to force divorcing parents to modify their behavior for the benefit of their children, a more stable long-term pattern of child care will generally be achieved if the parents are educated, guided, and enabled through mediation to make plans voluntarily that meet their idiosyncratic needs. In my experience, many parental divorce agreements about future child care are not implemented because eventually the parents do what they want and not what they feel they were forced to agree to do.

In the absence of major psychopathology, the likelihood of implementation of child-care plans is greater in proportion to the degree of freedom of choice of the parents in designing the contract. However, the mediator at the time of divorce should not merely enable the parents voluntarily to work out a plan for their children with which they feel comfortable. If the intercessor is a specialist in child development, he or she should provide information that increases the knowledge and understanding of parents about child care and the developmental needs of children as well as about the special problems commonly encountered by children of divorce. Although the intercessor should avoid imposing a plan, he or she should not hide from the parents the intercessor's opinion about the relative merits for their children of some of the options one or the other parent may propose.

Regardless of who initiates the intervention, the first task of the intercessor is to arouse the motivation of both parents so that they will invite him or her to continue working with them in formulating plans to terminate their marriage with minimal harm to their children. Making parents well disposed to the intervention is advisable irrespective of whether its auspices are in a voluntary agency outside the courts or within the framework of the court, such as a court clinic or welfare unit. All such interventions connected with divorce are likely to be perceived by the parents as being formally or informally linked with the court process. Thus parents usually feel obliged to choose arrangements for their children that they believe will be in conformity with the terms of the eventual court adjudication (Mnookin, 1978).

Planning a Preventive Program

In light of the foregoing, I propose that a comprehensive preventive program for divorcing parents and their children should provide a range of services to intervene, when necessary, in the lives of a very large heterogeneous population, composed mainly of normal parents and their children, but with a substantial minority of parents with psychiatric disorders. The program should center on the courts, through which all divorcing couples must pass, and extend into the community to programs and agencies that provide services in response to voluntary requests. These programs may operate within a variety of administrative auspices, which may or may not be under the control of the courts and may or may not have formal links with one another. However, no program should operate in isolation. Rather, programs for divorcing families should interface with other programs in the community in an effort to reduce the risk of psychopathology and maladjustment in children.

The service elements of such a comprehensive program should include the following:

Education. Information should be disseminated about the significance of divorce for children, the expectable reactions of children, and how problems may be handled. This information may be disseminated to the general population through the mass media. Brochures might also be provided by the courts to parents contemplating divorce. Information should be made available through in-service training programs and case consultation with relevant caregiving professionals such as judges, lawyers, family physicians, nurses, welfare workers, educational personnel, and clergy.

Guidance. Relevant information should be provided to all parents who initiate divorce proceedings through face-to-face meetings on an individual or group basis, in which problematic issues geared to the needs and capacities of individuals can be discussed.

Reconciliation. Marriage counseling should be provided in cases of marital disharmony to enable some parents to avoid divorce. Understanding the significance of divorce for their children may lead parents to change their decision regarding divorce.

Conciliation. Mediation should be provided, preferably by persons with expertise in child development, to enable divorcing parents to work out on a voluntary basis a mutually acceptable contract that will determine custody of children, visitation, and the division of parental responsibilities for children after divorce.

Reports to divorce court. Professionals should appraise family relationships and make recommendations to the court on child custody and contacts between children and parents after divorce.

Adjudication by divorce court. This procedure should include judicial appraisal of the effectiveness of child-care provisions in the divorce contract in safeguarding the rights of the children. Judges should be able to order additional specialist consultation if conflict continues or doubt exists.

Postdivorce surveillance. Services should be available in questionable cases for court-ordered long-term surveillance to ensure that provisions of the divorce contract are being implemented and are indeed benefiting the children. In other cases, follow-up monitoring on a voluntary basis should be available.

Postdivorce crisis intervention. Brief intervention should be available if requested by one of the parents or by a community professional. Such interventions are useful when new conflicts arise between the parents about the implementation of plans for child care or when plans do not appear to be serving the developing needs of the children. Intervention should attempt to prevent the escalation of hostility between the parents and should offer parents guidance on care of their children.

Methods and Techniques

Systematic presentation of preventive methods and techniques must await the evaluation of further experience. The final portion of this chapter will present a brief summary of methods I have found valuable.

Education

The following are the main issues and items of information that should be conveyed by a planned educational program:

The interests and needs of children often conflict with those of their parents with regard to divorce. Most children oppose divorce despite the fact that they suffer from parental conflict.

Children often spontaneously take sides without having been incited by a parent, which is regrettable in that it harms their healthy personality development.

Children often defend against a feeling of passivity and helplessness—aroused by not being a party to the decisions regarding the breakup of their home—by attempting to play an active role in reducing or aggravating the conflict. They may distort messages between parents or tell untrue stories about one parent to the other.

A divorced parent often fears that the other parent will harm the children. This fear may be aroused or exaggerated by the tendentious stories of the children or by feelings of hatred and suspicion between the parents. It may be helpful for an unbiased third party to judge the extent to which there is a factual basis for such fears.

It is crucial to safeguard the child's good relationships and to promote frequent contacts with the nonresidential parent. The residential parent should speak well of the other parent to the children.

If possible, children should stay overnight at least once a week with the nonresidential parent so that he or she remains involved in real parenting interactions, rather than those of a host only.

In rare cases, the nonresidential parent may be mentally disturbed. Interaction with the children may sometimes harm them and, if so, should be kept to a minimum and should occur only on the advice and under the guidance of a mental health specialist.

Prolonged conflicts over custody and access at the time of divorce may exacerbate and prolong bitterness, animosity, and vengefulness between the parents, which may foster partisanship among the children and thus endanger their mental health. Such conflicts should be resolved as soon as possible either by conciliation or by adjudication.

The more the details of a divorce agreement have been negotiated freely and without coercion by the parents, the more likely they are to be implemented. However, intermittent conflicts between separated parents in the years following divorce should be expected because of residual unresolved animosities or changes in family circumstances or due to development of the child's personality. A clause in all divorce contracts should specify that either party has the right to invoke *ad hoc* mediation or expert guidance by a mutually acceptable neutral intercessor, with the aim of interrupting escalations of hostile tension that might otherwise occur.

Parents intending to divorce should discuss the impending family breakup beforehand with their children in words and at a time that are geared to the age and developmental level of the children. If possible, parents should talk jointly to their children to demonstrate that they agree on their message. Parents should cover the following points:

- The parents intend to live in separate homes and to end their marriage because they have stopped loving each other and can no longer live together. The divorce has not been caused by anything the children have done.
- The parents intend to continue to love and care for them throughout childhood.
- The children will live in the home of one parent and will visit the other at regular intervals, except in the relatively rare instance of a viable joint custody arrangement. (The conditions relating to successful joint custody are outlined on pages 348–349). Both parents agree that the children should maintain contact with each parent; they know that a child needs continuing contact with both parents for healthy growth and development.
- The divorce will be permanent. If the parents stop quarreling after divorce and become friendly with each other, this will not mean that they will live together again.
- The parents realize that the children probably oppose their divorce, but the children cannot alter the situation and should not try to do so.
- The parents know that the children will feel upset, angry, sad, and insecure. The parents will help them master these understandable feelings, which most children succeed in accomplishing over a period of months.
- The children should stay out of the quarrels between the parents. They should not take sides. Even though the parents have stopped loving each other, they continue to love their children. Both parents want the children to love the other parent.

• The parents do not wish the children to carry messages from one parent to the other. They promise to try not to communicate with the other parent through the children.

Education of community professionals should take the form of in-service training seminars whose curricula should encompass the topics listed above. The goal should be for all professionals to be able to educate and guide divorcing parents and their children as part of their professional work. In addition, caregivers should refer clients to a mental health specialist for consultation or care if any of the following are evident:

• Signs of suspected psychiatric disorder in a parent, especially psychosis or severe personality disorder.
• Signs of psychological illness in a child that persist beyond the limits of an expectable adjustment reaction: scholastic failure, social isolation, inability to play, depression, prolonged regression and interference with personality development, fixed somatization, sleep disorders, excessive and prolonged antisocial aggressiveness and loss of impulse control, drug or alcohol abuse, delinquency, and promiscuous sexual behavior.
• Compulsive recruitment of a child as an ally by a parent by a campaign of incitement of the child and vilification of the other parent.
• Active partisanship by a child and his or her unbalanced vilification of a parent.
• A residential parent's interference with access of children to the nonresidential parent.
• Abandonment of the children by the nonresidential parent.

Conciliation

The leverage for influencing the parents to work out an optimal plan for the care of their children after divorce depends on their trust that the conciliator will not side with one parent against the other as well as their respect for his or her skills as a mediator, as an expert in child development, and as a specialist in the problems of children during and after divorce. The mediator should promote this type of relationship not by being cooly neutral but by being actively bipartisan. The mediator should demonstrate a warm involvement and solicitude for each parent as well as strive to help each achieve goals that are compatible with the best interests of the children. The mediator operates like a person playing solitary chess, alternately moving from one side of the chessboard to the other and playing the white pieces and then the black pieces.

It is helpful to meet first with both parents jointly to provide each with the experience that the mediator is sensitive to his or her views, and so that both parents can observe that the mediator behaves the same with the other. The mediator should point out that irrespective of the conflicts between the parents, both parents, and the mediator too, share a commitment to the superordinate goal of ensuring the welfare of their children.

In a short series of discussions, each parent is helped to express his or her point of view and to overcome emotional blocks as well as stereotyped perceptions and expectations that distort their communications with each other.

Coercive behavior should be interrupted to prevent one parent from being undermined or bullied by the other.

Firm control should be kept over the discussions to ensure that the parents focus on the current issues of working out a divorce contract, rather than giving in to their natural tendency to talk at length about past problems in their relationship.

Expression of negative feelings should be limited, and all overt and covert attacks should be interrupted. The emotional climate should be kept cool so that everyone can focus on the immediate task of planning.

Accepting that the two parents have different points of view, the mediator should point out that he or she does not intend to determine "objective truth" or to adjudicate between right and wrong. Rather, the mediator is there to help them identify issues related to the welfare of the couple's children on which they may be prepared to agree.

The mediator should clarify and reformulate the statements of each parent that represent productive options and modes of action and ensure that these are heard and understood by the other. If the "emotional noise" is too loud in joint sessions or if mutual suspicions and defensiveness are too great, the mediator should elucidate the point of view of each parent separately in individual sessions, and then report back in a joint session. However, the mediator should not act as a passive message carrier between adversaries; rather, he or she should reformulate and interpret the messages so as to highlight their task-oriented elements in language that is free from provocation and hostility.

Conciliation, like all mediation, should be a step-by-step process. The optimal tactic is to identify areas of agreement, formulate them, and then expand them. The most difficult areas of conflict should be dealt with last; and, if the couple cannot arrive at an agreement, unless the issue is existentially crucial, it should be set aside. As the couple find areas of agreement on various issues, the mistrust between the parties is eroded.

The children are likely to be active agents in shaping the conflict between the parents. The mediator should meet with the children jointly and, if it seems necessary, individually, then feed his or her impressions of the children into discussions with the parents. Occasionally, it may be useful to invite the children to take part in these discussions. The mediator should also provide information to both children and parents regarding expectable reactions in families during and after divorce.

As earlier suggested, the mediator should assume the role of expert regarding the probable significance for the children of the various options proposed by the participants. The mediator should attempt to broaden the range of options for the family and not impose his or her own plan. Points of view should be expressed openly and clearly; their choice of options should not be manipulated by "loading the dice."

Premature closure should be avoided. When a tentative plan has been developed, the mediator should encourage the family to spend some time "working it through" by imagining how it will be implemented in practice. The parents should also be urged to build a clause into their contract that will allow reevaluation of details of their custody, access, and coparenting plans after the divorce and that will provide a mechanism for either party to request mediation or counseling if things do not work out. It is beneficial for couples to understand that one or two occasional sessions of crisis intervention may be needed in the future to help them implement in practice what they have worked out in theory.

Reporting to the Divorce Court

In Israel a statutory regulation requires that in all cases of parental divorce a welfare officer should investigate the family situation and provide the court with an assessment of provisions for child custody, visitation, and other arrangements for child care. In complicated cases, the welfare officer may call for consultation by a psychiatrist or psychologist, and the judges themselves may request a supplementary report from a court-appointed mental health specialist.

In approximately 90 percent of cases in Israel, parents come to court with a plan for custody and visitation that they have worked out on their own or with the help of counselors or lawyers. Similar statistics have been reported in the United States, Canada, and Britain. In about 10 percent of cases, the parents have not been able to agree upon a plan and thus bring their conflict to the courts for adjudication. In my experience, many predivorce agreements by the parents do not adequately safeguard the welfare of their children. Therefore, reports by welfare officers and mental health specialists are an important mechanism for bringing to the attention of the judges problematic issues relevant to the future mental health of the children that might otherwise be missed in a busy divorce court. The following guidelines help govern investigation of these issues:

It is helpful to meet with the parents jointly as a first step in order to make an initial assessment of the nature of their relationship and of their capacity to collaborate after the divorce in parenting their children. Because the parents have usually been ordered by the court to see a professional, and have the children be seen as well, the first task is to establish one's role as an independent expert who has been ordered to make recommendations to the judges about the future care of the children. Despite the obligatory framework of the relationship, the couple are encouraged to collaborate freely since, despite their conjugal discord, each is motivated by love for the children. It will be better for the children and, in the long run, better for the parents, if a plan can be mutually agreed upon for recommendation to the judges. The parents are promised that the content of the report will be communicated to them before it is submitted to the court; attention will be paid to their reactions and modifications to the report may be made.

Permission should be requested to meet with the parents' lawyers. In my experience, permission was refused in only one case, which involved a father with a paranoid personality. After collecting preliminary information from the parents and their children, a joint meeting should be arranged with the lawyers that does not include the parents. It is helpful to appeal to the lawyers in their role as agents of the court committed to protecting the welfare of the children as well as representing and promoting the individual rights of their clients. I have found that most lawyers are interested in the needs of the children, whom they have usually not met; without infringing on their role as advocate for their client, they usually agree to collaborate informally with me, as court-appointed specialist, and with their colleague who represents the other parent in an effort to influence the parents to broaden their focus and to consider positively a plan that will benefit their children.

Because the attorneys know that the recommendations of the specialist will carry much weight with the judges, they may try to persuade the mental health professional to pay particular attention to the special needs and assets of their client and to the shortcomings of the other party. Such discussions can provide new insights into the complexities of the case, an enrichment of perception that may significantly modify the assessment. Moreover, such discussions may reduce the abrasiveness of adversarial courtroom tactics of the lawyers because they may have been sensitized to the possible negative effects of such tactics on the children.

Contact with the lawyers should be maintained throughout the case. Usually recommendations should be discussed by telephone or in a joint meeting or meetings before the report is written so that the attorneys have the opportunity to question the implications or side effects of the report and can suggest possible modifications. Mention of irreconcilable differences, if they exist, are included in the report.

The specialist should meet with the children as a group, with the entire family, with each child individually, and with each parent–child dyad. In these meetings, the specialist should not only collect verbal information about the personality, interests, and relationships of all the family members, but should pay particular attention to nonverbal behavioral cues regarding the nature of the relationships between each of the parents and each of the children. Especially noted is the sensitivity of each parent to the needs of the child and the parental capacity for nurturance, control, and protection, as well as the priority given to attending to the child's needs when they conflict with the needs of the parent. In meeting with the parent–child dyad, it is sometimes helpful to offer them a joint task, such as drawing a picture or working out a joint response to a thematic apperception test card. Such tasks allow the identification of differences between how the father and the mother relate to the same child.

A clinical-type interview with each member of the family helps to assess individual characteristics. If necessary, a clinical psychologist should be asked to provide an independent assessment of possible psychopathology and personality dynamics derived from responses to a projective test battery (Minnesota Multiphasic Personality Inventory, Rorschach, Thematic Apperception Test, and projective family drawings). The psychologist's assessment of parenting qualities and the possibility that intrapsychic or psychosocial factors will interfere with child care provides useful information for the report. In many instances, one spouse may accuse the other of being mentally ill; often such accusations are reciprocal. If the accusations appear to be justified, it is particularly useful to employ a standard test battery for both spouses, which is acceptable without loss of face, in that they undergo an identical investigation. In other cases, both spouses are referred for testing because the clinical interview arouses suspicion that one of them has an unrecognized mental disorder, sometimes previously undiagnosed cyclothymic illness, and more often a personality disorder. Referring both parents for testing, even when the mediator suspects a mental disorder in only one spouse, helps to avoid accusations of bias.

In cases in which a parent suspects psychiatric disorder in the other spouse, it is as important to present "objective" evidence that refutes this suspicion as it is to validate it, because resistance of a custodial parent to allow the other parent adequate access to the children after divorce may be linked with the belief that this may be actually harmful. In cases in which one parent may indeed be mentally disturbed, it is particularly important to assess the potential risk for the children and how such risk may be minimized.

Custody recommendations are often simple to make: ideally parents and children are in agreement; the siblings can remain together, living with one spouse, who is a healthy, competent parent. The children are able to remain in the family home or near their existing schools and friends. They can maintain regular contact with the other parent and with grandparents. In less than ideal situations, rational custody arrangements are nearly impossible to make. One needs the wisdom of Solomon to decide between a paranoid father and a passive–aggressive or hysterical mother, both of whom are far from ideal parents, but who demand custody of their children, perhaps for narcissistic reasons or as part of a feud with the other spouse. Or a difficult decision may have to be made between two healthy, competent parents, either of whom would be a satisfactory custodial parent. In such cases, especially when the conflict over custody is fierce, it is useful to assess which parent is more likely to fight the decision of the court and which parent will accept the inevitable and make the best of it.

The attitudes and wishes of the child may be the deciding factor in custody arrangements, irrespective of the specialist's assessment of the relative capacities of the contending parents. Strong partisanship in a child may override all other issues, regardless of whether it developed spontaneously on the basis of the child's appraisal of the relative merits of the two parents—linked with his or her perceptions of their behavior toward each other and toward the child—or whether the decision was influenced by one of the parents through a successful campaign of bribery, brainwashing, or incitement. However, adults should avoid abrogating their responsibility by giving children the power to choose which parent they will live with; intolerable guilt may result or irreparable damage may be done to the relationship between the child and the parent who is rejected. But even in a child as young as seven years old, and certainly in older children, when a child becomes actively and passionately partisan, there is little value in the specialist recommending, or the judge ordering, that custody be given to the parent the child hates.

In carefully selected cases, it may be helpful to recommend joint custody, that is, that the children live a substantial part of the time with each parent (for example, three to four days a week or alternating weeks with each parent). In such cases, children should have their own living space in each home. When this type of plan succeeds, the children avoid experiencing the loss of either parent, and both parents are able to experience the satisfaction resulting from fulfilling their parenting responsibilities. Types of joint custody—and certain unintended consequences of these options—have been reviewed by Elkin (1987) and Hagen (1987).

Joint custody succeeds only if the parents maintain friendly, cooperative relationships after divorce, with unimpeded communication and acceptance of joint responsibility for decisions regarding the care, control, education, health, and religious and leisure practices of their children. Moreover, their respective homes should be close to each other as well as to their children's schools and friendship groups. When these conditions do not apply, joint custody usually results in dismal failure and is often conducive to psychological disturbance in the children. McKinnon and Wallerstein (1988) recently reported on a monitoring program aimed at preventing some of the problems inherent in joint custody arrangements for young children.

Recommendations regarding parental access to the children should be governed by the general principle that the noncustodial parent have maximum *parenting* opportunities. Assessment should focus on the capacity and willingness of this parent to accept parenting responsibilities, including home facilities that allow the children to sleep over and supervision of eating, hygiene, sleep habits, homework, and leisure activities, and on the willingness of the custodial parent to promote such access. In cases in which the parents continue to be suspicious and vengeful after the divorce, especially when this situation is complicated by passionate partisanship in the child, it is unlikely that plans for regular parenting by the noncustodial parent will be implemented. If this situation is further complicated by psychosis or severe personality disorder in the noncustodial parent, it becomes a very difficult issue to decide on a recommendation that will be least harmful to the child. It is not always true that the experience of actual interaction will improve the child's image of the parent by the reality testing of his or her fantasies; such contact may in fact further traumatize the child. Fortunately, such extreme cases are rare. Even when a professional recommends regular contact—perhaps for theoretical or philosophic reasons—the child and the custodial parent will usually connive to prevent the plan from being implemented.

Postdivorce Intervention

Postdivorce intervention is crucial in any comprehensive preventive program. In many cases, the risks to the children are likely to increase after divorce. Parents who were in conflict during their marriage may continue or exacerbate their quarrels after divorce. They may begin interminable vengeful struggles with each other, often focused on issues of custody and visitation, that ostensibly were decided in the divorce agreement or court adjudication. Even in cases in which the divorce agreement was freely negotiated between both parties, collaboration in joint parenting of the children can be expected to involve difficulties. Such difficulties are inherent in the ongoing complications of caring for developing children who have no unitary home base—not to mention the incompatibility of personality or value systems of the parents that has led to the divorce. The likelihood of problems is increased in those cases in which the parental agreement about child care at the time of divorce was felt by one parent to have been signed under duress, either because of undue pressure experienced by one of the parties or by the overriding authority of the court.

Significantly, during its first two years of operation, 61 percent of the clients at Jerusalem Family Center requested help after the breakup of their home, about half within the first year and the remainder within two to ten years after their divorce. And of the clients who were seen initially before or during the divorce process, many have continued to maintain intermittent contact with the center on an open-ended basis in order to allow monitoring of the adjustment of the children and to allow parents the opportunity to seek guidance when they experience serious difficulties in implementing their mutually agreed-upon plan of child care. Our program contrasts in this respect with many programs in the United States, Canada, and especially Britain, that focus almost exclusively on mediating between divorcing parents to help them work out an agreement concerning custody and visitation, then terminate their intervention at the time of divorce with little provision for further contact.

This aspect of our intervention methodology is still being actively explored in order to define and describe those procedures and techniques that seem to be useful. The following preliminary formulations may well be modified, and will certainly be refined, in the light of further experience.

Establishing a framework for future interventions. In most predivorce cases, it is helpful to foster the development of a supportive relationship with each parent and child and to encourage clients to renew contact with the professional specialist* because of the complications relating to the split in their family. They are told that they will be seen individually or jointly at any time they wish. It is helpful to arouse the expectation that intermittent contacts may continue throughout the childhood and adolescence of the children and that the door will always remain open to them. If indicated, an effort is made to counteract the feeling that requesting help to overcome a crisis implies weakness or overdependency; rather it indicates a healthy acceptance of the realistic difficulties of caring for children after divorce and the realization that short-term support by an expert increases their capacity to master such difficulties in a wise manner.

Lower barriers for crisis intervention. Administrative arrangements should be made for any parent or child to be seen within a few days of asking for help. Crisis intervention is episodic, and the expectable two to four crisis contacts are usually concentrated within a two- to three-week period. It may be helpful to set aside an hour twice a week to be free to respond to crisis requests and to be available daily for telephone contacts at the office. I encourage parents in crisis to telephone me at home in cases of emergency; only rarely has the latter provision led to undue infringements on my private life, and in such cases the calls can be curbed. It means a great deal to people in difficulty to know that help is only a telephone call away.

In my office, my secretary has instructions to put through directly to me any call that seems to be a crisis contact, even if I am teaching or talking with another client. It is important for both students and clients to realize that an essential part of our work is immediate response to a request for crisis intervention, which in our center has highest priority.

Types of intervention. In contrast with the structured nature of the intake procedure, in postdivorce intervention the parent or child should have the choice whether to see me alone or with other family members. The contact is initially energized and structured by the client's felt need, usually expressed dur-

*The terms "specialist," "counselor," "intercessor," and "intervener" are used interchangeably in this section.

ing a short telephone conversation. After the first contact, the parents or children decide jointly with me who else should be seen. Convening a meeting with both parents or with the parents and selected members of the extended family may be suggested. Certain aspects of the visiting agreement may need to be reevaluated and renegotiated, parents and children may need to be guided in their interactions, or additional support from grandparents or influential members of the extended family may need to be mobilized to tide the parents and children over a current crisis.

The demands of postdivorce intervention are varied, and a wide range of intercession techniques must be available to allow the intervener to react appropriately to the demands of a particular situation. If both parents have a relatively healthy personality structure, techniques usually required are of the "enabling" type: education, guidance, and mediation. In cases in which one or both parents are psychiatrically disturbed and in which the crisis may be linked with a breakdown in implementing the terms of the divorce agreement because of parental psychopathology or with disturbance of a child because of disordered parental behavior during visits, it may not be enough for the intervener to utilize such purely nonauthoritarian techniques. The latter are founded on the approach of supporting and adding to the competence of "good enough" parents to work out their own solution of a family problem. It is important that we should not romanticize such an approach; in certain cases it just will not succeed, due to irrationality in one of the parents that cannot be significantly ameliorated by ordinary verbal persuasion and appeals to parental love and responsibility.

These irrational elements are often based on narcissistic blaming, paranoid fantasies, or psychotic ideation. The more salient they are, the more it is necessary for the intercessor to take on a more directive role in order to protect the well-being or mental health of the children. In cases in which the expertise and status of the intervener do not succeed in providing the leverage to counterbalance the irrational drives of the disturbed parent and in which referral for psychiatric treatment is not accepted or does not lead to the interruption of destructive patterns of behavior, the other parent should be advised to take court action to curb such behavior by judicial decision. The intervener may need to write a suitable report to the court, presenting recommendations regarding the case and their rationale. In only a few extreme cases, it may be necessary to foster an appeal to the courts (or report to protective services) for emergency authoritarian intervention to protect the well-being of the children. Sometimes merely informing the parents of the intervener's willingness to take such a step is sufficient to force the offending parent to conform.

Despite invoking the authority of the courts actually or potentially, it is possible to offer to continue in the role as a guide to both parents in the future. Such an extreme action places a great strain on the relationship with the sick parent, and it is understandable that he or she may then perceive the intervener as a personal enemy and cut off all further contact. Surprisingly, however, in several cases the healthy part of the parent's personality has been sufficiently strong that he or she responded positively to the offer of continuing help to the total family, and continuing guidance to both parents concerning their co-parenting responsibilities was provided.

Collaboration with community caregivers. As in all crisis intervention, it is important to mobilize the support of community caregivers, not only to focus their efforts to support parents and children in dealing with current issues but also to help them work out ways over the long term to enhance the social adjustment and meet the educational needs of the children. Relevant caregivers are likely to include teachers, counselors, and administrative staff of schools; social workers; community center workers; and family physicians. In order to provide continuing help to the family, other professionals may be asked for supplementary information about the functioning of the children and their family and be invited to keep the intervener informed about the progress or difficulties of the family. The caregivers' motivation is aroused to devote special care and attention to the children and their parents; they are also offered free specialist consultation by telephone or through face-to-face meetings if they encounter problems in their own daily work with the children. In my experience, school personnel, social workers, and family physicians have indeed requested subsequent consultation, and in effect we have developed an informal team operation.

Open group meetings. At our center, we have developed a mechanism that is particularly valuable in offering guidance to parents following divorce. I set aside one hour each week in the early evening during which I am available without prior appointment to any parent who wishes to ask me questions in a group educational setting about current or anticipated difficulties of or with their children. Originally, these weekly group meetings were designed as a forum for providing proactive guidance to parents considering divorce about the expectable reactions of their children and how best to handle them. Initially, a short lecture was given at each meeting, followed by questions from the audience. However, I soon discovered that in addition to parents contemplating divorce or in the throes of the divorce process, other parents who were encountering difficulties with their children months or years after divorce also came to the meetings—which were advertised as sessions open to parents who wished to discuss problems of children of divorce. Instead of repeating lectures to a new group every couple of sessions, the meetings were organized entirely on a question-and-answer basis and geared to the felt needs of participants, many of whom attended intermittently for several sessions. The result has been a most interesting educational group with a completely open-ended format.

In some instances, a parent involved in a particularly burdensome crisis before or after divorce has poured out private and personal details of the current predicament, despite efforts to get him or her to formulate questions in a generalized, nonpersonalized manner (befitting an educational rather than a therapeutic setting). Such parents may describe, for example, physical violence of the spouse or ex-spouse or the sudden desertion of the children by the other parent. In such cases, the questioner is urged to make an appointment for private guidance, although it is possible to discuss the general implications and complications of the predicament in a nonpersonalized way in the group setting. On such occasions, the other members of the audience have often spontaneously offered helpful suggestions and sympathetic reassurance and support to the questioner. As such incidents accumulated, the educational meetings began to take on the additional features of a mutual-help support group. In fact, a core subgroup of parents with long-standing problems involving their ex-spouse or their children have informally bonded together into a mutual support group. Some of these people attend the meetings every week, often without saying a word, apparently content to feel part of the group and to derive comfort from hearing about the problems of other parents and from listening to my comments. One parent said, "It helps me a lot to see my difficulties and those of my children within the perspective of the experience of other divorced parents. It gives me a sense of balance."

Common Issues and Their Treatment

The following issues have often been presented for intervention.

Parental interference with visiting arrangements. This was the most frequent reason for a call for help. The noncustodial parent, usually the father, accuses the mother of preventing the children from visiting according to the jointly agreed or court-adjudicated schedule. Often these accusations are justified, although the situation may be aggravated by the unwise behavior of a father, reacting to his frustrations by maligning the mother, whom he accuses of taking sides against him.

Intervention in such cases usually includes making the custodial parent aware that he or she is endangering the mental health of the children by preventing them from having adequate contact with the noncustodial parent, then exploring the reasons for behaving in this manner. If the custodial parent is acting on the fear that the noncustodial parent is psychologically disturbed and will harm the children, the basis of this fear is explored. As previously mentioned, if it seems necessary, a psychologist investigates the personality structure of the noncustodial parent by means of a comprehensive battery of psychological tests to validate whether the fears are in fact justified.

If the custodial parent's fears are not justified, the specialist meets with the parents jointly, helping both parties understand that a negative evaluation of each by the other is an expectable consequence of the animosity and distrust that occur after divorce. The parents are told that they must guard against their natural tendency to bias and to negative judgments based on preconceptions and that they must accept this tendency in the other. Both parents must make an effort to overcome their mutual suspicions if they are to implement their plans for the welfare of the children.

In my experience, if neither of the parents suffers from a major personality disturbance and the two have not waited too long before seeking help, such an approach usually succeeds within three to four sessions. If, however, a pattern of broken contact between the children and the noncustodial parent is established, the matter is usually not as easily remedied because antagonisms have been allowed to develop in the children. In cases of long-standing breaks in parental contact or in which parental psychopathology is a major factor, the noncustodial parent should be supported in seeking legal redress.

Child interference with visiting. Sometimes the custodial parent openly or covertly influences the children to oppose visits to the other parent. In other cases, the children may develop their own opposition to visits because of the negative attitudes of the custodial parent or because of the noncustodial parent's unwise behavior during visits. The child may become upset after visits, experience difficulties in school, or have behavior problems in the home that are clearly linked with visits. Understandably, the custodial parent seeks to protect the child by allowing him or her to avoid visits.

It is important to deal promptly with such situations. It is helpful to warn parents against such behavior at the time of divorce, helping them to understand that the adults must decide what is best for the child and that the question of regular contact with the noncustodial parent is not a matter for negotiation. When such a situation develops, the specialist should meet with the children alone to explore the basis for their objections. Usually they stoutly maintain that their attitudes have not been influenced by the custodial parent but are based entirely on the negative behavior of the noncustodial parent toward them or the custodial parent. Despite these accusations, it is usually easy to get the child to admit that he or she also loves the noncustodial parent and would not object to visits if the parent's behavior improved.

After meeting with the child, the specialist should explain to the noncustodial parent how the child feels. Almost invariably the response is that the child has been "brainwashed" by the custodial parent. Although admitting that this may be a factor and, moreover, one that the specialist will try to change, the specialist should attempt to persuade the noncustodial parent to be more sensitive to the needs of the child. Meeting with both parents jointly, the specialist should emphasize the importance of maintaining the visiting plan. Finally, it is helpful for the specialist to meet jointly with the child and the noncustodial parent to help them communicate effectively and find ways to make the visits more satisfying.

In the absence of parental psychopathology, results depend on the timing of the intervention. The longer the situation has lasted, the harder it is to change, particularly with an older child who has become fiercely partisan. In such cases, the authority of the courts may be of little help. In cases of salient psychopathology in the noncustodial parent, parent–child contact may have to be terminated or established under the supervision of the court or a court-appointed person.

Infringement upon privacy. Frequently, the noncustodial parent, usually the father, enters the home of the former spouse without being invited or telephones the children at home without the custodial parent's prior approval. In such cases, the custodial parent becomes increasingly angry over violation of privacy, whereas the noncustodial parent does not understand this anger and ascribes it to the custodial parent's lack of psychological balance. Usually these situations can be easily remedied in a joint meeting wherein the former spouses are encouraged to discuss ways they can communicate with the children and each other without violating the privacy of either person.

Differences in value systems in child care. Differing attitudes and practices of child care, a common focal point of parental conflicts leading to divorce, are sources of continuing conflict after the divorce. Parents may believe that their individual approach to child care and education is the correct approach and that the other parent's approaches are harmful to the healthy development of the children. Consequently, quarrels arise and hostility escalates.

In such instances, it is helpful to arrange one or two joint meetings during which the parents are encouraged to express their opinions and fears. The specialist should point out that when parents live under the same roof, it is important for them to resolve their differences and adopt a unified policy of child care so that the children do not become confused by inconsistent signals or attempt to play one parent against the other. When spouses divorce, each parent organizes his or her own home in line with his or her own values. As long as the parents do not allow the children to manipulate them, the children soon learn to behave in each home in conformity with the demands of the parent in charge, just as they also learn to conform to authorities in other settings. As long as each parent communicates values and expectations clearly and consistently, the children will not become confused. Moreover, as long as the parent's behavior is based on love, children can adapt to widely different patterns of upbringing without damage to their mental health. Despite their differences in behavioral style, most parents admit that the other parent loves the children and is devoted to them.

Disturbed child behavior. Family crises often occur in response to disturbed behavior in one or more of the children. Such requests should be evaluated quickly. If the parents' description of the child indicates a recent change, a diagnostic appraisal is indicated. Often, the child is merely manifesting characteristic signs of a predictable adjustment disorder, in which case the parents should be reassured and guidance offered. If the appraisal indicates that the child is suffering from significant psychopathology, the child and the parents should be referred for psychotherapy.

Sometimes an adolescent is out of control in reaction to his or her noncustodial father's partial or complete abdication of responsibility. Such situations are often aggravated by depression and a feeling of helplessness in the mother, who has to work long hours to maintain her one-parent home. In my experience, if the adolescent is violent toward his or her siblings, actively rebels against the mother's authority, and shows early signs of delinquency, little is to be gained by psychotherapeutic support for the mother and counseling of the adolescent. In such cases, I usually recommend placement in a residential school, which is relatively easy to arrange in Israel because the country has a well-developed network of residential institutions.

Courtship or remarriage of a parent. The specialist may be asked to offer counseling to a parent, and sometimes to older children, with regard to the sexual curiosity of the adolescent or to the adolescent's attempts to interfere in and control the sex life of the parents. Sometimes a parent may engage in a flurry of sexual behavior when free of the constraints of married life or in an effort to deny depression and respond to feelings of having been rejected by the former spouse. One or two counseling sessions is often sufficient to help these parents reinstate adequate controls and to stand firm against children who attempt to intrude unduly into their private life. Children, too, are usually receptive to such intervention.

When a parent announces his or her intention of remarrying (or does not make an announcement for fear of upsetting the children, but the children find out anyway), the children and former spouse often feel insecure, despite the fact that remarriage often stabilizes the life situation of the parent and thus potentially improves the welfare of the children. The children and former spouse should be encouraged to view remarriage in a positive light.

In such situations, it is helpful to meet first with the parent contemplating remarriage and discuss the likely complications and how to deal with them. Then the specialist should meet with the parent considering remarriage and the children to discuss the issues surrounding the remarriage plan, particularly the relationship of the children with the future stepparent and any stepsiblings, as well as possible fears of the children that the parent will withdraw his or her love. Fears concerning moving to a new home far from their present school and friendship groups should also be addressed.

Finally, we advocate a meeting with both parents and the prospective new spouse to offer guidance on possible problems and on ways of handling them. It is beneficial to meet jointly with the parents of both households to overcome communication barriers that might interfere with the care of the children.

Conclusion

This chapter addresses the problems posed by trying to prevent psychological disorder in children exposed to a major family stress—separation or divorce of parents—with the associated reduction in psychosocial support for the children caused by the parents' preoccupation with their marital conflicts as well as depression resulting from the breakdown of their marriage. This constellation paradigmatically reflects mental health risk—high stress and low psychosocial support.

In the first section of this chapter, a rationale for a proactive approach is proposed. The preventive worker must *take the initiative* in intervening in the life of divorcing families, often without having been invited to do so. This situation is an inevitable consequence of the model of primary prevention; the preventive mental health worker deals with a currently healthy population that is recognized to be at risk of future illness, although few of its members may be currently aware of the dangers that lie ahead. How then can we justify such uninvited intervention into what most people in a democratic society consider to be a private domain? How may we obtain societal sanction for such encroachment? How may we avoid the criticism of civil libertarians that we are adopting a parental approach or "playing God"?

This chapter emphasizes the need for careful circumspection in planning programs and developing preventive methods and techniques in order to ensure that we do not insensitively push people around and that we respect and foster their autonomy as much as possible. Simultaneously, we must build in safeguards to facilitate parents' ability to reject our intercession if we do not obtain their sanction for our playing an active part in their lives.

The second section of the chapter details a model for a comprehensive program of preventive intervention. Most children are upset by the divorce of their parents and its consequences; although only a minority become sick, it is a large minority—possibly as high as 30 percent. Clearly the traditional slogan of safeguarding "the best interests of the child" is an idealistic formulation; it should be replaced by "trying to do the least harm to the child." How can this be accomplished through a planned program that must grapple with the obstacles posed by the large size and heterogeneity of the population involved as well as with the knowledge that the potential hazards will continue at least throughout childhood and are not restricted to the immediate crisis of the divorce? Thus the model proposes building an organizational framework that provides for repeated intermittent professional support in response to need over many years, buttressed by nonprofessional support through mutual-help systems.

Finally, this chapter presents a brief description of a range of supportive methods and techniques, from which professional workers may choose those that are appropriate to the individual needs, resources, and limitations of their clients. My thesis has by now become traditional in population-oriented psychiatry: We must be prepared to deal with *all* members of the population at risk and to tailor our services to their idiosyncratic needs, rather than perfecting a method and then recruiting clients for whom the method is appropriate, while rejecting those for whom it is unsuitable. This approach involves developing a wide range of techniques and treating innovatively the needs of individuals and families with diverse ethnic and sociocultural life-styles.

Although the techniques described here are yet to be tested through rigorous, experimentally designed research in which a random sample of children of divorce and their parents who receive interventions are compared longitudinally with a control group, the anecdotal evidence from consultation with more than 350 children and their parents indicates that the approaches described here are promising. In light of high divorce rates and the magnitude of the stress experienced by children of divorce and their families, continued experimentation with and testing of preventive programs involving collaboration with attorneys, judges, physicians, mental health and social welfare personnel, teachers, clergy, and other caregivers are urgently needed. Even in the absence of definitive research findings, it is vital that we reach out to children and their parents before, during, and after divorce.

References

Elkin, M. (1987). Joint custody: Affirming that parents and families are forever. *Social Work, 32*, 18–24.

Fogelman, K. (1983). *Growing up in Great Britain*. London: Macmillan.

Hagen, J. (1987). Proceed with caution: Advocating joint custody. *Social Work, 32*, 269–231.

James, H. (1897). *Whar Masie knew*. London: The Bodley Head.

Kalter, N. (1977). Children of divorce in an outpatient psychiatric population. *American Journal of Orthopsychiatry, 47*, 40–51.

Kalter, N., & Rembar, J. (1981). The significance of a child's age at the time of parental divorce. *American Journal of Orthopsychiatry, 51*, 85–100.

McDermott, J. F. (1970). Divorce and its psychiatric sequelae in children. *Archives of General Psychiatry, 23*, 421–427.

McKinnon, R., & Wallerstein, J. (1988). A preventive intervention program for parents and young children in joint custody arrangements. *American Journal of Orthopsychiatry, 58*, 168–178.

Mnookin, R. (1978). *Bargaining in the shadow of the law*. Oxford, England: Centre for Sociolegal Studies, Oxford University.

Rutter, M. (1985). Resilience in the face of adversity. *British Journal of Psychiatry, 147*, 598–611.

Wadsworth, M. E. J. (1979). *Roots of delinquency*. New York: Barnes and Noble.

Wadsworth, M. E. J., & Maclean, M. (1986). Parents' divorce and children's life changes. *Children and Youth Services Review*, 8, 145-159.

Wadsworth, M. E. J., Peckham, C. S., & Taylor, B. (1985). The role of national longitudinal studies in prediction of health, development, and behavior. In D. B. Walker & J. B. Richmond (Eds.), *Monitoring child health in the United States* (pp. 63–83). Cambridge, MA: Harvard University Press.

Wallerstein, J. S., & Kelly, J. B. (1980). *Surviving the breakup*. New York: Basic Books.

Weiss, R. S. (1975). *Marital separation*. New York: Basic Books.

16

Crisis Prevention for Parents of Children with Handicapping Conditions

JUDITH GREENBAUM AND GERALDINE MARKEL

PARENTS OF HANDICAPPED CHILDREN need effective coping tools to anticipate problems and avoid crises in caring for their children. The education and training of these parents can provide such tools. We hope that the principles addressed in this chapter will guide professionals in their work toward this end:

- The presence of a handicapped child creates a dramatic impact on the family.
- The parents' primary goal is to ensure that their child reaches his or her maximum potential.
- The family of the handicapped child faces predictable crises relating to stages in the life cycle of the child, issues in family functioning, and gaps in services available to both the child and family.
- Parents can learn to prevent and/or manage crises regardless of their socio-economic and educational backgrounds.
- Research in psychology, social work, and education has yielded systematic procedures that can be used to train parents of handicapped children.
- Mental health professionals should have a repertoire of roles and skills, from which they can select, to help parents prevent or manage crises.
- A critical role of the mental health worker is to create an adaptive training system that educates parents to anticipate, prevent, manage, and learn from crises.
- Parent-education groups are the most efficient and effective method to train parents to prevent and manage crises.

Within an educational context, handicapped children have been defined as "mentally retarded, hard of hearing, deaf, speech impaired, visually handicapped, seriously emotionally disturbed, orthopedically impaired, or other health impaired children or children with specific learning disabilities" (Public Law 94-142, p. 488). In 1975, when this Act was passed, half of the more than eight million handicapped children in this country were not receiving appropriate educational services and more than one million of them were excluded entirely from the public school system.

Although the conditions of handicapped children vary widely, several researchers (Barsch, 1968; Greenbaum, 1980; Simeonsson & Bailey, 1986) found many similarities among families with handicapped children, regardless of the child's disability. Families of handicapped children, as well as the disabled person, share certain problems by virtue of their disadvantaged and devalued position (Wright, 1983). However, practitioners emphasize the importance of viewing each family and family member as having individual strengths and needs, not merely as members of a class of people (Gallagher & Vietze, 1986). It is important to understand that what actually handicaps a person cannot be determined by describing the disability alone (Wright, 1983). Societal attitudes and values, for example, or architectural, legal, and social barriers play as important a role as does the specific limitation of function in the handicapped individual's pursuit of life goals. Additionally, evidence suggests that as environmental alterations are made to meet the needs of a person with a disability and as services are provided to the child and the family, the severity of the problems emanating from the handicapping condition is modified and lessened.

Historical Overview

Throughout recorded history, individuals who were different because of a handicap were "destroyed, tortured, exorcised, sterilized, ignored, exiled, exploited, or considered divine" (Hewett & Forness, 1974, p. 12). Use of institutionalization to segregate handicapped persons from society was the rule until as recently as 1950.

In the literature published between 1945 and 1970, the birth of a handicapped child was generally seen as a tragedy for all involved. Common parental reactions to the birth of a handicapped child included grief, denial, guilt, shame, withdrawal, anger, hostility, recrimination, rejection, overprotection, acceptance, and integration (Wolfensberger & Kurtz, 1969). When a retarded child was born into a family, physicians generally advised the family to institutionalize the child, and the family usually complied. Families questioning either their physician's diagnosis or the recommendation for institutionalization were viewed as pathological. In the stereotypical family of that time, the birth of a handicapped child was perceived by the father as an insult to his masculinity and to his family name; the mother felt it was a punishment for an imagined sin and was overwhelmed by the burden of child care. Parents often drifted toward divorce as the mother devoted more of her time to the care of the handicapped child. The siblings were shamed and shunned by their peers as well as emotionally neglected by their distressed parents. In addition, the daughters of the family, who were made to share in the responsibility of child care, were distanced from their friends and the normal joys of growing up. The entire family became socially isolated (Wolfensberger & Kurtz, 1969). For these reasons institutionalization was recommended, although institutionalization itself often brought further grief both to parents and child (Turnbull & Turnbull, 1978).

With the founding of the Association for Retarded Children (now Citizens) in 1950, parents of handicapped children began to organize: first, to upgrade the institutions into which their children had been banished, then to push for publicly funded community services. The return of disabled veterans from World War II and the Korean War further raised the consciousness of society about handicapped persons. Using the Civil Rights movement of the 1960s as a model, parents of handicapped children and disabled adults banded together to ask for equal rights under the law.

After 1970, the litigation and legislation instituted by parent and consumer organizations provided handicapped persons with equal access to appropriate public education, recreation, vocational rehabilitation, civil rights protection against discrimination, the removal of physical barriers, and services and financial support for eligible persons.

Impact on the Family

Parenthood has been viewed as a stressful experience (LeMasters, 1965; Dyer, 1965); the parents of a handicapped child may well face additional stress because of the special demands involved in raising the child. Focusing on the family as a whole, Palfrey, Walker, Butler, and Singer (1989) suggest that socioeconomic status, traditional and nontraditional family style, and the educational attainment of the mother are important variables in the family's adjustment to the handicapped child. In their study of 1,726 special education students with a disabling condition, "28 percent of their parents indicated a direct stressful impact . . . on the family's daily lives in terms of jobs, housing, friendships and marital harmony," rising "to 60 percent for families of children with physical/multiple impairment" (p. 102).

The provision of services to this population created by the increased public awareness of the 1960s and the enabling legislation of the 1970s has improved the life of handicapped children and their families (Simeonsson & Bailey, 1986). In general, contemporary families experience less guilt, less withdrawal from social interactions, and less severe negative feelings compared with their counterparts prior to the 1960s. Contemporary families of handicapped children are more likely to search for help earlier (due to the provision of services at birth and the availability of home programs), are more likely to recover from their crisis (again due to the availability of services), are less depressed (due to the availability of support groups), are able to redefine their roles and initiate attitude and value changes, and are generally better able to accept and understand their child and situation. Whether the stress of having a handicapped child actually precipitates a crisis depends on the magnitude of the handicap, the perception of the handicap by the parents, the family's coping repertoire, and the services and support available to them. However, although parents may be less crisis prone today than they were in earlier years, the stresses that affect families of handicapped children may nevertheless induce a crisis situation.

Life-Cycle Crises

Family life-cycle theory describes stages and transitions that families experience over time. Life-cycle events, whether positive or negative, are considered stressful. They require a change in the routine life pattern of the family system (Turnbull, Summers, & Brotherson, 1986; Farran, Metzger, & Sparling, 1986). In the life cycle of a family with a handicapped child, predictable crisis episodes occur (Suelzle & Deenan, 1981), more or less corresponding to family life in general. These crises, centering on events related to the age of the handicapped child, may continue throughout the child's life. The following predictable life-cycle crisis stages have been identified: diagnosis, preschool years, school entry, late childhood, adolescence, adulthood, and aging parents. At each of these stages, families experience great stress, which often triggers a crisis reaction. Feelings of frustration, disappointment, anger, and grief threaten the emotional stability of individual family members. Values and beliefs are challenged, family functioning undergoes modifications, and social and community relationships change. Family and individual adaptation to these crises depend largely on the amount of support they receive, the availability of services to the handicapped child, and personality factors. According to some researchers, community services play a crucial role in mediating parental responses to these crises (Suelzle & Deenan, 1981).

Diagnosis

Diagnosis can occur at birth or any time thereafter as a result of traumatic injury or disease. Many parents and professionals consider the diagnostic crisis as being the most severe crisis. Much has been written about parental feelings regarding the birth of a handicapped child. Despite increased societal acceptance of the handicapped child, parents still experience shock, disbelief, hopelessness, helplessness, anxiety, and anger. Parents experience chronic sorrow that recurs at various times throughout the life of the child (Olshansky, 1962). In addition to these feelings, several cognitive–affective processes affect the parents' perception of the handicapped child, including expectancy–discrepancy, spread, and underprivileged status or stigma (Wright, 1983; Goffman, 1968).

At birth, most parents expect a normal, healthy child. With the birth of a handicapped child, parents are faced with a discrepancy between their joyous expectations and reality. Parents often report having dreams in which their child is "normal" (the wished-for child). It is only when parents no longer imagine the handicapped child as being nonhandicapped that expectancy–discrepancy issues begin to fade.

Parental attitudes and values, which are generally based on those of society, may also be severely tested if the child has a damaged or atypical physical appearance. For example, parents may find it difficult to look at an infant with an unreconstructed cleft palate.

For some time, parents may focus only on their child's handicap, needs, and problems. The term "spread" describes the power of one characteristic to define the entire person. For example, the parents of a three-pound premature baby may for many months focus only on the child's weight and may ignore how well their child is eating, how attractive he or she is, or how well the child holds up his or her head. It may take a long time for parents of a handicapped child to see the whole child as opposed to the handicapped child.

During the first eighteen months of the handicapped child's life—the span of the diagnostic phase when a child is handicapped at birth—parents are often overwhelmed with caregiving needs. The mother, who is usually the primary caregiver, experiences great stress. Feeding the child with a cleft palate or using a urinary catheter can be difficult and frightening. And performing these tasks while maintaining a normal routine for the rest of the family can be overwhelming.

Throughout this period, many parents find it difficult to communicate with physicians, therapists, and other service providers. Anger, triggered by this difficulty in communication, can color the parents' relationship with professionals for many years. Parents are asked to make decisions regarding medical interventions and therapies about conditions they scarcely understand. They may seek out second and third opinions, trying to make sense of conflicting evidence and advice.

Parents are often unable to find the help they need due to insufficient services. For example, an economically vulnerable family with a child who has bronchopulmonary dysplasia must have a telephone in case of emergencies. The physician will not release the child from the hospital until the family has a telephone. Where does the family turn if it cannot afford a telephone?

In dealing with these difficulties, parents can feel terribly alone. No one seems to understand how they feel, what they want and need. They do not know others who have gone through this crisis and cannot imagine how they and their family will survive. They live from hour to hour, day to day. They are unable to organize their lives or plan for the future. The whole family may be affected by this loss of control. For example, the four-year-old brother of a six-month-old mentally retarded infant woke up during a nightmare and cried, "Mommy, Daddy, I dreamt my house was falling down." Indeed, he described figuratively what was happening to the family during this crisis.

When diagnosis occurs later in the child's life due to traumatic injury or disease, both children and parents may experience these feelings and face these issues. The entire family must confront the discrepancy between the way the child is now compared with the way the child used to be. For many families, this experience is more difficult than giving birth to a handicapped child.

Preschool Years

Even if the parent is successful in accepting and integrating the child into the family during the child's first twelve to eighteen months, new challenges arise during the preschool years when the child enters the community. During this period, the extended family, friends, neighbors, service providers, and strangers meet the child for the first time, and issues of acceptance versus inferior status surface. Parents often perceive that their child is stared at, shunned, patronized, criticized, and denied opportunities that nonhandicapped children automatically enjoy. Parents, too, feel the stigma of inferiority as "parents of a handicapped child." They, too, are stared at, ostracized, and criticized by family members, friends, and neighbors: "It's such a downer to invite her any place," said the parent of a nonhandicapped child about the parent of a handicapped child, "I want to have fun!"

The financial drain on the family can be enormous, despite new legislation in several states that provides some financial support for families with severely handicapped children living at home and state and federally funded Supplemental Security Income (SSI) for persons who qualify. Children may need special clothing, food, and equipment; medical and therapeutic services not reimbursed by health plans; costly respite care; and travel expenses to medical centers. Moreover, many health insurance companies do not cover handicapped persons.

Parental overprotectiveness may surface at this stage in reaction both to the lack of help and understanding the parents and their child may have experienced during the diagnostic process and to the care needs of the handicapped child. Parents may feel that no one can take care of their child as well as they can—and they may be right.

Difficult decisions and sacrifices may be necessary. Mothers who may have been developing careers of their own must make tough decisions regarding their work and self-fulfillment, because the care of the handicapped child and the dearth of trained day-care providers willing to care for such a child may force the mother to stay home.

School Entry

For families with children who have learning disabilities or mild mental impairments, school entry may initiate a diagnostic crisis because the impairment becomes apparent only in an academic environment. For parents who have been aware of and coping with their child's problems, school entry means labeling their child as "different" in order to obtain needed services from the school. These parents do not want their child stigmatized and separated from the general school population and perhaps shunned and scapegoated by peers. Many parents hope that their child will outgrow developmental delays and feel it is too soon to describe their child as handicapped.

For the child, school entry may precipitate a crisis because it may be the first time the child has been away from his or her parents and with a group of other children. Because handicapped children are often excluded from preschool classroom experiences, they lack the emotional, social, behavioral, and communication skills necessary to adjust to school. They have difficulty concentrating on tasks, making friends, sharing the teacher's time, and delaying gratification. Although teachers attempt to impart these skills, the school entry process can be a painful one for both the children and their parents.

At this stage, children with handicapping conditions become less acceptable as playmates to other children. Up to age five, children tend not to perceive differences such as race or handicap between themselves and others. However, at school age the handicapped child has fewer playmates; moreover, playmates tend to be younger or older than the handicapped child. Parental concern about the acceptance of their child by his or her peers may continue throughout the child's life. As awareness grows, acceptance and friendship become key issues for the child.

Late Childhood

During this period the child's long-term potential and prognosis are more clearly defined. Scores on intelligence tests "stabilize" and become more predictive of school success. The parents of children with cerebral palsy may have to accept the fact that their child will not be able to walk efficiently and will probably need a wheelchair for mobility, despite extensive physical therapy. For the deaf child, parents may have to accept the fact that their child will probably never speak clearly enough for casual conversation and will have to use sign language for communication, thus limiting social interaction in the mainstream. The parents of children with learning disabilities may be forced to watch their child fall farther behind in school while becoming increasingly frustrated, special education notwithstanding. These parents and their children may experience a secondary diagnostic crisis as they face discrepancies between past and current expectations about the child's future. Maintaining realistic hope in this crisis can be difficult: parents must reexamine their goals and values and search for ways in which their input can make important differences in their child's life.

Parents of the near-normal child may experience greater stress at this time than do parents of the severely handicapped child. The former may feel that everything they do is crucial to the child's later independence, thus pushing themselves and others hard. Parents of the severely handicapped, on the other hand, may have accepted the general boundaries of the child's future. Despite the sadness accompanying such knowledge, parents may experience a certain relief in this acceptance of reality. Future reality, however, may be modified by vision, creativity, motivation, and new technology.

Concerns about siblings may surface at this time. Although research findings (Grossman, 1972; Simeonsson & Bailey, 1986) suggest that siblings are not necessarily harmed by being the brother or sister of a handicapped child and, indeed, may benefit, parents often feel guilty about the time they spend with the handicapped child and fear that the siblings will feel shortchanged. They also fear that the siblings will be teased or rejected in school by their classmates.

Adolescence

Adolescence, the transition between childhood and adulthood, marks a period of concern and struggle for all parents. Children with a handicap experience all the usual problems of adolescence in addition to problems exacerbated by the handicapping condition. The development of self-concept is a critical issue at this age. Appearance, physique, conformity in dress, behavior, and speech become particularly important (Wright, 1983). Wanting to move into adulthood and be independent, the child remains dependent; wanting to be like his or her peers, the child is "different"; wanting to be with peers, the peer culture is exclusionary.

Handicapped adolescents continue to need parental help. Moreover, the parents may find it difficult to loosen parental bonds and may become even more protective due to their perception of the heightened dangers of adolescence, such as drug use and inappropriate sexual behavior. Appropriate exploration and risk-taking may be hindered in handicapped adolescents. They may be treated by parents, school, and community as being much younger than their actual age.

Because adolescents who are handicapped perceive themselves as being relatively powerless, they often respond to frustration and anger in a passive– aggressive manner. The more parents, teachers, and physicians direct, order, or beg, the more the adolescent may rebel even when the situation is life-threatening.

Regardless of disability, adolescents with a handicap often lag behind their peers socially and/or academically. With learning-disabled and mildly retarded adolescents, the discrepancy between age and ability becomes more apparent, although they may be relatively age-appropriate socially. Physically handicapped, blind, or deaf adolescents who are bright may nonetheless lag academically because they need more time to accomplish academic tasks, such as reading and writing, as well as activities of daily living, such as dressing and eating. Vocational and career training may have been poorly planned and poorly implemented, often unrealistic as to the needs of both the students and the community in which they live. Relatively isolated in childhood due to physical and attitudinal barriers, many adolescents have not been able to develop the social skills necessary for creating and maintaining friendships.

Respite care for more severely dependent mentally impaired or chronically ill adolescents may become extremely difficult to find, leading to further isolation for the parents. The issue of perpetual parenting surfaces: severely impaired adolescents often continue to need the same level of supervision and care as does a young child. Guardianship proceedings for the dependent eighteen-year-old resurrect old feelings of sorrow. As nonhandicapped adolescents happily plan their education and careers, parents of dependent handicapped adolescents must deal with the expanding gulf between their children and others.

Adulthood

For disabled persons, unresolved adolescent issues often continue well into the adult years due to unresolved dependency issues, poorly developed social skills, lack of experience in risk taking, and lack of appropriate community resources. Only recently has society begun to focus on the needs of handicapped adults. Eligibility under federal special education laws ends at age twenty-one. In the economic recession of the 1980s, it was common to encounter well-trained and educated handicapped young adults with no place to work or live and without adequate financial support, transportation, recreation, or social opportunities. There are not enough group homes, adult foster-care facilities, and accessible housing. Attitudinal and physical barriers often prevent meaningful employment. Consequently, adult handicapped persons often remain dependent on their families.

To complicate matters further, the parents of handicapped adults are themselves aging. They have less physical and emotional stamina than is needed for the continued care or support of their handicapped adult child. Respite care for handicapped adults is almost nonexistent in most communities. Families with a dependent mentally impaired or chronically ill young adult may face hardships in their social and work lives. The role of caregiver becomes increasingly difficult. The issue of perpetual parenting must be confronted and resolved.

Coping

Some parents are able to cope effectively using their own resources; others need differing levels of help at various points of crisis in their lives. Still others may need intensive therapy. The mental health professional must decide whether intervention is needed and, if so, what kind. It is important that the parents maintain a sense of control over these crisis situations; mental health workers come and go throughout the child's life, but the parent is the child's support and advocate forever.

Coping depends on personal factors such as resilience, confidence, a sense of humor, willingness to redefine roles, attitudes and values, accessibility of services, and availability of family and community support. Acceptance of the handicap and the situation, which varies throughout the life of the child depending on life stages, family functioning, and environmental factors, is a key issue. According to Featherstone (1980), acceptance, an ongoing process, involves acknowledging the handicap and its long-term significance, integrating the child and the disability into the life of the family and its members, learning to forgive one's own errors and shortcomings, and searching for meaning in loss. On a more practical level, several researchers have reported that financial security helps the coping process; the ability to purchase needed services and respite care provides relief for family members (Featherstone, 1980; Grossman, 1972).

To summarize, in addition to the crises created by life-cycle stresses, further crises may be precipitated by recurring issues of chronic sorrow, dependence/independence, spread, stigma, expectation/discrepancy, and the need for respite care throughout the life of the child. Mental health workers can help parents prevent or manage crises by working proactively to anticipate the occurrence and recurrence of these problems, thus reducing the impact of stress (Farran et al., 1986); by helping parents understand life-cycle crises; and by providing information, behavioral training, and skill development.

Goals

Parents' goals for their handicapped child are similar to their goals for their nonhandicapped children: to function relatively independently as adults in keeping with their own values, needs, and interests. The mental health worker can help the parent become more self-aware, to set goals for the future, and to plan strategies for achieving goals (Brotherson & Turnbull, 1988). Parents should be encouraged to picture how they want their child to function as an adult and begin working early toward those goals. For example, if their goal for their child is as much independence as possible, they must begin using babysitting or respite care during the child's first few months of life, include the child in the family's routine outings in the community at an early age, and give the child responsibilities in the home.

Parents can be helped to examine and modify values and attitudes that inadvertently interfere with the welfare of their child. For example, parents might work toward valuing individual differences among family members so that the handicapped child can become no more "different" in the family from anyone else. All family members should be encouraged to communicate openly and to listen actively to one another's feelings so that feelings are shared.

The goals provide a focus for the parents, which, in turn, helps them and professionals decide on specific objectives and related training. In developing future goals and attempting to build a healthy family, parents gain a sense of purpose and control over their life by being able to connect their daily routines and activities with the strengths they wish to develop in their child. Families increase the likelihood of realistic progress and decrease the chances of wasting time, energy, and money. In so doing, they experience less stress and are able to enjoy their child.

The Mental Health Worker's Roles in Helping Parents

The mental health worker can assume many roles in working with parents of handicapped children. Although role variation may occur based on the setting (school, hospital, private practice, or community agency), six roles are critical in helping parents: listener, informer, facilitator, trainer, therapist, and advocate. In general these roles move from nondirective to directive, from informal to formal, and from less intensive to more intensive involvement with the parents. The roles provide a flexible repertoire of functions and related tasks in dealing with ongoing and rapidly changing needs. The worker should attempt to accurately analyze and select the role that will facilitate growth in the parent. A crisis situation, for example, diagnosis, may require the worker to assume various roles in his or her dynamic interactions with the parents (Lippitt & Lippitt, 1966).

In the *listener* role, the worker creates a climate of openness, credibility, and trust; legitimizes feelings; and through active listening begins discussing parents' needs and goals.

As an *informer*, the worker gathers information for the parents about their child's handicapping condition; knows what resources are available in the community; refers to parent groups and needed services; creates a professional community network; and provides continuing education to other professionals.

The *facilitator* role, which begins the dynamic interaction between parent and worker, often extends over a long period. In this role, the worker stimulates thinking, raises issues, and identifies both positive and negative issues. The worker helps parents use a systematic problem-solving process by enabling them to identify and prioritize their problems; outlines alternative solutions and consequences; sets up a monitoring system for the child and the family; and illustrates how to use feedback for decision making. Focusing on collaboration and mutual support helps parents begin using their own resources and become self-managing.

The *trainer* role, usually carried out in a group setting, focuses on educational needs. The worker helps develop parent groups, provides direct training and practice in child development, behavior management, communication skills, assertiveness, and stress management. Parents are helped to share their feelings so they can examine how negative thinking presents barriers to coping and feeds into helplessness. Work with the school and service agency is illustrated and practiced. This role is best fulfilled by creating an adaptive training system, which is described in a later section of this chapter.

The role of *therapist* is obviously a familiar one to mental health professionals. In a crisis-prevention framework, the role of therapist is not usually adopted initially. The therapist raises deeper issues and concerns, identifies underlying psychological problems, and proposes and implements a treatment plan. The worker must approach the initiation of therapy with great care; persons who are not ready for this approach will not benefit from it. The therapeutic role is often viewed negatively by parents who feel their primary needs are to obtain services for their children (Radin, 1974). As one parent said, "Can you imagine! The social worker wants to help me deal with my anger. I wouldn't have any anger if they would just give my child the services he needs."

Some parents, however, do have symptoms of underlying psychopathology that present significant barriers to ensuring the growth of their child. Although these parents may respond well to individual psychotherapy, a parent education group may also be appropriate. If parents function fairly well and are "good enough" parents, the therapeutic role need not be assumed (Bettelheim, 1988).

As *advocate*, the worker advises parents of their rights under the various laws serving handicapped children, helps parents design strategies to ensure the exercise of these rights, trains parents in assertiveness skills, negotiates, mediates, and accompanies parents to meetings. This role also involves encouraging other professionals to assume positive attitudes toward the parents. In some situations, parents can be referred to parent advocacy groups that can exercise more vigorous intervention when necessary (Sundel & Sundel, 1980).

The following dialogues between a worker and a parent illustrate the various roles that a worker can assume during the crisis of diagnosis:

Listener (at time of birth)
Parent: (crying) "She's so small, she's got all those tubes sticking out of her. I can't stand looking at her. I'm afraid she'll die. I can't handle this, Why couldn't I make a beautiful baby?"
Worker: (touching parent's hand) "I know you're scared; it is frightening. We're monitoring closely and so far she's O.K. Try not to blame yourself for anything. You didn't cause this to happen. We'll help you learn to take care of her."

Informer (soon after)
Parent: "Why does she have so many tubes in her? Doesn't it hurt? How long will this go on? Do they really know what they're doing?"
Worker: "I'm sure you have lots of questions—many of which I can't answer. Here is a booklet on premature babies that will give you some information. I'm going to schedule an appointment with the neonatologist so you can get some more answers. Let's write a list of questions you want to ask."
Parent: "Look, I'm overwhelmed. How can I get here every day with two other children?"
Worker: "I understand how you feel. My job is to help find you the information and resources you need. First, there's a babysitting service in the hospital. Second, there's a parent group in the hospital. It might be helpful to talk to another parent who's had a similar experience."

Facilitator (several weeks later)
Worker: "Have you had time to think about taking the baby home?"
Parent: "She's too tiny. I'm afraid. I can't possibly take care of her."
Worker: "Let's start with what we know about your baby. She is cute and looks just like her mom. She's breathing on her own, and the doctors think she's strong enough to go home. Yes, you've got a baby with problems. We don't know what the future will bring, but let's be hopeful. Meanwhile we'll all be working together. I'll find a public health nurse to come to your home to help you. You've been taking care of her in the hospital. Now, what seems so hard about caring for her at home? We can make a plan."

Trainer (several months later)
Parent: "My daughter is blind. I don't know what to do. I'm afraid to put her down because she might get hurt. She cries a lot and holds her breath."
Worker: "You're facing some difficult problems. I've referred you to your public school. They are responsible for providing a home teacher who can train you in working with your child. Also, you'd benefit from the parent group; it can help you learn to manage your child at home. What are some things that you've done that have worked?"

Therapist(whenever deeper issues become apparent)
Parent: "I just can't deal with blindness. I think it's the most horrible thing that can happen to anyone. I hate myself. I even hate my baby."
Worker: "I think we should talk about this. This sounds like a different kind of problem. Why don't we set up some meetings during which we can work on these feelings?"

Advocate
Parent: "I've called the school and they told me that their classes are full and they can't take my child."
Worker: "Remember the booklet I gave you on your legal rights as the parent of a handicapped child? With your permission I'll call the director of special education right now and set up a meeting."

Parent Training

Since the 1960s, researchers have demonstrated that parents can be trained to teach their handicapped children various skills, thus positively affecting their learning and school socialization (Brown & Moersch, 1978; Henderson, 1981; Turnbull & Summers, 1987). Such training is usually accomplished with systematic behavior management techniques (Berkowitz & Graziano, 1972; Johnson & Katz, 1973).

Early attempts at training children with a handicap (Wahler, Wenkel, Peterson, & Morrison, 1965) involved at least one highly motivated parent, one or two specific child behaviors, and considerable professional involvement in treatment, predominantly in a clinical setting. Later projects targeted complex behaviors, training parents in all aspects of intervention, greater attention to training in and for the natural environment, and the use of group formats (Robinson, 1975; Glogower & Sloop, 1976; Moreland, Schwebel, Beck, & Wells, 1982). Many training options and formats (Heifetz, 1977; Peed, Roberts, & Forehand, 1977; Bernal, Klinnert, & Schultz, 1980) now exist to help parents learn to alter their children's interpersonal, social, and academic behaviors in various settings. Still, maintenance and generalization effects can be problematic (Forehand et al., 1979; Koegel, Glahn, & Nieminen, 1978; Kelly, Embry, & Baer, 1979).

Frequently parents and children fail to generalize their skills to environments other than those in which they were trained. Improvement from training done in clinic or home may not be observed in school or community. To improve effectiveness, the practice of skills must be incorporated into training programs in addition to lectures, discussions, and films. Training should also include techniques such as modeling, coaching, behavioral rehearsal, and feedback. When it is possible, skills should be practiced in settings and situations similar to those in which the skills will be required (Forehand & Atkeson, 1977; Nay, 1979). For example, fathers were trained to care for their infants in the hospital with follow-up sessions in their homes (Dachman, Aless, Urazo, Fugua, & Kerr, 1986). In addition, the involvement of parents in all aspects of the training process facilitates maintenance and generalization. Therefore, self-regulatory and self-management skills should be targeted through self-selection of goals, self-recording and monitoring, self-evaluation and reinforcement. Follow-up, reinforcement, and support by nonprofessionals (other parents, siblings, volunteers) help provide the continuity of training that professionals cannot provide due to time and monetary constraints (Sanders & James, 1983).

The Adaptive Training System

A systems approach is used to train parents both individually and in parent-education groups. The worker establishes the system with a particular set of information, skills, values, and experiences. The goal of the system is to provide parents with the tools and coping mechanisms with which to prevent and manage crises as well as to ensure the child's progress.

To meet the individual and ongoing needs and interests of parents, the system must be adaptive. To attain adaptability, the worker must actively create mechanisms to collect and opportunities to use information on the progress of the parents, family, and the child. Feedback is used continuously to maintain or modify the training system (Markel, 1974).

Working with Individual Families

The system begins at the point at which the parent is currently functioning. The four-step circular process includes assessment, goal setting, strategies, and feedback.

Assessment: Where are we now? Based on clinical intake procedures, the first step is to identify how the family is feeling and functioning at this time. Under- or overestimation of family strengths and needs can lead to faulty planning and decision making. Determining how much the family understands of the child's situation and what coping mechanisms they can draw upon may require more than one or two interviews. Until these questions are answered correctly, the system will contain errors. The information must be constantly updated as the family situation changes.

Goal setting: Where do we want to go? The mental health worker incorporates knowledge of larger psychosocial issues and child-development theory with the family's values, long-term vision of their child, and feelings or attitudinal barriers they face. Short- and long-term goals are established cooperatively with the parents. The use of accurate information on the child's progress ensures that goals are relevant to the parents' values, appropriate in terms of the child's potential, and realistically based on family situations or available services. This process can begin in an informal and exploratory manner with more formalized goal setting at a later date.

Strategies: How will we get there? Using information gained from the assessment and goal-setting process, the worker and parents decide on a set of strategies. These strategies include (1) understanding and clarifying feelings, values, strengths, and weaknesses, (2) gathering information on, for example, child development or resources, and/or (3) improving skills such as preparing for a conference, controlling fears, asking questions, or managing conflict.

Feedback: How well did things go? Recording or monitoring mechanisms are established to collect information about progress toward the parents' goals and the impact of these goals on the child and family. Together, parents and worker judge the effectiveness of the strategies; adjustments are made based on the results.

It is important to pinpoint discrepancies that may exist between what is said and what progress has actually occurred (for example, "everything is O.K." versus parent misses appointments or child's temper tantrums increase). Training that meets the parents' real needs can be arranged only when feedback is accurate and timely. It is critical to monitor behaviors and trends if activities are to remain in focus. Modeling, cueing, and reinforcing parental record keeping is important. Record keeping may include notes on conferences, diaries, report cards, calendars, or photographs. Parents should be responsible for the record keeping, which is used as a framework for discussions and interactions between the worker and parents.

In order to obtain, analyze, and use feedback effectively, the parents and the worker should discuss information about each other's performance and that of the child. Figure 1 provides examples of questions that workers should ask parents.

It is important to have long- and short-term goals with feedback about the accomplishment of or progress toward each goal. Such feedback provides information on long-term objectives and demonstrates whether skills learned at home or in school have been maintained and/or generalized to other environments. Often the skills are inadequate, and when students enter the community or work environment, the inadequacies of their school programs become evident. The practitioner plays a critical role in helping parents (and children) establish realistic objectives related to community life and in monitoring progress toward these goals. In turn, such information must be used to influence the school or training program. For example, if social skills are a goal, they must be demonstrated and practiced in school, at home, at work, and in the commu-

FIGURE 1. Sample questions to ask parents.

- *What have I done that works?*

Describe how I have helped you pinpoint your important needs.
List the most and least useful things I have done.
Show me things you have used for monitoring your progress and/or your child's progress.
Can you suggest how I can be more helpful?
To what degree am I providing the information, support, or skill development you want?
What should be maintained or modified in my services to you?

- *What have you done that works?*

To what degree are you accessing the services and resources you need?
To what degree are you feeling you can cope with and manage problems and crises?
List ways you have changed or grown because of our meetings.
Describe the degree to which strategies have worked for you.
What should be maintained or modified?

- *How has the child progressed?*

What events or behaviors indicate progress or lack of progress toward goals?
List positive or negative feelings the child has about him- or herself. Can the child identify ways in which he or she has made progress?
How is current progress related to previous problems, crises, or barriers? What does this mean for the future?
What should be maintained or modified?

nity. In each situation, items for discussions with the parent should focus on the following questions: What type and degree of success is observed in social situations? When problems occur, how difficult is it to bring the child back into compliance? How consistent is this information with other sources? Is current training adequate? What training or modification should be considered?

Major problems occur if parents are not fully involved in the planning, no feedback procedures are established, information used for decision making is not based on the child's observed or actual progress, and progress is not related to relevant goals—for example, the child can do math on ditto sheets but cannot make change or add at work. In order to get the system to function effectively, the worker may need to (1) suggest samples of relevant and realistic objectives to parents, (2) identify relevant monitoring mechanisms to measure progress toward goals (especially in the community), and (3) demonstrate techniques of problem solving and decision making related to the goals and values of the parents. The worker's role is fulfilled when parents collect and use information about the child's progress independently to prevent or manage the predictable and ongoing crises in their lives. In essence, the parents become self-managed.

Working with Groups

The four-step model of assessment, goal setting, strategies, and feedback is also applicable to parent-education groups. The group should first discuss values and attitudes; second, identify ways in which positive feelings can help parents prevent and manage crises; and third, describe techniques for becoming independent decision makers. The overarching goal is for parents to gain a sense of control over their lives. To this end, the worker teaches skills related to service acquisition for children, effective communication with professionals, problem solving, self-management, conflict resolution, and crisis management. It is important for the worker to model group behaviors; resist getting into a treatment mode; avoid jargon; allow for disagreement; encourage assertiveness; encourage social interaction before, during, and outside group meeting; encourage helping behavior among group members; and encourage individuals to take responsibility for group interaction and group functioning. The worker should train the group as a whole to reinforce crisis-management and self-help skills of individual members. The worker can use feedback based on individual family plans, group and individual comments and suggestions, parent role plays, and the progress of children in order to anticipate as well as to identify strategies to manage crises and foster growth. The questions asked of the parents by the worker are the same as those for collecting and analyzing feedback from individual families: What did I do that worked? What did you do that worked? How is the child progressing? Finally, group feedback can expose patterns of service barriers and insufficiencies. The worker in the role of advocate can join with the group to bring these problems to the attention of educational and service agencies for remediation.

General Objectives for Parental Training

Whether dealing with individual families or parent-education groups, a systems approach requires a set of preliminary training objectives. These objectives can be divided into three separate domains: affective (feelings), cognitive (information), and application (skills). Figure 2 illustrates some general objectives for each domain.

The worker can use these general objectives in several ways. First, the objectives can be used as a checklist during intake interviews. Second, they can be used as a menu that parents can add to or select from during program planning. As each objective is written, feedback about its attainment and the form it will take must be considered. Specific objectives should be measurable so that

FIGURE 2. General objectives for training parents.

Feelings: Parents will

- Identify and consider positive alternatives to feelings such as guilt, mourning, anger, and helplessness.
- Describe and consider positive alternatives for dealing with psychosocial issues such as "spread," stigma, and expectation/discrepancy.
- Consider and discuss their own value systems in relation to their individual needs and those of their child.
- Discuss the benefits of developing a positive view that includes feelings of self-worth and control; a hopeful but reality-based view of the future; and a creative, proactive style of achieving their long-term goals.
- Monitor their feelings and the consequences of behaviors in order to identify needs and design plans for personal growth.

Information: Parents will

- Demonstrate their understanding of pertinent handicapping conditions and the impact of these conditions on the short- and long-term care of the child at home, in school, and within the community.
- Describe basic stages of child development and their implications for their particular child and family.
- Specify typical crisis stages and how they may be prevented, contained, or managed.
- Know how to locate information about their legal and human rights and their responsibilities regarding the education of their handicapped child.
- Know how to locate information about available resources.
- Know how to locate information about agencies and services related to Supplemental Security Income (SSI) and financial aid.
- Learn how to access for their handicapped child the programs, services, and opportunities available to all persons in their community.
- Know how to locate existing national parent groups and/or form their own support group.

Skills: Parents will

- Demonstrate their ability to communicate with medical, educational, and service agency personnel.
- Identify the needs of their child and/or themselves and access appropriate services.
- Demonstrate personal coping skills for maintaining a positive attitude and for dealing with failure, conflict, anger, and frustration.
- Demonstrate analytical and problem-solving skills when working toward the goals they have set for their child.
- Develop plans and demonstrate teaching and behavior management techniques to work with their child at home.
- Demonstrate strategies for personal growth (for example, managing time, prioritizing concerns, acquiring leisure and recreational skills).
- Demonstrate ways they are trying to build a healthy family.
- Utilize appropriate feedback in modifying goals, strategies, and plans.

feedback data can be collected to measure program success and, if necessary, modify the objectives and/or the program.

Traditionally, checklists have been used for feedback when parents must complete complicated multistaged tasks such as preparing for and participating in school conferences. Other methods of collecting information require that the parents demonstrate an understanding of and the ability to apply certain information. For example, parents can show their understanding of child development by designing a home teaching lesson for their child or an understanding of the communication process by using role plays during group meetings. The worker is responsible for designing relevant tasks and experiences, the demonstration of which proves that parents have achieved the objectives.

Checklists and exercises to guide parents with complicated responsibilities such as the preparation, participation in, and evaluation of a school conference can be prepared by the worker or adapted from already existing materials (for example, Markel & Greenbaum, 1985). Parent-training and advocacy groups have already developed training materials that are readily available (Parent Advocacy Coalition for Educational Rights (PACER), Minneapolis; Citizen's Alliance to Uphold Special Education (CAUSE), Lansing, Michigan).

Communication Skills

Because information on their child's progress is the basis for decision making, parents require accurate, up-to-date feedback. Many parents, as well as professionals, report that poor communication is often the greatest barrier to acquiring appropriate services (Heward, Dardig, & Rossett, 1979; Kroth, 1985). To develop effective communication skills, parents must develop competence in three critical skill clusters: getting, giving, and using information. More specifically, parents need to know how to get and understand information from medical, mental health, education, or service personnel; how to give information to ensure that professionals hear parent concerns and understand parent information and opinions; and how to use information for decision making and dealing with problems. Parents need to identify and prioritize problems, solve problems, negotiate for solutions, and resolve conflicts with professionals. With competence in all three clusters, parents will be better able to prevent crises (see Figure 3).

Poor communication between parents and professionals increases the likelihood of crises. Poor communication results in information that is inaccurate or incomplete and can lead parents to accept inadequate or inappropriate programs; can cause lack of cooperation between parents and professionals (noncompliance), which wastes time or leads to mismanagement of the educational or medical program; and can create unnecessary friction and conflicts, some of which end in litigation, and loss of time and resources for the child. In such situations, the child becomes a pawn in an adults' game and is often lost in the shuffle.

The adaptive training system is especially useful in teaching social or communication skills. The literature indicates that maintenance and generalization of training are enhanced when participants practice skills during training and when support, feedback, and reinforcement occur after training within the natural setting (Kent, O'Leary, Foster, & Prinz, 1977). Based on these findings, training of communication skills should include (1) having parents identify the situations in which they need to receive or give information and/or make decisions (for example, medical or educational conferences), (2) providing modeling, coaching, intensive practice, and positive feedback within training sessions, (3) using new parent-communication skills in simple, low-risk natural situations to build confidence and judgment, and (4) establishing follow-up and additional training. This step-by-step model is used over time with increasingly complex or difficult situations. Individual skills must be combined into clusters so that the parent can practice more complicated interactions. Interactions might include setting up situations in which parents must manage their own anger, confront the hostility of others, and resolve conflicts.

Training materials for many aspects of the communication process are available, some of which are specifically designed for parents of handicapped children. For example, as indicated earlier, checklists and exercises can be provided to guide parents with the complex responsibilities involved in the preparation for, participation in, and evaluation of a school conference or engaging in a behavior rehearsal (Markel & Greenbaum, 1985).

FIGURE 3. Communication: Parent competencies.

Receiving information: How to get and understand information from medical, mental health, education, or service personnel:

- Insist on enough time to prepare for the conference so a comprehensive set of questions or concerns is ready.
- Require others to respond in a focused manner with usable and complete information.
- Set a schedule for responses from various personnel; request time to understand, digest, and discuss information.
- Listen for and deal with discrepancies, ask for clarification, separate fact from opinion.

Giving information: How to ensure that professionals hear your concerns and understand your information and opinions:

- Outline issues about which you want to provide information.
- Be prepared to report a message in several different ways.
- Rehearse how to say no.
- Collect information documenting the effectiveness or ineffectiveness of programs.
- Provide examples.
- Discuss your feelings about productive and nonproductive aspects of the communication process.

Using information and dealing with problems: How to identify and prioritize problems, negotiate for solutions, and resolve conflicts with professionals:

- Identify discrepancies between what is said and what is done, things said in private and in public. Ask clarifying questions.
- Prioritize options, perhaps incorporating differing viewpoints of professionals (e.g., "if I were to follow the suggestions of the physician, I would . . .; but if I followed the advice of the psychologist . . .").
- Identify the professionals who are decision makers, those who are empowered to say yes.
- Align yourself with professionals who encourage rather than interfere with independent decision making by parents.
- Ask for, contribute to, and provide feedback on plans implemented for your child.

Parent-Education Groups

The parent-education group is an effective modality for training parents to manage or prevent crises in their families, locate services, work effectively with their child, accept their situation, and become competent self-managers (Farran et al., 1986; Heward et al., 1979; Turnbull & Summers, 1987; Kroth, 1985). Such groups have proven to be beneficial not only for parents of handicapped children but for parents of schizophrenic patients, premature infants, and teenage drug abusers, among others. Although such groups serve multiple purposes, parents see their primary need as informational. This is particularly true for low-income parents (Radin, 1974). The size of the group can vary. Parents may or may not be homogeneous in terms of any of the following factors: age of child, type and severity of disability, socioeconomic class, needs, interests, and experience. In groups in which parents come from different socioeconomic classes, particular attention must be paid to encouraging equal involvement of all parents in the group. Minority-group parents may need a "buddy" to encourage and support their participation, whereas non–English-speaking parents may need a translator to help them participate.

Although the educational group may include some therapy, it differs from a therapeutic group in many ways. It is more informal. Although it might meet on a monthly or biweekly basis, parents feel free to come and go as they prefer. It is an egalitarian group. The worker, serving as facilitator, performs various tasks. He or she organizes the group, arranges for speakers when asked to do so by parents, collects information for the parents, provides training and opportunities to practice new skills in a safe and controlled environment, and encourages and supports new approaches of parents. However, during the meetings, the worker should not act as the "leader"; rather, the worker should sit back, listen, and learn. Information, help, and strategies flow back and forth among all the members. Neither probing nor invasion of privacy should occur.

After a preliminary meeting with the mental health worker, parents are encouraged to join a group in order to meet others who share their concerns and are in various stages of coping. The extreme loneliness, hopelessness, and helplessness the parents feel can be greatly alleviated by participation in an educational group. Although the focus is on information and education, the group also provides the parents with opportunities to share feelings and to establish a support system, as shown in the following example:

> The worker in charge of a small early intervention program for children with multiple handicaps from thirteen through twenty-two months of age held evening meetings once a month on topics of interest to the parents. Most of the children in the program had been born prematurely and had remained in the hospital for a month or longer after birth. They had multiple problems, were still in need of supplemental oxygen, and were being monitored for sudden infant death syndrome (SIDS). Usually the mother came to these evening programs alone, leaving the father to take care of the infant. Only one or two of these parents had been out with their spouses socially since the baby had been born. They all felt that their infant was too sick to leave with an untrained sitter, and there were few, if any, trained sitters or respite-care workers available. At the beginning of the second or third meeting of the group, a mother jumped up to show off

her new toy, a beeper or pager such as physicians use when they need to be summoned in an emergency. The mother described how liberating this beeper was for her, because she knew that she could be in touch with her child's sitter at a moment's notice, which meant that she did not need "the perfect sitter" and felt more comfortable leaving her child with a responsible adult who was aware of her child's needs. Another parent said that she had found that nursing students from a nearby college were excellent sitters. Other parents suggested forming a babysitting pool, although this was seen as a last resort because all of the parents were in need of rest and relaxation. All the parents said they realized they had to push themselves to leave their child with a stranger, who probably was not as competent as they were in taking care of their child. They agreed that they needed to work on this in order to make their child less dependent on them.

Under the guidance of the worker, the parent-education group becomes a supportive, caring, nonjudgmental group in which parents can share negative feelings and be understood; develop positive feelings by watching other parent role models cope; and maintain hope in the face of sorrow, physical demands, and frustration. The group allows self-disclosure, risk taking, and spontaneity. Parents can learn to clarify and prioritize their own issues based on the experience of the group.

A new group, calling itself "Parent Survival," met every Tuesday morning from 9:30 A.M. (after the children had been picked up by the school bus) until 11:30 A.M. (when the mothers had to leave for home to give their child lunch). It was an informal, leaderless group that met at a different home each week. A worker served as facilitator. Some parents attended regularly, some rarely. For some mothers, the group was a social occasion and a time for relaxation. For others the group provided information and ideas from people with similar experiences. Occasionally, speakers were invited to talk about topics of common concern.

One mother, the parent of a severely impaired six-year-old daughter, arrived at a group meeting late, looking very agitated and disheveled. Everyone looked at her, because she had always been quiet and contained at previous meetings, "saintly," as another mother had wryly described her. She poured herself some coffee and took her seat. Suddenly, she started to cry uncontrollably. Through her tears she said, "I just wanted to run out of the house and run and run and never come back. It all just seemed so hard." The other mothers stopped what they were doing and went over to her and touched her, "Yes, yes, we've all felt that way." Some of them had tears in their eyes. She stopped crying and said, "You have?" "Yes, many times," came several replies. "I thought I was the only one who felt so bad. I felt so alone, I felt so guilty," the woman said. The group spent the rest of the morning talking with this mother about her problems and how they had shared and solved similar ones, offering advice on how to deal with the child and how to make the mother's life easier and more enjoyable.

Professionals traditionally discuss the importance of involving the family and child in community activities and excursions. However, families often find such activities difficult. Professionals may not understand parents' resistance to this idea or the emotional strain parents feel when they are placed in an unpredictable and uncontrollable situation with their child. Parents who share similar experiences can often help one another.

A parents' group was discussing the stress parents feel when out in public with their child. One parent described how sometimes she wished she were invisible. Several added that they would like to go out in public just once and not be stared at, even in a kindly way. One parent wished people would not be so helpful when she was shopping with her son. She wished that they would ignore her as they do everyone else. Another parent said that she always sees other babies when she takes her son outside for a stroll, and the comparison between them and her son is very hurtful to her. She does not have to deal with these feelings when she is home alone.

One parent related that people peek at her daughter in the stroller and inevitably ask how old "the baby" is. Most assume that she is eight to twelve months younger than her actual age of two years. Close to tears, she told how torn she is about answering. If she lies and says that the child is much younger than her real age, the mother would feel disloyal to her daughter. But if she answers truthfully, people ask all sorts of questions that she doesn't want to get into with strangers. Many members of the group had had similar experiences. After discussing various possible responses, one of the group members said that perhaps they should approach such situations in the way people approach the question "How are you?" She asked, "Don't we always respond, ']Fine,'] whether we are or not? We don't go into long explanations about how we are really feeling, especially to strangers." Another parent said, "It's O.K. to lie occasionally. We don't have to be perfect, we don't have to feel guilty." She added that when the little girl got old enough to understand, however, it would be important not to lie.

These issues can be understood only by parents of handicapped children or by experienced workers. When parents share feelings in a group situation, the worker need not be all-knowing; the parents serve as resources. The efficacy of such self-help groups has been apparent to participants. An estimated 500,000 self-help groups meet throughout the nation to serve 15 million people. Despite low budgets, informal structure, volunteerism, and little professional involvement, self-help groups of all kinds seem to be effective in helping people cope with problems.

Sometimes parents encourage one another to focus on the developmental needs of their child as a "whole child," not as a handicapped child.

At an early-intervention group meeting, the speaker, a parent of a twenty-four-year-old severely retarded young woman, brought pictures of her daughter to show to the group. She described her daughter as similar in many ways to other people in her family, having beautiful curly hair, wanting to listen to Elvis Presley all day, always knowing where other family members had left their keys or glasses, and enjoying being helpful around the house. The daughter also was stubborn and opinionated at times, and usually, but not always, able to make her wants known. The other parents at the meeting were then asked to talk about their own children, how they were similar to other members of their family, how they were unique, what they looked like. Some parents went on to share funny things that their child had done or said. Some parents found it difficult to describe their child. Many parents realized that for the first time they were not thinking of their child as a handicapped child, but as a *child*.

Parents can serve as role models for other parents, whose lives are filled with caring for a young handicapped child and who have little energy left over for family, friends, and outside interests. Parents of young handicapped children often cannot imagine themselves laughing, having a career, being an interesting person, having a fulfilling life in the future. Sometimes parents need to demonstrate to other parents their long-term development as "whole" people, not merely as caregivers. For example,

> A parent was asked by a school social worker to speak on the topic "Family Survival with a Handicapped Child." The parent, herself a "survivor," had had an interesting career and a warm family life. The parent shared with the group that she had learned through the years that parents must take care of themselves. This means consciously creating or maintaining strong personal relationships and developing outside interests in which they could immerse themselves. She told the group that she had learned to let some things go, such as housekeeping and cooking "from scratch," and that she learned not to be a slave to schedules and therapies (something a professional might hesitate to say). She also learned that she did not have to be perfect; she was not a saint, just a human being. She told the parents to talk to themselves as they would to a dear friend, to encourage themselves, tell themselves they are doing a good job, tell themselves that they should not feel guilty if they can't do everything that is asked of them. And finally, she urged others to seek professional help for problems that seem unsurmountable, as she had done several times in her life (Gordon, 1978).

Parents need to learn to distinguish situations and problems that require professional expertise and to realize that using professional resources is a sign of responsibility and strength, not of weakness or lack of skill. The parent-education group may identify a need to work with a specific subgroup of the family, such as siblings or fathers.

> At one parent-group meeting, as usual only two fathers were in attendance. When someone commented upon this, one of the mothers said that her husband was having a hard time dealing with their son's disabilities and that he left all the child care and meetings with the professionals to her. She related how difficult this was for her. Another mother echoed the experience. At this point, one of the fathers stood up and said he would be willing to talk to the fathers involved about how much their wives and their children needed them to take an active part in their lives. He turned to the other father and asked if he would join him.
>
> After warmly welcoming the idea, the group decided that a subtle approach was needed or the targeted fathers would be turned off. The two men hit upon the idea of a men's night out at a nearby bowling alley. Although the night would be devoted mostly to having fun, they could bring up their children's disabilities and openly discuss them. The bowling group met for many months, and several good friendships developed out of it. The fathers began to share their feelings, support one another, and become more involved in their children's lives.

As the parent-education group continues to meet, it may mature to the point where the parents wish to join with a larger parent-support group, such as the Association for Retarded Citizens or the Association for Children and Adults with Learning Disabilities; or it may gradually change into an advocacy group and join with other groups to work for social change in the larger community.

The changing needs of group members and other factors lead to attrition in any open-ended group. Parents leave the group for many reasons: They may be able to and wish to cope on their own; they may find other means of support; they may feel uncomfortable with the group or the mental health worker; they may be overwhelmed with other problems that have first priority. Services and/or community attitudes may improve to the extent that the effects of the child's handicapping condition are negligible. The group can be rejuvenated if the need arises. The worker should expect changes to occur as the group evolves and should not feel that his or her work has failed.

The Influence of Values and Attitudes on Crisis Management

The attitudes and values of parents and professionals affect their interactions. Parents may have negative views of helping professionals, including physicians. The mental health worker may be viewed as the gatekeeper to services, with whom parents must interact whether they like it or not. Parents primarily want services for their children, not therapy for themselves.

> In a group meeting, several parents of premature infants remarked that they had dodged the hospital social worker when they saw her coming to talk to them. Interested only in talking to their child's doctor or being with their child, they saw the social worker as an interference and a bother. However, these same parents stated that several weeks or months later they sought out the social worker because they needed to talk to someone about their feelings and concerns.

Mental health workers may also be viewed negatively because they are not seen as "one of us"; that is, they are not parents of a handicapped child and consequently have no personal knowledge of the parents' situation. Sometimes attitudes are the result of past negative experiences; in other cases they are related to the generalized anger parents may feel about their situation. Regardless, the worker must ask questions of the parents to ascertain negative attitudes that might interfere with the development of a trusting relationship. The worker must also be willing to forgo contact at a particular time in a parent's life, then initiate contact again when the parent is more open to the worker's help.

Professionals may also have negative attitudes toward parents, which involve being uncomfortable with the child's handicap or blaming the parents, however subtly, for the child's problems. Because mental health professionals influence those with whom they interact, not only directly with their skills and knowledge, but indirectly and subtly with their values and attitudes, they need to analyze their perceptions of handicapping conditions prior to interacting with parents or parent-education groups. Such self-examination should recur as a part of professional growth as the worker interacts with, trains, and learns from parents. For example, a worker may have difficulty looking at or interacting with a drooling adult who is mentally retarded, and consequently will not be able to hide his or her feelings from the parents. If a worker feels that blindness is the worst possible thing that could happen to a person, these feelings will be communicated to a blind child and his or her parents. Discomfort or feelings of revulsion will block positive communication between the parents and worker. The parent is likely to feel uncomfortable, devalued, and suspicious. Thus the worker must desensitize him- or herself to negative feelings and attitudes about physical appearance. Also, some workers feel that all parents of handicapped children are in need of therapy, which is not the case. The worker must learn to distinguish persons who need therapy from those who do not. Finally, the worker must develop his or her values and attitudes so that the parent feels respected and understood. The following vignette illustrates how observation and interaction with a young mother modified the worker's original expectations and led to growth for child, parent, and worker.

> M, a fifteen-year-old high school dropout, gave birth to a little girl whose cleft palate and cleft lip necessitated gavage feeding for several months. The social worker, in assessing the functioning of this family, initially assumed few strengths existed on which to build and that the future of mother and child was relatively bleak. However, after observing the young mother feeding and holding her baby in the hospital, the social worker began to rethink her initial assessment. The bond between the mother and child was clearly strong: she patiently fed her baby every day, brought toys and decorations for the isolette, and often asked the doctors and nurses for advice and information.
>
> When the social worker next met with the mother, the worker asked M if she would like to know more about her child's condition and things M could do to help the child. The mother eagerly said yes. The social worker gave her written material, apologizing because some of it was highly technical. The mother said, "I'll get a dictionary and if I can't find a word in it, I'll ask someone. I want to read as much as I can so I can help my baby. I want to know when the doctors are going to be able to fix her face. It hurts me to see her look that way." Soon the social worker discovered that the mother was reading at a much higher level than before and, according to the physician, the child seemed to be thriving. The worker continued to provide M with information on her child's medical condition and on how to care for the child at home.
>
> In discussing M's feelings about the child's appearance and her disappointment at not having the beautiful baby she imagined, the social worker pointed out that it was obvious that M loved her child.
>
> "Oh, yes," the mother replied, "but at first I cried every time I saw her."
>
> "But now you don't?" asked the social worker.
>
> "No, I'm sort of used to her, I guess, and when she smiles that crooked smile of hers, I just melt."
>
> "That sounds like progress to me," said the social worker, "What do you think?"
>
> When the child left the hospital at six weeks, M was pleased when the social worker suggested they take photographs of the child every month to have a record of the baby's progress. This mother was used as a role model in several parent-education groups.

Conclusion

Parents of handicapped children face predictable crises throughout their child's life, which, if anticipated, can be prevented or at least better managed. It is the mental health professional's responsibility to create a system to meet the parents' needs for information, services, coping strategies, and other skills. Parent-education groups provide an effective way to train parents to work with their children, communicate with professionals, and, in general, take charge of their lives. Although workers may fill a variety of roles from a crisis management perspective, the most critical role from a prevention perspective is that of trainer. As trainer, the worker can establish an adaptive system to meet the changing needs of parents and child, based on actual progress. Within the context of this system, the worker can provide access to information, resources, and strategies that only a professional can provide. A special feature of the parent-education group is its self-help nature. Parents can share, model, and support one another in ways that only parents who share similar experiences can do. The combination of professional input and parent participation provides a powerful and cost-effective way of helping parents realize their goal of helping their children achieve their maximum potential.

References

Barsch, R. (1968). *The parent of the handicapped child: The study of child rearing practices.* Springfield, IL: Charles C Thomas.

Bernal, M. E., Klinnert, M. D., & Schultz, L. A. (1980). Outcome evaluation of behavioral parent training and client-centered parent counseling for children with conduct problems. *Journal of Applied Behavioral Analysis, 13,* 677–691.

Berkowitz, B. P., & Graziano, A. M. (1972). Training parents as behavioral therapists: A review. *Behavior Research and Therapy, 10,* 297–317.

Bettelheim, B. (1988). *A book on child rearing: Good enough parenting.* New York: Random House.

Brotherson, M. J., & Turnbull, A. (1988). Transition into adulthood: Parental planning for sons and daughters with disabilities. *Education and Training in Mental Retardation, 23,* 165–174.

Brown, S. L., & Moersch, M. S. (1978). *Parents on the team.* Ann Arbor, MI: University of Michigan Press.

Dachman, R. S., Aless, G. J., Urazo, G. J., Fugua, R. W., & Kerr, R. N. (1986). Development and evaluation of an infant-care training program with first time fathers. *Journal of Applied Behavior Analysis, 19,* 221–239.

Dyer, E. (1965). Parenthood as crisis: A re-study. In H. J. Parad (Ed.), *Crisis intervention: Selected readings* (pp. 312–323). New York: Family Service Association of America.

Farran, D. C., Metzger, J., & Sparling, J. (1986). Immediate and continuing adaptations in parents of handicapped children: A model and an illustration. In J. Gallagher & P. Vietze (Eds.), *Families of handicapped persons: Research programs and policy issues* (pp.143–163). Baltimore: Paul H. Brookes Publishing.

Featherstone, H. (1980). *A difference in the family: Living with a disabled child.* New York: Basic Books.

Forehand, R., & Atkeson, B. M. (1977). Generality of treatment effects with parents as therapists: A review of assessment and implementation procedures. *Behavior Therapy, 8,* 575–593.

Forehand, R., Sturgis, E., McMahon, R. R., Aquar, D., Green, K., Wells, K. C., & Breinstein, R. S. (1979). Parent behavioral training to modify child noncompliance: Treatment generalization across time and from home to school. *Behavior Modification, 3,* 3–25.

Gallagher, J., & Vietze, P. (Eds.). (1986). *Families of handicapped persons: Research, programs, and policy issues.* Baltimore: Paul H. Brookes Publishing.

Glogower, R., & Sloop, E. W. (1976). Two strategies of group training of parents as effective behavioral modifiers. *Behavior Therapy*, 7, 177–184.

Goffman, E. (1968). *Stigma: Notes on the management of spoiled identity*. New York: Penguin Books.

Gordon, S. (1978). *Living fully: A guide for young people with a handicap, their parents, their teachers, and professionals*. Athens, Ohio: John Day Publishing.

Greenbaum, J. (1980). *Parent attitudes toward mainstreaming: A survey of parents of handicapped children*. Unpublished doctoral dissertation, University of Michigan, Ann Arbor, MI.

Grossman, F. (1972). *Brothers and sisters of retarded children: An exploratory study*. Syracuse, NY: Syracuse University Press.

Heifetz, L. J. (1977). Behavioral training for parents of retarded children: Alternative formats based on an instructional manual. *American Journal of Mental Deficiency, 82*, 194–203.

Henderson, A. (Ed.). (1981). *Parent participation—student achievement: The evidence grows*. Columbia, MD: National Committee for Citizens in Education.

Heward, W., Dardig, J., & Rossett, A. (1979). *Working with parents of handicapped children*. Columbus, OH: Charles Merrill Company.

Hewett, S., & Forness, W. (1974). *Education of exceptional learners. Boston:* Allyn and Bacon.

Johnson, E. A., & Katz, R. C. (1973). Using parents as change agents for their children: A review. *Journal of Child Psychology and Psychiatry, 14*, 181–200.

Kelly, M. L., Embry, L. H., & Baer, D. H. (1979). Skills for child management and family support: Training parents for maintenance. *Behavior Modification*, *3*, 373–390.

Kent, R., O'Leary, D., Foster, S., & Prinz, R. (1977). An approach to teaching parents and adolescents problem-solving communication skills: A preliminary report. *Behavior Therapy*, *8*, 639–643.

Koegel, R. L., Glahn, T. J., & Nieminen, G. S. (1978). Generalization of parent training results. *Journal of Applied Behavior Analysis*, *11*, 95–104.

Kroth, R. (1985). *Communicating with parents of exceptional children: Improving parent–teacher relationships*. Denver: Love Publishing.

LeMasters, E. (1965). Parenthood as crisis. In H. J. Parad (Ed.), *Crisis intervention: Selected readings* (pp. 111–117). New York: Family Service Association of America.

Lippitt, G., & Lippitt, R. (1966). *The counseling process in action* (2nd ed.). San Diego: California University Associates.

Markel, G. (1974). *The evaluation consultant and innovative elementary projects in an education system*. Unpublished doctoral dissertation, University of Michigan, Ann Arbor, MI.

Markel, G., & Greenbaum, J. (1985). *Parents are to be seen and heard: Assertiveness in educational planning for parents of children with handicaps*. Ann Arbor, MI: Greenbaum and Markel Associates.

Moreland, J., Schwebel, A. I., Beck, S., & Wells, R. (1982). A review of parent training literature (1975–1981). *Behavior Modification*, 6, 250–276.

Nay, W. R. (1979). Parents as real life reinforcers: The enhancement of parent training effects across conditions other than training. In A. P. Goldstein & F. H. Kanfer (Eds.), *Maximizing treatment gains: Transfer enhancement in psychotherapy* (pp. 370–382). New York: Academic Press.

Olshansky, S. (1962). Chronic sorrow: A response to having a mentally defective child. *Social Casework*, 43, 190–193.

Palfrey, J. S., Walker, D. K., Butler, J. A., & Singer, J. D. (1989). Patterns of response in families of chronically disabled children. *American Journal of Orthopsychiatry, 59,* 94–104.

Peed, S., Roberts, M., & Forehand, R. (1977). Evaluation of the effectiveness of a standardized parent training program in altering the interaction of mothers and their noncompliant children. *Behavior Modification, 1,* 323–348.

Public Law 94-142. United States Code, 1978 Edition, Title 20. Section 1401. P. 488. St. Paul, MN: West Publishing.

Radin, N. (1974). Socioeducation groups. In P. Glasser, R. Saari, & R. Vintek (Eds.), *Individual change through small groups* (pp. 89–101). New York: Free Press.

Robinson, L. (1975). Group work with parents of retarded adolescents. *American Journal of Psychotherapy, 35,* 397–408.

Sanders, M. R., & James, J. E. (1983). The modification of parent behavior: A review of generalization and maintenance effects. *Behavior Modification, 7,* 3–27.

Simeonsson, R. J., & Bailey, D. B., Jr. (1986). Siblings of handicapped children. In J. Gallagher & P. Vietze (Eds.), *Families of handicapped persons: Research, programs and policy issues* (pp. 67–77). Baltimore: Paul H. Brookes Publishing.

Suelzle, M., & Deenan, V. (1981). Changes in family support networks over the life cycle of mentally retarded persons. *American Journal of Mental Deficiency, 86,* 267–274.

Sundel, S. S., & Sundel, M. (1980). *Be assertive: A practical guide for human service workers.* Beverly Hills, CA: Sage Publications.

Turnbull, A. P., Summers, J. A., & Brotherson, M. J. (1986). Family life cycle: Theoretical and empirical implications and future directions for families with mentally retarded members. In J. Gallagher & P. Vietze (Eds.), *Families of handicapped persons: Research, programs and policy issues* (pp. 45–65). Baltimore: Paul H. Brookes Publishing.

Turnbull, A. P., & Summers, J. A. (1987). From parent involvement to parent support: Solution to revolution. In S. M. Pueschel, C. Tingey, J. E. Rynders, A .C. Crocker, & D. M. Crutcher (Eds.), *New perspectives on Down's syndrome* (pp. 289–306). Baltimore: Paul H. Brookes Publishing.

Turnbull, A. P., & Turnbull, R. (1978). *Parents speak out.* Columbus, OH: Charles E. Merrill.

Wahler, R. G., Wenkel, G. H., Peterson, R. F., & Morrison, D. C. (1965). Mothers as behavior therapists for their own children. *Behavior Research and Therapy, 31,* 113–124.

Wolfensberger, W., & Kurtz, R. (Eds.). (1969). *Management of the family of the mentally retarded.* Chicago: Follett Educational Corporation.

Wright, B. (1983). *Physical disability—A psycho-social approach* (2nd ed.). New York: Harper and Row.

AFTERWORD

Clearly, from the viewpoint of both clients and practitioners, brief crisis intervention works. Studies of planned short-term versus open-ended treatment have shown that "more" is not necessarily "better"; not only is "less" often good enough, but it can, in fact, be "best."

This sourcebook on crisis intervention in a brief treatment context is, of course, a product of our times. During the 1980s, practitioners came to the harsh awareness that the economic resources of the United States are not boundless; that our society is becoming increasingly polarized between the affluent and the poverty-stricken; and that the belt tightening on the part of third-party payers—the insurance companies and government agencies that fund mental health services—increasingly indicates that service delivery must be short-term.

Unfortunately, only the funding for mental health services is shrinking; the number of persons needing help for a multitude of problems constantly grows. The community mental health services system—built with dreams of hope for a new and better life for the emotionally distressed and mentally ill in America—is now being dismembered by funding cuts. The Community Mental Health Centers Act of 1963 mandated the establishment of twenty-four-hour emergency and crisis intervention services at federally funded community mental health centers, and this legislation had fostered the growth of crisis intervention services. Although the number and scope of community mental health center services have been drastically curtailed, in most communities a network of reasonably accessible crisis intervention services remains. As indicated in this volume, brief crisis therapy—provided under the auspices of hotlines, outpatient mental health clinics, hospitals, family counseling services, and other social, health, and educational agencies—makes a significant difference in peoples' lives, helping to improve their psychosocial functioning. Thus, some reason to be hopeful persists as we contemplate the future of crisis intervention services.

A Look into the Future*

Crisis intervention is no longer the experimental fad many considered it to be thirty years ago. This sourcebook attests to that fact. Thus, we predict that in years to come brief crisis intervention will be regarded not only as a generally accepted but also as a *preferred* mode of delivering mental health services to clients under stress. Just as brief crisis treatment is now the method of choice at most university student counseling services, so, too, similar adaptations of time-limited crisis-oriented therapy for persons in stress are likely to be increasingly

---

*This section is adapted from Parad, H. J. (1986, November). *Crisis intervention: Past, present, and future*. Keynote address, First Australian Conference on Crisis Intervention, Adelaide, South Australia.

regarded as the treatment of choice in mental health programs for children, adolescents, and adults (including the aging) in a variety of child guidance, family service, hospital, and clinic settings.

Experimentation with brief crisis therapy will continue in many other settings such as child-care centers; employee assistance programs in the workplace; and schools, where the need for brief individual, family, and group crisis counseling will grow as school enrollments rise.

In light of the accelerated interest in family and group therapy and the accompanying recognition of the role played by significant others in crisis resolution, the crisis counselor of the future will probably be increasingly oriented to innovative interactional and network approaches. We hope that mental health workers dealing with health crises in hospitals will have flexible work schedules so they can do more family crisis therapy with family members and significant others during evening visitation hours when family members are likely to visit the patient in crisis.

Because of their vital role as caregivers at times of crisis, police, firefighters, disaster aid workers, paramedic rescue workers, and similar personnel dealing with large numbers of people under stress will play an increasingly important role as crisis counselors. They will need further training and consultation by professionals experienced in crisis intervention.

As economic restraints become tighter, cost–benefit requirements will ensure that brief therapy, approximately six to sixteen sessions in length, will be the wave of the future. Although not all brief therapy is crisis-oriented, many clients receiving brief therapy will be under severe stress and their therapists must be knowledgeable about crisis intervention.

Dramatic reports on drug abuse, sexual molestation, child and spousal abuse, and teenage suicide in the media will draw heightened public attention to these crisis experiences, creating further demand for around-the-clock hotline crisis intervention telephone services.

Increases in the population of older adults, combined with the growing sophistication of life-support medical technology, will further enhance the importance of sensitive crisis intervention and crisis consultation services to patients, their families, and medical personnel, all of whom are dealing with death and dying, often making agonizing life-and-death decisions about whether to maintain or withdraw mechanical life-support systems.

In the future, time-limited crisis intervention will be taught as an integral part of graduate mental health courses on psychotherapy and counseling, rather than as a separate course.

In addition to the foregoing trends, which we feel have reasonable likelihood of coming to pass, we would like to offer several hopes for the future.

We hope that the practice of preventive crisis intervention (similar to the examples detailed in Part III) will attract more attention from mental health professionals.

We hope that, despite the economic constraints plaguing researchers today, a renewed thrust to engage in systematic, rigorous research will engender a more precise, cumulative literature on the processes, outcomes, limits, and possible misuses of brief crisis intervention services. Knowledge regarding the structuring of time in crisis intervention needs to be refined. What is the optimal number of sessions for typical clients in crisis? What are the uses and limits of the single-session crisis interview? Is six still the modal number of sessions in most crisis intervention programs?

A number of other topics deserve special attention: criteria for different types of interventions with diverse ethnic groups; how the client and worker actually perceive and relate to time-structuring procedures; the risks and advantages of crisis induction, a technique used by some professionals to accelerate change; specific ways in which eclectic action-therapy techniques (for example, psychodrama and sculpting) can be blended with other, more traditional approaches; how to deal with impasses in brief crisis therapy when the usual task-centered, problem-solving techniques don't work; better understanding of the common and specific therapeutic elements that contribute to a successful outcome; the costs and benefits of prearranged follow-up interviews; and the differing effectiveness of individual, family, and group crisis modalities. Also needed are carefully controlled experimental studies of open-ended versus time-limited crisis intervention approaches.

To summarize, we believe crisis intervention will be increasingly utilized in both traditional and nontraditional settings; it will be theoretically and technically *eclectic*, integrating psychodynamic, cognitive, behavioral, humanistic, and existential perspectives; it will be *interactionally oriented* to include significant others; it will be *preventive* in scope; and, we hope, it will routinely include *systematic follow-up* studies to investigate the pros and cons of its effectiveness with diverse populations at risk.

Given the financial limitations within which mental health professionals now operate, it is unlikely that many comprehensive rigorous research efforts will be mounted in the near future, though the need for systematic research is urgent. However, even in the absence of such research, it is clear that crisis intervention is now an established component of ongoing services in most mental health and social welfare programs. It is here to stay and it will grow, we hope, in a way that relieves suffering and maximizes human potential throughout the world.

INDEX